# George Seferis

# George Seferis
## Waiting for the Angel

### A Biography

Roderick Beaton

Yale University Press
New Haven and London

Copyright © 2003 by Roderick Beaton

Designed by Adam Freudenheim
Set by SNP Best-set Typesetter Ltd., Hong Kong
Printed in Great Britain

Library of Congress Cataloging-in-Publication Data
Beaton, Roderick.
   George Seferis : waiting for the angel : a biography / by Roderick Beaton.
      p.   cm.
Includes bibliographical references and index.
   1. Seferis, George, 1900–1971.   2. Poets, Greek (Modern) – 20th
century – Biography.   I. Title.
   PA5610.S36Z634 2003
   889'.132–dc21                                                    2003004902

ISBN 0–300–10135–X (hbk.)

A catalogue record for this book is available from the British Library

10 9 8 7 6 5 4 3 2 1

This book is for
Nick and Mike

Upon the stone of patience we still wait
for heaven's miracle to make all well
still waiting for the angel like the age-old
drama, the hour of evening when the open

roses fade... Scarlet rose of wind and fate,
you are but memory, a heavy rhythm
o rose of night you passed me by, a storm
of purple, storm at sea... The world is simple.

'Erotikos Logos', V (1931)


The angel
three years we waited for him intently
watching very closely
the pines the shore and the stars.
Becoming one with the plough's blade or the ship's keel
we sought to find once more the primordial seed
so the age-old drama could begin again.

*Mythistorema*, 1 (1935)


Strange, I see here the light of the sun; the golden net
where the things of the world writhe like fish
as a great angel winds it in
along with the nets of the fishermen.

'Agianapa I' (1955)

# Contents

List of Illustrations                                                    viii

Preface                                                                    xi

## I
## 'The Spectre of Odysseus'

1   Exile from Paradise (1900–1918)                                        1
2   A Student in Paris (1918–1925)                                        31
3   Servant of Two Masters (1925–1931)                                    65
4   Wayfarer the Seafarer (1931–1934)                                    101

## II
## Poetry in a Mean-Spirited Time

5   The Scales of Injustice (1935–1937)                                  133
6   'A Generation Sacrificed' (1938–1941)                                158
7   The Second Exile (1941–1943)                                         193
8   'The Pain-Perpetuating Memory of Pain' (1943–1944)                   225

## III
## 'Light, Angelic and Black'

9    Descent into Hades (1945–1950)                                      257
10   Paradise Found (1951–1955)                                          293
11   '. . . And Lost Again and Again' (1956–1961)                        329
12   A Time for Renewal (1961–1971)                                      369

Acknowledgements                                                         406
Greek Names, Transliteration, Translation                                409
Abbreviations and Sources                                                411
Notes                                                                    416
Guide to Further Reading                                                 494
Index                                                                    497

# List of Illustrations

## Plates

(unless otherwise indicated, copyright George Seferis Photographic Archive, Cultural Foundation of the National Bank, Athens, reproduced by permission)

1. Despo Tenekidou, Stelios Seferiadis, probably taken about the time of their marriage in 1897
2. Stelios Seferiadis, Paris, 1 August 1918 (his 45th birthday)
3. Despo Seferiadou (Tenekidou), portrait by E. Ioannidis, c. 1917 (private collection, reproduced by courtesy of Elli Mylonas)
4. GS aged 2 or 3 (portrait photograph)
5. 'George, wide-eyed and serious . . .' GS, Ioanna and Angelos, c. 1916
6. and 7. Skala: 'There, the people, sailors and villagers, were my own people.'
8. Suzon Clauzel and a friend, signed photograph, 19 June 1919
9. GS (left) with unidentified friends, 'posed with extravagant daring on the roof of Notre Dame cathedral,' 25 October 1920
10. Angelos Seferiadis, Notre Dame, summer 1922
11. Marie-Louise Pouyollon, Jacqueline Pouyollon, Le Vésinet, July 1924
12. GS and Jacqueline, Le Vésinet, July 1924
13. GS with Petros Adamos (left), at 121 Boundaries Road, Balham, London, September 1924. 'I talk English even to the cat'
14. Loukia Fotopoulou (Lou), in her basement flat, the 'cistern'
15. GS (right, hat in hand) was official guide to Edouard Herriot (centre) on his semi-official visit to Greece in August 1929
16. Ioanna Tsatsou, shortly after her marriage in 1930 (Archive of Konstantinos and Ioanna Tsatsos, reproduced by permission of Despina Mylonas)
17. GS with Sotiris Stamelos, 'a living embodiment at once of Homer and of Makriyannis,' Skiathos, July/August 1930
18. GS with Loukia Fotopoulou (Lou), 1930, about the time when he wrote to her: 'I'm not sure how long the magic really lasted'

19. Andreas Londos, husband of Marika (later Maro Seferi): '. . . a striking resemblance to the movie-star Clark Gable' (c. 1934) (courtesy of Anna Londou)

20. Marika Zannou (later Maro Seferi) and her sister Amaryllis Dragoumi (right), Poros, 1938. It was Amaryllis who introduced Maro to GS

21. Henry Miller (left) and George Katsimbalis (the 'Colossus of Maroussi'), Hydra, November 1939

22. Henry Miller, Hydra, November 1939: ". . . putting on his black spectacles as though to work with an oxy-acetylene flame . . .' ('Les Anges Sont Blancs')

23. Alexandrian friends. Left to right: Timos Malanos, Maro, Nanos Panayotopoulos (Nuzha, 1943)

24. Maro in the Botanical Gardens, Cairo, 27 June 1942. With evacuation from Egypt looming, hopes that her daughters could join her from occupied Greece had just been dashed

25. George Kartalis (right) with GS, Cairo, 23 August 1943

26. 'The snow here is never-ending . . .' GS outside his house in Atatürk Bulvarı, Ankara, January 1949

27. 'Descent into Hades': GS outside the 'little house' in Skala (now restored as the Yorgo Seferis guest house); his grandmother's house is in the background (2 July 1950)

28. GS (right) with Rex Warner, Woodstock, Oxfordshire, 1952

29. GS and Evangelos Louizos, St Hilarion, Cyprus, 8 November 1953

30. At the Acheiropoietos monastery, Cyprus, 6 December 1953. Seated (left to right): GS, Lawrence Durrell, Antoinette Diamanti, Maurice Cardiff. Standing: the Cardiffs' son, the painter Adamantios Diamantis

31. '. . . a younger incarnation of the "Colossus of Maroussi" as Katsimbalis had been thirty years before . . .' George Savides (left) with Katsimbalis and Maro, Rhodes, September 1955; photo by GS

32. 'Our Seafaring Friend': D.I. Antoniou, Beirut, 1955; photo by GS

33. At the United Nations, 12 November 1956. Left to right: Constantine Karamanlis, GS, Evangelos Averoff-Tosizza

34. GS pays his respects to Archbishop Makarios, arriving in Athens from captivity in the Seychelles, 17 April 1957

35. GS with Harold Macmillan, London Airport, 7 August 1958

36. 'M. Zorlu [foreign minister of Turkey, right] and M. Averoff [foreign minister of Greece, left] had exchanged "Turkish delights" in New York . . . George was horrified' (London, February 1959)

37. Konstantinos ('Kostakis') Tsatsos and George Katsimbalis, 1960 (Archive of Konstantinos and Ioanna Tsatsos, reproduced by permission of Despina Mylonas)

38. GS and Maro at the London embassy, 51 Upper Brook Street, 1961 (courtesy of the Greek embassy, London)

39. GS with Anne Philipe, Delphi, May 1971

## Other illustrations

*Frontispiece*: GS in the garden of the house at no. 20, Agras Street, Athens, 1970 (copyright as for plates)

Title-page of *Turning Point* (1931), including the first appearance of the mermaid device (King's College London, Maughan Library: Foyle Special Collections)                                                                 100

The *calligramme* which opens *Logbook II* in the first, calligraphic edition of 1944 (courtesy of Edmund Keeley)                                              224

'Wherever I travel, Greece wounds me.' Cartoon, copyright Kostas Mitropoulos, reproduced by permission (first published in *Tachydromos*, Athens, April 1966)                                                          368

# Preface

Poet, essayist, diarist, novelist, prolific letter-writer, in all he wrote George Seferis bore authoritative and humane witness to the century into which he was born (in 1900). The voice that speaks through his writings is above all a *Greek* voice: Seferis's perspective on the history and culture of his time is always shaped by the consciousness that he was writing in a living language whose successive phases can be traced back through more than three thousand years. The Greeks are a people small in number (approximately fifteen million today, around the world), with an exceptionally long recorded history. It is no accident that, when in 1963 Seferis became the first Greek ever to win a Nobel Prize, the citation specifically paid tribute to him as the most worthy representative 'of the Greece of today.'

As a poet, Seferis won international acclaim between the 1940s and the 1970s for his thought-provoking lyric voice and powerful evocations of what Lawrence Durrell termed the 'spirit of place.' Through his impact on Durrell, Henry Miller, and other British and American writers, Seferis brought about a revolution in the way later generations have viewed his country: no longer as a museum-piece of the past but as a place of vibrant, dionysiac energy.[1] In Greece itself, no other writer has exercised such a dominant influence since the Second World War. C.P. Cavafy, whose work is probably better known today, has been the object of imitation and pastiche, but Seferis has had successors; Seferis' poetry stands in a clear historical line between the great voices of the past (Solomos, Kalvos, Palamas, Sikelianos, Cavafy himself) and almost all the major figures since.[2]

It is as a poet that Seferis first established this reputation; but during his lifetime he was already highly regarded for his essays on literary and cultural topics. Since his death, the successive publication of nine volumes (so far) of diaries, several collections of his letters and a completed novel has added a rich background, revealing a writer and thinker more versatile, across a wider expressive range, than even his warmest admirers had been allowed to suspect while he was alive. With these successive publications, the somewhat austere spokesman of humane values has progressively acquired a more human side.

But this is still only half the story. For almost forty years of his life, Seferis served his country as a professional diplomat. He rose to a high level in that profession, ending his career as Ambassador to London; he also occupied key positions, not strictly diplomatic ones, during times of historic crisis for his country. Before, during, and just after the Second World War, and again in the 1950s, during the conflict between Greece and Great Britain over the future of Cyprus, Seferis exerted himself to the utmost to influence the outcome of events according to his own deeply held convictions. As a critical observer of the events in which he was involved, Seferis possessed a devastating clarity of vision; he could tease out the consequences of a policy or a set of events far into the future, usually with deadly accuracy. Out of these experiences, over the years, he would hone his starkly uncompromising views of the forces that govern world affairs: forces ignored at their peril, he believed, by those who think that they hold power in their hands.

While Seferis was alive, and for long afterwards, almost nothing of this was known to his readers, often even to his friends, beyond the stark biographical facts of his career. Even today, while the bibliography on his writing runs to well over two thousand items, in several languages, little has been done to examine what Seferis did in his professional career, how the experiences gained in that career affected his writing, or how both may be grounded in the developing consciousness and beliefs of the private man.

For all these reasons, a biography of Seferis is both timely and a particular challenge. A huge amount of material on and by Seferis now exists in print; part of his unpublished archive became accessible in the Gennadius Library, Athens, in 1975; almost all of the rest was opened in January 2000. Not everything which a biographer would wish to consult is yet available; as with any important figure, there will always be openings for new discoveries and new interpretations. But with so much material now in the public domain, to which additions are constantly being made piecemeal, often in newspapers and periodicals where they can be hard to track down, it is high time that the attempt was made to draw together the many threads of the complex personality and achievement of Greece's first Nobel laureate.

This is what I have tried to do in this book.

Seferis did not make the biographer's task an easy one. He did everything he could to separate the identity of the poet and man of letters from that of the higher civil servant. From his twenties to his sixties, he complained of being the 'servant of two masters.' From the time when he first published a book of poems, he rigorously divided himself into two public personae: 'Seferis' is a literary pseudonym, at once transparent and distinct from the family name of the diplomat, 'Seferiadis.'

The story of Seferis's life is the story of this divided self. In writing it, I have taken a deliberate stand: this biography is not the story of 'Seferis' the poet, or of 'Seferiadis' the diplomat, but, so far as it is possible to reconstruct it, the story of the man who was both. For that reason, in the chapters that follow, I call him by the version of his first name that he used in English: George.

Seferis himself had ambivalent ideas about biography in general and his own in particular. In his semi-autobiographical novel, *Six Nights on the Acropolis*, he warns against the danger, in words borrowed from Dante, of 'treating shadows as though they were solid things;' he subscribed to the view of Mark Twain, that 'Biographies are but the clothes and buttons of the man – the biography of the man himself cannot be written.' Already, when he was twenty-five, he had written in his diary:

Man is always double: he who acts, and he who sees himself acting; he who suffers, and he who sees himself suffering; he who feels, and he who observes himself feeling. When I say 'I,' what do I mean, self A or self B? And this shows that true sincerity is almost impossible.[3]

On the other hand, this was a writer who frequently adopted the confessional first person in his published work; whose one completed novel, and many of whose essays, are heavily indebted to his own personal diary; who from at least the age of sixteen until the eve of his death kept a series of diaries, amounting to more than two thousand printed pages; who in later life invested heavily in time and effort to edit these diaries for eventual publication; and who meticulously maintained a personal archive so extensive that the final stages of cataloguing it were still going on thirty years after his death.

Seferis left us two consciously constructed and, I believe, arbitrarily divided selves. The biographer, by the very nature of the task, is bound to construct another. But this is what writers do. As Seferis put it, in his last collection of poems:

The white paper is a harsh mirror
it returns to you only that which you were. . . .

all that you have been collapses without substance
unless you entrust yourself to this void.[4]

In taking on this task, I have inevitably had to be highly selective. In addition to the published sources (of which a full bibliography, to the year 2000, is expected shortly), I have had unrestricted access to all but a handful of files in the George Seferis papers (Gennadius Library, Athens). This archive contains manuscript drafts of almost everything that Seferis wrote, many thousands of letters received, several sets of letters to family and friends, and a meticulously maintained set of carbon copies and drafts of some fourteen hundred private letters written during the last thirty years of his life. There are also hundreds of press cuttings, many of them with Seferis's annotations, reviews of his books, and documents both private and professional.[5]

Extensive though it is, the Gennadius archive is still not comprehensive. Important collections of letters are in the private archive of Ioanna and Konstantinos Tsatsos; since the death of Ioanna Tsatsou in 2000, it is likely that more material will come to light. Most of Seferis's large collection of books, many with his annotations, are in the Vikelaia Municipal Library, Heraklion, Crete; a catalogue of them has been published. There is also a series of files, not yet catalogued, of his diplomatic papers there. A small amount of material has found its way to the Greek Literary and Historical Archive (ELIA) in Athens; some of Seferis's correspondence in English, notably with Eliot, Durrell, Miller, and his translator Edmund Keeley, is now in the library of Princeton University. Documents relevant to Seferis's diplomatic career are held at the Public Record Office, London and the Archive of the Foreign Ministry, Athens (very little is as yet accessible in the latter). I have consulted all of these, and been helped in the course of my work by these and other institutions, as well as by a great many individuals. Full details appear in the Acknowledgements and the section 'Sources and Abbreviations.'

Finally, finishing this biography completes a personal 'odyssey' which goes back almost forty years. It was in 1965 that I first heard the musical setting of Seferis's poem 'Denial' played on the jukebox of a café on the island of Mykonos. I had just returned from a visit to Delos, and narrowly missed, by a matter of days, being one of the 'welter' of tourists crowding the motor boat on which Seferis and his wife Maro made the same trip, through the same choppy seas, that September.[6] Not yet an undergraduate, I bought the

*Collected Poems* when they first came out in the bilingual edition, translated by Edmund Keeley and Philip Sherrard, in Britain in 1969. Since then, I have been reading and re-reading Seferis, writing about him, lecturing about him, occasionally translating him, and for the last twenty-five years teaching him to university students in Britain.

One of the greatest pleasures of writing Seferis's biography has been in trying, so far as possible, to follow the footsteps of the much-travelled exile. It is an unsettling experience to walk through the streets of modern Izmir, as Seferis himself did in 1950, with an 1898 guidebook in hand, trying to get your bearings in the vanished streets that were once home to many thousands of Greeks. The tiny fishing hamlet of Urla Iskelesi (called Skala in Greek), thirty kilometres along the coast, has not lost the air of dereliction in which Seferis found it when he returned, once only, at the age of fifty. A sign of the long overdue détente between Greece and Turkey is the street name, near the harbour: *Yorgo Seferis sokağı*; just opposite its end, the 'Yorgo Seferis' guesthouse, opened in 2000, is a loving restoration of the house in which he spent the happiest times of his life: his childhood summers, at the start of the last century, until he was twelve.

I cannot claim to have followed Seferis everywhere he went. Parts of the Middle East, that play a small part in his story, would have been difficult to reach during the years while I was working on it: Baghdad and the vanished site of Seleucia on the Tigris, most of all. Of greater importance in Seferis' life are a number of places and archaeological sites in northern Cyprus, including Salamis and Engomi, each the subject of an important poem. As a British tourist, I could cross the 'Green Line' that since 1974 has divided the island, into the self-proclaimed 'Turkish Republic of Northern Cyprus.' But in Cyprus I do not feel like a tourist, and I have not so far found it possible to go where my Greek and Greek-Cypriot friends and colleagues may not. It is to be hoped, at the time of going to press, that this situation may soon, at last, be about to change.

For entirely different reasons, I have not tried to retrace Seferis's itinerary to Pretoria and Cape Town, or as far east in Turkey as the '*angolo francescano*' in Ankara or the rock-cut monasteries of Cappadocia. Unexpectedly moving moments, on the other hand, came on suddenly finding myself in the rue Bréa, near the Luxembourg Gardens in the Latin Quarter of Paris; and in following the road across the island of Aegina, at dusk, from the now derelict Floros House to Perivola, that a thirty-six-year-old Seferis must have taken to meet his future wife, Maro.

In all these places, and in libraries, handling pages handled, and written, by Seferis, I have been constantly reminded of one of his best-known poems, 'The King of Asine.' There, searching the ruins of an archaeological site, the poet is haunted by an absence; nothing remains of its three-thousand-year-old king, except to 'touch at times with our fingers his touch upon the stones.'

*Roderick Beaton*
*King's College London*
*July–December 2002*

# I

## 'The Spectre of Odysseus'

And there appears before me, again and again, the spectre of
     Odysseus, eyes reddened by the brine of the wave . . .

He tells me the difficult pain of knowing the ship's sails billowing
     with remembrance while your soul becomes a tiller.
And to be alone, in the darkness of night, directionless like chaff on
     the threshing floor.

The bitterness of seeing your companions overwhelmed among the
     elements, scattered: one by one.
And how strange it is to find courage in speaking with the dead,
     when the living who are left to you are no longer enough.

('Reflections on a Foreign Line of Verse,' Christmas 1931)

# 1

# Exile from Paradise
# 1900–1918

Who knows, if my life has become as it has and has unfolded along
two parallel roads – one road of obligations, patience and
compromises, and another road trodden without concessions, freely,
by my deepest self – this is because I knew and experienced, during
those years, two cleanly separated worlds: the world of the house in
the city and the world of the house in the country.

(*Manuscript Sept. '41*)[1]

## Infidel Smyrna

Smyrna in 1900 was one of the great commercial centres of the Levant,
and the second city of the Ottoman Empire. It was in those days a multi-
cultural, polyglot place. Out of a population of nearly a quarter of a million,
the largest group were Orthodox Christians whose first language was Greek.
Turkish-speaking Muslims made up between a quarter and a third. There
were also significant communities of Armenians, Jews, and more or less
permanent settlers from western Europe, called by Europeans 'Levantines'
and by the local population 'Franks.'[2]

The Greek community lived cheek-by-jowl in solidly-built houses
crammed together in a maze of narrow streets behind the Quay, the wide
promenade and tramway that ran northwards past the busy passenger port
to the Point. Muslim Turks made up the governing classes and the very
poor. The city's mosques and administrative buildings were grouped just
south of the harbour, at the foot and on the lower slopes of Mount Pagos,
which rises above the city to the south and whose slopes are crowned by the
ruins of a Byzantine fortress, called in Turkish Kadifekale, or Velvet Castle.

Inland from the Greeks lived the Armenians, with their own cathedral
dedicated to St Stephen. The Armenians, like the Greeks, were entrepre-
neurs and together with them made up the bulk of the thriving middle
class. In the southern suburbs were two substantial Jewish quarters, one
on the lower slopes of Mount Pagos, the other beyond the headland
that marked the southern limit of the Quay, in Karatash. The Jewish

community, then at its peak, numbered twenty-five thousand. The Levantines (or 'Franks') were mostly Catholic, their *lingua franca* French or Italian. They lived in neat and elegant streets to the north of the Greeks and Armenians, in the districts known as Bellavista and the Point, and also in the exclusive village suburbs of Bournabat (the modern Bornova) and Cordelio (Karşiyaka), on the opposite side of the bay.[5]

The main commercial artery in the lower city was the winding, crowded Rue Franque, lined with two- and three-storey shops and businesses. Here Levantines, Greeks and Armenians owned arcades of shops; George's mother's family, the Tenekidis, owned one such arcade on the Rue Franque. The grandest buildings in the city, however, were those which lined the mile-long Quay, from the harbour to the Point: portentous, severe, stone-built with abrupt frontages on to the cobbles where the horse-drawn trams went past, and where hundreds of row-boats were daily tied up waiting to ferry passengers to and from the liners lying off in the bay. Seen from the sea, the most conspicuous buildings, moving left from the Custom House at the edge of the harbour, were the Grand Hotel Huck, the even grander Hotel Kraemer, which some time about 1900 added a fourth storey to its massive square elevation, the Sporting Club with its distinctive tall arched windows and white marble exterior, the stubby, blank-faced French consulate and, next to it, the Smyrna Theatre, which had a sophisticated repertoire of European drama, revue and opera. Inland from the Quay, the lower city was dominated by the seven-storey belfry of the Greek Orthodox cathedral of St Photini, whose great bell had been a present from the Tsar of Russia and could be heard all over the city. Not for nothing was Smyrna nicknamed, in Turkish, in those days: *gâvur Izmir* (infidel Smyrna).

The streets and markets of the lower city were crowded, noisy and colourful. Daily camel-trains from the interior of Anatolia brought spices, flowers, fruit and vegetables in season, crossing over the single-arch Caravan Bridge that spanned the Meles river, nearly dry in most seasons, to be sold in the Street of the Great Tavernas. Dried figs, raisins and tobacco were among the most important exports of Ottoman Smyrna.

In the streets and bazaars, all the languages of Europe and many of the Middle East would be heard daily. But the multi-culturalism of an Ottoman city at the beginning of the twentieth century was not the same as the multi-culturalism of, say, London or New York today. Each community was very tightly organised around its religion, and its members lived together in a clearly defined, and usually homogeneous, neighbourhood. Opportunities for fraternisation across these boundaries were limited, and intermarriage impossible unless one of the partners changed religion. This in turn would require not just a change of faith but of an entire way of life, habits, neighbours, friends, sometimes of job, and even of language.[4]

It was into this city in 1900, that George Seferiadis was born on 29 February according to the old, Julian calendar then in use among the Christians of the Ottoman Empire, or 13 March according to the Gregorian (western) calendar.[5]

The house in which he was born had three storeys, an interior courtyard with a well, a glassed-in balcony facing the street, with a view of the sea, and its own basement store-rooms. It occupied a corner plot diagonally across the road from the back of the Sporting Club, on the Parallel, the first street inland from the Quay. When George returned to Smyrna in 1950, the Sporting Club was still standing, but he could find no trace of where the family house had stood.

The only building on this part of the Quay which survives from that period today is the French consulate. The Sporting Club was the second building to the right, looking from the direction of the sea. The Parallel, like the Quay, is one of the few streets in this part of the city whose line has been preserved in the post-1922 streetplan, although almost all the buildings which once lined it have vanished; it is now named Cumhuriyet Bulvarı (Republic Boulevard). What must have been the Seferiadis family house is clearly marked on a 1905 plan; its site now lies on the edge of the tree-planted campus of one of modern Izmir's two universities. The University bears the name '9 September' – to commemorate the date in 1922 on which Turkish republican forces under the command of Mustafa Kemal entered Smyrna, to bring the cosmopolitan city of *gâvur Izmir* to a terrible end.[6]

### Greeks of the East

The name Seferis first appears in the family records in the early nineteenth century, when Seferis A(y)inabeyoglou married the daughter of a local Ottoman official in Caesarea, the modern Kayseri in south-central Anatolia. 'Seferis' here appears to have been a given name. At this time family names were the exception rather than the rule; the second name is either a nickname or a patronymic. George seems to have understood his ancestor's second name to imply that his paternal ancestors came from the island of Aegina, close to Athens ('son of the lord of Aegina'); but there is no other evidence to connect his father's family with the geographical area of present-day Greece. Other possible derivations of the name are from

5

Turkish *ayina* (mirror), or perhaps *ayi* (spring). The only other family names preserved from this period, Tsartinoglou and Kasisoglou, are also evidently Turkish; so is the name 'Seferis' itself. *Sefer*, in Turkish, is an Arabic borrowing, related to the word that has come into English as 'safari.' Its principal meanings in both nineteenth-century Ottoman and the modern language are: 'Journey, voyage, campaign, state of war.' George was certainly aware of the first two of these meanings, which in years to come would resonate deeply with his own condition as an exile from his homeland and as a diplomat, bound by his career to move from place to place.[7]

The evidence of these names, together with the geographical provenance of the family, suggests that before the Greek revolution against Ottoman rule in 1821, George's forebears on his father's side had been deeply rooted in the Anatolian heartland, and indeed in the Turkish language. In 1820 or 1821, the first Seferis baptised his first child, a boy, to whom he and his wife Nazli gave the conspicuously more Greek name Prodromos, meaning 'forerunner,' the title of John the Baptist in Greek. Some time after this, Seferis A(y)inabeyoglou bequeathed to his six children his given name in the form of a surname. This was a common practice at the time, as was the addition of a patronymic suffix. Most Greek surnames today have been generated in this way: the endings *-akis* and *-opoulos* are diminutives in the modern language, *-oglou* is carried over from Turkish, while *-adis* or *-idis* (the last vowel can also be transliterated as 'e') harks back to the names of ancient heroes. Odysseus Laertiades, for example, in Homer's *Odyssey*, is the son of Laertes. In this way, Prodromos, the first-born son of Seferis A(y)inabeyoglou, became Prodromos Seferiadis. It was George, when he published his first volume of poems in 1931, who would reverse the process to become, once more, plain 'Seferis.'

Beyond the names, not much is known about the Seferiadis family during the nineteenth century. One of Prodromos' brothers apparently married a relative of the Ecumenical Patriarch of the Orthodox Church, which has its seat in Constantinople; clearly a sign of social distinction for the family. In all there were either four or five brothers and sisters, but details have been preserved only of Prodromos' own family and that of his brother Anastasis. Prodromos must have married late in life, since his two sons were born when he was in his fifties and his wife, Charikleia Angelidi (or Analidi) died young, of a 'malignant fever,' in June 1880.

Stelios (Stylianos), the poet's father, was born on 1 August 1873. The death of his mother when he was only six seems to have marked Stelios for life. Like his more famous son, George, Stelios was also a poet, and his collected poems, which he published in Athens late in life, are prefaced by a short dedicatory poem commemorating the loss of his mother. Prodromos himself recorded the births, marriages and deaths of his family with laconic, moving formality, in the flyleaf of an 1867 encyclopaedia which did equivalent duty to an English family Bible.[8]

Despite this early tragedy, Stelios seems to have been an eager, perhaps a flamboyant, certainly a hard-working soul. While still at school, he had met and fallen in love with his future wife, Despo (Despina) Tenekidou. Before he was twenty he had become a regular correspondent of at least one Smyrna newspaper and had published his first poems. A photograph from about the time of George's birth shows Stelios Seferiadis leaning his head earnestly against his wife's cheek, his neat, bright features focused past her, his eyes wide and brimming. The pose is traditional in photographs of newly married couples at the time, but there is still something individual in the young man's ardour and enthusiasm.[9]

George's friend, the novelist George Theotokas, who studied under Stelios Seferiadis much later, in the early 1920s, remembered him at that time:

> He was a man of lively temperament and very sociable, always beaming at his visitors, immaculately dressed, without a crease, his grey beard perfectly groomed. He was a lover of women and ostentatiously solicitous towards them, with the exaggerated civilities of the time before 1914. He appreciated honours and titles, high society and important connections. In society he behaved like a man of the world, an affable European; with his family, though, I realised he could be different: austere, an authoritarian Anatolian-Greek father of the old school. He made particular demands on his children . . . and often flew into a rage if things did not turn out as he wanted.[10]

Stelios had studied law for six years in France, first at Aix-en-Provence, then in Paris. At the beginning of 1897, he was awarded his doctorate from the Sorbonne. In the same month, he returned to Smyrna, clearly intending to make the city his home. On 2 February of that year, the now 76-year-old Prodromos Seferiadis recorded on the flyleaf of the family encyclopaedia:

> Sunday. My [*this word heavily deleted*] firstborn son Stylianos took as his wife Despo Tenekidou daughter of George. The nuptials took place at

7

the Tenekidou household . . . I wish them health, harmony and happiness and may they live many many years with all blessings.[11]

It is hard to read between such formally laconic lines. The formulaic good wishes with which the entry ends are repeated identically in the entry recording the marriage of Prodromos' other son, Michael, a year and half later. But on that occasion the festivities took place at the Seferiadis household, not that of the bride. The deletion of the pronoun may signal a rift between Stelios and his father, who was old enough to have been his grandfather. If this was so, it was a pattern to be bitterly repeated in the next generation, between Stelios and his own sons.

Whatever Prodromos Seferiadis may have thought of his son Stelios' marriage, the family of his bride was both more prosperous and more socially established in the region. On the paternal side, George's mother's family came from the Aegean island of Naxos. Yorgakis Tenekes (Little George the Tin-Man), was the fifth of eleven children born to Kyriakos Tenekes, or Tenekidis, and his wife Charikleia Maravelia. It is not clear which generation added the Hellenic suffix to the Turkish name Tenekes, or when the migration from Naxos to Smyrna took place. This was the only branch of the family that had a definite connection with the geographical area of what is now Greece. Yorgakis Tenekidis, George's maternal grandfather, after whom he was named, established himself near Smyrna, in the town of Vourla (now Urla), where he had substantial holdings of land. Half the houses and much of the surrounding farmland around the harbour of Vourla (George's beloved Skala) belonged to Yorgakis Tenekidis. After Yorgakis died in 1886, all this became the property of his widow, the poet's maternal grandmother.

Evanthia Michalaki Tenekidou had been born into the Pastamantzoglou family, which also came from the interior of Anatolia, this time from Ankara. (Later, in Athens, this distinguished family, one of whose scions would become a diplomatic colleague of George, modified its name to Pesmazoglou.) Despo, born in 1874, was the eldest surviving child of this marriage, which produced eight children, of whom three died in childhood. By the time that George was growing up, the Seferiadis and Tenekidis families were doubly linked, since Despo's sister, Maria, married George's uncle Socrates.

George's parents presented a striking contrast. Where Stelios was handsome, extrovert, a fervent idealist in both politics and the arts, uncompromising in the demands he made of himself and those close to him, Despo

Tenekidis appears plain, plump, and rather passive-looking in the few photographs that have been preserved. A portrait painted when she was probably in her early thirties, on the other hand, shows not only a strong facial resemblance to all her children, but an obstinate strength of character that each of them, in very different ways, would inherit, or seek to emulate.

Writing on his birthday, six years after her death, George would remember his mother in his diary:

> A saintly woman with a boundless capacity for love. She would love without those effusions of sympathy that ruin everything . . . I can never think of her in a drawing room; I always see her either on the seashore or among the vineyards and the trees.[12]

George's sister, Ioanna, writing half a century later, used equally devotional terms:

> So immediate and heartfelt was her solidarity [with others], so understated as though she was asking forgiveness. She identified herself with whoever was in distress. She was terrified of offending his human dignity, his pride. She knew all the families of the village . . . She regularly did the rounds and visited them. She watched lovingly over the health of their children, their schooling . . .[13]

Despo was deeply religious, with that profound lack of intellectual or moral *angst* that is characteristic of many Orthodox faithful. Ioanna describes her mother's daily devotions before the icons in the family house, as unusually punctilious. Despo's letters to George are full of simple, heartfelt exhortations in which God and His mercy are often invoked, and always heavily underlined. Although it has been little noticed, there is a devotional strand of simple, religious humility which runs through much of George's poetry; it is not unreasonable to see this as the poetic legacy of the self-effacing Despo.[14]

George was not the first child born to Stelios and Despo Seferiadis. The couple had been married for just under two years when, on 16 January 1899, Stelios' father, Prodromos, recorded in the family encyclopaedia: '1 a.m. Birth of a daughter baptised Maria-Ioanna.' Four months later the next entry reads: '7 May death of Maria-Ioanna.'[15]

It is usual in Greek families for children to be baptised with the given name of a grandparent, on the paternal side first, then the maternal. Apart from Despo's younger sister Maria, there is neither a Maria nor a Ioanna recorded on either side of the family. Whatever the reason for the choice of name, Stelios and Despo persevered with 'Ioanna' when their next daughter was born. This was a not uncommon practice in this, and other, families of the time. Ioanna records this family tragedy at the beginning of her memoir, although without mentioning the name of the dead child, and wonders whether this was the hidden reason for a sense of melancholy that the surviving children inherited.[16]

George's conception most likely took place within a month of the death of Maria-Ioanna. His very existence, then, may be seen as testimony to Stelios' implacable determination to fulfil whatever goal he had set himself, a characteristic of his father's which George throughout his life would deeply resent. The encyclopaedia records that Despo gave birth to a son on 'the night of 28 to 29 February, 1900, at 1.30 a.m.' Five weeks later, on 6 April, in the 'Metropolis of the Church of Smyrna,' that is, in the Cathedral of St Photini, the first of the three surviving Seferiadis children was baptised George (Yeoryios in formal Greek, more usually written and pronounced Yorgos). The birth of George is the last entry in the encyclopaedia in the hand of grandfather Prodromos. Against the date 17 June, of the same year, 1900, George's uncle, Michael, has written: 'My good father died. May God grant him rest close by Him.'[17]

George was the only one of the Seferiadis children to be named after a known relative: George (in the diminutive form, Yorgakis) had been the name of Despo's father, who had died in 1886. It may possibly be a reflection either on the relative status of the two families, or on the relations between Stelios and *his* father, that the name chosen for the couple's eldest child should have come from the maternal side, not the paternal. In common with Greek custom, George was also given his father's name, in the genitive case, as his middle name, or patronymic: Stylianou (son of Stylianos, the formal equivalent of Stelios).

Next to be born was Ioanna, in 1902, followed by Angelos, the youngest, in 1905. Close together as they were in age, these three were to remain emotionally close and deeply loyal to one another throughout their lives. George, in 1967, would publish the poems that Angelos had left behind on his premature death, with an introduction which tenderly evokes the brother whose short life seems to have been so needlessly blighted. And Ioanna in turn, in 1973, two years after George's death, would publish her memoir of him, with the proudly possessive title *My Brother George Seferis*. Ioanna's memoir remains the principal witness to George's early years, as well as to her tenacious devotion to him. Ioanna was not only the longest lived of the three (she died in September 2000), but also probably the happiest. The stories of all three Seferiadis siblings are closely interwoven.[18]

### 'The world of the house in the city'

Photographs of George aged two and three (portrait photos, for which the little boy has been over-groomed and over-dressed) show a round face framed by thick dark hair, with incipient curls. His eyes and the set of his face have a sultry look, suggestive in equal measure, perhaps, of awe and resentment – attitudes with which George would often confront the 'world of the house in the city' in later life.

His father, Stelios, had by this time embarked on a career as a barrister, negotiating with success the labyrinthine complexities of both the law and its political ramifications in Ottoman Smyrna. Greek affairs were settled according to Greek national law in the Greek consular court. Affairs involving the Orthodox Church and its very considerable property were decided in an ecclesiastical court, whose basis was the old Byzantine legal system preserved by the Orthodox Patriarchate. There were the Capitulations, according to which citizens of several European states were entitled to pursue claims and be heard according to the legal system of their homeland. There was, of course, Ottoman civil law and the Islamic code, the *sheriat*, either of which might be applied in different circumstances; and there were mixed courts, in which differences across these boundaries might be settled.[19]

In addition to his legal practice, Stelios applied himself vigorously to his hobby, which was literature. In 1902 he won the newly instituted Pan-Ionian Prize, judged in Athens by a formidable triumvirate of judges, for a collection of his poems. A year later he wrote a one-act play, *Mad for Love*, though it is not clear whether this was either performed or published. In 1907, his version of Sophocles' tragedy *Oedipus The King*, translated into demotic Greek (the spoken, informal register of the modern language), was given a warm reception when it was read aloud at his old school, the Evangelical. But when the same translation came to be performed, three years later, at the Sporting Club, an exclusive venue, and also just across the street from the Seferiadis home, it provoked a near-riot. Stelios seems to have been unafraid of controversy; many upstanding Greek citizens and members of the Sporting Club were scandalised at the temerity of a poet who dared to recast the hallowed, but largely incomprehensible, Greek of Sophocles into the 'vulgar tongue' of every day. In Athens, earlier in the same decade, attempts to do the same thing for St Matthew's Gospel and for Aeschylus' trilogy of tragedies, the *Oresteia*, had provoked such violence that several people had been killed.[20]

The public life and career of the professional barrister and amateur poet invited hazards of another kind, too. A probably harmless poem signed by Stelios Seferiadis, published in the New Year's Day edition of the newspaper *Armonia*, in 1906, caused the newspaper to be closed down for forty days: the censors had read into this poem seditious references to the Ottoman capital, Constantinople, and to independent Greece. Although in this case the censor may have been over-zealous, this is not the only evidence that Stelios was known, already by the time George was old enough to go to school, as a prominent supporter of Greek irredentism, and therefore, from the point of view of the Ottoman authorities, of sedition.[21]

On 16 May 1904, the Aronis School celebrated its fiftieth anniversary. This had been Stelios' school for a time; soon George, in his turn, would become a pupil there. After the invited Ottoman dignitaries had departed, the party continued behind closed doors, with Christos Aronis, the owner and headmaster, and some of his distinguished Greek friends paying tribute to the 'patriotic' (that is: Greek) character of the education provided at the school. Stelios and another local amateur poet each recited a poem written for the occasion. Unfortunately, the poems caught the eye of the censor when the proofs of the newspaper *Amaltheia* were passed to him. Midhat Efendi, who had been one of the invited dignitaries, complained to the editor that *he* didn't remember these poems being recited. The affair was smoothed over by the pretence that the poems had been inspired improvisations delivered as the poets were taking their leave of the headmaster, and the school hastily backed up this version of events.[22]

Even at this relatively benign period in the relations between Greeks and Turks in Anatolia, these spirited exhibitions of poetic ingenuity carried real risks for Stelios. Commenting on the situation as it would soon develop, George summed up in retrospect: 'we knew what it meant to be enslaved.' It is perhaps in relation to this background that the veiled political commentary of many of his own later poems should be understood, as well as the extreme caution that surrounded it.[23]

Stelios, according to Ioanna, was a perfect father at this time, spending hours carving model boats for George and improvising heroic tales from history and legend for the three children. But even Ioanna, who adored her father, chooses this point in her memoir to introduce the intolerable pressure that Stelios would bring to bear upon his son, in later years, to excel in his studies. Although she does not say so explicitly, this probably indicates that the pressure had already begun in these early years in Smyrna.[24]

School, for George, began at the age of six. The Aronis School at that time occupied a homely three-storey building with a tiled roof, shutters fastened back from the windows, and a glassed-in balcony, opposite the garden of the French consulate. It was therefore barely a stone's throw from the Seferiadis house on the Parallel.[25]

The Young Turk revolution of 1908 brought about a number of changes to the education system for Ottoman subjects. Up till then, the only schools in which the state had an interest had been Islamic schools. The Young Turks, with their programme for modernising the empire, began to prescribe for secular education as well; in 1909, the teaching of Turkish was made compulsory. When this happened, the headmaster and proprietor of George's school, Christos Aronis, sought and obtained French patronage for his institution. This meant that he and his teachers were answerable not to the Ottoman state, but to the *Mission Laïque Française*. French had already been the second language of the Aronis school. From the start of the 1909–10 session, when George had completed three years there, the school was re-baptised the *Lycée Gréco-Français Chr. N. Aroni*, with a bilingual letterhead. Some subjects could now be studied entirely in French; as well as the Greek national leaving certificate, students could take the Baccalauréat. When the time came for George to transfer to the Gymnasium (or high school) section, in September 1913, he might have been expected to follow in his father's footsteps and go to the more prestigious Evangelical School, but Stelios decided to keep his son where he was. Given the unsettled conditions of the time, and Stelios' own connection with the French consulate, this may have been no more than common prudence. But it may also have been because George had up to this time proved a reluctant and not especially gifted pupil.[26]

George's earliest surviving school report, for 1909, gives his best subjects as Nature Study and French, with a grade of seven on a scale on which ten is the top mark and an average of five or below is a fail, requiring the pupil to repeat the year. Analytical month-by-month reports sent to his father in subsequent years show that from his fourth year in the junior department onwards, George took almost half his subjects in French: including geography, history and writing. In 1912, these monthly reports regularly place George ninth in a class of thirty-five; in May 1913 he came thirteenth in a class of twenty-nine. In June of that year, his last report before entering the Gymnasium (high school) section of the *Lycée* gives his average as 6.5.

13

His best subjects were history (studied in Greek, 8.5) and *Compositions, Versions et Thèmes* (in French, 8). His lowest marks (5) were for mathematics, physics and geography.[27]

When his last junior school examinations were over, qualifying him to enter Gymnasium, George in a symbolic gesture set fire to all his schoolbooks in the courtyard of the house in Smyrna.[28]

French played a formative role in the education of all three Seferiadis siblings. Perhaps from the time when George first went to school, the family had a French governess, a Madame Dubois, who taught him the fables of La Fontaine. Ioanna, always a more natural diplomat than her brother, in her memoir of George's life regularly smooths over points of friction or unpleasantness. Ioanna's account erases the French governess entirely, but not her mother's antipathy to live-in (female) teachers in general. Despo, according to Ioanna, insisted on bringing up her children herself. It is possible that the extrovert and handsome Stelios, a fluent French-speaker, was not to be trusted with the Frenchwoman in the house – or at least that Despo thought so.[29]

George's first extant letter, dated 2 June 1908, when he was eight, is addressed to his father, who had stayed behind in Smyrna while the rest of the family moved out to the country. Blotched and poorly spelt, it is a touching account of the family's arrival there, including attempts to show off with flourishes in formal Greek, and signed with his full name, in the formal register: Yeoryios Stylianou Seferiadis. Before long, George would be writing to his father in French at least as fluent and grammatical as his written Greek.[30]

In September of that year, presumably just before the start of the school year, Stelios was ill in Smyrna and Despo had gone to be with him, leaving the children in the care of a relative or employee called Anna. A letter to Despo, from all three children and Anna, includes George's tender good wishes for his father, in formal Greek: 'With all my heart I will beg God to make my beloved father well soon. Tell him, little mum [*mamaka*], that I am a good and sensible boy and that I am being very diligent [the last word misspelt].' With this letter is another, undated but referring to the same occasion, addressed to Stelios, in which George writes in French. Veering between the intimacy of the singular pronoun *tu*, and the formal *vous*, with a touch of mischief, and partly, no doubt, also to show off his mastery of tenses, the eight-year-old George fires off a barb which conforms uncannily to Freud's theory of the Oedipus complex:

14

Annie is sure that I will be able to take fourth-year lessons and my dear mama is going to lose her husband and *I* will be very happy if she does lose him. And you my dear papa, would *you* be happy?[31]

Since George was about to enter his *third* year of school, the probably sarcastic reference to 'fourth-year lessons' suggests that Stelios was already pushing him academically beyond what he felt was his natural limit. In hindsight this light-hearted, but also precocious letter, which ends in terms of effusive affection, can be read as prophetic of the deepening bitterness between father and son in years to come.

It was not, however, the city of Smyrna to which George for the rest of his life would return in memory, and in writing, with the deep devotion of an adherent meditating on a paradise lost. Indeed he would look back on the city in which he was born and grew up without affection, even with hatred. He only once so much as mentions Smyrna by name in a poem. George, in his imagination and in his deepest allegiance, belonged not to the city where he was born, but to the fishing village some thirty kilometres west along the coast, where he spent his early summers until the age of twelve. This was the present-day Urla Iskelesi, known to the Greeks of a century ago as Skala tou Vourla (Vourla Harbour), or simply: Skala.

## 'The world of the house in the country'

Looking back from the perspective of late 1941, when the German invasion of Greece had displaced him to a second and much more distant exile, George gave life, in words, to the Skala of his memories:

... Skala tou Vourla ... was for me the only place that, even now, I can call home [*patrida*] in the most rooted sense of the word: the place where my childhood years burgeoned.

Smyrna meant school, which was intolerable, rainy Sunday afternoons behind the window-panes: a prison. An incomprehensible world, alien and hateful. Skala was what I loved. When I look back sometimes at those years, there is, I think, no face, no landscape, no corner that I can remember with affection. Skala was an entirely different matter. In the same way as on the stage of the medieval Mystery plays the earth is horizontally marked off from heaven, Skala was a circumscribed region, enclosed; it was like entering a garden from the *Arabian Nights*, where all was joy. There, the people, sailors and villagers, were my own

15

people. The roads, the trees, the shores, were the roads, trees and shores of a country that belonged to me.[32]

In poems from the 1930s to the 1960s, Skala, though never named, is repeatedly invoked as 'the other world' or 'the other life,' an ideal place that once was intimately known but now is beyond reach. In his later travels as a diplomat George returned to Smyrna on three occasions, spending in all something like twenty days there. He would return to Skala just once, for a few hours, in July 1950. Then, he would describe the experience as unrepeatable, and compare it to Odysseus' descent to the underworld.[33]

His sister, Ioanna, too, in her memoir recalls Skala as a 'magical place where we could live in the imagination.' She describes the way the land gently embraced the sea, the shape of the bay and the group of offshore islands that the three Seferiadis children saw as peculiarly their own; in their grandmother's garden was a huge plane-tree, and a well, with its wheel for drawing up water. Depicting the excitement at the beginning of summer when the carriage came to transport the family from Smyrna to Skala, Ioanna, always more extrovert and sentimental than her brother, says outright what George more suggestively implies in so many of his poems and other writings: 'the gates of paradise had opened to us.'[34]

16

In a letter to his English translator, Rex Warner, George would offer a more briskly factual account, in the slightly quaint English of his later years:

the place where my family used to spend the summer holidays in those happy days (a very small village – 100 souls or so) was named Skala; our house was on the sea front. From the windows I could see the islands . . . and the sea which was splendid; on my right hand I had the Island of St John linked with the mainland by a jetty, where we used to walk in the afternoons. It was used for quarantines of the ships going to Smyrna and in times of contagious diseases many ships were anchored off the island; in September Skala was used as port of export for dried raisins produced by the mainland – from the back window of our house one could have a nice view of the vineyards stretching up to the hills of *Vourla* the main town of the neighbourhood (30.000 souls in my time); splendid lads (almost all of them indulging in the hobby of smuggling tobacco) speaking wonderful vernacular greek.[35]

For the rest of his life, George would remember the simple, direct speech of the peasants and fishermen of Skala with affection and admiration; years later, he would credit this 'wonderful vernacular Greek' as the first formative influence on his poetry.[36]

At the time, the young George was probably not much interested in the ancient history of the place. But he could not help being impressed when 'one day . . . villagers working in our vineyard unearthed a whole painted sarcophagus in terracotta.' He would have known already, no doubt, that Skala in ancient times had been the site of Clazomenae, one of the many Greek cities of that coast. Later, he would attach particular significance to this, since the most famous son of ancient Clazomenae had been Anaxagoras, one of the earliest philosophers, the 'Pre-Socratics,' in whose ideas he would find the distant origins of his own modern humanism.[37]

When George returned to Skala in 1950, many of the solid, square stone-built houses that had belonged to his grandmother's family were still standing but in ruins. Half a century later still, surprisingly little has changed today. Urla Iskelesi has been left untouched either by mass tourism or by the uniform developments of holiday homes that have disfigured much of the Turkish Aegean coastline in recent years. The little harbour, with its brightly painted fishing boats, is like any traditional Aegean harbour, Greek or Turkish; a new mole extends well beyond the old white-painted lighthouse that would have marked the limit of the harbour when George, Ioanna and Angelos were children. The island of St John now houses a hospital for infectious diseases, and is still out of bounds to visitors. The group of three smaller islands, further off, still punctuates the seaward horizon, merging into the haze of a still summer day.

Only one building on the harbour front survives, as a ruin. But its covered arcade facing the water is recognisable from photographs of the 1900s of the Seferiadis children messing about in boats. In these, George looks much happier than in the stiffly formal portraits that were no doubt taken in the city. Until the early 1990s, a row of six houses from that period still stood, facing the harbour. It was one of these that George recalled in his letter to Warner; when the summer wind, the *meltemi*, blew it carried the spray against the windows of the upstairs bedroom; waking on autumn mornings, he could tell from the colours in the room whether the sea outside was calm or choppy. The 'little house,' or the 'house at the back,' which George's grandmother bequeathed to him in her will, and on whose outside wall he carved his initials at the age of ten, stands in the street parallel to the harbour-front, at a short distance from the sea. Derelict when George revisited Skala in 1950, it has now been lovingly restored and in 2000 was opened as the Yorgo Seferis guesthouse, with a commemorative plaque to mark the centenary of his birth. Since 1997, the narrow street opposite, that leads towards the sea has borne the name *Yorgo Seferis sokaği.*[38]

Two doors along from the Yorgo Seferis guesthouse is the house, much modified and with its ground floor turned into a bar, in which George's grandmother lived until her death in 1909. The well and its wooden well-head, in the rear garden, though somewhat reconstructed, are recognisable from Ioanna's description from memory, and from George's account of his visit in 1950; but the huge plane-tree, whose benign shadow becomes a potent force in some of the poems of *Mythistorema*, had already gone half a century ago.[39]

The terms of belonging that George uses to describe his relationship to this place, and particularly to the simple people, fishermen and villagers, who lived there, are almost feudal. The same can be said of his grand-mother, Evanthia Michalaki Tenekidou herself, as he later remembered her: 'If sometimes I feel the need to give, I think that I owe it to this patrician lady.' No wonder the young George, spending his summers here until the age of twelve, should have felt that he belonged to this place, and that this place belonged to him.[40]

Although George's strict separation of his childhood into two 'worlds' would find expression only later, it is very likely that behind it lies another, perhaps more fundamental, division, that he may have felt at an instinctive level at this time. Smyrna, the world of school, compromise, and rainy Sundays which he hated, was also his father's world; it must have been in that world that the naturally left-handed George was first forced to hold a pen in his right, as he would do for the rest of his life.[41] Skala, his 'own' world, was a world ruled by women, and particularly by the matriarchal, majestically regal presence of his maternal grandmother. George's powerful need for, and attraction to, women of commanding beauty and strong character began early.

Almost all the early memories that George would record later in life relate to Skala: the silver watch that his grandmother gave him; his first sight of a ship's compass, from an old sailing vessel, that exercised a 'mysterious fascination;' the paddle steamer that plied between Smyrna and Skala, whose Armenian captain was a notorious drunkard.[42]

Perhaps the earliest among these memories is of a family visit to a provincial bishop at Sokia (Söke), about fifty kilometres south of Smyrna and reached by a branch line of the Aydin railway. On this occasion, what stayed in George's memory was the sight of a gang of chained prisoners, in the railway station, pissing against a wall. Given the religious character of this visit (he also remembered the 'steps of the Bishopric'), this was pre-sumably an expedition initiated by his mother. By contrast, George's only recorded memory of the family home in Smyrna, apart from the 'rainy Sunday afternoons,' was of the servants singing passages from *Erotokritos*, the epic love story in verse that had been written in Venetian-ruled Crete at the end of the sixteenth century, and which George would revere all his life. But when he incorporated this memory into a poem, many years later, he would transfer it to the 'old seafarers, bent over their nets,' who belonged to his memories of Skala.[43]

An annual event that George must have witnessed and participated in, at Skala, each year until he was twelve, was the celebration of the birth of St John the Baptist, on 24 June. This was at once a religious festival and the occasion for traditional, secular celebrations to mark the Summer Solstice. The festivities began the evening before, when the Greek quarter of Smyrna and the many of the towns and villages round about must have resembled a traditional English Guy Fawkes Night. Old, unwanted furniture and rubbish were piled up in the open spaces between the houses, each family competing to build the most impressive bonfire. Once the fires had begun to die down, everyone, 'young and old,' was expected to jump over the burning embers, muttering a good-luck charm against bedbugs and lice. This ritual, which has widely dispersed parallels in both the modern and ancient worlds, was believed to have been effective against the plague.

St John's Day itself was marked by two further customs. In the ritual of the *klidonas*, household objects belonging to members of the family were left out overnight in a bowl of water, under the stars. Distantly related, perhaps, to the English custom of ducking for apples, *klidonas* is the name both for the ritual and for the bowl full of objects. When, on 24 June, each object was lifted out in turn, one of the assembled family would improvise a rhyming couplet which was supposed to predict the future of the object's owner, in love or marriage. On the same day (also known as the Day of the *Klidonas*) another custom was to melt pieces of lead and throw them into a bucket of water. Once the sizzling had stopped, the shape in which the lead solidified was supposed to predict for unmarried girls the identity or trade of their future husbands.[44]

These traditional rituals, which in later memory were to form an organic link between his own earliest years and the ancient prehistory of Greek and European civilisation, came to assume a permanent place in George's poetry, from 'Fires of St John,' written in 1932, to 'Summer Solstice' in 1966.

## Shadows of war

Before 1912, there is no evidence that Stelios Seferiadis was professionally involved with the Greek state or its political interests among the Greek population of the Ottoman empire. Stelios' nationalist sentiments were no secret in Smyrna, but nor were they unusual among Ottoman Greeks of his class and background. It was probably not until 1912 that this began to change.[45]

The island of Samos, whose coastline comes close to the Anatolian mainland, some fifty kilometres south of Smyrna, had a largely Greek Orthodox population and had become an autonomous principate within the Ottoman empire as long ago as 1832. In 1908 the 'progressive' (that is Greek nationalist) wing of the island's tiny parliament had sparked a minor revolt against the continued presence of Ottoman troops. In the summer of 1912 the instigator of this revolt, Themistocles Sofoulis, who had had to flee the island, returned clandestinely and began to land volunteers from other Greek islands and Crete. At this time Italy was at war with the Ottoman empire over Italian colonisation in Libya, and had just occupied the Dodecanese islands to the south. Britain, France and Russia, the guarantor powers of Samos' ambivalent status within the Ottoman empire, were anxious to avoid the spread of hostilities, or indeed the premature dismemberment of the empire.[46]

Britain and France each sent a battleship to Samos, to impose a blockade. The three powers tried to contain the situation through their vice-consuls on the island, and their consuls stationed at Smyrna. Stelios Seferiadis seems to have arrived at the start of hostilities, in the company of the Russian consul, around 12 August. The next six weeks saw some heavy fighting, which was won by the Greeks, and the evacuation of the Ottoman garrison under the protection of the British and French ships. It is not clear whether Stelios remained on Samos throughout this time. He was certainly present in the council chamber of the Samiot parliament, along with the Consuls-General of the three powers, who had come from Smyrna for the occasion, on 8 October, when Sofoulis' *fait accompli* was on the one hand given official international recognition, on the other was referred to the final arbitration of the Great Powers in consultation with the Sublime Porte, the Ottoman government in Constantinople. Stelios, on this occasion, is described in one source as the 'legal counsellor of the French consulate in Smyrna.' Since the French Consul-General was the senior of the three, his was the definitive speech, and Stelios acted as interpreter.[47]

The intervention of the powers in the Samos conflict in 1912, in which Stelios Seferiadis for the first time served in an official capacity, was singularly ineffectual. It came too late to prevent Sofoulis from taking over the island for Greece in August and September; the assembly of the consuls on 8 October coincided with the outbreak of the First Balkan War in Macedonia. From then on, local difficulties in Samos were an irrelevance on the geopolitical stage.

From Stelios' point of view, however, this first foray into the arena of international politics had ended with the best possible result. The union of Samos with Greece was proclaimed on 11 November. By this time the forces of the Ottoman empire were in full rout in the Balkans; the Great Powers had given up any attempt to restore the status quo. But Stelios himself had acted as an intermediary, not an instigator, and for all his patriotic sentiments, he had been employed neither by the Greek state nor by the revolutionaries on Samos, but by the French consulate in Smyrna, acting in concert with Great Britain and Russia.

Nevertheless, his involvement with Samos seems to have marked a watershed for Stelios. It was in that year that he gave up his legal practice. At the same time, he published a treatise (in Greek), which questioned the legality of the boycott in international law, implicitly challenging a recent action by the Ottoman government against its Greek subjects. Stelios was also now writing patriotic poems which celebrated the achievements of the Greeks and their Balkan allies in the First Balkan War; it is not clear whether these were published at the time. How he was officially employed during the next year and a half is not certain. It is more than likely that, having come to the attention of the French Consul-General, he continued his association, whether officially or unofficially, with the French consulate in Smyrna.[48]

It was perhaps in this connection that Stelios and Despo spent about a month in Paris, in late September and October of 1913. George addressed a number of postcards and letters to them there. This had been the first summer, as both George and Ioanna would later recall, that the family had not spent at Skala.[49]

What Stelios and Despo were doing in Paris, or which of their numerous family members were looking after the children in Smyrna, is not recorded. Life was more difficult for Christian subjects of the Ottoman empire now than it had been for centuries. Defeat in the First Balkan War in December 1912 had provoked a bloody *coup d'état* in Constantinople at the end of January. These events brought to power in 1913, for the first time in Ottoman history, a government neither ecumenical nor tolerant of diversity, but staunchly Turkish nationalist. This was the government of the Committee for Union and Progress, headed by the triumvirate that would shortly precipitate the empire into the First World War, on the side of the Central Powers: the pashas Enver, Talât and Cemal.[50]

Writing to his mother in October 1913, George complains: 'Here the Turks are against the Greeks and whenever they see a Greek book in any schoolboy's hands they tear it up.' It must have been not long after their parents' return from Paris that an incident occurred that both George and Ioanna would still recall many years later. One evening, there came a knock at the outer door. George went to open it; Angelos and Ioanna, hearing the knocking, came out on the upstairs landing. Uncle Socrates quickly entered the courtyard, with a lady clinging to his arm. The lady was veiled, dressed in black. 'Call your father,' Uncle Socrates told George, and led the lady, who had not so much as greeted him, straight into the dining room. Despo was downstairs too, and adjusted the lady's veil, before turning to the stairs to shoo the younger children out of sight. The next day, they learned that the 'lady' had been a mule-driver in the family's employ, who was wanted by the Ottoman authorities. The fugitive spent the night under the Seferiadis roof, before being dressed as a coalman and smuggled aboard a steamer bound for Piraeus.[51]

It seems there were many such memories. Three fishermen, presumably from Skala, who worked for the family, had been murdered on one of the deserted islands where in earlier years Uncle Socrates had taken the children to picnic in his boat.[52]

It was in this atmosphere that George finished his first year of Gymnasium in June 1914. But this summer, like the previous one, there was no question of the family moving out to the relative isolation of Skala. Stelios Seferiadis, since his high-profile involvement in Samos two years before, seems to have believed that his family was at risk. On 29 June, the Archduke Ferdinand, heir to the throne of the Austro-Hungarian empire, was assassinated by Serbian nationalists in Sarajevo. Just over a month later, on 4 August, war was declared between the Triple Entente, consisting of Great Britain, France and Russia, and the Central Powers (Germany and Austria-Hungary).

At this point neither Greece nor the Ottoman empire was involved; nationalist tensions in the empire had been rising steadily since late 1912, but the start of the First World War in Europe did not immediately affect the already deteriorating relations between Greek Christians and Muslim

22

Turks. Stelios, that August, may have foreseen the entry of the Ottoman empire into the war on the side of the Central Powers, although this was not seen as inevitable in the capitals of Europe until September.

Whatever the precise reason, 'within a week' of war being declared on 4 August, the Seferiadis home behind the Sporting Club was closed up indefinitely. None of the family could have any idea of when, or even whether, they might return to the home in which the children had been born. It seems that Stelios, the ambitious lawyer just turned forty, saw the move as definitive, a new beginning. Despo, more deeply rooted in her family, their connections, and land, would cling tenaciously to these things as, in different ways, did the children, ever afterwards. That August, the whole family embarked for Piraeus, and the Greek capital, Athens.[53]

### Home from home

While elsewhere in Europe the nations marched to war, in the autumn of 1914 the Seferiadis family settled into a first-floor flat overlooking the corner of the Pedion Areos (Field of Mars), at 10 Kodringtonos (Codrington) Street, Athens. Many streetnames in this part of Athens commemorate distinguished foreigners who were once of service to the nation. Admiral Sir Edward Codrington (1770–1851) had been in command of the allied fleet in 1827 at the battle of Navarino, the decisive engagement that ensured the establishment of an independent Greek state. Today Kodringtonos Street is lined with five- and six-storey apartment blocks in post-war concrete and glass. The Seferiadis family apartment would have been housed in a detached villa of two or three storeys, with a stucco front and some ornamental plaster-work, roofed with orange tiles, perhaps with a fringe of tiles moulded like acanthus leaves, in imitation of classical buildings. Several such houses, many of them in a depressing state of repair, can still be seen in the neighbourhood.

23

George was enrolled that autumn at the Model High School (*Protypon Gymnasion*), a tram ride away in Eleftherias Square, just off Piraeus Street below the Acropolis. Ioanna started at a private girls' school at the lower end of Akadimias Street; Angelos in the junior department of George's school. A photograph of the three, taken at this time, shows George wide-eyed and serious, wearing collar and tie and the square-cut suit he probably wore to school. Ioanna, hair cut short, is already a beauty with a mischievous air of knowing it. Angelos in a sailor-suit, looking askance away from the camera, facially resembles his sister more than his brother, but seems touchingly vulnerable, lacking their self-assurance.[54]

The headmaster of the Model High School, Dimitrios Goudis, was by all accounts a charismatic teacher with idiosyncratic educational ideas. One of these was to publish a series of booklets containing his pupils' compositions; as a result, George's first published work saw the light of day when he was only fifteen. The booklet containing the summer examination essays of Goudis' second-year pupils is dated 1915, and carries, in pride of place, George's essay on the topic, 'First Day of Vacation.' The language is the formal Greek of the time (*katharevousa*). The piece is lushly written and sprinkled with classical allusions of the sort that were doubtless encouraged at the Model High School. George's first foray into print is a dutiful, somewhat forced exercise: white sails billowing 'from the mighty breath of Aeolus' are compared to seagulls' wings 'striking the ethereal foam of the pure-white waves.'[55]

In later life, George would be as reticent about his schooldays in Athens as about his 'intolerable' school in Smyrna. In his geometry exercise book from his first year at the Model High School, he copied out the dictum, in ancient Greek, which Plato had placed above the gate of his Academy in the fourth century BC: 'let no one ignorant of Geometry enter here.' Below this appears a piece of rhyming doggerel which, if it is original, must be George's earliest surviving verse:

> Archimedes said
> and so did Euclid:
> geometry in plane
> is somewhat plain.[56]

Other things that he learned had a more lasting impact. During his final year with Goudis, George read Sophocles' tragedy *Antigone* in the original ancient Greek, in a depth that was probably rare in Greek high-school education at this time. Other ancient texts which he read, during these years, for the first of many times, were the *Apology of Socrates* by Plato and several books of Homer's *Iliad.* He also read Latin literature (Ovid and Cicero). Although he would have studied Latin to a high standard – a requirement for lawyers in Greece, since Greek law derives, via the French *Code Napoléon*, from Roman law – George does not seem to have studied Latin literature in the original at school.[57]

It was probably also at school that he first read the Greek poets of the age of Romanticism, and also of the national struggle for independence, Dionysios Solomos and Andreas Kalvos. It is not clear what other poetry he would have read in the modern form of his own language. It was almost certainly during his high-school years that George read all of Victor Hugo, and he was also intimate, by the time he was sixteen, with the poetry of Lamartine and Rostand. By this time, too, he must already have made the acquaintance of his beloved *Odyssey* of Homer and the medieval Arabic collection of tales, the *Thousand and One Nights*, the two books above all others to which he returned again and again throughout his life.[58]

In Athens, the Seferiadis family was largely cut off from its extensive network of family and friends in Anatolia. For the first time in their married life, Stelios and Despo had to rely on his income alone for the upkeep of the family, since wartime conditions in the Ottoman empire made it impossible for them to draw on the substantial assets of the Tenekidis.[59]

Stelios now set about establishing himself in his new surroundings with his customary vigour. Since his involvement in Samos in 1912, he had become well enough known to those with the power of patronage in his profession to be elected unanimously to a chair of International Law at the National and Capodistrian University of Athens, at that time the only university in Greece. Political patronage carried risks, however; and in free Greece Stelios was as unprepared to compromise his principles as he had been back in Smyrna.

25

In the autumn of 1915 the prime minister, Eleftherios Venizelos, was effectively sacked by King Constantine. Venizelos saw the balance of advantage for Greece in entering the war on the side of the Entente; Constantine, whose pro-German sympathies were probably exaggerated by his opponents, stuck out, in the face of intense British and French pressure, for strict neutrality. This was the beginning of the National Schism, which during one world war brought Greece to the brink of civil conflict, sowing the seeds of the actual civil war that would break out during the second.

Stelios, like most Greeks from the Ottoman empire living in Greece, identified strongly with Venizelos. It was unthinkable for Greece to enter into the world war on the same side as the traditional enemy, the Ottoman empire; and so effective was Venizelist propaganda that Venizelists for years afterwards continued to believe that this, rather than his declared policy of neutrality, had been the intention of the king. Venizelos stood for continuation of the successful war of 1912, that had brought huge territorial gains for Greece in the north and in the Aegean. By committing early to the Entente, Greece would be able to capitalise on an Ottoman defeat, to realise its century-old ambition of liberating the remaining Greek Orthodox population of the Ottoman empire.

Committed to these principles, and to the bestowers of patronage who shared them, Stelios Seferiadis was electable to a university chair so long as Venizelos held power. The university term would have started in October. On 22 September (Old Style), Venizelos was forced by the king to resign.[60] Stelios' appointment was not ratified by the Ministry of Education (as all university appointments in Greece have to be, to this day). Another four years would pass before Stelios would take up the post to which he had been elected in 1915. Two months later he left Greece and the family for which he now had an urgent need to provide, to establish himself in private legal practice in Paris.[61]

Stelios must have arrived there at the beginning of December, because on the 11th of that month he wrote a touching but stern response to George's first letter since his departure:

> I want you to come first, first in everything. Be careful that in whatever you do, whatever you study, whatever you write and whatever you say, always think it over twice.[62]

26

A year and a half later, in July 1917, Stelios would be more demanding still:

> Superfluous to say and to commend to you that, during this time when we are far apart, *you* are the head of our family. *You* must give everyone courage, as well as setting a good example, and give every possible support.[63]

George may have found his father uncomfortable to live with, but there is no doubt that all the family missed Stelios greatly. Whatever their internal stresses, the Seferiadis family up till this time gives every appearance of having been extremely close. After December 1915, except for short periods, and despite heroic efforts, the family would never be united again.

A more congenial surrogate for the absent Stelios appeared in George's life, in the form of Nikos Aronis. A friend of the family from Smyrna, Nikos was the son of George's old headmaster, Christos Aronis; in 1915 he was in Athens, in his second year of a law degree at the University. Aronis was five years older than George, although he survived him by many years to publish his reminiscences of their friendship, which during George's high school and university years had been close. Aronis remembered George from his father's school in Smyrna, but their friendship began in Athens, when Nikos moved into the Seferiadis household and for a time even shared a room with George. Ioanna had her own reasons for all but writing Aronis out of her memoir of her brother's early years; but even she concedes that at this point he was George's best friend.[64]

With Aronis and his friends, George soon began going to concerts and the theatre. Together they attended evening lectures at the University on such subjects as Greek poetry, ancient and modern, archaeology and folk-lore, and went to hear Kostis Palamas, the doyen of Greek poets, then in his prime, lecture at the Parnassus society. On the day after Epiphany, 7 January (Old Style) 1916, the Seferiadis children performed a play before Despo and several distinguished neighbours. *The Failed Emancipation*, according to the hand-written programme, was a 'satire' by N. Aronis; the leading lady was a schoolfriend of Ioanna's, Melpo Stai, who was about to become George's first love and the object of his first poems.[65]

In a note dated 1918, George wrote, 'My first verse was a tear for my first love.' His infatuation with Melpo followed a pattern to be repeated in later, more serious affairs. He addressed her by a nickname which was a variant of her given name: the grammatically irregular 'Melpa.' He wrote poems addressed to her or inspired by his feelings for her. The moment of truth came that summer: Ioanna recalls creeping up the back stairs to eavesdrop on George's solemn declaration of love in the form of a poem. Melpo rebuffed him, and George decamped in dudgeon to forget his sorrows, with Aronis and another friend, on the island of Aegina.[66]

There, during August, with these friends George had an 'unforgettable' time, picking up girls on the harbour front and improvising verses in their honour. He wrote affectionately to his mother in time for her nameday (15 August). A week later he wrote again, this time trying to persuade Despo to allow Ioanna and Angelos to come to Aegina as well, but this she would not allow. It is possible that either this summer or the next, when George was again on Aegina with Aronis, he may have worked off his bitterness and frustration at Melpo's rejection by accompanying his older friend to a brothel.[67]

'I belong to the generation of the [National] Schism,' George would write many years later. 'That crisis is engraved on my flesh.' On 22 September 1916, not long after George and his friends had returned from Aegina, the ousted premier Venizelos set up a provisional, pro-Entente government in

Greece's second city, Thessaloniki. Greece now had two governments, one in Athens loyal to the king, the other in Thessaloniki loyal to Venizelos. The British and French delivered a humiliating joint ultimatum to the government in Athens, demanding disarmament and a complete diplomatic break with the Central Powers. This the royalist government refused, and an economic blockade of Piraeus began in November. For the next few months, conditions at home must have been grim for Despo, with Stelios out of reach in Paris and with a family to feed.[68]

To make matters worse, on Friday 18 November fighting broke out in the streets of Athens. The supporters of Venizelos clashed with troops and police loyal to the king, in the so-called *Noemvriana*, or November Events. George was 'reminded astonishingly of the behaviour of the Turks back in Smyrna.' He and Aronis, at the risk of their lives, as Aronis recalled almost seventy years later, would run the gauntlet of the snipers on the rooftops, and the animosity of the royalist crowds, to buy what vegetables they could find, to supply the household.[69]

A month later, on 13 December, a huge crowd gathered in the Field of Mars, for the public excommunication of Venizelos by the Archbishop of Athens and All Greece, Theoklitos. With Aronis, George watched from a window along the route, as the crowds poured through the streets, priests and clergy at their head, all carrying stones to hurl at Venizelos' effigy. George's family was staunchly Venizelist, though he himself, he later insisted, was 'not fanatical,' and added, 'I am a man of dialogue, not of the raised fist.' What shocked him then, and left its mark on him throughout his life, was the vicious fanaticism that had been on display that November in Athens; he never forgot the demands that had been published in the press, that 'Venizelists should be forbidden to walk on the pavements . . . or that it was not proper for priests to baptise the children of Venizelists.'[70]

The November Events baptised George in the turbulent waters of internal Greek politics. Thereafter, try as he might, he would never regain the state of political innocence that he would always associate with Skala – not even in his last years, after he had retired from the diplomatic service. In Athens, whether or not George was ready to realise this yet, he had found his second home, the one to which he would always afterwards return.

### Into exile

George graduated from the Model High School in May 1917; he had attained the solidly respectable average of 8.35. He wrote to his father that he was frankly happy: 'like a tree being pruned,' he would never again have to study mathematics, logic, history. Unlike a tree, though, he added gloomily, he did not expect to blossom.[71]

The following month, the endgame between Venizelos and King Constantine was played out. The king went into exile and Venizelos, prime minister of a reunited Greece, now committed Greece officially to the First World War on the side of the Entente. The likelihood that Stelios would soon be able to earn his living in Athens had never been greater. It is the more surprising, therefore, to find him writing irritably to Despo, in August: why does she still delay in bringing herself and the children to Paris? Is it because Ioanna is unwell? Ioanna had had pleurisy, though she herself remembered this as being in 1915. Ioanna must eat as much as her mother, the letter continues. He, Stelios, has sent them money. The letter ends: 'Kiss the children for me with much much love and thousands of kisses. Stelios.' There is no greeting for Despo herself.[72]

Stelios probably knew Venizelos personally before this. A few months later, he was photographed among the prime minister's entourage on the steps of the Greek embassy in Paris. At the start of the new year, 1918, Stelios was writing to George again, apologising for disappointing him in not coming to Greece with Venizelos; he had, he explained, large financial affairs in hand. At this point Stelios seems to have been expecting to return soon to Greece and his family; there is no further mention of them joining him in Paris.[73]

Ioanna elides this curious hiatus in the life of the family. She says that George was enrolled at the Law School of Athens University, but was pre-empted by his father, who summoned them all to Paris instead. She paints an all-too-believable picture of her mother's sleepless nights before embarking on this journey, with three children, during a world war which few then realised would be over a few months later. What Ioanna does not say is that this state of indecision lasted for at least a year. Nor does Ioanna, or anyone else, explain what it was that finally persuaded Despo to brave the mines and enemy submarines in the Mediterranean, to sell up everything in Athens at the beginning of June 1918, and take the family to join Stelios in Paris after all.[74]

It is clear from his letters that Stelios loved his children dearly. His absence in Paris was due to his determination to provide for his family, not to evade his obligations to them. The tone of his letter to Despo in August 1917 suggests that this mad dash across a continent in wartime may have been seen by both husband and wife as a last-ditch attempt to salvage, if not their feelings for one another, then at least their family life. The cause

29

of the breakdown of the Seferiadis marriage is not known, and Stelios and Despo would never formally separate. But it became clear before long that even this desperate remedy was doomed.

If George did enrol at Athens University for the session after he left high school, there is no record of his ever having attended classes there. Indeed, the period of George's life from the end of August 1917, when the whole family returned to Athens after spending a month with Nikos Aronis in Aegina, and the following June when the exodus for Paris took place, is almost a complete blank.[75]

The press cuttings that he preserved from this period suggest that George was caught up in his father's enthusiasm for Venizelos' internal triumph and the progress of the war in Europe. An unusual rapport between father and son, no doubt aided, in part at least, by prolonged separation, came about in April 1918: Stelios sent his son a ballad on his nameday, and George sent a verse reply in what is probably a dutiful, rather than mischievous, pastiche of his father's somewhat conventional style. It is the only recorded occasion on which father and son ever conversed as poets.[76]

The decision finally taken, Despo relinquished the apartment in Kodringtonos Street, in June 1918, and the family set out to cross war-torn Europe. The ship that took them as far as Corfu was called the *King Constantine*; there, they had to wait for an Italian ship that would take civilians across to the nearest Italian port of Gallipoli. The captain would not allow them to go below because of the risk of submarine attack. From Gallipoli they travelled, via Rome, on crowded trains that were packed with troops. On 21 June they crossed into France. George regaled Aronis with several details of this journey, including his resort to schoolboy Latin in order to persuade an Italian priest to open the train window. At their first stop in the French Alps, at the spa town of Aix-les-Bains, some five hundred kilometres short of their destination, a letter awaited them from Stelios: Paris was under bombardment by the Germans, it was unsafe for them to proceed any further. Stelios wrote that he would come and fetch them.

It is not clear how this latest hiatus was resolved. On the national holiday of 14 July, while German shells were still falling in the centre of Paris, in a luxury apartment close to the Etoile, at 34 avenue Wagram, the family was at last reunited.[77]

# 2
# A Student in Paris
# 1918–1925

Day dawns, evening comes, we sleep, we wake up, we wait with
longing for tomorrow, we're disgusted with yesterday, we're
running, running, out of breath and we never arrive anywhere and
we return back and run all over again, and all the time we're
waiting, without ever arriving...

(Pocket-diary: Paris, 29 January 1920)[1]

### The family divided

The apartment in avenue Wagram was spacious and luxuriously furnished
in period style. Stelios had apparently been able to rent it for a song,
since everyone who could had abandoned Paris because of the German
bombardment. Later, George recalled those first summer months in the
strange city as being like:

> a Charlie Chaplin stage-set... It was the age of the first jazz. I was buying
> hazelnuts from a barrow when I saw one of those shells burst, at the far
> end of a boulevard.[2]

Ioanna, in her memoir, relates how the three children would gather after
supper in George's room, where he would read to them Greek and French
poetry, and sometimes his own. During these first months, while waiting
to enrol and start classes in Law at the Sorbonne, George seems suddenly
to have revelled in his vocation as a poet. Before this, there is no evidence
that he had written any poetry at all, apart from his formal reply to his
father's nameday ballad, between the year of his infatuation with Melpo,
1916, and the family's arrival in Paris. Even the press cuttings that he
preserved, from 1916 to 1918, are exclusively to do with politics and the
progress of the war. It was only from this summer onwards that he began
to cut out and mark items from the newspapers on literary topics.[3]

As early as July and the family's first days in Paris, George began with
translations. He chose Edmond Rostand, best known today as the creator of

Cyrano de Bergerac. The style of these first translations of poems by Rostand, into rhyming Greek, is not very different from that of Stelios, who had himself published translations from French poetry. However, these are not merely translations. The heroine of a ballad from *Musardises* is transposed to become 'renowned in Skala;' the narrator takes the road to Vourla; the heroine is contrasted to the 'ladies of Smyrna' and is herself translated into the landscape of George's childhood as 'Margaroula.' Homesickness is written into the heart of this engagement with a new life and a foreign language.[4]

But he was not content with translating. His first published poem, that appeared in a Greek magazine in Paris three and a half years later and never again during George's lifetime, must have been written during the first flush of his discovery of Paris and of a vocation. Entitled 'Sonnet,' and faithful to that form, the poem is signed, with evident nostalgia, 'Yorgos Skaliotis': George from Skala. Homesickness is present here, too, and takes a darker form; in the poem's bitter final line, even the 'kiss of love' is charged with death.[5]

The unreal feeling of those first months did not last long. By the end of August, the bombardment was over, the Germans about to retreat; with the end of the war in sight, Paris began to become a real city, full of people. In September, George was still writing furiously: a short story and at least two poems have been preserved from that time. But the darker tone that was already emerging in 'Sonnet' now takes over. The longer of the poems is entitled 'Last Words of Someone Who Committed Suicide.' The manuscript is prefaced by a short note to his sister:

> *Beboula* [his nickname for Ioanna], I'm sending you this because you asked me to, it's done in an evening and needs a lot of corrections that I haven't the heart to make now.[6]

The other poem is a wistful reminiscence of an unfulfilled love. Preserved along with it are drafts of an embarrassingly sentimental letter addressed to an unknown woman, whose name he did not even know. This, too, was quite possibly a literary exercise.[7]

That same month, September 1918, George wrote to his friend Aronis, who was working in the Government Ration Department in Thessaloniki:

> I weep – why? I don't know why, because I've got some evil demon inside me that pushes me towards the heights, towards the azure heaven,

32

towards the air, towards love, yes love . . . [But] fate is unkind, I have to study, to bury my life in frozen books that await me: deaf to music, blind to poetry, scholastic in love. Ten days ago I decided to suffocate the poetry I have inside me so as to get it out of my system. My poetry is a form of conscience that beats me without mercy. I suppose I'll stop going even to the theatre, because when I see something good, it gets me by the throat because I'm envious, I'm envious and [that makes me] afraid.

Attached to the fragment of this letter is preserved an empty paper file with the superscription: '1918 September. From today I bury my poetry in here,' and an indication that this resolution may have lasted until June 1920.[8]

Within three months of coming to Paris and affirming his vocation, something had gone badly wrong. No doubt, as this letter indicates, George was under pressure from his father, as he had been since his schooldays in Smyrna, to direct his energies towards academic work and his future career. But his first term at the Sorbonne would not begin until November. Evidently he was dreading the prospect. But the signs of growing depression in the fragmentary writings of that September may have deeper roots.

Ioanna's memoir characteristically elides unpleasantnesses, especially within the family. But even she, writing of the siblings' summer evenings spent reading together, adds, without comment: 'Those were our good moments.' On what happened next, Ioanna is uncharacteristically clipped, and offers no explanation:

33

In the autumn of '18, George rented a student room near the Sorbonne. Angelos carried on [reading and writing] Greek with Mother, so as not to fall behind. I was despatched as a boarder to a French boarding school at Auteuil. The family was dispersed.

George moved out of the family home in November, presumably at the start of the University term; he later remembered his first winter, in an unheated room in a boarding house in the Latin Quarter, as the coldest and most alienating time he had ever experienced. This drastic reversal of expectations, suddenly carried through, fits into a pattern and bears mostly the signature of Stelios. In her telescoped, and on some points inaccurate, account of that winter and the following spring, Ioanna makes no mention of family life.[9]

It is clear, though, from letters that she wrote to George at the time, that the relationship between Stelios and Despo had reached breaking point that autumn; the chilling phrase 'the family was dispersed' is to be undestood literally. By early November 1918, Stelios was writing to George to give him a temporary address in Bordeaux. This unexplained, and almost certainly only brief, absence from Paris marks the first of an indefatigable series of travels, on public and private business, that would become the punishing rhythm of Stelios' life for many years to come; it would not be long before the strain would begin to take its toll on Despo's health.[10]

George's bitterness against the pressures exerted by his father, and the polarisation in his mind between his studies and his vocation, as it emerges in the letter to Aronis, could only have been exacerbated by the disintegration of his parents' marriage. The world of Skala had always been the world of his mother's family; the 'world of the house in the city' had been his father's. It was perhaps now that the separation of these two worlds became an article of faith for him. For the time being, with his poetry 'buried' and his first term as a law student about to begin, it was Stelios' world of the city that was in the ascendant.

The end of the world war was now approaching. In Macedonia, in Mesopotamia, and now on the Western Front, Entente forces had begun to break through. First to sign an armistice was the Ottoman empire, on 30 October; Austria and Germany followed on 11 November. Soon the leaders of the victorious nations would gather in Paris, to determine the shape of a new Europe, in which nation-states would take over from the defeated empires.

On the day of the armistice in Europe, the Paris-based Greek newspaper *Neos Kosmos* (*Le Nouveau Monde*) carried the announcement of a new ministry that Venizelos was setting up in the Greek government. The Ministry for Unredeemed Greeks was clearly designed to prosecute Greece's long-cherished claims in the east. Secretary to the Ministry, the newspaper announced, was Stelios Seferiadis. At about the same time, or a little later, Stelios' appointment to the University of Athens, that had been blocked on Venizelos' departure from office in 1915, was announced. During the first months of 1919, Stelios would be thrust into the political limelight; while Venizelos cut a charismatic figure at the Paris Peace Conference, the hardworking, and staunchly irredentist Stelios Seferiadis would be never far from his side.[11]

Alone in his freezing boarding-house room, during the first months of 1919 George subjected himself and his life to a searing scrutiny. He was tormented by homesickness; this seems not to have been specifically for Skala but rather for the familiar Aegean world, that included Skala, Aegina, and even Athens. 'It hurts me to think . . . of the glances and fair hair of

Greece,' he wrote to Aronis, but then impatiently scored through what he had written. In another letter, he compared himself scathingly to his friend:

you've managed to achieve something in your life, you've struggled and come out on top, while I from the time I left school haven't managed to do anything, for the time being I'm a round, round zero.[12]

George was surely unreasonably hard on himself here: Aronis was five years older, a graduate in his first job. But George went on to insist that, if he were to meet Aronis again in Greece in the summer, he would first have to have proved himself worthy in some way.

Before that could happen, two events would intervene, to change irrevocably the pattern of life both for the Seferiadis family, and for their native city of Smyrna.

One morning that spring, Ioanna was surprised to find George waiting for her in the school quadrangle:

'What's the matter? What are you doing here?'
'Mother's had a slight cerebral stroke. Don't worry, she's better. But you'll have to stay and be with her. We can't leave Angelos [with her] on his own.'

This was the beginning of the terminal decline of their mother's health; it also set its seal on the break-up of the family in Paris. As soon as she was well enough to travel, Despo took Ioanna out of school and left with the two younger children, by train and ship for Athens. In his pocket-diary against the date 2 May 1919, George noted: 'This evening my mother, my sister and my brother left for Greece. Will I ever see them again?[13]

During those first days of May, matters were coming rapidly to a head over the future of Smyrna. At the Peace Conference, Italy had been pressing territorial claims in south-western Anatolia. Now, in a unilateral action, Italian troops began landing on the south Anatolian coast, at Antalya. To counter this development, the prime ministers of Britain and France, Lloyd George and Clemenceau, and President Wilson of America authorised the landing of Greek troops to secure Smyrna and its hinterland against the Italians. On Friday 15 May, a Greek occupying force disembarked at the harbour of Smyrna. Here, at last, was vindication for Venizelos' costly strategy of joining with the Entente against the Ottoman empire. Although the occupation of Smyrna was technically little more than a policing operation, to pre-empt Italian expansion in the region, it was hailed by Greeks

everywhere, and most vociferously by supporters of Venizelos, as the beginning of the realisation of the 'Great Idea,' to 'redeem' the Greek population of the Ottoman empire for the Greek state.[14]

Two days after the historic landings in Smyrna, George wrote excitedly
to Despo:

> Maybe I'll manage it, I'll come to Skala and we'll celebrate the Feast of
> the Assumption [15 August]. . . . You'll have heard the most welcome
> news. Our Smyrna has been liberated. Let's hope she'll remain defini-
> tively liberated. . . . Venizelos is over the moon, he embraced and kissed
> Dad. Dad came and told me last evening. I was sleeping, it was as though
> I saw it in my sleep.[15]

This letter was addressed to Athens. By the time it arrived there, Despo
and the children had already left. They reached Smyrna before the end of
the month, hard on the heels of the Greek troops.[16]

### Left Bank blues

Three days after his family left Paris for Smyrna, George noted in his diary:
'I'm mad. I'm in love with her without knowing it. I scattered daisies in
my room.' She was Suzon, the daughter of his landlady, Mme Clauzel.
Ioanna, with understandable indignation, described Suzon many years later,
as 'beautiful, blonde, older than him, grasping . . . the type of cunning
woman who will offer the minimum necessary to suck a man dry.' It was
not until the summer of 1920 that George would confide fully in Ioanna,
but when he did, she concluded that Suzon's treatment of him had been
nothing short of 'criminal.'[17]

The type of the older woman, the beauty, the woman of strong character, is one that would continue to haunt George's adult life. And it must be
said that it was only this once, when his spirits and his fortunes were at
their lowest ebb, that he came to grief. But with Suzon he came to grief
badly. Something of the extreme touchiness with which he conducted his
later affairs with women may well have been the consequence of the total
humiliation he experienced, at the age of nineteen, at the hands of Suzon.

George's infatuation was complicated by the existence of 'another.' Suzon
seems to have taunted him with her feelings for this other man. George
took this seriously, and brooded about his rival. On the other hand, Ioanna
knew, or thought she knew, all the dramatis personae of this unhappy melo-
drama. The 'other' was a fellow-Greek, a boarder at Mme Clauzel's who

36

had since returned to Athens, where Ioanna could soon report on his activities. Brother and sister had evidently known Suzon's former lover in Paris, and in their letters refer to him as something of a figure of fun. Later in life, George would have professional dealings with his old rival from Paris; there is no evidence that he bore him any lasting animosity.[18]

It took George less than a fortnight to recognise what surely was the truth about Suzon: 'She doesn't love me. Perhaps she's even stringing me along.' A month later, shortly before the middle of June, the relationship reached a crisis: 'I've fallen, I've rolled I've plunged in the mire[;] perhaps the fault was not all mine. I had the love, she the instinct. It's all over now.' But of course it was not all over, although the pocket-diary is a blank for several months after this. At the beginning of August he was writing to Ioanna, who by this time was back in the familiar house at Skala, with Angelos and their mother, to say he wished he could come and join them: 'I swear to you it's not by my own choice that I'm staying in Paris.'[19]

Ioanna, in her memoir, remarks sadly that George never did confide to her his reason for staying in Paris that summer. Partly, no doubt, it had to do with Suzon; he seems also to have been short of money, and Ioanna implies that Suzon had a greedy eye for her lover's purse-strings. Perhaps, too, the strict conditions George had set himself, in his letter to Aronis earlier in the year, may have played a greater part than any of his family knew.

Meanwhile, Ioanna, her mother and Angelos had spent the first part of the summer in Smyrna, staying at Uncle Socrates' house on the Quay. It was not until August that the house at Skala was ready for them. In September, Stelios arrived in Smyrna, on his way to take up his appointment at the University of Athens. The family was now re-united, all except George; soon they would move back together to Athens. But the marital truce was precarious. Within a week of Stelios' arrival in Smyrna, Ioanna reported to George that their parents had begun quarrelling again. She had other news for him too: Nikos Aronis was in town; there was a rumour, she coyly added, that she and Nikos were now unofficially engaged. Melpo, George's first love, was in Smyrna too, now a charming young lady. But nothing could fill the aching gap in Ioanna's thoughts, since George himself still had not come. At the end of September, she wrote to him a melancholy letter: sitting alone in the 'little house' at Skala, that had belonged to George since his grandmother's death, she had been reading and re-reading his poem about suicide, and feeling lonely and desolate without him.[20]

To these letters from his sister, George replied with an air of melancholy bravado. He could not, he assured her, conceive even a line of poetry. But before long he was sending her a comic ballad making light of his travails with Suzon, and a translation (from French) of Keats's poem 'La Belle Dame Sans Merci,' no doubt chosen for its subject matter. As autumn turned into winter, matters went from bad to worse. Since Stelios had left Paris in September, George now, for the first time, had no member of his family near him. In November it snowed heavily; he was suffering badly from the cold. He could not afford the price of a heated room, he wrote to his mother; in December he bought an electric radiator. There was friction with other boarders; some were Italian or took Italy's side over the race to occupy Anatolia. Just after New Year, he confided that he had had a terrible row with his landlady.[21]

What had happened was this. On the day when he had written to his mother that he could not afford to change his lodgings, George had made up his mind that he would do exactly that: so as to get away from 'her.' After three days tramping round the Latin Quarter 'with a heavy heart,' he found a suitable place and put down a deposit. He then broke the news to Mme Clauzel that he would be leaving. Suzon had hysterics. George spent that night walking the streets, unable to make up his mind. At midday the next day, he went back to the *pension* he had found and cancelled the rent he had just agreed, forfeiting fifty francs of his deposit. The entry in his pocket-diary for the day after that reads only, 'We made up.'

But Suzon, having won the battle of wills, proceeded to humiliate her lover as never before. The entries for the following days record some of her insults verbatim; the most wounding was surely: 'Only a Greek could treat me so disgustingly.'[22]

New Year, 1920, found George in the depths of misery and self-loathing. He was ashamed of his inability to change his life, and of his lack of progress in his studies. He several times expressed a visceral disgust with life itself, in the form of women and blood. His pocket-diary for 1920 contains entries only up to the first days of February. Although Suzon continued to exercise some hold on his affections during the next two years, and he did not make the break from Mme Clauzel's boarding house until the end of the academic year, it seems that the acute phase of the crisis was now over.[23]

The summer before, George had passed his first-year Law examinations without distinction, though with some promise of better things, as one of his professors confided to Stelios. At the beginning of July 1920, he took the examinations for the second year; again his grades were only middling.[24]

By this time, Stelios was back in Paris, once again accompanying the Greek prime minister, Venizelos. Just over a year after the Treaty of Versailles had laid down the terms of peace between the victorious powers and defeated Germany and Austria, a new treaty was being negotiated among the victors that would lay down similar terms of peace for the Ottoman empire. The Treaty of Sèvres, signed on 10 August 1920, was both a personal triumph for Venizelos and the fulfilment of a substantial part of the irredentist aspirations that had dominated Greek political life for almost a century. In the distribution of former Ottoman territories, France, Italy and Greece were each given control of large regions. The straits of the Bosphorus and the Dardanelles, together with Constantinople, the Ottoman capital, were to be part of an internationally controlled zone. Greece would consolidate the gain, already made the previous year, of Smyrna and the surrounding *vilayet* of Aydin, subject to a plebiscite to be held in 1925, and would also gain the eastern part of Thrace.[25]

The town of Sèvres, just outside Paris, is home to the porcelain that bears its name. To commemorate the signing of the Treaty, a set of picture post-cards from the museum was printed. Stelios addressed three of these to George, each with the hastily scribbled legend: *Sèvres 10 Août 1920*, and his signature. At this point Despo and Ioanna were also back in Paris, having travelled separately from Stelios; George now took the opportunity to disengage himself from Mme Clauzel's boarding house and Suzon, and moved into the small apartment he had found for his mother and sister for the summer. According to Ioanna, who may have been confusing this with a moment during the deliberations at Versailles the previous year, Stelios summoned the whole family to watch the officials leaving. George standing pale and proud, said to her, 'in there, they're setting the seal on our humanity.'[26]

Two days after the signing of the treaty at Sèvres, Stelios accompanied Venizelos to the Gare de Lyon in Paris. As Venizelos was about to board his train, on the first leg of his return journey to Greece, two Greek ex-army officers approached, drew handguns, and fired several shots. The prime minister, according to one account, 'collapsed, covered in blood, into the arms of . . . Stelios Seferiadis.' Venizelos was not seriously hurt, but the attempt on his life, on 12 August 1920, would provoke a violent backlash, with far-reaching consequences.[27]

In Athens, Venizelists went on the rampage that summer and autumn. At the height of the disturbances, a leading opponent of Venizelos, the charismatic nationalist ideologue, novelist and diarist, Ion Dragoumis, was murdered by members of the security forces in the outskirts of Athens. Then on 25 October the death of the young King Alexander, the result of a freak accident, would pave the way for his father Constantine, exiled since his earlier débâcle with Venizelos, to lay claim to the throne he had lost three years before. The parliamentary election, that Venizelos had already called for 14 November, unexpectedly became a renewed trial of strength between supporters of Venizelos and of his arch-enemy, the former king. The outcome was the crushing defeat of Venizelos at the polls. After a correspondingly large vote for the return of Constantine as king, in a referendum held three weeks later, Greece by the end of 1920 had a head of state who was seen in the capitals of the victorious powers as a former ally of the Kaiser.[28]

The victors in the election were quick to turn on prominent supporters of Venizelos. Stelios, a member of the Permanent Court of Arbitration at The Hague, in addition to his other duties, did not return to Greece until a month after Venizelos' fall. When he did, it was to learn that he had been ousted from the University.[29]

In the meantime, far away in the centre of Anatolia, in Ankara, Mustafa Kemal, a brilliant military strategist and a hero of the Ottoman defence of the Dardanelles in 1915, had already broken away from the moribund government in Istanbul to declare his 'National Pact.' Kemal had set up a provisional capital in the interior of Anatolia, at Ankara, and was rallying support among Muslim Turks to defend the integrity of their Anatolian homeland. The fate of the treaty of Sèvres, and of the Greek-Christian population of Anatolia, now fatally exposed, would soon be sealed.

In Paris, during the first half of 1921, George was supposed to be preparing himself for his final degree examinations. His academic year had begun with a brief idyll with a Norwegian girl, Kirsten Andresen. He confided in Ioanna about this affair, and even sent her a copy of the poem he wrote, in French, addressed to Kirsten after her departure in December. But the poem itself is far from flattering, and George was almost brusque in his insistence, to Ioanna, that he had given of himself without commitment, knowing that their time together would be short. Kirsten continued to write to him for six months after this, and sent him photographs of her life in Norway; but this time it was George's turn to be hard-hearted.[30]

By this time he had found for himself a circle of high-spirited Greek friends, with whom he would stay in close touch throughout the rest of his time in Paris and for some years afterwards. They included the flamboyant

George Poniridy, who was studying music and working hard to become a composer, and the slightly built Petros Adam, or Adamos, who would later become an anthropologist. There are photographs of George with this group, posed with extravagant daring on the roof of Notre Dame cathedral. In this company, and no longer living under Mme Clauzel's roof, he seems at last to have found his equilibrium in Paris. But it was never more than precarious.[31]

In May 1921, Ioanna wrote to George from Athens. Stelios was on his way back to Paris. In warning him what to expect, she also confided the hope that she and her mother might come to join them later in the year:

> *en famille*, naturally. That's what mother says; say nothing to Dad, though, not yet, and then you're not to be made miserable if old habits kick in and Dad starts on you, complaining. . . . Then, my Yorgoulo [*her pet name for him*], between mother and father it's all over. It's like a broken vase that you fix for the moment, all it needs is a touch and it'll fall in smithereens. It's almost out of the question for either of them to live together . . . Naturally, they can't separate, that would be absurd and quite beside the point.[32]

With Stelios once more in Paris, George soon found the pressure more than he could bear. Within weeks, he was writing to his sister in despair. He cared nothing for the law, only for literature. 'I've got so much inside me that's working on me, it hurts,' he wrote to Ioanna; 'if I do write, I'll be the best.' In the meantime, he longed more than anything: 'for a little rest . . . to be beside a calm sea, with open horizons. To calm down, to lull myself for a while with love . . .' But it was not to be. The strain seems to have brought him to the point of mental and physical exhaustion. Ioanna thought he was actually ill and begged their father to ease off. When the date of his final examinations was set for the last week of June, George failed to appear. To his father he explained:

> I'm not ready and I'm overtired. . . . Try as I might (for you) I couldn't take part in the examinations. So I'll have to ask you to help me pass in October.[33]

The next four months George spent in resentful isolation at 1, rue du Lycée, in the village of Sceaux, then a small place a few kilometres up the Seine from Paris. Here Stelios paid him a visit once a week, except when called away to London or the Hague.[34]

As proof of his good intentions, George had left behind in Paris all his 'literary books,' taking with him only the *Iliad*, the *New Testament*, and the poems of the ancient lyricist Anacreon. He spent that summer revising his law books, bitterly resenting his father and the enforced suppression of his natural self. Ioanna, who was distraught not to receive a letter for so long, had to wait until almost the end of August for this news. He wrote reassuringly to his mother; his examinations had now been set for the end of October; 'how bored I am with them,' he added. He even wondered about coming to Greece afterwards: 'but it seems a bit difficult with the political situation, and I've absolutely no desire to be sent to jail in Greece.'[35]

This was a reference not to the new government (which did not, after all, imprison its opponents), but to the unresolved matter of George's military service. Since the Greek occupation of Smyrna in 1919, young men of his age had begun to be called up. A year earlier, he had been anxious about this obligation; while he had no desire to serve in the army, he did not wish to be thought a 'softie' (*kourabies*).[36]

Now, in 1921, since mid-July, while George had been sweating it out with his law books in the solitude of the outskirts of Paris, many of his contemporaries from Smyrna and Greece, volunteers and conscripts, were being thrown into battle in the interior of Anatolia. The new Greek leadership, deprived of the support that Venizelos had been able to elicit from the Great Powers, had resolved on a desperate gamble, to strike at Kemal's nationalist stronghold of Ankara. In the searing heat of an Anatolian summer, Greek troops had pushed as far as the Sakarya (Sangarios) river, just sixty kilometres short of Kemal's provisional capital. There the bloodiest battle of the Asia Minor campaign (or Turkish War of Independence) was fought, before the Greek High Command had to concede that its supply lines had been stretched too far, and drew back to a line some two hundred kilometres east of Smyrna and the sea.[37]

The only lasting effects, on George, of that summer spent in isolation at Sceaux, were to consolidate his resentment against his father and for the first time to make him overweight. 'I was never out of my bedroom-slippers all summer,' he explained to his mother.

George was called for examination in the last week of October 1921. He passed. Now he had his *licence*, he was a graduate in Law. To his mother he complained: 'The title means nothing to me. Not so Dad.' Stelios had already begun taking him about and introducing him everywhere as a lawyer. One of the examiners had been Stelios' colleague André Weisz, who had earlier consoled him on his son's poor showing at the end of his first year. The day after the second examination, Weisz wrote to Stelios to tell him that he had found his son little short of brilliant. George's performance in international law testified to his excellent preparation of this material. Stelios, who was by now a well-known authority in this field, at least could feel vindicated.[38]

George, after his sojourn in Sceaux, was now back in Paris. But there was to be no question of him either returning to Greece immediately, or turning to literature, as he had hoped. By November he had moved into a student room in the Latin Quarter, and embarked upon the first stage of a doctorate in law. Furiously he complained to Ioanna: 'will I be able to find the time I need for my own work, or am I going to die peddling the law?'[39]

## In the steps of Jean Moréas

It is not clear to what extent George's resolution, expressed back in September 1918, to 'bury' his poetry was ever seriously kept. It was decisively revoked in June 1920. Even before this, he had begun sending new poems to Ioanna. One of these, which she reproduces in part, and describes as 'astonishing,' is a prayer of penitence addressed to the Virgin Mary, who is all but conflated with his mother; Despina, the formal equivalent of Despo, means 'Mistress' and is a title of the Virgin. Like many of George's poems of these early years, this one is not remarkable in itself, but stakes a claim to territory that he would later make his own: in this case the tone of religious devotion, the mingling of the sacred with the personal and profane, and the first tentative steps towards a free-verse form that George had probably, by this time, begun learning from the example of Jules Laforgue, one of the most radical figures in French literary Modernism, whose influence would also be acknowledged by T.S. Eliot.[40]

In the same month that he came out of hiding as a poet, June 1920, George took out a reader's card at the Bibliothèque Nationale, valid until December: it was not legal books that he went there to read. Among the French classics he read Racine; among the moderns: Laforgue, Valéry, Remy de Gourmont, Rimbaud, Moréas, Claudel, and Gide. His discovery of Proust's monumental novel-in-progress, *A la recherche du temps perdu*, he would later date to the autumn before. Soon, he would start keeping and often annotating cuttings of articles from the press on literary topics; the names that occur most frequently at this time are those of Valéry, Gide and Brémond. But the one figure who towered above all the others in George's

43

imagination was Jean Moréas, and this for a very simple reason. Moréas, who had died ten years previously, had been the only Greek ever to win a place in the French poetic pantheon.[41]

When towards the end of 1920, he was asked to address a lecture to the society of Greek students, whose secretary was his friend Petros Adamos, Georged opted without hesitation for Moréas as its subject.[42]

It was probably while he was working on this lecture, that George for the first time set out, in a letter to Ioanna, his programmatic view of poetry, tradition, and his own place in it. He told her:

> I could write in French and perhaps I shall but I don't want to, because I love Greece. [But] in Greek it's impossible for me to say what I want [to say]. Then in poetry, in art more generally, it's not enough that you write, you have to map out a tradition and base yourself on that...
>
> Art is a road made by artists. In Greece the artists are like telegraph poles along the side of the road, each one alone. All this needs to be looked at carefully. Which I plan to do, in all its facets. For the moment it's enough for me to feel and to make notes...[43]

44    George's first decisive step along this road was taken on the evening of Friday 18 March 1921, when he delivered his lecture on Moréas. Starting at nine o'clock, it must have been a long evening: the manuscript runs to eighty-seven pages; even in printed form it occupies almost thirty of close type. Though never published by George himself, this was the first and one of the longest of his essays on literature and culture that in later years and after his death would prove scarcely less influential than his poetry.[44]

George's lecture on Moréas is a remarkable achievement for an under-graduate student who had had no formal training in literary criticism beyond what he might have been lucky to have had at the Model High School in Athens. Jean Moréas had been baptised Ioannis Papadiaman-topoulos; he had taken his French name from the region of his birth, the Peloponnese, also known as the Morea. In sketching the trajectory that had led from there to the enigmatic denizen of late-night cafés in Left-Bank Paris at the turn of the century, the lecture highlights details of Moréas' career that could almost be George's own. Moréas' father, like Stelios Seferiadis, had been at once a lawyer, who distinguished himself in public life, and a poet. Moréas' father, too, was capable of ordering his son from one end of Europe to the other; but Moréas in his mid-twenties had done something that George would never do: when his father had sent him to study law at Heidelberg, Moréas had refused, and gone to settle in Paris instead, to devote himself to poetry. Another notorious characteristic of Moréas provoked a comment from George that would prove prophetic of his own public career:

> This arrogant pride of his affords his enemies the opportunity to denounce him as vain and vacuous, but it is such a beautiful thing when pride is the product of [the ancient Greek maxim] *Know Thyself*.[45]

Moréas had been an exhibitionist in dress, behaviour and conversation, something that George would never be; though there is, perhaps, a temporary hint of even this in the moody, defiant elegance of the photographs from his Paris years. But proud George was and would be all his life: touchy to excess in the face of criticism, whether aesthetic or ideological, he would take refuge in a public haughtiness that would only exacerbate his isolation and sense of hurt; many of his friendships were blighted by an offence, real or imagined, that he could never fully forgive.

Elsewhere in the essay, George drops further clues that reveal just how closely he identified with his subject. Introducing Moréas' first published work, he adds the comment: 'In any case, almost always the first verses are tears for first love.' In private, he had used this exact phrase to recall his own first verses, written for Melpo at the age of sixteen. Another seeming generalisation is probably also a deeply felt comment on himself:

> So you might see in him some of the quirks of a spoilt child, [but] don't poets perhaps always remain children until they die? Not so very much spoiled, though, by society.[46]

But George was not content with a factual resume of his subject's life. The career of Moréas, he told his audience, presents a 'great problem':

> . . . how could he reject his entire past, so as to come and re-embark on a new literary career, in a place utterly alien, if not entirely from the point of view of culture, then certainly from that of language[?]
>
> The answer is difficult. I at least do not propose to play the part of Oedipus confronted by this new sphinx.[47]

The sphinx's riddle and its correct solution – man – that saves Oedipus' life, according to the ancient Greek myth, would become a lifelong point of reference for George. Here, it is likely that just as for Oedipus so for George; the real answer to the riddle is: himself.

The concluding part of the lecture offers two solutions to the riddle of Moréas' life and career. Firstly, and uncontroversially, Moréas achieved greatness in his poetry with his late work, *Stances*. His achievement had been to insert into the intensely civilised but alien culture of France an aesthetic absolute that George identifies with the ancient artistic achievement and contemporary landscape of Greece. *Stances*, according to George, was the nearest that the expatriate Moréas ever came to reconciling the competing claims of his two cultures, Greek and French. Ten years later, George would pay a different sort of homage to this achievement; when he finally settled upon a title for his own first volume of poems, it would be a near-translation of the French *Stances* back into Greek. The Greek title of this volume, for which the standard English translation is *Turning Point*, is *Strophe*, which also means 'stanza.'

George's second answer to the 'riddle' posed by Moréas is less convincing as literary history, but even more revealing when applied to himself. This was to appeal to the notorious 'language question' in Greece. Brought up and living in a society that distinguished sharply between the spoken, living form of the language ('demotic') and a formal register (*katharevousa*) full of archaisms and dead rhetoric, a poet of the calibre of Moréas, George concluded, must have found himself driven to express himself in a foreign tongue. It was the same diagnosis, and the same solution, applied to the case of Moréas, as George had already applied to himself in his earlier letter to Ioanna.[48]

These two attempts to solve the puzzle presented by Moréas culminate in the lecture's startling peroration:

> Greece lives, to the extent that she is able to give birth to great poets. ... I believe that if she has not managed to provide suitable soil for the tree that [once] burgeoned upon her land, ... in years to come she will be able not only to give birth, but also to suckle and to nurture the Poet, the Messiah, who will seize [back] from the hands of the barbarians the beauty, the gold-flaming torch, that they have stolen from us.[49]

Whether any of his audience knew it or not, the future George Seferis had proclaimed, with no trace of false modesty, the mission of his life. A Greek poet, writing in Greek, and rising above the formidable obstacles that had driven Moréas to find refuge in a foreign city and a foreign tongue, would claim back for the modern Hellenes the creative flame that their distant ancestors had once bequeathed to the world.

Not long after the lecture on Moréas was delivered, Stelios' return to Paris and the ensuing *débâcle* over George's final examinations that summer put a stop to these pursuits until November. Not long after that, in January 1922, his first published poem appeared in the Paris Greek-language newspaper, *Vomos (Altar)*.[50]

Buoyed by this first foray into print, George seems for the first time to have dreamt of publishing a book of poetry. To Ioanna, in February 1922, he wrote: 'I'm thinking of a series of poems to be called *Nocturnes*... A beautiful edition with very few copies printed...' His eye had been caught, a few days before, by the shop-front of Sylvia Beach, who specialised in highly priced, quality editions of unusual new works in very small print runs. George had never heard of the author of *Ulysses*, and some years would pass before he would read James Joyce's masterpiece; it was the Greek flags with which the volume was festooned in the window that had drawn the attention of George and his group of friends. But it was an encounter that would have important consequences. The rare, high-quality edition, *hors de commerce*, would ever afterwards appeal to him, and a number of his own books would be published in this way. And the idea that he, too, like Joyce, might create an avatar of Homer's Odysseus for the modern world may first have entered his mind on that February day of 1922, seeing his own national flag used to promote Joyce's experimental novel of modern Ireland.[51]

### Death of a city

Ioanna's hopes of rejoining her brother in Paris in the winter of 1921 had come to nothing. That autumn Despo and her younger children had moved into an apartment block near the centre of Athens, on the corner of Kyvelis and Mavromataion Streets, close to the National Museum. This became the family home, and George's when he returned to Greece, for the next twelve years; its wide roof terrace the backdrop to several photographs of family and friends during that time.[52] Early in the new year, 1922, family correspondence was again turning upon plans for a reunion in the summer. It had already been decided that Angelos, who would be seventeen in July, would follow in George's footsteps and study in Paris; Ioanna, despite her earnest entreaties, had to be content with the University of Athens Law School.[53]

Anxiety about the political situation in Smyrna also begins to surface in these letters, during the spring of 1922. The military stalemate in

Anatolia had not changed since the summer, but politically the Greek occupation of the *vilayet* of Aydin was unravelling fast. In March, the British, French and Italian foreign ministers met in Paris. The meeting ended with a communiqué that effectively recognised that the Treaty of Sèvres was dead; the basis for a new and lasting peace settlement would have to be the evacuation of Greek forces from Anatolia.[54]

Shortly after that, George wrote to his mother, trying his best to reassure her:

> But why are you worrying yourself about nonexistent things? Whatever happens, Smyrna isn't going to be left to the Turks. So you see, the only thing that can happen is at the most autonomy [for Smyrna] – bad news, of course, from the national point of view . . .[55]

This no doubt reflected Stelios' opinion. But Stelios does not seem to have enjoyed any regular official position at this time. His letters to George indicate a new and serious anxiety about money. It was probably for this reason, rather than because he foresaw the collapse in Anatolia, that Stelios wrote to George asking him to approve the sale of the house at Skala that his grandmother had left him in her will. This is also, perhaps, revealing of the state of relations between Stelios and Despo, since under the Greek administration of Smyrna it would have been an easy matter to liquidate assets owned by the Tenekidis family. There seems to have been no question of doing this, however, in order to meet Stelios' financial obligations.[56]

This was not the only difficulty at this time. In the spring of 1921, according to her later memoir, Ioanna had kept from George her growing anxiety about their mother's health. Despo had been suffering from dizziness and poor spirits. Now, in May 1922, in a letter that begins with a warning not to read it to their father, Ioanna announced to George:

> Mother's health is a very delicate business. . . . This year . . . she needs something more than just to be careful. I don't know if Dad has realised how serious this business is. The millionth part of what she lived through in '18 would do her terrible harm. You understand, don't you?[57]

Stelios, meanwhile, had continued to travel from his base in Paris. In April he was briefly in Germany, representing Greece in some capacity that George found 'futile.' Perhaps as a consequence of this visit, and apparently without consulting the other members of the family, Stelios abruptly

48

despatched George to Dresden at the beginning of July, with instructions to spend the summer learning German. Despo and Ioanna were to join him there. Stelios would come too, if he could, but confided to George his difficulties in finding sufficient work to meet all the family's financial needs.[58]

It is possible that engineering the reunion of his family in Dresden, in recently-defeated Germany, where even the most penurious foreigner was a rich man compared to the local population in those years of hyper-inflation, was another attempt by Stelios to remedy his financial difficulties that summer. If so, it was a desperate one, and it backfired badly.

George, sent on ahead to arrange accommodation for his mother, his sister and Angelos, succumbed in just over a week to an acute case of culture-shock and took the train back to Paris, apparently believing he would be in time to forestall the others' arrival. But Ioanna and Angelos, travelling with their invalid mother, arrived in Dresden to find him already gone, and a letter and telegram waiting for them. In the letter, George confessed to having done something extremely foolish. Ioanna's memoir characteristically smoothes over the incident, with the ambiguous comment, 'He wished to achieve a *fait accompli.*'[59]

As a result, the family was briefly reunited in Paris that summer, although not under the same roof. Ioanna was thrilled to be close to her brother once again (they had not seen each other for two years). Angelos now moved in with George for the university year, a prelude to studying medicine at the Sorbonne. Despo and Ioanna stayed for only a few weeks, then left with the intention of spending September in Smyrna and Skala, before returning to Athens for the winter.[60]

The boarding house where George and Angelos now had rooms was at 15 rue Bréa, Paris VI. It is a short, narrow street of prim, tall shuttered houses that cannot have changed much since 1922. A short walk through the Luxembourg Gardens would take the brothers to the Latin Quarter and the Sorbonne.

On 3 September 1922, George wrote to his mother: 'Now that you've left I realise how necessary you [two] are to me.' She mustn't worry about him, he goes on:

> The evening you left, all of us who were at the station, Dad too, came back on foot to my boarding house. Dad came up to my room and he liked it as a room and as a boarding house, as a result he wants to stay here too. . . . Angelos is fine, I'm taking care of him. Today he's going with Dad to get a suit cut. . . . Write to me the moment you get to

49

Smyrna and tell me everything. All the details you can, about the situation.[61]

The envelope is addressed:

> Monsieur Soc. Séfériadès
> pour Madame Despo Séfériadès
> Quais 134
> Smyrne
> Asie Mineure

It is marked *'Retour à l'envoyeur'* (return to sender) and on the back: *'parti'* (departed).

While George's letter to his mother had been on its way, the end of the three-thousand-year-old Greek presence in Anatolia had come swiftly. On 26 August, Kemal's forces launched a hammerblow attack on the entire length of the Greek lines. Within two weeks, the remnants of the Greek forces, those that had not been killed or captured, had bypassed Smyrna to the south and were evacuated by Greek ships from the headland of Çeşme, opposite Chios. On Friday 8 September, the last Greek ships left the harbour of Smyrna, carrying among others the unloved High Commissioner, Aristidis Stergiadis. The date, 9 September, when Turkish Republican troops entered Smyrna, is still commemorated as a milestone in the formation of modern Turkey.

Four days later, after an orgy of looting and killing throughout the Christian parts of the city, a series of fires broke out in the Armenian quarter. The fires spread swiftly, and raged for three days, leaving the entire heart of the city burnt out. American, French, Armenian and Greek eyewitness accounts tell of arson by Turkish soldiers, whether acting on orders or not. Reprisals against prominent Greeks, among them the senior representative of the Orthodox Church, Archbishop Chrysostomos, were horrific. By the end of the month, on the orders of Kemal, there was barely a Christian left in the ruins of the city. Greek women, children and old men were evacuated in chartered merchant ships in a belated humanitarian enterprise. Greek men of military age were regarded as prisoners of war, rounded up and marched off into the interior, where many died working in labour gangs or through random acts of reprisal. Of the city's other communities, those with foreign passports were given refuge by the foreign warships that stood off in the bay, under orders to observe strict neutrality; the Jews, who had generally enjoyed better relations with Muslim than with Christian officialdom, were unharmed. The Armenians were effectively wiped out.[62]

All this, George, his father, and Angelos could learn only day by day as it happened, from rumours, from the terrifying reports in the French press, and no doubt also through official contacts that Stelios still had in Paris. When the news of the Turks' arrival in Smyrna first broke, George must have believed that the two people he loved most in the world, his mother and his sister, were trapped there. By the time the fires had stopped smouldering in Smyrna, and in Paris the full extent of the destruction could be read in the newspapers, he knew that Despo and Ioanna, at least, were still in Athens and unharmed. He wrote to them there, a letter raw with grief, bewilderment and anger. Twisting and turning through its disjointed phrases is the thought of what must have happened to their relatives.

There is nothing of the 'poet' about this letter. It is a letter that any young man, whose life had been turned upside-down by such events, might have written to his mother. Touchingly, incongruously even, it plucks the hope of renewed family life, love and the possibility of happiness for those who mean most to him, out of the destruction.

51

Monday evening

Dear mum

Your first letter came two days ago with the newspapers on the eve of the catastrophe almost. From then events have tumbled out of control, the Turk has entered our Smyrna, burnt it and is massacring us. How can I describe for you the days, the agonies we're suffering here in a foreign land and what an inhospitable foreign land it is. . . . Thankfully, you two are now safe. You and Ioanna are the most important thing. Our only terrible anxiety now is our relatives in Smyrna. Dad has cabled you. No reply so far. He went to *Le Temps* to ask about Uncle Kokos. They don't know anything. We're driven mad. Write to me as soon as you can with details. . . . I'm sitting writing to you because I must write to you. I can't gather my thoughts, everything comes to me as though in a dream and then I think of you and your nervous disposition and so sensitive, my poor little mother what kind of a state can she be in? . . . Can the human mind find room for such a thing, in the twentieth century, the century of humanity, a city of three hundred thousand people can be made into a graveyard in just four days. Cable me at once: where is Uncle Kokos, Uncle Socrates, Aunt Elli? Where have they ended up – because

I can't bring myself to imagine that they didn't get out somehow, write to me what they're thinking about the future. Write to me everything about the state of Greece, hysterical, false Greece that without the least heroism, the least self-sacrifice, without the least protest even, could sacrifice her children by the hundred thousand. . . . Angelos has a room next to mine, a clean little room, it's warm and we have our meals together, every lunchtime and evening Dad comes round after we've eaten, and we have coffee the three of us, we think about you and talk. He's wretched too. He's thinking of taking an *appartement* and sending for the two of you to come and all live together for the time being in Paris. Who knows if all this mightn't even be to the good if we can draw together tightly as a family once again. That's why you shouldn't be sad, if people are together with love and health everything else can be mended. . . . If there's the least thing you need, send us a telegram. Take care of Ioanna and tell her to write to me. I kiss you and I kiss her. George.[63]

Shortly after this, a telegram arrived at the rue Bréa: SAUVES SEFE-RIADES. The whole family had come through safely. Within a few weeks, the house behind the Archaeological Museum in Athens was overflowing with refugees bearing some degree of kinship to the Seferiadis or Tenekidis family, some of whom Ioanna and her mother had never seen before. Despo's charity and compassion were already legendary. In the immediate aftermath of the catastrophe she did indeed, as George had feared, suffer what sounds like a nervous collapse; the doctor came and bled her, she was confined to bed, unable to stop crying. But as soon as she was on her feet, she was indefatigable in seeking out relatives and family retainers among the thousands of refugees who had suddenly flooded Athens and Piraeus, and distributing what little she had – even, according to Ioanna, her bed.[64]

George was not the only one, when the scale of the disaster became known, to point a furious finger of blame at those who had brought his country to this pass. In Greece, King Constantine was quickly ousted by a military *coup d'état*. A pro-Venizelist revolutionary government, after a summary trial, on 28 November executed six political and military leaders held responsible for the disaster. This act, carried out against international pleas for clemency, guaranteed, more than any other, that bitterness between supporters and opponents of Venizelos would continue to poison Greek political life throughout the entire interwar period. George, however,

52

cut out and sent his mother a long article from the *Journal des Débats* on the execution of the 'Six,' in which the action was regretfully approved, with the laconic comment: 'first rate.' And years later, reflecting on these events in the wake of Greece's defeat and occupation in another war, in 1941, he would remain unforgiving.[65]

That same month, November 1922, George sent to Ioanna two letters and a poem in which he tried to come to terms with what had happened. The poem, another in the projected series of 'nocturnes,' is a fairly crude attempt, as is understandable in the circumstances. But in the letters, self-conscious though they are, for the first time there emerges a measured, almost fatalistic tone; several of their phrases and images anticipate lines of poetry written much later:

> . . . I think of all the things I could do, I think of my hands cut off, no one loves me but you, and I've so much to say, . . . and the world is so alien, so dressed-up, I don't know how I could talk to anyone about it all. . . . Have you ever noticed, little sister, how much emotion is concealed in hoarse voices? I'd like to have verses that would be like the drops welling up, out of an overflowing heart.[66]

53

In Athens, things were worse than ever. The house in Kyvelis Street was now so packed with relatives, camping in the kitchen and the hall, that Ioanna took her mother to stay with a friend in the fashionable suburb of Kifisia, on the slopes of Pendeli. Stelios, who was presumably in close touch with Venizelos in Paris, announced to George in November that he had been appointed to a committee in charge of reparations, and so would be likely to stay in Paris for the next two years. The new government seems to have favoured Stelios more immediately, however, since at the beginning of the New Year he was back in Athens, and once again teaching at the University.[67]

It was during these months, when the permanent loss of his homeland was a fresh wound, that George met the first great love of his life.

### George in love

Her name was Jacqueline Pouyollon. She was eighteen when George first met her, on 5 January 1923. According to Ioanna:

> Father happened to meet up again, that winter of 1923, with old Parisian friends, her mother, Marie-Louise. The acquaintance was renewed. This

cultured and open-hearted woman asked to meet George and Angelos. She invited them to her home.[68]

This is Ioanna, in 1973, at her most teasingly bland. In fact, either Marie-Louise or her husband, or both, seem to have been friends of Stelios from his student days in France; a letter by George, in 1932, would refer to this 'family linked by friendship with my own for more than thirty years.' M. Pouyollon is absent from the surviving correspondence and photographs; although mother and daughter depended on him financially, Jacqueline's father seems not to have lived with his wife and daughter. George would meet him only rarely, and would have harsh words to say of him.[69]

The new acquaintance with mother and daughter did not come quite out of the blue. Although Ioanna's account obscures the fact, it was cemented by the kindly presence of Despo's sister, the penurious and kind-hearted Aunt Agla, who gave piano lessons and occasional concerts in Paris. Two sets of photographs in which the family appears were taken at the house of Agla Tenekidou at Le Vésinet, outside Paris. A further connection between the families was that Jacqueline was also a talented pianist. A month after George's first meeting with Jacqueline, he and Angelos went boating with the Pouyollons and Aunt Agla in the Bois de Boulogne. The photographs taken on that occasion show everyone wearing furs against the cold; but there is an additional stiffness in the body language of the figures that is touching, almost comical. Stelios had already, in his latest letter to George, sent his 'greetings to all – Marie-Louise, Jacqueline . . .' It would not be long before George was sending photographs of his new friends to his sister, and urging Ioanna to write to Jacqueline, as Despo was already corresponding with Marie-Louise. During the succeeding months, George's letters to Despo represent Marie-Louise as a second mother to Angelos and himself. In June, Despo would express her heartfelt thankfulness that 'Marie-Louise is an angel from <u>God</u>, I can feel it: she has you [two] in her heart.'[70]

All this would be explained if the new relationships between families were being cemented with a view to a possible marriage. Interpreted in this way, Aunt Agla would have provided the essential link between a father on his own in Paris and the family of an eligible girl. It may be that at this low point in the fortunes of the family and of their homeland, after the expulsion of the Greeks from Smyrna, Stelios had decided, in his usual impulsive way, that the best prospects for the future lay in George making a life and a career for himself in France.

54

Marriage was certainly in the air at this time. The previous summer, during her brief sojourn with her mother in Paris, Ioanna had been outraged to find herself, accompanied by George, taken to tea by Stelios with a potential suitor at the Ritz. Although Ioanna had remained on close terms with Aronis, it seems to have been Stelios who prevented this match from going ahead. When Nikos announced to George his impending marriage, he added, 'Between brothers there's no need for forgiveness,' thus tacitly acknowledging the bond that informally had existed between himself and Ioanna. Nikos and Androniki Aronis were married in April 1923, and soon afterwards arrived in Paris, where George introduced them to Jacqueline and her mother. Ioanna places Aronis' marriage a year early, in April 1922, but perhaps revealingly comments that it 'set [George] thinking.'[71]

Three months after his first meeting with Jacqueline, George wrote to his sister: 'she resembles you, that's why I like her so much, she too has her congenital wounds.' In photographs, Jacqueline does have more than a passing resemblance to Ioanna, though partly this has to do with style of dress. She is tall, almost as tall as George, with short thick dark hair and incipient curls. Hers is a slightly masculine beauty; she has a strong chin and broad face; there is a sultry intensity about her eyes.[72]

Aronis, who must have met her in May or June, would describe    
Jacqueline, many years later, as 'blonde, blue-eyed, a pianist, with very refined feelings and a deep, tender love for George.' According to George, she was a brunette; the photographs give no help with the colour of her eyes. But there seems to be no question about her musical talent, or about her feelings for George. His for her are harder to gauge.[73]

Just before he had written that letter to Ioanna describing Jacqueline, he had tried to give literary expression to what was happening to him. Two versions of an unfinished short story, or prose poem, written that March, wrap his first meeting with Jacqueline in a cloud of emotional anguish. In this fictionalised version, George adopts the persona of 'Alyis Vayias.' The first part of this name suggests pain [-algy]; the second, the Greek name for Palm Sunday, hence, again, pain and sacrifice. This alter ego is the child of a heroically suffering race and of a father with the most terrifying gaze. Alyis Vayias is a lover of freedom, but 'at the age of 23 has been ruined by ancestral slavery.' Clearly, the recent trauma of Smyrna, and classically oedipal feelings about his father, are closely involved here. The girl is given a Greek name, Krinoula ('little lily'): he idolizes her as a saviour, but he cannot be happy in her presence; built into his incipient love is the pain of parting. Ioanna, who would become a staunch advocate of Jacqueline in all that followed, implicitly concedes what may well have been the truth about the relationship, right from this early stage:

> He would seek out Jacqueline, and he would avoid her. This only made his loneliness the greater. He needed peace and quiet. He needed that solid love that knows only how to give, without making demands.[74]

Undoubtedly George was attracted to Jacqueline; but he seems to have had almost a horror of the responsibilities of marriage. Ioanna is surely also right that for George to have married Jacqueline would have meant the end of the very specific ambition that he had spelt out at the end of his lecture on Moréas: to become a *Greek* poet. He did write some verses in French, that he sent to his sister, both before and during his relationship with Jacqueline; but, however much it may have seemed a temptation in the circumstances of 1923, there had never been any question of his following all the way in the footsteps of Moréas.[75]

This was a love affair that would leave its mark on both participants for life; curiously, very few traces remain of the times that they must have enjoyed together. They seem to have talked about poetry and music. Ten years later, George would recall how he had read to Jacqueline the notoriously difficult poem by Valéry, *Jeune Parque*:

> Next day she said to me, 'I dreamt that I was *Jeune Parque*.' This made such an impression on me that I still remember it. The girl was 17 [sic] years old and she had explained *Jeune Parque* to me.[76]

But even during the eighteen months that George remained in Paris after he met Jacqueline, the amount of time they spent in each other's company must have been very limited. During the spring of 1923, Marie-Louise took her daughter to the family's second home in Nice for two months. Then George was preparing for intermediate examinations towards his doctorate, and according to Ioanna desperately tired. The examinations were postponed. Only when they were over, in early July, did Ioanna allow herself 'the hope, at their first meetings after the exams, that a happiness would light up his soul.'[77]

A watershed seems to have been reached on the eve of Bastille day (14 July). George, Angelos, the Aronis couple and their friends all took part in the traditional all-night street party in their neighbourhood. Marie-Louise and Jacqueline came to join them. The singing, drinking and dancing went on all night; even George, never more than a dutiful dancer, for once 'had wings on his feet.'[78]

The impression of parental stage-management is hard to avoid in what happened next. Almost immediately, Marie-Louise took Jacqueline away to a spa, until October. George broke a two-month silence to write letters to Despo and Ioanna that are overflowing with misery, but unenlightening on its cause. Stelios now stepped in, to take both his sons to the Brittany coast for a fortnight. It is the only known instance of Stelios taking a holiday; indeed Ioanna's account even suppresses the fact that he went too. Whatever had happened on Bastille night, it had not dampened the ardour of Jacqueline's feelings for George. Though none of their correspondence has so far been traced, a series of photographs of herself, taken at the spa, and dated to August, must surely have been sent to him during their enforced separation.[79]

In the second half of September, Stelios left Paris to take up his duties once again at the University of Athens. George and Angelos were once more on their own. Almost immediately, George came down with paratyphoid, and was taken to hospital. He kept the news from his mother and Ioanna until he was better. It was now that Marie-Louise and Jacqueline returned to Paris; together with Angelos, mother and daughter gathered round and helped him convalesce. Marie-Louise, he wrote to his mother on 17 October, had been a 'saintly friend, . . . at once a mother and a nurse.' Three days later, it is likely that George and Jacqueline became lovers.[80]

George was now about to begin his last winter at the Sorbonne. His relationship with Jacqueline had entered a new phase, and a new impasse. She wanted marriage; he did not. Soon the affair would begin to be transmuted into something infinitely more painful and, in its way, even longer-lasting.

On 31 August, 1923, the recently installed dictator of Italy, Benito Mussolini, bombarded and briefly occupied the Greek island of Corfu. On the international stage, these were the first shots in a campaign that, in 1940, would bring Greece into World War II, with tragic consequences for both nations. In the hothouse of student life on the Left Bank, the 'Corfu incident,' as it came to be known, soon became a touchstone for hostilities that had been latent since the race to occupy Smyrna in the spring of 1919.

George's brother Angelos had been studying medicine at the Sorbonne for a year. Early in Angelos' first year, George had written to their mother that his brother was happy, learning to cut up frogs, and very proud of his first surgical instruments. Now, during the autumn of his second year, an incident took place that is revealing of Angelos' character, and also of his close affinity to George.

> In the anatomy lab of the Medical School, a bullying Italian fascist, with whom Angelos was having words: 'You're a coward and a big-mouth, you're a cheat,' the Italian shouted, 'like all Greeks!'
>
> '*I'm* a coward and a big-mouth, like all Greeks?'
>
> 'Yes, you, the lot of you!'
>
> Angelos picks up a dirty scalpel, where it had been lying on the marble autopsy bench, and *frap,* he'd cut through the vein of his left wrist. Then, thrusting his bloodied wrist into his adversary's face, he said: 'You then, who aren't a coward or a big-mouth, can *you* do that?'[81]

Aronis, who tells this story, was with George at the hostel he shared with his brother when Angelos came home, white as a sheet and with his arm in a sling, and told this story.

58

> George . . . remonstrated with him for his ridiculous behaviour: like a Japanese Samurai, [he said,] to wipe out the insult in his own blood. Nevertheless, he embraced his brother tightly and kissed him, and in this way showed his unconfessed pleasure at a spontaneously rash act motivated by a sense of honour.

This story reveals a characteristic that both brothers shared, and may have been inherited, in particular, from their mother. George, always more circumspect, more closed-in, but far stronger than his brother, was usually able to contain this self-destructive response to adversity. But there would be occasions in the future when George, too, would turn against himself the anger and frustration that had been roused by adversaries whom he despised.

Angelos Seferiadis, the youngest of the family, had all the patrician temperament of the Tenekidis family, but neither the financial nor the intellectual resources to sustain it in the world that was emerging from World War I and, for Greeks, the aftermath of the 1922 defeat in Anatolia. It was not long before Angelos abandoned medicine; it was, according to Ioanna, anatomy that finally repelled him. Angelos never did find his true *métier*, though his brother was always convinced that he had had it in him to be a poet.[82]

By early in 1924, it was understood in the family that as soon as George's studies were over, he would be returning, after all, to Greece. Before the terrible events of September 1922, Stelios had been planning for his son to take the examination to enter the Foreign Ministry in Athens. The prospect of marriage to Jacqueline, raised the previous year, might have changed all that. But George was not prepared to take that step. Just after New Year, he wrote to his mother that he was planning to leave Paris for good in February, in time for his birthday; then at the end of February: 'I've decided in any case to finish with Law this year, that means May at the latest.'[83]

In June, George was still in Paris, and noting in his pocket-diary that he had 'finished with International Law.' Ioanna says that he completed his doctorate at this time, but this is chivalrous on her part: she herself later became a Doctor of Law; George did not. In his pocket-diary, that summer, George wrote sarcastically, 'I'll pass the two [remaining] examinations for my doctorate in November. . . . *Bonne blague!*' But by November, he had already left Paris, allowing his registration at the Sorbonne to lapse: 'it's now certain I can't return to Athens with any more qualifications than I've got already,' he conceded crossly to his father.[84]

The higher qualification might have been desirable, but was not a requirement for entry to the Foreign Ministry. Proficiency in a second foreign language, on the other hand, was. Two years earlier, Stelios had tried to persuade George to go to Germany and learn German, but that had gone badly wrong. At some point in the early summer of 1924, Stelios hit upon the solution of England. George would spend the summer learning English. To his mother he confided that he was not looking forward to the new experience: 'I don't know more than two or three words of the language at all and this makes it very difficult for me.'[85]

George's feelings for Jacqueline, as the moment of parting approached, became more enigmatic than ever. According to Ioanna, at this point the lovers 'would wander for hours on end, without speaking, over the bridges and through the parks of Paris.' In April, when Marie-Louise again took Jacqueline away for a prolonged stay in the country, George wrote in his pocket-diary: 'who knows? who knows?' On the same day, he began a poem, entitled 'In Memoriam, The Ballad of Departure,' that he would finish six months later, in England. He seems to have taken no positive step to consolidate their relationship; but he was tormented by the enforced separation that Stelios would see fit to prolong until the end of the year.[86]

59

At the beginning of July 1924, there was a reunion at aunt Agla's house at Le Vésinet. Stelios, George, and Angelos were present, as well as Jacqueline and Marie-Louise. Photographs were taken, and sent to Despo and Ioanna in Athens. By the end of that month, George's books had been boxed up and were on their way back to Greece; Jacqueline and her mother had left to spend August in the country. On 1 August, he saw off Angelos and the Aronis couple at the Gare de Lyon, on their way back to Greece. The next day, Saturday, from the other side of Paris, George and his friend Petros Adamos set out from the Gare St Lazare for Dieppe, and the crossing to Newhaven.[87]

## Fog

George's first introduction to the country that was to play such a large part in his life in years to come was an inauspicious one. To his mother, he wrote: 'The journey was appalling. Everybody the colour of straw and the steamer bobbing like a cork.' Many years later, writing to a younger male friend, he recalled his first experience of England:

> I'd missed the sea terribly and so had opted for the longest crossing: four hours, I think it was. This was August, but the moment we were out of the harbour, the storm hit us, with hail and everything. I, needless to say, stayed out on deck, I'd missed the sea so much. When I got off, soaked to the skin, at Newhaven, I was beckoned over by a very polite gentleman, who took me behind a wooden screen and ordered me to show him my privates, and went on, in that English accent they have: *tirez le prépuce*.[88]

For the rest of August, George and Adamos stayed at the home of one C.M. Robinson Berwyn, whom they called 'Roby' for short, at York Avenue, Hove, outside Brighton. Roby he described to his mother as 'the teacher of a friend;' at Hove, George and Adamos had to speak English all day. According to a story he told his wife, many years later, it was the fifteen-year-old daughter of the household who took pity on him, after he had tried to teach himself from a bilingual French and English edition of Shakespeare.[89]

A month later, George and Adamos left Hove and moved into lodgings at 121 Boundaries Road, in Balham, a suburb of southwest London between Wandsworth and Tooting. They lodged with an Irish family, by the name of Brady. Years later (writing to a friend, in English) George would remember them as 'terribly "sentimental" and "poetic".' On a different occasion he recalled:

> There was a large dark tree in front of my window. I had gas lighting and kept warm with an open coal fire. I stayed up late, reading poets I couldn't understand, or writing.[90]

The house is a typical London suburban two-storey house, built around the beginning of the century, in red brick, on a corner plot. In those days its walls were covered by a deciduous creeper, whose bare branches George described, with a forced ingenuity perhaps worthy of the Bradys, as like 'the hairy chest of a crucified orang-utan.' There are still trees in the road, though there is no longer one outside number 121. At the back of the house is the traditional brick-built lean-to kitchen, that gives on to a tiny patio garden. Among a group of photographs taken by the kitchen window, is one in which George looks soulful, sitting in a wicker chair. In another, he is standing, holding the cat – to his mother he wrote that he talked English even to the cat – beside the raffish-looking Adamos, who only comes up to his shoulder.[91]

Adamos left in early October, and on the 12th wrote to George a lively letter from Paris.

> Yesterday at two in the afternoon I went to rue Vital [Paris XVI: the Pouyollons lived at no. 57]. There were just the two of them. Jacqueline went out later . . . George: courage! We talked about you until quarter past four; you're a stinker you don't deserve to be looked after so well but we're all obliged on account of your obesity, *poor little thing* [*this phrase in English*].[92]

By this time George was keeping a numbered tally in his pocket-diary of letters written or received; it can safely be assumed that his correspondent was Jacqueline. On 1 October the number was just six; on the same day he noted the precise time at which Marie-Louise and Jacqueline should have returned to Paris from the country. By December these letters were being recorded at the rate of two a week.

It is not clear what active steps George took, apart from talking to the Bradys' cat, to work on his English. He invested in a number of dictionaries, grammars, guide-books and novels; but a letter from Stelios, at the end of October, urging him to enrol for a course or find a teacher for the language, implies that after two months in Balham he had done neither. He went to concerts. In the first days, he and Adamos sought a cure for homesickness in the few El Greco paintings in the National Gallery. A small portrait of a saint, probably 'St Jerome as Cardinal,' George thought must have had for its model a Cretan boatman, though it was surely the fishermen of Skala that he really had in mind. Among other lasting impressions were a line from a popular song, heard on a phonograph, one dank sunset in Epping Forest, 'A sunny day we shall go . . . ;' 'monstrous chimneys belching out the smoke of civilisation;' and the flickering, magical shapes of the coal fire in the Bradys' hearth.[93]

It was while he was staying at Balham that George made his first attempt to write a novel, and also wrote the first of the poems that he would later publish under the name of Seferis. A letter to Angelos suggests that the novel was well advanced; he had been motivated by 'all the disgust I've felt at [Greek student life in] Paris recently.' This was *In the Boundless Chess-Game of the 'Concorde';* a few pages are preserved in George's published diary for the following year. These fragmentary drafts, and the letter to his brother, mark the début of the alter ego Stratis, George's fictional persona from now on, later to appear in poems as Stratis Thalassinos (the Seafarer).[94]

62

To Angelos, that October, George also vividly described his first experience of the legendary London 'pea-souper.' Under the condition that would today be called 'smog,' George felt that he and all the other inhabitants of the city were living in the depths of the sea; jokingly, he wondered whether the trombones of the Salvation Army band had been responsible for provoking the phenomenon from on high. Even the beggars in London struck him as formally dressed: 'these men with unbearably sad music seemed to have been the victims of an accident that had happened yesterday; victims of something out of the natural order,' he would describe them many years later. The song, 'Say it with a ukulele,' would become the epigraph of the poem 'Fog' (the title in English), that bears the dateline 'Christmas 1924,' and includes all these impressions.[95]

The manuscripts reveal that 'Fog' was the last in the series of 'nocturnes' that had been begun in Paris, and was at first subtitled, 'a self-portrait of London.' It uses a strict metrical form with rhyme; in other respects, it anticipates aspects of George's maturity: the failure of communication ('what can I say to her? – tell me, / Christ, on my lonely path') and the helplessness of the people in the fog, as vulnerable as thrushes in a universe in which 'their angels are the pox.'[96]

The mood of bitter helplessness to which this poem gives expression has spilt over from a series of draft letters to Stelios, written during the same month. The cause of this crisis was his father's decision, that seems to have taken George by surprise, not to allow him to return to Paris to spend Christmas with Jacqueline and Marie-Louise. In a fury of frustration, George rounded on his father in mid December:

I wrote and told you precisely why I wanted to leave here before the holidays. You've understood exactly the opposite. You think I want to go to Paris to have a good time. When I can't even afford to eat. You thought I was being led astray by women. For reasons that are absolutely my own, sweet things make me melancholy. . . . Please bear in mind that it wasn't at all out of disrespect that I didn't ask your advice. You'd told Marie-Louise I'd be there for New Year. She'd written to me to ask if that was true. Also I'd written to *you* to tell you when I was thinking of coming to Paris. . . . I shall stay here as long as you want and more. I've no reason to go to Paris.[97]

From the same letter comes the outburst, 'I'm bored with words and words that remain only words.' In the poem this would become: 'Words for words, and yet more words.' Though it is far from being a love poem, at a personal level 'Fog' powerfully articulates George's angry sense of impotence in the face of his father's will, his impatience to get back to Paris and Jacqueline, but also the terrible paralysis of his own will as he succumbed to the unnaturally fallen and seemingly irredeemable state represented by the apocalyptic London fog.

Just into the New Year, on 7 January, George boarded the boat train at Victoria Station, for Paris (Gare du Nord) via Dover and Calais. He stayed for five weeks at a hotel in the Boulevard Montparnasse. These were the last weeks that he and Jacqueline spent together as lovers. On the 29th, Despo wrote her last letter to him: the family, in Greece, were awaiting news of how he would travel back. She also refers to a letter received from Marie-Louise, 'very emotional about your departure.'[98]

On 11 February, George was in Marseille, and boarded the *Pierre Loti* for the five-day voyage to Greece. The irony of the ship's name would not have escaped him. Pierre Loti had been a popular French writer and orientalist whose pro-Ottoman sympathies had provoked Stelios, during George's first year in Paris, to a vociferous attack in print.

Now with the years of exile in Paris behind him, George sailed aboard the *Pierre Loti* into the harbour of Piraeus at 7 a.m. on Monday, 16 February 1925.

His mother was waiting for him on the quayside. 'Lord,' she murmured, 'dismiss thou thy servant...'[99]

# 3
# Servant of Two Masters
# 1925–1931

Horror: always the two masters. From here on, all my
contradictions. I don't want to become a lawyer, or a journalist,
or a bohemian. The only talent I have is to want to make poems,
patiently, obstinately, working for months and years like a Chinaman
or a manic artisan.

(*Days 1*; 1 March 1927)

## Keeping faith

The Athens to which George returned that February was very different
from the city he had left almost seven years before. The city's wide, tree-
lined boulevards and smart cafés, in the early years of the century, had used
to be compared to those of Paris. Now, since the uprooting of the Greeks
from Anatolia (sealed and made permanent by the Treaty of Lausanne, in
July 1923), the population of Athens and the port of Piraeus had more than
doubled. Terrible shanty towns, built of corrugated iron and mud-brick,
without sanitation or water, had sprung up all round the city. Every open
space in the city centre, from the docks at Piraeus to the new settlements
on the outskirts, was filled with temporary encampments, dusty in summer,
exposed to rain and wind in winter. Refugees and the signs of destitution
and despair were everywhere.[1]

George cannot have been unmoved by these visible reminders of the loss
of his homeland. But years later, he recollected only: 'the little Ford buses
adorned with the most extraordinary names, the roads all dug up, the
outdoor silent cinemas.' The political upheavals that had followed the
disaster in Anatolia, the counter-revolution in Greece, and the execution

of the 'Six,' left him equally indifferent. By the time George returned to Greece at the beginning of 1925, Venizelos had tried and failed to form a stable administration; a plebiscite had abolished the monarchy and declared Greece a republic; parliamentary government was in disarray, and four months later, in June, succumbed to the *'opéra bouffe* military dictatorship' of General Pangalos. George seems to have been less interested in politics at this time than at any other in his life. Writing fifteen years later, he recalled: 'there was not a single personality in all the political world that had any appeal;' he felt only 'indifference and sometimes revulsion at the mechanisms of the politicians.' A new force in political life was the Greek communist party, that had been formed in 1924. George was unimpressed by these new political radicals, and in the next few years would not be above lampooning them in private.[2]

It is at this point that George's posthumously published diaries begin. *Days 1*, as the chronologically earliest volume is now known, might have been expected to afford a new and more direct window on his life and experiences than exists for previous years. Tantalisingly, the reverse is true. This volume of his diary was reworked on at least two, probably three, later occasions, and the originals destroyed. There is little, in *Days 1*, of the unforced, frank, engaging and engaged manner that characterises later volumes from 1935 onwards. Probably, even in its original form, this was a self-consciously introverted, literary attempt to catch the fleeting moments and chance *aperçus* that seemed to George important in his formation as a writer. The influence of the fictional diaries of Gide is manifest, and would come to be compounded in the process of reworking. In the form in which the material exists today, it has been divided up between *Days 1*, which purports to be a diary, but from which almost all personal, biographical details have been expunged, and a semi-autobiographical novel, *Six Nights on the Acropolis*, that is in large part made up of the diary of George's fictional alter ego, Stratis, and would not achieve its final form until the 1950s.[3]

Other evidence for this period is scarce. There are few extant letters, since George was now living at home with his family, and the friendships that later elicited his richest correspondence were still being formed. Ioanna devotes much less space to the period after his return to Greece. So it is more than usually difficult to part the veil that George drew, with the advantage of hindsight, over the formative years that culminated in his first public appearance as 'Seferis.'

For six years, in Paris, George had been bitterly nostalgic for his own Greek world. There was no returning, now, to Smyrna and Skala; but after the defeat in Anatolia, Athens had become the undisputed centre of that world. It was here, in Athens, that George now felt that he belonged. It was here that he would fulfil the promise with which he had concluded his lecture on Moréas, back in 1921. But after so long abroad, the process of adjustment was painful. Worse, it seems to have been little short of demeaning: 'The race, its atavistic attitudes, the Greek tradition, I've had it all up to here. Unbearable pain. Maybe I got it wrong from the start?'

This was only one of many such expressions of bitter disillusionment in his diary:

> Just look at the superficiality of people [here], their ignorance, their spitefulness, their lack of awareness. Our intellectuals guzzle art like goats let loose on grass.[4]

It would not be long before George was to formulate one of his enduring aphorisms about the essential contradiction of the Greek character:

> In Greece there exist two races: the race of Socrates and the race of Anytos, Meletos and Lykon [the philosopher's accusers when he was tried and condemned to death by the Athenians in 399 BC]. The first makes for the country's greatness; the second does the same thing negatively. So long as the first exists, the second has to exist as well. But now the first has gone completely, and that's that.

A little later, once he had embarked on *Six Nights on the Acropolis*, he would announce as the novel's central theme: 'the sickness of Athens, the sickness that emanates from Athens.'[5]

In years to come, a friend in the merchant navy explained to him the incurable nostalgia of the sailor: 'As soon as we're at sea, we sicken with nostalgia for land, and as soon as we tie up in port, we're constantly anxious to be on our way again.' These words no doubt impressed George so much, because he recognised something of his own experience in them, and never more so than during these first years after his return from Paris to Athens. Back where he had so much longed to be, he found himself missing the sophisticated world that he had left behind; above all, he missed the intricate subtleties of the French language.[6]

It was surely for this reason that George threw himself, within a year of returning to Greece, into a frenzied round of literary translation; it was an almost desperate bid to bridge the gap in culture between Paris and Athens. Indicative of his literary interests at this time, most of what he translated was prose rather than poetry. Only one of these translations, of the subtle and ironic meditation on the pursuit of abstract ideas, *La soirée avec M. Teste* by Valéry, ever saw the light of day. When it appeared in the journal *Nea Estia* in 1928, it was George's first substantial publication, and also the only one to be signed 'G. Seferiadis.'[7] He went on to tackle two early fictional works by Gide, belonging to the self-satirising genre to which Gide had given the name *sotie*. One of these, *Paludes*, on which George drew heavily in his own experimental fiction, survives in a fair copy dated 24 August 1926. At about this time he also translated the *Lettre de Madame Emilie Teste*, and a handful of poems, by Valéry, and some essays by Montaigne. Many of these translations he destroyed a few months later.[8]

In his diary, George explained his motives in two ways. Translating was in part a linguistic and an intellectual exercise; but also, in translating from the vastly more sophisticated resources of literary French into the spoken form of his own language, George set out to test, and if possible to extend, the expressive possibilities of demotic Greek as a vehicle for sophisticated literary expression.[9]

It was not only through this intense literary engagement that George kept faith, during his first two years back in Greece, with the world that he had left behind in Paris. He was corresponding with Jacqueline and her mother, Marie-Louise, often at the rate of two letters sent or received per week. Nothing of this correspondence, which must have been carried on in French, is known to survive, with the exception of two studio photographs of herself that Jacqueline sent him in July 1925; but its frequency can be traced through the laconic pages of the pocket-diaries for 1926 and 1927. From the same source, there are indications that some of this correspondence was being passed via the intermediary of his friend Poniridy, in Paris, presumably to avoid attracting unwelcome attention at home.[10]

This is in marked contrast to the traces of Jacqueline that have been allowed to remain in *Days 1* and *Six Nights on the Acropolis*. In each, with her identity only lightly disguised, she appears as no more than a memory, albeit a particularly tender one; there is no sign of struggle, and hardly any indication of a continuing commitment after George had left Paris and returned to Greece. A diary entry for August 1926, a year and a half after his return, reads:

> The most powerful passion I have, the passion to express myself, has been an unquenchable source of misery for me. It was this that made me unthinkingly injure the woman I loved.[11]

This is not merely an understatement; the tense of the last verb (in the preserved form of *Days 1*) is directly belied by the pocket-diaries. Not only was George still in love with Jacqueline; he seems now to have entered upon a commitment to her more wholehearted than he had felt able to make when the two had been together in Paris. This, at least, is the most likely significance of the entry in his pocket-diary, against the date 5 March 1926: *ML: Lettre officielle. J____* (the last letter heavily written, and smudged). Although no other evidence confirms the implication that George and Jacqueline were now engaged, later letters preserve the traces of his stubborn determination to keep faith.[12]

Writing to his sister after it was over, George recalled the 'superhuman effort' of his first two years back in Greece: 'How much you have to forget yourself, or alter your natural condition, so as keep hold of *real* contact at a distance.' He described the effect, then, as being 'like living through a crisis of mysticism.' It was surely during these years that the image of Jacqueline began to be transformed, in George's mind, into the ethereal, idealised, partly devotional figure that appears in later poems. With the same hindsight, he would recall more bluntly: 'I've had tragic experience of parting in my life, while the effort of concentration seared and withered every other passing, free tenderness within me.' An unavoidable consequence was, at the time, not so much mysticism as narcissism: 'Introspection (as in the years [nineteen] twenty-five to twenty-seven) is altogether useless,' he concluded. It is in this form, as narcissism or introspection, that the 'crisis' of those years is most fully explored in *Days 1* and *Six Nights*, although both obscure its cause.[13]

'Do you know who Narcissus was? Someone who could see himself drowning but couldn't make a move to save himself.' So declares the fictional Stratis, in *Six Nights*; but the observation was already present in George's own diary, as early as the end of 1925. The condition that George experienced during these two years was to find its most lyrical expression in retrospect, in poem 15 of *Mythistorema* (1935):

Have mercy on those who wait with so much patience
lost among dark laurels beneath the heavy plane-trees
and those who all alone talk to wells and springs
and are drowned in the ripples of the voice.[14]

It was an impossible situation, and it could not last. *Six Nights on the Acropolis,* though it gives at once both less and more than the full story, is about how it ended.

When George had been sent to England in the summer of 1924, Stelios had thought it possible that his son could pass the entry examination for the diplomatic service at the beginning of the following year. Then in November, when he had been urging George to stay in London until after the Christmas holiday, Stelios had proposed the summer competition, of 1925, instead. But again there was a postponement. It was now that George transcribed into his diary part of the passage from St Matthew's Gospel (in the demotic translation of Alexandros Pallis, here given in the Authorized Version):

70    No man can serve two masters . . . Therefore take no thought, saying, What shall we eat? or, What shall we drink? or, Wherewithal shall we be clothed? (For after all these things do the Gentiles seek:) for your heavenly Father knoweth that ye have need of these things.[15]

Jesus' words from the Sermon on the Mount are here wrenched out of context, so that the two masters (God and Mammon in the original) are not identified, and the famous saying is juxtaposed, instead, to the role of God the Father in making all human dispositions. The words of the Bible, as quoted by George and applied to his own circumstances, seem to be saying: *it is impossible to be equally devoted to a career and to poetry, but I have no choice in the matter because everything is in the hands of Stelios.*

The next competition was due in January 1926. Stelios had often acted as an examiner for the Ministry on these occasions. He could not, of course, examine his own son; but two days before the appointed day, he subjected George to a 'mock' exmination. The candidate was insufficiently prepared, Stelios decided; and the ordeal was postponed again.

Ioanna presents this final postponement, which in the event lasted almost a year, as a bitter blow to George. Despo was now terminally ill; he had wanted to give his mother the satisfaction of seeing him pass this prestigious hurdle. His own laconic comment records merely annoyance at his father's interference. In reality, there was probably a good deal of deliberate procrastination on George's part: these repeated postponements may well have been his means of passive resistance.[16]

Certainly this was the time, during the spring and summer of 1926, that George was most occupied with literary translation from French. He was also reading prodigiously – and not for his examination. Most of this reading, which occupies a prominent place in *Days 1*, was in French. Among the French classics he read Rabelais, Montaigne, Villon; he subscribed to the *Nouvelle Revue Française*, the creation of André Gide, and read or re-read more widely than ever in contemporary fiction and poetry. It was now that he first encountered the ideas of the philosopher Alain (pseudonym of Emile-Auguste Chartier), as they were set out in the recently published *Système des Beaux Arts*, and (through French) the work of the German poet Rainer Maria Rilke.[17]

At the same time George began systematically to read Homer's *Odyssey*, in the French parallel-text prose version by Victor Bérard. In Greek, he read for the first time the two masterpieces of prose that had been written in the vernacular ('demotic') during the nineteenth century, but had remained unknown until the twentieth. *The Woman of Zakynthos*, by Greece's 'national poet,' Dionysios Solomos, is a satire that draws on the tone and imagery of the biblical *Apocalypse*; the historical *Memoirs* of General Makriyannis bear witness to the Greek war of independence in the 1820s and its aftermath. Both served George ever afterwards, not just as stylistic models, but (the latter especially) as the repository of a simple and profound moral conscience that he would always attribute to the Greek people.[18]

During the summer of 1926, George, Ioanna, and their mother moved out of Athens to escape the heat, to a house in what was then the country, at the village of Vrisi outside Kifisia. Stelios did not join them, but came to say goodbye, in June, before taking ship for Marseille and Paris. It is impossible to tell what, if anything, remained of the old ardent enthusiasm of the youthful photograph that shows Stelios with Despo, his arm around her and their heads touching. That June day in 1926 was the last time that he saw her.[19]

On 22 August, the unloved dictatorship of General Pangalos was ousted by a *coup d'état*. George noted in his diary: 'here, a dictatorship collapsed the other day . . . , almost silently, like a pile of straw.' By this time Despo had taken a further turn for the worse. She had not left her bed for weeks.

Angelos was away in the Aegean. It was George and Ioanna who consulted doctors, and brought a specialist out from Athens. The specialist diagnosed kidney failure and gave Despo two months at most to live. Ioanna now wrote to Angelos, who arrived on the day she died. Stelios seems to have written that he could not leave Paris before the middle of September. Her children took it in turns to watch over her, sleeping fully clothed between watches. On the night of 9 September, it was Angelos' turn. Ioanna woke to hear her brothers whispering, should they wake her? Against this date and the place, 'Kifisia,' in George's published diary, appears a blank space.[20]

Despo should have been buried in Athens, and, according to Greek custom, the next day. George set out with his mother's body in its coffin, insisting that Angelos stay with his sister in the house, so that she would not be alone. It was a day of riots and martial law in the city, following the recent *coup*. The minuscule cortège was stopped along the road, and made to turn back. It was the first time, according to Ioanna, that George used the expression, to refer to the Greek authorities, that would later become almost a refrain for him: 'We just can't be taken seriously.' The three siblings had to bury their mother, instead, at Kifisia.[21]

In later life, both George and his sister were always reticent about their mother. Despite this, Despo's profound, simple, 'patrician' humility in face of a divine order of things in which she believed absolutely, became as fundamental a legacy for George as it more obviously was for Ioanna. The word 'miracle,' that would come to have key significance in his later poetry and thinking, enters his writing on the eve of his mother's death. An insight that would be developed in poems from *Mythistorema* (1935) to the *Three Secret Poems* (1966) first appears on Despo's last nameday, 15 August. Although the published diary entry makes no mention of his mother or her condition, the insight that appears for the first time, against this significant date, is surely the crystallisation of a lesson that the temperamentally resentful George believed he could learn from the example of his mother's life:

> ... the most important thing isn't to change our life, dreaming of another more interesting one, but to give voice to the life that we've got, just as it was given to us: this humdrum, humble, human life, in which everything we could possibly ask for *has* to exist. It's in this life that belongs to us, that no one can take away from us and is unique (since it belongs to no one else) ... that we've got to learn to see the miracle.

A few weeks after his mother's death, George was wondering, in his diary, whether angels might exist in Greece today, and if so, what they might look like.[22]

George's examinations for the diplomatic service finally took place on Sunday and Monday, 19 and 20 December 1926. The spaces against these dates in his pocket-diary are heavily marked with asterisks; throughout the previous four weeks he had marked off a daily countdown. There were three vacancies at the Ministry on this occasion. Ioanna says that there was a long list of eager candidates. George was examined in French, diplomatic history, in diplomatic, consular, public and commercial law, in Ottoman legislation, political economy, geography, typing, and English. He learned the result at midnight at the end of the second day: he had come second. His first act on learning the news was to send a telegram to his friend George Poniridy in Paris, for him to pass on to 'ML;' that is, to Marie-Louise and Jacqueline.[23]

A week later he presented himself for the first time at the austere building with tall, neoclassical portals, just off Syntagma Square in the centre of Athens, that still houses part of the Ministry of Foreign Affairs. For the next two years, he would be assigned to the cryptography department. Today, outside the building in the now pedestrianised Zalokosta Street, a bust of George Seferis surmounts a large plinth of rough-hewn marble. It is a much older man, in pullover and tie, who looks with pained sadness downwards past the pen held in his hand. Inside, a room was named after him in an official ceremony in May 2000. It is unlikely that the twenty-six-year-old George, ambitious as a writer and resentful of his new professional duties, would ever have imagined such a form of public recognition, here of all places.[24]

73

### Lou, Salome and the 'cistern'

George had been keeping faith with Jacqueline and her mother, Marie-Louise, by letter for just over two years, when suddenly everything changed. According to Ioanna:

> A true woman, with a taste for music and a cultivated sensibility, fell in love with George. She was married, a little older than he was . . . Above all, she did not expect him to be faithful to her. And George accepted her love with gratitude.[25]

This was Loukia Fotopoulou, whose name George would soon abbreviate to 'Lou.' In due course she would also acquire the literary aliases Salome and Bilio.

Loukia Fotopoulou was something very unusual in Athens at the time: a highly educated woman, living apart from her husband, struggling to earn a living by writing reviews and articles on classical music. She had been in Paris during some of the same years as George, studying music, but their paths do not seem to have crossed there. Her musical tastes (deep love for Debussy, Ravel and Stravinsky, distaste for Wagner) were soon to prove formative for George. An obituary stresses her spontaneity, vivacity, extrovert concern for others, strength of character, and physical fragility. She does not look fragile in the few photographs that show a broad-shouldered, rather masculine-looking woman, though there is evidence in George's letters to her that her health was not good.[26]

All of this is consistent with the character of Salome (also known as Bilio) in the novel *Six Nights on the Acropolis*. She too is small in stature. She has auburn hair and a harsh voice, her conversation is unpredictable; she is passionate, with a 'bitter sense of pleasure.' Like her counterpart in real life, the fictional Salome has been married and is separated from her husband. She has relationships with women as well as with men, jealously guards her sexual freedom, and in a key strand in the novel's plot, effectively procures one of her girlfriends for the hero.[27] It might be thought that these last details are more at home in the world of fiction than of fact; certainly there is much that is purely literary in the way that they are elaborated in the novel. But George acknowledged that the real-life Lou also had lesbian relationships. And during the summer of 1927, he seems to have made up for his two years of loyal celibacy with a bout of promiscuity; jottings in his pocket-diary at that time imply that at least one of these casual girlfriends may have been procured for him by Lou.[28]

It seems that George first became attracted to Lou during the summer of 1926, while his mother was dying at Kifisia. A chance meeting on the bus into Athens, one hot July afternoon, is refracted in different ways in *Days 1*, *Six Nights*, and in the first draft of the poem 'Automobile,' the earliest of the poems of *Turning Point* to be written after George's return to Greece. This short, bitter poem elaborates a full-blown fantasy of loveless modern sex, in which it is only the bodies that hurtle together on the car's imagined trajectory, while the lovers' hearts are scattered to right and left, never meeting. In what is probably the uncut version of the diary entry, preserved in the novel, this scene provides the setting for the first meeting between Stratis and Salome.[29]

The sequel came ten months later, next spring. In the novel, Stratis and Salome become lovers suddenly, in her basement flat, on the evening of

Good Friday the following April. In George's pocket-diary for 1927, across the pages covering the first five days of April, is a series of scribblings, only partly legible, but showing signs of haste or emotion, and without parallel in these diaries. Some appear to be lines of doggerel. It was not Easter-time in Greece, but the diary is French: against Sunday 3 April is printed: *La Passion*. The word has the same double meaning in French as it does in English, and may well have been sufficient to suggest to George the symbolic juxtaposition of the Orthodox Good Friday ritual with the passion of the lovers hidden away in Salome's basement flat. Much is made of this, in the episode of the novel; the same symbolism underlies the poem that a few years later George would write for Lou, *The Cistern*. An isolated entry in *Days 1*, against Saturday 2 April 1927, consists of four lines of verse whose imagery closely foreshadows that poem. Lou, in real life, did live in a basement flat, not far from the Seferiadis family home, on the other side of Patission Avenue; from this time on, the word 'cistern' became George's private codeword for a sexual assignation.[30]

Then in the pocket-diary, beginning with 5 April, the numbers indicating letters to or from Jacqueline and Marie-Louise have been heavily scored out. The last letter from Jacqueline ever to be recorded in this way was written on 16 April, and received by George on the 22nd (this was Good Friday in Greece). The entry for the following day records the last in the parallel series from Marie-Louise. Thereafter the name 'Lou' first begins to appear in the pocket-diary. Evidently, immediately after the events of those first days of April, George had written to Jacqueline and to her mother, and broken off the relationship.[31]

75

That summer Ioanna was in Paris and met Jacqueline for the first time. The picture of grief that she paints becomes fully intelligible only in the light of these developments:

> As soon as I set eyes on Jacqueline I felt sorry for her. Perhaps because I knew what I knew. Perhaps because her large eyes had concentrated in them all the sadness there is. She spoke little, didn't complain; when she spoke his name, a warmth of love spread through the room. I don't remember what she said, but the memory of that grief has never left me.[32]

But Ioanna's narrative entirely suppresses the break that had come just two months before this. According to Ioanna, Jacqueline remained the principal object of George's affections, 'in spite of separations and his relationships with other women,' until the very eve of her marriage several years later. In reality, it was Ioanna herself who, from this time onwards, would continue to keep faith with the girl whom her brother had abandoned. But George, when the moment of crisis came, had behaved more honourably than his sister gives him credit for.[33]

*Six Nights on the Acropolis* telescopes into a little under six months the emotional switchback of the first three years of George's affair with Lou. Salome is the most fully realised character in the novel; but her relationship with Stratis is ambivalent from start to finish. From Stratis' point of view, the principal value of this relationship is that she breaks the spell of narcissistic introspection in which he had become trapped. Other aspects of the fictional relationship are less happy for the hero. Salome is almost always the dominant partner; often Stratis is afraid of her. Another character describes her as 'a dangerous woman; she won't let anything stand in her way: *amorale.*' There is something aggressive, perhaps even predatory, about her sexuality. Elsewhere, Stratis compares her to a labyrinth, and the novel contains other sinister references to the myth of the Minotaur, and to the sexual rapacity of Minos' queen Pasiphae, although these are not directly linked to Salome herself. All these attributes come together in the fictional name, Salome. The parallel is explicitly drawn with the Biblical story of Herod's daughter dancing naked and demanding the head of John the Baptist, as retold by Oscar Wilde in his French play, *Salomé*. Many years earlier, George had first referred to this story in the context of his relationship with Suzon; in the novel, Stratis does so with reference to Salome.[34]

There is no way of telling how much, if any, of this amounts to an accurate portrait of Loukia Fotopoulou, but it probably does reflect the way in which George saw her at this time. There is evidence to confirm this, from outside the fictional world of *Six Nights*. George's diary for the end of 1927 includes a long passage translated from the Latin novel of the second century AD, *Metamorphoses*, better known in English as *The Golden Ass*, by Apuleius. There are references to Apuleius also in *Six Nights*; in *Days 1* a coded link to Lou is supplied by the note that accompanies the translation: 'waiting in the cistern.' The pages that George translated come from the beginning of Book 2, and tell how the hero, Lucius, a gullible young man on a visit to a strange town, is seduced by his fascination for magic into a passionate affair with a witch, whose recompense is to change him into an ass. The significance that this story must have had for George, at the time, becomes clear as soon as the Greek form of the hero's name,

*Loukios*, is set alongside the name of the witch: *Fotis*. Loukia Fotopoulou has become, in George's imagination, the beguiling witch who has the power to make an ass of him.[35]

Elsewhere, the diary assigns magical power of a rather different sort to a thinly disguised Lou. This time she appears as 'Princess Lu;' here, as in their later correspondence, George's nickname for her is playfully thought of as Chinese. A narrative of an excursion with 'Princess Lu' in the pinewoods above Kifisia takes on a supernatural and mysterious dimension, when the little princess takes to the treetops, swinging higher and higher until there is nowhere left for her to go, and to the observer's horror she plummets to the ground. His first instinct is the base one, to take the train straight home. When, instead, he brings himself to look for the body of his lost companion, he finds only a dead sparrow, that must have been there since the morning. A few years later, George would work this theme of the inspired but impossible dance, that leads to death, into the published prose poem, 'Nijinsky,' which has also been read as a key statement of his poetics.[36]

The first poem that George addressed to Lou (under the alias Bilio) catches both the intensity of physical passion and the sense of despair that follows the all-too fleeting moment. The manuscript is dated 14 February 1928, suggesting that it was originally a Valentine. There was also an epigraph, later deleted, which comes from the *Odyssey*: four lines devoted to the hero's dalliance with the nymph Calypso. As recounted by Homer, Calypso's charms were at once erotic and supernatural; they also had sufficient power to cause Odysseus to forget his faithful wife, Penelope, and postpone his epic voyage home to Ithaca for seven years.[37]

All in all, then, George seems to have regarded the new force in his life at this time in highly ambivalent terms: slaking the sexual thirst of his years of loyalty to Jacqueline with deliberate abandon, but at the same time jealous, perhaps even afraid, of the power that the older woman now exercised over him.

There is one final aspect of the relationship that did not find its way into the novel, but that loomed large from the beginning and would become obsessive in George's later, preserved correspondence with Lou. This was secrecy. Loukia Fotopoulou, although living apart from her husband, was in the eyes of the world a married woman. In the social circles in which George moved, and especially for a young career diplomat, the *mores* of the time were rigid. While it was accepted, even expected, that men would have short-lived affairs, after marriage as well as before, social decorum demanded absolute discretion about these. A long-term affair, involving commitment, was acceptable only if it ended in marriage. Both her age, and the fact that she was married already, ruled out Lou as a suitable marriage partner for George.

For all these reasons, the affair had to be kept dark. Even George's closest friends, it seems, were in ignorance. He could give full rein to his passion only hidden away in the 'secret lair,' the 'cistern' where:

> The night does not believe in dawn
> and love weaves death a living shroud
> just so, the way a soul's set free
> a cistern gives the lesson: silence
> amid the passions of the city.[38]

Looking back on three years of this relationship, at a moment when he was trying to end it, George offered Lou his bleak summary of what they had enjoyed together:

> We didn't meet often, once in a week or ten days, because that was the way society was. Two or three hours [together], and then we'd forget. . . . Remember how afraid we were that people would talk, what might become of us if they did. Once or twice at the beginning we talked about it . . . Since then, no confession, no complaint would come in the way of those precious hours that belonged to us. We had two or three years of secret, silent love; I'm not sure how long the magic really lasted. . . .[39]

### The four Georges

While all this was going on, George was forming or consolidating the three most enduring male friendships of his life; all three of these new friends were also called George.

The break with Jacqueline seems to have provoked a reappraisal of his other important relationships from Paris days. Poniridy came to Athens on a visit in July 1926; George already thought he was outgrowing his friend, whom he found 'fast and lazy.' They seem to have met for the last time in 1932. Adamos fades out completely after the end of 1925 (although, with the others, his name appears on the distribution list for *Turning Point* in 1931). Aronis, who in old age would be touchingly proud of his early friendship with the 'Nobel man,' concedes that after their respective returns from

Paris they were never close again, though they met on a few occasions; George mentions Nikos for the last time in his diary in 1931. As he entered the second half of his twenties, George was learning rapidly, both about himself and about what he valued in his friends. One of these lessons seems to have been to keep his emotional life and his friendships separate in future. All three of his earlier friends had known Jacqueline and Marie-Louise well, and had been privy to his feelings. It would have been difficult, after the break, to feel the same way about them either. Now, obedient to the lesson of the 'cistern,' George kept his life strictly compartmentalised.[40]

The first, and in some respects the greatest, of these new friends was George Katsimbalis. Katsimbalis' father, Constantine, spent a large part of his life in Paris. A man of means, a lover of literature, of good food and wine, his amatory conquests had included the poet the Comtesse de Noailles. In Paris, 'Old' Katsimbalis had become a close friend of Stelios Seferiadis. When George and the rest of the Seferiadis family arrived in 1918, George remembered meeting 'Old' Katsimbalis at the Hotel du Louvre, among his earliest acquaintances there. Years later, George Katsimbalis, in his turn, would recall Stelios Seferiadis with affection: 'I'll never forget the emotion with which he helped me close my trunk . . . when I was on my way to Smyrna in 1920 and he gave advice and blessings to the young second lieutenant who was about to set foot for the first time in the holy land of Ionia.' This was before the two Georges had met.[41]

Temperamentally very different from George, the young Katsimbalis was an ardent supporter of Venizelos, and remained an unashamed, life-long nationalist. He had twice carried these convictions to the point of action, serving as a volunteer, first on the Macedonian Front from May 1917 until the end of the First World War, and then in the Anatolian campaign, in which he rose to become captain of artillery. It is not entirely clear to what extent his subsequent disabilities were the result of wounds received in the fighting. But it was characteristic of George Katsimbalis' larger-than-life personality that the 'big stick' (*mangoura*) which was ever afterwards necessary for mobility, should soon have become a legendary symbol of his dominance over Greek literary life from the 1930s to the 1950s.[42]

George met the young Katsimbalis for the first time, in Paris, some time after May 1922. Some years later, he would recall waiting for the bus in the rue des Médicis, while Katsimbalis regaled him with anecdotes of the fierce Cretan gunners of his platoon, who used to write home to their families in the traditional verse of the island's folksongs. The two seem to have been friends, but not especially close, by the time that George left Paris for London in 1924. It was only after Katsimbalis returned from Paris to Athens for good, at the end of 1927, that their close friendship began.[43]

The Katsimbalis house in Athens stood at the corner of Syntagma Square, where the family owned some of the most valuable land in Greece; they also had a sizeable estate outside the city, in the fashionable suburb of Maroussi (Amaroussion), not far from Kifisia. The family house at Maroussi, standing alone on a small hilltop on the edge of the Mangou-fana wood, and open to the elements, had been baptised by the poet Zacharias Papantoniou with the name 'Trianemi' (place of three winds). Within a few years, Trianemi had become the hub of a significant section of the Greek literary and intellectual world. Ioanna particularly loved Tri-anemi, and gives an affectionate account of it. It was there, too, some years later, that the legend of the 'Colossus of Maroussi' would be born, when Henry Miller accompanied Lawrence and Nancy Durrell to Athens in the autumn of 1939, and all three fell under the spell of Katsimbalis.[44]

Miller's exuberant account surely has almost as much of Miller in it as of Katsimbalis. The dimensions of the man are heroic:

80
> He was a curious mixture of things to me on that first occasion; he had the general physique of a bull, the tenacity of a vulture, the agility of a leopard, the tenderness of a lamb, and the coyness of a dove. He had a curious overgrown head which fascinated me ... His hands were rather small for his body, and overly delicate. He was a vital, powerful man, capable of brutal gestures and rough words, yet somehow con-veying a sense of warmth which was soft and feminine. There was also a great element of the tragic in him which his adroit mimicry only enhanced.

Katsimbalis' great passions, according to Miller's portrait, were Greece and food; and Miller relays a good deal of his idiosyncratic, fluent conversation on both topics. But Miller was aware, too, of a darker side to Katsimbalis. Once again, the colours are no doubt exaggerated, and it is noticeable how Miller separates these two portraits which, taken literally, hardly seem to be of the same person:

> There were a lot of things he couldn't do any more – the war had banged him up a bit. But despite the bad arm, the dislocated knee, the damaged eye, the disorganized liver, the rheumatic twinges, the arthritic distur-

bances, the migraine, the dizziness and God knows what, what was left of the catastrophe was alive and flourishing like a smoking dung-heap.[45]

There was yet another side, that Miller probably never saw, and that might not have interested him greatly if he had: his 'sober, productive, punctilious side,' in the words of George's American translator Edmund Keeley. Wholly committed to literature, and to the development and promotion of a specifically *Greek* literature, Katsimbalis never wrote anything himself. His creative personality was all in his talk. But he did invest enormous energy, and the financial resources at his disposal, to support and encourage the creative work of others. The most spectacular beneficiary of this energy and talent, in years to come, would be George. The entire influential movement in Greek literature known as the 'Generation of the Thirties' bears the stamp of Katsimbalis' personality and his authority.[46]

Katsimbalis was at once a Maecenas (a wealthy and influential patron) and an Ezra Pound (publicist and unpaid literary agent) to his friends; in return he was unrelenting in his demands on them. Katsimbalis emerges from their correspondence as the only man from whom George would accept criticism, though he did so grudgingly. Katsimbalis was indefatigable in another way, too: this most extrovert and inspired talker would set himself, in his private hours, one of the most thankless tasks in the service of literature, to compile exhaustive bibliographies of modern Greek writers. Today, Katsimbalis is rightly seen as the father of modern Greek bibliography; his bibliographies of his idol Kostis Palamas, but also of Sikelianos, Seferis, Kazantzakis, Cavafy (whom he loathed), and others, are still standard works of reference today.

Looking back on this friendship after it had endured for nearly half a century, George emphasised:

> Katsimbalis has that wonderful quality of being without evil intention in his heart. He might criticize somebody, but in a good-hearted way. And he believed that our country, our little country, was able to do something. He had that sort of belief.[47]

Another new friend, who entered George's life a little after Katsimbalis, was George Theotokas. Novelist, playwright, essayist and diarist, Theotokas would also make his mark on Greek literature. He was five years younger than George, and a native of Constantinople. While at Athens University, Theotokas had studied Law under Stelios Seferiadis and alongside George's brother Angelos; he had risen to be president of the Students' Union. Ioanna, too, remembered Theotokas from the University; he had struck her, then, as 'sympathetic, shy, he blushed easily.' Then in London, in the summer of 1929, she encountered Theotokas again; he gave her a manuscript to read. This was *Free Spirit*, published in Athens a few months later under a pseudonym. *Free Spirit* is an intemperate broadside which lambasts most modern Greek poetry and fiction, and proclaims the dawn of a new age: Greek literature is to embrace internationalism and the modern world, and free itself from the cliques and political polarisation that, according to the author, had bedevilled Athenian cultural life for years.

In this manuscript, Ioanna seems at once to have recognised a kindred spirit to her brother. It was she who introduced them, when they were all back in Athens, that autumn. George, as Theotokas would later recall, had the reputation of being 'isolated and unapproachable;' Theotokas, as the younger man, came to the meeting with a degree of awe. Soon, as they became friends, George would invent roles for them both, taken from Stendhal's novel, *La Chartreuse de Parme*: the older George, the professional diplomat, becomes the wily and worldly-wise Conte Mosca; the younger, Theotokas, his protégé, the romantic hero, Fabrice. Although the relationship would never again be as confiding as during its first three years, and would become more distant after the Second World War, the two maintained these roles for more than three decades until Theotokas' death in 1966 when George published his obituary for his friend under the title 'Conversation with Fabrice.'[48]

Already balding, with short dark hair brushed straight back, and a physique not unlike George's own, Theotokas at the end of the 1920s brought out the playful side of George. It was for Theotokas that he wrote the light-hearted poem, 'Syngrou Avenue, 1930.' This was George's first poem in free verse. It had been provoked by Theotokas' call, in *Free Spirit*, for new poets to discover new ways in which to hymn the modern Athens of aeroplanes and the new arterial roads that were then being built; one of these was the avenue that links central Athens with the sea at Faliron, after which the poem is named.[49]

Together George and Theotokas fantasized about a distant future. In the year 1965, George was going to be a member of the Athens Academy; Theotokas, after having turned his back on the lofty ideals of his youth, and become locked in conflict with the Greek royal family, the house of Glücksburg, was going to be President of the Republic. There are some uncanny presentiments here: in the event, 1965 was indeed the year of a damaging constitutional clash between King Constantine II and his prime minister; George that year was indeed proposed as a member of the Athens Academy, but refused to make the necessary obeisances in order to be elected; a decade later it was to be, not Theotokas, but another member of George's circle, Ioanna's husband Konstantinos Tsatsos, who would become President of the newly declared Republic.[50]

By the end of the 1920s, Seferis, Katsimbalis, and Theotokas were so close, and so closely embroiled in plotting the literary revival of their country, that they came to think of themselves as the 'three Georges.'[51]

There was, however, a fourth George. This was George Apostolidis; in photographs he poses square-shouldered, with a moustache, and something of the air of an Italian tenor on stage. Apostolidis had trained as a lawyer in Paris, although he and George met only after both had returned to Greece in the second half of the 1920s. Like Katsimbalis, Apostolidis was a year older than George; like Theotokas, he came from Constantinople. At the end of 1926, Apostolidis established himself in a legal partnership in Athens. He had a lifelong interest in French theatre; lacking the intellectual rigour of George's more literary friends, he shared George's enthusiasm for the ideas of the French philosopher Alain, in particular the 'hands-on' concept of the artist as artisan. Perhaps linked to this approach, and unlike the other two Georges, Apostolidis was ungrudging in his admiration for everything that George wrote. With Apostolidis, George was able to relax his guard more than with his other friends; in these early days they went swimming together and patronised a fashionable Athens night-club. Even Apostolidis seems to have known little about Lou, but he was the only one of George's male friends, after the break with Jacqueline, in whom he would occasionally confide something of his feelings about women.[52]

Perhaps for all these reasons, George often described Apostolidis as his closest friend. This uncomplicated warmth of feeling seems to have been undiminished by the years. In the late 1950s, Apostolidis would labour tirelessly, while George was away in London as ambassador, to oversee the legal and technical aspects of building his permanent home in Agras Street, next to the Stadium in Athens. In general, George found it difficult to rely on people; Apostolidis was probably the only person in his life, outside his immediate family, on whom he felt that he could rely absolutely.[53]

## New horizons

In March 1928, George volunteered for a five-day mission to Istanbul as a diplomatic courier. It was his first experience of flying, and he recorded his impressions in detail in his diary. The seaplane took off from Faliron Bay. From a height of five hundred metres, he looked down on the signs of human activity, like 'skin diseases on the earth,' and the seagulls flying far below. Crossing the islands of the northern Aegean, the aircraft flew low enough to terrify the sheep grazing on the hillsides.[54]

In the city that the Greeks knew as Constantinople, George found himself suddenly confronted by his 'childhood years welling up' before him. It was his first experience of the new Turkish Republic of Mustafa Kemal, who among many other drastic changes had moved the capital from Istanbul to Ankara. Something of George's jaundiced state of mind, a year into the new relationship with Lou, is carried over into the poem that he wrote at the time of this visit, 'The Companions in Hades,' his first poem with an overtly Homeric theme. The speakers in this poem are the dead companions of Odysseus, who according to Homer 'foolishly' lost their lives on the voyage.[55]

The summer of 1928 was a fevered time in Greece, and nowhere more so than in the house among the pine-trees, between Kefalari and Kokkinaras, on the slopes of Penteli, above Kifisia, where George, Ioanna and Angelos retreated from the noise and heat of Athens.

In the political sphere, Venizelos had re-entered politics in May. Almost immediately, the elderly Cretan statesman was swept to power at the head of a caretaker government, to oversee elections in August. Venizelos' electoral triumph on 19 August, coming after years of ineffectual squabbling and military interventions, inaugurated the only period of stable parliamentary government that Greece would experience between the two world wars. It would last for four years; among its effects on the Seferiadis family would be to elevate Stelios to the highest offices of his career, including a term of service as a member of the newly formed Council of State, a form of Supreme Court.[56]

At the same time, the Greek literary world was shaken by the suicide, on 21 July, of the poet Kostas Karyotakis. 'A poet of exceptional sensibility . . . whose fate it was to leave behind an *oeuvre* that counts as a high point in our literature,' was George's somewhat constrained tribute many years later. Karyotakis, a civil servant like himself, had served the same two masters as he did; Karyotakis' last poem mounts a scathing assault on the boredom and small-mindedness of Greek provincial life and the mindless bureaucracy that regulated it. Although Karyotakis had produced three collections of poetry and ended his life before the first appearance of George Seferis in print, the difference in the two poets' ages was only four years.[57]

Within a year of Karyotakis' suicide, George's friend Theotokas would be holding him up as a negative example to the poets of the coming decade, in *Free Spirit*. George left no record of his feelings at the time, and ever afterwards distanced himself from the example of Karyotakis. But the shorter poems of the collection *Turning Point* are matched only by those of Karyotakis in their mood of hard-edged bitterness and self-mockery, encapsulated in often experimental but always strict forms, using metre and rhyme. George had himself discussed the possibility of suicide with his sister in his student days; he would cut out and keep occasional newspaper cuttings about attempted suicides until shortly after this. In Karyotakis' end, George must have seen mirrored a frightening possibility for the self that he still was in 1928.[58]

In their summer retreat in the cool of the pines at Kokkinaras, according to Ioanna all three Seferiadis siblings were in love. Fever literally took hold at the beginning of August, when first George and then Ioanna went down with dengue, a condition whose principal symptom is a dangerously high temperature.[59]

It was while in the grip of dengue fever that George first conceived the literary alter ego, Mathios Paskalis. The name apparently was inspired by a cinema poster that he had seen some years previously, in Athens; the film was based on the novel by Luigi Pirandello, *Il fu Mattia Pascal*. George never did read the novel; it was the name that stayed with him, probably because in the form in which he rendered it into demotic Greek its components recall the dictum of the ancient tragedian Aeschylus: 'learning through suffering' (*mathos pathei*). In addition, 'Pascal' or 'Paskalis,' from the same root as the noun *pathos*, derives from *Pascha*, meaning 'Easter.' Just like the earlier guise in which George had first tried to come to terms with his feelings for Jacqueline, Alyis Vayias, Mathios Paskalis is condemned by his name to suffer.[60]

The poem 'Letter of Mathios Paskalis' is dated 5 August 1928. It was the first day after his delirium that George was well enough to hold a pen. The fictional persona is clearly in a disordered state; the long lines of the *verset claudélien*, without internal metre, are only just kept under control by the strict rhymes in which they end. The poem is addressed to a woman called 'Verina,' apparently an alias for the object of that summer's transient passion, while Lou was away at a fashionable sanatorium on Mount Pelion.[61]

The poem is about escape. It begins with the 'skyscrapers of New York,' that of course George had never seen, and continues:

85

Verina, we have been wasted by life and the skies of Attica and the
    intellectuals who scramble up on their own heads
and the landscapes that have been reduced to striking poses of drought
    and hunger . . .

It ends with a romantic yearning for distant places:

Oh, to be in a bare-rigged ship lost in the Pacific Ocean along with the
    sea and the wind
alone and without wireless and not even the strength to struggle
    against the elements.[62]

This poem is not the only evidence for George's widening horizons in
the late 1920s. Beginning this summer, he applied himself to adapting into
Greek poetic forms from the Far East that had captured the imagination of
poets in western Europe during the preceding decades.

This interest may have been in part suggested by the conceit that disguised Loukia Fotopoulou as the exotic Chinese Princess Lu. The Japanese
haiku fascinated George, with its austere form, limited to seventeen syl-
lables. One of the earliest of these that he preserved was a dedication to
Lou, that recalls the fantasy of the flying princess:

All of the forest
in a single pine-needle.
Lou, your gift to me.[63]

At the end of 1931, he was promising to send more of these to Lou; since
1928, he told Katsimbalis a little after this, he had written fifty haikus.
Sixteen of these found their way into *Book of Exercises*; another nine are
preserved in *Days 1*. Another such formal experiment, in the more complex
form of the Malay *pantun*, was held over from *Turning Point* at the last
minute. Although George does not appear to have taken these 'exercises' in
exotic verseforms very seriously, he was the first to introduce them into
Greek poetry.[64]

But during that summer of 1928, in the wake of the dengue fever,
George had still not found his voice as a poet. Even the future direction of
his literary vocation was uncertain. He had just appeared in print as the
translator of a prose work by Valéry (*La soirée avec M. Teste*); he was at
work in earnest on a novel, *Six Nights on the Acropolis,* which he had prob-

ably begun in the immediate aftermath of his first involvement with Lou, the previous year. Only a handful, and some of the least characteristic, of the poems that he would later publish under the name of Seferis yet existed. All this was about to change.[65]

### Turning point

That autumn, once he had recovered from the fever, George took a month's leave from the Ministry. Perhaps prompted by Ioanna, who had recently also been disappointed in love, his thoughts began to return to Jacqueline.[66]

> The mood of a day that we lived ten years ago in a foreign place
> the glow of a primordial moment that took wing and vanished like an
>      angel of the Lord
> the voice of a woman forgotten with so much care and so much effort;
> an end inconsolable, frozen into marble the sunset of one September.

So begins the poem now known as 'The Mood of a Day.' Its original title had been 'Starting Out.' George was reflecting on the time in Paris when he had first avowed, and then almost immediately been forced to suppress, his vocation as a poet. But the woman must be Jacqueline, and further on the poem bursts out: 'Where is the love that at one stroke severs time in two and confounds it?' For answer, the poem's final stanza elaborates upon a chilling image suggested by the *The Narrative of Arthur Gordon Pym* by Edgar Allan Poe, to which its epigraph also alludes: 'We plainly saw that not a soul lived in that fated vessel!'[67]

For the becalmed explorers in Poe's narrative, desperate hope of rescue turns to horror, when they realise that all the crew of the ship bearing down on them are dead; they have been cheated by the outward semblance, only, of life. In the poem, George fixed on this scene as an image for the empty prolongation of life once the vital spark has gone. The contrast between living presence and the dead, discarded husk it leaves behind is central to George's poetry, and much of his thinking, from this time on. It is first articulated in this poem, the first of a group that pronounces the epitaph on his relationship with Jacqueline.

By the autumn of 1928, if George had persuaded himself, 'with so much care and so much effort,' to forget Jacqueline, Jacqueline herself was not yet ready to forget him. The following summer, Ioanna accompanied Stelios to England and America. On the way, she stopped in Paris and called on Jacqueline: 'she was in such a terrible state, I was really worried. She wanted

87

to come to Greece, to see him again.' This no doubt alarmed George. His response, as Ioanna gives it in edited form, sounds stiff and defensive:

> You can't imagine how painful to me is all that you write to me about J. I mean, I turn my attention to the painful points within me, that have never stopped hurting . . . In the end that's the profession of being human . . .[68]

Probably he begged Ioanna to use her influence to dissuade Jacqueline from coming. But the sophisticated world he had left behind in Paris was soon to be starkly juxtaposed to George's new life in Greece, in an entirely unexpected way. It was not Jacqueline who arrived in Greece that summer, but Edouard Herriot, former prime minister of France and now mayor of Lyon. George was assigned to be his official guide. No doubt a consequence of the recent shake-up in Greek politics, this was the first time the Foreign Ministry had set him a task that touched his imagination. George would exert himself to the full.

Edouard Herriot was an internationalist in outlook, a personal friend of Venizelos, and at this time associated with the efforts of his successor in office, Aristide Briand, to promote the most-far reaching scheme in its day for European integration, the 'Briand plan.' On 13 August 1929, George arrived in the northern city of Thessaloniki and set off by car in an official cavalcade to welcome the official party at the frontier. Shortly afterwards, the Athens newspaper *Eleftheron Vima* carried an interview with Herriot on the future of the Briand plan. The headline for the interview strikes a chord in the early years of the twenty-first century:

> Difficulties in effecting the Briand Plan. Europe unless organised risks becoming a colony of America. Need for economic cooperation among European states.

The itinerary was a gruelling one: by car from Thessaloniki, by the mountainous inland route (Kozani, Elassona, Larissa), then over the Agrafa mountains to Delphi. There followed four days in Athens when Herriot spent some time in official talks, thereby giving George his only partial break during the visit. Then it was by sea to Delos, back to Piraeus and again by sea through the Corinth Canal to Patras for the ancient sanctuary of Olympia; then a fleeting visit to Crete, where George was powerfully

88

impressed by his first sight of the pre-Hellenic Minoan civilisation. Last came a whistle-stop tour, again by car, of the archaeological and historic sites of the northeastern Peloponnese (Mycenae, Epidauros, Nafplion), until at last the visitors departed, by ship for Venice, on the evening of 2 September.

Something of the significance that this visit had for George can be gauged from the fact that he kept everything relating to it: itineraries, tear-off pages from a desk-diary, photographs, maps, press cuttings, even menus. He also kept the effusive letters of thanks he received from Herriot and members of his entourage afterwards. It was George's first role of responsibility, and for all his declared antipathy to the 'treadmill' of the Ministry, this was clearly something different. A year later, when Herriot published his rather plodding, sentimentalised account of his pilgrimage to Greece, the book was dedicated to Venizelos, and included a tribute to 'Georges Séfériadès, jeune et charmant compagnon.'[69]

George had acquitted himself well. But the experience had done nothing to reconcile the differences in culture and perception that had been troubling him since his return from Paris, nearly five years before. An unbridgeable conceptual gap separated the perspective of an educated foreigner, even a declared philhellene like Herriot, from that of the Greek who actually lived in this land. The moment that was ever after to lodge itself in George's memory came at Olympia. The French politician, brought up in the humanist-classical tradition of northern Europe, dismissed George's attempt to interest him in the Christian basilica that had been built over the site of the workshop of the sculptor Pheidias. 'I'm not interested in anything later than the third century [BC],' Herriot had commented brusquely — and presumably it was not for the junior diplomat in attendance to contradict him.

Many years later, when he was again speaking in French on an official occasion, in wartime Alexandria, George referred back to this moment, in order to stress his own sense of Greek history and culture as a totality, just as French history and culture, from the middle ages to the twentieth century, were routinely seen as a totality. He had been shocked, he declared then, by the words of his distinguished interlocutor, who 'had just like that turned out the lights on an enormous extent of two thousand two hundred and something years.'[70]

In the months that followed, in the autumn of 1929, according to Ioanna, George was 'tormented by the idea of Jacqueline.' The discarded opening of the poem 'Erotikos Logos' (or 'Love's Discourse'), soon to become the centrepiece of the volume *Turning Point*, confirms this. It was five years since his parting from Jacqueline to go to England:

> How strange to think that five years have gone by
> in the abyss of parting, or imagine:
> five times the trees have blossomed in your garden
> and dropped five times their fruit upon the earth.[71]

A few days before these lines were written, and seemingly as a kind of prelude to the larger work, George had produced the poem which, thanks to the musical setting by Mikis Theodorakis, many years later, would become his best known and is today almost an unofficial national anthem among Greeks worldwide. The poem's title, in the standard translation, is 'Denial;' its elusive, fleeting evocation of blighted love might better be rendered as 'Renunciation.'

The simplicity of this three-stanza poem is deceptive. Its language wistfully undermines conventional poeticisms; each of its full rhymes hauntingly places despair at the heart of hope, fatally lodged there by the very
90    sounds of language. The beach where the lovers lie (like the 'cistern'), is secret (*kryfó*), but the water there is undrinkable (*glyfó*); 'her name' (*onomá-tis*) written on the sand is wiped away by the sea-breeze (*bátis*); the passion (*páthos*) of commitment to a whole way of life is nothing but a mistake (*láthos*). It ends:

> Such heart we put into our lives,
> such passion, love and long-
> ing when we started; wrong!
> And so we changed our lives.[72]

That winter, the poem 'Erotikos Logos' was left unfinished. Despite the almost angry certainty of the final line of 'Denial,' George was not yet ready to carry through that final act of renunciation, either in life or in art.

In June 1930, Ioanna married. The event seems to have taken many people by surprise. In a photograph taken at this time Ioanna appears as tall and slim, with a simple elegance; the mischievous grin of her late teens has now become moulded into graceful coyness. She was also intellectually able. Like her father before her, Ioanna timed her marriage to coincide with the end of her studies and her doctorate in law; she had in the meantime been working part-time in a law firm. Working women were a rarity in Athens then, at least among the well-to-do classes; and Ioanna, the elegant and vivacious daughter of a Councillor of State, had all the qualities to make heads turn in the relatively small world of Athens society. What caused surprise, in the spring and summer of 1930, was her choice of husband.[73]

Konstantinos Tsatsos (Kostakis to his family and friends) was three years her senior. He had been born into a well-to-do mercantile family with commercial interests in Trieste, which at the time had been the principal sea-port of the Austro-Hungarian empire. His memoirs bear witness to an inferiority complex about these origins that hardly seems supported by the facts; Tsatsos was not the social inferior of the Seferiadis family, or of many of those with whom he later associated in political life. He was, though, acutely conscious of his short stature (he had stopped growing in his early teens, and as an adult was barely five feet tall), and of what he would later describe as the physical ugliness of which he first became aware as an adolescent. But Kostakis Tsatsos had spirit, and more, to compensate for these disadvantages. Precociously intelligent, with a love of learning and literature, he had entered Athens University at the age of fifteen. Although only a year older than George, he had already been earning his spurs working as a cryptographer for the Greek delegation at the Paris Peace Conference, at the time when George had been in his first year at the Sorbonne. Tsatsos had gone on to study philosophy at Heidelberg, a background that a few years later brought him into fruitful contention with George. At the time when he met Ioanna, he was working as a lawyer in the family firm; soon he became Professor of Philosophy at Athens University. Throughout his life Tsatsos was a prolific writer and translator. After the Second World War, he entered politics, and several times held office in governments of the Right, rising to become President of the Republic from 1975 to 1980. He was also, perhaps by way of compensation for his looks, throughout his life a self-confessed and dedicated womanizer.[74]

Tsatsos' marriage to Ioanna was his second; he had been still married to his first wife when they met. George liked him better than he had his sister's previous suitor; he and Kostakis were to remain good friends and intellectual sparring partners for the rest of George's life. When Ioanna returned from America with her father, and announced that she was going to marry Kostakis, George was probably as surprised as anyone. He does not seem to have been especially enthusiastic. 'I hope it will be for Ioanna's hap-

91

piness. Kostakis is a splendid fellow and I pray for luck to lend a helping hand,' he wrote to their brother Angelos, shortly before the wedding. The wedding itself earned only half a dozen lines, caricaturing one of the female guests, in the edited form of George's diary. The couple left for an extended honeymoon on the island of Skiathos. Just over a month later, at the end of July, George went to join them there.[75]

The fortnight that he spent on Skiathos, with his newly married sister and brother-in-law, seems to have been one the happiest interludes in George's life. He made friends among the island's boatbuilders and fishermen, whose vivid speech and practical skills reminded him intensely of Skala. One of these, Sotiris Stamelos, would become in George's eyes a living embodiment at once of Homer and of Makriyannis, his ideal of the innate moral wisdom of the Greek folk. Sotiris was eighty years old, a violinist in the traditional folk style and an endless source of stories. Like Homer's Odysseus, Sotiris had his Penelope, the girl he had loved and lost, and who in old age was his inseparable companion outside marriage. 'An example of the aristocracy of poverty,' as George called him, this dignified peasant had been put in prison by the Turks in his youth; while there, he had tattooed himself with the shapes of the boats of his island. Sotiris is commemorated in *Days 1*, in *Six Nights on the Acropolis*, and in Ioanna's memoir. Later, he provided part of the inspiration for the old tale-spinners who are Homer's avatars in the poem 'Reflections on a Foreign Line of Verse' (written at the end of 1931). Later still, the old man's tattoos, as a symbol of constancy and endurance, would appear in the epigraph to the poems of George's exile during the Second World War, *Logbook II*.[76]

At the same time, George re-read Homer's epic tale of homecoming, the *Odyssey*, from beginning to end. If not actually on Skiathos, it was also at this time that he first read Joyce's modern odyssey, *Ulysses*, whose first publication had attracted his attention in Sylvia Beach's bookshop in Paris. The foundations were being laid for the poems that five years later would be published under the title *Mythistorema*.[77]

In this idyllic atmosphere, George also began to take stock of his emotional life. When he had been almost a week on Skiathos, he wrote a long, carefully worded letter to Lou. It is the first of three 'letters in vain' that he would address to her during the next few months. This one, it appears, was not sent; the affair, according to the letter, had already been over before he left Athens.[78]

The break with Lou was to prove only temporary. But confronted daily with the 'happy ending' to his sister's romance, and no doubt also with Ioanna's continued championship of Jacqueline, if George was ever going to waver in his renunciation, it would be now. As the story is told by Ioanna, he said to her, just the once, at a moment when they were alone, 'Jacqueline should be here.' An indication of his emotional state during these two weeks can be gleaned from the blatant wish-fulfilment with which *Six Nights on the Acropolis* ends.[79]

On an island that suggestively conflates Skiathos in 1930 with Skala, as George remembered it from childhood, Stratis in the novel is fully liberated in sexual fulfilment with Salome, now known by the less threatening name of Bilio. Conveniently, she then goes back to Athens, where she dies; the news is brought to Stratis, still on the island, by the woman who in the fiction is the antithesis of Salome/Bilio. This is Lala, the idealised lover for whom it turns out that Salome had been preparing Stratis all along. There is no close counterpart to Lala, or to much of her story, in real life. But Lala is often given the physical and temperamental characteristics of Jacqueline. In addition, she is surrounded by a partly mystical aura; imagery associated with her recurs in poems that have a connection with Jacqueline; her name in the novel's first draft was 'Lili,' and this is directly connected to the alias for Jacqueline that George had used in his short story about her back in 1925: 'Krinoula' (little lily). Part of the wish-fulfilment at the end of *Six Nights* is the same as had first found expression then, at the very beginning: Jacqueline is turned into a Greek.[80]

Years later, recalling that summer and the crisis in his relationships with Lou and Jacqueline, George found the means, in fiction, to fulfil both, against the idyllic backdrop of 'Bilio's island.' But, in the real world, he could not rely on the plot mechanisms of fiction to resolve his dilemma for him. He had broken off with both Jacqueline and Lou. Now he must choose between them.

Since the previous December, George had been assigned to the League of Nations desk at the Ministry. He had probably made at least one official trip to the headquarters of the League, at Geneva, that May. A longer visit was in prospect for the autumn, and he wrote to Ioanna from Athens, just after his return from Skiathos in mid August, with the news that this had been confirmed for the following month. From Geneva he could take the train to Paris, and see Jacqueline. And this, perhaps persuaded by Ioanna, perhaps on his own prompting, is what he did.[81]

But already, by the time he met Jacqueline again, at the end of September, the interlude of Skiathos was over and George was back on the emotional roller-coaster as never before. A coded entry in his diary reveals that within two weeks of coming back from Skiathos, having supposedly ended everything with Lou, he was once again enjoying the favours of her basement flat: 'August. The cistern: against all expectation, unbelievable day.'[82]

On 5 September he left Athens, accompanying Foreign Minister Andreas Michalakopoulos and an official of the Ministry, Vassilios Papadakis, to Geneva for the Eleventh Assembly of the League of Nations. George was Secretary to this delegation. Soon after he arrived in Geneva, he wrote another 'letter in vain' to Lou, presumably once again breaking off the relationship.[83]

A short diary entry for 21 September begins: 'On the train from Geneva to Aix-les-Bains. On my way to see ruins, my own ruins, tightness about the heart.' Aix-les-Bains was the frontier station, where he had waited, with his mother, sister and brother, for word from Stelios, back in 1918. But it seems that George's nerve failed him on this first attempt. It was not until the following weekend that he spent forty-eight hours with Jacqueline and her mother in Paris. To Ioanna he wrote immediately afterwards:

> Little sister, what can I say to you and how can I tell you the story. . . . I wished you could have been there, to lift the weight from me a little. . . . I poured out all the tears of my body. It was like a veil falling from my eyes, and showed me a lot of things that have been dormant and gathering strength all these years. I'm cut to ribbons. I'll try to go to Paris again, even just for a day . . .

The following weekend was the last before the delegation was due to return to Greece. Again, he spent it in Paris. There is no record of what was said. But something of George's feelings can be caught from a later letter that recalled the time spent in Geneva as a nadir:

> The climate made me ill. I'd been reduced to seeing personal enemies in the swans and the bicycles. On the Pont des Bergues I felt between two fires.[84]

Swans would ever afterwards, in George's poetry, 'become a symbol for me of everything I loathe.' 'I've always used them as very harsh, vengeful creatures,' he noted many years later. The precise origin of this image is irrecoverable; but a clue may be preserved in *Six Nights*, where Stratis describes his first sight of Salome's naked body: 'with the suppleness of a swan, all over.'[85]

94

Back in Athens, as soon as he next had leave from the Ministry, George threw himself into finishing 'Erotikos Logos,' the poem that had been left uncompleted the year before. Poignantly, this poem captures the possibility of an impossible happiness, that had briefly hovered over the summer in Skiathos. Across the larger canvas of its twenty-four stanzas, divided into five sections, it reaffirms the act of renunciation that had been declared at the end of 'Denial.' That summer and autumn, George had thought that it might still be possible to go back; now he knew that it was not.[86]

The poem's language is dense, often allusive; the rich rhymes and the effects of assonance and alliteration make for suggestiveness, in the manner of the French Symbolists, rather than the lapidary incisiveness of George's later free-verse poems. In the first, second and fifth parts, it is fate that is addressed, not the loved woman. It was fate that made love possible; it is fate that now causes involuntary memory to rise like a coral reef to the surface of the mind, and lead the poet back to what has since been lost. The woman is addressed only in the poem's third, central section, which is also the longest. He imagines the words of her reply:

> 'Like waves inside a seashell comes to me the adverse
> far-off, impenetrable world's lament
> but moments too of stillness when bright-forked desire
> is all my thought, desire and none but that.

95

> 'Perhaps in memory you see me risen, naked
> as when you came, my dear, familiar stranger
> to lie down by me and deliver me for ever,
> as was my wish, from the swift rattling wind.'[87]

Finally, just as in the earlier 'Mood of a Day,' the moment of erotic epiphany is out of reach: 'Where now the two-edged day that changed our lives?' What hope can there be for 'souls so numbed from nurture on the lotus?' This surely recalls George's comparison of his affair with Lou to Odysseus' dalliance with Calypso. 'Erotikos Logos' closes with a paradoxical affirmation of loss, a willed renunciation of what cannot be recovered, and an acceptance, tinged with the language of religious faith, of life as it is: 'the world is simple.'[88]

### The Poet George Seferis
'Erotikos Logos' was finished on 30 December 1930. 'I sweated blood, working ten hours a day!' George recorded in his diary. The remainder of

the fourteen poems that make up his first published collection fell into place very quickly during the first months of the new year. From March to May 1931, he wrestled with the arrangement of the volume. He settled for a three-part structure with 'Erotikos Logos' as the centrepiece; it was not until 1950 that the shorter poems were grouped together into a single section, as a counterweight to the longer poem which becomes the culmination of the collection, in the standard edition today.[89]

At the same time, he considered a whole range of possible epigraphs, including the one that a year later he would use for *The Cistern:* the words of El Greco that, as George understood them, affirm the autonomy of art and the right of the artist to rearrange what he sees for aesthetic effect. A title for the volume gave even greater trouble. Among the possibilities that George toyed with at this late stage were, 'Exercises,' 'Dissonance,' 'Expiation,' 'Homage,' even the eschatological 'Second Coming.' The eventual title seems to have emerged from a plan to structure the volume's three parts in the antiphonal manner of the choruses in ancient tragedy: a 'strophe' is mirrored by the 'antistrophe' that follows. Finally, *Strophe* stood alone: the volume is named after a verseform, be it the 'strophe' of the ancient chorus, or the 'stanza' of the modern lyric. In this way George paid tribute to the *Stances* of Moréas; but as its authorised translation into English and other languages testifies, this title owes at least as much to life as it does to art. George's first volume of poetry is known abroad as *Turning Point.*[90]

There was yet another urgent matter to be decided, before the book could be printed. 'I'm looking for a pseudonym,' George noted in his diary in March, a mere two months before *Turning Point* was published. Ioanna suggests that the name 'George Seferis' had already emerged from his intense discussions with her the previous autumn. But as late as 5 March 1931, the last of the poems to be written, 'Rocket,' in the manuscript still bears the signature 'George Seferiadis.' On its first appearance, and ever afterwards, the literary pseudonym 'Seferis' would be accompanied by a visual device: George's own drawing of a mermaid with a forked tail, the fins of the tail almost meeting above her head so as to form a circle. What is probably a prototype for this image appears on the improvised cover that he made, out of an old legal binder of Ioanna's, for his copy of the soft-bound French translation of Joyce's *Ulysses*. Although this cannot be proved, it is tempting to link the inspiration for this device with George's summer idyll on Skiathos, and his parallel reading of the 'odysseys' of Homer and Joyce.[91]

The months between the completion of 'Erotikos Logos' and the appearance of *Turning Point* seem also to have seen the first foundations laid for what would become George's next two books of verse. His diary for January contains the draft of an unfinished poem, to be called either 'Journey' or 'Aeolia;' this has plausibly been seen as the first serious germ of the mythical journey that would become the theme of *Mythistorema* (1935). On the day that *Turning Point* was published, George noted in his diary that work on both this poem and *The Cistern* had stalled. This was the first mention of the poem that would become his second (and even slimmer) volume a year later.[92]

*Turning Point* was distributed to the bookshops on 25 May 1931, and 'sent to the critics' three days later. A handsome little booklet of forty-eight pages, with a dark red soft cover, it had been printed in two hundred copies at George's expense. Half of these were distributed to family, friends, literary and other acquaintances; even the foreign minister, Andreas Michalakopoulos, received one. There were two distribution lists. The first is headed by Stelios, Ioanna and Angelos; immediately below them come Jacqueline and Marie-Louise, then George Apostolidis, followed immediately by 'L. Loukidi' (Lou's married name). The second list details the distribution of fifty copies printed on high-quality paper. These were the ones destined for 'the critics.' George was assiduous in ensuring that the work of this unknown poet would reach the hands of the most influential literary figures of the day. These included Cavafy, Drosinis, Sikelianos, Pallis, Vlastos, Varnalis, and the French academic Hellenists, André Mirambel, Hubert Pernot and Louis Roussel.[93]

In later years, George was always rueful about his lack of commercial success as a writer, before he achieved fame. Five months after publication, by which time he was far away in London, he wrote to ask Theotokas about sales: 'I think *Turning Point* has sold about 20 copies, maybe a few more,' came the reply, along with the dubious consolation that Theotokas' first book had sold eighty in an only slightly longer period. A total of ninety copies were sold before George withdrew the remainder, on the eve of the Second World War, in preparation for the first edition of his *Poems*.[94]

In the small world of literary Athens at the beginning of the 1930s, what mattered was not sales or popularity but the response of the critics. Not all of those who noticed the arrival of *Turning Point* liked it; none, including even Theotokas, was unreservedly enthusiastic. On the other hand, only two reviews were wholly negative. One of these was a short notice written from a traditionalist perspective by the poet Napoleon Lapathiotis; the other, by

97

a Marxist critic, found the poems 'reactionary.' Thirteen reviews appeared between the end of May and the following October, an impressive tally for a first book by an unknown writer, and indeed the most that any of George's books ever received on its first appearance.[95]

Almost all the reviewers were impressed by the technical mastery of the verse; many were struck by the poems' originality. Most tried to find a context for the new poetic voice by placing it in the tradition of French *poésie pure*, the extreme abstraction of art from life advocated by Henri Brémond and Paul Valéry. This was hardly surprising; George was already known as the translator of the most uncompromising manifesto for this trend, and even his friends would concede, then and later, that his first published poems owed a debt to Valéry. But George reacted angrily against having this label, as he saw it, uncritically stamped upon his work; another, that of the 'ivory tower,' was often used synonymously and annoyed him even more. Many years were to pass before George could wholly emancipate himself from this critical reception of his work – and indeed from the characteristic voice of his first two collections.

The most influential response to *Turning Point* came in the form of a private letter to George from the venerable and undisputed great man of Greek letters at this time, Kostis Palamas, now in his early seventies. The unseen hand of Katsimbalis may be detected here: Katsimbalis' admiration for Palamas knew no bounds; Katsimbalis' father was a friend of Palamas (though so, by this time, was Stelios Seferiadis). Whether or not it was Katsimbalis who prompted or encouraged Palamas to write, it is hard to miss the sure hand of the publicist in the prompt publication of the letter in the columns of *Nea Estia* in September. Palamas warmed instinctively to the poet's control of language and metre, but also gently took him to task. A poem, Palamas insisted, could be a form of riddle, as Goethe had it; but the pleasure of solving the riddle had to be within the reader's grasp. Palamas twice uses the word 'cryptographic' to describe the poems of *Turning Point*, and complains that he cannot find the key to unlock the code.[96]

Palamas is unlikely to have known that the poems' author had recently completed two years' service in the cryptographic department of the Ministry of Foreign Affairs; one of George's professional duties there had been to oversee the printing of a 'dictionary of cryptography.' During the same period, the break with Jacqueline and his affair with Lou had generated in him an obsession with secrecy about his emotional life. From *The Cistern*, that would be finished the next year, to *Six Nights on the Acropolis*, completed more than twenty years later, George would develop his own codes to enable him to do this. The rest of his career as a poet would be a constant struggle between the need to 'express my emotion,' 'to speak simply,' as he would later put it, and a deeply felt instinct to preserve the sources of that emotion inviolate. His first two published collections were criticised for being cryptic; his last was to include the word 'secret,' 'cryptic,' or 'private' in its title.[97]

The previous winter, George had been introduced by Katsimbalis to a young man with a critical flair for poetry and no means of financial support. This was Andreas Karantonis, whom Katsimbalis – by a mixture of bullying and cajoling, and with the active connivance of George himself – now set to write a whole book whose very title was already a *fait accompli*: *The Poet George Seferis*. Karantonis' book was finished in record time, and published, at Katsimbalis' expense, in December, just over six months after *Turning Point*. It was an achievement of breathtaking cheek on Katsimbalis' part: the book by Karantonis is many times longer than the collection of poems it sets out to bring before the public. The blatant, if often astute, direction of the project by Katsimbalis, always from behind the scenes, is apparent in the published extracts from his correspondence with George during this period.[98]

This was Katsimbalis' masterstroke. It ensured that George's small collection of poems would remain in the public eye; it provoked its own share of controversy, and in doing so set the seal on the critical reception of *Turning Point*.

Afterwards, George never doubted that the publication of his first book had indeed marked a turning point in his own life. Another coincided with it almost exactly: it was in the same month, May, that he received notice of his first foreign posting. He had completed his initial period of service at the Ministry, and was about to begin his consular service abroad. On 8 August 1931, after seeing Ioanna's first child baptised with the name of their mother, Despina, he left Piraeus by sea, bound for England.[99]

George had served his apprenticeship, in full, to each of his two exacting masters.

ΓΙΩΡΓΟΣ ΣΕΦΕΡΗΣ

# ΣΤΡΟΦΗ

*Σὴν χάριν*

ΑΘΗΝΑ

1931

The title-page of *Turning Point*, including the first appearance of the mermaid device.

# 4
# Wayfarer the Seafarer
# 1931–1934

No matter what happens, no matter what should befall us, whether
. . . God will protect us or not, the question is this and only this:
what will we have done? . . . What will we have done with our
freedom, with our love, with our suffering? It's a question that will
always press in on us, a cycle from which we will never be able to
break out, . . . the question will be always there: What did you take?
What did you give?

(Fragment of a dialogue with Stratis Thalassinos, 1933)[1]

### Alter ego

A photograph sent by George to Ioanna, in February 1932, shows him in a
bowler hat and heavy, dark overcoat, buttoned up, standing stiffly beside a
traffic light in Piccadilly Circus, London. Above him and behind him, out
of his line of sight, soars the winged statue of Eros, which celebrates the
fickle nature of sexual love, and is the real centrepiece of the photograph.
As he commented to Ioanna: 'I look awful but Eros has come out well.'
Clearly composed with a humorous, rueful eye, this photograph offers a
striking visual counterpart to the earthbound, bereft state of 'waiting for
the angel,' with which, not long before this, the poem 'Erotikos Logos' had
ended. A week after sending these photographs to Ioanna, George wrote to
Katsimbalis, echoing the poem's closing words: ' "The world is simple" –
only when you've just finished a poem.'[2]

George's hair was beginning to recede; a portrait photograph of him,
from the same year, shows a more pensive, heavy-jowled face than ever. In
London, for a time, he was concerned enough to keep a tally of his weight,
which fluctuated around fifteen stone (210 pounds).[3]

When he arrived in London, on 17 August 1931, after a brief sight-seeing
tour by car with a French colleague in southern France, it was exactly
the same season as when he had first come to England, on the first stage of
his protracted separation from Jacqueline. Now it was with Lou that he
was about to begin a long and intense correspondence; history seemed

set to repeat itself, as George once again determined to keep love alive at a distance.

The story of his two and a half years at the London consulate is very much the story of this relationship, its vicissitudes, and the secrecy with which George pursued it. He corresponded at length, and often revealingly, with each of the other three Georges in Greece throughout this time, as well as with his sister; but it is in the letters addressed to Lou that he frankly and without reserve probed his own deepest feelings, and recorded the tortured process of his artistic self-discovery. The second volume of George's posthumously published diaries, *Days 2*, consists in large part of extracts from these letters.[4]

London itself would not have changed very much since 1924, except that the Great Depression was beginning to bite. In the streets, the dole queues would have been a new, and dispiriting experience. Great Britain abandoned the international gold standard in October 1931, just two months after George's arrival. In Greece, the Venizelos government had no choice but to follow suit. During the next few months, the value of the drachma plummeted by 47%. The humiliating efforts which followed, by Venizelos and his ministers, to raise funds from wealthy Greeks living abroad, cannot have left the London consulate untouched. The salaries of diplomatic employees were reduced by six per cent at the start of the new year; from the following May, George was paid in paper currency. He was to feel this new stringency keenly. But the main cause of financial constraint, which he could not confide to his family or friends, was his determination, throughout his time in London, to give what support he could to Lou.[5]

Apart from the consequences of the economic collapse, the political issues of the day seem largely to have passed George by. Even the uprising by the Greeks of Cyprus against British colonial rule, in October 1931, left no trace in his correspondence, except with Ioanna and, probably, his father. The events of that October in Nicosia would cast a long shadow, and George would find his abilities and his convictions tested to the utmost by their sequel, many years later. Ioanna gives the impression that the Greeks of Cyprus held a special place in her brother's affections from this time on; but almost certainly this was the result of hindsight.[6]

George was now working as secretary at the Greek consulate. In those days the consulate occupied a narrow terraced house at 131 Gower Street, next door to the University College Medical School, and opposite the neo-classical pediment of the UCL main building.[7] His working day began at 10.20 am and lasted until only three or four in the afternoon. The work itself, he told Theotokas, had 'a lot to do with shipping and a bit with tourism.' To Lou he described it as 'the most inane form of service I've ever done.' To Apostolidis he wrote that the only friends he had in London were his professional colleagues; with the notable exceptions of the Ambassador and the Consul, they were 'good people and very kind' to him. The 'mindless consular service' had 'the colossal advantage of only occupying my hands and leaving me free time.' In any case, he added revealingly, 'I haven't come here to shine as an aspiring diplomat.'[8]

George now began to separate his professional life from his deeper interests more rigorously than ever. 'For me it's an unbroken rule,' he explained in a letter to Katsimbalis, after six months in London, 'not to mix my literary work with the service. I systematically avoid starting or continuing a discussion of matters of art or thought with professional colleagues.' In his professional life, he was conscientious, and sensitive to the opinions of his superiors. To Theotokas he confided that

if ever I had the chance to serve my country, seriously and to some purpose, I'd be ready to do my utmost. But before that could happen I would have a) to believe in the people who make things happen, and b) to feel that I really had something to offer.[9]

103

There can have been little in George's professional career, up to this point, that would seem objectively to justify such a declaration, though in the event it was to prove prophetic.

But now, in the second half of 1931, newly arrived in London, George had other preoccupations. At the end of September, he moved into a two-room furnished flat in Hampstead, at 8 Antrim Grove, NW3. The house belonged to an elderly widow and her daughter; his rooms were cleaned by a maid, who carried with her an aroma of beer and bacon. It is a leafy part of London, socially a considerable step up from Balham, where he had stayed on his first visit, seven years before. The other side of Antrim Grove has been rebuilt since the 1960s; Number 8 looks much as it must have done then: a demure, semi-detached house with bow windows to the front and a tiny front garden, almost hidden behind the traditional English privet hedges. George's rooms were probably on the attic floor.[10]

It was to Lou that he sent a plan of the rooms and their furniture, as he once used to do for Ioanna with each of his Paris lodgings. At this early stage of their correspondence, he and Lou were experimenting with fictitious personalities under whose alias they might express themselves more freely. George was amused by her invention of 'Mrs Ralli' and encouraged her to carry on with it. He continued, 'As for me, if I can't write to you direct, you'll be hearing from a joker who follows my life and I'm going to baptise with the name Anastasis Vayias. Mr Vayias is the *pendant* of Mrs Ralli.'[11]

Under the very similar pseudonym of *Alyis* Vayias, George had given provisional literary form to his feelings in the first phase of his relationship with Jacqueline. He seems to have realised at once that this would not do for the new circumstances. Anastasis Vayias was quietly dropped. In his place, four days after that first letter to Lou from Antrim Grove, a more durable alter ego for George was born.[12]

This was Stratis Thalassinos. 'Stratis' had already emerged as the name for the central character in George's early attempts at prose fiction; it is a common Greek name, the familiar form of 'Eustratios.' 'Thalassinos' was a new addition; this is not a proper name but a noun or adjective, meaning 'seafarer,' or 'seafaring.' Putting the two together brings out the latent similarity of 'Stratis' to the demotic Greek word *strata*, meaning a road or journey, and therefore very close in meaning to *sefer* in Turkish. 'Mr Stratis Thalassinos,' as he would appear during the next few years in letters, poems and prose sketches, has a name that can be translated, 'Wayfarer the Seafarer.'[13]

Many years later, George would write to Katsimbalis that it had been 'under that large dark tree' opposite his sitting-room window that Stratis Thalassinos had been born. The first of a series of prose sketches which bear the name of this new-minted character is dated 17 October 1931. Stratis Thalassinos is introduced in the third person; he is sitting in a room identical to George's own, as he had just described it for Lou, and looking out at the tree across the road. 'Mr Stratis Thalassinos' is disposed to 'write sociological observations about the place in which he finds himself':

> English windows . . . have no shutters. So an Englishman who lives on the ground floor can never have permitted himself to think of having a naked woman with him. They must do their love-making under the table.[14]

It is not clear whether 'Mr S.T.' was ever seriously used as an alias in George's correspondence with Lou. A few weeks after this, he was urging her to tear up all his letters, 'except for the one from Stratis Thalassinos which isn't a letter, because I plan to work on that idea.'[15] But if it was the sight of a tree at dusk on that October day that first brought Stratis Thalassinos into being, this whimsical, portentous, skittish, sometimes visionary, always unpredictable 'other' would be more often associated, thereafter, with the optical illusions of an English fireside, which had so impressed George on his earlier visit to London.[16]

At the end of his first year there, he could single out only two good things: 'the flame and the river.' The Thames, with its docks and ocean-going ships, the navigation lights on tugs and barges that passed beneath the bridges, had immediately appealed to him as 'the only place [in London] I love purely and simply.' 'Mr Stratis Thalassinos' had been the gift of the fireside flame. Between that evening in October 1931 and the following summer, Stratis Thalassinos would be responsible for two sequences of five poems each, that George would later publish: 'Five Poems by Mr S. Thalassinos' and 'Mr Stratis Thalassinos Describes a Man.'[17]

Something else that probably encouraged George to persevere with this alternative version of himself was his friendship, which began at this time, with a real seafarer who was also a poet. This was the twenty-five-year-old Dimitris Antoniou (D.I. Antoniou, as he signed his poems; 'Tonio' to his friends). George had encountered him once before in Athens, at the house of the poet Palamas. Now serving as navigation officer on a long-distance cargo ship, Antoniou turned up at the door of George's office at 131 Gower Street, one foggy winter afternoon early in December.[18]

Although apparently a man of few words, Antoniou impressed George deeply on that occasion with his talk of life at sea. This young ship's officer 'carried more books with him than clothes,' his cabin aboard ship was piled high with empty cigarette packets: the manuscripts of the poems that before long he would publish with the encouragement of George and Katsimbalis. Henry Miller's portrait of Antoniou, a few years later, well captures the aura with which the two literary Georges invested their 'seafaring friend':

> I envied him the islands he was always stopping off at . . . I like the idea of being alone in the little house above the deck, steering the ship over its perilous course. To be aware of the weather, to be in it, battling with it, meant everything to me. In Antoniou's countenance there were always traces of the weather. . . . I like men who have the weather in their blood.[19]

A lifelong bachelor, Antoniou seems to have dedicated his life to the sea and to poetry. He came from the Dodecanese, which means that at this time he may have been an Italian subject (hence, perhaps, his nickname). Photographs, taken later in life, show a thickset man, his short hair brushed straight back, with full eyebrows, a firm set to the mouth and chin, and a coldly penetrating gaze.[20]

George probably spent no more than a few hours in Antoniou's company, before his ship sailed from London. Thereafter they corresponded rarely, though they would often meet back in Athens, in Katsimbalis' circle, and on a number of occasions George would make a point of travelling on 'Tonio's ship.' Probably what George admired in Antoniou was the projection of his own 'seafaring' self, that at the time of their chance meeting was struggling to emerge in the persona of 'Stratis Thalassinos.' This would explain why Antoniou provided the inspiration, and may have been to some extent the private addressee, of at least three poems of *Mythistorema*. 'Bottle in the Sea,' the title of poem 12, was Antoniou's shorthand expression to refer to his own poems. Poem 13 recalls details of that evening in fog-bound London, when together they came upon the figures of Christ, Stanley Baldwin and a mermaid, done in coloured chalk by a pavement artist. Transposed into the plural, the 'friends' who took ship, in poem 5, and the helplessness of those left behind, to 'write clumsily and with effort on paper / of ships or mermaids or shells,' may also suggest an idealised version of that meeting with Antoniou in December 1931.[21]

### Words of revelation

Around the time of his meeting with Antoniou, in December 1931, George wrote to Lou:

> Sometimes I have the impression that I'm blindfolded in a byway of my life; there's a corner to turn, but I won't realise it until who knows how many years later. I suddenly imagine a word at random, without any effort, from a friend, would bring me great peace – perhaps.[22]

This was not wholly prophetic. At least the first of three such 'words,' that would each strike George with the force of a revelation at the end of 1931, was already to hand. He had just finished the last work of the philosopher Alain, published that autumn, *Vingt Leçons sur les Beaux-Arts*. 'It's been years since I've read a book with such enthusiasm,' he wrote to Lou. At once, he seized on the phrase: 'The artist who loses his own self is the one who has not dared to believe in his own self.' These words by Alain evidently spoke directly to George's perplexity at the time. But this was only the beginning.[23]

It would be Alain, in his resistance to Valéry and the ideal of 'pure poetry,' who would eventually show George the way out of the impasse into which the reception of *Turning Point* had thrust him. It was also Alain who defined the poet's invisible task as the 'response of the human body in communication with all things': the tactile emphasis on the body and on the reality of things would soon become fundamental to George's poetics. So too would the distinction between the innate style of the artisan and the mechanical products of the age: 'there cannot but be something of the ancient and savage about the beautiful; from which comes the authority, everywhere recognised, of ancient models and ancient forms.' Some years later, George would translate this passage from the same book by Alain, in his public debate with Konstantinos (Kostakis) Tsatsos:

> The true and the sincere are not sufficient [for the artist]; or rather, true sincerity for a poet is not at all in his spirit, but rather in the confidence which he places in his own blind nature, which accords with great nature through a kind of march or dance...[24]

107

The highest 'nature' of the poet is blind, according to Alain, just as George himself, in December 1931, felt 'blindfolded.' But although he cannot consciously perceive it, the poet, is united, as an artist, to a universal force.

The second revelation was perhaps somewhat dramatised as George recalled it many years later:

> It was shortly before Christmas, 1931; I was looking at Christmas cards in a bookshop in Oxford Street. Then, for the first time, among the tinted lithographs, I took in my hands a poem by Eliot. It was 'Marina,' from the series *Ariel Poems*:
>> What seas what shores what grey rocks and what islands
>> What water lapping the prow
>> And scent of pine . . . [25]

In reality, the discovery cannot have been quite so abrupt. To Katsimbalis, George wrote, not long after this:

> Now, as to T.S. Eliot . . . , I started with him as soon as I got here. He's surely one of the most important people in English literature today,

along with Joyce, Huxley and the late D.H. Lawrence. . . . But alas, I'd only read one poem by him before I came here.[26]

Indeed, Eliot had even been mentioned in a review of *Turning Point*, that had appeared at the beginning of July. But if the discovery of Eliot's poetry may have been a more gradual and considered process than it appears from George's later recollection, there is no doubt that 'Marina' did strike him, that Christmas, when it was first published, with the force of a revelation.[27]

The poem's nautical imagery derives from Eliot's idealised memories of Cape Ann in New England; although George could not yet have known this, there was already a remarkable biographical link between the two poets, despite their very different backgrounds. In 'Marina,' George could not have failed to pick up the echo of his own childhood reverence for the boatmen and fishermen of Skala. Eliot's poem draws on the story of a father's quest for his lost daughter, as told in Shakespeare's play *Pericles, Prince of Tyre;* this provides a further link with the Aegean world familiar to George. The daughter, the loved person in the poem, is elusive, through the fog, most nearly glimpsed 'Under sleep, where all the waters meet.' The elderly voyager, imagining that which he cannot reach, asks at the end of the poem to 'Resign my life for this life, my speech for that unspoken,' and the poem ends on a note of hope: 'the new ships.'[28]

In the first flush of his enthusiasm for 'Marina,' George hoped to meet Eliot, through a Greek acquaintance of Katsimbalis. But the acquaintance became ill, the promised letter of introduction was delayed; by the time it arrived, in February 1933, Eliot was in America. It would be almost twenty years before George and Eliot met face to face.[29]

The third, in the series of revelations at the end of 1931, seems to have been triggered by an article in the *Times Literary Supplement*. It was a reference to his compatriot El Greco that first caught George's eye. But the article also mentioned the fifteenth-century mystic, St John of the Cross, as one of the greatest Spanish poets; George was intrigued enough to order a book on the subject by the philosopher Jean Baruzi, which had just been reisssued. He admitted to his brother-in-law Kostakis Tsatsos, who was an academic philosopher as well as a lawyer, that the book had turned out to be much bigger than he had expected; he had read only those parts which 'concern the substance.'[30]

What George read, in Baruzi's French paraphrase of the commentary to a line of *The Dark Night of the Soul*, and translated into Greek during the last hours of the year, was this:

He who learns the finest 'particularities' of a vocation or an art 'goes always in darkness,' rather than [guided] by his original knowledge, because, if he did not leave [that knowledge] behind him, he would never reach the point of liberating himself from it.[31]

It was an insight that George would repeat, in slightly different words, again and again throughout his life, and perhaps most movingly in the interview that was published in the French newspaper, *Le Monde*, only a month before his death:

Tradition tells us that the poet, Homer, I mean, was blind. But it seems he must have seen an enormous amount of things in his life, and it was after having seen all that that he became blind. *That* is the poet, *that* is the artist, he walks blindly, he walks in the dark.[32]

By that time the lessons of St John of the Cross, of Eliot, and of Alain (about the 'blindness' of the poet), would have become fully interwoven in George's thinking.

To his friends, George was defensive about the significance of this latest discovery. 'Where on earth did you dredge up that ancient mystic from?' complained the rational sceptic Katsimbalis. George justified himself by insisting that 'for me this is the word of a poet and a craftsman.' It was as a fellow-artist that St John of the Cross appealed to him, and he invoked the dictum of the more philosophically acceptable Alain: *Il faut prendre toujours le chemin le plus long* ('One must always take the longest way'), to which George suggested adding: *l'inconnu* ('the unknown'). To Kostakis, too, he found it necessary to temper his enthusiasm: 'I have so little inclination towards mysticism.'[33]

Only when writing to his sister did George go deeper. The mystical dimension that he had discovered in St John of the Cross and in Eliot's religious poem, *Ash Wednesday*, struck a chord with what he had already experienced during his years of keeping faith with Jacqueline. It was to sum up that experience, in hindsight, that he now used the phrase 'a crisis of mysticism.' Ioanna's partial account of that relationship obscures as much as it reveals, but her conclusion is probably not wide of the mark: 'Even if he had no inclination towards religious mysticism, he did work profoundly with his erotic mysticism, by other routes, to reach a similar state of mind.'[34]

'Erotic mysticism' might well suggest the devotional aura with which a loved woman is addressed by George, in poems from the early prayer to the

Virgin Mary that also invokes his mother (sent to Ioanna in 1920) to the *Three Secret Poems* of the 1960s. But a uniquely frank letter to a male friend, Theotokas, written a few months after this, gives a sharper edge to the convergence of the mystical with the erotic in George's experience at this time:

> I'm sure you've often and beautifully made love (I mean in the physical sense). It's always impressed me (I'm not speaking about the simply organic function, the one that's like purgation) how intensely one has, immediately after the spasm, the impression of having died and been reborn. It's an infinite and minuscule moment of interruption of being, the person you are is for a moment cut, at one stroke, into two (excuse me if I refer to myself), the one half on one side in the kingdom of Hades and on the other side, the other half suddenly living a new life.[35]

This was not a wholly new reflection for George: the words used here echo the apocalyptic line from the poem of 1928, 'The Mood of a Day': 'Where is the love that at one stroke severs time in two and confounds it?' It is a theme that would reappear in a haiku (a form associated with the 'princess Lu'), and reworked many years later in '*Thrush*' and in the complete version of *Six Nights*. In all these instances, the erotic epiphany is grounded in the specific relationship with Lou. It was very probably in the light of these experiences that George later generalised a definition of 'eternity.' Not to be confused with endurance, or resistance to time, eternity for George would emerge as a subjective and intensely lived experience, paradoxically rooted in organic life with its limited duration:

> ... eternity ... appears to be an interruption, an opening up of our temporal life, a lightning flash that strikes us in the present moment, and not an endless unfolding of time to infinity ...[36]

A crucial step towards this later insight was taken in the poem that George finished during the first months of 1932, in the immediate wake of the artistic and 'mystical' discoveries of the last month of the previous year.

### The Cistern

Despite the fact that it was dedicated to Apostolidis, *The Cistern* is Lou's poem. It was written for her; in large measure it was written about her;

George shared draft versions with her before anyone else, and humbly accepted her critical suggestions while it was in progress. He had first conceived the idea of a sequel to 'Erotikos Logos' almost immediately after finishing the earlier poem. The title and the overall structure, in twenty-four stanzas, had already taken shape during the first months of 1931, while George had still been in Greece and preparing *Turning Point* for publication. If 'Erotikos Logos' had affirmed his painful renunciation of Jacqueline, its sequel would celebrate the new, and secret, love that had begun in Lou's basement flat.[37]

But progress was slow. In October, soon after moving into his rooms at Hampstead, he took it up again. To Lou he wrote that 'today I find *The Cistern* incomparably superior to "Erotikos Logos." ' But once again the new poem had stalled; he turned aside to experiment with the 'joker,' Stratis Thalassinos. It was in the light of his end-of-year experiences that George returned to the poem, in February 1932. By the ninth of that month he had drafted eighty-five lines (out of a total of a hundred and fifteen). The poem was finished, apart from minor reworking, by the beginning of April; it was now that he hit upon the idea of publishing it on its own, in a limited edition *hors de commerce*.[38]

It was while he was putting the finishing touches to *The Cistern* that an 111 event occurred that threatened to upset the fragile equilibrium of George's inner life, from which the poem derived. On 21 March, he wrote to Ioanna, in some agitation, that he might possibly have to write to her soon, in the greatest secrecy; she may tell Kostakis, but no one else must see his letters. Jacqueline and her mother were due in London in a week's time. The same week, Angelos wrote to George, from Paris, to give him the address, near Hyde Park, where they would be staying.[39]

Jacqueline was considering a proposal of marriage; she would not give a definite answer until she had seen George. According to George, who thought her behaviour 'immensely arrogant,' her aim in coming to London was 'to show me . . . that I've been in love with her for years and whatever [*sic*] I've loved up to today, I've loved because I was seeking *her*.' For once, under this pressure, George revealed to a friend something of his feelings for Lou:

> . . . from the time that we broke up, another woman has come into my life and given me all that one human being can give to another, with unaffected generosity. I feel I'd be the greatest bastard ever, if I did anything to hurt her [i.e. Lou] in the slightest . . .[40]

George held to his resolution. But he was badly shaken. Even to Katsimbalis, with whom he never discussed his emotional life in letters, he confessed, when it was over, 'These last few days, I've been racked by "crisis." It needs much courage.' To Ioanna, the same day, he wrote, 'I've aged many years, these last 15 days.' But at least there was now a clear understanding between himself and Jacqueline: 'everything's over between us, cut and dried, finished . . . We're free now, each of us, vis-à-vis the other.'[41]

Even while the 'crisis' had been going on, George's letters to Lou had continued uninterrupted; he was afraid, he wrote to her, that she might have thought him cold and distant. A diary entry, dated not long afterwards, already relegates Jacqueline's visit to the past. He had been moved by the warmth of her voice; he wished her well, but her problems were no longer his. A remark quoted in French shows that they no longer used the familiar *tu*.[42]

It had been no more than a painful raking over the embers. The break lay five years in the past. What Jacqueline made of *Turning Point* is not recorded, though it is unlikely that she could have understood much of it. When George drew up the distribution list for *The Cistern*, a few months later, neither Jacqueline nor her mother would be included.

112

*The Cistern* is generally reckoned to be George's most sustained 'musical' composition, and also his most impenetrable. It uses a difficult (and non-tra- ditional) five-line stanza, with a regular pattern of half-rhymes, replacing the full rhymes of 'Erotikos Logos,' and accompanied by even richer use of assonance and alliteration. The metre is no longer the traditional Greek fifteen-syllable, but the eleven-syllable with no fixed stress pattern, which ever since Dante had been the standard metre of Italian poetry, and which had earned a regular place in Greek verse only in the nineteenth century.[43]

The poem begins boldly, with its central symbol: 'Here, in the earth has taken root a cistern.' Karantonis, to whom George sent an 'explanation,' now lost, almost certainly had authorial authority for his assertion that 'the *cistern* is here the architectural symbol of death.' This suggests that it was in the intensely cryptic, involved lyricism of this poem that George first began his modern exploration of the paradox that lies at the heart of Homer's *Odyssey*: namely, that the key to achieving the hero's goal (*nostos*, or homecoming) can only be found by travelling first to the world of the dead. But, although he confessed this to none of his friends at the time, the 'cistern' was also George's codeword for a secret sexual assignation. It is entirely in keeping with the dense texture of the poem, and of the particular brand of 'erotic mysticism' that comes through in the letter to Theotokas, that the cistern should stand simultaneously for death and for sex.[44]

A conspicuous part in *The Cistern* is played by the traditional Good Friday ritual in which an effigy of the dead Christ, surrounded by flowers, is paraded through the streets on a catafalque (the *Epitaphios*). In *Six Nights*, Stratis and Salome first consummate their love in her basement flat on the evening of Good Friday, then go out and join the religious procession. Although the full version of *Six Nights* was written long after *The Cistern*, there are many similar details between the poem and the fictional episode. At the end of the latter, Stratis says to Salome, 'We've damned ourselves today,' which can also be translated, 'We've been to hell today.' This is immediately connected to the epigraph for *The Cistern* that George retained until the very last moment: three lines from the *Inferno* of Dante. These describe the poet's state just after he has passed the lowest pit of hell: leaving behind the sight of Lucifer, he begins his rapid ascent towards the sun, but still in a state of shock, caused by all that he has seen in the underworld.[45]

In this way, the subterranean cistern, which is at once the grave and the secret bedchamber, alludes not only to Homer's underworld where Odysseus learned the way to achieve his homecoming; it is also the Christian place    113 of punishment to which Christ descended between the crucifixion and the resurrection. George's letter to Theotokas, comparing the act of love to a mystical experience, also enclosed a fair copy of *The Cistern*. Although its significance was lost on its recipient, that passage in the letter provides the frankest gloss on the poem that George ever offered. The 'death and rebirth' of the sexual act are enacted in *The Cistern*, whose private symbolism was at the time shared only with Lou.[46]

Ten days after the departure of Jacqueline and her mother from London, George wrote out a fair copy of *The Cistern* and sent it to Apostolidis, with the injunction, 'You'll oblige me, if you'll write me your opinion. It's tormented me so much, I've no idea if it's garbage or if it's a – masterpiece.' He had the reassurance that he needed, almost by return of post: 'Do not have the slightest doubt of any sort that it's a masterpiece.'[47]

George's other friends were not so sure. Theotokas liked the poem but was frankly baffled; Karantonis was deferential, but presumed to express his reservations at length. Katsimbalis found the poem loose, lacking in rhythm and coherence. While technically excellent ('the eleven-syllable verse a miracle of musicality'), as a whole 'it drags,' he wrote to George; it leaves 'even the most well-disposed reader cold and unmoved.'[48]

George was never one to take criticism lightly, even from his friends. With Katsimbalis, it became almost a quarrel. Roused by George's hurt defence of his poem, Katsimbalis went on to accuse him of 'disjointed raving . . . [the poem] contains many ill-conceived or descriptive elements . . . must be reworked . . .' Certain expressions 'are as much to be avoided as the Devil avoids incense, unless you want to be accused of counterfeiting Valéry.'[49]

In the heat of this exchange, Katsimbalis launched into a dazzling diatribe, in which his reservations about *The Cistern* became the catalyst for an impassioned set of demands that would have far-reaching repercussions, not just for George's development as a poet, but for the whole literary movement in Greece that before long was to become known as the 'Generation of the Thirties.' In this letter, Katsimbalis urged George to set aside his foreign preoccupations and write about Greece as a Greek:

> How much longer are we going to . . . hide ourselves away in murky cisterns? How much longer are we going to consign our souls and our youthfulness to the depths, instead of elevating them into a sublime burnt-offering upon a mountain peak under the incandescent sun? . . . George, George, I feel you've betrayed us, and you too have been swallowed up by the land of Franks *[i.e. France, but also Western Europe]*. Forget the (so-called) man of your century and set yourself to express something of your country and its nature, which is your nature too. That's what we expected of you, those of us who expected something of you. Burn your Frankish books, chuck them away on the seashore . . . Tread firmly, and tread, above all, the land of your country. . . . Above all, you've got to *see*, with your own eyes, what is Greek and full of light; you've got to take off those dark, alien spectacles which blind your sight and don't allow you to see *even the truth of what I'm saying to you now* . . . It's an absolute necessity for you to rid yourself of the cultural company you've been keeping, among the foreigners who put fetters on your ankles and won't let your own personality shine through . . . I thought it my duty to shout this to you from the housetops.[50]

114

This was Katsimbalis' 'big stick' at its most fearsome and eloquent. It would not be wielded in vain. The poetic landscape it champions, though not the atavistic nationalism implicit behind it, would come to dominate George's next book of poetry, *Mythistorema*. Among other complaints in the letter was that George was behaving like Greek artists in the last century who used to come back from abroad, to paint Greek landscapes in the colours of Dutch canals: 'who even remembers them today?' scoffed Katsimbalis. Both the 'base art' of imitating foreign models, and the line 'No one remembers them. Justice,' would find their way almost directly into *Mythistorema*.

But first, in the face of opposition from some of his most trusted friends, George determined to go ahead with the publication of *The Cistern*. Defending this decision to Ioanna, a week before the poem appeared, he wrote, 'Katsimbalis . . . has just written in his latest letter, "you've betrayed all of us who believed in you." I think I'd have been betraying them if I *hadn't* done what I've done.'[51]

Only two people had wholeheartedly admired *The Cistern*. One was Lou, whose support George could not publicly acknowledge; the other was Apostolidis, to whom he dedicated it. *The Cistern* was duly published, in fifty numbered copies, on 20 October 1932. Each copy was signed, but the author's name was not printed on the cover; the mermaid device alone proclaimed the continuity from *Turning Point*, and the sixteen-page booklet bore the imprint: 'Not for Sale.' The distribution list was headed by Katsimbalis, followed by George's family. Next came 'Loukia,' immediately followed by her cousin Melpo Axioti (later a leading experimental novelist), leaving the poem's official dedicatee to trail in eighth place.[52]

## Crisis

In July, the Greek consul in London was transferred at short notice, and George found himself on his own in charge of the consulate. He moved into Gower Street on 11 July, thereby saving himself the rent and the wear and tear of travelling from Hampstead every day. He had rarely been so listless in his life: 'I can't do anything without love, without enthusiasm.' But 'enthusiasm' was not quite the word he was looking for, and he substituted the word which means 'devotion,' in the religious sense. It was impossible, he found, to talk about literary matters in London:

here the best craftsmen *[i.e. writers]* are considered to be either ridiculous or obscene, and those who take an interest in them are called *high-brow* – an untranslatable, apotropaic term. I once shocked a respectable person when (for something to say) I mentioned Byron! How can you breathe a word about Lawrence or Joyce, when their books are banned?[53]

At the end of July 1932, George was summoned to Paris to see his father. He does not appear to have made contact with the Pouyollons on this occasion. With George Poniridy, his old friend from Paris days, he went to revisit old haunts but, as he probably truthfully lamented to Lou immediately afterwards, he had had no 'beautiful creature' to keep him company. Probably, Stelios wanted to discuss his plans, which were now well advanced, to buy a plot of building land in Athens. There appear also to have been worries about Angelos, who had left Paris for Heidelberg without completing his doctorate.[54]

A month later, George learned that Jacqueline's father had died suddenly, leaving Jacqueline and her mother destitute. He immediately put through a telephone call to Paris (a costly and far from easy business in those days): talking to Jacqueline was 'heavy but bearable.' He telephoned again. This time:

> I had the feeling I was unravelling a strand of barbed wire with my bare hands. Remnants of feelings still bitter, because they're the remnants of a life that we shared.

116  From that moment, he found Jacqueline's pain too much to bear, but also hated himself for his 'cowardice.' He could not bring himself either to go to Paris to see her, or to write. Instead, a few months later, he presumed on his acquaintance with Edouard Herriot, who was once again prime minister of France, to ask if a position could not be found for mother and daughter. In his diary, and to Apostolidis, he had bitter words for the man who might, in different circumstances, have become his father-in-law. Meeting Jacqueline again, back in April, after seven years, had reminded him of how people who have been close have acquired something of each other. 'The worst thing,' he commented in his diary, 'was that those things that she'd taken from me, I could see, were the very things which open the way to life's tragedies.'[55]

For most of the next year, George's thoughts were taken up obsessively with his relationship with Lou. The poem 'Fires of St John,' written at the beginning of July 1932, and attributed to Stratis Thalassinos, looks back nostalgically to the midsummer rituals of Skala. From then until next Easter he seems to have written nothing.[56]

Planning for Lou to visit him in London began in August. England at this time was bound by sexual taboos even stricter, and more hypocritical, than those of Athens; the proprieties of the diplomatic service were stricter still. George's obsession with secrecy now reached new heights; there were constant instructions and changes of plan. George could be peremptory in such matters. Lou could not, of course, visit him at the consulate, he warned her in September; he would find lodgings for her nearby. She must travel 'incognito,' and not with other Greeks; she could, if she wished, write articles about concerts in London, but must not conduct any interviews. To her suggestion that they might meet in Paris instead, he curtly replied in the negative.[57]

Apostolidis had announced to George that he would be getting married in December; George knew the bride, and wrote to both to congratulate them. Apostolidis was planning an extended honeymoon: 'our first objective is you,' he wrote enthusiastically to George. 'We'll be in Paris around 15 December and then, either you can come and see us, or better still we'll come and spend Christmas with you in London.' When this letter reached George, he was expecting Lou to arrive any day. He wrote hastily: 'London is wretched at this time of year;' it would be much better for them to come in the spring. Not even Apostolidis was allowed to know about Lou's impending visit; when George did, in the event, spend four days in Paris with Lou over New Year, he concealed the fact from his friend, who must have been there at the same time.[58]

George's sensitivity about the relationship had been exacerbated, in the meantime, by a letter from Theotokas. News of the affair, though not of its most recent turn, had finally broken in Katsimbalis' circle. Theotokas launched into a lurid tirade, which purported to be an account of George's private life before he had left Athens. Not only, thundered Theotokas, in a wicked parody of a barrister in the divorce court, did you engage in illicit relations with a married woman:

you brought even adultery into disrepute... This woman, who had sacrificed everything for your worthless self, you deceived with another woman, to wit: a virgin, whom you tried to lead astray with promises of *poésie pure*, in order to satisfy vulgar Anatolian appetites. The virgin in question, however, stuck to her guns [*elle a tenu ferme*], as the expression is. She put you up against the wall and without circumlocution made you a proposal of legal matrimony . . . And you, what did you do? You did what cowardly fortune-hunters like you usually do. You packed your bags... And beat it in all haste, one dark night, leaving home by the back door, without farewells, leaving an irreparable trail of destruction behind you.[59]

Theotokas' broadside seems to have been motivated not so much by malice as by schoolboyish glee: George's friends had been irked by his 'refusal to confess where and how and when dammit you have intercourse with a woman.' It was the very closeness with which George had kept his secret that provoked the brash vulgarity of its exposure. The insult must have been compounded, for him, by the fact that Lou was actually in London at the time, though presumably Theotokas did not know this; worse, only a few months previously, George had let down his guard sufficiently to try to express to his friend the feelings that lay at the heart of *The Cistern*. George never fully forgave Theotokas for this, and for a full year afterwards refused even to write to him.[60]

Lou spent the last six weeks of 1932 in London. George took her to the museums, where they spent happy hours together. A visit to Kew Gardens in December, at the deadest time of year, suggested an apt metaphor for this phase of their relationship: in his diary he noted those names of exotic orchids in the hothouse which derive from mythological associations of the Greek goddess of love.[61]

On New Year's Eve, in the inside cover of his pocket-diary for 1933, George wrote, 'Happy [New] Year and lots of good cheer! Stratis Thalassinos and Lou.' But there had also been quarrels; the last days of her visit were dogged by flu. Her decision to leave London the next day may have taken him by surprise. He went with her as far as Paris, where they parted four days later, he to return via Folkestone to London and a bout of flu, she by train and ship to Athens.[62]

Within days of Lou's departure, George was frantically awaiting letters from her ('you *could* have written from the ship and posted it in Piraeus'). The only thing that might keep him from a kind of desperate introversion, of the sort that he had experienced during his years of keeping faith with Jacqueline, he wrote, was:

a living body very close to me that will let me hold it tightly like a lifebelt, that will have me when with passion, love, force I enter into it as fully as I can.[63]

At the end of January he declared himself faithful to her: 'I can't be the least bit unfaithful to you, it's no good chasing butterflies, as you put it.' But only a week later he began a letter to her:

I woke up this morning with the decision to write to you to take good care to forget me and to remove me from the programme of your life.

What this letter conveys is not a 'decision' at all, but a desperate condition of indecisiveness. Another, the very next day, lurches from a passionate, despairing cry: 'I can't shake off the thought of you . . . You've filled every corner of my loneliness,' to the bleak sign-off: 'Lou, forget me.' But within days he was wondering feverishly about leaving the service so as to return to her in Athens.[64]

He had reached a state of crisis. What he was writing to her, he knew, was incoherent. He felt drunk, as though he had drained a bottle of whisky; he could no longer work; there was no one with whom he could share his feelings. 'If this goes on,' he confessed to Lou, 'I'll have to find any mechanical means of forgetting. Enough.'[65]

Nine days after that, George was reporting, in the language of *The Cistern*: 'Silent embraces, like the seed in the earth.' It was the beginning of an extraordinary interlude of calm and happiness:

It's as though I'd been paralysed and suddenly felt I could walk . . . , as though I'm no longer a servant, I don't belong to anyone. Strange desires to destroy something, to tear myself to shreds.[66]

Between 11 February and 5 March, George wrote to Lou almost every day, sometimes more than once on the same day; in the middle of this period he began a new sequence in his numbered letters to her. In words whose opening phrases, more than thirty years later, would be echoed in his last book of poetry, the *Three Secret Poems*, he extolled:

Love in the greatest light of the earth, without the shadow cast by any tree of sentiment. The sky [*or* heaven] is made of light, the earth is made of light and the horizon is free – nothing else. It's difficult for a human being to reach this point. It's a work of humility. I've come face to face with what I was looking for, all these years. The effort that remains is worth it.[67]

Shortly after that, came an affirmation that would be true of George all his life:

I've developed in conjunction with love. That's my zodiac sign. I mean, the great and basic and most profound problem inside me is the problem of love. My stance towards the world is a stance of: either love, or not-love.[68]

Exactly what happened during those February weeks in London is impossible to make out in any detail. At one level, it is both likely, and in character for this relationship, that George had found 'mechanical' release in 'chasing butterflies' after all. But there is no doubt that the object of these declarations is Lou herself. Thus liberated, he seems to have found it possible to ask her unambiguously to drop everything she was doing in Athens and rejoin him in London; even so, as would emerge from the sequel, there was to be no more formal commitment made on either side.

While it lasted, it was a kind of protracted epiphany: 'I can't experience anything in between the two extremes: love and death.' It was a lesson that built on the 'erotic mysticism' of *The Cistern* and perhaps went beyond it. To Ioanna, who could have had no idea what had provoked it, he declared, 'I've come to believe and to conclude, the opposite of what many people do, that a person who knows that he will die cannot experience despair.'[69]

### 'The day that could not die'

The period of high-wire elation came to an abrupt end on Friday 3 March 1933. Recalling these events a few months later, George wrote to Lou:

> I was so childish as to believe that I'd brought off something really important and that when I wrote to you to come, you'd have flown to me at once. Your answer was that letter . . . which began, 'stop, can't you, stop.'[70]

Her 'unjust letter,' as he called it, provoked two contrasting responses on successive days. The second, the product of a sleepless night, was petulant, personal, and angry. Apparently, she had called him 'crazy' and a 'child,' and set down some of his faults. But George's very first response was on a different level entirely:

> My own strength, mainly, is that I can be patient. . . . My life up to now has been patience – and almost nothing else. This morning I read the papers of a sailor who'd been killed in an accident last Saturday. I was looking at his certificates: *Conduite: exemplaire. Cause de décharge: fin du voyage*. That's the way I was thinking about myself too (with the tendency I have to generalise the most trivial things): at the end of my voyage there'll be some certificates somewhere, *conduite exemplaire*. It's

another question whether there'll be some curious junior consul to read them.[71]

'I know that life is a very difficult voyage,' he went on, 'and it takes a great deal of patience.' He then apologised to Lou for his recent behaviour; he asked her to think, instead, of achieving day by day the condition of 'serenity.'[72]

The humble sailors, lost one by one like the companions of Odysseus, in the course of a mythical voyage after elusive glories and impossible hopes, would come to be enshrined in poem 4 of *Mythistorema*. The speakers in poem 15 come to terms with what they cannot have: 'The life that was given to us to live, we have lived.' The final poem of the sequence ends with the same word that George had used to Lou in this letter, to signify the exhausted acquiescence in which their personal adventure must now end: serenity.[73]

Imagery that would later be taken up in *Mythistorema* appears again and again in these letters from the first half of 1933:

It's as though I'm on a voyage; when I'll arrive and where I'll arrive I no longer even ask myself. At the same time, life in its daily routine continues along its insignificant road with trivial matters.

121

On another occasion: 'Don't make any plans, that's the way our lives are. Impersonal. It's necessary for one to be always ready without expecting anything.'[74]

The northern fog and the unexpected violence of the swans in poem 1 of *Mythistorema* recur in the letters and diaries from London that are included in *Days 2*. The flowering almond-trees which, in the penultimate poem of the sequence, represent hope yet to be fulfilled, can be traced to George's return visit to Kew Gardens that March, just a week after he received Lou's 'unjust letter,' in which she refused to join him.[75]

At the same time that Lou's bombshell shattered the manic elation of late February, events in the wider world were such as to make an impact on even George's inward-turned consciousness. In Greece, the four-year period of political stability that had been ushered in by Venizelos' election victory of 1928, had ended with the inconclusive election of 25 September 1932. Since then, Greece had been effectively without a government. A new election was called for 5 March. Venizelos and his allies were defeated by the rival People's Party; a failed *coup d'état* the following night, by General Nicholas Plastiras, who had headed the caretaker government and was fiercely loyal to Venizelos, exacerbated tensions still further. This was the political climate in Athens which prompted Katsimbalis (always the more fervent of the two in his political allegiances) to write to George, before the result of the election was even known, of the 'probability of a civil blood-bath.' It was a prophecy fulfilled in the next decade. But the interference in the electoral process by Plastiras (who had also master-minded the *coup* that toppled the royalist government after the disaster of 1922) was one of a series of milestones that would lead to the total collapse of civil order in Greece during the 1940s.[76]

It was not only in Greece that events took a frightening turn in the first week of March, 1933. In America, the recently installed president, Franklin D. Roosevelt, was taking sweeping new powers over the banks; even fabulously rich America was abandoning the gold standard. And in Germany, in the wake of the Reichstag fire, elections on the same day that Venizelos finally lost power, 5 March, confirmed the Nazis as the ruling party and opened the way to Hitler's absolute rule. 'In such a world,' wrote George to Lou a week later, 'only fanaticism can flourish, and when fanaticism flourishes, the conflagration isn't far off.' It was the first sign of something awakening in him, that had lain dormant since the loss of his homeland eleven years before.[77]

With the immediate crisis in his personal life now over, George's preoccupation with Lou reached a new impasse. One solution would have been for Lou to have divorced her husband and married George. But on this he was brutally adamant: 'if we get married it will mean I'm blocked, if not absolutely destroyed, in my job.' His views on marriage, in principle, he had set out for Apostolidis not long before. One obstacle was his 'Siamese twin,' a phrase he had earlier used to refer to the alias 'Mathios Paskalis' and now applied to Stratis Thalassinos; by this George meant, presumably, his obligations to his art. Another was 'the feeling that you're producing replicas of yourself, as if the original weren't enough.' George's indifference to producing children seems to have been unshakeable throughout his life, and was probably related to the same cause. As he wrote in a late poem, 'Our words are the children of many people.' But for Lou, as for other women in his life, this must have seemed an attitude of despair.[78]

In May the decision was reached that Lou would, after all, come back to London to join him. By this time, George had begun writing again. In April he had started to translate *The Waste Land.* At the same time, the sequence of short poems eventually published as 'Notes for a "Week"' was begun on Monday of Orthodox Holy Week, and would at first be entitled 'Mr Stratis Thalassinos's Week.'[79]

The London setting of these poems, and the hints of a sinister mythology at work beneath the surface of daily trivia, are elements barely assimilated from Eliot (particularly from *The Waste Land* and *The Hollow Men*). Their original association with Holy Week links the personal strand in them to *The Cistern*, but the tight musical form of the earlier poem has been irrevocably broken; the 'Notes for a "Week"' are written in a loose free verse; one of them is in prose. Love is no longer possible, and the redemption implied by the closed symbolism of the earlier poem has been dissipated:

> I saw her die many times
> sometimes weeping in my arms
> sometimes in the arms of a stranger
> sometimes alone, naked;
> that was how she lived with me.
> Now I know that nothing lies beyond
> and so I wait.[80]

123

On the eve of Lou's arrival, at the end of June 1933, George wrote to promise her 'great joys of body and soul.' After this there are no more letters, either preserved or listed. The relationship would not definitively be over for another three years; but 'Notes for a "Week"' suggest that George had at last recognised the impasse into which he had driven both himself and Lou. To Apostolidis, in July, he wrote that he was again finding it impossible to write; England had now brought him to the same depth of depression as he had experienced three years before in Geneva, when he had made his tearful visits to Jacqueline.[81]

The second half of that year is almost a complete blank. How long Lou stayed, and how this second visit ended, are not recorded. It is probable that the long twilight of the affair also left its mark upon *Mythistorema*. The first to be written of these poems, and the only one of them to be written in London, ends, 'will we be able to die properly?' Others invoke 'the agony of the day that could not die;' the friends, who become a burden to us, because 'they no longer know how to die;' 'the smiles, that do not move on, of the statues.' Wells that were once life-giving (a recollection, perhaps, of *The Cistern*) are now without water, giving back only:

> A hollow, stagnant echo, the same as our loneliness
> the same as our love, the same as our bodies.[82]

It was the exact antithesis of the epiphany of that February. It was surely this impossible phase of his relationship with Lou that George was remembering, a year later, when he summed up his experience of England:

> Let's say that I lived that whole time in an aquarium that gave me nothing else but the smell and the sense of fog in the throat, the oppressive green of the unending summer day, and the thirst (that latterly became a sickness), the agonising thirst for a condition at once indefinable and unreachable.[83]

George's last months in London were dogged by uncertainty about his immediate future; it was a pattern that would be repeated many times in the course of his career. Perhaps as a consequence of the change of government, the Ministry first announced his transfer back to his birthplace, to the consulate at Izmir, but this was soon rescinded. It seems to have been Katsimbalis who broke the news to George, in October 1933, that his superiors now proposed to send him to Cardiff. To Ioanna, he complained, 'I didn't enter the Service to become a harbourmaster for four years.' Ioanna happened to have a good friend who was the niece of the new Foreign Minister, Dimitrios Maximos; for the first time, probably, but certainly not the last, Ioanna's devotion to her brother, and her influence in high places, would be decisive in determining the moves of George's diplomatic career.[84]

By early November 1933, he could at last be confident that his transfer to Athens was only a matter of time. Indeed, he seems to have been ready to leave London that month. He was sufficiently mollified with Theotokas, thanks to the mediation of Lou among others, to respond enthusiastically when Katsimbalis sent him the first volume of his friend's novel, *Argo*. George at once dashed off to its author an affectionate six lines of louche doggerel; on the surface, at least, the rift was healed.[85]

The publication of Theotokas' novel marked another milestone in the genesis of *Mythistorema*. *Argo* had been conceived as a *roman fleuve*, an ambitious panorama of Athenian life in the 1920s. Driven by an impersonal, daemonic passion, derived from Dostoyevsky and Gide, each of the novel's main characters is doomed to be frustrated: the voyage of these modern Argonauts, it is already clear in the closing pages of this first volume, has no Golden Fleece at the end of it. In a letter to George,

124

Theotokas explained: 'It's a *musical* necessity that urged me to end the book with the word *serenity*. The idea of serenity is the final, half-extinguished note of the first part.' In his first reaction to *Argo*, George praised the 'desire for a pattern, . . . the "figure in the carpet",' in the phrase of Henry James.[86]

Within a month of that exchange of letters, George had drafted the earliest of the poems to which, a year later, he would give the title *Mythistorema [Novel]*. In his own very different, and much more laconic way, George's 'novel' in verse would explore similar territory to Theotokas in *Argo*: a modern quest, that at times alludes specifically to the myth of Jason and the Argonauts, and would also end with the same word: *serenity*.

When the time came for him to leave London, George was not sorry to go. He handed over the London consulate to his successor on 20 January 1934. To Katsimbalis he had already announced that on his way back he would spend ten days in Paris.[87]

The two-and-a-half weeks that George spent in Paris, at the beginning of 1934, cannot have been a happy time. There was rioting in the city; the laconically recorded fact that he went to a clinic there, rather than in London, raises the possibility of a venereal infection. He could not have been insensitive to the similarities between this journey and that of nine years earlier, when he had left London to spend a month with Jacqueline 125 and her mother in Paris, at almost exactly the same time of year, before catching the steamer from Marseille to Piraeus. Now, at the beginning of 1934, he saw the Pouyollons for the last time.

George left Paris on 7 February. In the course of a disturbed night on the train, he dreamed of Jacqueline as a Greek peasant girl, and the Paris suburb of Passy as a village. He recorded his dream two days later, on board ship. The cosmopolitan passengers on deck were playing records of light opera on a phonograph. The juxtaposition of this image with an unreachable ideal would become the essence of poem 8 of *Mythistorema*. Four years later, on the anniversary of this entry, George would note in his diary:

'*Et je trouve qu'il est beau de mourir dans sa religion.*' [And I find it a beautiful thing to die in one's religion.] I remember that phrase, in January '34 in Paris, and the dull warmth of her voice. For us laymen, too, I don't see what else there can be.[88]

Both the tone, and the unexpectedly religious terms which here sum up the impossibility of what might have been, all these years ago, set the scene for George's final, poetic farewell to Jacqueline. Poems 7, 14 and 15 of

*Mythistorema* are dominated by memories of Jacqueline, now distanced and sublimated into an almost religious calm. These poems were written as a group in November 1934, together with the poem then entitled 'Fairy-tale of Blood,' which puts the case more bitterly and was finally excluded from *Mythistorema*. All four seem to have been written out of the mood of melancholy which overcame George that autumn when the news reached him, via Ioanna, of Jacqueline's marriage.[89]

## Voyage's end

Stelios' original decision to buy a plot of land in Athens and build a house big enough for himself and his family had been prompted by the economic crisis of 1931. Ioanna had helped choose the site, on the edge of the Plaka district, in the centre of Athens. This was at number nine, Kydathinaion Street, opposite the twelfth-century church of the Transfiguration of the Saviour, and not far from the foot of the Acropolis. The plot was long and narrow, sandwiched between the neoclassical villa built in 1842 by the Berlin-trained architect Kleanthes, which today houses the Centre for Asia Minor Studies, and a group of old houses which have long since been replaced in post-war concrete. By the time that George returned to Athens in February 1934, the house was finished; it was to remain his principal home in Athens for the next three decades, and today still belongs to the descendants of Ioanna and Konstantinos Tsatsos.[90]

126

Stelios had planned the accommodation on three floors. George's part of the house was on the ground floor; it gave directly on to a small patio and the narrow garden. Ioanna, Kostakis and their children lived on the top floor; Stelios kept for himself the grand, heavily furnished rooms on the middle floor. Angelos, when he was in Athens, and until his marriage four years later, seems to have had his own room, like George, on the ground floor. An internal staircase at the rear linked the separate establishments; although greater formality seems to have surrounded Stelios on the middle floor, there was constant coming and going of the siblings above and below.[91]

Once more, just as in 1925, George was back among his family and friends. As before, the process of readjustment left few direct traces. The letters that occupied such a large part of his life in London abruptly come to an end; the course of relationships disappears from view. Even diary entries are very sparse for the next two years.

His work for the Ministry, at this time, seems to have engaged George's interest no more than it had in London. After a six-week hiatus, he was assigned to the Minister's office for a few months; then to Protocol, the section which deals with incoming diplomats from abroad. Political life at this time was dominated by the aftermath of a second assassination attempt against Venizelos, the summer before; the government of Panayis Tsaldaris and the ruling People's Party was implicated in a cover-up, and by the end of the year was scandalously postponing the trial of the culprits. Looking back on this time, George thought it would have been quite reasonable for the populace to 'have dragged half a dozen ministers out of their arm-chairs, taken them down to the jetty at Faliron and thrown them into the sea.' Politically, it was a time of stalemate; in retrospect, and probably also at the time, George drew a parallel between the criminal irresponsibility of those in power now, and the actions of another anti-Venizelist govern-ment that had led the country into the disaster in Anatolia in 1922, in the wake of a previous assassination attempt against Venizelos. From George's strongly Venizelist point of view, history appeared to be repeating itself.[92]

The foundations for *Mythistorema* were now almost all in place. But only one of the poems that would eventually make up the published sequence of twenty-four had yet been written; there was as yet no conscious plan for the volume, in anything like its present form. 'Faintly at first,' something new began to appear, following a brief visit to Delphi in April, two months after George had returned to Greece. The sanctuary of Apollo at Delphi had been a place of pilgrimage in ancient times. The poem that he now wrote begins: 'We who started out on this pilgrimage . . .' The theme of the cyclical journey, with which he had been toying since at least the time when he had finished *Turning Point* back in 1931, was now firmly established. So was the plural subject, 'we,' that brings an entirely new, communal dimen-sion to *Mythistorema*.[93]

That summer, Ioanna rented an old house on the harbour of the island of Spetses, half a day by steamer from Piraeus. She, Kostakis and their children spent the summer there; the company included Angelos and George's cousin Elli, to whom he had dedicated the poem 'Reflections on a Foreign Line of Verse.' George came to join them, on his first leave from the Ministry. Now that he had parted for the last time from Jacqueline, Lou was still part of his life; but the hothouse intensity of the 'cistern' had vanished with the last of the London fogs; the door stood open to new relationships. Tsatsos recalled that vacation on Spetses, not without a touch of malice:

As for the faithful follower, George, he got to know a charming Russian girl and had, as usual, spread his wings in love. Give him a book, a bit of sea and lots of female company, and the world was full for George.[94]

It was probably while he was staying on Spetses that he drafted, in early September, no fewer than four poems in the space of three days; one of them refers to Hydra, a short distance away, where the painter Nikos Hatzikyriakos Ghika was a family friend. By the time George returned to Athens, exactly half the poems that would go to make up *Mythistorema* had been written in draft. It was now that the distinctive landscape that dominates the volume began clearly to emerge: a sparely evoked, sunburnt, mostly timeless Aegean landscape of rocks, earth and pines. Water is scarce and the sun is as unforgiving as the ancient Furies. It is against this pitiless backdrop, in several of these poems, that history is condemned endlessly to repeat itself.[95]

Towards the end of 1934, Katsimbalis' long-nurtured plans to found an independent literary journal came to fruition. Theotokas recalled how he, Katsimbalis, George and two other founder-members came together at the house of the novelist Thanasis Petsalis. The eventual editor, whose name would appear on each issue of *Ta Nea Grammata (New Letters)*, Katsimbalis' hard-working and biddable protégé Andreas Karantonis, was not even present. Although the six agreed to launch the journal as a joint venture, with subventions from each, it was probably understood from the start that the guiding spirit was to be that of Katsimbalis. Before long, it would be Katsimbalis who was taking all the decisions, and putting up most of the money. It was agreed that the first issue would appear as soon as possible in the new year.[96]

Possibly the momentum of this venture had its effect on George's plans for his own next book. In December 1934, he noted in his diary that work on his new project had stalled half way. Then it seems to have struck him, quite suddenly, that he had already written all the material that he needed; all that was required was to find a satisfactory arrangement for it. Crucial was the title, which came to him one day in December, when he was passing by a bookshop window. But still he was unsure of himself. He was determined to publish, but worried how best to present a collection of poems so thematically fragmented and formally daring; these would be the first poems that George published in free verse, still a rare novelty in Athens. One version of an abandoned preface is openly defensive: he apologises for publishing an unfinished work. A second, more defiantly, and indeed surprisingly, resurrects the alibi of Stratis Thalassinos for the same purpose.[97]

These prevarications were soon abandoned, and replaced by the bald statement that 'explains' the unusual choice of title for a volume of poems:

> It is its two components that made me select the title for this work: MYTH, because I have used fairly obviously a certain mythology; HISTORY, because I have tried to express, with some coherence, a situation as independent of myself as the characters of a novel [*mythistorema*].[98]

It was only now, in the final stage of preparing the volume for publication, that the structure of the work emerged. Out of a probable twenty-nine poems drafted between the spring of 1933 and March 1935, twenty-four were selected, numerically repeating the organisation of the Homeric epics, and also of George's own previous larger-scale compositions, 'Erotikos Logos' and *The Cistern*. The arrangement of the poems, imposed at the same time, confers a strong sense of a beginning and an ending. The impression of cyclicity was further reinforced with the dateline 'December 1933–December 1934.'[99]

*Mythistorema* was published in March 1935, in a hundred and fifty copies, hard on the heels of Katsimbalis' new journal, *Ta Nea Grammata*. 'Progress,' George remarked ironically in his diary, remembering the two hundred copies in which his first book, *Turning Point*, had been printed.[100]

In his personal life, the completion of *Mythistorema* marked the end of an odyssey that had begun with his displacement to Paris and the avowal of his vocation in 1918. Twice George had followed the same trajectory as the mythical heroes of these poems, 'towards the north;' twice he had faced the painful adjustments of return. In his deepest relationships, he had found a fateful pattern repeated; he now saw the same process at work in human affairs at large, and more particularly in the history of his country. In *Mythistorema*, the voyage, at once personal and communal, ends not with the achievement of any goal, but in a stoical mood of acceptance:

> Here end the works of the sea, the works of love.
> Those who some day will live here where we end

should the blood darken in their memory and overflow
let them not forget us, the feeble shades among the asphodels,
let them turn towards Erebus the heads of the victims:

We who had nothing shall teach them serenity.[101]

# II

## Poetry in a Mean-Spirited Time

... it often seems to me
that it is better to be asleep than to find yourself thus without
      companions
and insist so. And what can you do in this state of suspension, what
      say?
I do not know. And what is the use of poets in a mean-spirited time?

(Friedrich Hölderlin, *Brot und Wein,* VII, translated into Greek from
the French translation by Jean Pierre Jouve, and used as the second
epigraph to *Logbook,* 1940)

# 5
# The Scales of Injustice
# 1935–1937

Here we found ourselves naked, holding
in our hands the scales that tipped towards the side
of injustice.

(*Gymnopaidia*: 'Santorini' [October–December 1935])


## George in the world

In Athens, on the evening of Friday, 1 March 1935, it was Carnival time. Traditionally, during the day, children go to parties in elaborate fancy dress; at night the streets are full of good-natured revellers. The narrow streets of Plaka, between Kydathinaion Street and the Acropolis, would have been full. George had good reason to be in celebratory mood. Katsimbalis' new journal, *Ta Nea Grammata*, had been successfully launched, with himself given pride of place, second only to the acknowledged doyen of Greek letters, Kostis Palamas; *Mythistorema* was in press and would appear later in the month. And he had that day received notification of his promotion at the Ministry, to First Secretary.[1]

Early that Friday evening, officers loyal to Venizelos seized control of the fleet and of two army barracks in the centre of Athens. By nine p.m. the Makriyannis barracks, just south of the Acropolis, had been surrounded and a gun battle was raging. Within hours, heavy artillery had moved into the streets, the revellers had dispersed, and the cannon on the top of Lycabettus hill had sounded a national emergency. The gunfire would have been clearly audible from Kydathinaion Street.

Ever since 1922, the *coup d'état* had become almost a regular interruption to normal life, almost like a grotesque extension of Carnival. But this was different. It was the second time since Venizelos' final defeat at the polls two years before that General Nicholas Plastiras had mounted a putsch in his name. Only this time the elderly Venizelos, the wily arch-parliamentarian who had charmed Lloyd George, had given his blessing to the rebels.

The *coup* petered out in chaos. Eleven days later, it was all over. Venizelos himself fled the country. But already it was becoming apparent where the real power in Greece now lay. Generals Kondylis and Metaxas, in the name of an elected government, which they would themselves topple seven months later, had faced down General Plastiras, who acted in the name of an already powerless Venizelos. Panayis Tsaldaris, the prime minister, was known even to his supporters, according to George, as 'the Moth.' When the revolt crumbled, Plastiras would soon join Venizelos in exile. In the course of the next sixteen months, ineffective and ailing political leaders would find themselves more and more out of touch with the country. Huge purges in the military ensured future loyalty to the winners after the March revolt. The future for democratic institutions had never looked bleaker; soon, they would be suspended altogether.[2]

It was during these months that George for the first time became fully engaged, as a writer, with the political fate of his country. It was a reflection of the times, as well as of his own naturally guarded temperament, that the manner in which he did so would be densely veiled.[3]

Although his diary is silent about it at the time, George, his friends, and his family found themselves ostracised as supporters of the now disgraced Venizelos. Ioanna reports that close friends refused to greet her in the street; the Seferiadis-Tsatsos household in Kydathinaion Street, though not itself implicated in the plot, was part of a support network for persecuted Venizelists. A good friend of the family, the veteran republican politician Alexandros Papanastasiou, was one of those who stood trial for their lives during the summer of 1935. Ioanna records her relief at his acquittal. George never forgot the systematic persecution he experienced at the Ministry at this time, although he never elaborated on it. Later, looking back, he had harsh and well-weighed words for the ineffective politicians, among whom he included even Papanastasiou, who 'seemed to have lost his grip.' It was the 'fanaticism' of the forces now in the ascendant that appalled him, rather than any specific political programme; in many ways, the events of 1935 repeated the polarisation of 1916, when George had been a newcomer to Athens and had witnessed the burning of Venizelos' effigy by supporters of the king.[4]

Against this background of political turmoil, for the long university vacation Ioanna, Kostakis and their two young daughters found refuge in the old village of Zagora, in Thessaly, near the end of the road where Mount Pelion meets the sea. Kostakis was intent on finishing his book on the poetry of Palamas; Ioanna wanted only peace and quiet and not to hear talk about politics. George was to join them there in August.[5]

But first, he fulfilled what he called a 'vow to himself': his seafaring friend, Dimitris Antoniou (Tonio) was now plying the Aegean on a passenger ship, the *Akropolis*, owned by his family; George was determined to 'see him in action at his post.' It was no more than a thirty-six-hour trip: outwards from Piraeus to Naxos, Paros and Santorini, returning via Syros. But the whole day, while he was at sea, George never left the bridge. Then, in the calm of Mount Pelion, legendary home of the centaurs, from where Jason had set out with the Argonauts in search of the Golden Fleece, he wrote, and dedicated to Antoniou, the first of three poems in which that brief voyage round the Aegean would become a powerful political metaphor. This is 'Sirocco 7 Levante,' whose title is the nautical term for the course of a ship heading out of the Saronic Gulf into the Aegean.[6]

At the same time, and drawing on the same brief voyage, he drafted what would become one of his most famous opening lines. In the standard translation, this is rendered: 'Wherever I travel Greece wounds me;' but the Greek carries further nuances: 'Travel wherever I might, it is Greece that causes me pain.' From the ancient legends of Pelion, the poem goes on to connect this pain with the shirt of Nessus, which once worn could not be taken off, and contained a deadly, flesh-eating poison. 'In the Manner of G.S.,' as the poem was eventually titled, would not be finished until a year later. It builds upon the voyage with Antoniou to elaborate a bleak vision of Greece as a ship without a helmsman, bound on a voyage that had left citizens and political leaders alike behind.[7]

During those weeks spent with Ioanna and Kostakis on Pelion, George was deeply moved by the silence and the scents of the mountain, by the stars, and the proximity of the sea. While there, he made a systematic study of Dante's *Divine Comedy*, which he had first begun to read in his late twenties. He also read Freud's *Interpretation of Dreams*; a note in his diary connects the importance that Freud attributed to 'dreamwork' with a statement by the early Greek philosopher Heraclitus of Ephesus, who lived in the sixth century BC. It is the first mention of Heraclitus by George; in his later thinking and writing, both Dante and Heraclitus would emerge as powerful bulwarks against the forces of disorder in the world.[8]

At the beginning of September, George returned to Athens. Just over a week later, violence broke out in parliament: 'the henchmen of [General] Kondylis beating up generals in the ante-chamber of the cabinet room, while the prime minister [Tsaldaris] hid under the table,' as George would later scathingly recall. A month after that, on 10 October, the hapless Tsaldaris was stopped in his car by members of the military and politely invited to relinquish office. Then, on 3 November, a plebiscite was held on

135

the restoration of the monarchy. Under conditions of martial law, with compulsory voting and different coloured ballot papers for 'yes' and 'no,' 97.87% of the valid votes cast were found to be for restoration. King George II of the Hellenes landed, amid fanfares and a hastily declared public holiday, at Tzitzifies, at the southern end of Faliron Bay, on 25 November 1935. From there he was conveyed to the city centre along Syngrou Avenue, the wide, straight boulevard in whose construction, only a few years before, first Theotokas and then George had seen a symbol of the new, cosmopolitan (and republican) Athens of the 1930s.[9]

George vented his disgust privately to Theotokas, in his first indisputably political poem, 'Syngrou Avenue II,' which bears this date. The date and the poem's title would later mark the first entry in a separate series of diaries that are now known as 'political,' in itself another watershed. 'Syngrou Avenue II' was never intended to be published. The disgust that it expresses builds upon a series of running jokes shared with Theotokas at the time. Its central idea, the rather tasteless one that the cradle of European civilisation has been taken over by a barbarian king of the jungle, with the trappings of monkey, parrot and totemic idol borrowed from the 'Negro rooms at the British Museum,' is inspired by Theotokas' patronising admiration for the native resistance to the invasion of Abyssinia (Ethiopia) by Mussolini.[10]

George's antipathy to the monarchy was deeply rooted. His was a view shared by many displaced Greeks from Anatolia, who blamed King George's father, Constantine, firstly for his refusal to join the Entente in a war against Turkey, and then, in 1921 and 1922, when the country was already at war with Turkey, for losing that war. Not all supporters of Venizelos in the 1930s still thought like this, but George was unwavering. Commenting on these events a few years later, he blamed the leaders of the 1935 *coup* for its botched execution, but stopped short of repudiating their aims. 'I had no party, leader or companions,' he went on. He could not forgive even Venizelos. But this was not because of that statesman's unconstitutional recourse to the military in supporting Plastiras' *coup*. It was Venizelos' pragmatic recognition of the monarchy, in the last months of his life, that made the 1935 putsch, in George's eyes, after the fact 'an act without faith, an act of folly.'[11]

The poems which most fully and seriously articulate George's newfound anger at what he saw as communal injustice were published in *Ta Nea Grammata* early in the new year, 1936, with the overall title *Gymnopaidia*. This title alludes not only to the dances 'in a strict and heavy rhythm,' which in antiquity took place on the island of Thera (the modern Santorini), to which the poems' epigraph alludes; it is also the title of a group of piano pieces by the French composer Erik Satie. George shared with Lou an admiration for Satie as a modernist; he had originally intended this title for one of the prose pieces attributed to 'Mr Stratis Thalassinos,' written in London as far back as 1931 or 1932.[12]

'Santorini,' the first of the pair, is the third of the three poems inspired by the brief voyage with Antoniou the previous July. That had probably been George's first visit to the volcanic island, whose most striking feature is the giant, broken caldera into which ships sail. The fact that volcanic activity has caused smaller islets to appear and disappear again in the submerged caldera, in historical times, provokes the central image of the poem. The landscape becomes a metaphor for the communal life of the country; instability extends to the very land itself. In a marked shift from the mood of acceptance and 'serenity,' with which *Mythistorema* had ended only a few months before, in this poem, 'the scale was weighted towards the side / of injustice.' In the second poem of *Gymnopaidia*, entitled 'Mycenae,' the sense of a generation doomed to re-enact a cyclical pattern of violence is carried over from *Mythistorema*, but intensified with a new note of grim foreboding for the future.

137

It was here, in contrast to the poem written privately for Theotokas, that George made his first public comment on the return of the monarchy:

> the inexhaustible purple
> that evening of the return
> when the Solemn Ones [Furies] began to hoot
> across sparse-growing weeds –
> I saw snakes cross-wise twined with vipers
> twisted over the evil generation
> our fate.

These lines are rich in allusions, whose sinister significance is even more immediately apparent in Greek. But the political subtext of this poem seems never to have been noticed, and this for a very simple reason: *Gymnopaidia* in the standard edition carries the dateline 'October 1935,' that is, a month *before* the return of King George to Greece. In typescript, the dateline reads: 'October–December 1935.' George the dissident could be diplomatic in covering his tracks.[13]

Certainly, this was the impression of one of the first pioneers from the

English-speaking world who found himself directed, early in 1936, to George as a leading 'Modern Greek' poet.

Bert Birtles was an Australian journalist. He had strong communist sympathies, and two years after his visit to Greece would publish the first eye-witness account in English of political conditions there at the time. Birtles and his wife Dora were introduced to George, probably in mid-February. They were not impressed. Seferiadis, Birtles writes,

> kept politics out of his writings, although in fact politics were more or less his profession . . . He was still in his thirties but it seemed to us that the life of diplomatic ease had already left its subtle marks upon him. About him was an air of self-preservation and we could not but notice a studied tendency to intellectual evasion. This might have been agnostic but I wondered if it would end . . . in some form of retrograde authoritarianism, religious or political. He was . . . unwilling to see Fascist implications in Eliot's poetry . . .[14]

This was written long before mainstream readers entertained such misgivings about Eliot; George's response was not surprising for its time. But the evasiveness noted by Birtles would often in future be a stumbling-block to the wholehearted acceptance of George's work by the left. At the time, he kept no record of the encounter. When Birtles sent him his book, two years later, George probably enjoyed the Australian's spirited and disrespectful eye-witness account of the arrival of King George at Faliron. But, alone and politically leaderless as he described himself at this time, George could only have been mistrustful of Birtles' breezy certainties.[15]

On 18 March 1936, Venizelos died in exile. A state funeral was held in his native Crete. George took ship with Antoniou, aboard the *Akropolis*, to attend. Souda Bay was filled with ships; official preparations and the public grief of the islanders seemed to emanate across the water, to give the sea 'a mythological appearance I'd never seen on it before, I who have looked at the sea and loved all its legends.'[16]

Less than two months previously, parliamentary elections had once again produced an inconclusive result. The balance of power was now held by a handful of communist members of parliament; this situation was as unwelcome to the newly returned king as it was to the generals, Kondylis and Metaxas, who had engineered his restoration. The future for parliamentary government in Greece was now bleak indeed.[17]

138

However, these prospects can have been only one among many topics for spirited conversation on the top floor of number 9, Kydathinaion Street. It was here that Ioanna and Kostakis hosted the dinner parties and late-night talking sessions that would extend the range of George's acquaintance, developing to embrace many of the intellectual and political leaders of the country during the coming decades. Katsimbalis' circle was of course welcome. Among the regular visitors were the novelist and journalist Stratis Myrivilis, the author of the searing account of life in the trenches on the Macedonian Front in World War I, *Life in the Tomb*. Myrivilis, before long, would include an affectionate portrait of the society of 9, Kydathinaion Street, thinly disguised, in a novella. Poets who frequented the Tsatsos' apartments on the top floor included the Italian-educated George Sarantaris, the philosopher-poet Demetrios Capetanakis, whose brief career in England later helped lay the foundations for George's own success in that country, and Michalis Akylas, who was also a short-story writer. None of these three young men was to survive the coming war. By contrast, Odysseus Alepoudelis, whom George also came to know in this circle, would long outlive him, and under the pseudonym of Elytis would become the only other Greek writer, after George, to be awarded the Nobel prize in the twentieth century. Elytis had recently published his first poems, under Katsimbalis' aegis, in *Ta Nea Grammata*; he and George soon became good, although never especially close, friends.

139

The company often included the veteran language reformers, Alexandros Delmouzos, Manolis Triantafyllidis, and Evangelos Kakouros. The economist Yangos (Ioannis) Pesmazoglou, a cousin of George's on his mother's side, was also often there. Political philosophy was represented, at its theoretical end by Cornelius Castoriades, at its practical by Panayotis Kanellopoulos, a close friend of Kostakis, shortly to found his own party and become the first of the very few politicians on whom George could pin his faith, for a time, in the future of his country. Among several future government ministers, and even prime ministers, it was in this circle that George first came to know and respect the German-trained philosopher-turned-politician, George Kartalis, whose fortunes would be linked to his own in the closing stages of the Second World War, and Evangelos Averoff-Tosizza, the foreign minister with whom he would work closely, and also quarrel irreparably, over the fate of Cyprus in the late 1950s.[18]

It was here, too, at one of these dinner parties on the top floor of the house in Kydathinaion Street, early in 1936, that George met the third and greatest love of his life.[19]

### Coup d'état / coup de foudre

She was Maria Zannou, known to family and friends as 'Marika.' She was a striking beauty, athletic-looking and slim, with long gold-blonde hair that she always wore tightly braided. Like Lou, Marika was already married; she also had two young daughters. She was a year younger than George.

Marika's father, Miltiades, had been born into the well-to-do Zannos family in Constantinople. When he had been still a child, the family moved to Athens, where Miltiades qualified as an engineer. It was while working on a viaduct to carry the national road from Athens to Lamia that Miltiades fell suddenly and irremediably in love with the young and beautiful daughter of the French architect for the project. This was Marie Pascal, more than twenty years his junior. In insisting on this match, outside his religion, Miltiades called down his mother's curse on his head. Marika was their fourth child; Marie Pascal died giving birth to her; for this reason she was baptised with the Greek form of her mother's name. For grief, Miltiades refused even to see his youngest child, and shipped her off to her mother's relatives in their rural chateau in the Drôme, not far from Lyon. Her father changed his mind some years later, when he learned that her French grandmother was preparing her to enter a convent, and brought her back to Greece.[20]

140

The first woman that George had seriously loved, Jacqueline, had been French. If part of what had attracted him to Lou had been that she was 'his first *Greek* woman,' she, too, had nonetheless lived and studied in Paris. Now came Marika, who was half Greek and half French; French was literally her mother tongue, and had been Marika's only language until her return to Greece, at the age of either five or seven. As a result, Marika had little formal education in Greek, as is evidenced by her spiky, individualistic handwriting, and sometimes also by her spelling. All her life she would be bilingual; George would refer affectionately to the characteristic way she pronounced certain sounds in Greek.[21]

Marika had been twenty-two, living on the island of Poros, and engaged to be married, when she met and fell in love with an officer serving at the island's naval base. This was Andreas Londos, who in photographs shows a striking resemblance to the movie-star Clark Gable. To the consternation of her family, Marika abandoned her fiancé to marry Londos after the briefest of engagements. Soon afterwards, he resigned his commission to take his bride travelling round Europe for a honeymoon that lasted seven months and used up a considerable inheritance.

Since then, Londos had worked in various capacities, but had no regular income. He played cards for high stakes, lived well beyond his means, and would give way to legendary rages. By the time that Marika met George, the marriage was falling apart in mutual acrimony. Londos had a long-term girlfriend, as well as numerous occasional attachments; it was no doubt in the hope of widening her own interests that Marika allowed herself to be taken along to Kydathinaion Street by her sister that evening at the beginning of 1936. The life Marika had led up to now could scarcely have been more different from that of George. Before long, he would be wondering, in letters to her, if she wouldn't miss 'the life you're used to with your kind of people, yachts and parties, wouldn't you be bored?' On the other side, George's family and many of his friends were clearly disconcerted by Marika's forthright temperament and total lack of intellectual pretension. Theirs was to be, in many ways, a match of opposites.[22]

But at the time of that first meeting, it was the elder sister, Amaryllis, with whom George had more in common. Amaryllis was four years older than George, a flamboyant character, well-read, a famous beauty and emancipated. She was married to a stockbroker, Nikolaos Dragoumis, known as Nelos, whose father, at the end of the previous century, had built the fine neoclassical villa overlooking the sea on Poros from which Marika had set out after her marriage to Londos. The name of this house, which still stands, little changed from that time, is *Galini* (Serenity), a name that cannot have failed to appeal to George when he first visited it in the summer of 1936.[23]

141

Amaryllis at this time had joined the circle of Loukia Fotopoulou. In early summer, George and Amaryllis began a correspondence which is half teasing, half flirtatious on her side, by turns indignant and intrigued on his. Undoubtedly he was flattered by her admiration; but Amaryllis was too vivacious to be overawed by 'the poet George Seferis.' Beneath all this, there is no doubt of Amaryllis' warm and genuine affection for him. When she learned that the Tsatsos family were spending the summer on Aegina, and that George would be joining them there, she wrote to him from Poros to remind him that Marika was also on Aegina, although she also warned him that the social life of the Londos household left her sister too busy to write letters.[24]

It was almost inevitable that George and Marika would meet again on Aegina. The two households were only about a mile apart. The world of well-to-do Athenians, in those days, was a small one; Marika's younger daughter, Anna, was a classmate at school with Despina, Ioanna's daughter. In this way, the scene was set for the new *coup de foudre*, whose effects would shake both families in the years to come.[25]

For that summer, Ioanna had chosen an old, rambling house with a lushly planted garden, full of exotic trees, and dominated by the scent and shade of a giant cypress. At the end of the garden was a clearing with a view out to sea. The Villa Floros is now semi-derelict, its grounds overgrown, though the descendants of some of the trees are still there, and Mediterranean pines still cast a generous shade. The surrounding area has been built up with modern bungalows, whose gardens are rampant in summer with jasmine and bougainvillea. The house at Perivola, where Marika and her daughters were staying, can also still be seen: just beyond the brow of the hill where the road south from the town comes in sight of the sea.[26]

The atmosphere in the Tsatsos household, that August, was highly charged. Soon after the birth of the younger of their children, Kostakis seems to have reverted to his womanizing ways; in time, his marriage to Ioanna would develop into a durable alliance of two powerful and complementary personalities, founded on mutual support in bringing up a family and in public life, as intimacy waned. Now, Kostakis indulged his 142 fantasies and pursued infidelities with serial abandon. Ioanna, unlike her husband, would always maintain perfect discretion about her own private life; it is idle to speculate about the precise nature of particular attachments, but Ioanna was, at various times after this, close to several charismatic and powerful men who had important roles to play in national life, and also crucially in George's. That summer of 1936, Ioanna had fallen under the spell of the poet Angelos Sikelianos.[27]

Sikelianos was a generation older than the Seferiadis siblings. His sister had been married to the brother of Isadora Duncan, and through the same circles he had met his first wife, the American heiress, Eva Palmer. Everything about Sikelianos was larger than life, and so had been his youthful ambitions. The Delphic Festivals which he recreated, with the support of his wife, in 1927 and 1930, had been intended, in all seriousness, to reconstitute the ancient pagan sanctuary of Delphi as the ecumenical spiritual centre of the world, as it had been for the Greeks of antiquity. The festivals had been a financial, though not an artistic, failure; among the casualties had been Sikelianos' marriage to Eva. Both as a poet and a man, Sikelianos was grandiose and grandiloquent: he possessed something of the charisma attributed to the Italian writer and fascist Gabriele d'Annunzio, with the important difference that in Sikelianos' case its manifestations were wholly pacific and benign. His mysticism has been compared to that of his older contemporary, W.B. Yeats. The full-bodied Romantic rhetoric of much of his verse kept younger poets, including George at this time, at an awed distance, though Sikelianos had responded to *The Cistern*, sent to him at Katsimbalis' insistence, with characteristic gallantry.[28]

After Palamas, who at seventy-seven was a generation older still, Sikelianos was acknowledged to be the greatest living Greek poet. That spring, Katsimbalis had organised a series of public lectures to commemorate the fifieth anniversary of Palamas' first book of poems. Relations between the two greatest living poets were notoriously strained, so it was a real tribute to Katsimbalis' persuasive powers that one of these lectures was given by Sikelianos.[29]

The lecture was held at the Parnassus Society, not far from the old Parliament building, on the evening of 3 April 1936. George went in a group which included Ioanna, Kostakis, Katsimbalis and Theotokas. It was the first time that Ioanna had heard Sikelianos in full flow; following his words, she felt as though she was actually watching the poet-creator in hand-to-hand combat with God. Should she write to him? she asked George, clutching his arm. Gravely, he replied, 'We ought to encourage artists.' Ioanna wrote, and Sikelianos sent her a poem in reply.[30]

143

That August, Sikelianos paid elegant court to Ioanna on Aegina. One day he arrived from his estate on the neighbouring island of Salamis, in his own motorboat, piled high with a cornucopia of fruit, and even an icebox. Later in the month, he stayed on the island, perhaps at the house of his friend, the poet and later novelist, Nikos Kazantzakis. A month after that, Sikelianos would send Ioanna the manuscript of the poem 'Autumn 1936,' which as well as being a veiled commentary on the political situation, is perhaps a love poem.[31]

George and Marika, in private, called him 'God.'

Away from the peace and quiet of Aegina, the political crisis that had begun with Plastiras' failed *coup* the previous March was rapidly worsening. Early in the summer, parliament went into recess, having failed to form a stable administration. General Ioannis Metaxas, the leader of a tiny right-wing party, had been entrusted by the king with forming an interim government, to last until the autumn. Labour unrest now intensified; in May, a strike by tobacco workers in Thessaloniki led to a mass demonstration, at which several demonstrators were killed. A general strike for the whole country was called for 5 August.

The day before, Metaxas, with the approval of King George, dissolved parliament, introduced emergency legislation, and suspended much of the constitution. Greece had suddenly become the latest in a long list of European countries in which democratic government had been first discredited and then usurped. It was a bloodless but highly effective *coup d'état.* Martial law was declared in Athens, and strict censorship imposed on the press. Within weeks, the arrests had begun. Among the first to be rounded up and sent into internal exile on barren islands in the Aegean was Kostakis' brother Mistos (Themistocles), who had been a Liberal MP in the last parliament. The new authoritarian regime was soon known by the date on which Metaxas had seized power: the Fourth of August. Before long its ideologues would be proclaiming the birth of the 'Third Greek Civilisation,' in undisguised emulation of Hitler's Third German Reich.[32]

Eleven days after the *coup*, on 15 August, George arrived at the Villa Floros, on Aegina, to begin a month's vacation. Looking back from the distance of a year, he remembered the first time he met Marika again, soon after his arrival:

We got to know one another one August noon on the beach. We were drying off, stretched out side by side. She had a dark-coloured veil over her face, it was wet. I bent over her to kiss her. She let her head loll, seeming indifferent; teeth clenched, lips cold. Then suddenly she pulled away the veil, it was like opening a book. We climbed the mountain naked in the sun. She was mine, as she is now, as she will be always, as once in our bed . . . [she said], 'Nothing separates us any more.'[33]

144

Less than a week after that, he and Marika spent their first whole day alone together. Over half a century later, she would tell the story with a freshness that conveys something of what the thirty-six-year-old George must have admired in her:

It was 21 August, a Friday. We set out the two of us for the Temple of Aphaia on Aegina. We started at crack of dawn from Perivola, where I was staying. We took a rugged path and, leaving the Peak on our right, came to Aetochori. It was still dark and the villagers were lighting fires on the slopes. At the village a woman had lit her oven and gave us warm bread, olives and ouzo. Later we went down towards the east side of the island until we came to the sea. Ayia Marina was below us. We went down and plunged into the sea. The place was perfectly deserted: rocks and caves. Later we climbed up barefoot to the Temple; outside the empty house of the custodian we found a jar of water. We washed off the salt, that was burning on our bodies, we drank and quenched our thirst. There was no end to the water in that jar. As it got dark, we heard the chug of a motorcar and then the mighty laugh of Angelos Sikelianos, who had come with George's sister, Ioanna, to find us.[34]

That day, and the benign presence of the Peak of Aegina, would be commemorated in George's poems, beginning later that year, and continuing up to the *Three Secret Poems* of thirty years later. The intensity of those snatched hours on Aegina, and of a brief visit to Amaryllis and her family on Poros, is caught in the group of poems called 'Sketches for a Summer,' written soon afterwards; it also extends achingly into the diary entries and love-letters of the next fourteen months, during which time the future of the relationship hung in the balance.[35]

On 17 September, his leave over, George sailed back from Aegina to Piraeus with Marika. The brief entry in his diary for that date marks the first appearance of his own, more folksy variant of her name: 'Maro,' pronounced with the stress on the second syllable. For more than half a century after that, until she died in her hundredth year, in March 2000, Maria Zannou would choose to be known in public as 'Maro.' But on that September day in 1936, any such hopes for the future seemed suddenly to have been dashed. Waiting for him on his desk at the Ministry, George found a notice of his imminent transfer to the southern Albanian town of Korça.[36]

### Letters from 'my village'

That same day, he wrote to Katsimbalis, who was in Paris. On Aegina, George declared, he had finally come to see the truth of what Katsimbalis had written to him all those years ago, when he had urged him to put 'murky cisterns' behind him, and respond to the Aegean summer in all its glory. 'Now I understand what you meant, in my own way,' he wrote to his friend. He had come back from Aegina full of plans for writing all winter. Suddenly, everything had been blighted by the news of his transfer. The Under-Secretary for Foreign Affairs, Nikolaos Mavroudis, to whom George was ultimately answerable, was at the moment in Geneva; 'Old' Katsimbalis had influence with him. In the strictest confidence, he asked Katsimbalis if he could persuade his ailing father to intervene with Mavroudis to keep him in Athens. The desperation behind this letter is palpable; but typically, George made no mention of the real reason for it.[37]

145

A spontaneous offer to mediate with Mavroudis came from Maro's sister, Amaryllis. For the first time addressing George in the informal, singular form, 'I hope,' she wrote, 'that you've recovered a bit from the *coup* of the first moment, and however things are now, you'll have got things a little organised in your head.' If Amaryllis did exert herself on his behalf, it seems to have been to no avail.[38]

Katsimbalis wrote from Paris to say that his parents were of the opinion that George's transfer would be for the good of his career, and declined to intervene. George was now beginning to suspect what may well have been the truth: that the 'good of his career,' in his family's eyes, would be served by removing him quickly from the company of yet another married woman. To Katsimbalis he wrote furiously: 'My travels I owe to one person alone and I know who that is.' This can only refer to Stelios, who had indeed been the cause of several painful displacements in George's life before this, and who heartily disliked 'the little gazelle,' as Maro was nicknamed in the Seferiadis family. Maro herself always believed that Stelios had been behind George's sudden move that autumn, and that she had been the reason.[39]

Whatever the true motive, Mavroudis was unrelenting. George would repay him shortly afterwards in a poem, if it is true that the scarecrow-like 'hollow man,' depicted in the wastes of an Albanian winter in 'The Old Man,' is intended to represent the Under-Secretary who held George's fate in his hands. Later, he would describe Mavroudis as 'a crafty, lazy and vindictive old man, with very limited horizons, who hated anything that created problems and distrusted everything.'[40]

While waiting for his transfer to be confirmed, and still doing everything in his power to avert it, George began to recreate the summer that was just past, in 'Sketches for a Summer.' The first of these continues the veiled but strong political commentary of his poems of the previous year: it contrasts the 'free wave of the sea' in summer with the glum inhabitants of autumn, 'saluting lines of the dead, standing to attention.' Several others are love poems to Maro. They also include the short 'Epitaph,' whose imagery recalls both the coals and fog of London and the cypress-trees at Kifisia, in which the 'Princess Lu' had been transformed into a bird. Dated in his diary to October 1936, this brief poem marks the final ending of George's relationship with Lou.[41]

On 21 October, the decree posting George to Korça as consul was published. Now that summer was over and the families were back in Athens, it cannot have been easy for him to spend time with Maro. When they met, one rainy morning in the National Gardens, close to Syntagma Square in the city centre, he was shocked at how tense and miserable she looked. With just a week to go before his departure, they met again, at a derelict factory compound on the edge of the city, near the Kifisos river: it was here that in the early years of the century the Zannos family had produced a well-known make of brandy and liqueurs. As a child, Maro had spent some of her happiest hours in the open grounds surrounding the villas of the owners. Seeing this dismal remnant of childhood through the eyes of Maro, George found himself confronted sharply by his own memories of Skala before 1914. He wrote an atmospheric account of the visit and these impressions in his diary, and sent it to Maro a few months later.[42]

But the deep melancholy that hangs over George's recollections of these meetings had as much to do with the future as the past. For the third time in his life he was about to entrust, unwillingly, his deepest emotional commitment to the trials of long-distance correspondence – an irony which he noted grimly in a letter to Maro.[43]

Two months, almost to the day, after his return from the summer idyll on Aegina, George was changing trains amid the rain and mud of the desolate railway junction of Platy. It is here, in the coastal plain of Macedonia, that the line from Athens to Thessaloniki and the rest of Europe crosses the local line that winds up into the highlands of West Macedonia. He had just had his last sight of the sea, that now more than ever he considered to be his own natural element. All that day it rained. The transition from the Aegean coastline to the interior of the Balkans is sudden and total. This is a landscape of forests, still lakes and rolling, widely spaced mountain ranges; to George's 'islander's' temperament, it was immediately alien. The placid surface of the lakes he found sinister; a few years later, a poem would link that landlocked stillness with unexplained violence. That first day, the mountain tops were hidden in cloud; in a poem of the following summer he would describe, with memorable exactitude, their 'skin wrinkled like an elephant's belly.'[44]

At Florina, the end of the line, he was met by a consular official with a car, for the long, slow drive further into the mountains to the Albanian frontier and his destination. The light was fading, as the road wound upwards through a ravine. Beechwoods rose steeply on either side, the slopes carpeted with fiery-tinted autumn leaves. The whole scene, he wrote to Maro on the day after his arrival, reminded him of her: these were her colours. He captured the moment in a poem, that would many years later be set to music by Mikis Theodorakis:

I kept hold of my life I kept hold of my life travelling
among the yellow trees beneath the slanting rain
on silent slopes where leaves of beech drift deep,
no fire on the peaks. Darkness is falling.[45]

The town of Korça (Korytsa in Greek) lies in the centre of a plain dominated by the Moraves mountains to the east. A small river, the Drenica, runs
past its southern edge. George found only two places of interest nearby, to
which he took regular walks: one was the hillside village of Mporje, where
he admired the little fourteenth-century church of the Ascension with its
frescoes; the other was Drenova, a mining village but also the start of the
mountain game reserve now known as the Drenova National Park. Korça
itself, with its well-preserved Ottoman buildings, cobbled streets and
mosques, as well as a substantial Greek population, interested him not at
all, though he took some fine photographs of its outdoor market, which
he also vividly described. He referred scornfully to the place as 'my
village;' and was unmoved by the attempt of that incorrigible irredentist,
Katsimbalis, to lift his spirits: 'Don't start grizzling again and the nostalgic
sighs. Korytsa [Korça] is also *Greece*, a piece of Greek soil and Greek
148    nature.'[46]

As consul, George must have had to deal with the day-to-day business,
and occasional tensions, of the sizeable Greek minority in this part of
Albania. But this aspect of his work and environment is almost entirely
absent from his diaries and correspondence. The Greek consulate must
have been something of a lightning conductor for nationalist claims on
what some Greeks, even today, call 'Northern Epiros;' this was doubtless
the reason for the surveillance and checks on his mail by the Albanian
authorities, of which he frequently complained. He could have thrown
himself into the local politics of the Greek community in Korça. He was
certainly neither unaware of its history and aspirations, nor indifferent to
them. But he kept himself studiously aloof. In his letters and his diary, it
was overwhelmingly the foreignness of Albania that he stressed again and
again.[47]

In Korça, George found limited consolation in smoking, drinking, and
listening to his collection of jazz records. With a skittishness that is sometimes heavy-handed, he described his diplomatic colleagues of other nation-
alities (French, English, Italian, Serbian), and caricatured the backwardness
of Albanian society. Since French was the common diplomatic language,
he had dealings with the French teachers seconded to the *Lycée Français*;

the Albanians, he noted, accused them of spreading communism. It is possible that among their number he encountered Enver Hoxha, a teacher at the Lycée at this time, who for forty years after the Second World War came to rule the most closed and hardline communist state in the world; if so, the meeting seems to have left no impression on either man. When, in May, a rebellion against King Zog was brutally put down in the towns of Gjirokastra and Tepelena, George made light of the events, except insofar as they interrupted his correspondence with Maro.[48]

During the long, snowy winter and spring in Korça, his thoughts were all of Maro, and the Aegean summer that they had spent together. To Apostolidis, now suffering from tuberculosis and confined to a sanatorium in Switerzland, he confided something of his feelings:

> I've never missed a woman, the way I miss this woman. I've never missed anyone or anything so much . . . I've tried to position this love, how can I explain it, like something autonomous, outside myself that I can submit to, but also keep my distance from it. I can only manage it for a few hours at a time. Then my strength gives way . . . Everything's against us.[49]

149

Between his arrival in Korça in November and the following July, George wrote eighty-eight letters to Maro. Some were addressed, for form's sake, to the Londos family home in Kolonaki, on the southern slopes of the Lycabettus hill; they contain nothing to which a husband could take exception. But most were sent under cover, in envelopes addressed to Maro's sister Amaryllis, who was now a trusted, if by no means uncomplaining, confidante of the couple.[50]

Some of the preoccupations that emerge in these letters — with secrecy, with physical longing, with convoluted and changeable plans to meet — are reminiscent of George's earlier letters to Lou from London. But the tone of this correspondence could not be more different. Gone is the introverted posturing of 'Mr Stratis Thalassinos.' There is scarcely a trace of self-pity in these letters; when he indulges in black moods, he also makes a point of apologising; for, perhaps, the first time in a relationship, it is George who is confident and high-spirited, it is *he* who is constantly rallying *her* and encouraging her. He is no longer ground down by adversity or the uncongeniality of his surroundings, as he so often had been in London; from Korça his frequent complaints of boredom are expressed with tearing high spirits. This new sense of fresh air blowing through George's letters from

Albania (and not only those to Maro) surely owed much to the forthright, direct character of the woman with whom he was in love.

In contrast to the London years, too, that winter and spring at Korça were intensely productive. Partly, this had to do with the fortunes of the journal *Ta Nea Grammata*.

Katsimbalis had been in Paris since the previous summer, attending the sickbed of his father. When 'Old' Katsimbalis died at the end of March 1937, George wrote an affectionate obituary for him. The prolonged absence of its guiding spirit, as much as the new censorship imposed by Metaxas, was making severe difficulties for the journal. It had almost closed down at the end of the previous year. In order to keep it going, Katsimbalis wielded his 'big stick' from Paris: George must write something for every issue.[51]

From Korça, he obliged with a steady stream of poems, beginning with 'In the Manner of G.S.,' that he had finished in August or September, and the 'Sketches for a Summer.' By the summer of 1937, he had completed the last of the poems that would make up his largest single volume of poetry, *Book of Exercises*. Although this was not published until 1940, the selection, arrangement and final editing of the volume were all done at Korça, and finished by September. By this time, George was also launched on the poems that would go to make up his next collection, *Logbook*.[52]

At the same time, and also partly to oblige Katsimbalis, from Korça he now began systematically writing essays. Until now, George had only twice appeared in public as a literary critic. The first time had been in Paris, with his lecture on Moréas, the second the introduction to his translation of T.S. Eliot's *The Waste Land and Other Poems*, that had appeared the previous July. Now, he began the series of essays, drawing on a tradition stretching back from Eliot to Montaigne, that continued for the rest of his life.[53]

Prompted by this activity, during his months at Korça George began laying the groundwork for a far-reaching investigation of the Modern Greek literary and cultural canon, which, although never completed in any systematic fashion, provides a thread of coherence linking many of his published *Essays*. Key figures in this canon, with which he began to engage seriously at this time, were General Makriyannis, whose *Memoirs* he had first begun to admire ten years earlier, and the Alexandrian Greek poet C.P. Cavafy, the literary predecessor with whom he would have the greatest difficulty, in future, in coming to terms.[54]

For once, the frustrations of love at a distance were proving fruitful for George. But with summer approaching, and his feelings for Maro undiminished by separation, the relationship was now heading for a crisis.

### 'Everything's possible, even "happiness"'

Ever since arriving at Korça, George had been bombarding the Ministry in
Athens with requests for leave. Hopes of coming back for Christmas had
been dashed by Mavroudis himself, who was reported to have said, 'Listen
to that, he's only been gone a month and he wants to come back already?
No way!'[55]

When a second application for leave was rejected at the beginning of
February ('not even for 24 hours'), George pleaded the need for urgent
dental treatment. This stratagem was more successful, and enabled him to
spend the month of March 1937 in Athens, seeing Maro as often as was
practicable. Later plans to meet in Macedonia, either in Thessaloniki, where
Maro's friend Sofia Mavrogordatou, the daughter of the novelist Penelope
Delta, was in the lovers' confidence, or in Verria, came to nothing; Maro
seems to have resisted firmly his proposal to spend part of his summer leave
on Aegina.[56]

Then in June, after a hurried exchange of letters and telegrams, George
absented himself, apparently without leave, and spent four days with Maro
at the seaside village of Tsangarada, north of Volos on Mount Pelion. He
was barely back in Korça, when Maro's letter arrived. In his diary he noted
merely: 'disaster.' Londos had made a scene on her return; Maro had confessed everything. The cuckolded husband had threatened to throw her out
of the house and bar her from seeing their two daughters. George's response
to her anguished letter is measured, practical and supportive. It also shows
his own instinct for self-preservation, which had been well developed
during his clandestine relationship with Lou:

> Write and tell me if my trip has been discovered. Then take my letters,
> seal them up, and give them to my sister. You'll tell her they're personal
> papers of mine, for her to look after. You don't want them in your house,
> now.[57]

From this point events moved rapidly. Within days, George was writing
to Maro again. A decision must be taken. He saw only two possibilities:
either to end everything now, in which case he would do everything in his
power to make things easier for her, even though it would go against all his
instincts; or they could begin to make plans to live together. That same
night, a telegram arrived from Maro, 'I'll do anything, to live with you;' but
not, apparently, unconditionally. Only three days later, after another letter
had come from her, did he take up what appears to have been *her* proposal.
He wrote to her:

We'll get married, not because we have to, but because that way it's easier to live in society. What binds us won't be marriage but our love. This, too, I want you to know, if you make this your decision: if you become my wife, you'll be free and I'll be free. If we stop loving one another, we won't stay together. . . . So, we'll get married. This isn't a decision of now. I took it from the moment when I sat down, one afternoon back in January, to write to Andreas.[58]

On that occasion, she had dissuaded him from writing to Londos. Now, he knew that he had to confront the aggrieved husband. But still he vacillated: if Maro was going to leave Londos anyway, what would be the point? Either way, it was now imperative that he come to Athens. Maro and her daughters were once again staying at Perivola, on Aegina, where Londos would join them at weekends. By the middle of the month, George was still waiting for the Ministry to approve his urgent request for a week's leave. All further decisions, by Maro or himself, were deferred until then. It was not a new situation in George's life, and the outcome was very nearly as disastrous as it had been before. But this time, as he wrote to Apostolidis, when his leave at last came through and he was about to set out for Athens to confront Londos:

The whole affair gives me the sense of heading out into open waters. A breath of fresh air . . . What I'll come back with, I've no idea. I've thrown the dice up to heaven; I'm waiting for them to fall; everything's possible, even 'happiness.'[59]

George left Korça on Saturday 24 July. After two days on the train, he reached Athens late on Sunday. The next day, Maro and Londos returned from Aegina for a formal meeting at their family home. What happened was recalled by Maro many years later:

After they had met [alone], Andreas told me that it was up to me to decide, but that on one thing, at least, they had agreed absolutely: the correct style of dress for a *gentleman* [in English]. As soon as George had gone, Andreas put it to me straight: if I went with George, I'd lose the children. I decided to stay, although it hurt me terribly. Next day I phoned Kydathinaion Street and told George that I was leaving for Aegina and we would not meet again. He replied hoarsely that he had been expecting it.[60]

In fact, she did not speak to George; George was out when Maro telephoned (on the Wednesday). It was Ioanna who took the call. To Ioanna, George wrote stiffly, five days later:

The matter of M[aro] has ceased absolutely to be of any interest to me. Because the message wasn't: which solution was the right one, but which way ought we to have gone about finding this solution. I didn't like this behaviour and it's destroyed a lot of things to do with that matter.

By this time (Monday 2 August), he had destroyed all Maro's letters and instructed his family never to speak of her again. The note to Ioanna was hastily dashed off as he was about to leave Athens. His destination was the sanatorium on Mount Pelion, above Volos. This was a fashionable summer resort for well-connected Athenians; the proprietor of the sanatorium, George Karamanis, and his wife Anna, had long been friends of George and all his circle. He did not travel alone.[61]

Ioanna, in her memoir, says of that summer only that George had 'many problems':

153

I saw little of him. But he sent me [from Pelion] a delightful diary written on pages of his notebook. But that is another story. A secret that might have turned into something but did not.

What seems to have happened is that George's family seized the opportunity afforded by Maro's decision, and took immediate steps to push him into a suitable marriage. In the 'diary' to which Ioanna refers, actually a series of letters, and in his pocket-diary, George refers to his companion either anonymously as 'Girlfriend,' or as 'Clélia,' a name borrowed from Stendhal's La Chartreuse de Parme, from which he had already quarried aliases for himself and Theotokas. She came from a distinguished local family, from the region of Volos, and would certainly have made an eminently suitable match for George. In his correspondence with his sister, this possibility is cryptically conveyed in the phrase 'St John.' Ioanna would have understood at once the allusion to the midsummer ritual of St John's Day at Skala, and in her letters urged him on.[62]

What Ioanna found 'delightful' about these letters from Pelion was presumably their sprightly, almost adolescent cheerfulness, and a sexual frankness which harks back to a much earlier period in the relationship of brother and sister. But in the context of all that George had so recently been writing to Maro (little, if any, of which he had been prepared to share with his sister), what Ioanna found delightful turns into the thinnest veneer of bravado over an abyss of despair and bitterness.[63]

On Pelion, George found the old-world atmosphere of the sanatorium suffocating. He visited 'Clélia' at her mother's house in Volos. The house was old, with a little courtyard at the front, sixteenth-century engravings on the walls, and a library in the style of the 1890s. These and other details he noted in his diary for 11 August; they also passed into the poem that he finished shortly after his return to Korça, 'Piazza San Niccolò.'[64] A key to this intensely personal poem is the postscript to George's letter to Ioanna dated the previous day: 'Clélia's house is just like Proust's house at Cambrai.' 'Piazza San Niccolò' opens with the first sentence, untranslated, of Proust's monumental novel, *A la recherche du temps perdu*, and its title links the location, a church in Volos, with the liberating power of involuntary memory experienced by Proust's narrator, Marcel. But the poem evokes, instead of Marcel's release, a suffocating sense of imprisonment in a circumscribed and outdated way of life. Privately, for George, this must have been his image of marriage to an eligible young girl whom he barely knew. In the poem, hope, or transcendence, lies far away:

154

> To find the cool freshness of the mountain you have to climb
>     higher than the belfry
> and higher than the hand of St Nicholas
> some 70 or 80 metres are not too much. . . .
> Yet it is there, a little higher than the belfry, that your life changes.
> It is no great matter to climb but it is very difficult for you to change
> as the house is inside the stone church and your heart inside the
>     house that grows dark
> and all the doors locked by the great hand of St Nicholas.[65]

In the world of this poem, it is only in 'the ease of sleep,' where 'the waters run,' that 'the bitterness of parting fades;' there is probably an allusion here to the line of Eliot's 'Marina,' another poem about an unattainable ideal: 'under sleep where all the waters meet.' But at the personal level, the 'parting' here can only be the parting from Maro. The ascent into the 'cool freshness' of Mount Pelion, away from the claustrophobia of 'Clélia's' ancestral home, and the change in himself that would be much more difficult than the ascent, all correspond to George's intense hopes for a life, that might have been, with Maro.

George sailed from Volos for Thessaloniki on 15 August, and arrived in Korça the next day. He had been away for exactly three weeks; he had asked for, and been granted, only one week's leave. Possibly he had already arranged this before he left, in the expectation of spending the extra fifteen days with Maro; or there may have been intervention in high places, to enable the idyll with 'Clélia' to reach a conclusion satisfactory to George's family. Either way, the official document recording his resumption of duties at Korça is dated 3 August, two weeks before he actually returned.[66]

Already, his pocket-diary was laconically recording letters to or from his 'Girlfriend.' On his arrival at Korça, he found a letter waiting for him from Maro. Hard on its heels came another from Ioanna, with a postscript from Kostakis. 'Marika' had written to him in a moment of weakness, because they had not even said their farewells. Already she had thought better of it. If George insisted on a reply, he should send it under cover of his brother-in-law, who would convey it to the Londos household. This George did.[67]

Back at his post, George threw himself into his duties with what vigour he could muster. He finished preparing *Book of Exercises* for publication, and wrote three bitter poems, of which 'Piazza San Niccolò' was the first. Maro wrote again, at the end of August, asking to see him. He did not reply, but wrote, ten days later, to her sister instead; Amaryllis diplomatically expressed surprise at hearing from him, perhaps laced with anger, but made no mention of Maro. The exchange of letters with his 'Girlfriend' continued until the middle of the month.[68]

George now learned that his desperate efforts to secure a transfer back to Athens were perhaps about to be rewarded after all. His father had already written that he was expecting to see him shortly; then on 20 September, he was able to tell Katsimbalis, in strictest confidence, that he thought he would be in Athens early in October; to Apostolidis he added that he had no idea whether for a short or a long stay. The telegram from Mavroudis arrived ten days later; it was not an immediate transfer, but the purpose of the summons seems to have been to prepare the ground. If Maro was right in her suspicions, and behind these manoeuvres lay the unseen hand of George's father, then Stelios had relented too soon. Before he left Korça, George was once again in regular contact with Amaryllis. It must have been through her sister that Maro knew to expect him. He arrived in

Athens on 7 October. Maro was at the railway station. 'I fell into his arms,' she said, many years later. 'Sobs.'[69]

It is impossible to know what expectations George can have had when he set out from Korça that October morning of 1937. Even after the break with Maro, he can have had no desire to prolong his exile in his 'village.' But there is no evidence that he had any inkling, until after he had arrived in Athens, what the price of his repatriation would be. It was not until two weeks later, that an order of the day from Theologos Nikoloudis, Under-Secretary for Press and Tourism, and one of the most outspoken ideologues of the Metaxas regime, co-opted George Seferiadis on to a committee dealing with the drafting of new laws in his department.[70]

Despite its modest title, and its formal subordination to the Foreign Ministry, the Under-Ministry of Press and Tourism was the ideological heart of Metaxas' authoritarian 'New State.' It enjoyed formidable powers under the emergency legislation passed in the wake of the 4 August *coup d'état*. The committee on to which George had been co-opted must have been to some degree responsible for the new round of censorship laws which would be brought in, the following February. Already, all publications in Greece were subjected to rigorous censorship; there was strict control over the information given to foreign news organisations. Nikoloudis, a former journalist and newspaper editor, made no secret of his admiration for the Third Reich, and was reputed to run his department in open emulation of Goebbels' propaganda ministry in Berlin.[71]

156

By the time he left Athens six weeks after he had arrived, to wind up his tenure at the consulate in Korça, George had agreed to serve Nikoloudis as Director of the Foreign Press Section of the Under-Ministry. He left Albania for the last time on 2 December, and took up his duties formally five days later. George's personal antipathy to his new boss was well-founded, and would emerge clearly later. At the time, he left no record of his feelings, or indeed of his motives, in accepting this appointment.[72]

The only account that George ever gave of how he came to the Press Ministry dates from 1943. Then, under the pressure of allegations that he had been an ideological supporter of the Metaxas regime, he insisted that he had not sought this post, but had been 'appointed by decree.' No doubt, in the strict sense, this was true. But there is no evidence that George made any representations against taking up this appointment, as he had done over his recent transfer to Albania, or before that, when the Ministry's decree had consigned him to the consulate at Cardiff. He could have stayed in

Albania, where indeed his Ambassador took a warm view of his abilities and protested strongly at being deprived of his services.[73]

The explanation must surely lie in the resumption of his relationship with Maro. George's pocket-diary for the two weeks following his definitive return from Albania contain entries in Maro's handwriting, probably made much later, marking the dates when they were together. By the start of the new year she had left her husband for good, and moved into a small flat that George rented for her, close to the ancient stadium (and to the site of their future home). This proved a shortlived measure; before long, Maro was reunited with her daughters, in drastically reduced circumstances, in Plaka, just around the corner from Kydathinaion Street.[74]

To achieve this, in the face of overwhelming odds, both George and Maro had had to pay a price that was yet to be reckoned. Maro, in moving out of the family home, in the face of Londos' threat to deprive her of her children, had taken the first step towards the sacrifice she would be called upon to make three and a half years later, which would cast its shadow over the rest of her own life and the lives of her daughters. And George, for reasons that had patently nothing to do with political sympathy, had accepted a job which in the eyes of many, then and later, would implicate him in the workings of the Metaxas regime.

157

# 6
## 'A Generation Sacrificed'
## 1938–1941

A generation sacrificed . . . A generation that has inherited from the first war an anxiety unknown before, the feeling that every foundation . . . has been eroded, has turned to dust; . . . that knows it doesn't have long before the next war that's coming.

(*Days 3*: 6 September 1935)

### Ministry of Propaganda
In later life, George was adamant that his work at the 'propaganda' ministry, during the Metaxas years, had had nothing to do with the exercise of censorship within Greece:

> A diplomat was required to maintain contact with foreign Embassies and foreign correspondents. . . . I was to assume only those duties which belonged to the purview of the Ministry of Foreign Affairs, without, that is to say, having any involvement with matters concerning the domestic press, wireless broadcasts, or the other activities of the Under-Ministry.[1]

In fact, during a three-week period in 1938, he was formally deputed to stand in for his opposite number who had responsibility for internal censorship; in a letter to Nikoloudis marked 'strictly personal,' George objected that the distinction between 'formal' and real responsibility was meaningless in practice, and demanded to be released from duties 'in which my conscience as a civil servant forbids me to continue.' There is no reason to doubt that this request was granted. But even before this episode, George can hardly have found his new job congenial.[2]

A bland outline of what must have been his job description, at the time when he started, can be read in one of the Under-Ministry's many self-congratulatory publications, that appeared shortly afterwards:

> The Under-Ministry of Press and Tourism attaches supreme importance to the surveillance and enlightenment of the foreign Press. It has tried

by objective means to enlighten so far as possible those foreign newspapers that in a variety of ways have manifested an interest in Greece, and a special concern is the briefing of foreign correspondents visiting our Country.

In this manner, it can be said that Foreign public opinion, through its most reliable news media, has been enlightened in relation to the importance of the work now being achieved by the Government of the Fourth of August, and also that, as a consequence, the prestige of Greece in international public opinion has risen as never before.[3]

One of George's first duties was to attend the wedding of Crown Prince Paul and Princess Frederica (the future king and queen of Greece), on 9 January 1938. Immediately afterwards, the press office was mobilised to play down the event. Metaxas, having exploited the king's prestige and distrust of his subjects in order to gain power for himself, was now busy sidelining his royal patron. George, on this occasion at least, with his strong aversion to the monarchy, must have experienced a bitter satisfaction in carrying out the orders of his masters.[4]

But this was a rare convergence. For the royal wedding, the regime had brought back from exile or retirement many of the politicians who had been muzzled since the *coup* of 1936. Able to communicate with one another for the first time in eighteen months, the former leaders of the democratic parties quickly conspired together and published a quixotic memorandum condemning the 'New State.' Metaxas' response was swift, brutal and effective. A hundred and fifty former politicians were arrested and deported to remote islands.[5]

There followed a second round of emergency legislation, which tightened the grip of the regime in all walks of life. The government now openly described itself as a 'dictatorship.' The law of 11 February provided for the establishment of 'concentration camps' for political dissidents; a 'certificate of civic responsibility' became a requirement for most types of employment; 'declarations of repentance' were introduced. Hard on the heels of the second emergency law, on 22 February two new press laws gave yet harsher teeth to the measures against free speech in Greece; these must have been essentially the work of Nikoloudis, and their wording had been passed by the committee of the Under-Ministry to which George had been co-opted in October. As one later historian summed up the consequences, 'After 1938 press censorship became stricter and hardly any news from Greece was accurately reported in foreign countries.'[6]

159

George's direct comments on these events are few. The time when he regularly kept a detailed private record of his struggles in the professional sphere was still some way off; his 'service' diary for the years leading up to 1940 occupies just over a page, and reveals almost nothing of his feelings at the time. His personal diary is scarcely more informative. 'It is easier for a camel to pass through the eye of a needle,' he noted, a week after taking up his duties at the Under-Ministry, 'than for a Greek politician to understand Greece.' But George's new masters also despised the politicians they had ousted; if his target was in fact Metaxas and the political leaders of the 'New State,' this entry does not say so unambiguously. At the start of the new year, 1938, he reflected on his country, that not only caused him pain, in an allusion to the opening line of the poem 'In the Manner of G.S.,' but 'degrades us.' Even the laconic injunction to himself, 'Don't belong to any [political] party,' is less than categorical, at a time when all party-political activity was banned.[7]

George may have chosen to express himself cautiously, or not at all; but he was not equivocal. One of the politicians deported at the end of January was Andreas Michalakopoulos, whom George had served when he had been foreign minister. He had accompanied Michalakopoulos in the delegation to represent Greece at the League of Nations in Geneva, and included him, not long afterwards, on the distribution list for *Turning Point*. When Michalakopoulos became ill in custody, and died shortly after being released, it was a serious embarrassment to the regime. The death in such circumstances of a former foreign minister and prime minister was hushed up at first; then a mockery of a 'state' funeral was rushed through with the utmost secrecy.[8] Returning home from the obsequies, George wrote in his diary:

> In order to speak at all, in a debased age, it's perhaps necessary – perhaps you can't do otherwise – to speak in its language. This doesn't mean that you accept it.[9]

George did not accept it; he accepted neither the 'debasement' that he found degrading about the Metaxas regime, nor the language of its propaganda that he was obliged to speak in his professional capacity. Looking back with recent hindsight, George would conclude that Metaxas' 'greatest fault' had been:

> He had promoted in his immediate circle a contempt and a fear of independent opinion, a sneering at freedom, the habit of the methods of the

160

police cell, a dependence on informers; the composite methods of fascist states daubed with Greek local colour out of tourist brochures.[10]

But by the time these words were written, Metaxas would be dead and George far away in exile. The strongest evidence for his attitude at the time, when he had been newly co-opted to serve that culture, comes from two poems that he began in February 1938.

The very next day after the announcement of the second emergency law, 12 February, George drafted the poem 'The Last Day.' It begins with a grimness that is not only seasonal: soldiers present arms, a funeral march goes past. Trivial conversations are overheard; no one knows what to do any more, on a day when 'By dawn tomorrow, nothing will be left to us; all to be surrendered; even our hands.' The poem continues:

My friend was singing as she walked by my side, a broken song:
'In spring, in summer, slaves . . .'
It made you think of aged teachers who'd deserted us.[11]

The song alluded to is a traditional one, associated with the uprising of the oppressed Greeks against their Ottoman overlords in 1821, out of which the modern nation had been born; the 'aged teachers' are those who had inculcated, for generations, a national pride based on the values of freedom and self-sacrifice. The song, in this 'broken' form, reduced to disjointed essentials, and ignored by the passers-by, is no longer a call to arms, but rather a cryptic warning that Greeks are once again, and all unawares, degenerating into their former condition of subjection.

When George came to prepare his next collection, *Logbook*, for publication, in 1940, he held this poem back, fearing the intervention of the censors. With characteristic caution, he inserted handwritten copies of 'The Last Day' inside the copies of the book destined for trusted friends; when the poem first appeared in print, it would be thanks to the initiative of Katsimbalis, in 1944, under a different censorship regime, and apparently not without difficulty then either. Since 1950, 'The Last Day' has taken its place in cumulative editions of George's *Poems*; but even there the published dateline 'Athens, Feb. '39' must be a deliberate mistake, intended to direct the reader's attention away from the specific historical circumstances of its composition, and to highlight more strongly, instead, its broader theme of foreboding about the coming world war, which George had foreseen since at least 1935.[12]

Thirty years after 'The Last Day' was written, when another dictator-ship had taken power in Greece, George would read this poem at Harvard University to an audience that included Greek Americans and students from Greece. It ends (in the Keeley and Sherrard translation, read by Edmund Keeley on that occasion):

> I'm sick of the dusk. Let's go home,
> let's go home and turn on the light.

A student voice from the back of the room yelled, in English, 'Yes. Let's turn on the light in Greece.' Many in the audience joined in, with hearty applause, clearly responding to the poem's veiled political comment. George himself, as Keeley recalls, was startled.[13]

The other poem of that month is 'The Return of the Exile,' dated, in manu-script, 26 February 1938. Just four days after the announcement of the new press laws, this was also the date of a royal decree announcing George's pro-motion and imminent transfer to the consulate in his birthplace, Izmir. Within days the transfer had been rescinded; he would stay at the Under-Ministry for another three years. But briefly, and not for the first time, George must have had to confront the possibility of returning to the places he had last seen as a child. This is one of the strands that go to make up this deceptively simple poem. But at a more immediate level, the return-ing exile is George newly returned from Albania; the land to which he returns is the Athens of the Fourth of August.[14]

So soon after the deportation of the politicians and the announcement of new authoritarian legislation, George can have had no choice but to brief foreign journalists, that February, with the soothing reassurances and half-truths that are the stock-in-trade of one of the two voices that are heard in this poem. The 'Return of the Exile' is a dialogue between the self-serving, self-deluding follower of orders (the obedient servant of the 'New State') and the moral and political conscience of the poet. The voice that greets the returning exile drips with reassurance, but before long the suave cer-tainties and the cloying sentimentality have become sinister. 'You will get used to it,' this voice repeats insistently; the threat is half-unveiled.

At first, the returning exile experiences something not at all unusual, in going back to a place remembered from childhood: everything is far smaller than he remembers it. But as the dialogue progresses, in place of gradual recognition comes increased alienation. The very landscape seems to have shrunk. How can he live in this 'sheepfold'? Why are the people all on their *knees*? Soon the whole scene shrinks still further. 'With every word you speak, the smaller/at every moment grows your stature,' the exile complains, in a line that surely carries more than a frisson of self-knowledge from George's experience at the Under-Ministry. At last, the exile is left alone:

> And now I hear no sound at all
> my last friend has sunk out of sight
> how strange it is that everything
> around here bit by bit sinks lower;
> along this way come mowing down
> thousands of chariots with whirling scythe-blades.[15]

Even the poet's voice has been split into two; in the name of a Hellenic ideal, Metaxas' 'New State' has created a desert in which only the archetypal enemies of Hellenic civilisation can flourish: barbarism and tyranny.

It is apparent that the strong political statement contained in these two poems was not intended to elicit a political response. Why was George so guarded about this?

163

An instinct for caution can only provide part of the answer; the experience of his father, writing topical poems for the Greek newspapers of Smyrna before 1914, in a dangerous game of cat-and-mouse with the Ottoman authorities, may have played a part. But George's background as an artist, and particularly his debt to the French Symbolist movement and its English-language inheritors, seems also to have left him with a deep horror of anything that might smack of preaching from the pulpit. The indirectness of his political testament in verse, in this and many later poems, was due at least as much to an overriding aesthetic imperative, as to any consideration of expediency or self-preservation.

This stand is explained in the essay written just over a year later, in which he set out his fullest views on the nature of poetic language. In 'Monologue on Poetry,' George presents himself as a craftsman in words. A key term in the essay is 'precision;' probably this was due to his recent immersion in the poetry and essays of Ezra Pound. It was now that he definitively laid to rest the shadow of the 'ivory tower,' that had never been deliberately chosen by George, but had dogged him since the publication of his first poems: 'art,' he declared, as an article of faith, 'is the supreme means to help people approach one another.'[16]

The poet, George asserts in that essay, carries an enormous responsibility, but this is not primarily a social one; it is rather responsibility to the language that he inherits and will pass on, enriched or impoverished, to future generations: 'the ultimate purpose of the poet is not to describe things but to create them by naming them.' If the world that we inhabit and recognise is shaped by language, then the precision to which the poet aspires is not merely an aesthetic goal; it is also a moral one. Although he could not spell this out in print, George had had first-hand experience, through his work at the Under-Ministry of Press and Tourism, of the sinister power of propaganda and the manipulation of language for the purposes of an authoritarian regime. The terrible power of language in the world, so easily abused by the censor and the propagandist, is also the poet's to command, if he has control of his medium. This is why George insists that poetry has a supreme duty to be 'true,' and to be 'precise' – not in the sense of faithfully representing something that is already there, but rather in the way that God, at the end of each day of Creation, surveyed his handiwork and 'saw that it was good.'[17]

Seen in this way, the veiled political content of many of his poems, from 1935 onwards, could not be directed to any functional goal; the truth that George claims for poetry is of a different nature from that of even the sincerest and most honourable statement of belief, or call to arms. Paradoxically, but not irrationally, the political 'truth' of these poems is there for posterity, not for the exigency of this or any other moment.

164

### Beyond the 'New State': Hellenism

Already, during the political disintegration that had followed the failed Venizelist *coup* of March 1935, George had alluded bitterly to the 'people of this generation that belong to a state that has become small, as Greece has since 1922.' With his Venizelist, irredentist upbringing and Anatolian background, George could never forget that the Greek language and Greek culture, for centuries before the disaster of 1922, had spread throughout the Balkans, the eastern Mediterranean and much of the Middle East. The old 'Great Idea' of expanding the physical frontiers of the Greek state had gone for good; but what George found most contemptible about the Metaxas regime was its narrow focus on the 'New *State*.' Venizelos and a few like-minded politicians, according to George, had acted from the perspective, not of the state, but of the nation, which had never been confined within geographical boundaries. 'Now that the Nation has been huddled within the limits of the state centred on mainland Greece, the activity of those people who are worth something is bound to be limited too,' he had written while he was in Korça.[18]

Looking back with hindsight on the Fourth of August dictatorship, what George would condemn in Metaxas almost as much as his authoritarian methods was his opposition, while a senior army officer before 1922, to the irredentist vision of Venizelos. This distinction between nation and state became an article of faith for George, at the time when he was beginning to carry out his duties at the Under-Ministry of Press and Tourism:

Greece becomes a secondary matter ... Whatever of Greece obstructs my thinking of Hellenism, let it be destroyed. If it was right for this country to expand its borders [*the policy of Venizelos and others before 1922*] ... it was so that Hellenism could develop, in a corner of the earth – this idea of human worth and freedom, not this archaeological idea.[19]

These thoughts were brought sharply into focus in April 1938, when George headed a three-man Greek delegation to the third conference of the Press of the Balkan Entente, in Istanbul. His enthusiasm for the visit, and even his sincere admiration for the courtesy of the delegation's Turkish hosts, come through clearly in the letters he wrote to Maro, who was obliged by diplomatic protocol to stay behind in the little flat in Mousourou Street, since she was not his wife. He preserved a number of mementoes of the occasion, including a photograph of himself looking very earnest and solemn behind a rostrum, in the midst of neoclassical décor and painted flowers in the Beylerbey palace on the Bosphorus.[20]

While there, he took time out to admire the early fourteenth-century mosaics of the Kahrye Camii, the mosque, now a museum, that in Byzantine times had been the Church of the Chora, an acknowledged high-point of late Byzantine art. The proud vestiges of a Greek-speaking, cosmo-politan empire that had lasted for a thousand years made a striking contrast to the petty authoritarianism of the 'Third Greek Civilisation' that George had left behind at home, as he noted in his diary and (obliquely) in a three-line poem written on his return.[21]

It was now that the occasion arose for him to develop these ideas in print. His brother-in-law Kostakis Tsatsos had just published a long philosophical essay, which included a section critical of the 'younger generation' in the Greek arts. George seized the opportunity with relish.

The heated public exchange that now began was to last for almost two years. It has all the trappings of high controversy; according to Ioanna, all of literary Athens was divided into opposing camps. In reality, as Ioanna also readily acknowledged, it was a somewhat staged confrontation: the two men were living in the same house, and would often meet on the stairs to read out impassioned passages to one another or to Ioanna. In the summer months, the dialogue continued in the open air, at Kifisia. George admitted afterwards that at every turn he had had the spectre of the censors breathing down his neck. What he wanted to say was not easy to express and keep within the laws of the 'New State.'[22]

The key sections of the essay are the last two, which confront the 'Greekness' of a work of art. 'Greekness' was a term much in vogue in Athens in the late 1930s; by it was meant, in effect, a form of national stereotyping. By 1938, it was not only adherents of the 'Third Greek Civilisation' who had come to take refuge in this abstraction and apply it as a yardstick for what was 'genuine' in the arts in Greece. Tsatsos was certainly no admirer of Metaxas or the régime; his brother had been sent into exile in the Aegean, a fate that would be shared by Kostakis himself before the last round of the 'dialogue' had seen print. But Tsatsos was an academic philosopher; and although he claimed to be a follower of Kant, his basic position seems pre-Kantian: a neoclassical insistence on *a priori* theoretical criteria against which aesthetic, moral or political actions can be judged. One of these criteria, for Tsatsos, was 'Greekness.'

166

George responded as a practitioner, not a theoretical philosopher. *A priori* criteria were not for him, he insisted, and he raised the obvious objection to 'Greekness' as a measure of aesthetic worth:

> ... I interpret this to mean that we are to consider the 'Greekness' of a work of art as an aesthetic criterion which can condemn it or save it, regardless of its other virtues or vices.
>
> This principle I reject.[23]

'Greekness,' for George, was a wholly artificial, and potentially pernicious, abstraction; he only ever used the word in actual or implied quotation marks. Very often in the past, he went on, we Greeks have brought back ideas and objects from Europe that we think derive from ancient Greek civilisation, and have set ourselves slavishly to imitate them. As an example, he held up the nineteenth-century 'purification' of the language, against which his father's generation had fought. Another example was the neoclassical edifice that houses the Athens Academy:

The example of the buildings of the Academy is not unique. We all know it. But we fail to notice that most of the times when we speak about the Greekness of a work of art, what we are speaking about are the buildings of the Academy.[24]

The work of the Danish architect, Theophil Hansen, and completed in 1887, the buildings of the Athens Academy derived from traditions that are primarily northern European; it is only in quite superficial aspects that they resemble a classical temple. It was this imitation of an empty form that George held up to exemplify his contemporaries' obsession with 'Greekness.' But the most telling example of this false, and in George's eyes, pernicious imitation of the external, superficial appearance of the classical and Hellenic, was the one that he could not name, but is clearly present by implication in the 'Dialogue on Poetry': the 'Third Greek Civilisation' itself.

It was now that George invoked the alternative, and more historically grounded, term 'Hellenism.' In English, the distinction between 'Greekness' and 'Hellenism' looks at first sight like hairsplitting. But 'Hellenism' has a rather different meaning in Greek from the same term in English. The English term, since the nineteenth century, has most often been used to refer to the nature or character of ancient Greece, that is, to a *quality*, as in the phrase 'Romantic Hellenism,' or in Matthew Arnold's influential opposition between the 'Hellenic' and the 'Hebraic' roots of modern civilisation. In Greek, however, 'Hellenism' has a clearly defined and long-established meaning, as the totality of the Greek people, either at any one time or throughout history. This meaning may be extended to define the civilisation, or culture, of that people; but 'Hellenism' in Greek always defines a collective entity, never a quality in the abstract.[25]

167

Hellenism, in this cultural sense, George reminded his readers, had once upon a time been carried throughout the known world by the conquests of Alexander the Great:

And in that vast Diaspora it naturally had a significant impact. Hellenism was worked upon, shaped, given new life by temperaments sometimes Greek and sometimes not, until the Renaissance; and from that time on . . . by temperaments not Greek at all, that were active outside Greek lands.[26]

As a result, since the time of the Renaissance, Hellenism had become appropriated by the culture of western Europe; it had become 'European Hellenism.' This was a theme that George had first taken up in his student days, in his lecture on Moréas; then, he had envisaged the repatriation to Greece of the ancient poetic legacy that had become bastardised in the west. What he called for now was a subtler, and more difficult, process: for his own and subsequent generations to build on what they have inherited from the West, to create their own, distinctive *'Greek* Hellenism.'[27]

The key to all George's thinking about nationalism, and the nature and power of tradition, lies in the passage that follows this. The abstract qualities, the 'ideas,' that, in future, would more and more come to define 'Hellenism' for him, are not given *a priori*, but historically. His is a dynamic concept, and as such this 'Hellenism' differs radically, in kind, from the 'Greekness' of Tsatsos, and also of the 'Third Greek Civilisation':

> [Greek] Hellenism will acquire a physiognomy, when today's Greece acquires a cultural physiognomy of its own. And its features will be precisely the synthesis of characteristics of the true works that will have been produced by Greeks. In the meantime, we should . . . counsel the young to seek after truth, . . . not by asking *how* they can be Greeks, but with the faith that since they *are* Greeks, the works to which their innermost selves actually give birth cannot but be Greek.[28]

168

This was what George had recognised, although he does not say so in the essay, in the 'enduring decay' of that 'aged city,' Constantinople (Istanbul), when he had gone there in April. In the mosaics of 'trees, textiles, roofs, movements' that he had seen in the Church of the Chora, George had recognised the artistic products of craftsmen who had shared his own Greek language, and so were part of that same Hellenism. An example that he does give, in the essay, is of a painting by El Greco that he had first seen in the National Gallery in London, in 1924: 'the astonishing impression of "Hellenism"' given him by a 'couple of brushstrokes' on the shoulder of a miniature saint. Tsatsos misunderstood this, and thought that George was talking about a *quality*, the 'Greekness' of El Greco's painting. But he was not: the impression he described here is that of kinship which comes about through a shared language and tradition.[29]

From this time on, George's deepest loyalty lay with a 'Hellenism' understood as an accumulated and accumulating cultural heritage that knows no boundaries in time or space. The aesthetic and ethical characteristics which he progressively ascribed to this 'Hellenism,' and which increasingly, in future, would come to define it for him, are those that it has acquired and disseminated along its historical trajectory; they have not been laid down in advance. Nor are they the innate property of a privileged race. George does, in this essay and in its sequel, the 'Monologue' of the following year, on occasion adopt the then current terminology of the Greeks as a 'Race.' After the outbreak of the Second World War, when he addressed these issues before a non-Greek audience, in 1944, and again in his Nobel prize acceptance speech in 1963, he would stress his 'horror at racial theories;' the continuity that he claimed for Hellenism was linguistic and cultural, not biological.[30]

If, before long, George came to make sweeping claims for Hellenism, equating it at times even with 'humane-ness' itself, this was not because he believed that these values are intrinsic to his people or part of a genetic inheritance, but because speakers of the Greek language had been the first to articulate them for posterity; since then, Greek-speakers, among others, had striven to keep that knowledge alive. One may question the historical validity of some of these claims; but George's concept of Hellenism as accumulated culture, rather than as biological continuity, would prove to be quietly influential in Greece in the later twentieth century and beyond.    169

## Towards world war

In the summer of 1938, Maro took her daughters to Pelion. George, who had last come here under very different circumstances a year ago, no doubt preferred to keep his distance from the sanatorium run by Karamanis and his young and beautiful wife, Anna. Under the supervision of Anna Karamani, a hostel for children had been opened nearby. Ioanna and Kostakis had brought their children there too, and were staying in the neighbourhood; George, for once, did not join them. Sikelianos, however, was an unmissable presence. Tsatsos records the bond of sympathy he forged with that 'sacred monster,' during quiet afternoons when the women were absent. Maro, whose sharp eye missed nothing, informed George that ' "God" has his eye on the Nereid of Pelion and has given up the Muse of Aegina. . . . This time it looks to be the real thing.' The elderly Sikelianos had transferred his attentions from Ioanna to Anna Karamani, who duly eloped with him four months later, to become, before long, his second wife.[31]

Maro did not stay long on Pelion. For a month, from mid July to mid August 1938, she and George were together, while he, in all probability, was putting the finishing touches to the 'Dialogue on Poetry.' For part of that time, they enjoyed the rustic poverty of a seaside hovel at Tolo, near Naf-plion in the northeast Peloponnese. While there, they spent a morning at the Bronze Age site close by, identified by the Swedish archaeologists who had excavated it in the 1920s as Asine, mentioned by Homer in the 'Cata-logue of Ships' in Book II of the *Iliad*. There is a photograph of Maro, acting the 'little gazelle,' climbing on the cliffs that surround the promon-tory of Asine. The poem that George began immediately afterwards, and then put aside, would become one of his best known, and ten years later would furnish the title for his first book in English translation: *The King of Asine and Other Poems.*[32]

Ioanna, no doubt reflecting the disfavour with which the family contin-ued to view her brother's relationship with Maro, records that George's downstairs flat now had its own separate entrance at number 9a Kydathi-naion Street. But the independence gained was limited. Convention, as well as financial considerations, laid down that an unmarried man should live under the parental roof; an independent household, in the form of a house or flat, was to be expected on marriage, as part of the dowry. Maro and her daughters were now living just around the corner, in a run-down penthouse.[33]

170 Stelios, that summer, was in Paris, and soon to be compulsorily retired from the University of Athens. At about this time he met the woman who, a little over a year later, would become his second wife. None of his family ever forgave Stelios for this late marriage. Thérèse Lefort was perhaps about fifty at the time, and in the eyes of his family, his social inferior.[34]

These events, coming on top of Stelios' implacable dislike of Maro, pre-cipitated the final rift between father and son, now beyond all healing. When Stelios, perhaps intending a gesture of farewell to Greece, the fol-lowing year published the collected poems that he had written in his youth, in an edition of 520 numbered copies, he gave number 2 to George, but without inscribing a dedication. The book is now in the Library of George and Maro Seferis, at the Vikelaia Municipal Library, in Heraklion, Crete; many of its pages remain uncut.[35]

Like many of his contemporaries, George saw in the Munich agreement of September 1938 the harbinger of the war it was supposed to avert. While Hitler and the British prime minister, Neville Chamberlain, negotiated outside Munich, George was summoned from Kifisia to the ministry at one-thirty in the morning; he stayed at the Athens Press Agency, ready to brief foreign correspondents about the Greek response should war be declared.

Then word came, around five in the morning, that Chamberlain had retired for the night. 'Europe,' George wrote in his diary, 'or what we've been brought up to think of as Europe, if it hasn't quite expired, is ready to expire. And with it a great part of our lives is now at an end.'[36]

Proof that the Munich peace was unlikely to be lasting came to the southern Balkans earlier than elsewhere. On Orthodox Good Friday, 1939, Mussolini invaded Albania. That country, as George knew from direct experience, had in practice been an Italian protectorate for years; now towns were bombed and King Zog I, the one and only king in Albanian history, fled for his life to Greece. George felt himself to be 'The wrong man in the wrong place' (the phrase appears in English in his diary).[37]

During a hectic ten days in May 1939, George fired off his latest salvo in the continuing public dialogue with Tsatsos, the 'Monologue on Poetry.' As soon as it was finished and despatched for publication in the next issue of *Ta Nea Grammata*, he set sail, by way of Istanbul, for Constanţa in Romania, and the Romanian capital, Bucharest. It was Romania's turn to host a meeting of representatives from the four countries that made up the Balkan Entente (Greece, Romania, Turkey and Yugoslavia). He had made a similar trip back in February. Now, in Bucharest in May 1939, George found a kindred spirit in the poet Takis Papatsonis.

171

Papatsonis had begun publishing poetry ten years ahead of George. He had also been ahead of him in translating, for the first time, Eliot's *The Waste Land* into Greek. One of the first Greek poets to write in free verse, Papatsonis was deeply religious, as George, at least in any overt way, was not; Papatsonis' poetry is intellectually dense and demanding; though rewarding, it has always had a limited appeal to Greek readers because of its extensive use of the Roman Catholic tradition. Papatsonis, like George, had a lifelong career in the higher echelons of the civil service, in his case in the Finance Ministry. As poets, the two had crossed swords in public before this, and would again. In 1932, a hostile review of *Turning Point* by Papatsonis had elicited a furious 'open letter' from George, which Katsimbalis refused to allow him to publish, forcing instead a grudging reconciliation between the two. In the late 1940s, Papatsonis would step out of line again, with a public critique of Katsimbalis' circle that was to have lasting repercussions right through the 1950s and 1960s, not least for George.

But amid the official delegates of the Balkan Entente, and in an unfamiliar capital city, the two poets made common cause. George wrote to Maro:

The only person here whose company is bearable is Papatsonis. He's cultured and truly intelligent. At least you can have a good time with him. We play hookey together in the evenings, when we can, and talk about poetry.[38]

For some years afterwards George and Papatsonis shared a joke about the 'Moldo-Wallachian horse.' The giant equestrian statue of King Carol I of Romania, which stands in the centre of Bucharest, did not, like the horse in Jean Cocteau's *Orphée*, say M.E.R.D.E., according to two light-hearted poems that George wrote for Papatsonis shortly afterwards.[39]

Throughout the hot summer months of 1939, the deepening crisis in Europe kept George close to his desk. In July, he declared that Athens was 'intolerable;' he found himself forced to live 'like a hedgehog.' Maro went to stay with her Zannos relatives at Trapeza, not far from Patras on the north coast of the Peloponnese. There he joined her briefly when he could – not without some trepidation, the first time, about the reception he might expect from her family. Londos also visited for their elder daughter's birthday. George did not want Maro to be there when Londos came. In the event, Londos 'behaved like a beast.' This was perhaps the time when the terms of the divorce were settled. It was probably also about now that Londos wrote to George, in insulting terms, demanding that he marry his former wife so that her future would be secured financially.[40]

In Europe, it was the last month of peace. At Maroussi, on a starry night 'marred by the moon,' Katsimbalis, his wife Aspasia, and George recited Aeschylus. Late that night, in his diary, George made explicit for the first time an idea that would become a cornerstone of all his later thinking:

> Feelings that I find in Aeschylus, that reassure me: the security and the balance of justice, without sentimentality, without moralising, without psychology. Like a law of the universe, clear, uncorroded. And the authenticity of that voice, its authority. The greatest order *(taxis)* that I know.[41]

The idea that justice and moral law might be extensions of, and integrally bound into, the unalterable physical laws of the universe, was something that Aeschylus, in fifth-century BC Athens, had inherited from Europe's first philosophers, the 'Pre-Socratics' who had flourished on the same Asia Minor coast that had been George's home. One of these was Anaxagoras of Clazomenae; back in 1919, Ioanna had kept George enthu-

172

siastically abreast of the archaeological excavations of Clazomenae, beneath their beloved village of Skala. Another of this group of philosophers was Heraclitus of Ephesus — first mentioned by George in 1935, when he was beginning to wrestle with the theme of political injustice, and whom increasingly he would invoke in later writings.[42]

From the August 1939 issue of an English magazine, *The Month*, George cut out and kept an article entitled 'Thought's Earliest Problem.' The article quoted a fragment from another Pre-Socratic philosopher, Anaximander of Miletus: 'Of those who hold that the first principle is one, moving, and infinite, Anaximander . . . said that the infinite is principle and element of the things that exist. He was the first to introduce this word "*principle*".' George marked the author's gloss upon this passage, and wrote next to it: 'Aeschylus.' It was in all probability this article, perhaps read aloud by Katsimbalis, that had turned the minds of the company towards Aeschylus that evening at Maroussi. The notions of order against chaos, a moral law of the universe, and the historical coincidence that these concepts had first been articulated in his own language, and against the same landscape where he himself had spent his earliest years, would become George's strongest bulwarks against the forces of dissolution that now, in August 1939, were about to be unleashed upon the world around him.[43]

On the day that the German foreign minister, von Ribbentrop, flew to Moscow to sign the non-aggression pact between the German Reich and the Soviet Union, 22 August 1939, Loukia Fotopoulou died suddenly, in a village in Attica; the news stunned all of George's circle. Three days later, in his diary, George wrote his epitaph for Lou, without attribution or explanation. It recalls the fragility and the dazzling flight of fancy of the little Princess Lu who had soared into the treetops at Kifisia, but when she fell, there was only a dead sparrow on the pine-needles below:

> A body so small
> how did it open up such a chasm
> the way the rings from a stone thrown into water
> spread out to infinity;
> only, there is no water.[44]

The next entry in George's diary is dated 30 August: 'General mobilisation in Poland.' Echoing the warning of the French Marshal Foch at the time of the Versailles treaty, in 1919, he added: 'The end of the twenty-year armistice.' The forces of the German Reich entered Poland on 1 September 1939; two days later, war would be declared in Europe.[45]

But first, in George's life, came an altogether happier invasion than the one that everyone feared.

## The world comes to Athens

Lawrence Durrell and his wife Nancy had been living for several years on the Greek island of Corfu; recently they had been joined there by Henry Miller, footloose between Paris and America, and determined not to let a world war come between him and his vocation as a writer and consciousness-raiser. Corfu would have been vulnerable in the event of an attack by Italy, so on the eve of hostilities, the three set out for Athens.[46]

Durrell at this time was scarcely known as a writer; he had published small collections of poetry and two novels, one of which was banned in Britain. Miller, on the other hand, had already achieved international notoriety for the outspoken sexual frankness of his novels, *Tropic of Cancer* and *Tropic of Capricorn*. Miller's exuberant memoir of the five months he spent in Greece at the end of 1939, *The Colossus of Maroussi*, includes a thoughtful portrait of George:

> Seferiades is more Asiatic than any of the Greeks I met . . . He is languorous, suave, vital and capable of surprising feats of strength and agility. He is the arbiter and reconciler of conflicting schools of thought and ways of life. He asks innumerable questions in a polyglot language; he is interested in all forms of cultural expression and seeks to abstract and assimilate what is genuine and fecundating in all epochs. He is passionate about his own country, his own people, not in a hidebound chauvinistic way but as a result of patient discovery following upon years of absence abroad. . . . [He] is a cross between a bull and panther by nature . . .[47]

Miller recalled a first meeting with George late one night in Syntagma Square, in the company of Antoniou, but this was probably narrative licence. It was, according to George's diary, on the afternoon of Saturday, 2 September, while in Berlin the ultimatum from Britain and France was ticking away, that Katsimbalis and his wife Aspasia invited the Durrells, Miller, and their mutual friend Theodore Stephanides to tea on the veranda of Trianemi, the Katsimbalis house at Maroussi. Katsimbalis had not finished his siesta when the visitors arrived; Stephanides, who was bilingual, had been primed to translate some of George's poems for Katsimbalis to read aloud to them. By the time George joined them, some time later, the reading was over:

174

So when I arrived, it was to find everyone warmly disposed. They are, I think, the first Anglo-Saxon writers I've met. Durrell is a short, solid young man: a sharply satirical mind. . . . Miller, a known name – but I haven't read anything of his – is all-American, much more direct, his talk packs far more of a punch.[48]

The sudden irruption of two such high-spirited mavericks from the Anglo-Saxon world was a breath of the purest fresh air to George. Miller, he would recall many years later, had been 'the first man I admired for not having had any classical preparation on going to Greece;' and would add, 'There is such freshness in him.' Under the mutual spell that Miller and Katsimbalis cast over one another, George found the perfect antidote to the crabbed intellectual and physical boundaries of the 'New State' that he loyally served. But his admiration for Miller seems never to have been uncritical. Almost ten years later, when his brother Angelos was in California and in need of friends, George was cautious in his recommendation to seek out Miller: 'whatever objections one may have about him, he's a very powerful personality.'[49]

Both the admiration and the unspoken reservations are acknowledged in the poem that George wrote, and dedicated to Miller, after they all went together to visit the painter, Nikos Hatzikyriakos Ghika, at his home on the island of Hydra, at the beginning of November. It was presumably for this reason that the first Miller learned of the existence of this poem was when a translation of it appeared fifteen years later; George's explanation, then, of his 'oversight' is not entirely convincing.[50]

For Miller, it was the start of a tour of the northeastern Peloponnese and the nearby islands, under the guiding tutelage of Katsimbalis. George accompanied them only as far as Hydra for the weekend. The weather was mild and the sea calm; George and Katsimbalis, according to Miller, were 'jubilant: they had not had a holiday for ages.' Miller gives a highly-wrought account of passing by the island of Poros, that seven years later would leave its mark on George's poem '*Thrush.*' On Hydra, described in the *Colossus* as 'a rock which rises out of the sea like a huge loaf of petrified bread,' George photographed Miller leaning against the upturned keel of a boat, with a backdrop of masts and sails in the harbour. Almost bald, his eyes completely hidden behind large black sunglasses, and with something of the air of a Tibetan monk, Miller has his teeth bared in an open grin.[51]

Before, during and after that trip to Hydra, Miller had been talking a great deal about Balzac, whose biography he had been writing in Paris. A fortnight later, back from his trip with Katsimbalis, he lent George his notes, which opened George's eyes to a strangely eccentric account of the nineteenth-century French literature that was so familiar to him. Shrewdly, George recognised that 'This man who hates the Americanised way of life, exactly typifies the American experience.' Miller's notes sent him back to Balzac's novel *Louis Lambert*, from which George quarried the phrase 'Les anges sont blancs,' as the title of his poem for Miller, with an epigraph from the novel.[52]

The poem commemorates Miller's arrival in Greece, during the days 'when the map of Poland was changing shape like an ink-stain on blotting paper;' but its focal point is the visit to Hydra, which also appears in the published dateline. It ends with a recognisable portrait of Miller that day:

> . . . this man with the toothmarks of the tropics on his skin
> putting on his black spectacles as though to work with an
>     oxy-acetylene flame
> said humbly, carefully, stopping at every word:
> 'The angels are white, incandescent white and the eye is
>     shrivelled that would look at them
> and there is no other way, you must become like stone when
>     you seek out their company
> and when you seek the miracle you must scatter your blood
>     like seed to the eight corners of the winds
> because the miracle is nowhere else but circulating inside the
>     veins of man.'[53]

It is a starker, more terrifying version of a lesson that George had learned many years before, from his mother on her deathbed: that the 'miracle' is to be found, not through seeking exotic alibis, but in the midst of 'this life that belongs to us.' It had been in the aftermath of that death, that George had first asked himself what angels would look like if they existed in Greece today. The answer that the poem attributes to his American friend throws everything back, once again, on the hero who would emerge from all his later work: *man*.

Miller spent no more than a few weeks in Athens, in the course of a whistle-stop tour of Greece that lasted until Christmas. But before he left for the United States, where apparently his father was dying, he made a present to George of the journal he had kept during his months in Greece.

176

'Can you imagine somebody doing a thing as generous as that?' George asked Edmund Keeley many years later. 'The only manuscript of his notes for the book he will write given as a gift to a friend before he has written the book?' Their meeting had obviously meant a great deal to both men, and they continued to keep in touch for many years afterwards, though more frequently and spontaneously on Miller's side than on George's. But Miller never did fulfil his promise to come back to Greece. He and George never met again. Their trajectories, in any case, were very different; it was the moment that left its mark.[54]

With Durrell it was a different matter. Durrell would stay on in Greece until the last possible moment; Durrell also knew some Greek, and before long he and George would be translating one another's poems. It was through the extrovert Durrell that George began to make new friends among the British and other expatriates who now flocked to Athens, during the first months of the war in Europe.

Among these were the shy, elegant and 'depressive' poet Bernard Spencer, who after the war would collaborate on the first book-length translation of George's poems into English, and the novelist and future biographer of Cavafy, Robert Liddell, both of whom worked for the British Council, where Durrell joined them in November. Another English poet whom George must have met in this circle was Robin Fedden, cultural attaché at the British embassy. Before long the group was joined by R.D. (Reggie) Smith and his wife Olivia Manning, who would later give a vivid account of life in this short-lived wartime hothouse of expatriate Britons in the third volume of her *Balkan Trilogy*.[55]

More exotic characters were the Polish count, Max Nimiec, and Henry Reynold de Simony, who according to George was allegedly a Knight of Malta, with the privilege of riding into churches on horseback. 'Max,' as everyone called the count, claimed to have escaped from Poland to Corfu with only a rucksack on his back, and to have been helped on his way by Serbian gypsies. Also affectionately remembered in *The Colossus of Maroussi*, Max was terminally ill, but had so much money, that he could not take out of Greece, that he had resolved to live out his last months in desperate splendour. He gave wild parties, told stories, and on one occasion, recalled by both Miller and George, attempted to drive his 'flimsy little English car which looks like an overgrown bug' up the steps and into the lobby of the King George Hotel on Syntagma Square. German Intelligence had Nimiec marked down as a British spymaster. In June 1940, de Simony stood godfather to the Durrells' daughter, christened Penelope Berengaria (the middle name being perhaps the godfather's privilege to bestow); George was present and described the occasion in a letter to Miller. Three months later, it was the Knight of Malta who brought the news to George that Max Nimiec had died of a heart attack while dancing at the Argentina cabaret, a favourite haunt close by the Under-Ministry of Press and Tourism in Filellenon (Philhellenes) Street.[56]

It was only natural for these new arrivals to gravitate into the orbit of the ever-hospitable Katsimbalis. Theodore Stephanides, a friend of the 'colossus' since Paris days, had been for several years the guardian angel of the Durrell family on Corfu, and was now back in Athens. Stephanides had British nationality and spoke Greek with a slight English accent. The naturalist Gerald Durrell, brother of Lawrence, would describe him:

> With his ash-blond hair and beard and his handsome aquiline features, he looked like a Greek god, and certainly he seemed as omniscent as one. Apart from being medically qualified, he was also a biologist, poet, author, translator, astronomer and historian.

Stephanides had worked with Katsimbalis, in the past, to translate the poetry of Palamas into English. George, who had first met him in Paris, almost twenty years before, now wrote of Stephanides, with a new appreciation, 'he is one of the best people for honesty and integrity that I know.'[57]

New additions to the circle included the younger poets Nikos Gatsos, Andreas Kambas, and the surrealist Nanos Valaoritis, an enthusiastic admirer of George, who exerted himself in London, after the war, in paving the way for George's success in English translation.[58] Another was the Frenchman Robert Levesque. A younger protégé and confidant of André Gide, Levesque had been teaching in Greece for two years. George first met him when Gide visited Athens; so full were his impressions of the great man who had influenced his own early work, that it was only when Gide's journal came to be published, soon afterwards, with a tribute to Levesque on its very last page, that he remembered the slight young teacher from the Institut Français whom he had first met at the same time. Thereafter George and Levesque developed a good, though never close, friendship. After the war, Levesque proved as indefatigable as George's new English friends in promoting George's poetry, through translation into his own language.[59]

In Europe, the last months of 1939 and the first of 1940 were the time of the 'phoney war.' A sense of unreality prevailed, while the expected air raids and land battles failed to materialise. In Greece, the perceived threat came from Mussolini's Italy, which had already annexed neighbouring Albania. But for the time being the Duce kept out of the war. In Athens, as in other neutral capitals, it was a time of intense diplomatic and propaganda activity. Since the declaration of war in Europe, the nature of George's job at the Under-Ministry of Press and Tourism had changed overnight.[60]

## War of nerves

'The period of neutrality was a difficult one and, for me, very hard,' wrote George, a year after it ended. Within months, the strain of his work at the Ministry had brought his nerves close to breaking point. The official policy was one of strict impartiality towards all belligerents. George agreed that this was the only thing to do, but almost at once found his office besieged by the press attachés and other officials of the respective embassies, complaining that the day's coverage in the Greek press had shown a bias towards the opposing side. George was not directly responsible, of course, for what was written in the strictly controlled Greek newspapers, but the Under-Ministry was, and it was his responsibility to defend the official line. On one occasion, he had to call on the German Ambassador, to explain to him why a speech would not be reported in the Athens German-language newspaper. The ambassador behaved with dignity, George reported; but the next day he had to listen to a furious rant in German, of which he understood not a word, from a Nazi party official who came to his office. It was one of several such occasions. German diplomats, George noted, stopped using the international diplomatic language, French, until after the fall of France in June 1940; in the meantime, he had to conduct business with them through an interpreter.[61]

179

'Strict impartiality' would have been hard to maintain in these circumstances, even if George himself had been strictly impartial in his sympathies, which he was not. His instinctive distaste for the Nazis went back to the moment when Hitler had come to power in Germany. From his time in Korça, he had never forgotten an account of one of Hitler's Nuremberg speeches, reported on the radio: 'the German people is free from original sin.' For George, this was the equivalent of the act of *hubris*, the pride that seeks to defy the human condition, that in ancient Greek tragedy would invariably call down a terrible punishment from the gods. A German propaganda film that showed the bombing of Poland, in September 1939, provoked his deep disgust.[62]

No doubt it was not accidental, either, that the new friends he was making, in the international community, were mostly British and French. The single German who confided in him was half-Jewish and no friend of the Nazis; although he paid George the compliment of translating one of his poems, George could not help having misgivings about Helmut von den Steinen, although he later accepted that these had been misplaced.[63]

As early as November 1939, the press attaché at the British Embassy, David Wallace, noted in a dispatch to London: 'The Under-Secretary [*sic*], Mr Seferiades, has translated T.S. Eliot into Greek and is well-disposed but of little account.' George's sympathies might be in the right place, from the point of view of the British Foreign Office, but he was in no position, at this stage in his career, to influence the policy of his government.[64]

The Nazis, only a few months later, were taking George more seriously. At the beginning of June 1940, he attended his last meeting of the Balkan Entente; while he was away in the Yugoslav capital, Belgrade, the press attaché at the German embassy tried to persuade Nikoloudis that George was in the pay of the British. Not long afterwards, a memorandum from the Nazi Security Service, the SD, alerted the Foreign Ministry in Berlin:

180 Seferiadis can be considered chiefly responsible for an anti-German and therefore pro-British attitude in the Greek press. . . . He also influences the [Under-] Minister for the Press in this direction. . . . It is to be supposed that with the elimination (*Ausschaltung*) of Seferiadis a significantly more pro-German attitude on the part of the Greek press with regard to German interests would be achieved.[65]

It was no false sentiment that guided George's conduct, or that shaped the cool assessment of political realities on which it was based. In his diary, just after Paris had fallen, he wrote: 'In a war where, *for me*, there can be no victor, I can't feel truly involved by this or that event.' What he meant by this unexpectedly bleak statement emerges from the commentary on this period that he wrote, in exile, just over a year later.

I don't think it required a lot of brains to see that submission to the Axis would have meant the end of Greece.

'But if the Axis wins?' people kept saying.

If the Axis were to win, and we were defeated on the side of England, I didn't think we'd suffer much worse than we would have if we'd submitted from the start: we'd seen so very many dismemberments of states that had given themselves up without a fight. Then again, if the British were to win and we were their enemies, they would be the ones to dismember us, in order to buy God knows what advantages, either while the war was still going on or after it was over.[66]

It was a shrewd, and unsentimental, assessment. It is noticeable that what counted for George, at this moment of truth, was not the moral claims or ideology of the belligerent states, but the old-fashioned Venizelist principle of national self-determination. How best could Greece hope to survive the geopolitical upheaval with the least damage to her integrity?

Early in 1940, George made up his mind to publish, in the spring, all the poems that he had written that he wished to preserve. 'Who knows what lies in wait for us after that?' he noted in his diary. It would be, he informed Theotokas, at the time of the fall of France, his 'testament.' Not only did George now plan to reissue, in a single volume, all the poems that he had published up to *Gymnopaidia* in 1936; he went ahead at the same time with two new volumes: *Book of Exercises*, the large and heterogeneous collection of poems written over the previous decade, that he had assembled before he left Korça in 1937, and his newest work, to be titled *Logbook*.[67]

181

This title may have been in part a late homage to Valéry: *Extraits du Log-Book de Monsieur Teste* forms part of the series of prose meditations, of which George had translated at least two back in 1926. But it must have been during his first months at the Foreign Ministry, the following year, that a letter had crossed his desk containing an extract from a real ship's log, 'We are stationary in the same position awaiting orders.' This phrase, which also appears in George's diary and in *Six Nights on the Acropolis*, provides the first of two epigraphs for *Logbook*. The second consists of George's translation, via French, of four lines by the German Romantic poet Friedrich Hölderlin, reproduced on p. 131. The anxiety expressed in those lines was a perennial one for George; it can never have been felt more acutely than at this historical moment. Neither could the irony of quoting these words, from a *German* poet, in 1940.[68]

For his two new collections, George had secured the services of a tiny family business of typesetters, the brothers Tarousopoulos. The print-shop was in an old house on the shore, on the outskirts of Piraeus, between New Faliron and Kastela; opposite, when he first went there, the fishermen's boats had been drawn up for the winter. The house was built round a small courtyard; an enormous cage was filled with exotic birds that went wild whenever the sea was stormy. The practical art of printing exercised a strong fascination for George; in the brothers he recognised the combination of skill and humility that he always admired in traditional craftsmen and artisans, a role-model that he would often invoke for the poet, too. George spent a good deal of time at the Tarousopoulos print-shop, and was no doubt exacting in the demands he made on the brothers. At first, he had entrusted the new edition of his *Poems* to a more prestigious firm, but later withdrew it, when he found that the firm had German connections; that assignment, too, ended up with Tarousopoulos.[69]

It was out of one of these early sessions at the print-shop that George came to complete the poem that more than any other would bring him international recognition. 'The King of Asine' had been begun shortly after the stolen holiday with Maro, at Tolo, in the summer of 1938, but then he had abandoned it. Now, with the page lay-out for *Logbook* agreed, it emerged that he would be left with two blank pages. This was on Thursday 1 February 1940. Between the end of that Thursday afternoon and Saturday, and without reference to his drafts of the poem from almost two years before, George hammered out the final form of 'The King of Asine' in three successive versions. It was, as he described it to T.S. Eliot many years later, with probably only slight exaggeration, 'the work of a night.'[70]

Later in the year, he looked back on 'The King of Asine' as his only poem of 1940. It occupies the final position in *Logbook*; within weeks of its publication, George would be wondering, in his diary, 'Why do so many people like this poem? Curious.'[71] In its final form, the poem bears all the consciousness of the end of an era. Standing among the vestiges of a three-thousand-year-old citadel, with the sea empty and still at his feet, the poet wonders: what might be recoverable today of the king who had led his minor contingent to the Trojan War, and failed to leave a hero's fame behind him? Only the name of his tiny kingdom, Asine, is preserved by Homer: 'one word in the Iliad and that uncertain.' Remembering the gold masks uncovered by Schliemann at Mycenae, the speaker concedes that the elusive, once-living king can now be nothing more than a 'void behind the mask.' But this void, whose contours the mask preserves, is paradoxically always with us: 'a dark point travelling like the fish / in the serenity of the sea at dawn and you can see it.' The imagery of loss for a moment becomes more personal. Although the other person present in the poem is undoubtedly Maro, it is Lou whose recent death haunts the speaker in the middle of the poem.[72]

Then comes an outburst that seems to sum up the whole of George's

182

determination, in early 1940, that come what may, something of the life just ending, for all its faults and weaknesses, *deserves* to be preserved and kept alive.

> do they exist, the movement of the face, the pattern of tenderness
> of those who have become so strangely diminished in our lives
> of those who have remained as shadows of the waves and thoughts
>   with the boundlessness of the sea
> or maybe no, there remains nothing but only the heaviness
> the nostalgia for the heaviness of a living being
> there where we now wait, insubstantial ourselves, bending down . . .

Finally, as the sun penetrates the underground passage in the walls of the citadel, a bat flies out; its inaudible squeaking evokes the souls of the dead, from earlier in the poem, that have not, perhaps, after all, been wholly lost. The poem ends:

> Might that be the king of Asine
> that we've been seeking so assiduously on this acropolis
> touching at times with our fingers his touch upon the stones[73]

183

At Easter, 1940, George spent what would prove to be his last holiday for six years. He and Maro stayed with the family of her sister Amaryllis, on the island of Poros, at the Dragoumis family house called *Galini* (Serenity). His lyrical description of the place, that Easter, may owe something to the numinous enthusiasm with which Henry Miller had endowed it, as they passed by on the expedition to Hydra back in November. George's diary juxtaposes an idyllic interval of peace, shared with Maro, with the symbolism of the Easter ritual and darker thoughts inspired by the tiny seaside cemetery which cannot have failed to remind him of Valéry's *Cimetière marin*. The long diary entry ends: 'A strange world, invisible, haunted, lies behind all these things.'[74]

But the relationship with Maro, like the peace itself, was living on borrowed time. By now, Maro must have been divorced from Londos. For the summer, she took her daughters to Trapeza, to stay with her Zannos relatives. She had cleared out the flat, round the corner from Kydathinaion Street, and left her belongings with George.[75]

At the end of July, she wrote to him from Trapeza: there were decisions to be taken urgently about the future. The immediate problem was money.

Londos, far from contributing to the upkeep of his daughters, had borrowed substantial sums from Maro since the separation. The key to the situation was Londos' rich aunt, who now intervened. If Maro was about to start living openly with her lover, the aunt insisted, then her daughters could not be allowed to remain with her. The aunt would pay for them to be sent to boarding school, instead. But there was an alternative. If George were to marry Maro, then the Londos family would be satisifed and the children could continue to live with her after all. Explaining this to George, and no doubt cautious of his likely reaction, Maro added that she did not believe it. But the real point of the letter seems to be just this. If she had had money of her own, Maro added, the situation might have been resolved differently. But the children should not be made to suffer just because she had been too lenient with Londos over money.[76]

George's reply was long and measured, and almost certainly not what Maro had been hoping for. He too had been thinking about these things for months, he explained to her. He had no money either, far less than he might have been able to expect, a year or two ago: 'that's to say, before my father created the commitments that he created last winter.' This is clearly a reference to Stelios' second marriage, which seems to have had repercussions for his children's expected inheritance. Indeed, Stelios hovers as a threat over this whole exchange with Maro. But if George did not have the money to support Maro and her daughters, in the summer of 1940, his father's behaviour can have been only part of the reason; another must have been the substantial bill that he had shortly to settle with the Tarousopoulos brothers for the three volumes of his poems.

George's letter continued with a carefully worded response to Maro's proposal of marriage: 'Despite all that [the financial difficulties], the best thing would be if we were to get married.' It was almost a re-run of the exchange of letters to and from Korça three years before. The irony cannot have escaped Maro, when she went on to read:

OK, if you like, I've this to propose to you: we'll get married. But, if we get married, we get married the two of us, not you and I and Mr Londos. And for that to happen . . . you've got to choose between me and the children. For the children to live with us isn't possible for many reasons, which you know.[77]

Back in the crisis of July 1937, Londos had faced Maro with the ultimatum: 'the poet or your children.' Now here was the poet himself, forcing the same impossible choice on her once again. George even went so far as to make conditions. She was to cease all contact with 'Mr Londos;' if they had to meet, it must be with third parties present. The aunt must make provision for the children directly, rather than through Londos; presumably the reason was that if Londos were to renege on his responsibilities in future, George would not become liable for the maintenance of his wife's children.

Throughout these exchanges, there is no question about the depth and sincerity of George's feelings for Maro. But the forty-year-old bachelor was as resistant as ever to the formal obligations and practical responsibilities of marriage.

It was Maro who found the solution, after what must have been a fraught three days in Athens at the beginning of August. The children would stay with Londos' sister, Lia, whom Maro trusted, in Kolonaki. That way the threat of boarding school, that particularly appalled Maro, was averted. Since in effect this meant that Londos had custody, while Maro had access and would not be far away, the immediate crisis seemed to have been averted. In the event, it was merely postponed.[78]

By this time, in early August 1940, almost all of northern Europe had fallen to the German Reich. Italy entered the war in July. Metaxas still held to his policy of neutrality, but everyone knew that its days were now num- 185 bered. The war of nerves suddenly intensified. On 11 August, the Italian press made much of an alleged incident on the frontier between Italian-occupied Albania and Greece. Then on the morning of the 15th, off the island of Tinos, where the shrine of the Virgin is a place of pilgrimage on that day, the cruiser *Elli* was hit by three torpedoes fired from an unseen submarine; the ship sank in a few minutes, in full view of the holiday crowds. George spent the rest of the day at the Ministry. A German representative asked him to relegate the sinking to second lead in the Athens foreign-language newspaper, then added:

'But tell me, truly, don't you know whose submarine it was?' And when I told him we did not: 'But don't you have suspicions?' he persisted. 'As to suspicions,' I replied, 'we're *neutral*.'[79]

At the end of August, George's three books of poetry were at last ready for collection from Tarousopoulos' print-shop. *Poems I* was printed in 525 copies; much the largest print-run of any of George's books to date, it exceeded by five the number of copies of his father's collected poems that had appeared the previous year. Notionally, according to their colophons, these three books had been published at monthly intervals between March and May. In reality, all three went into circulation on the last day of August, two weeks after the sinking of the *Elli*. George had been only just in time with his poetic 'testament.'[80]

At home, Stelios was now back in Athens and living in the middle-floor flat of the house in Kydathinaion Street. Presumably Thérèse, his wife, was with him, though there is no mention of her in George's diary or correspondence at this time. Maro was still at Trapeza. There was no more discussion of marriage in his letters with Maro; but she was in all probability the cause of a furious argument with his father about the ownership of his own, downstairs flat, at the end of September. Afterwards, George confided miserably to his diary: 'After fifteen years of work, I don't earn my living; I mean, the cost of food, rent, clothes. Humiliating thought: if only I was rich.'[81]

But however pyrrhic it had been, he must have won a victory of sorts in this battle of wills with his father, since the very next day, Maro wrote from Trapeza to say that she would be arriving at the end of the week. She would leave her children with Londos' sister in Skoufa Street, in Kolonaki, and come on her own to join him. For the first time, Maro was about to move in with George. He wrote back to her with feverish anticipation:

> I've got the most dreadful hard-on, my love, and I can't think of anything else but how I'm going to fuck you for a whole night without stopping.[82]

A month later, George spent most of Sunday, 27 October, at the Ministry. Then before going to sleep at two o'clock in the morning, he read for a while from the memoirs of his beloved General Makriyannis, the participant-witness to a very different war, the war of independence that had been fought in the 1820s. He was awakened by the telephone at three thirty. It was now Monday, 28 October 1940.

> I got dressed and went out at once. At the Under-Ministry of Press two or three civil servants. Grazzi [the Italian Minister] had seen Metaxas at three. He had given him a note and told him that at 6, Italian troops would begin to move [into Greece from Albania]. The prime minister replied that this was tantamount to a declaration of war, and when Grazzi left, at once called in the British Minister.

Afterwards, George was convinced that if Metaxas had given a different answer, and had called in not Sir Michael Palairet but his German counterpart, there would have been congratulations and relief all round the ministerial table. No one had known, until it happened, which way Metaxas would jump. Even Metaxas himself seems to have been unsure of the response he would meet from his ministers.

The task now fell to George and Nikoloudis, working together, to draft the official declaration of war to be signed by the king. It seems to have been George's initiative to stop all news telegrams from German correspondents from leaving the country, since Germany was Italy's ally. The officials at the telegraph office, he observed caustically, 'were still neutral.' What excuse were they to give, one of them demurred? 'Tell them the lines to Berlin are down. And if they make a fuss, send them straight to me,' George demanded, and rang off.[83]

The sirens sounded at six that morning. Within hours, the story of the Italian ultimatum, and Metaxas' reply, had become a legend. Metaxas had said: *ochi* (no). Today in Greece, 28 October is one of the country's two national days, and has ever since then been known in Greek as *'Ochi'* Day.

187

### Greece against the Axis

With that single word, Metaxas had succeeded in uniting the Greek people behind him, as none of the verbose speeches glorifying the goals and achievements of the Regime of the Fourth of August had ever had the slightest chance of doing. The doubters were on the fringes: among the highest echelons of Metaxas' own government, and among the country's tiny Communist Party, whose members were mostly in jail and in any case hamstrung, for the time being, by Stalin's alliance with Hitler.

Technically, as George wryly noted, the war that now began was a war not against fascism or the Axis, but against 'the armed forces of Italy.' Over-enthusiastic Greek journalists could still be reprimanded, and reminded that 'we too are a fascist state.' 'In Greece there is no such thing as a fifth column,' a friend in uniform was lectured by his commanding officer. 'Of course not,' quipped back the friend (who was probably Katsimbalis) under his breath, 'because *we* are all in the opposition.'

But for most people, the divisions of the interwar period were swept away in the all but unanimous determination to defend Greek soil against the invader. As George summed up the feeling, a year later:

at the base of the pyramid people knew very well what they were fighting against, they were fighting against enslavement, any and every form of enslavement that came with the Axis.[84]

For George, as for many Greeks at that time, irrespective of political background or belief, that historic 28th of October marked 'not the validation but the abolition of the 4th of August;' privately, he blamed Metaxas for failing to realise this and capitalise on it. To fight against the common enemy, junior officers with a Venizelist past were reinstated, but not senior ones. Kostakis Tsatsos, sent into internal exile in September 1939 for an ill-judged outburst of democratic sentiment, had already been allowed to return. Tsatsos' close friend, the young liberal politician Panayotis Kanellopoulos, who had been exiled since 1937, was also pardoned, and went off to fight at the front with the rank of corporal. But George continued to marvel that the war, that had enormous popular support, could be prosecuted at all by the 'ministerial lackeys' of the Fourth of August regime.[85]

Not only, however, was the war prosecuted; the Greek counter-attack was a spectacular success. Within weeks, the invading Italian forces had been driven back beyond the Albanian frontier. In the mountainous terrain of southern Albania, some of which George knew well, and in the most appalling winter conditions, the Greek army would continue to push the Italians steadily back until the spring. It was the first successful land action against the Axis during the Second World War. Suddenly, the Greeks were heroes.

188

Many of George's friends and family were now in uniform. Theotokas, after a farewell lunch together in January 1941, was photographed in his corporal's uniform, standing beside George in wide overcoat and bowler hat, outside the National Library. Two months later George's brother, Angelos, now married and who had just baptized his son, had also been called up. Katsimbalis, semi-invalid though he was, returned gloriously to the colours. 'Katsimbalis the civilian,' George wrote to Henry Miller afterwards, 'seemed a dwarf compared with that extraordinary *stature*. He had to make everything to measure[:] boots, belts, even his sword I suppose. He was too big for anything ready-made. He was serving in the ac[k]-ac[k]s, happy that he could get good retsina in the neighbourhood.' Stephanides was in the Royal Medical Corps. Antoniou's ship had been commandeered, and would soon be lost; Antoniou complained stoically that the *Akropolis* had not been built for the weather through which he now had to navigate on behalf of the Navy. Andreas Londos, too, was back in the Navy, after almost twenty years, and would spend much of the war at sea. George himself was called up in February, although he was a year over the age limit. The Foreign Ministry, in any case, intervened quickly to keep him at his post.[86]

At the same time, others were coming forward as even less likely volunteers. Kostakis Tsatsos and two other university professors wrote to Metaxas personally, asking to enlist. Tsatsos even bought all his equipment, but no answer was forthcoming, and the professors continued to give their lectures. One day in December, Angelos Sikelianos marched into Nikoloudis' office and asked to be allowed to go to the front. He must, he said, be accompanied by his young wife, who loved him and said she would die if he went on his own. George, who was in attendance, and knew Anna Sikelianou from her days as the wife of George Karamanis, at the sanatorium on Pelion, butted in, quoting the title of a swashbuckling historical novel: 'The heroine of the Greek War of Independence.' 'No, my friend,' Sikelianos rejoined witheringly, 'The heroine of Sikelianos!' Sikelianos did not go to the front, but he did publish several morale-boosting poems that winter that read as though they had been written there.[87]

But even while the victories lasted, through that winter and into early spring, there was a darker side. Odysseus Elytis fought in Albania as a Second Lieutenant and was badly wounded. George Sarantaris, another intimate of the Katsimbalis and Tsatsos circles, and close to both George and Elytis, was also wounded while fighting on the Albanian front, and died later of his wounds.

Maro, now living with George in the ground floor flat in Kydathinaion Street, was working as a nurse at a military hospital. Many of the wounded were brought back from the front with frostbite, and had to have limbs amputated. George was deeply moved by Maro's accounts of her patients, most of them young villagers with little education or experience of the world. George had always been inclined to idealise the simple man, the man of the people, exemplified for him by the fishermen of Skala, and the violin-playing avatar of Odysseus, Sotiris Stamelos on Skiathos. His concept of the 'people' (*laos*), that would play an important part both in his political dealings and in his writing during the next three years, drew strongly on these earlier experiences; he recalled some of them in his diary at just this time. These memories were now crucially honed by Maro's plain, harrowing tales of the wounded and dying soldiers she tended. One of these, known only by his first name, Michalis, would find his way into the poem 'Last Stop,' that George would write as the war in Greece was about to end.[88]

189

From a professional point of view, George found it a relief that the war of nerves had given way to open conflict; the evasions of neutrality were a thing of the past. His office had been moved from Filellenon Street, soon after the outbreak of hostilities, to the corner of Stadiou and Korai Streets, opposite the University. He was now responsible for giving a nightly press conference. This would begin with George reading, in French, the official bulletin of the day that he would have prepared himself. He would then take questions. For the first time in his life, with the news of the first Greek successes in Albania, he relished his job: 'I don't stop, day or night, except to sleep a little. I wish for nothing else but even more work.'[89]

It would not be long before the intensity began to take its toll. Once already, while the war of nerves had been still going on, George had found himself dreaming about the map of Albania, and awoke to misquote W.B. Yeats: 'Responsibilities begin in dreams.' By February, he was waking himself up, talking in his sleep about the business of the Ministry. He remembered this period, for the rest of his life, as one of the rare times when his inner self was invaded by external pressures and the preoccupations of his job. But in his diary he reminded himself that it was not the war itself that was having this effect on him; it was 'those lepers, the pollution that pollutes the war.'[90]

190

By this time, although the military campaign was still going well, there was once again chaos at the heart of the Greek government, and George was close enough to know what was going on. Metaxas, who had been in poor health for some time, died on 29 January 1941. There was no one of comparable stature in the cabinet. It was, apparently, the sinister Chief of Police under Metaxas, Konstantinos Maniadakis, who engineered the appointment of a relatively minor figure, the banker Alexandros Koryzis, to succeed Metaxas as prime minister. While the British continued to pin an essentially quixotic faith in King George, Greece was now all but leaderless.[91]

What appalled George most was the evidence of growing panic he saw in the government around him:

They're overwhelmed by an indescribable fear of the Germans. Wherever you turn, at the ministries and headquarters, it's the same. Desperate lack of spirit. Nikoloudis keeps walking up and down his office, brandishing his stick and cursing the Government. It doesn't occur to him that he *is* the government.[92]

The fears of ministers were not unfounded. By early March, it was apparent that the might of the German Reich was being directed towards the Balkans and the support of Hitler's ally, Mussolini. Bulgaria joined the Axis on 1 March 1941, and German troops began crossing the Danube the next day. Two weeks later, when the Yugoslav government caved in to intense German pressure, it was overthrown by a popular uprising. On the 14th, George noted in his diary, 'Ever better news from Yugoslavia.' But ten days after that the Yugoslav uprising had been crushed, and Yugoslavia, too, had succumbed to the will of the Axis.[93]

All the strength of the Greek army had been directed against the Italians, in the northwest of the country. The border with Bulgaria to the north had strong defences, known as the Metaxas Line; but they were relatively weakly manned. On 22 February, British Foreign Secretary Anthony Eden had arrived in Athens, by air from England, with the Chief of the Imperial General Staff. As a result, at the same time as German troops were moving into Bulgaria, a modest British and Commonwealth contingent had begun arriving in Greece from Egypt.[94]

On Sunday 6 April, German forces mounted a massive attack against Greece on two fronts, one from Bulgaria, the other from Yugoslavia. George, at his evening press conference, spoke 'off the cuff, without quite knowing where I was going to end up.' But his speech earned him emotional congratulations from among the assembled Allied correspondents. The preserved text (a translation from the original French into Greek officialese) does not seem quite 'off the cuff;' but it does contain phrases and ideas that would reappear, after the war, in '*Thrush*' and other later poems:

> Of course, we know – we have been told it so often – that there is a new order in Europe. Of course, this 'new order' means that the weak must be destroyed, that the most disgusting lies may be used in order to destroy the small peoples of Europe, that *all the means of modern science* must be used systematically to root out those people whom they wish to enslave.

We Greeks, George continues, are a small people, but we have much experience. This is a war against 'the forces of evil.'

> When these press conferences began, I explained to you the *moral* reasons for our decision [to fight on 28 October]. The same reasons hold good today. We believe that *justice* will prevail in the end.[95]

This is not only the professional rhetoric that the occasion requires, though of course it is that as well. For the rest of his life, both in the political sphere and in his writing, George would continue to struggle to articulate a concept of justice that would indeed be sufficient to prevail over the 'means of modern science' and the superior forces of destruction in the world.

Despite brave resistance along the Metaxas Line, the vastly superior German forces broke through, to take the northern city of Thessaloniki on 9 April. Soon, the army fighting in Epiros and Albania found itself cut off from the rear. Further stands by British and Commonwealth troops at the Aliakmon line, and further south, near Thermopylae, the site of a similarly doomed battle in 480 BC, were overrun, with heavy casualties.

On the day that Thessaloniki fell, Maro said to George, over their evening meal, 'Perhaps we should get married.' By now, there were constant air raids on Athens. Two nights earlier the whole city had been rocked by the gigantic explosion of a munitions ship in the harbour of Piraeus. The decision that George had put off, the previous summer, was taken in a few words, and probably a little earlier than his laconic diary entry records: a certificate from the ministry granting him leave to marry 'Miss Maria Zannou daughter of Miltiades' is dated the same day.[96]

192 Next day, George sought out 'two or three grumpy priests.' Then he went upstairs and spoke to his father. It must have been a difficult interview; indeed it is almost the last occasion on which George records speaking to Stelios at all.

At six-thirty on the evening of Thursday 10 April, George and Maro were married in the Church of the Transfiguration of the Saviour, on the opposite side of Kydathinaion Street. It is not clear who else was present; Stelios, for one, was not.

'Our best man,' as George grimly recalled later, 'was Hitler.'[97]

# 7
# The Second Exile
# 1941–1943

On a chilly night in Jerusalem, while the Germans were at El Alamein, half a dozen of us sat in the poor light of a hotel dining-room reading poetry to each other. 'Think of it,' said the Greek Seferis from his dark corner, 'exiles reading poetry to each other.' Many of the poets out here are refugees; all are exiles. Seferis . . . is haunted by the conviction that he should have remained in Greece with his friends. The sense of a missed experience, that no alternative experience can dispel, haunts most of us.

(Olivia Manning, Cairo, 1944)[1]

## Evacuation

The decision by the Greek government to abandon Athens was taken on Wednesday 16 April. The week that followed saw unprecedented panic among the government and its servants; ministers and their staff squabbled bitterly over who was to be evacuated and who was not. On the afternoon of Good Friday, 18 April, Alexandros Koryzis, Metaxas' reluctant successor as prime minister, committed suicide; for several days it was King George who assumed control of the country, while on every side the government and armed forces disintegrated.

It was the intention of the king, and of those ministers and generals who had not completely lost their nerve, to re-establish the government in Crete. Crete, it was thought, with British support could be held indefinitely. Those who left Athens would be abandoning their homes and families to the advancing enemy; but there was no concerted plan at this stage to abandon either the country or the fight against the Axis.[2]

Maro, according to George, had been clear 'from the start, that we ought not to remain.' On the first day when the evacuation was agreed in cabinet, George let his minister, Nikoloudis, know of his intention to leave with the government. These things George noted in his diary. But the diary makes no mention of the terrible decision that was now forced on Maro, and which she had probably already taken before the sudden wedding the previous week. Their marriage meant that now she, too, could leave with George for Crete. But her two daughters would be left behind. In the far less extreme circumstances of the previous summer, George had warned Maro that he would not be prepared to take responsibility for her daughters. Now, even had he wished to, there was almost certainly no way in which he could have done so.[3]

Maro, in the meantime, had confided in a very grand and charismatic elderly lady, Penelope Delta. Described as 'the Louisa May Alcott of Modern Greek letters,' Delta had been the wayward child of the Benakis family, one of the wealthiest of Greek families established in Alexandria. She was now in her late sixties, and confined to a wheelchair. Maro had come to know her through the eldest of Delta's three daughters, Sofia Mavrogordatou, who had been an early confidante over Maro's affair with George. As well as being a successful writer of children's fiction with a strongly nationalist flavour, Delta's own life had been a tearjerker romance, involving thwarted love and suicide attempts. Delta seems to have been particularly moved by Maro's story, because it so closely mirrored her own passion, thirty years before, for the charismatic writer, diarist, patriot and political figure, Ion Dragoumis. Then, Delta had found herself confronted with the same ultimatum that Maro now faced: to choose between the man she loved and her daughters.

194

Delta urged upon Maro the choice that she had been unable to make herself, in the moral climate of a different time. She, Delta, would look after Maro's daughters, leaving Maro free to follow George. The girls would be welcome on the Deltas' extensive property at Kifisia, which included several houses and spacious grounds. What Maro could not know was that Penelope Delta, in a final gesture of romantic patriotism, would kill herself with an overdose of opium when the Germans entered Athens. By the time this happened, Maro would be far away.[4]

Now, even with the personal decision taken, it was no easy matter for George and Maro to leave. Nikoloudis was only grudgingly prepared to include his Director of Foreign Press among the entourage of what was left of the 'propaganda' ministry. On Good Friday, dodging frequent air raids, George and Maro, with a group of more junior diplomats, made their way across Attica to the small port of Oropos, opposite Euboea. But this first attempt to leave ended in farce. The ship was dive-bombed while waiting to depart; the captain steamed round in circles, taking evading action. The damage was slight, but late that night, without explanation, everyone was ordered ashore. It was now that George learned, by telephone, of Koryzis' suicide. Nikoloudis was out of the government; formally, for the next three days, there was no government. Everything would have to start over again.[5]

In the scramble that followed, George had now to insist that he was on the Germans' 'blacklist.' He could have had no idea, of course, of the memorandum that had been sent from the *Sicherheitsdienst* to the German Foreign Ministry, while Greece had still been neutral; but its existence proves that the warnings he received, at the time, through intermediaries, were accurate. Quite how he arranged for himself and Maro to sail from Piraeus, a few minutes before midnight on 22 April, on the SS *Elsi*, remains unclear. In his diary, George records that he had even approached David Wallace, the British press attaché, who then turned up on the same ship. Explaining these events two years later, he was at pains to point out that he owed his inclusion in the evacuation to the patronage neither of Nikoloudis, nor of the senior official of the Foreign Ministry present, Vasilios Papadakis. Instead, he had had to pay for his own and his wife's passage.[6]

The ship was not molested on the twelve-hour voyage. George put this down to the fact that the forward hold was full of German prisoners of war. The last of the British expatriates were also on board, including Reggie Smith and his wife Olivia Manning. Her fictional account of the voyage concludes the last volume of the *Balkan Trilogy*, and is as indignant about the high-handed, snobbish behaviour of the British officers and high-class evacuees as was George in his diary.[7]

Souda Bay, the large natural harbour close to Chania, which was then the capital of Crete, was full of bombed and burning wrecks when the ship arrived there at noon next day. It was George's nameday. British, Australian and New Zealand troops were disembarking from Egypt; the Battle of Crete was only a month away. Accommodation in Chania was cramped and, at first, primitive; it was almost impossible to sleep at night because of the air raids. During the day, at Government House, when the Stukas came over, it was the duty of a policeman to sound a car horn by way of alarm, unless the anti-aircraft guns on the roof opened up first; at the end of the raid the church bells would begin tolling for the dead.[8]

There was once again a Greek government, although its effective jurisdiction was limited to the island. There was an irony in this, which was lost on none of the Greeks. Crete had been the homeland of Venizelos; a fierce tradition of local patriotism still attached itself to his memory, and to the republican principles fervently held by many of his erstwhile supporters. Chania had seen, only three years before, the only serious revolt against the Metaxas dictatorship. It was as much as anything in recognition of these facts that the new prime minister, who had been sworn in the day before the evacuation, was both a Cretan by birth and a Venizelist who had himself suffered the displeasure of Metaxas. This was Emmanuel Tsouderos, who like his ill-fated predecessor was a banker, but was blessed with greater skills of self-preservation.

Since the rest of the cabinet remained much as before, the royal family and the ministers of the government were understandably not at their ease in Crete. An added reason for hostility was that most Cretans of military age had been called up, during the previous six months, to fight in Epiros and Macedonia, where the officers commanding them had just negotiated an ignominious and unauthorised surrender. 'They feel there's been a great betrayal,' George commented in his diary, 'and that the previous government sold out everything.' He also noted, almost gleefully, that the hated chief of police, Maniadakis, went everywhere with an armed escort; the most jittery people on the island were the policemen, who were not Cretans but had been drafted in from other parts of Greece.[9]

George was deeply moved by the sight of the 'old warriors who come down from the mountains, another race,' with faces 'as wrinkled as an olive trunk,' broad white beards, and no doubt wearing the traditional black *vraka*, or baggy trousers, long black boots, and black headscarf. His happiest moments were spent with his landlord, who in the intervals between air raids, would recite episodes from the romance of the late sixteenth century, *Erotokritos*, that George had first heard as a child in Smyrna. He loved the strong dialect of the islanders, and the assurance with which they spoke: the exact opposite of the professional world that was visibly falling into ruins around him. In these surroundings George's admiration for the 'people' (*laos*) knew no bounds:

> what the *laos* did, it did *on its own*. During six months of war, there were two completely different things: on the one hand there was a flowering, an *anonymous* resurrection; and on the other was the cancer of the Grande Bretagne Hotel [GHQ in Athens], with its dark corridors and gestures of despair.[10]

These were soft, still days; the spring rains were not yet over; outside the town the slopes were filled with the scents of citrus blossom and wild herbs, which George went gathering with Maro. He would have liked dearly to stay in Crete, but the climate of despair had followed the government from Athens.

196

In Government House each ministry was crammed into a single room; at one stage George was informed that he had been appointed cabinet secretary, but he had yet to see any sign of a cabinet meeting and doubted whether he would. He continued working for Nikoloudis, but there was little work to do. When a thinner than usual issue of the official *Government Gazette* appeared in Chania, the first since the evacuation, George took the credit for overseeing its publication. The air of impending departure deepened daily. On 10 May, several ministers left for Egypt, Nikoloudis among them. In his diary, George wrote a brief, and bitter, obituary for a working relationship that had lasted three and a half years; prematurely, as it would soon transpire.[11]

The senior official of the Foreign Ministry was now Vasilios Papadakis. This was someone with whom George had had professional dealings before; he had been the senior Foreign Ministry official on the delegation to the League of Nations in Geneva back in 1930, not a happy memory for George. Then Papadakis had preceded him at the Under-Ministry of Press and Tourism, but with a much wider brief which, unlike George's, had included censorship of the domestic media. Papadakis was a true acolyte of the Fourth of August regime; George even recalled the ridicule Papadakis had provoked by flaunting the uniform of the Metaxas youth movement.[12]

George remained convinced that it was Papadakis who had made difficulties for him in leaving Athens, and was now plotting to surround himself with yes-men in order to curry favour with the new prime minister, Tsouderos. Certainly, Papadakis was in the ascendant, and George did not like him. Two days after Nikoloudis' departure, a journalist from Heraklion was appointed Director-General of the Press Ministry. George took this to mean that his responsibilities there were now at an end.[13]

The British were organising the evacuation of all Greek government personnel from Crete. George sounds sourly sceptical, in his diary, about the determination even of the British to defend the island, after his own government had scuttled away. He was wrong about British intentions, but his misgivings about the outcome were to prove fully justified.[14]

A huge ocean-going liner, the *New Zealand*, was waiting alongside at Souda, among the smoke and debris. When they were shown to their cabin by a Malay steward, Maro commented to George, 'What a beautiful voyage we could have had on a ship like this . . .'

The sunset over Chania was the last Greek sunset that either of them would see for three and a half years.[15]

### Into the unknown

The ship, with its ragtime band, pianola at the bar, and dinner served in the smoking room by uniformed stewards, belonged to a vanished age. But the sense of venturing into the unknown, while danger lurked out of sight, brought George sharply up against the memory of the first time he had travelled abroad in wartime. Life-jackets had to be carried at all times; some people wore them, and looked like characters out of an Elizabethan painting. An escort of warships accompanied the *New Zealand* on its way through the still waters of the southern Mediterranean. It was, George thought, just a continuation of that earlier voyage, in 1918. Nothing had changed. He thought, too, of his poet-friends who had been left behind: Antoniou, who was missing after his ship had been sunk; Elytis, of whom he had last heard in a military hospital in Ioannina that had been destroyed by the Germans; though both, in the event, were to survive.[16]

His first sight of Egypt was a depressing one for someone as attuned as George to the Aegean landscape, whether of Smyrna or Athens. It was the flatness of the horizon that struck him; the tallest things in sight, as the *New Zealand* entered the harbour of Port Said, were the ships and houses. The cheerful Greek consul, who ate with them at their hotel, assured Maro that she would soon be back with her children. In response to their looks of surprise, he explained: 'in a few weeks the Germans will have taken everything and you'll go back to Greece.'[17]

The Greek new-arrivals were now despatched by train to Cairo. The Egyptian capital would become the nearest to a stable base that George and Maro would have during the Axis occupation of Greece. But that was still for the future. On this first, fleeting visit, George was less impressed by the pyramids than he was by an exotic pelican in the zoo, whose hangdog expression reminded him of Tsouderos; soon, he came to associate the city with mud in the streets, the smell of horse-dung and a 'mouldy taste;' Cairo held no attraction for him.[18]

But Cairo was not to be their destination either. On 20 May, the day that German paratroopers began landing in Crete and the Battle of Crete began, George and Maro arrived in Alexandria. It was a relief to George to be back in sight of the sea; but the Windsor Hotel, on the Corniche, where they were housed, had been transformed into a smaller version of the Grande Bretagne in Athens. Most of the Greek government and its civil service were here; the atmosphere of constant in-fighting disgusted George; 'leeches and sharks,' he called them.[19]

198

On the other hand, Alexandria itself was a wholly new experience. Or rather, it was the discovery of a place at once familiar and strange, since in some respects Alexandria was the image of Smyrna as it had been in his childhood.

Founded by Alexander the Great on the Mediterranean coast, and away from Egypt's traditional artery, the Nile, Alexandria in antiquity had always been more a Greek than an Egyptian city. Since the early nineteenth century this had become true once again, as Greek merchants moved in from all over the Ottoman empire. During that century, Alexandria had become the centre of the lucrative trade in Egyptian cotton; in the 1940s it still had a mixture of populations not dissimilar to that of Smyrna at the beginning of the century. Again like Smyrna, many of its central streets were lined with buildings in the grand European style of the late nineteenth century. Even today, although the Greeks were mostly forced out during Nasser's reforms of the late 1950s, the centre of Alexandria preserves its old-world, European flavour; two or three of the famous old-style cafés, that in the 1940s were run by Greeks, such as Pastroudi's and the Trianon, still function and have been refurbished in the old style. Many of the imposing tenement blocks that housed the Greek community have been replaced in shoddy concrete; others can still be seen, in a dispiriting state 199 of repair. The Windsor Hotel no longer exists (at least by that name), but the Cecil, with its mock-Moorish windows and balconies, still overlooks the Eastern Harbour and the Qaitbay fortress where the Pharos of Alexandria once stood.

In Alexandria, George at once felt himself to be:

in a corner of the greater Greek world. It was something to think, heading homewards, that I was treading the same street that began with the Gate of the Sun and ended at the Gate of the Moon and that somewhere along the Rue Nébi Danial, a crazed mob [of Christians] killed [the pagan philosopher] Hypatia [in AD 415].[20]

These landmarks would appear again, in the first poem that George would write after leaving Greece, 'Days of June '41.' So, too, would the site of the tomb of Alexander the Great, which is supposed to lie at the intersection of these two streets, but has never been found. In the poem, those weeks of May and June in Alexandria are juxtaposed to images of the Battle of Crete, which George and Maro followed through the daily news bulletins at the Windsor Hotel:

the beautiful island bloodied
wounded; the peaceful island, the powerful island, the innocent.
And the bodies like broken branches
and like roots torn up.[21]

Alexandria was not only the city of its founder and a part of the wider world of contemporary Hellenism. It was also the city of the greatest of all modern Greek writers, C.P. Cavafy.

Cavafy, for George, had long been the problematic 'other.' In almost every way his own antithesis, the Alexandrian Greek master of irony, whom E.M. Forster had once famously described as 'a Greek gentleman in a straw hat, standing absolutely motionless at a slight angle to the universe,' had at first been dismissed by Katsimbalis' circle, including all three literary Georges. Back in 1932, Katsimbalis had written to George a spirited but deeply unkind account of an encounter on the bus with the elderly and terminally ill Cavafy, on his final visit to Athens. Before long, George had come to recognise Cavafy's poetry as a problem to be explained; once embarked on writing essays for Katsimbalis and *Ta Nea Grammata*, he had made his first conscientious attempt to sort out his ambivalent responses. Cavafy was a problem with which George was to wrestle for many years; the book on Cavafy which he had first begun to plan in Korça would never be finished. But it was in the wake of this experience of Alexandria, when George found himself suddenly thrust into the world of the older poet, that he made his most sustained efforts to unlock the 'secret' of his deceptively lucid predecessor.[22]

Fortunately, he had a well-qualified guide. Timos Malanos was a cotton merchant, who had lived most of his life in Alexandria; literature was his hobby and his passion. Malanos had known Cavafy in the poet's last years, and been the first to publish a book about his poetry. Three years older than George, Malanos was spare and lean, with something of the air of an Edwardian Englishman, and the richly textured pronunciation of the Egyptian Greek. George had first met him back in 1935, when Malanos had been visiting Athens, and Katsimbalis had introduced them. They had maintained a polite, occasional correspondence since. Now, at the end of May, in Alexandria, they met again, along with another businessman and amateur man of letters, Nanis Panayotopoulos, whom George had also met some years before, with Katsimbalis in Athens.[23]

It was deeply invigorating, for George, to escape from the political hothouse of the Windsor to the Trianon café for an afternoon in this company.

Of the two men, it was the genial Panayotopoulos with whom he felt the more in sympathy. About Malanos, even at that early meeting in Egypt, when for the first time they had begun using first names and the informal singular, George had his reservations: 'a terrible *aesthete*,' he stressed, and was irritated by the literal-mindedness of Malanos' comments on *Logbook*, of which George had just loaned him a copy. But Malanos was indispensable to him as a guide to the 'mysterious' world of Cavafy's poetry, and scarcely less so to the mysteries of contemporary Alexandria. Malanos took him on a tour of Cavafy's city, including some of the sights of the backstreets that made George think of Blake's illustrations of Hell.[24]

By the beginning of June, the Battle of Crete had been lost. The Greek navy, such as had survived the last six weeks, had arrived in the Western Harbour of Alexandria; there were also several thousand Greek combatants who had fled Greece, and would soon be formed into regular army brigades. Apart from these small forces, the king and his government were without subjects. Since Egypt, nominally independent and neutral, was in practice under British control, this meant that the Greek government was too. At once, steps were taken to distance the government-in-exile from the legacy of the Fourth of August. The first of these had been taken already, in the 201 appointment of Tsouderos as prime minister, even before the departure from Athens; technically, the process was completed six months later, in statements by the king and Tsouderos in London; but in the eyes of many, this was a shabby, half-hearted affair, and the aura of right-wing dictatorship continued to hang over the government long after the last of Metaxas' associates had left it. Now, at the beginning of June 1941, it was decided to move the seat of the exiled government to London. Several of its more ideologically unsavoury members were to be shed along the way, despatched with the title of Minister Plenipotentiary to parts of the globe where they could do no harm.[25]

One of these was Nikoloudis, who was to open an embassy in South Africa, and proposed to take his senior civil servant, George, with him. Perhaps as a form of reaction to the intense strain of the preceding months, George confronted the new situation with a fatalistic lassitude such as he had not shown since his darkest days in Paris or at the London consulate. He had no desire to go to South Africa, nor to work once again for 'one of the most impulsive, conceited and self-centred characters' he had ever known. He would much have preferred to return to the Foreign Ministry; but he could not or would not work with Papadakis, who was in charge (the

Fourth of August had a long way yet to unravel). Too late and at a bad moment, he tried and failed to put his case directly to Tsouderos. Almost everyone, from the royal family downwards, would be sailing on the same ship from Suez. But before he returned from Alexandria to Cairo, en route for Suez, it had been confirmed that George's destination would be Pretoria.[26]

Before embarking, he had a brief reunion in Cairo with the Durrells, whom he had last seen when they passed through Crete. Durrell, his wife Nancy and their one-year-old daughter had escaped from the southern Peloponnese on a caique just as the Germans were closing in. Recalling these meetings, George wrote to Miller, not long afterwards: 'Larry, I love him. He has wonderful moments.' One of these moments would result in the poem 'Mythology' by Durrell, that George later translated and included in his own next book of poems. In Cairo he also saw Robert Liddell and Bernard Spencer, who like Durrell had worked for the British Council in Greece, and had now been assigned to Cairo. With them, evacuated on the same ship from Greece, was the childhood friend of the Seferiadis siblings, Elli Papadimitriou, now a committed Marxist. These, together with Robin Fedden, whom George must also have known in Athens, were soon to become the main players in one of the strangest literary ventures to come out of the Second World War, the magazine *Personal Landscape*, which in turn would pave the way for *The King of Asine and Other Poems* by George Seferis, in English.[27]

The Greek exiles, including George and Maro, sailed from Suez on 27 June. Several thousand miles to the north, German tanks were sweeping eastwards into the Soviet Union. Nothing, it seemed, could stop Hitler now. Even the official news bulletin, posted on the ship as it crossed the equator, announced that 'the outlook indeed is grim.'[28]

There was once again a bizarre aura of luxury on board ship. The dinner-gong made George think of pre-Raphaelite paintings, or the 'invisible troupe' that in Cavafy's poem is the harbinger of death for Mark Antony. Tsouderos, the prime minister, seemed to him more than ever 'without substance,' and reminded him of the ghost of Hamlet's father. George had never been in such close proximity to the royal family before; the experience did nothing to lighten his prejudices. Ought one to bow every time one crossed their path? He noticed that they spoke among themselves in English and French, using Greek only occasionally. 'For them, I suppose,' he growled in the privacy of his diary, 'we're the natives.'[29]

The voyage to Durban lasted ten days. After the sweltering doldrums of the Red Sea, it was winter in the southern hemisphere. The royal arrival was greeted with a twenty-one-gun salute; a band of Scots Guards struck up the Greek national anthem; a Greek cargo ship that had turned up even here, was decked out fore and aft. It was a strange arrival, in a land where so many of the people were black but (here, in the harbour) wore European clothes. Unfamiliar trees and plants had, as yet, no names. It was heartening to hear birdsong, for the first time after the days at sea. The war seemed far away; there was no black-out.[30]

In Johannesburg, on its high plateau in the heart of gold- and diamond-mining country, what struck George first was the freezing cold; this was July, the hottest month of the year in the world he had left behind. The official party began to thin out; the royals departed, though for another month he would have to share a hotel with the prime minister and his entourage. It would not be until the beginning of September that Nikoloudis' new embassy would be ready to open its doors in the South African capital, Pretoria. By this time, George had conceived a powerful dislike for Tsouderos, whom he described as 'two-faced, a petty politician through and through . . . , timid, highly-strung and devious.' When the government in exile departed, on its way to London, at the end of July, he hoped they would not meet again until Greece was liberated.[31]

Here George was surely protesting too much. He was well aware that by staying behind in South Africa with Nikoloudis, he was throwing away his original hopes, that by leaving Greece he could continue to help the war-effort. The Pretoria embassy was a backwater; professionally, there was nothing for him to do there. While Tsouderos had been in Johannesburg, it would still not have been too late for George to put his case. He was mortified that another colleague was being sent to the embassy in America, where there was a real role to play. Clearly, he had been outmanoeuvred by Papadakis, who had effectively 'neutralised' him (George's word). But in what he called his 'service diary,' George also conceded his own failure; at the same time he revealed an honourable, if perhaps slightly naive, understanding of the relationship between government ministers and their senior civil servants:

> They made me feel bitterly how weak I am at pushing myself forward, at claiming my due. I thought that a minister, when he decides on an appointment (and how few there are of us who've followed Tsouderos) has the obligation to enquire, at least to find out something about the man appointed. I was wrong. Ministers just want you to wear their livery.[32]

203

There is genuine self-knowledge here; behind the first sentence, in particular, it is hard not to hear the voice, also, of Maro. What exactly *had* George achieved by leaving Greece and bringing his wife to the other side of the world; what was he to do now? He and Maro discussed this subject endlessly; but neither in George's diary, nor in the few pages of a journal that Maro kept in Pretoria, is her side of the discussion recorded. On the same day that he made these comments in his service diary, George paid his first visit to Pretoria; 'ghastly,' he described it frankly on his return. That evening, he explained to Maro that it was perhaps better this way after all. Surrounded by people that he despised, he could not have given his best in the service of his country; perhaps now, as things were, with 'a little serenity,' he would be able to do 'something more worthwhile.'[33]

He had not written a poem for over a year. It was time to begin.

## Among the agapanthi

On 2 September 1941, George and Maro moved into a small flat in a huge, old-style apartment block on Kerk Str. Oost, one of the main arteries of central Pretoria; 'the quietest house I ever had,' he would describe it, when they left again. Just opposite was the government complex, on its hill, surmounted by twin belfries whose bells chimed the hours – the only sign of life that George observed in what he chose to call the 'Venusberg,' probably in ironic allusion to the opera *Tannhäuser* by Wagner, his least favourite composer. It was half-an-hour's walk to the Greek Legation, now functioning at 975 Pretorius Street.[34]

During the weeks that followed, he worked as he had never worked before, except while he had been finishing 'Erotikos Logos;' sometimes as much as twelve hours a day – and this had nothing to do with the professional duties that occupied him for four or five hours each day at the embassy.[35]

It began at the end of the second week in Pretoria. George and Maro were talking after supper. Suddenly, Maro records, he pulled his chair over to the desk, signalled to Maro to sit beside him, and began to write. As he wrote, staring straight ahead of him, he drummed out rhythms with his free hand. He wrote quickly, making no alterations. All this time he smoked one cigarette after another. Maro dared not light one herself, for fear of breaking the spell. He threw into her lap the finished page. It was the poem, then untitled, 'Days of June '41,' that recaptured the voyage from Greece, the days spent in the footsteps of Cavafy and of Alexander the Great, in the company of Panayotopoulos and Malanos in Alexandria, and the Battle of Crete. At the bottom of the page, he had written the date and, for the first time at the end of a poem, the word 'Pretoria.' It was like waking from a trance, as he wrote in his own diary, to find that he really was in this remote place.

If Maro made any comment, neither of them mentions the fact. Whether prompted or not, George now took another sheet of paper, and was writing again, more slowly this time, with longer pauses while the pen remained aloft, his head nodding slowly. Then came a second page delivered into Maro's lap. It was, as she recognised at once, his considered answer to the subject of so many of their conversations of the last few months. The circumstances of its writing explain the title of the poem that comes second in *Logbook II*: 'Postscript.'[36]

It is written in the form of a prayer; its refrain: 'O Lord, not with those people.' 'Those people' are the 'insubstantial people' of the ship from Suez to Durban; vain and ineffectual but with power over the speaker's fate. Their eyes are 'bleached without eyelids,' their voices too feeble to reach beyond their 'yellowed teeth.' It is a grim caricature of Tsouderos and his entourage. To them are counterpointed an idyllic memory of children playing on a green slope, which is also a source of healing herbs. The force of the juxtaposition is effective for any reader; but Maro knew that the children were her children, Mina and Anna, and the cousins with whom they had used to play during the summers at Trapeza, where she would use wild herbs gathered from the hillside to cure their minor injuries and stings. Now, the poem continues,

205

> we breathe
> with each morning a little bit of a prayer
> that finds the shore by voyaging
> through chasms of memory . . .

The poem itself was that prayer, George's acknowledgement of what Maro suffered, and why: 'O Lord, not with those people.' The version of the poem that he gave to Maro that evening ends, after this refrain: 'but let thy will be done.' In the published version, this has become: 'Let thy will be done otherwise.'[37]

Childhood was very much on George's mind that September. So, too, was the need to take stock, to understand and explain himself. How did he come to be in the situation in which he and Maro now found themselves? It was now that he recalled his own childhood, and began to write the remarkable political testament known as *Manuscript Sept. '41*. Here, for the first time, he explicitly drew the dividing line between the self that belonged to his beloved Skala, and his other childhood self that had inhabited the city of Smyrna, with its drudgery and compromises. Maro catches something of the atmosphere of the small flat at Kerk Str. Oost, at the time when George must have embarked on the *Manuscript:*

> When he talks about the skippers and the people of his village [Skala], his voice and his eyes take on a different expression, the way they do when he tells a story about his mother, who I think was the person he's loved the most in his life.[38]

In the poem 'The Figure of Fate,' which is dated 1 October, the child born on a dark, windy February night is clearly George himself; but the role of father has been taken over by one of the weatherbeaten skippers of Skala (he uses the same word as Maro records from this conversation). These lines may perhaps recall the loss of Despo, his mother, in the middle of the night, in the house among the trees at Kifisia, back in 1926:

> because you became separated one night in the wood from the
> woman
> who gazed with fixed, staring eyes and had lost the power of
> speech . . .[39]

The *Manuscript*, on which he continued to work until December, although beginning in the confessional mode of autobiography, is chiefly taken up with the political life of Greece, and George's own personal relation to it. More than half of it consists of an acute dissection of the contradictions and occasional absurdities of the final phases of the Metaxas regime, which he had experienced at first hand. The *Manuscript* is addressed to no one, unless implicitly, perhaps, to Maro. Its theme is 'what it means to be enslaved;' it weaves together George's early memories of the Greek community of Anatolia under pressure from its Ottoman rulers before the First World War, with the condition of Europe under Axis domination at the end of 1941. The *Manuscript* concludes:

> I have written these pages with no other purpose than to put my conscience in order. The only more general conclusion I can draw and that troubles me is the astonishing gulf that separates the people from the cabal of its rulers, irrespective of what party they belong to. Where this will lead us, I do not know.[40]

206

As well as the *Manuscript*, six of the thirteen poems that would make up *Logbook II* were written during just over four months in Pretoria. The poem in which George most seriously came to terms with his South African exile is the one that he wrote towards the end of this time, 'Stratis Thalassinos among the Agapanthi.' The strange flora that he had noticed on first coming ashore at Durban now had names; the dark blue agapanthus lilies had been given (by European botanists) a name made out of the Greek words for 'love' and 'flower.'

It was Maro who first pointed it out: 'This is the country of violet-coloured flowers: jacaranda, dahlias, bougainvillea, agapanthus.' George connected this, '*in abstracto*,' with the skin-colour of the blacks, to construct 'an idea of the colony we're living in.' In a general way, George seems to have found the South African blacks more admirable than their colonial masters, but seems not to have met any as individuals. Maro tells a story about how he had to extricate the embassy from the embarrassing case of a Greek who was in trouble with the police for preaching equal rights in the black townships. The story ended with smiles all round; afterwards, Nikoloudis' wife was appalled that a Greek, of all people, should do such a thing. 'But why,' retorted George, 'don't you want anybody ever to have any liberal ideas?' Before leaving South Africa, he would inveigh caustically against the crude racial theory of one Dr Ley, whom he had encountered in Athens and found his behaviour more depraved than that of the races whose depravity he claimed 'scientifically' to have proved.[41]

But if George was indignant about the arrogance of the European colonists in this country, the name of the indigenous dark-blue lilies was the touchstone for his own sense of exile. The long-stemmed flowers set him thinking of asphodels, that according to Greek mythology grow in the Elysian fields. But here there could be no communication with the dead, that is: with the past of his own culture. Stratis Thalassinos, the 'modern Odysseus,' cries out impotently for help, while catastrophe looms and his companions have been bewitched by the enchantress Circe – in a mythological allusion that may be politically charged, in her *palace*.

These new poems, together with his political act of stock-taking, were by no means all that occupied George during the feverish burst of activity that began that South African spring of September 1941. He also experimented in more light-hearted ways. Finding the limericks of Edward Lear in a Johannesburg bookshop reminded him of the ribald doggerel to which Durrell had introduced him in Athens. During his first few months in South Africa, he said that he wrote a limerick every day, 'for my health;' he sent

207

many of the more printable ones to his friends. To Durrell he wrote, including an example in English, and apologising for the roughness of the 'translation':

I think that limerick writing is a good exercise for lonely men, and suppose that the genre has been created in England because all of you are lonely like islands. But the interesting thing is that it brings forth a sort of individual mythology:

> There was a young girl from Uganda
> Who sat under a jacaranda
> An old man with an umbrella
> When he saw this *kopella*
> Waved his carnation from a veranda.[42]

Another discovery was the *calligramme*, a precursor of 'concrete poetry' pioneered by Guillaume Apollinaire during the previous world war, in which the words of a poem form the lines of a sketch, representing the subject visually. Of six *calligrammes* published posthumously, four belong to that October, three of them even to the same day. Both the form of the *calligramme*, and the idea of the poem as calligraphic handicraft, would be carried forward into *Logbook II*. Two poems of that collection, in its first edition, would be presented in this way.[43]

Since at least his twenties, George had always liked to think of the poet as a kind of artisan, a craftsman working with his hands. In the depths of his new exile, where books in Greek were a scarce and precious commodity, he discovered a whole new delight in the laborious work of copying out poems by hand. As he wrote with rueful pleasure to Malanos, when he and Maro had begun copying the *Odes* of Kalvos from a borrowed edition, 'Say what you like, we've arrived, whether we like it or not, in the blissful years before Gutenberg's invention [of printing].' Then, in just over three weeks, in October and November, he copied out by hand all one hundred and fifty four poems of the Cavafy 'canon,' adding notes on each. At the same time he drafted a prologue for his planned book on Cavafy; in it he included a variation on the phrase from the letter to Malanos: 'We've finally reached the years when the abolition of printing has been invented.' For George this rather tortuously expressed paradox seemed to sum up something about the war years. When the time came to publish his own *Logbook*

208

1. Despo Tenekidou, Stelios Seferiadis,
probably taken about the time of their
marriage in 1897

2. Stelios Seferiadis, Paris, 1 August 1918
(his 45th birthday)

3. Despo Seferiadou (Tenekidou), portrait
by E. Ioannidis, c. 1917

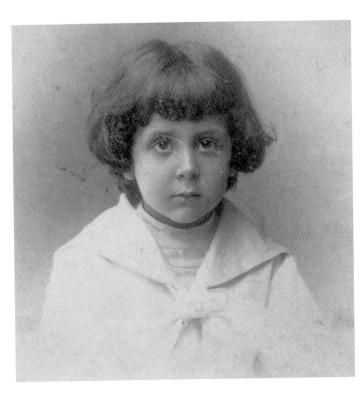

4. GS aged 2 or 3
(portrait photograph)

5. 'George, wide-eyed and serious...' GS, Ioanna and Angelos, *c.* 1916

6. and 7. Skala: 'There, the people, sailors and villagers, were my own people.'

8. Suzon Clauzel and a friend, signed photograph, 19 June 1919

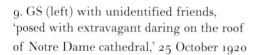

9. GS (left) with unidentified friends, 'posed with extravagant daring on the roof of Notre Dame cathedral,' 25 October 1920

10. Angelos Seferiadis, Notre Dame, summer 1922

11. Marie-Louise Pouyollon, Jacqueline Pouyollon, Le Vésinet, July 1924

13. GS with Petros Adamos (left), at 121 Boundaries Road, Balham, London, September 1924. 'I talk English even to the cat'

12. GS and Jacqueline, Le Vésinet, July 1924

14. Loukia Fotopoulou (Lou), in her basement flat, the 'cistern'

15. GS (right, hat in hand) was official guide to Edouard Herriot (centre) on his semi-official visit to Greece in August 1929

16. Ioanna Tsatsou, shortly after her
marriage in 1930

17. GS with Sotiris Stamelos, 'a living
embodiment at once of Homer and of
Makriyannis,' Skiathos, July/August 1930

18. GS with Loukia Fotopoulou (Lou),
1930, about the time when he wrote to her:
'I'm not sure how long the magic really
lasted'

19. Andreas Londos, husband of Marika (later Maro Seferi): '... a striking resemblance to the movie-star Clark Gable' (*c.* 1934)

20. Marika Zannou (later Maro Seferi) and her sister Amaryllis Dragoumi (right), Poros 1938. It was Amaryllis who introduced Maro to GS

21. Henry Miller (left) and George Katsimbalis (the 'Colossus of Maroussi'),
Hydra, November 1939

22. Henry Miller, Hydra, November 1939: '... putting on his black spectacles as though to work with an oxy-acetylene flame...' ('Les Anges Sont Blancs')

23. Alexandrian friends.
Left to right: Timos Malanos, Maro,
Nanos Panayotopoulos (Nuzha, 1943)

4. Maro in the Botanical Gardens, Cairo, 27 June 1942. With evacuation from Egypt looming, hopes that her daughters could join her from occupied Greece had just been dashed

5. George Kartalis (right) with GS, Cairo, 23 August 1943

26. 'The snow here is never-ending...'
GS outside his house in Atatürk
Bulvarı, Ankara, January 1949

27. 'Descent into Hades': GS outside
the 'little house' in Skala (now
restored as the Yorgo Seferis guest
house); his grandmother's house is in
the background (2 July 1950)

8. GS (right) with Rex Warner, Woodstock, Oxfordshire, 1952
9. GS and Evangelos Louizos, St Hilarion, Cyprus, 8 November 1953

10. At the Acheiropoietos monastery, Cyprus, 6 December 1953.
Seated (left to right): GS, Lawrence Durrell, Antoinette Diamanti, Maurice Cardiff.
Standing: the Cardiffs' son, the painter Adamantios Diamantis

31. '... a younger incarnation of the "Colossus of Maroussi" as Katsimbalis had been thirty years before...' George Savvides (left) with Katsimbalis and Maro, Rhodes, September 1955; photo by GS

32. 'Our Seafaring Friend': D.I. Antoniou, Beirut, 1955; photo by GS

33. At the United Nations, 12 November 1956. Left to right: Constantine Karamanlis, GS, Evangelos Averoff-Tosizza

34. GS pays his respects to Archbishop Makarios, arriving in Athens from captivity in the Seychelles, 17 April 1957

35. GS with Harold Macmillan, London Airport, 7 August 1958

36. 'M. Zorlu [foreign minister of Turkey, right] and M. Averoff [foreign minister of Greece, left] had exchanged "Turkish delights" in New York ... George was horrified' (London, February 1959)

37. Konstantinos ('Kostakis') Tsatsos and George Katsimbalis, 1960

38. GS and Maro at the London embassy, 51 Upper Brook Street, 1961

39. GS with Anne Philipe, Delphi, May 1971

*II*, in Alexandria in 1944, he would use the new photo-offset system, to reproduce his calligraphic, illustrated manuscript. Below the title, in that now rare edition, appears the phrase from his unfinished book on Cavafy.[44]

Out of the same months in Pretoria came the abortive project, hatched through correspondence with Malanos, with George's junior colleague Alexandros Xydis, and others back in Alexandria, for a new literary magazine, to be known as *Eunostos*, a title that can be loosely translated: 'happy homecoming.' Planning for *Eunostos* lasted until the summer of 1943, by which time George's energies would be fully occupied elsewhere. But something of the impetus behind the project probably helped fuel the launch of *Personal Landscape*, whose first issue, published in Cairo in January 1942, included part of one of George's letters to Durrell.[45]

Summer had come to Transvaal at last, it was the season when Pretoria emptied. Nikoloudis and his wife had joined in the general exodus to Cape Town. On the morning of Saturday, 24 January, George was alone at the embassy. He called Maro at home on the phone: 'Maro, telegram from Tsouderos in England, in code, for me. From what I've decoded so far, we're going to Cairo.' The career diplomat who had been left in charge of the government press office in Cairo, Constantine Kollas, urgently needed someone with more experience of press matters to assist him. No one else on the strength of the Foreign Ministry had experience to match George's – '*unfortunately*,' the message continued. There was a personal barb even here; the message was signed 'Papadakis [for] Tsouderos.' In his diary, which elides these details, George wondered what 'reasons can have brought about the change in their attitudes towards me.'[46]

It would still take another three months for their departure from South Africa to be arranged. The first step was to persuade Nikoloudis to release him. Hurriedly, George and Maro prepared to leave for Cape Town. When they got out of the state-of-the-art, air-conditioned 'Blue Train,' after the thirty-six hour journey from Transvaal, he was thrilled to smell the sea. Nikoloudis was not best pleased at the news; he reacted, George said, as though he had been stabbed in the back. Diplomatic niceties had to be observed before the former propaganda chief would give his reluctant blessing to George's departure. In the meantime, he and Maro stayed in Cape Town. They went swimming; they took the cable-car to the top of Table Mountain; they went to the Botanical Gardens. George, according to Maro, was 'lighthearted, cheerful, lovable.' But he found the landscape alienating: the flat-topped mountains of Cape Province seemed to him 'decapitated;' he clung obstinately to the 'mania of the Greek who always wants to measure things on a human scale.'[47]

All this time, news from Greece had been frustratingly hard to come by. Maro was allowed to send telegrams to her daughters, limited to twenty words each, at the rate of no more than one per month, through the Red Cross. A letter to George from Ioanna, sent via the Red Cross in August, had taken until Christmas to reach him. Another, that he sent to his brother Angelos, at the beginning of March 1942, would be date-stamped on arrival in Athens in late November. A series of letters from Apostolidis, in a sanatorium in neutral Switzerland, apparently never reached George in Pretoria. Even between South Africa and Egypt, postal communication was slow and not always reliable, no doubt because ships were sunk by enemy action. It was during his first months in Pretoria that George established the habit of always keeping either a draft or a carbon copy of all his personal correspondence.[48]

Back in Pretoria from Cape Town, in March, George received a letter from a diplomatic colleague, who had also been a regular visitor to the top floor of the house in Kydathinaion Street. It was only now that he learned of the courageous stand taken by his brother-in-law, Kostakis Tsatsos, that had cost him his job at the University back in October. Tsatsos had defied a ban on boycotting classes on the anniversary of Greece's entry into the war. George was deeply moved by this story. Then a month later, came horrific details of the famine that had left thousands of people dead in the Greek cities and towns, during the exceptionally hard first winter of the occupation.[49]

In these conditions, while waiting to leave South Africa, George found it impossible to settle to anything, or to write. On 13 April, he and Maro closed up the flat and moved back into the hotel in Johannesburg where they had stayed when they first arrived; a farewell dinner with Nikoloudis and his wife was strained. A colleague took them by car to Durban, a two-day drive; from there they embarked at six in the morning on a giant Sunderland flying boat, moored in the harbour.[50]

It was an epic, four-day journey from end to end of the African continent in wartime, by way of Lourenço Marques, Beira, across the Zambezi to Mozambique; then, after a short night on the ground, to Lindi in Tanganyika, Dar es Salaam, inland over Kilimanjaro, to sleep for almost a whole night in a stifling hotel on the shore of Lake Victoria, not far from Kampala. Their room had been provided with a Gideon Bible, and

George began translating the *Song of Songs* for Maro until they both fell asleep. It was the harbinger of a labour of love that he was to take up again after almost twenty years (this time, translating from the Greek of the Septuagint). Then, in Khartoum, he had his last sight of the Southern Cross, low on the horizon on one side, while on the other he could make out the familiar contours of the Great Bear. The moment marked 'the threshold of our world.'[51]

George and Maro reached Cairo late on Saturday 25 April 1942. After all the delays in setting out, he had been brought from South Africa in record time. No one in Cairo seemed to know quite why.

### Displaced persons

George and Maro could now feel relatively close to home. In Egypt, where so many new exiles were continuing to arrive from occupied Greece, news from home was relatively plentiful. It was probably now that George first learned of the hyper-inflation in occupied Greece that was making the drachma almost worthless. Although the acute conditions of famine had eased with the end of winter, food there was still scarce. The black market flourished. Sporadic acts of resistance brought savage reprisals. Ioanna, he probably also heard for the first time, had set herself the harrowing task of       211
comforting the families of those who had been executed. Many years later, she published her diary of those years: a moving testimony to courage and fortitude, and a touching memorial to so many friends and acquaintances who had died suddenly and violently.[52]

Maro had news of her daughters. After the suicide of Penelope Delta, her friend Sofia Mavrogordatou, Delta's daughter, had been in charge of Mina and Anna, on the Deltas property, which was relatively well provided for, at Kifisia. Maro had not been settled in Cairo long when she received word from Sofia Mavrogordatou that she was putting the girls on the first ship for Egypt. This must have seemed an unlikely prospect, as well as a risky one, since Greece was under blockade. It was soon shelved, in any case, when Egypt itself came under threat of attack by Rommel in June.[53]

Of all the escapees who had arrived in Egypt from Greece since the start of the occupation, the most politically significant so far was Panayotis Kanellopoulos, who by coincidence had reached Cairo a week ahead of George. Two years younger than George, the new arrival 'brought youth, vigour, . . . a sense of awakening, optimism.' Kanellopoulos was not an experienced politician; before founding his own party in 1935, he had been an academic. But while his political background was liberal-republican,

Kanellopoulos' direct experience of Greece under the Axis gave him, for a time, enormous prestige in the eyes of both the Greeks and the British. The British ambassador to the government in exile, Sir Reginald (Rex) Leeper noted in a confidential memorandum to the Foreign Office, a little later:

> M. Kanellopoulos is not a great practical mind, but his honesty and his patriotism are as unquestionable as his energy, and he has become at least more conspicuous a figure than any other politician of his generation.[54]

It was a measure of how far the exiled government had travelled since the days of the Fourth of August regime that, within weeks of his arrival, Kanellopoulos had been made Vice-President of the Council, that is, Deputy Prime Minister. Although Tsouderos was at the moment in Egypt, to oversee this and other changes to his government, the official seat of the government in exile remained London. Kanellopoulos was set to become the senior member of the government based in Cairo; soon he would also be Minister of Defence.[55]

George had his own reasons to welcome both Kanellopoulos' arrival and his sudden elevation. Ever since student days, Kanellopoulos had been a close friend of his brother-in-law, Kostakis Tsatsos; George had been introduced to him at Kifisia in 1928, during the summer of the dengue fever. Kanellopoulos had occupied himself, during three years of internal exile under Metaxas, by writing a history of European civilisation in nine volumes; George confessed his doubts about a project on such a scale, but Kanellopoulos' work has had its admirers ever since, including C.M. Woodhouse, who at this time had recently been parachuted into occupied Greece, and would remain a lifelong friend of both Kanellopoulos and George. Before his exile, the tall, lean, voluble aspiring politician had been a familiar figure in the house at Kydathinaion Street. Here was someone in a position of authority in whom George could place his personal trust. The previous year, George had found himself incapable of pressing his case with Tsouderos; now he sought out the new Deputy Prime Minister at Shepheard's Hotel and at the defence ministry.

Their conversation was clearly at least as much political and professional as it was personal or intellectual. George complained to Kanellopoulos that the press office and the Cairo embassy were in chaos. He was supposed to be helping Constantine Kollas run the Press Office, but his superior had no idea how to use him. By the end of June 1942, George was more desperate than ever to find a role in which he could be useful. He put it to

Kanellopoulos that he might work directly for him; he even offered the services of Maro; 'she's cool-headed and determined,' he said. But Kanellopoulos did not appear to take up his offer.[56]

As summer drew on, these were weeks of growing uncertainty in Egypt. The Libyan port of Tobruk fell to Rommel in June 1942; yet another evacuation was in prospect. Against this background, George wrote his first poem since returning to the northern hemisphere. The poet who in his younger days had often been accused of baffling his readers with riddles, of taking refuge from the world in the aesthete's ivory tower, now declared:

> I want nothing else but to speak simply, to be given this grace.
> Because our song has become overloaded with so many kinds of
>    music that slowly it is sinking
> and our art has been overlaid so heavily that the gold has eaten
>    away its face
> and it is time we spoke the few words we have because tomorrow
>    our souls set sail.[57]

Dated 20 June 1942, the poem is entitled 'An Old Man on the River Bank.' George was only forty-two; but photographs show his hair thinning and on his face an expression of being harassed by heat and worry; six months later, he began an entry in his diary: 'I don't think I've ever felt so old.' The river in the poem is recognisably the Nile; the implicit setting Cairo. Reflecting from the distance of Alexandria, on the sea, George's thoughts would return, some months later, to the imagery of this poem:

> Rivers always leave you behind, as they flow, with what you've got: bitterness, troubles, despair. The sea brings deliverance. A person on the riverbank: one of the most depressing images that exist.[58]

For George, the air of official panic that gripped Cairo in the last days of June had a terrible familiarity. On the wide sweep of lawn that, in those days, led down from the British Embassy to the edge of the Nile, huge bonfires were set up; it was said that half-burnt secret documents rained down on the city for days: to the British, these events were known as 'the Flap.' George thought the decision to close the Greek embassy, and the consulate in Alexandria, was premature. Most of the Greek officials and politicians from Cairo found themselves, after a cramped exodus across the Suez Canal under constant air raids, in Jerusalem, where George and Maro would spend the next month. 'We're the eternal refugees,' he commented in his diary on the eve of their departure from Cairo. But what he complained of most was not the continual displacement, but the waste.[59]

While in the Western Desert Rommel's advance was halted at El Alamein (the decisive battle there was not fought until October), George visited the sights of Jerusalem. At the Holy Sepulchre, he marvelled at the accumulation of epochs and centuries, the exact opposite of the Acropolis of Athens, that already in the nineteenth century had been stripped bare of all the later accretions and excrescences to the ancient temples. On the way out, his eye was caught by a display outside a souvenir shop: 'crowns of thorns' for sale.[60]

His only poem from Palestine derived from an expedition to Jericho, the Jordan, and the Dead Sea on 10 July. 'Stratis Thalassinos on the Dead Sea,' in its first version, opens with a refrain that is translated almost directly from Eliot's *The Waste Land*: 'Jerusalem, unreal city.' The change in the published version is small but significant: the Greek word that now replaces 'unreal,' *akyverniti*, means 'without government, unruled; adrift.' There is no English word that exactly captures this metaphor, which recalls the ancient ship of state, to convey the very precise diagnosis of social and political flux which in George's poem replaces Eliot's far more abstract disaffection. Later, the phrase became the title of the classic trilogy of novels by Stratis Tsirkas, set during the war years in Jerusalem, Cairo and Alexandria, and known in English as *Drifting Cities*.[61]

Again, in this poem, as with the agapanthi in South Africa, George adopted an alias. At first, this was to have been Mathios Paskalis; in the published version, he once again resurrected his seafaring alter ego from London years: Stratis Thalassinos. It is a poem about refugees, the restless condition of universal homelessness of which the signs had been everywhere for the last few weeks, and the collapse of a civilisation.

'Stratis Thalassinos on the Dead Sea' was written before much was known about the fate of the Jews in Europe. But George would certainly have known about the British policy, at this time, of strictly limiting Jewish immigration into Palestine. There may be an allusion in the poem to the recent fate of the Jewish refugees refused entry to Palestine and subsequently lost aboard the cargo ship *Struma* in the Black Sea, an event on which George also commented in his diary at this time. Above and behind the 'ungoverned,' or 'drifting,' city and the chaotic flux of the countryside stands the aloof presence of the British. George's confidence in his country's

214

allies was not unbounded; he had seen them abandon mainland Greece, then Crete. In the aftermath of the fall of Tobruk, while the fate of Egypt hung in the balance, he had noted in his diary, 'the only thing that distresses me is that upon the stupidities of the English generals will depend whether half the population of my country is wiped out, or all of it.'[62]

At one of the Biblical sites he visited on 10 July, George was struck by the notice, in block capitals: THIS IS THE PLACE, GENTLEMEN. 'Gentlemen' reminded him of other circumstances, particularly the brusque call in British pubs, at closing time: 'Hurry up please it's time,' which Eliot had incorporated into *The Waste Land.* The word, he said, always seemed to be wielded like a boulder dropped on your head. The phrase, in English and in block capitals, also found its way into the poem, where it serves as another refrain. It was not the last time that a public notice in English would serve George as a forceful counter-weapon of satire against the bland assumptions of authority that he associated with the British empire.[63]

Many of these sentiments were shared by his English writer-friends, who had also been displaced by the 'Flap.' Olivia Manning's recollection, that provides this chapter with its epigraph, must actually recall the genesis of 'Stratis Thalassinos on the Dead Sea.'

By the end of June 1942, the 'Flap' was officially over. Displaced persons and institutions were drifting back to Cairo and Alexandria. On the 27th a telegram addressed to Kollas from Tsouderos, in London, advised the reopening of the press office in Cairo, 'with a skeleton staff under Mr Seferiadis.' A week later George and Maro were back in the Egyptian capital. It soon transpired that Kanellopoulos had not ignored his plea for a useful role. Kollas was ousted, and George became 'Press Director, Middle East,' a post that he formally took up on 22 September. Ironically enough, Kollas was despatched to Pretoria, to replace the archpriest of the Fourth of August, Nikoloudis, whose official career now came to an end. George cannot have been displeased by any of these developments.[64]

### 'Mountebanks, Middle East'

George worked well with Kanellopoulos; no doubt it was he who sent along his friend Lawrence Durrell to help the Deputy Prime Minister improve his English. Soon, though, he began to notice that Kanellopoulos lacked a sense of humour or the ability to listen. The Press Office was starved of funds and logistical support; it was not until December that George could persuade Kanellopoulos to complain to London; but London, he had already noted, had devised the 'excellent system of not replying.' He quickly came to realise that not only his own role, but that of the Greek government too, was subject to strict controls by the British. In particular, the British controlled all official communications with occupied Greece; any discussion in the press of Greek national interests was also subject to strict censorship. As George summed up the situation at the end of his first two months: 'extravagance and waste, of people, of resources, even of money.'[65]

But if professional and political contact with Greece was in the hands of the British, it was all the more vital for the exiles to seek whatever means they could to learn news of their own families and friends. An acquaintance who reached Cairo early in 1943 told George the story of his brother Angelos. Only just recovering from an operation for stomach ulcers, at the end of the previous summer, Angelos had been arrested by the Italians. He had spent six weeks in custody before being released. It turned out that the arrest had been a mistake; it was another Seferiadis who had attracted the attention of the occupying forces with his left-wing views. It was an inglorious tale, and one that was to have deadly repercussions later in George's brother's life.[66]

Maro, too, found an unexpected means to keep in touch with her daughters in Greece, through her estranged first husband. Andreas Londos was now in charge of an élite naval group, the equivalent of the Special Boat Squadron, which worked closely with the British navy to make raids into the enemy-controlled Aegean. This work brought Londos often to Alexandria; from there he would send photographs of the girls, taken in Greece, to Maro in Cairo. In this way she learned that Mina and Anna had finally left the protection of the Deltas family and were back with Londos' sister in Kolonaki. There, Londos would send them dangerous, and coveted, gifts: gold sovereigns and even fresh fish. It seems that despite George's earlier misgivings, Maro and Londos met on a number of occasions; at least once, Londos even came to see George himself, on official business, in Cairo.[67]

Towards the end of 1942, British propaganda statements had seemed to recognise the postwar rights of Bulgaria and Albania on an equal footing with those of Greece. When the mild remonstrances of Tsouderos in London were brushed aside, George and Kanellopoulos became furious. These were enemy countries; Bulgaria was even one of the three occupying powers in Greece. In the context of the war, in the first weeks after the decisive battle of El Alamein in October 1942, these were perhaps trivial concerns. But they were sufficient to provoke the first crisis between the Greek government in exile and its British hosts. At the end of 1942 Kanellopoulos flew to London. George thought it would be the 'crucial test of his [Kanellopoulos'] firmness and endurance;' his own view was that Kanellopoulos should resign unless British statements on the 'national question' were rescinded, though he drew back from saying so outright.[68]

But it was trouble in a different quarter that was to bring about Kanellopoulos' downfall, in the first months of the new year, and also to put George's own position and reputation in jeopardy. In occupied Greece, the previous September, the National Liberation Front had been formed (known by its Greek initials, EAM). This was the organisation behind the largest and most effective of the resistance groups, the National Popular Liberation Army. ELAS, as the latter was known, also by its Greek initials, enjoyed cautious British support, and had cooperated with British officers parachuted into Greece to blow up the Gorgopotamos viaduct in November 1942. The existence of EAM and its military wing, ELAS, as well as the increasing dominance of communists among their leadership, were becoming known among the Greeks in Egypt, and particularly in the two infantry brigades which, a month before the Gorgopotamos action, had distinguished themselves at El Alamein. Kanellopoulos had been invited to join EAM while still in Greece, but had refused. Now, as defence minister, he had an almost impossible balancing act to perform: many of the junior ranks in the brigades wanted the government to repudiate the legacy of the Fourth of August. The more radical of them were also beginning to demand alignment with EAM in Greece and the dismissal of officers whose political sympathies were either fascist or royalist or both. While the British had no love for the Metaxas inheritance either, Churchill in particular remained steadfast in his support of the Greek king, partly for traditional reasons, but also in recognition of what was seen as the king's loyalty to British interests during 1940–1. For his part, Kanellopoulos, in his memoirs, would defend his refusal to dismiss, on the grounds of their political beliefs, officers who had won battle honours in Albania or at El Alamein.[69]

217

The first signs of trouble came on 24 February 1943. By the first week of March, open mutiny had broken out in the two Greek brigades stationed in Egypt and Palestine. On 7 March, Kanellopoulos was heckled and his car stoned when he visited a military hospital; his driver suffered a knife wound and was captured by the rebels, who ended up having to treat him. The British intervened to contain the mutiny; 'the situation is well in hand,' as George ironically quoted an official statement of 12 March. The political fall-out was that Kanellopoulos resigned, and most of the higher echelons of government, including the prime minister, Tsouderos, were brought back from London so as to be closer to the action in Cairo.[70]

George had already begun to make enemies of his own. He was personally attacked in the strongly conservative Cairo Greek-language daily, *Fos* (*Light*), on a trivial pretext. Another conservative Greek-Egyptian, a newspaper editor who also had a post at the embassy press office, was apparently conspiring to oust him and take over his job. Although his diaries do not make this explicit, George was surely paying the price for his close association with Kanellopoulos, whom many Greeks, particularly the rank and file in the services, now saw as too right-wing, while the British, on the other hand, blamed him for having leant too far towards the liberals.[71]

The week before the new government was sworn in, George was in bed with flu. His absence from the office was considered in some quarters to be tactical, and may well have been. In the darkened seclusion of his hotel room, George mused on the fall of his friend. 'Kanellopoulos,' he wrote in his service diary, 'could have been an inspired poet – by that I don't mean a good poet.' Kanellopoulos was not, in George's perhaps surprising opinion in view of their closeness, fundamentally democratic. George privately reaffirmed his faith in 'the human dimension, as in the ancient city-states and in [the *Memoirs* of] Makriyannis.' It was this faith that he saw as lacking in Kanellopoulos.[72]

But with Kanellopoulos out of office, George was now at the mercy of both their enemies, as well as of what he saw as the arch-duplicity of Tsouderos: ' "*Divide* and rule." His weapon is to break things down; everything he does smells of putrefaction.' The decision to move George out of his post, and away from Cairo, seems to have been taken in the new government's first week of office. At first there was talk of Tehran, where in the end another, closer, associate of Kanellopoulos would be sent instead; by the middle of April a decree had been issued appointing George to the embassy in Ankara, with the rank of Counsellor. While Cairo was the Allied headquarters for the whole Middle East, and was soon to become the effective seat of the Greek government in exile, the embassy to neutral Turkey was a graveyard for minor or unwanted officials.[73]

It was not, however, the prospect of yet another move that provoked an unprecedented manifestation of fighting spirit in George. It was the discovery that his removal was being justified by labelling him a fascist and fellow-traveller of the Metaxas regime. In the peculiar circumstances of the time, the accusation probably meant little and would have been soon forgotten, not to say forgiven, in the service. Others, including Kanellopoulos, were being routinely smeared in the same way; in another context George had noted, with wry amusement, that 'fascist' in Cairo had come to mean no more than a term of abuse; someone had called Miller's *The Colossus of Maroussi* a 'fascist book,' meaning simply that he had not enjoyed it. In such company, George surely need not have worried.[74]

But George was incensed. The time had come for him to declare openly the political principles that he had hammered out and refined in private since 1935; in particular his wartime faith in the simple people of his country, and his contempt for those who claimed to rule in their name. He demanded a personal interview with the new Deputy Prime Minister. Georgios Roussos was seventy-five, which made him older than George's father. A lawyer with an impeccable old-liberal, Venizelist record as both ambassador and government minister, Roussos had long since retired to Alexandria, where he had become a figurehead for liberal republicanism, particularly among the well-off Greek business community. Leeper described him, for the benefit of the British Foreign Office, as 'old and a sick man and his mind is tortuous and in general it may be said that M. Roussos would be an unsatisfactory element in any Government.'[75]

This was the Deputy Prime Minister to whom George said:                         219

Mr Roussos, from my father I've been accustomed to hearing that you are a man of honour and justice. I call upon that man now. They can transfer me, they can do what they like with me; but I cannot permit my name to be sullied. . . . Now it is being said that I stayed with Nikoloudis [in Pretoria] because I am a fascist. I will react against this by all means in my power.

Roussos knew nothing of the case, but was not unsympathetic; all he had heard of George, he said, was that during the recent crisis his sympathies had appeared to be 'democratic.'[76]

Once again, George could have been appeased at this point. But having started, he would not stop. While on a daily basis he and Maro began their preparations for the move to Turkey, it was almost certainly during those same weeks that George set about what he must have conceived as a grand finale to his time in Egypt.

Back in March, he had been asked to prepare a speech to mark the death of the poet Palamas, who, at the age of eighty-three, had succumbed the previous month during the famine in occupied Athens. It was a simple, short address, hastily written out in the midst of other work, the first literary lines that George had written since returning to Cairo from Jerusalem the previous summer. Given on 10 March, the speech seems to have been well received, a fact that may have suggested to George an appropriate means of hitting back at his accusers now, on his own ground. There is no evidence that his next appearance as a public speaker was similarly commissioned; on the contrary, it seems to have involved the crucial mediation of Malanos and several others, apparently including even Roussos himself. George's second public speech was delivered at the Rialto cinema in Alexandria, to an audience of fourteen hundred, on 16 May; three days later he repeated it in Cairo; on that occasion the audience was 'unfortunately' only about five hundred. The subject of this talk was George's old hero, Makriyannis.[77]

The lecture, in the form in which it was soon afterwards published, was an emotive performance; it was also the first time that George had spoken out in public about matters of politics and history. Makriyannis is presented as the ideal case of the simple man of the people, innocent of book-learning or the scholastic tradition of its purveyors, a man of deep principle and direct utterance, which together confer on his *Memoirs* the authority almost of a sacred text. George makes much of the fact that his hero had taught himself to write, as an adult, for the express purpose of bearing witness to the struggle for independence in which he had played a significant part; he makes just as much of the General's misfortunes after the war had been won. One of the ringleaders of the bloodless revolution of 1843 which forced the German-born King Otto, the first king of Greece, to grant a constitution, Makriyannis had earned the undying enmity of the throne and the king's courtiers. Thrown into prison, beaten, and condemned to death, he had been reprieved and allowed to die in his house beneath the Acropolis of Athens, tormented by the wounds he had received in the struggle to wrest the citadel from its Turkish garrison thirty years before; George even invoked the shrunken, wizened appearance of Makriyannis' deathmask in the Ethnological Museum in Athens.

This essay has more often been read for its literary appropriation of Makriyannis as an authority-figure for George's generation than for its political content. Certainly, there are strategic literary claims made too. But the real thrust of the lecture was political from the first. George constantly reminded his audience that Makriyannis and his generation had fought against hopeless odds, in the name of freedom, and won; deftly he wove together the Greek struggle for independence in the 1820s with the war

220

that was now going on. His theme could not have been more patriotic; at the same time his handling of it was subtly, but unmistakably, partisan. Makriyannis, as hero and victim of injustice at the hands of a German-born king and a toadying political class, was held up before the audience as 'the conscience of an entire people.'[78]

The audience for this lecture, when it was first given in Alexandria, included Crown Prince (later King) Paul, who said to George afterwards, 'I didn't know these things.' Tsouderos and several members of the cabinet were also present; at the luncheon that followed, 'they looked daggers at us.' One of them asked George sardonically if he thought this would speed up his departure for Ankara. In Cairo, where no serving ministers came to hear him, he recorded colleagues from the Foreign Ministry 'edging away from me like rats from a sinking ship.' At least one, whom he took to be a Tsouderos man, understood the lecture as a direct attack on the prime minister.[79]

On the other hand, Kanellopoulos, from whom George seems to have distanced himself in recent weeks, wrote in his diary:

> Hardly ever has a lecture made such an impression on me. The subject was splendid − old, topical, and timeless − and Seferiadis was superb. A pity that the audience was relatively small. Thousands of Greeks ought to have heard Seferis talk about Makriyannis.

221

Not content with that, Kanellopoulos went to George's hotel three days later to congratulate him − and stayed for three and a half hours, reading to him the rest of his diary.[80]

But even now, George was still not satisfied. The day after he gave the lecture on Makriyannis for the second time, in Cairo, he wrote and typed out a seven-page letter to the new Deputy Prime Minister. Here, in the ugly language of official communications, George sets out more clearly than anywhere else the sequence of events that had brought his career to its present crisis, and also laid bare his political convictions at the time. The letter is not, of course, an unbiased document; it was written at a particular time and for a particular purpose; it begins and ends with the writer's barely contained rage at what he calls the whispering campaign against him. George does not contest his transfer to Ankara, but does insist on clearing his name. Though the injustice done to him hardly ranks with the tribulations of Makriyannis, clearly he felt that both were due to the same generic causes. His 'political ideas,' he declares, are certainly not in favour of dictatorship, nor are they aristocratic-republican; I favour people's rule [*laokratia*]. That is to say, I believe that the so-called upper class in Greece has been bankrupt for years and that the only policy that has hopes of succeeding is that which will be able to create new party members and new leaders arising from the heart of the people [*laos*]; that policy which . . . will try to liberate our people in social, economic and national terms. These are, in summary form, my political convictions, which I have not concealed, either now or in the past, and which readers of my literary work are in a position to diagnose . . .[81]

There is nothing in this statement to distance George's views at this time from the policy of the communist-dominated EAM. These opinions had surely not been fully formed before the outbreak of the European war, quite likely not even until he had arrived in Egypt. Though the deeper, and subtler, convictions expressed in the lecture on Makriyannis would never change, this was the only occasion on which George ever expressed himself in favour of 'people's rule.' But for the next year, his sympathies would be with the left-wing guerrillas fighting in Greece, and their supporters in

222 Egypt.[82]

He delivered this letter to Roussos, by hand, on 22 May, a week after his triumphant lecture on Makriyannis in Alexandria. Clearly, Roussos was impressed. Two weeks later the Deputy Prime Minister telephoned George personally, to tell him he would keep his job; a document of the same date abolished what was left of Metaxas' once notorious propaganda ministry and replaced it with the Central Press Service, answerable directly to the Deputy Prime Minister, Georgios Roussos. George was immediately appointed Director-General of the new service.[83]

He had survived one round of intrigue, but in order to do so had given hostages to fortune that would be used against him in the yet more serious crises of the following year. George's sense of deep disgust at the whole ordeal is carried over into the poem he wrote when it was over, with the Cavafian title 'Days of April '43.' The setting, given by the dateline, is the Greek government offices (today's Greek consulate) on Sharia Emad-el-Din. Surrounded by the noise and filth of Cairo, where the discarded melon-skins in the streets in the poem have the same metaphorical force in Greek as banana-skins in English, the solitary, unnamed hero 'goes forward,' an expression which recalls the earlier poem, 'An Old Man on the River Bank':

... carrying on his work and all the while
a thousand mangy dogs shred his trouser-legs
and leave him naked.
He goes forward, staggering, while fingers accuse on every side,
and a dense wind whips up round him
garbage, mule-dung, stench and slander.[84]

With the successful British and American landings in Sicily on 9 July 1943, the war entered a new phase. Soon, in September, Italy would capitulate; the only direct reference George made to these events was to report a newspaper headline on 26 July, the day after Mussolini had been arrested and imprisoned. Egypt was no longer in the front line. For months, in Cairo, there had been speculation about a new front in Europe. It came as a bitter blow to the Greeks to discover that the liberation of their country would not, after all, be a strategic objective for the Western allies.[85]

Less than two weeks later, George came across a group of workmen in his office block, in the act of striking a small stage-set that had been left behind by former tenants of the building. 'Why,' he wondered in his diary, 'does a particular impression *function* poetically, more than any of a thousand other daily impressions?' This one functioned, and on Friday 6 August he wrote the poem known in the standard translation as 'Actors, Middle East.' The Greek word is more disparaging: the Greek exiles, in this poem, are not actors, but mountebanks. The poem uses rhyme and regular metre to deadly satirical effect. It begins, 'We put up stage-sets, then we knock them down.' A caricature of a set of makeshift curtains, above which rises a royal crown, appears on the cover of one of George's published 'service' diaries of the period; the imagery of this poem would be taken up again in the frontispiece of the 1945 edition of *Logbook II*, by the left-wing artist Yannis Tsarouchis.[86]

While his countrymen squabbled among themselves in the make-believe world that Cairo had become, the war had moved on. Greece and Greek affairs, in Cairo, at the beginning of August 1943, had become a side-show; a stage-set to be conveniently struck and tidied away.

223

Τῆς Μαρῶς.

ΠΑΡΑ ΕΙΚΟΝΕΣ ΣΥΛΛΟΓΙΖΟΜΑΙ ΠΩΣ ΤΟΥΤΑ ΠΟΥ ΚΑΠΟΤΕ ΠΟΥ ΓΡΑΦΩ ΔΕΝ ΕΙΝΑΙ ΕΤΟ ΔΕΡΜΑ ΤΟΥΣ ΠΟΥ ΚΕΝΤΟΥΝ ΟΙ ΦΥΛΑΚΙΣΜΕΝΟΙ Ή ΠΕΛΑΓΙΣΙΟΙ.

The *calligramme* which opens *Logbook II* in the first, calligraphic edition (printed in the standard edition as the volume's dedication): 'For Maro. Sometimes I think that these things I write are nothing other than images tattooed on their skin by convicts or sailors.'

# 8
# 'The Pain-Perpetuating Memory of Pain'
# 1943-1944

And if I speak to you in fairytales and riddles
it is because they're sweeter in the hearing, and the horror
cannot be talked about because it is alive
because it is unspeaking and goes forward;
dripping by day, dripping into sleep
the *pain-perpetuating memory of pain*.

(*Logbook II*: 'Last Stop,' October 1944)

## Political and personal landscapes

It was not only in the West that the fortunes of war were decisively shifting during the summer of 1943. The German advance into Russia had been halted at Stalingrad; since January, Soviet forces had been pushing steadily westwards. George was not alone in wondering, at the end of that summer, what it would mean, for a Balkan country such as Greece, to be liberated by the Soviets.

Political tensions among the Greek exiles, and still more disastrously within Greece itself, were about to explode into internecine conflict. George first diagnosed the symptoms of the coming civil war in the unlikely surroundings of Shepheard's Hotel, the most elegant and fashionable venue in Cairo, at the end of August 1943.[1]

The catalyst for this observation had been the arrival in Cairo of an official delegation from the resistance organisations operating in Greece. The delegates had been flown out by the British, amid the greatest secrecy, from a specially constructed airstrip in the Greek mountains. They arrived on 9 August, and the next day were closeted in intense discussions with the British Ambassador, Sir Reginald (Rex) Leeper and other officials. The first inkling that George had of their arrival was the day after the meeting, when he was astonished to see, in the office that housed the Greek Foreign Ministry, the son of a well-known Venizelist politician, now a prominent member of EAM, 'as though descended from heaven.' The day following, he received a mysterious telephone call: George Kartalis would come to see him at his hotel that evening.[2]

George Kartalis was seven years younger than George. He came from a political background and had studied law and economics in Switzerland, Germany and at the London School of Economics; according to C.M. Woodhouse, who worked closely with him in the British Military Mission to occupied Greece, Kartalis 'could easily pass for an Englishman, a rather fruity aristocratic Englishman.' During the Metaxas years, Kartalis had fallen foul of the regime, and had become a frequent visitor to the top floor in Kydathinaion Street. The small band of partisans known as EKKA, after its initials in Greek, had become active, since early in 1942, in the Parnassos area of central Greece. Its military leader was Colonel Dimitrios Psarros, a veteran of the Greco-Italian war; its political guiding spirit was Kartalis. It had been under the roof of Kostakis and Ioanna Tsatsos, with their blessing and support, that much of the early planning for EKKA had gone on. It was this armed group that Kartalis had been brought by the British to Cairo to represent.[3]

No doubt, that evening, Kartalis had much to tell George about his family back in Athens. But Kartalis' main purpose was surely to brief him on the meeting that had taken place two days before, and the events in occupied Greece that had led up to it. Armed skirmishes had already broken out between ELAS, the military wing of the communist-dominated EAM, and the smaller independent groups, of which EKKA was one. The purpose of the meeting in Cairo, George would now have learned, had been to try to establish firm working relationships among the different resistance groups, and between each of them and the government in exile. In reality, however, there was only one thing that united all the resistance groups, and this was their opposition to the monarchy. The delegation had tried to force this issue with Leeper. But British policy remained firmly behind King George of Greece; the meeting had ended in stalemate. Its only effect had been to drive the rival groups farther apart, and to make more obvious than ever, to someone in George's position, how badly out of touch the exiled government was with its nominal subjects in Greece.

The arrival of the delegation from the resistance, as George commemorated it immediately in a poem, was like 'music,' 'the sound of a flute, / the sound of a distant drum' from the high mountains of home. It brought a breath of the freshest air to the dead and desiccated land of bones that was at once the Egyptian desert and the stale, moribund world of the exiled government. But the poem ends with a despairing cry for help; George understood all too well that the message from the mountains was not necessarily one of hope.[4]

During the days that followed, George visited the partisans in the eighth-floor flat where they had been housed. His diary describes them lying around in enforced idleness, in their underpants, while British officers and batmen came and went. Kartalis became ill, with a high fever; it took George's influence with Roussos to have him moved to the Greek Hospital. George went out socially with two other delegates, both communists; they were joined by Kanellopoulos. But it was Kartalis who impressed George as having the strongest intellect. 'He talks guerrilla warfare, politics, and psychoanalysis, all at the same time. Sometimes he seems so volatile, so divided in himself, it makes you want to scream.' Kartalis was also the only one who thought to ask 'the very simple question,' which by now was uppermost in George's mind too: 'How far are the allies going to let the Russians advance?'[5]

In the middle of September, the delegation was flown back to occupied Greece, with as much secrecy as when it had arrived. In his diary, George recorded his relief when he heard that Kartalis had reached Greece safely. If, as seems likely, the two Georges had not been particularly close before, a bond of some strength had been forged during the weeks that the delegation had been in Cairo. It is sometimes suggested that Kartalis had had a relationship with George's sister Ioanna; if there was any truth in this, it would most likely have dated from the early days of EKKA in 1942. There is no means of telling what George might have learned, or have guessed, from his conversations with Kartalis; but part of what bound the two men now, politically, was most probably the esteem in which each of them held Ioanna Tsatsou.[6]

With the delegation gone, the routine of George's life in Cairo returned. In October, news came from Greece of full-scale civil war in the mountains, between the communist-dominated forces of ELAS and its largest rival, known by the initials EDES. George, commenting in his service diary, was even-handed in apportioning blame, but reserved a large share of it for the British. It was they who had always insisted on monopolising communication between the mountains and the exiled government; this was the result.[7]

That autumn and through the crises that would follow in the spring, George found time for his own work. He began to plan the collected edition of his *Essays*, eventually published in Cairo at the end of March 1944. The edition was financed by two sisters, retired teachers who had made a small fortune by opening a milk-bar for British soldiers and expatriates in the city. The

227

sisters had been moved to this act of beneficence by hearing George lecture on Makriyannis.[8]

A more unusual publishing venture was the photographic reproduction of five handwritten poems by Sikelianos that had been circulating in a clandestine edition in occupied Athens, with the title *Akritika*. Roughly equivalent to *Frontier Songs*, this title alludes to a popular heroic tradition that goes back to the Byzantine middle ages. When a copy reached his office, George was inspired to disseminate Sikelianos' poetic act of defiance among the Greeks in Egypt. To this end, he enlisted the help of Malanos, and of an Armenian art photographer, Apkar, to whom Malanos had introduced him on his first visit to Alexandria. The result, using photo-offset technology that was new at the time, was a handsome reproduction of the volume in a hundred and fifty copies, produced in Alexandria and published in Cairo. George added his own handwritten preface, in which he hailed Sikelianos as the 'greatest Greek poet since the death of Palamas.'[9]

At this time, too, he was in regular contact with several of the group of British writers who since 1941 had been collaborating on the magazine *Personal Landscape*. The editors were Lawrence Durrell, Bernard Spencer and Robin Fedden, all of whom George had first met in Athens at the time of the 'war of nerves.' Each issue of *Personal Landscape* had opened with an item headed 'Ideas About Poems.' At the end of January, George wrote to Durrell, 'Your *Ideas about poems*, gave me this *Idea about poems*, which I feel obliged to communicate, very confidentially, to you.' Durrell responded, as no doubt he was meant to, with an enthusiastic offer of publication. The penultimate volume of the magazine, for 1944, opens with the 'Ideas about poems' of 'Mathaios Pascal.' Under this transparent mask, George proposed the genial theory that:

228

> Poems do not live alone. . . . Usually and normally poems form large crowds subject to special *sociological laws* . . . These social happenings in 'poemical' societies do not correspond necessarily to the accidents of our own human societies.[10]

This sense of a solidarity and kinship of poems, capable of transcending the boundaries and divisions of the world in which their authors have to live, was deeply felt by George at this time, and brought him close to the preoccupations of the British members of the group, who were also exiles. Years later, receiving the Foyle prize in London, he recalled this period when 'the goodwill and humour of *Personal Landscape* were among the few things that gave me comfort.'[11]

There was a practical side, too, to this interaction of poems. The previous year George had translated Durrell's poem 'Mythology;' soon, he would honour the translation with a guest appearance in the first edition of his own next book of poems, *Logbook II*.[12] Durrell returned the compliment, broadening the 'poemical society' further with the collaboration of Spencer. In the densest exchange of letters that exists between Durrell and George, during the early months of 1944, drafts of several of George's poems, in translation, passed back and forth from Cairo to Alexandria, marked extensively in Durrell's red ink. 'We are having trouble,' Durrell wrote to warn George, 'translating you so that you don't sound like Eliot.' The immediate result was the appearance of 'The King of Asine,' which Durrell described to George in another letter as 'a very great work,' in the same issue of *Personal Landscape* as contained 'Mathaios Pascal's' ideas about poems.[13]

George's temporary convergence and 'poemical' interaction with the work of the *Personal Landscape* poets was perhaps the single most important extraneous factor in establishing his future international reputation before the Nobel prize. Otherwise, though, it seems likely that he gave more than he took. George was the oldest of the group; the powerful combination of myth with the 'spirit of place,' established throughout the eight issues of *Personal Landscape*, surely owes much to his example, as well as to the conversation of Katsimbalis, in the mythical dimensions given it in the *Colossus of Maroussi*. It was precisely this combination of myth and a numinous sense of place that Durrell was to develop, after the war, in his best-known work, including *The Alexandria Quartet*. After a long period of critical neglect, the work of these exiled British poets during the Second World War, and particularly of Durrell, Spencer, G.S. Fraser, and Keith Douglas, would be claimed, at the end of the century, as 'the central [British] poetic achievement of the decade,' which 'should be acknowledged as a source of the dominant strain in postwar British poetry.'[14]

229

The fulcrum of these cross-cultural developments, which would reach far into the future, was George's friendship with Durrell, never closer than in the spring and summer of 1944. Durrell described George in a letter to Miller at this time as 'my best friend in Egypt,' but added:

> we almost never meet. It's as if meeting people who have real human demands to make of one is too tiring – or perhaps too guilt-making since we are both involved in this web of idiocy and panic – and I don't see what sort of political future waits for Greece.[15]

George, with his greater political acumen and firsthand experience, by this time had a good idea of what the political future held for his country, and was now more bitterly critical than ever of official British policy towards it. This was the reason, although he kept it to himself, why in May 1944 he refused to take part in a collaborative volume with Durrell, Liddell, R.D. Smith, Olivia Manning, and Harold Edwards dedicated to *The Age of Eliot.* 'My reaction: to send them to the devil, . . . after everything we've seen these last few months,' he wrote in his diary.[16]

For George, the good fellowship of 'poemical societies,' and the largely apolitical vigour of his English friends, could be little more than a welcome distraction. As early as February 1944, he had written to Durrell:

I don't want to care any more about personal landscapes or personal preservatives, whatever you call them; the only thing you can give me is . . . some knowledge of the English tongue. I need it in order to explain to this english speaking era which we are entering the rights of my *personal* Country.[17]

George's own poetic landscape could never be merely 'personal.'

230

### Greek against Greek

The year 1944 had begun with George and Maro moving out of their crowded, cramped hotel into a flat close to the Greek government offices in Sharia Emad-el-Din. 'For the first time since June '42,' he noted in his diary, 'a home of our own. For how long, I wonder?'[18]

As the government that he served drifted steadily towards dissolution, George was kept busier than ever. The flow of information was one of the few areas in which the government had a huge and daily task; in practice, this meant the control of information. But his heart was less and less in it; when Roussos, who had helped him clear his name, was dropped from the government at the end of January, George began seriously to think how to 'rid myself of this job, that's becoming dirtier by the day.' He was now reassigned to the Foreign Ministry as Press Director; his job and responsibilities remained the same. It was from this period that his younger colleague, Angelos Vlachos, would later remember him as 'pessimistic and grumbling about everything and everybody': 'The situation made him bitter but he responded with passivity.'[19]

Then in March came the crisis. On the 17th, George must have been among the first in Egypt to learn of the formation, only a week before, of a provisional free government in Greece. Known by its Greek initials PEEA, the new government was dominated by EAM, whose military wing, ELAS, controlled by far the largest share of territory liberated by the resistance. Greece now had no fewer than four seats of government. In Athens there was the quisling government of Ioannis Rallis, which was of course wholly subservient to the Germans. Then there was the official government in exile, with its prime minister in Cairo, which in practice was scarcely less subservient to the British, a fact further emphasised since its titular head was King George II, two thousand miles away in London, which made a third seat of government. Now, in the Greek mountains, came the new provisional government. The government in exile, whether in Cairo or in London, had always had a problem with legitimacy. Constituted as it had been out of the rump of the authoritarian regime of the Fourth of August, it had never enjoyed a popular mandate, and had almost no direct contact with its notional subjects in Greece. Now, faced with a rival about which little was known, but which seemed to have the enormous advantage of being in close touch with the people it claimed to govern, the exiled government and its British backers faced their greatest crisis of the war.[20]

George's office was allowed to announce the formation of the new government only on 26 March, the day after the official Independence Day celebrations; but rumour was ahead of him, and the celebrations were overshadowed in Cairo and Alexandria by jubilant demonstrations in favour of the provisional free government in Greece. The minister for the navy, Sophocles Venizelos (the son of Eleftherios), sent for George on the 30th to give him the text of a radio broadcast he was due to make at the weekend on the subject; George asked him if Tsouderos had approved it. 'The British,' George told the minister, 'want to know if the Greek government is unanimous.' When the broadcast went out on Saturday 1 April, it was obvious to George that Venizelos was stabbing his prime minister in the back. Afterwards, George asked Venizelos what had happened to the deputation of officers from the Greek army, navy and air force that had called on Tsouderos the previous day to demand cooperation with the provisional government in Greece. 'They've been arrested,' was the reply.[21]

Two days later, George was summoned to Tsouderos' office, and handed the draft of an announcement. 'The president of the Greek government, Mr E. Tsouderos, . . . has decided to submit his resignation to His Majesty the King . . . and has requested the King to accept his resignation and assign the presidency of the government to Mr S. Venizelos, Minister for the Navy.' Tsouderos asked for comment. George pointed out that if he had already submitted his resignation to the king, then the first part of the announcement could not stand. 'All right, then, *has submitted,*' conceded Tsouderos – 'as though,' George adds, 'he was only then seeing the reality.'[22]

On 5 April, George released to the Egyptian Greek-language newspapers the king's acceptance of Tsouderos' resignation; Venizelos was now charged with forming a government. But Venizelos had already resigned on his own account. The reason, according to an official order of the day released to the navy, was that the king had insisted on Tsouderos remaining as prime minister. George was in no doubt that Venizelos was the author of this order of the day, which was as inflammatory as it was untrue. The Greek armed forces in the Middle East now came out in open mutiny.[23]

This was a much more serious crisis than the one that had brought down Kanellopoulos the year before. With silent sarcasm, George once again recorded, in English, the laconic words of his official informant: 'Situation well in hand.' The now headless Greek government in exile did not have the situation in hand at all. Venizelos seemed to George to panic. 'He has a graze on his forehead. Short as he is, he looks like a schoolboy emerging from a bout of fisticuffs.' Since Venizelos refused to form a government, the entire cabinet resigned, and called on Roussos, who was old and ill, to take over. But no sooner was George about to release Roussos' reluctant statement accepting office, than it was suddenly embargoed by the British. The king had announced his imminent departure from London for Cairo, and assigned the premiership to Venizelos, who had already refused it. While the entire Greek political class in Cairo, in and out of government, manoeuvred to evade responsibility, George noted with despair the worsening situation in the armed forces, where the first casualties had been reported among the mutineers.[24]

As he summed up his feelings on 5 April:

> . . . the only thing that's going forward is this chaos of ours that's blowing up, blowing up with astonishing rapidity, without any of those who've a part to play in this tempest even trying to stop it. On the contrary, each one unleashes his own flask of evil winds. The two extremes are working together marvellously and we're like the Girondins, . . . condemned to the guillotine by both sets of fanatics.

As the situation continued to unravel, George was convinced that, of the two extremes, it was the 'far right' that had the upper hand. Within days, known supporters of the left in Cairo, including some of his friends, were being rounded up and deported to Asmara in Eritrea.[25]

The arrival of King George in Cairo, on 11 April, solved nothing, and the crisis dragged on. George was enraged to be handed communiqués by the British embassy, on behalf of the Greek government, only to find that the ministers of that goverment did not even know what was in them. His liaison officer at this time was Captain David Balfour, who before the war had been an Orthodox monk on Mount Athos with the name of Father Dimitris, and was now working for the Intelligence Service. George railed against

> this tragedy which has been created by half a dozen bastards who would-n't have been up to selling peanuts in the Zappeion gardens and have turned up here to rule the fortunes of Greece for no other reason than that they can stumble over five words of Greek and belong to a great power.

It was, he had declared, a few days previously, again in the privacy of his service diary, 'quite intolerable to find myself suddenly the megaphone or the alibi of Mr Balfour, or whoever else of his ilk, who's going to direct the Greek affairs of my section from behind my back.'[26]

For GHQ Cairo, which was after all a military organisation with a military purpose in wartime, the suppression of the mutinies in the Greek infantry and navy was of more urgent importance than understanding their political causes. George seems to have been unaware of the potentially far more serious threat, from the British point of view, of unrest among the Egyptians which came to a head at the same time as the Greek mutinies; seen in that context, their suppression served a political purpose to which the Greeks were only incidental. On the day of the king's arrival in Cairo, George recorded in his diary his outburst to a colleague, in which he spelt out the reponsibilities of the British, as he saw them, for this new 'Anglo-Greek war':

> Who organised the partisans? Who brought the delegation from the partisans only to behave so disgracefully towards them afterwards? Who made such a mess of the business of the King? In such difficult times they've managed to create an amount of ill-feeling among the Greeks that even their worst enemy wouldn't have wished on them. . . . We've warned them, we've told them in every possible way, ever since the Albanian campaign we've never stopped telling them. It's had no effect.[27]

233

On 22 April, three Greek naval ships in the harbour of Alexandria that had refused to put to sea were stormed by a force of cadets loyal to Admiral Voulgaris, the commander of the fleet who had been co-opted into the government as the new minister for the navy. Two days later, the First Infantry Brigade, whose camp had been surrounded for three weeks by British tanks, surrendered their weapons. The mutiny was all but over. From the newspaper *Fos*, George transcribed the account of the obsequies for those who had been killed during the storming of the ships at Alexandria:

*Six coffins were draped with the colours of the glorious Royal [Hellenic] Navy . . . Copious flowers and garlands were placed on these six only. Three other coffins were bare, unadorned, without a single flower, displaying for all to see the implacable retribution . . .*

George commented: 'Pillorying the dead. Worse: a mistake. If only they'd read Aeschylus: "the pain-perpetuating memory of pain" – the fools.' In the violent suppression of the April mutinies, George saw a violation of the immutable law of balance in nature which, at the beginning of the war, he had found in the Pre-Socratic philosophers and in Aeschylus.[28]

234  But it was no longer a solution for George to side, as he had tended to do since leaving Greece, with the left. On the very same day, he learned for certain that, in Greece, Kartalis' close friend Dimitrios Psarros, the military leader of the resistance group EKKA, had been murdered after his group had been ambushed and scattered by ELAS. Before long, further details of actual or alleged atrocities by ELAS would provoke George to 'sorrow and anger.' Here, too, the Heraclitean 'measure' had been overstepped; here too was inhumanity. There was also the integrity of postwar Greece to consider. Prompted, perhaps, by that prescient remark of Kartalis, the previous August, about the extent of the Russian advance into the Balkans, George several times noted in his diary, while the mutinies were still going on, the fundamental differences between the British and their Soviet allies that they were bringing into the open. The danger of a clash between the victorious powers, with Greece as the hapless backdrop, was already becoming apparent to him. He blamed Russian propaganda for encouraging the mutineers and their supporters with false hopes; he blamed his communist friends for believing them.[29]

On Tuesday 25 April, after the suppression of the mutinies and the fall of an interim government which had been briefly headed by Venizelos after all, there was 'once again a crisis without a Government, who knows for how many days.' In putting it like this, George was less than generous to the *deus ex machina*, as many now regarded him, who had just entered the stage. This was George Papandreou, who had opportunely arrived from Greece ten days earlier, and to whom the king had that day given a mandate to form a government.[30]

Papandreou had the advantages of a commanding presence and a liberal-republican background that included a range of ministerial experience under the elder Venizelos. Papandreou's recent statements combined a left-of-centre political stance with a tough stand against the communist-dominated EAM and its military wing ELAS. Having made the obligatory adjustment to his position over the monarchy, Papandreou quickly won the endorsement of both the British prime minister, Winston Churchill and, in America, of President Roosevelt. In Cairo there was the inevitable jockeying about who would serve and under what conditions, but by his second day in office, there was no longer any doubt that Papandreou was in firm control.

The new prime minister's combination of toughness and flexibility was thought by many at the time to offer the best, if not the only, solution to the problems that now faced the Greek government in exile; the opinions of later historians tend to endorse this view. George disliked Papandreou from the first. The reason for this was not primarily political. There was nothing in Papandreou's eight-point programme for the establishment of a transitional coalition government to oversee the liberation of Greece, to which George could consistently have taken exception, unless perhaps the question of the future role of the monarchy, that had been expressly shelved. But George would inveigh sarcastically against the 'Lebanon Charter,' as this programme became known, and what he saw as the absurd position of Papandreou once it had been signed by all parties the following month: on the one hand owing his power to an anti-communist platform; on the other, throughout the summer of 1944, through a combination of expediency and strong British pressure, obliged to seek an accommodation with EAM.[31]

George's first two meetings with Papandreou, as he recorded them in his service diary, have a strong element of caricature. The new prime minister emerges as pompous, vainglorious, inconsistent and incapable of attending to detail. During the following months, George could scarcely mention Papandreou in his diary without a dig at the longwinded posturing of his speeches, his 'voice histrionically throbbing,' his 'ranting like a drunk.' During these first days, George's diary placed greater than usual weight on

235

the negative whispers that he picked up in corridors. His Greek colleagues were openly mocking Papandreou, he claimed; it must have been from a British source that he heard the comment, quoted in English: 'a straw-man, not a strong man.' Within days, George had become convinced that Papandreou was 'just another Tsouderos.'[32]

From none of this could one guess that George Papandreou, whether likeable or not, would prove himself during the next quarter century one of the few democratic politicians of undoubted stature in Greece, coming closest among his generation to inheriting the mantle of Venizelos, and bequeathing to the country a parliamentary dynasty that would dominate the country's political life in the last decades of the twentieth century and beyond. The reason for George's antipathy was personal and professional: one of Papandreou's first actions on assuming the premiership had been, in effect, to sack him.

George probably over-reacted when Papandreou told him, on his first day in office, that he was suspending the entire personnel of the Press Office. The day after, having been asked by the new prime minister for a confidential memorandum on his staff, George mounted, instead, a strong defence of himself and of his office collectively. At the same time, he tendered his resignation. On 28 April, he stopped signing official documents. Instead, he composed three lengthy memoranda. One was a formal letter to Papandreou reiterating the nature and difficulties of the work he had been doing in Cairo, and demanding a response to his offer of resignation. Another was the written memorandum on the Press Office that Papandreou had demanded the day before. The third was a formal request to the Foreign Ministry to transfer him to other duties. George then went for an anti-typhus vaccination and retired to bed for twenty-four hours. While there, he polished the text of his three official letters, before despatching them by hand of his trusted friend and junior colleague, Alexandros Xydis. George's resignation as Press Director was curtly accepted by Papandreou on 3 May.[33]

Just as had happened the previous year, when he had been about to lose his job, George was now subjected to rumours and smears in the Egyptian Greek press. In the 'new wind' that was blowing through the Greek civil service since the suppression of the mutinies and the arrival of Papandreou, he found himself cold-shouldered by colleagues in a way that reminded him of the anti-Venizelist reprisals of 1935. Months later, he would acknowledge that there were people in high places 'who still haven't forgiven me for my lecture on Makriyannis, the same ones who pushed for my dismissal by Papandreou.' Having all but lost his job a year before because of his alleged sympathies with the right, George had now been ousted for leaning too far towards the left – and this, ironically, at the very moment when he had ceased to trust EAM.[34]

A week after his resignation, he recorded an exchange with his French opposite number:

> 'Strange,' he said, 'up to now your office has been accused of being conservative, now of being leftwing, it's strange – I don't understand it.'
>
> 'Perhaps you should understand it's because we've done a good job,' I said.[35]

The events of April 1944 had brought George as close to breaking point as he ever came. He suffered from insomnia for the first time in his life, and had to use sleeping pills. During sleepless hours, he had set himself to copy out, in a calligraphic hand, with illustrations, the poems that would become *Logbook II*; 'it remains a psychological mystery to me how I managed to do this thing,' he would write in his diary, shortly afterwards. Whether in the heat of these events, or more likely earlier, he had conceived his own next publication which was now almost ready along the same lines as that of Sikelianos' *Akritika*: a calligraphic manuscript reproduced by photo-offset technology. For the title page of the volume, he drew a more naturalistic version of the mermaid with the forked tail that had been printed on all his publications since *Turning Point*; emblematic of the times is the fact that her arms are truncated at the wrists, a cruel visual realisation of the image in poem 3 of *Mythistorema*, 'my hands disappear and come towards me / truncated.'[36]

More than ever, after the events of April, George seems to have experienced the need to explain and justify himself. In the previous crisis, he had addressed himself to Roussos, the deputy prime minister. But there was no one, now, among the politicians to whom he could turn and expect a hearing. Ironically enough, he was now on relatively friendly terms with Tsouderos, but there would have been no point, now, in trying to defend himself to the ousted prime minister, who had once reminded him of the down-at-heel pelican in Cairo Zoo.[37]

The unsuspecting victim of George's ire turned out to be his Alexandrian friend, Timos Malanos. The quarrel that now erupted was both revealing, and long-lasting in its consequences. The pretext was apparently trivial. On 9 May, George received a letter from Malanos. This was the letter that contained the proposal to collaborate on a volume about Eliot; it begins with a glancing reference to recent events. 'Happily,' wrote Malanos, before turning to more congenial topics, 'there is also Literature.' 'I disagree with you profoundly,' George rounded on his friend by return of post, and proceeded to elaborate the grounds of his disagreement in two further long letters, written on successive days.

Literature, George insisted, is not, by its very nature, something that can exist 'happily' or 'unhappily':

> Art is not the great forgetting, art is the great consciousness, and it isn't a consolation, it's a torment, it's a struggle. . . . Art for me is something out there and I serve it, because I cannot do otherwise.[38]

Art, George rammed home his argument, is an uncompromising public duty. But so too was his 'other job,' his professional one. You, he rounded on Malanos, are a man of letters and you also work for your living, but you do so only because you have to; you owe no obligation beyond what you're paid to do:

238

> I, on the other hand . . . serve my country, whose people are taxed in order to pay me. This service too I have carried out and do carry out in no amateurish way, but seriously, very seriously. . . . I have colleagues who exert themselves to secure large dowries, to use their position for social ostentation, or even to land sinecures. I have not done this. If I had had any such inclination, I could have taken care to stay in Pretoria, where I had the spare time that literature (*happily*) filled. Instead I came to Cairo. . . . To this 'other job' of mine, you must know, I've devoted great care and competence . . . and if something goes wrong in this work, it's not some commercial blip . . . , it's something that affects those 'common interests' that I've assumed the obligation to serve with dignity and with pride. . . . This is why, my dear Timos, the last six years I've worked harder at my public service than at least 90% of my colleagues, day and night. . . .[39]

The 'aesthete' Malanos may have wondered why his friend should find it necessary to justify his *professional* conduct to him, of all people. But George had not finished yet. The next day he returned to the attack. Echoing, in starker terms, what he had already written for *Personal Land-*

scape, about the congress of poems in ' "poemical" societies,' George insisted: 'For me, art is not an isolated recreation. It consists in interaction with others.' As a craftsman, only, he might crave solitude in order to confront the technical demands of his craft; 'but this does not mean that I turn my back on life.' Bitterly, he accused Malanos of taking refuge from the world in literature, in the 'ivory tower' which George, slightly disingenuously, now declared that he himself had left behind him 'around 1928.' Furiously repudiating this stigma that had been attached to his own first published work, George declared:

> It might surprise you if I tell you that the event that has affected me more than anything is the Asia Minor disaster [of 1922]. Another event, that has affected me a good deal (I mean to an exceptional degree, fundamentally) is this war and the ordeal of my country and my family caught up in this whirlwind. . . . Perhaps it will enlighten you further if I add that from the age of 13 I've never ceased to be a refugee.[40]

On the surface, the rift with Malanos was soon healed. But both men were by nature obstinate, and both could be equally touchy. Malanos gave due warning when he replied, 'You don't shut me up just by being clever. I can be clever too.' The offending phrase, Malanos protested, had been written in a spirit of friendly consolation, and George had taken it upon himself to preach a sermon. Five years later, George's outburst would still rankle with Malanos. Announcing to George his forthcoming book on his work, Malanos would explicity revive the terms of their quarrel in 1944:

> I'm well. As well as an intellectual can be. But happily there is poetry, there is literature. I know you don't like this phrase, but I find it consoling. Perhaps at the end of March [1950] I'll be able to send you my little book on the poet Seferis.[41]

When he did, it would sever their relations for good.

George's outburst to Malanos, that May, has an importance far beyond the relationship of the two men. It shows just how far George had travelled from the reluctant 'servant of two masters,' who had so bitterly grudged the time and effort expended on his legal studies in Paris and on the undemanding duties of his first years in the service of the Foreign Ministry in Athens and London. In the aftermath of the events of April 1944, and of everything that had led up to them, he found it necessary to justify himself

239

equally in the service of *both* exacting masters. These letters to Malanos capture a rare moment of revelation, for George, in which the deepest allegiances and motivation of the 'I' of Skala and the 'I' of Smyrna, of the private poet and the public servant, turn out to be not antithetical but similar, if not identical, after all. It was the most explicit realisation by George of a process that had begun in the mid 1930s, with *Mythistorema*, and still more with the first politically charged poems that had followed it. It was a process that would reach its culmination in the poems of the next two years, 'Last Stop' and *'Thrush,'* and be continued a decade later in the poems that he dedicated to the people of Cyprus.

### Doodlebugs, London

George now had no official role, though as a senior civil servant he remained in Cairo, on the strength of the Foreign Ministry. The Lebanon Conference of 17–20 May 1944, attended by high-level delegates from both the provisional government in Greece and the exiled government in Cairo, at last produced the government of 'national unity' that most interested parties had been demanding since the end of March. George was one of the reception committee when the delegates arrived from Beirut, after the conference, at the aerodrome outside Cairo. Among them were Kartalis, with fresh details of the murder of his friend Psarros, and other excesses by communist forces in Greece. Also with them was Angelos Angelopoulos, a committed member of EAM who was married to George's cousin Elli (Seferiadi), and who brought him news from home.[42]

The talents of the thirty-six-year-old Kartalis were widely recognised, although he was too much the individualist to make, or to keep, many political friends in Cairo. The government of national unity included a new portfolio of Press and Information, to which Kartalis was appointed as Minister on 8 June. This was the ministry under which George's former office now came. In the circumstances, George could hardly return to the post that he had left so acrimoniously only a month before, even if Papandreou would have allowed it. Instead, he was at once co-opted, informally, to become what Kartalis called, in English, his 'oriental secretary.' It seems to have been Kartalis' initiative to arrange an official visit to London as soon as possible, to try to explain the position of the new Greek government to Churchill and his Foreign Secretary, Anthony Eden, as well as to the British parliament and press. Despite objections from Papandreou, Kartalis made it a condition of his going that he should be accompanied by George.[43]

The journey was not without risks; London was now under attack from V1 flying bombs, known popularly as 'doodlebugs.' Before he went, George sent his calligraphic, illustrated manuscript of the poems he had written since leaving Greece to the photographer, Apkar, in Alexandria. Then, on his way to the airfield, he left with Maro a note for Malanos, asking him to call on Apkar to collect a 'surprise.' Just as he had hastened his poetic 'testament' through press in the months before the war came to Greece, so now, in the worst case, *Logbook II* could still be published for posterity. He was anxious, too, about leaving Maro on her own; it was the first time. 'Fortunately, she's being brave about it,' he noted in his diary.[44]

It was a twenty-four hour journey to London, by air, with a brief stop and change of aircraft at Rabat, in Morocco. During the flight, George read Kafka's *The Castle*, and thought its theme appropriate to the mission on which he was engaged with Kartalis, to gain the ear of the highest powers of the British empire. The second leg of the journey was markedly uncomfortable, in the bomb-hold of a converted Liberator where, despite extra clothes and two blankets, George woke up frozen, to hear one of the RAF attendants announcing, 'We are over England.' They landed in a cold English summer dawn, at an undisclosed location, which turned out to be outside Swindon. The journey through flat green fields to Paddington seemed to George to take him back in time. He recorded the comment of the lieutenant-colonel in liaison, a Scotsman, who accompanied them on the train: 'England never changes. England is always sleepy.' Paddington, when they reached it, was full of women and children being evacuated: these were the early days of the V1 attacks.[45]

At first, the visit went well. Thanks to able briefing and liaison work by C.M. (Monty) Woodhouse, who had succeeded Brigadier Myers as commander of the British Military Mission to occupied Greece in December 1943, Kartalis had a series of meetings with political figures all the way up to Churchill. His press conference on 1 August was widely reported and according to George a real success. But for all his political and intellectual sympathies with Kartalis, George was struck once again, in the close proximity brought about by their mission, by a fundamental weakness in Kartalis' character. 'A man of exceptional abilities who spreads himself too thinly, wastes his energies, then falls apart. He must find it difficult to keep serious people close to him,' George commented in his diary – surely a damning indictment of any would-be political leader. Twice, in his diary, George called Kartalis a 'nihilist.' Immediately on arriving in London, Kartalis had taken up with a girlfriend from his days at the London School of

Economics, and would often disappear for the night. Later in the visit, George recorded his companion's seemingly manic changes of mood, from boundless energy to terrible fatigue; Kartalis needed regular doses of drugs, George noticed, and by the end of the visit was running a high fever, for the second time in their acquaintance.[46]

During these weeks in London, it was not all business for George. Thanks to some of the friendships he had made since, he was now able to make the contacts in the literary world that had been denied him as a young consular official back in the early 1930s. A link was the poet and philosopher Demetrios Capetanakis, who had belonged to the Kydathinaion Street circle before he moved to England early in the war. Capetanakis had attracted the attention of John Lehmann, the independent-minded publisher whose series 'Penguin New Writing' would soon become enormously influential in Britain. At this time, in 1944, Capetanakis had just died, tragically young, from leukaemia; Lehmann decided to host a lunch at the Savoy Hotel to raise funds for a posthumous book of Capetanakis' poetry in English. George was invited, and enthusiastically supported the project. Lehmann recorded this first meeting:

242

> I was impressed by his charm, by his immense knowledge of everything that was going on in poetry all over the world, and by the look of brooding, philosophical reflection in the large dark-brown eyes under the domed brow.[47]

There came an anxious moment during lunch, when a doodlebug passed close overhead. None of those present, according to Lehmann, behaved so indecorously as to take cover under the table. It was the start of an acquaintance that would be crucial in launching George as a poet in English translation after the war. Also in London, he met Cyril Connolly, the influential editor of *Horizon*, the poet Stephen Spender, the writer Dilys Powell and her husband Leonard Russell, who was editor of the *Sunday Times* books page.[48]

George and Kartalis were invited to spend a weekend with the family of David Wallace, at their country estate. Wallace had been British press attaché in Athens at the beginning of the war, when he had worked with George, not always easily; their paths had crossed again since, in Cairo. On their departure from Egypt, George and Kartalis had shared a darkened lorry with Wallace, who had been in uniform, on a mission to occupied Greece as representative of the Foreign Office. Now the green hills of the park and the easy hospitality of Wallace's aristocratic family afforded George a sense of playing truant from school, and made him feel at ease. Less than a month after George's visit to his family in England, Wallace was killed in Greece.[49]

In London, George and Kartalis were staying at the Ritz, in Piccadilly. Their suite was on the fifth floor: 'very close to the flying bombs, I suppose,' George observed in his diary when they arrived. To Maro, he wrote that they were on the first floor, and made no mention of the doodlebugs. In his diary, he noted with clinical precision the sound of the rocket's engine: 'like a motor-cycle, until suddenly it cuts out;' the tall plume of black smoke, without fire, that was caused by vaporisation when it exploded. Close to where one had fallen, the trees were devoid of green, as though their leaves had been stripped with a knife. On one of his first nights at the Ritz, he lay awake until after three, counting the explosions in the vicinity of the hotel. He then slept through the rest of the raid, which continued until morning. The waiter who brought him his breakfast told him it had been 'one of the worst nights since the war began.' He found it consoling to compare notes with the head-porter of the Ritz, who turned out to be a Greek from Crete and also called George. Everyone's nerves were bad.[50]    243

It was not a good time to be visiting London. Despite the warm official reception given to Kartalis, the political timing of the visit turned out to be unfortunate too. Since the D-Day landings, just over a month before, most people in Britain had had their attention concentrated on the Allied advance in France. The political future of Greece, after the German retreat which was now generally reckoned to be imminent, was a small matter by comparison. Even within the political world of Greek affairs, Kartalis' mission was upstaged by two events about which he and George learned only belatedly, and at second hand. The first was a Russian delegation to the mountain headquarters of the provisional government in Greece, an event to which Kartalis had to make an off-the-cuff response before he had had time to consult with the government in Cairo. The second, and more important, was the sudden breakthrough in relations between Papandreou and EAM, which was announced on 7 August. To George's intense frustration, the day was a Bank Holiday Monday in England; offices were closed and everybody of importance was away in the country. The plan, until now, had been for Kartalis to follow up his success in London by going on to America; George already knew that he would not be accompanying him: 'those close to the palace have begun to find that I'm not the most suitable adviser for Kartalis,' was his sardonic comment on his immediate recall to Cairo. There had even been talk of Kartalis going to Moscow, but this seems to have been vetoed by the Foreign Office.[51]

By the time Kartalis and George had been three weeks in London, the entire position and composition of the Greek government of national unity, based in Cairo, had shifted. Nobody in London had seen fit to brief Kartalis about the imminent rapprochement between Papandreou and EAM, which was being vigorously brokered throughout the time when Kartalis was there; Kartalis' continuing hostility to the communists was more intellectually consistent than Papandreou's flexibility, but it was Kartalis who now found himself isolated: too far to the left for the comfort of most of his colleagues in Cairo, but also resolute in his refusal to work with the communist-dominated EAM, at a time when cooperation was the official policy of Papandreou, the communists, and the British.[52]

The only thing left for the Minister of Press and Information to do was head back to Cairo, taking his 'oriental secretary' with him; there was no more talk of either Washington or Moscow. If an unstated aim of Kartalis' mission to London had been to outmanoeuvre his prime minister and gain political ground with the British, it had backfired badly. A few months later, George was certainly not an impartial observer when he thought that Papandreou was afraid of Kartalis; but a recent political assessment confirms that Kartalis at the time did have all the credentials to have mounted a serious challenge to the prime minister. It can be assumed, in the light of everything he wrote about Papandreou, that if there had been such an agenda, it would have had George's strong approval and support. There is perhaps a hint of this in the fact that, in London, at the same time as he was lamenting the fact that all the official code-books for exchanging telegrams with Cairo were known to have been broken, George was also receiving messages for Kartalis from political friends in Cairo, using an improvised code of their own.[53]

On his return to Cairo, almost the first person George met, after Maro, was his brother-in-law, Kostakis Tsatsos, who had escaped from Greece. A telegram in London had led him to expect his brother Angelos to be with him; it turned out to be his cousin, Alekos Seferiadis, who had made the journey with Kostakis via Syria. Another new arrival was the young poet Nanos Valaoritis, who had travelled by way of Izmir and brought for George the first number of the latest (and final volume) of *Ta Nea Grammata*, that Katsimbalis had managed to bring out under the Occupation. Soon, Valaoritis was on his way to London, where George put him in touch with his recent contacts in the literary world. The foundations were now fully in place for the collaboration of Durrell, Spencer and Valaoritis that would result in George's first book to be published in English.[54]

In Greek government circles, the confusion during the second half of August was greater than ever. At first George thought he was being sent to the embassy in Beirut; then he was recalled to the Foreign Ministry, employed there directly for the first time since the end of 1937. It was a strange sensation after so long; but there seemed nothing for him to do. The antipathy that he felt for the new Under-Secretary for Foreign Affairs, Philippos Dragoumis, who was a close associate of Papandreou, appears to have been mutual. Within days, he was again told he was being transferred to Beirut. The liberation of Greece was awaited daily. When the news broke that the government would be moving, not to Greece, but temporarily to southern Italy, George was unsure even whether to believe it. After a further round of crises, in the course of which three ministers resigned, George learned that he would be going to Italy after all. It would not, he conceded in his diary, be the most comfortable, but 'may God grant it turns out the quickest route home.'[55]

September began with hectic preparations for departure. As they would be sailing from Alexandria, there would be a chance to arrange with Malanos for the printing, from Apkar's photographs, of the calligraphic manuscript of *Logbook II*. The ship waiting for the Greek exiles in the western harbour of Alexandria, the *Durban Castle*, was intolerably crowded, with three and a half thousand people on board. They embarked on Saturday 9 September, but did not sail for another two days. The first night at sea, George stood on deck, watching the stars. The shape of Scorpio, and its 'violet-coloured' heart, Antares, he thought had been following him, or he had been following it, ever since South Africa. In his diary, he promised himself to write 'something with the title: "Beneath the constellation Scorpio."' This would have been a perfectly possible title for the poem that he began during that voyage, and would eventually become the fitting finale to *Logbook II*, with the title 'Last Stop.' The 'heart of Scorpio' would return, two years later, as an emblem of the war that was now over, in '*Thrush*'.[56]

## Cava dei Tirreni

The final seat of the exiled Greek government turned out to be the village of Cava dei Tirreni, in the hills above Salerno, south of the Bay of Naples.

After so long in Egypt, this seemed to George a strangely displaced homecoming. Here was a familiar landscape of sea and mountains; the first rains of autumn were the first real signs of changing seasons that he had seen since leaving South Africa. With Maro, he made excursions to Naples and the ancient sites nearby. At Paestum, that in antiquity, before the rise of Rome, had been the Greek colony of Poseidonia, the three Doric temples reminded him of Aphaia, in Aegina, and made him feel 'astonishingly . . . at home in this Mediterranean terrain.' In the streets and houses of Pompeii, preserved through the centuries by the volcanic ash that had destroyed the town almost two thousand years before, George felt less a stranger than he had in many inhabited towns and cities where he had been recently. At Amalfi, the medieval trading port tucked into almost sheer cliffs, he recognised the Byzantine workmanship in the mosaics in the church of Sant'Andrea; here, he was back in his own 'climate,' in Europe, after the 'inhuman life of exile.' It mattered to George to find himself back in a Christian country after his years in the Middle East; twice in his diary at this time his thoughts even strayed idly towards the idea of becoming a monk.

Italy was like Greece but was not Greece; Greece itself remained 'like an island of Utopia,' still out of reach. George saw these weeks in Italy as a kind of preparation; everywhere he went, and particularly in the shell-damaged streets and tenement blocks of Naples, he saw 'Greek landscapes with images of horror which I imagine await us there.'[57]

Politically, too, Cava dei Tirreni was a strange limbo. The Greek government and civil service were billeted in two adjacent hotels in the town's main street. A plan to fly the Greek flag from each was vetoed by the British, no doubt with an eye to local sensitivities. Separate villas, higher up the hillside, housed the prime minister and the British embassy. George found himself all but ostracised by the minister to whom he was responsible. Philippos Dragoumis was the brother of Ion, who had been assassinated in 1920 in a revenge attack for the attempt on Venizelos' life shortly before. George's junior colleague Angelos Vlachos would later describe Dragoumis' 'perfectly white hair and the dreamy, unwavering look in his pale-blue eyes,' and continuing paranoia about his brother's (Venizelist) assassins. George, and presumably also Maro, dined at the Foreign Ministry table; he said that he felt constantly treated like Judas at the Last Supper. On the first day, Dragoumis assigned him to duties that could have been done by a clerical officer. He had no access to the 'watertight compartments' of the Ministry itself, or to any information other than what came through

246

public channels. It was poor consolation when a friend pointed out that watertight compartments only come into use when a ship is sinking; George knew well enough that 'for today's patrons I'm far too left-wing;' his real offence was his continuing closeness to Kartalis.[58]

Kartalis, after the government's move to Italy, seems to have played the maverick more than ever. A press conference in Rome on 24 September, attended by all the correspondents covering the Italian front, was inevitably, and probably correctly, understood by Papandreou and his close associates as an attempt to upstage the government. George reported only the reactions at Cava dei Tirreni, but since Kartalis had gone to Rome in the company of George's close professional associate and personal friend, Alexandros Xydis, it is clear that he, too, must have been privy to Kartalis' plans. Whatever Kartalis might have hoped to achieve, immediately after the press conference his brilliance swung to despair; it was the same manic mood-swing as had troubled George about him in London. After a face-to-face confrontation with Papandreou on his return from Rome, Kartalis announced to George on the last day of September that he was giving up politics and going back to Cairo, where his wife now was. George did everything he could to dissuade him; in his service diary he records his chagrin: 'I, who am no politician, am fated to try to help people of my generation who sink. And these are the best there are.'[59]

247

A week later he was still trying to help Kartalis, and to goad him back into action, in a series of letters sent through different channels. The tone of these letters is both conspiratorial and, uniquely in George's preserved correspondence with political figures, reveals a jocular affection reminiscent of the friendships of his youth.[60] First with Kanellopoulos, now with Kartalis, George had placed his hopes and his trust in a politician of his generation who was both an intellectual and intimate with members of his family. For both, he had been prepared to break ranks with the service and its official policy; in both cases he paid the penalty in opprobrium and ostracism that he deeply resented. Throughout the years of his exile, George's political insights had been always acute and often prescient. He had followed, almost day by day, the political failure of the republican-democratic middle ground on which he had always stood. The 'bankruptcy' of the old politicians, that he had proclaimed in his letter to Roussos a year and a half before, and reaffirmed now at Cava di Tirreni, was about to lead to chaos and then to civil war. All this George could see, more clearly than most.[61]

But in his own political allegiance and antipathies, the evidence is that he was guided, scarcely less than were those of the political class he despised, by family loyalty and a strong sense of personal injury. He could not forgive Tsouderos for having ignored him; he could not forgive Papandreou for the high-handed way in which he had sacked him as Press Director. But these were the effective political leaders of the government that George served during these years, while Kanellopoulos and Kartalis, both of them men of greater intellectual integrity and more congenial temperament, turned out to be fatally flawed. A political obituary for Kartalis, written just over half a century after these events, reads like the obituary for George's own political hopes: 'On the eve of liberation, the politics of polarisation had come to dominate to such an extent as to leave no room for politicians with independent ideas.'[62]

This was the background to the last two poems that George wrote before his return to Greece. One, dated the same day as his conspiratorial letters to Kartalis, is a vicious satire against the political hothouse that surrounded him at Cava dei Tirreni. Its title is a pun on the title of the poem by Mallarmé, *L'Après-midi d'un faune*, on which Debussy had based an orchestral prelude, and might loosely be rendered, 'Fawning in the Afternoon.' In strict rhyme and metre, the poem's jogging rhythm follows in the wake of traditional Greek songs of Constantinople and Smyrna; in the free-for-all of Cava, all that matters to today's fawning politicians, while their country is still being crucified, is booty from the NAAFI stores.[63]

'Last Stop' is George's far more serious meditation on the strange final interlude of what he called, in letters written at the time, an 'odyssey.' In a moment of revelation, also recorded in his diary, on the first night of October 1944, the moon had come out and 'the village on the opposite slope seemed turned into enamel.' Behind the conversational informality of the poem's opening ('Few are the moonlit nights that have pleased me'), lies a coded, telegraphic summary of almost the whole of George's career as a poet: from the summer sea of Aegina when he had been sixteen, through the phantasmagoric 'six nights' on the Acropolis, to the night 'marred by the moon,' when, with Katsimbalis at Maroussi, he had found comfort in reading Aeschylus as war was about to break out. As a personal summation, 'Last Stop' marks a moment of completion.[64]

Also exposed starkly in the moonlight is the collective consciousness (and perhaps also conscience) of all the fellow-travellers in the 'Noah's Ark' that had travelled from Egypt to Cava dei Tirreni on their way to their liberated homeland:

We come from Araby, from Egypt, Palestine and Syria;
the little state
of Commagene, snuffed out like a small lantern
is often in our thoughts,
and so are mighty cities that endured throughout millennia
only to become grazing ground for water-buffaloes
and fields for sugar-cane and maize.
We come from desert sands and from the seas of Proteus
our souls wrung out by public sins,
each one clutching rank or title like a songbird in a cage.[65]

Humankind, in 'Last Stop,' turns out to be weak but constant, a victim of the violent, inhuman forces of war, but also of the 'deceit and guile' against which Makriyannis, in his time too, had warned. This is a time to remember the victims of war: 'our minds are a virgin forest of friends killed.' The phrase from Aeschylus, 'the pain-perpetuating memory of pain,' that in Pretoria had summed up an all-consuming nostalgia for home, had acquired a more sinister, political reference with the 'pillorying' of the dead in the April mutinies; it reappears near the end of the poem, now with a very Aeschylean hint of terrible things that cannot be spoken, and the threat of worse to come.[66]

249

As well as looking back to the war that was ending, 'Last Stop' also articulates, in this guarded way, George's prescient fear of civil war to come. The 'heroes,' finally, who are invoked at the end of the poem are in the plural, and serve to affirm George's positive political faith: in the collective 'people.' Heroism in this war is condensed into the example of 'Michalis,' one of Maro's patients from the days when she had been nursing in Athens at the start of 1941, who had discharged himself and gone out into the black-out 'with his open wounds.' To Michalis the poem attributes the lesson that George had learned, back in 1931, from the Spanish mystic St John of the Cross, and now adapted with a reprise of the verb whose repetition forms a line of continuity through several poems of *Logbook II*: 'Heroes are the ones who go forward in the dark.'[67]

The final act, for George and Maro, began on Wednesday 18 October, the day when most of the government disembarked at Piraeus, and Papandreou made a triumphant speech in Syntagma Square. The civil servants had been left behind, and were still at Cava; George complained that even their wirelesses had been taken away. Now, at last, came the familiar chaos of mass exodus, by train to Taranto, then embarkation on the SS *Worcestershire*.

Lifebelts had once again to be carried throughout the voyage. The obliging Indian stewards reminded George, as on the earlier voyages, from Souda to Port Said, and from Suez to Durban, of 'the Asiatic dignity of the Empire.'

The mountains on the horizon were either Zakynthos or Cefallonia; it was his first sight of Greece after exactly three and a half years. Early next morning, the ship sailed past Hydra, Poros and the Peak of Aegina, all of them highly charged with memories from the immediate pre-war years. 'Look, Robin,' he pointed with teasing wonder, putting an arm round the shoulder of the Scottish classical scholar, A.R. Burn, one of the British service personnel who were also on board, 'they are still there. They have not taken away a single island.'[68]

George was the first on the ship to make out the Acropolis of Athens through binoculars. It was, he wrote, on Sunday 22 October, 'the most beautiful, the most light-hearted day in the world.' Against the following day, in his diary, appears the one word: 'Home.'

**Bitter homecoming**

The Germans, in their retreat, had declared Athens an 'open city,' but had blown up the entire docks and harbour installations at Piraeus. Although physically undamaged, the Athens to which George and Maro returned bore all the deeper scars of occupation that George had dreaded to find. In three and a half years, Hitler's 'New Order' had systematically looted the country; by the end of the occupation the drachma had been devalued by a factor of 27 million; Athenian landlords, when they could, exacted rent in foodstuffs. Until the Italian armistice, in September 1943, control of the capital had been shared between Italian and German occupying forces; in the last year the Germans had tightened their grip, and recruited Greek anti-communist volunteers to combat the growing power of ELAS on the streets. Violence and sudden death had escalated, from the arrests, interrogations and summary executions of the early months, to the near-anarchy that had come to prevail in Athens during the final summer of the occupation.[69]

250

Maro was now reunited with her daughters; she was shocked at how thin they had become. At Kydathinaion Street, George found there had been changes. Stelios, with his French second wife, had found the means to return to Paris soon after Greece had been overrun. Angelos' wife had left him early in the occupation; since then, he had moved into the middle floor. In his own flat downstairs, George was deeply touched to find that, of the bound copies of his poems that had been stacked up round the walls when

he had left in 1941, none were left when he returned. 'The enemy occupation had given the Greek public the opportunity for concentration and
reading,' he would marvel, in an interview more than twenty years later.
The truth was perhaps more prosaic. Ioanna relates how on at least one
occasion she had had to empty the house of anything either valuable or
compromising. Given the regular traffic that passed between Kydathinaion
Street and the armed partisans of EKKA, until their violent disbandment
by ELAS in April 1944, it would not be surprising if the high-quality paper
that George had supplied to the Tarousopoulos brothers, on which to print
his poems, had found its way to the slopes of Parnassus to be made into
cartridges for Psarros and his men. If this was so, it would have been
entirely typical of Ioanna never to have disabused her brother about the
fate of the literary 'testament' he had left behind.[70]

During the first weeks after the liberation, tension ran high throughout
Greece, and nowhere more so than in Athens. The government of national
unity, under George Papandreou, had finally secured the cooperation of the
communists only in early September. For its authority, Papandreou's
government relied heavily on the backing of ten thousand British troops
that had accompanied it from Italy. This fact was particularly conspicuous
in the capital, and was not equally welcomed by all. The bonds that held
the government together were paper-thin. George later summed up the
feeling of these days, in a letter to Henry Miller:

> although the word murder was [on] everyone's lips, I couldn't help but
> thank God for each moment I was allowed to stand on my feet under
> the open sky. A state of utter despair and an absolute readiness for
> happiness.

'Then,' the letter dryly continues, 'the civil war broke out in Athens.'[71]

On 3 December 1944, a mass demonstration was called by EAM in
Syntagma Square, in the city centre. The government, from which the communist members had just resigned, banned the demonstration, but
the ban was ignored. That Sunday morning, shots fired into the crowd from
the police post on the corner of the square left ten people dead and more
than fifty injured. The 'first round' of the Greek civil war had been fought
in the mountains during 1943 and the spring of 1944; the third, and
bloodiest, round was still some way off. The shooting in Syntagma Square
that day sparked off the 'second round,' more commonly known in Greek
as the *Dekemvriana,* or 'December Events.'

For decades afterwards, the perception of what had happened that December would be starkly polarised: from the point of view of the Right, the street-fighting had been an organised attempt to seize power by EAM-ELAS; in the eyes of the Left, it had been part of a deliberate plan by the Papandreou government and its British backers to crush the forces that had done the most to liberate the country from the Axis. There is still no authoritative history of the Greek civil war; but such consensus as exists, in hindsight, suggests that had the Left seriously planned to seize power in December 1944, as many people expected, they could not have been stopped from doing so. The instigators of the violence on that Sunday appear to have been individual policemen, who might well have felt they had more to fear than just numbers from a crowd whose demands included a thorough purge of former collaborators with the enemy.[72]

It was the beginning of more than a month of open warfare in the capital. The Papandreou government had lost control; effective power was assumed by the commander of British forces in Athens, Lieutenant-General Sir Ronald Scobie. The British prime minister, Winston Churchill, himself instructed Scobie: 'do not hesitate to act as if you were in a conquered city where a local rebellion is in progress.'

252   A British guard-post was set up on the opposite side of Kydathinaion Street from number 9; one of the ground-floor rooms of the Seferiadis house was politely requisitioned for a field hospital. Outside there were snipers; dead bodies lay for hours where they fell. The water had been cut off, and the electricity; the bread shops had been shut for days. The curfew kept everyone indoors for all but two hours in the middle of the day; one morning on his way to the Ministry, George passed a pool of blood on the pavement. In the Royal Gardens, behind the parliament building, there was a stench of unburied corpses. There was shooting day and night; Spitfires circled the Acropolis and strafed areas of the city under ELAS control.

Almost at the beginning of the 'December Events,' George had written in his diary:

As I woke up today I was thinking that idyllic Plaka has become the site of the first battle between the British Empire and Soviet Russia. It really was the first battle between the Western world and the East.[73]

The term 'cold war' did not yet exist; Churchill had yet to diagnose the existence of an 'iron curtain' drawn across Europe. But it was to the clear perception of this new reality, that would dominate world politics for the next forty-five years, that George awoke on that morning of December 1944. All that he had feared and prophesied, ever since that August evening of 1943, among the dinner jackets and velvet gowns at Shepheard's Hotel in Cairo, had finally come to pass.

And all the while, as George also noted in his diary, it was an unseasonal December; the sun shone, the days were 'exceptionally beautiful, delightful, supposing one were able to look at them.' It was a juxtaposition of beauty and horror, of light and dark, that would never leave him. Out of the experience of these two months, at the end of 1944, would come the central paradox of George's next published poem, *'Thrush'*: 'Light, angelic and black,' and farther in the future, the hard-headed intimations of renewal and redemption that distinguish the poems and essays of his last decade.[74]

253

# III

# 'Light, Angelic and Black'

At dawn on 16 September 1955, . . . *I was in the isle that is called Patmos.* . . . I was drawn back to other moments when I had experienced the Greek light: to that terrible blackness that I felt very strongly behind the azure, when I returned to my country in October '44... The Furies were lying in wait behind the sun, just as Heraclitus imagined them. A mechanism of self-destruction was there, in motion, obliterating every manifestation of good will.

(Prologue to the *Apocalypse,* translated into Modern Greek, June 1966)[1]

# 9

# Descent into Hades
# 1945-1950

If you can imagine the ugliest thing against the most perfect sky of our planet, you'll understand if I tell you that I have experienced the sharpest tragedy a human being could experience. The light itself was bleeding. Then life took its course again among disabled men, disabled minds, and disabled houses. . . . Every thought of good will came to waste.

(Letter to Henry Miller, 7 December 1948)[2]

## A second Venizelos?

On Christmas Day, 1944, Winston Churchill arrived in Athens by air, accompanied by his foreign minister, Anthony Eden. George observed tartly in his diary: 'The [British] empire seems moved to take Greek affairs seriously. For the first time in our history, it puts its prime minister's person on the line.'[3]

That evening, aboard a British battleship moored in Faliron Bay, Churchill was introduced to Archbishop Damaskinos of Athens and All Greece. Standing nearly seven feet tall in his priest's hat, with the rugged obstinacy of his peasant forebears, the archbishop deeply impressed the British prime minister with his grasp of political realities. George preserved the typed note he received from Rex Leeper, the British ambassador, dated 26 December:

> In accordance with the statement issued by Mr. Churchill last night, you are invited to attend a Conference to discuss the present situation in Greece. The Archbishop of Greece will preside. Mr. Churchill will address the Conference. If you are able to accept please be at the Grande Bretagne at 3.45 today.[4]

Churchill addressed the assembled Greek politicians and officials forcefully and at length. The meeting was acrimonious and lasted for two days. Telegraphically, in his diary, George noted the reactions of colleagues in the corridors and offices of the building while it was going on. By the time Churchill and Eden left Athens, the first step towards a political resolution of the fighting had been taken. Pending a resolution on the future of the monarchy, Archbishop Damaskinos was appointed temporary Head of State with the title of Regent.[5]

George had already met Damaskinos. Ioanna's relief work during the occupation had brought her into contact with the charismatic archbishop; she had had her own office at the archbishopric since early in 1943. The working relationship between two such conspicuous individuals seems to have aroused comment at the time; the rumour that Ioanna had been the archbishop's lover is still repeated today. There is naturally no direct evidence. But it may be to this that Tsatsos was referring in his memoirs, when he linked his own departure for Egypt in summer 1944 and subsequent decision to enter politics immediately after the liberation, to a 'deep trauma from a personal event' and the need 'to overcome the humiliation I had experienced in my private life.'[6]

On the day that the regency was announced, 30 December 1944, George and Ioanna went together to visit the archbishop at home, in the northern suburb of Psychiko. Damaskinos, who suffered from angina, received them in bed:

> He has the solid commonsense of a peasant; he has that strength, at least. He's a republican, but not fanatically so; also an advantage. . . . He was . . . far too large for the narrow room . . . His eyes were shining . . . with good humour. He knows no foreign languages; only, when he was in [internal] exile [under Metaxas], . . . to pass the time, I suppose, he memorised a French dictionary.[7]

Five months after that visit, on 24 May, 1945, George was summoned to the offices of the regency, now established in a mansion on Kifisias Avenue in Halandri, not far from Psychiko. Damaskinos asked him to become Director of his Political Office; in effect, his private secretary.[8]

There is no evidence that George actively sought this position with Damaskinos; indeed, his diaries show that he had been looking forward intently to being 'demobilised' in the first months of 1945. But it is hard to believe that the summons to Halandri could have come entirely out of the blue. The position of personal trust and influence in which George now found himself was very like the one that he had first tentatively hoped he might occupy under Kanellopoulos, in Cairo, and had later enjoyed with

Kartalis. Once again, George found himself closely allied with a rising political figure, in whose abilities he was prepared, for a time, to have faith; only this time, that figure was Head of State, with potentially far greater power to influence events. And once again the bond of mutual confidence had been established through the circle of Ioanna and Kostakis Tsatsos.[9]

Perhaps reflecting the blend of awe and affection appropriate to a revered member of the family, George's private nickname for Damaskinos when he started working for him, although the archbishop was only a decade older than he was himself, was 'Grandpa.'[10]

By the second week of 1945, the fighting in Athens was over. According to the Varkiza Agreement, concluded in early February, the communists agreed to lay down their arms, though on humiliating terms that would only store up trouble for later. Since the events of December, George's sympathies had undergone an understated but significant shift. If the new struggle of the times was to be between the British empire and Soviet Russia, between liberal West and communist East, then he could no longer throw in his lot with EAM or 'people's rule,' as he might have contemplated doing eighteen months before. Soviet communism, with its authoritarianism and the rigid conformity to the party line that characterised many of its adherents in Greece, had never held any appeal for him. Before long, George's new distance from the left, though never spelt out, would be duly noted against him in left-wing literary circles.[11]

259

His attitude to the British had altered too. In Cairo, George had often bitterly resented the pro-monarchist policy of the Foreign Office, as well as the high-handedness and interference of its representatives with whom he dealt daily. Now, the service diary that he kept during the regency reveals him working closely, and sharing confidences, with some of those same representatives. Chief among them was Sir Reginald (Rex) Leeper, who had been ambassador to the government-in-exile in Cairo and at Cava dei Tirreni, and was now accredited to the government in Athens. Leeper's blatant interventionism had begun, by this time, to attract criticism even in London. But during the regency, and until Leeper's recall in March 1946, 'Rex' and 'George' were on first-name terms. George shared the British ambassador's profound irritation with the Greek political class; and Leeper, in private, turned out to be much more republican in his sympathies than George could have imagined in Cairo.[12]

The changed political climate of 1945, and his own realignment within it, had a long-lasting effect on George's literary relationships as well. Newly posted to Greece from Britain were several lively spirits who quickly came under the spell of Katsimbalis and George; indeed it seems to have been almost a form of pilgrimage to seek out Miller's 'Colossus.' The cartoonist and columnist Osbert Lancaster arrived in Athens, while the December fighting was still going on, to take up a two-year post in charge of the British embassy press office. Under the aegis of the British Council, which had been operating in Greece before the war, there were now four British Institutes in different parts of the country. The new Representative at the British Council was Steven Runciman, Byzantinist and future historian of the Crusades, whose later memories of George were 'of laughter, of appreciation of the natural beauties of the world and the man-made monuments of the past, and of all the whims and traditions of history.' Director of the British Institute in Athens, for the same two years, was Rex Warner, a classical scholar and novelist, who would become one of George's most trusted translators. Together with C.M. (Monty) Woodhouse, who was back in Greece, temporarily seconded to the embassy, and Patrick (Paddy) Leigh Fermor, the travel-writer whose most famous exploit had been the abduction of a German general from occupied Crete in 1944, they became staunch members of Katsimbalis' circle, and lifelong friends of George and Maro.[13]

260    Before long, a spate of travel books, scholarly works, fiction and translations by these British writers, beginning with Lancaster's *Classical Landscape with Figures*, as early as 1947, and continuing with the work of Edmund Keeley, Philip Sherrard, and the American Kimon Friar, who had yet to appear on the scene, began to transform the way in which the educated Briton or American perceived Greece. All of them profoundly guided by George, and by Katsimbalis, they sought to direct their readers' attention to the modern realities of Greece, or to the medieval or recent history of the Greeks – and this at a time when 'Greece' still predominantly meant a civilisation that had ended more than two thousand years before.

It was in this new climate, and with many of these individuals as protagonists, that the British Council in 1945 launched the *Anglo-Elliniki Epitheorisi*, or *Anglo-Hellenic Review*, a Greek-language cultural magazine whose conception was clearly a by-product of the politics of the time. With Katsimbalis as its editor, however, the *Anglo-Hellenic Review* soon established itself as the successor to the now-defunct *Ta Nea Grammata*; for ten years it became the most widely read Greek literary periodical, bringing together many of the leading Greek writers with names well-known in English.[14]

While these new friendships were being cemented in Athens, George's young poet-friend, Nanos Valaoritis, was in London, soon to begin working for the BBC Greek Service. George had put Valaoritis in touch with the literary impresarios whom he had met on his brief visit to London with Kartalis the previous year: John Lehmann and Cyril Connolly. Thanks to articles and translations by Durrell and others of the *Personal Landscape* group in Connolly's magazine *Horizon*, Valaoritis was able to report to George, shortly after he arrived in London, that 'Here in England, you're the best-known Greek poet.' By the end of 1945, Lehmann was ready to float the idea, at a dinner-party that included Valaoritis and Stephen Spender, 'for a Seferis [book] in English.' Three years later, this would appear as *The King of Asine and Other Poems.*[15]

By the time that George assumed his duties with the regent, in May 1945, the world war had just ended in Europe. 'I feel nothing,' George noted in his diary on VE Day, and went on to describe a blind man playing the National Anthem on an accordion in Kydathinaion Street. When three months later the war in the Far East ended, with the dropping of atomic bombs on Japan, the events left no clear trace in either his personal or his service diary.[16]

261

By this time, in Greece, a second post-liberation government had already come and gone; its successor was soon in deep crisis. There was still no immediate prospect of any Greek government winning the legitimacy of a popular mandate, still less of the constitutional issue of the monarchy being resolved. Then in July, the political world of Athens was thrown into turmoil by the defeat of Churchill and the Conservatives in the British general election. Archbishop Damaskinos resolved on a visit to London, where he appeared to be held in high esteem by the new Labour government, and in particular by Eden's successor as Foreign Secretary, Ernest Bevin. The regent would be accompanied by George.[17]

The two weeks that George spent in London with Damaskinos, from 6 to 22 September 1945, marked the high point of his hopes for the regency. Leeper, Monty Woodhouse, and Harold Caccia, all on the staff of the Foreign Office, and with all of whom George was now on excellent terms, were in attendance. In a private conversation with Woodhouse, George observed that the British government ought to be seen to give something to Greece in return for its continued intervention in Greek internal affairs. Woodhouse wondered about the Elgin Marbles. No, said George, people's minds today were on territorial claims. He was thinking, no doubt, of the islands of the Dodecanese, in the south-eastern Aegean, that had been seized by Italy in 1912, and were now about to be ceded to Greece in settlement of a long-standing claim. George named Cyprus, which was then a British colony. Woodhouse was cautious, but personally sympathetic, and so was Leeper. Having taken these soundings, George urged Damaskinos to make a formal request to the British government. Within days, the regent was declaring that he would not leave London without a guarantee for the union of Cyprus with Greece; prime minister Clement Attlee, to whom Damaskinos put the request verbally on 10 September, said that he 'quite agreed;' a press communiqué was even drawn up for the regent to deliver on his return to Athens. But despite George's hopes that the Labour Foreign Secretary, with his background in the trades-union movement, and Damaskinos, the 'peasant from Central Greece,' would see eye to eye, the regent's meetings with Bevin were not a success, and nothing more came of the request.[18]

The crux of the London visit that September was the meeting between Damaskinos and King George II of the Hellenes that took place at Claridge's Hotel on 13 September. Technically, the question to be resolved was whether to postpone the referendum on the future of the monarchy that had been agreed at Varkiza, and if so, for how long; but the underlying issue was the one that had poisoned Greek internal politics for thirty years, and Greek relations with Great Britain throughout the war: should the king return at all? Official British policy was still, as it had been under Churchill's wartime coalition, in favour of the king's return. But on the morning of the historic meeting, it was Rex Leeper, as George recalled, who 'tried to nudge me into persuading Grandpa to break with the king.'[19]

Such thoughts can never have been far from George's mind; it was in all probability in the expectation that Damaskinos would emerge as a second Venizelos, that George had been willing to serve under him. But to Leeper he at once pointed out the danger: a contest between Damaskinos and the king would replicate the National Schism of 1915, when Venizelos had defied King Constantine, the present king's father. George would have liked nothing better than for Damaskinos to repudiate the king. As he hinted strongly to Leeper on this occasion, only one thing was missing: if there really was, as Leeper was suggesting, British and international support for Damaskinos, why was there no sign of any corresponding pressure on the king to step down?

It was a turning point for the regency, and also for George. Damaskinos met the king alone. The king received the regent with a speech, written out in advance. When he returned, the archbishop showed George the notes he had made. Leeper's official account to the Foreign Office, which may have come through George, ends dryly: 'no agreement was reached.'[20]

George's own impression was one of dismay. Damaskinos had been far too conciliatory with the king for George's taste.

Today I'm full of doubts. What is Grandpa up to? − is he paying lip service like a bishop under Ottoman rule, or does he think this is the way to compel the British to intervene with [King] George? Sometimes I can't make him out.

The entry in George's service diary continues with a deeply pessimistic scenario, of the

civil war that we feel constantly hanging over our heads in Greece − the war like the one last December that we must, must do everything we can to avoid, and which a referendum on the constitutional issue would bring very close to us, [because] it would exacerbate passions and thrust into the arms of the communists a significant number of supporters who aren't communists at all, but just republicans.[21]

263

When he flew back to Athens with 'Grandpa' ten days later, after a brief stop in Paris for a wreath-laying ceremony at the Arc de Triomphe, nothing had been resolved to George's satisfaction. The request for Cyprus had been shelved (indefinitely, as it turned out); Damaskinos had secured British agreement to delay the referendum on the monarchy until after parliamentary elections, but beyond this had steadfastly refused to take the initiative as George, and perhaps Leeper, had hoped.[22]

Back in Athens, it was a difficult time at home in Kydathinaion Street. In the summer of 1945, Stelios and his wife arrived on a visit from Paris. George, now occupying his father's empty flat on the middle floor with Maro, had to move back downstairs at short notice. In his diary, George made no secret of his irritation at this latest enforced move, after so many. But worse was to come on his return from London. In October, the quarrels between father and son over the ownership of their respective parts of the house, interrupted, but not resolved, by the war, were resumed more bitterly than ever.

Stelios was now determined to move out of Kydathinaion Street for good. With his customary impetuousness, but now a sick and irritable old man, he seems to have set about disposing of his children's patrimony, literally over their heads. When Stelios left Athens for the last time, with Thérèse, not long after this, the grandest of the three flats in the Kydathinaion house, the one separating George and Maro, below, from Ioanna and Kostakis above, had been rented out to strangers. George felt this as a violation, quite apart from the nuisance caused by the new neighbours. 'The myth of the father devouring his children, the "Cronus complex," if the expression exists, has never been more true,' he complained in his diary. When, a year later, he was ready to begin his poetic retrospect on the war years, '*Thrush,*' there is perhaps an echo of this very personal anger and sense of dispossession in its very first line: 'The houses that I had were taken from me.'

After this, George would still write to his father on occasion, although it is clear that the main channel of communication between Kydathinaion Street and Paris from now on was Ioanna; but George was never to see his father again. For the family, it was the final dispersal. Not long after the departure of Stelios, George's brother Angelos left for the United States, never to return.[23]

The government, that autumn, was in continuous crisis, and George was at the heart of it. The main political parties from the pre-Metaxas era, the Liberals and the People's Party, had come back in a zombie-like existence that was only emphasised by the extreme age of many of the protagonists who jockeyed for portfolios in a series of short-lived 'service' governments.

Leader of the Liberals was Themistocles Sofoulis, now eighty-five, whose exploits on his native island of Samos in the first decade of the century had first brought Stelios Seferiadis on to the international stage. The right-wing, monarchist People's Party, whose very name was an anachronism in these days of peoples' (i.e. communist) republics, was headed by Constantine Tsaldaris, the nephew of its pre-war leader who had defeated Venizelos in 1933. Nicholas Plastiras, prime minister for four months at the beginning of 1945, had led the successful *coup d'état* in the wake of the defeat in Anatolia in 1922, and the unsuccessful ones in 1933 and 1935 that had paved the way for the military to take power in the prewar years. Tsouderos, who had been prime minister for three years but never contested an election, served in varying capacities in several of these governments, as did other figures more or less tarnished by the ineffectual bickering of the wartime government in exile. Even those younger figures, Kanellopoulos and Kartalis, in whom George had once placed his trust and with whom he remained on friendly terms, seem to have succumbed to the behaviour of their elders. Kanellopoulos was even prime minister for twenty-one days during November (Leeper took George for a bet on fifteen); Kartalis at the time was furious. Both served in a series of cabinets; neither made any impact on the slide towards political anarchy.[24]

At the height of the political crisis, in October 1945, it was George, according to his own account, who persuaded Damaskinos to take over the premiership and head a government. This was a bold step, and one from which the archbishop soon drew back, not least because of the public outcry that followed: memories were too strong of the way in which Metaxas had come to power in 1936. George and Leeper were by no means the only ones in Athens to see in the archbishop the best hope of creating a government that would tackle the enormous economic and political problems now facing the country. Had Damaskinos played the strong suit which George was convinced he possessed, it would have been a solution to the post-war crisis in keeping with George's (and the regent's) Venizelist and republican principles. George still believed that it needed only a word from the British Foreign Secretary, the 'open sesame,' as he called it, at once to persuade Damaskinos, and to remove British backing for King George. On that word, George believed, depended the fate of Greece. But that word was not forthcoming.[25]

265

In the months after October, George's disillusionment with the regent deepened. In his service diary, 'Grandpa' becomes first 'the Old Man,' a term that in George's private mythology had earlier been attached to his father, and then to the pre-war Under-Secretary and arbiter of his fate, his old enemy Mavroudis. By spring the following year, George had dropped any nickname, affectionate or otherwise, and was referring only to 'the regent.' Politically, during the prolonged crisis at the end of 1945, Damaskinos had proved himself fatally indecisive; worse, George found him 'stubborn and short-sighted.' The world of Athenian high politics could be embarrassingly small, too. One evening during the autumn crisis, George scoured the city looking for the regent, who was wanted urgently at the British embassy. Eventually he found him, when he had given up the search and returned home – closeted with George's sister on the top floor at Kydathinaion Street.[26]

By this time, all George's deep-seated disgust at the antics of the governing class of his country had returned; on 28 October, the fifth anniversary of Greece's entry into the war, he was already thinking of looking for another job.[27]

Five months later, on the last day of March, 1946, the first parliamentary election in Greece for just over ten years was held. It was boycotted by the left, a tactic with a long and disastrous history in Greek politics. As a consequence, the choice before the electorate was between right-wing monarchists and right-wing republicans. Only half of those eligible to vote did so, but the popular mandate, such as it was, was overwhelmingly for the royalist People's Party. All that remained was to draw up a timetable for the promised referendum on the monarchy, but nobody now doubted that King George would return. The regency, at least as George had conceived it at the beginning, was over in all but name. The date fixed for the referendum was 1 September.[28]

With the royalist Right now in the ascendant, George was furious, but not surprised, to find in the summer of 1946 that his next step up the promotion ladder had been blocked. He blamed his old arch-enemy in the service, Alexis Kyrou, whose family owned the far-right newspaper *Estia*, and who on the eve of the Second World War had been one of the few senior figures in the government to come out openly in favour of the Axis. As was dryly noted by George's former diplomatic colleague, and editor of his service diary, Alexandros Xydis, George's 'service with the regency, along with his service in the Middle East, counted against him, instead of being additional grounds for his promotion.'[29]

266

When the votes in the referendum were counted, sixty-eight percent were for the return of the king. During the sixteen months that he had worked with Damaskinos, George had been at his office each day at eight, and would often not return to Kydathinaion Street until five the next morning. On 28 September, 1946, the day after King George returned to Greece and the regency offices on Kifisias Avenue closed their doors for the last time, George drew up his private balance sheet of those months. He regretted none of the advice that he had given; if it had been followed, he maintained, it would have been better for the country. Despite the distracting conditions in which he had had to work, he had made no serious mistakes. Even the most fanatical opponents of the regency had found nothing for which to blame him personally. As a point of principle, he had neither sought nor received favours; even in the glaring matter of his promotion, he had not asked Damaskinos, or anyone else in a position of influence, to intervene. 'And so,' he concluded,

> ends this service too, just like others before it, with a certain romanticism, as some would see it, but I would say with my own realism.

As he was writing, the cannons were booming from the top of Lycabettus and the streets were full of people rejoicing at the return of the king. 'May God lend a hand,' he wrote. 'I have done what I could.'[30]

Historians today do not generally lay so much stress on the king's return, among the causes of the third and final round of the Greek civil war, as George did at the time. The referendum was at least a genuine expression of the popular will (unlike that in 1935), and was not boycotted by the left, as the parliamentary election had been. In the event, King George would prove neither more nor less successful than Damaskinos had been in concentrating the minds of politicians on the real business of economic reconstruction and of rebuilding confidence between left and right. The regent had been powerless to prevent the 'white terror,' a campaign of intimidation, violence and imprisonment waged ever since Varkiza by the security forces – which still included many former collaborators with the Germans – against the left and its sympathisers. George must have known of this, but never so much as mentions it. The greatest fear in the regent's mind, and probably also in George's, had been of a royalist *coup d'état*, a threat that never materialised. More than the return of the monarch, it was the economic damage to the country, about which little had been done since liberation, and the isolation of the left, that would combine to bring the communists out in arms a year later. But from his own perspective, and given his own background, it was entirely consistent for George to be deeply pessimistic about the future, once the return of the monarchy was assured. In his own eyes, from the early summer of 1946 onwards, he and those in whom he had placed his hopes for a political solution had failed, just as they had failed before in the Middle East.[31]

267

### 'A small shipwreck'

At first, during the months of his gruelling service with the regent, George had had little time for other things. At the behest of the Ministry, he had served on the boards of the National Theatre and the national radio station. He had written a handful of poems, none of which he published. In March, he lectured at the Parnassus Society, on the Cretan romance *Erotokritos*, one of the high points of his own version of the Greek literary tradition; the text soon appeared in Katsimbalis' *Anglo-Hellenic Review*. Wearing spectacles for the first time in public, he had the sensation of seeing the world from inside a diving suit.[32]

At the beginning of February 1946 had come a heavy snowfall, an unusual event in Athens, and with it Lawrence Durrell, on his first visit since the war. For Durrell, it was an emotional reunion with George and the 'Colossus.' Durrell's grasp of Greek politics was as shaky as ever, and he was quite wrong to suppose that his friends had 'done the frightened rabbit so fashionable among the Venezeli[sts] and become royalists.' Another reunion came in April; George Apostolidis returned from the sanatorium in Switzerland, where he had been since before the war; together he and George had their first swim of the season, at Vouliagmeni, at the beginning of May.[33]

Later that month, a semi-official visit by the French poet Paul Eluard, one of the founding figures of Surrealism, who had become a prominent member of the Communist Party, brought the tensions of the Athenian literary world close to the surface. Meeting the great man at the French embassy, and hearing him lecture at the Attikon cinema, George was not disposed to be impressed. But the introductions were made by Sikelianos and Kazantzakis, for the former of whom George now had enormous respect; good friends of his were dancing attendance on Eluard. These included Robert Levesque, who since the war had been touring the Middle East with Gide, but had also found time to publish a volume of George's poems in French; another was the poet Elytis, who always stood aloof from politics but had been an admirer of Eluard since his youth. George found himself repelled by the atmosphere of Party solidarity that gathered round the distinguished visitor: 'you wonder how many of those who applaud like maniacs would have stayed [to hear Eluard], if he hadn't been politically one of theirs,' he noted in his diary.[34]

But there was an unexpected sequel. On the last day of Eluard's visit, George and Maro went with him in a group to the Sikelianos country retreat on the island of Salamis, a short distance from Athens. There they swam, and George climbed up to the Faneromeni monastery, where Archbishop Damaskinos had been held under house arrest for three years under Metaxas. Against the brilliant background of sea and sun, and in the relaxed company of his own friends, George saw the real human being, the poet, suddenly emerge in Eluard, unencumbered by the dogma and the party claques. 'Attic nature had put everyone in his proper place, relentless, as always,' he marvelled, as he described that day in his diary. It was most probably this specific moment, and no mere vague generalisation, that George would have in mind, some years later, when he wrote, 'I believe that there exists a humanising function in the Greek light.'[35]

During that summer of 1946, while in Athens the regency wound down, George's thoughts once more began to turn towards his long-delayed 'demobilisation.' Even as a new political era dawned with the detonation of the first hydrogen bomb in the Pacific, he felt a desperate longing for the Greek countryside, 'even for a single tree.' Already, swimming at Vouliagmeni, he had experienced the 'magic' of the sea, and had the sensation of being close to 'the dividing line into another world.' Then came the day with Eluard and his friends on Salamis. A week after that, on a Sunday spent walking in the woods at Kineta, not far from Athens, he came to experience this 'humanising function' of the landscape in almost anthropomorphic terms, as though the shapes of mountains and sea were about to resolve them-selves into the features of a longed-for human presence. It was, he said, a 'revelation,' and went on, echoing his own pre-war attempt to grapple with the idea of eternity: 'Dilation of the spirit within that other world.' The paradox that had already taken root in George at the time of the street-fighting of the previous December, now returned to him forcefully and found its first expression in the phrase that ends this entry in his diary: 'The black and angelic Attic day.'[36]

Two days later, George found himself once again confronting the idea of eternity, this time in a very different context. It was probably in an official capacity that he was present in the National Archae-ological Museum while some of the most famous statues of classical antiquity were being unearthed from the foundations; they had been buried there, for safety, at the beginning of the war. Surrounded by the cheerful atmosphere of an archaeological excavation, here in this august and rather severe building, he saw these ancient glories in an off-duty moment:

> The arm of some larger-than-life god, turned in towards the thigh, protruded below the scaffolding; a naked woman with her back turned to me had a grey workman's basket stuck over her head, leaving me with a view of only her beaming buttocks.

The famous bronze Zeus, or Poseidon, that had been found in the sea off Artemision and holds his hands outstretched, either to throw a thunderbolt or wield a trident, was 'lying on his back, on top of a packing case, like any tired workman.' George was able, as few visitors to the Museum can have been allowed to do, to run his hands over the bronze; juxtaposed, like this, to the real workmen digging and hauling on ropes, the ancient figure was at once intensely human, but at the same time the work of a craftsman 'conscious that he was giving life to a god' – though George at once brought

269

this divinity back down to earth by adding: 'who had committed a lot of adultery among mortals.'

Suddenly, the 'resurrection' of these statues from beneath the floor of the Museum seemed to fuse together the human with the divine. The language George uses in his diary recalls both Aphrodite, goddess of love, rising from the waves ('Anadyomene') and the Christian 'Second Coming.' It was too much for him at that moment to express, but his imagination rushed out of the Museum to embrace the landscape and the sea that he had missed so badly for so long:

> I know that all my life will not be enough for me to express what I've been trying to say these last few days; this union of nature with a simple human body – this insignificant thing, that is also more than human.[37]

Through May and June, George jotted down isolated lines and fragments of verse. Then in August, for a week spanning the religious holiday of the 15th, he and Maro were able to escape from Athens. They went to Poros, to Maro's sister Amaryllis, who had been widowed early in the occupation. George felt as if he were only now, truly, returning to the Greece he knew. On their last day there, he went with Maro by boat to swim from an island in the channel that separates Poros from the mainland of the Peloponnese. The boatman stopped to show them the wreck of a small naval supply ship, that had been scuttled at the time of the German invasion. Only the top of its funnel now reached above the water:

> We looked at it from above. The water was lightly ruffled and the way the sun played on it made the sunken ship – you could see it fairly clearly – with its broken masts, flutter like a flag, or a faint image in the mind.[38]

The name of the scuttled ship was *Kichli*, the ancient Greek word for a thrush. It would soon become the title of his next poem.

King George II returned to Athens on Friday 27 September 1946. The following Wednesday, as soon as he had handed over the last documents relating to the regency, George sailed out of Piraeus. He had secured a two-month period of leave, his first for nine years. His destination was once again Poros; Maro was already there, staying with her sister. The name carved above the doorway of the grand, 'Victorian' villa on the edge of the sea could never have seemed more apt: *Galini* (Serenity).[39]

Despite the powerful sensation of homecoming that George had experienced, coming here in the summer, Poros was not quite home to him. The week spent with Maro's sister Amaryllis in August had been his first immersion, since the war, in the kind of rural Greek life by the sea that he had known as a boy. But the name 'Poros,' as he explained in a letter to Durrell soon after arriving there in October: 'means passage, passage to where? So here I am asking this question. After the neutrality, after the war, after the "liberation," here I am asking this question.'[40]

If Poros, in George's own private mythology, was rather a means than an end, a stage on a journey, it was nonetheless a place of potent memories. He had come here with Maro, from Aegina, that summer of 1936; it was perhaps here that they had first become lovers. Here, too, they had come for their last snatched moment of leisure, during the 'war of nerves,' at Easter 1940. And before that, George and Katsimbalis had come this way with Miller and Durrell, on their way to visit Ghika on Hydra, where Miller had not only looked like a Tibetan monk but had held forth on the subject to his hosts. Miller's overwritten account of passing by Poros, in the *Colossus of Maroussi*, was one of the passages in the book that George most admired; he had translated it for Maro and their friends in Egypt:

Let the world have its bath of blood — I will cling to Poros. . . . That was a moment that endures, that survives world wars, that outlasts the life of the planet Earth itself. If I should ever attain the fulfilment that the Buddhists speak of . . . I say now let me remain behind, let me hover as a gentle spirit above the roofs of Poros . . . I can see the whole human race straining through the neck of the bottle here, searching for egress into the world of light and beauty.[41]

That day had probably been George's first introduction to the broad-brush ideas on oriental mysticism that first Miller and then Durrell would help to popularise after the war. Now, in the summer and autumn of 1946, George read, and carefully annotated, at least one book on ancient Chinese philosophy. In it, he found corroboration for the concepts of love and justice that he had derived from Aeschylus and the presocratic philosophers. At the same time, he was becoming intrigued by 'problems of Zen.'[42]

George had come to Poros, this time, to write a lecture for his friends at the British Institute, that he had agreed to give in December; the subject: Cavafy and Eliot. But he had never felt comfortable with Cavafy or his

Alexandrian-Greek world; it was a relief to turn to Eliot, and re-read the *Four Quartets.*[43]

At the end of the first week, he was still working almost aimlessly. The days were cloudy and wet; there was a melancholy feeling of early autumn, in the scents that wafted into the house from the surrounding pinewoods, in the sound of the wind over the sea. He found relief in physical tasks, such as chopping wood or rowing in the bay. Maro's daughter Mina was with them. Amaryllis and her children were away in Athens. In the middle of the month, they all came out for what seems to have been a noisy weekend. Then, on the day when everybody was due to return to Athens, leaving George and Maro to the peace of the house called 'Serenity,' he was awakened at six in the morning by their shouts, 'The sun! The sun!'

The weather had turned. Once everyone had gone, and the sun was up, George went out on the wide balcony, with its flagstones and balustrades, to look out over the bay, the naval dockyard, the conical shape of the town of Poros above its twin harbours, and the mountains of the Peloponnese beyond the still waters of the channel. It was a moment of extraordinary stillness and clarity: 'the sea,' as he described it, 'had no surface.' He had the sensation

272

that if the slightest chink were to open up in this closed vision, every-thing could *empty* from the four corners of the horizon and leave you naked and alone . . . without that astonishing exactitude of vision.[44]

Next day, Tuesday, he began to write. Cavafy was put on one side. He found it necessary to close the shutters, to shut out the brilliant light of late autumn, in order to work. Everything that had been stored up in him for so long, all his experiences of wartime and its aftermath, poured out of him 'with the tumult of a violent spring in northern climates.' After nine days, on the last day of October, he spent the entire afternoon chopping wood, until his hands stank of pine-resin. Then he bathed, and sat down at his desk.

'I've finished the poem,' he wrote later that night. 'Title: *"Thrush."* I don't know if it's good; but I know that it's finished. Now it has to *dry.*'[45]

When it first appeared, as a slim volume, in March the following year, *'Thrush'* was coolly received. Even George's friends found the poem obscure; uncharacteristically, he was persuaded to explain. To Levesque, his French translator, soon after its first appearance, he wrote a short letter 'clarifying' certain aspects of the poem. To Katsimbalis' younger cousin, Zissimos

Lorenzatos, he sent an edited version of his diary covering the period when the poem had been written. To Katsimbalis himself he sent an open letter, later included among his *Essays,* entitled 'A Scenario for *"Thrush".'* George was well aware that a writer is not necessarily an authoritative reader of his own work, and each of these 'explanations' is framed with appropriate caution. But all three would be in the public domain within three years of the poem's first publication, and since then have inevitably become part of the way in which *'Thrush'* is read.[46]

From the 'scenario,' almost all readers have clung to the gloss on the poem's protagonist: 'a certain Odysseus.' Following the story of the Odyssey, according to this 'scenario,' the hero finds himself, after years of wandering, in a house. This house is not his home, his longed-for island of Ithaca; but after he has dallied for some time with the mistress of the house, the enchantress Circe, it is she who gives him the directions that will finally bring him to his goal. First he must go to the underworld and learn from the dead. This was a legacy of the myth that George had already exploited to powerful effect at the end of *Mythistorema.* Only by passing through that experience of darkness will Odysseus find his true home, which, in the 'scenario,' is no longer Homer's Ithaca, but 'the light.' The letter to Levesque, written earlier, makes no mention of this mythological frame- work; there, the 'essence of the poem' is 'the drama that consists in the opposition, the confrontation of absolute light . . . with life (my life, the life of my country, of all of us).'[47]

The poem begins with 'the house by the sea.' The bare, unfurnished, temporary resting-place in which the speaker finds himself, now that the war is over, is not really the house called 'Serenity,' that appears in the published dateline. In reality, George found the Dragoumis family home on Poros a little overbearing, with its lush 'Pompeian-red' stucco and rather precious, *fin-de-siècle* ornaments and furniture. The house in the poem is more reminiscent of the half-furnished homes and offices in which he had lived and worked throughout the war years. In this composite house, the protagonist muses on the past; on the dead that have passed this way; on people from his own past life. 'You know, houses can turn obstinate, when you strip them bare.'[48]

Part II introduces two of these characters from the past. One is compared to Homer's Elpenor, the youngest of Odysseus' companions, who fell to his death when drunk; but he is a modern, rather Parisian-sounding Elpenor: he talks with a cigarette permanently between his lips, and he is not drunk. The other is an avatar of Circe, Homer's enchantress. On this part of the poem, George's 'explanations' are more distracting than illuminating.[49]

Elpenor speaks in an impassioned monologue. Like George's own younger self ('at the end of your youth'), he struggles to make himself understood in language of intense lyricism: he has seen the ancient statues, in the moonlight, bend and turn into living bodies. Circe replies curtly, and repeatedly, 'The statues are in the museum.' It is hard not to connect Elpenor's vision here ('cutting through time') with the recent experience in the National Archaeological Museum that George, too, had found beyond his power to express. The dialogue is followed by the announcement of war, and so must be imagined as belonging to the pre-war world. The failed dialogue between the tormented visionary and the older woman, who is here given the name of an enchantress, may draw, in hindsight, on aspects of George's relationship with Lou; there are many details, in this part of the poem, that hark back both to that relationship and to George's writing at that period of his life.[50]

The third part opens with the voice of Elpenor once again. Now among the dead, he hands on to the speaker the poetic talisman, a lemon-branch: 'it will flower in other hands.' 'For me, art is not an isolated recreation. It consists in interaction with others,' George had written furiously to Malanos, repudiating the legacy of the 'ivory tower.' The legacy of the 'sensuous,' introverted Elpenor, a version of George's own former self, would flower and bear fruit only through interaction with others. The phantasmagoric moonlight that dominated Part II now gives way to blazing sunlight; the narcissistic, aesthetic, Elpenor-figure, with his resemblance to the lover of Lou and the author of George's own early poems, hands over to the poet of *Logbook II* and of *'Thrush.'*[51]

Now, in the final part, the protagonist contemplates the 'small shipwreck,' the 'Thrush,' lying on the seabed, much as George had already described it in his diary. Looking down through the water at the sunken ship, he hears, as Odysseus did in the underworld, the voice that is to guide him on the final stage of his journey. This time, it is the voice of Socrates, the rational philosopher who had been condemned to death by the Athenians in 399 BC. Almost immediately comes the triumphant paradox: 'Light, angelic and black.' In the final section of the poem, it seems possible, after all, for the mythological sons of Oedipus, instead of fighting to the death, to be reconciled; their sister Antigone, instead of being buried alive, is crowned with the sun, though it is a 'crown of thorns.' 'The heart of Scorpio has set,' the poem declares, thus fulfilling a promise George had

274

made to himself while watching the constellations on board ship, just after leaving Egypt. Out of the 'laughter of the waves' (an expression translated from Aeschylus), the ancient goddess of love, Aphrodite, is reborn. Behind this epiphany of love perhaps stands the memory of that noon, ten years ago, when Marika Londou had come out of the sea and lain down, with 'a dark-coloured veil over her face,' and shortly afterwards she and George had become lovers. The poem continues with a quotation from the pagan Latin hymn, 'whoever has never loved will love;' and adds, 'in the light.'[52]

It was a future that would not happen in the real world, and when he wrote 'Thrush,' during the last nine days of October 1946, George knew very well that it was not likely to happen. If he was indeed thinking back to that summer, of the *coup de foudre*, ten years ago, he knew that it had not happened then, either. The 'dark behind the light' had already been there, waiting, in the form of the newly established dictatorship of Metaxas. It is perhaps in recognition of this, that the poem ends, not with the blaze of affirmation, but with a return to the empty house in which it had begun. There, wonder at the miracle is but one side of the coin ('angelic and black'); along with revelation comes the premonition of loss:

275

    and you are
in a great house with many windows open
running from room to room, scarce knowing from where to
    look out first
because the pines will disappear and the reflection of the
    mountains and the twittering of birds
the sea will empty, shattered glass, from north to south
your eyes will empty of the light of day
just as suddenly and all at once the cicadas stop.[53]

The ending of 'Thrush' is finely ambivalent. Like everything else that George wrote, it is deeply embedded in private experience, but it transcends that experience to become a richly evocative commentary, at once on a specific historical moment in the life of his country, and of the historical process, as George perceived it at work in human life. The voice 'crying in the wilderness,' the rational voice of the modern Socrates, the voice of a Cassandra, condemned always to prophesy truly but never to be believed: this voice, that was George's own, had tried, and failed, repeatedly throughout the past six years, to influence the political course of events. What could not be achieved in the world of political forces and events, could still be achieved in words, on the page, in this poem.[54]

## Of cliques and claques

With *'Thrush'* finished, the aura of fulfilment was slow to fade. George still had a second month of leave ahead of him. The lecture on Cavafy and Eliot was soon finished; the book on Cavafy, begun in Pretoria, was progressing well. Given more time on Poros, he thought he might have finished it.[55]

For much of November, the sun continued to shine; George, in his diary, continued to meditate on the light of his country, with almost religious awe. '*Deep down*,' he wrote on 5 November, 'the poet has a single theme: his living body.' Two decades later, it was in all probability these days, just after *'Thrush'* had been finished, that he was remembering, when he wrote:

> Once, at the end of autumn, it seemed to me that, with the clarity of a thunderbolt, god had passed . . . close by me. And I said, 'Deep down I am a question of light.' It was an experience that can come in reality very rarely in someone's life and illuminates it entirely; it cannot be conveyed in words.[56]

276

There is surely no contradiction between these two statements, introduced by the identical phrase: *deep down*. On his last day on Poros, probably with reference to the same experience, George wrote: 'I don't know if I shall ever be able to express this basic thing, as I feel it, this foundation of life. I know that with the light I must live.'[57]

There was also a less serious side. George was still enjoying the unaccustomed physical exercise of hewing wood, and dashing off skittish verses. The very next day after finishing *'Thrush,'* he wrote to Amaryllis in Athens, urging her to invite John Lehmann and his English friends to come and stay at *Galini*. They came a fortnight later. As there was no transport available, the Royal Hellenic Navy put a gun-boat at their disposal. 'Now the local powers that be [a reference to the naval base on Poros] have changed their attitude towards me; they take me seriously,' quipped George, in the privacy of his diary. As well as Lehmann, the party included Rex Warner, Maurice Cardiff (another friend from the British Council), and Katsimbalis. 'When we reached Poros,' Lehmann recalled:

> we found the poet awaiting us in genial mood. He discoursed to us learnedly, wittily, endlessly, and showed us his remarkable collection of

walking-sticks, many of them *objets trouvés* from his walks inland and along the shore. He looked . . . relaxed.[58]

By the time they left, the 'Seferis book' was about to become a reality. It was in the same relaxed mood, just after that visit, that George wrote to Katy Katsoyanni, the confidante of the orchestral conductor Dimitri Mitropoulos, summing up the achievements of his leave in joking style:

Mathios Paskalis . . . has been highly active of late. He has become a sculptor, a fixer of nervous wrecks, a writer for the shadow-puppet theatre . . . , and a versifier easily to be despised . . . Naturally, he has become greatly ambitious, and is preparing himself to receive the Nobel [prize for literature] . . .[59]

According to the gossip of the day, Sikelianos was under consideration by the Swedish Academy for the prestigious prize; a counter-bid had been made on behalf of Kazantzakis. In his diary, not long before this, George had noted his astonishment at the Greek temperament: Sikelianos had confided to him a proposal from Kazantzakis – that they might share the prize between them.

277

All this must have been among the topics for spirited conversation during that Indian summer on Poros. With a book of his poems about to be published in English, and with Warner ready to sit down and translate *'Thrush,'* 'Mathios Paskalis' was surely on the way to his apotheosis.[60]

Back in Athens at the end of the year, George found himself overwhelmed, almost at once, by 'the fever of the sick city.' The Ministry had yet to find a role for him. In February, there was a strike throughout the civil service over pay; George does not mention how this affected him, but he had begun the year worrying about money. It was not until April that he would be assigned to regular duties, in the UN section of the Ministry, and even that would be only temporary.[61]

On the wider stage, during the first months of 1947, the future looked more bleak than ever. In the north of the country, in the mountainous areas of the Peloponnese, and on some of the islands, the newly formed Democratic Army, the successor to ELAS, and loyal to the central committee of the Greek Communist Party (KKE), was taking the field in defiance of the government in Athens. Soon, a third of the rural population and half the area of the country would be under its control. The British government had announced its intention of stopping all economic aid to Greece, and drastically scaling down its military presence, on 31 March. In a speech to the US Congress on 12 March, President Harry S. Truman announced the policy of containing the expansion of Soviet influence, that would ever afterwards be known as the 'Truman doctrine.' The future of Greece, for the next twenty-seven years, would depend on the US. There was no way, now, of averting the third and most deadly round of the civil war, that had already begun in the mountains and would continue until October 1949.[62]

In Athens, during 1947, a vicious little civil war of another kind was waged in the daily press and literary magazines. This, too, was fought in three rounds, and George was at the centre of each of them. On 26 February, he was awarded the Palamas Prize for poetry. It was the first time the award, established at the time of the poet's death, in 1943, had been made. The prize money, a million drachmas, would hardly solve all George's financial problems; it was the equivalent, at the time, of about two hundred US dollars. The award provoked an outcry that had little to do with the literary qualities of the entries submitted.[63]

Then on 2 May, George gave a talk at the British Institute, at the opening of the first ever exhibition of paintings by the 'naif' painter Theophilos Hatzimichael. Theophilos, as he is generally known, had been one of the discoveries of the 1930s; for George, as for other members of Katsimbalis' circle, he represented the true 'man of the people,' a counterpart in the visual arts to Makriyannis. The poet and critic of the older generation, I.M. Panayotopoulos, who had been awarded the Palamas Prize for criticism at the same time as George won the award for poetry, chose the opportunity for a belated attack on Katsimbalis' circle. 'Cliques,' wrote Panayotopoulos, in the April-June issue of *Grammata (Letters)*, 'are a cancer in our national life.'[64]

278

The lecture on Theophilos turned out to be only a pretext. What had really incensed those on the outside of the 'clique' was its success in reaching a non-Greek audience. The third round of this civil war in miniature was fought in the summer and autumn of 1947 over the publication by Levesque of a book called *Domaine grec*, that aimed to introduce contemporary Greek writing to a French readership. Levesque had shared the privations of Athens throughout the occupation, and was devoted to Greece; *Domaine grec* was the second of three books that he would produce in as many years, all dedicated to modern Greek literature and culture. Later, Levesque would engagingly confess what was loudly alleged at the time: that he did not know Greek and had relied on the writers whom he translated, and especially on an unnamed Katsimbalis. In the small and now viciously polarised world of Athenian literati, *Domaine grec* proved to be dynamite. The very existence of the book proved that Katsimbalis and his 'clique' had been able to monopolise the way that modern Greek culture was perceived abroad.

Here, too, politics was never far from the surface. The right branded Levesque a communist, since he was close to Gide and Eluard; the left thought they could have done a much better job themselves. As Levesque was vilified by both sides, so was George. The right hounded him because his left-wing sympathies during the war made him, in their eyes, a communist; the left cold-shouldered him because he was not.[65]

Almost a year later, the furore had still not died down. 'Your very existence by itself annoys them and drives them mad even if you're not publishing and aren't even in Greece,' wrote Katsimbalis to George, the following May. But by the time Katsimbalis' letter reached him, George was far away, and his fortunes had taken two further turns for the worse.[66]

### Into the cold

At the Ministry, in the summer of 1947, George's future was still unclear. His promotion was blocked, for the second time, in June. It seems to have been in response to this that the ambassador in Ankara, Pericles Skeferis, with whom George had served in Albania and in the Middle East, sent a telegram to Athens requesting his services. Skeferis (the stress is on the first syllable) had an urgent vacancy for a Counsellor. This was the rank immediately above George's present one; almost certainly, it was a friendly gesture on Skeferis' part, intended to force the Ministry's hand, so that George would have promotion as well as a posting. Skeferis was one of the very few superiors George ever had with whom he seems to have enjoyed mutual trust and respect. But all that happened was that George was relegated to the diplomatic backwater of Ankara with, for the time being, no more than his present salary and status.[67]

Exactly a week after the exchange of telegrams with Ankara, George was taken ill. The doctor diagnosed kidney trouble, and confined him to bed. X-rays showed a stone in his right kidney. He was back at his desk by the middle of July, but it was necessary to have the stone removed before taking up his posting in Turkey. George went into the Evangelismos Hospital, in Kolonaki, at the end of October. After the operation, the wound was painful and slow to heal. George can still have been far from well when he sailed with Maro for Turkey, on 4 February 1948.[68]

279

The Turkish capital, Ankara, surrounded by the bare, high Anatolian plateau, impressed George as a 'cubist mushroom of a city.' It had become a capital city only in 1923; since then its buildings had multiplied even faster than those of Athens. Despite this, there was a housing shortage, and for their first five months George and Maro had to live in a hotel. The intense cold affected his health; snow lay on the ground for several months; the last snowfall came during Orthodox Holy Week, at the end of April. A poem written at the darkest time of his second winter sums up much of George's experience of Ankara. It begins: 'The snow here is never-ending.'[69]

Ankara was a very different world from that of the Aegean coast where George had been born and brought up, though he no doubt remembered that his maternal grandmother's family came from the region. Twice, in the past, he had been posted to the consulate in his birthplace of Izmir (Smyrna), but on each occasion the appointment had been rescinded before it could be taken up. Mentally, George must already have confronted the probability that one day he would come face to face with the ghosts of his past. Within a month of arriving in Ankara, he had written to his mother's sister, Stefania (Beba) Farkouch, who had married a Turk and now lived in Budca, a few miles outside Izmir; to Beba he outlined his first, tentative plans to revisit the place 'that I've such longing and such dread to see again.' More than two years would pass before these conflicting feelings were sufficiently resolved for George to undertake what he later called his 'descent into Hades.'[70]

He was glad to be away from Athens, and its atmosphere of 'fanaticism.' According to Angelos Vlachos, who served with him throughout his time at the Ankara embassy, George 'had gone into a species of hibernation. In the functions of the embassy he took minimal interest and spent all his time reading.' Although in a few letters from Ankara, George refers to having 'a lot of work,' what Vlachos perceived was probably not far from the truth. At one level, the delayed promotion, which finally came through that spring, may have contributed to this attitude. But George, although he was unlikely to say so to a junior colleague, had exerted himself, for years, far beyond the routine demands of a minor embassy; in the Middle East, and then in Athens, working under Damaskinos, the stakes had been of the very highest. Now, in Greece, the civil war had entered its most prolonged and violent phase. The civil war, as he told T.S. Eliot a few years later, had been 'the most terrible ordeal of all.' But with the exception of the letter to Miller that provides this chapter with its epigraph, there is not a single explicit reference to these terrible events in George's diaries, poems, or letters written while the 'third round' of the civil war was going on.[71]

No such taboo applied to that other, literary, civil war in Athens. Ruefully adopting the terminology of their enemies, George now addressed Katsimbalis, in letters, as 'Leader,' that is, of the 'clique.' The latest intervention, in April and May 1948, came from George's friend, the poet Takis Papatsonis. This was not a personal attack, like the others. Papatsonis thought it was time to cast down the twin idols of Katsimbalis' circle: the legacy of the French Symbolist poets, and a particular version of an indigenous, popular Greek spirit, as George and others admired it in the works of 'naif' artists like Makriyannis and Theophilos. For Papatsonis, the true tradition of Hellenism had been carried for centuries, and throughout many lands, by the medieval, Christian world of the Byzantine empire.[72]

George reproached his friend bitterly for this public attack, as he saw it; but he did not really take issue with its substance. For years he had been troubled by the disjunction between the broad historical and geographical extent of Hellenism on the one hand, and the narrow physical (and intellectual) frontiers of the Greek state on the other. Indeed, not long before this, he had even wondered, half seriously, if this narrowing of frontiers were not the root cause of the symptoms of civil war in Greece. Now, far outside those boundaries, in a foreign country where Hellenism had left its visible, historical traces, it was not long before George was writing to Katsimbalis: 'I'm trying to look, so far as I can without prejudice, at Byzantium. I'm going carefully.' To Katsimbalis' cousin, Zissimos Lorenzatos, with whom he had a lively correspondence at this time, he wrote: 'I'm trying to understand what Byzantium is. Something very different from how it looks from Athens.'[73]

281

It took a good part of the summer of 1948 for George and Maro to move their belongings into the house they were finally able to rent, at number 373, Atatürk Bulvarı. The house was small, but it had a garden with fruit trees and a rampant climbing vine, where their two cats could roam. George had had a car shipped out from Greece, and was learning to drive. For the first time since his marriage, he had an office at home where he could withdraw to work. His name for the secluded garden was '*l'angolo franciscano*' (the Franciscan corner), after it had reminded an Italian colleague of a Franciscan monastery; this became the title of a poem in which he also described it.[74]

While this upheaval was going on, *The King of Asine and Other Poems* was at last published; it had been delayed by the shortage of paper in postwar Britain. The book received no fewer than fifteen reviews, almost all of them exceptionally enthusiastic. Valaoritis wrote to George excitedly from London: it was the best critical response Lehmann had had to any of the books he had published so far. Within the year, Katsimbalis had gathered the reviews and printed the best extracts, in Greek translation, in the *Anglo-Hellenic Review*. It was a triumph. But George knew better than anyone how precarious were its foundations. As he wrote to Rex Warner, who had contributed a warm introduction to the book:

> I cannot help being amused when I read certain reviews published in respectable London papers, which seem to assume that I am an accomplished writer in my country — and on the other hand, little commentaries from no less respectable Athens papers, like the Estia, which affirm that my poems are bound to cause a hailstorm of rotten tomatoes.[75]

After that, the rest of 1948 was a difficult time. In Paris, Stelios had suffered a stroke at the end of the previous year; he could write only a few lines at the bottom of letters dictated to Thérèse. Now, not content with renting out his own part of the Kydathinaion Street house to strangers, Stelios insisted on selling it outright, 'for the price of a loaf of bread,' according to George. Threatened with the final, and irreparable 'dispersal' of the family home, Ioanna, who was the only one of the three siblings on the spot, acted decisively and bought out their father's share of the building. In doing so, she seems to have offended George deeply; precisely how is not clear. It was the only time in their lives that brother and sister quarrelled; it lasted for six months.[76]

That winter, while the 'steppes' of Anatolia were deeply covered in snow, George was once again ill. With Maro's help he occupied himself in making fair copies of the diaries that he had kept since returning from Paris to Greece in 1925. Almost the first thing he had done, on moving into the house on Atatürk Bulvarı, had been to bring his current diary up to date. Now, during this bleakest of winters, he began systematically editing and copying the daily traces of his life during the past quarter of a century. It was a laborious task; and it would continue to occupy him, off and on, until the eve of his departure from Turkey. It was prompted, in part at least, by timely thoughts of his own mortality, and also by a sense of bitterness about the chances of posthumous fame for a poet in the modern world.[77]

When the long Anatolian winter finally gave way to spring, George's spirits began rapidly to improve. Preparing the ground for their more exten-

282

sive travels the following year, he and Maro took time off to visit the old Ottoman capital of Bursa (Prousa in Greek) on the Sea of Marmara, and Istanbul (Constantinople in Greek, or more familiarly, *I Poli* – 'The City').

While at Bursa, he wrote a poem that pays tribute to Beethoven's string quartet, known as '*Canzona di ringraziamento*' – the composer's thanks to the Deity for having come through an illness, 'in the Lydian mode.' George, on the shores of ancient Lydia, gave thanks to the Deity in his own way. In the picturesque backwater that was modern Bursa, whose mosques and mausolea evoked the splendour of one of the holiest cities of the Ottoman empire, and in the shadow of the mountain known to Greeks and western classicists as 'Bithynian Olympus,' George was struck forcibly by what he called 'the fluctuations and the extinction of the power of Caesar.' Writing to Lorenzatos, he continued: 'nothing provokes greater feelings of melancholy than an expended power.'[78]

Later in the year, in Constantinople, poking round the ruins of the city's fortifications, built by the emperor Theodosios in the fifth century (and in those days in a much poorer state of repair than they are today), George again found himself wondering at this 'relic of a spent power.' In the Kahrye Camii, the former monastery of the Chora, whose fourteenth-century mosaics had so impressed him back in 1938, he met the American art historian Thomas Whittemore, who was working on their restoration. He was appalled at the poor condition of the Vlachernae palace of the Byzantine emperors, and at the way the railway tracks weave in and out of the shore walls along the Sea of Marmara.[79]

But it was not the might of the Byzantine empire, nor of the Ottoman that had followed it into oblivion, whose end struck George with the greatest pathos that autumn. Touti, the older of the couple's two cats, had died a year ago; George honoured her with a mock-heroic epitaph. But Ramazan, the younger, died the day after their return from Istanbul to Ankara. He had waited for them, it seemed to George, before climbing into the trellised vine to die. George was deeply affected by this 'miniature death.' In a poem completed twenty years later, he would pay tribute to:

> Ramazan the way he stared out death,
> for days on end in the snows of Anatolia
> in the frozen sun
> staring for days on end, the little household god.[80]

283

As he prepared to round off his own half-century, the following February, George was more preoccupied than he had ever been with life's passing. At the same time, on the other side of the scale, books of his poems were in print in French and English; in Athens he had just brought out a second edition of his translations of T.S. Eliot, with a new introduction. A new collected edition of his *Poems, 1924–46*, would soon be ready to go into circulation in Athens, in two thousand copies. The last marked-up pages went off to Katsimbalis, who was overseeing the publication, on 9 January. He had even taken up work again on the unfinished book on Cavafy, that he had abandoned almost two years before.[81]

Then in the early hours of 19 January 1950, on the other side of the world, his brother Angelos died suddenly, in his sleep.[82]

**Among the dead**

The historic little Army post Presidio of Monterey is sometimes deceptively called 'the country club.' Built on the site of an eighteenth-century Spanish fort, it enjoys a bland California climate and a view of the nearby Pacific. Today, however, its yellow barrack walls house one of the country's highest-powered schools – the biggest and most intensive language center in the United States.

This was how *Newsweek*, at the time, described the US Army Language School, established on the outskirts of San Francisco soon after the Second World War. Angelos Seferiadis had come in the summer of 1948 to work in the Greek department that had been opened there soon after the announcement of the 'Truman doctrine' the previous year.[83]

Life had not been easy for Angelos in the United States. The youngest of the Seferiadis siblings had never been one to accept the 'short-cuts' that even George would concede that life sometimes demands. Following the war, Angelos spent two years in New York, where he worked for the Greek-language newspaper *National Herald*, and may also have been briefly employed in the press department of the Greek consulate. Soon after his arrival there he was befriended by Ann Arpajoglu, an Anatolian Greek working on the paper; Ann had lived in America for many years and was now an American citizen. By early 1948, Angelos' position in New York had become wretched; with the Greek civil war now at its height, he was the target of repeated accusations, emanating from official sources, that he was a communist.[84]

284

Ann, now in charge of the Greek department at Monterey, stepped in at this crisis in Angelos' life to bring him to California. Announcing his brother's death to George by letter, she introduced herself as the person who had been closest to Angelos in America. From the exchange of letters between George and Ann during the months after Angelos' death, it is clear that she had cared for him deeply. In these letters, Ann presented Angelos as the 'scapegoat for the Greek tragedy of the last fifteen years;' a victim of conspiracy and fate; eventually she confided to George that 'it was you they envied, Angelos they persecuted.'[85]

As a result of these accusations, less than a month before Angelos' death, the Federal Bureau of Investigation had come to the school to question him; he had been denounced, according to Ann, by the Greek consulate in San Francisco. It was, she wrote to George, 'the unkindest cut of all.' By the time the FBI report came through, exonerating him completely, at the end of January, Angelos was dead.[86]

Ann believed firmly that at the time he died Angelos' fortunes had been set, at last, to rise. Soon, she informed George, he would have had a work permit and a home of his own; he would have been able to fulfil his dream and bring his young son out from Greece. He was a poet, too, and had aspirations to publish his first book of poems. George always had faith in his brother's poetic abilities, and many years later brought out this collection of poems with his own affectionate afterword.[87]

285

But on the night of 18–19 January, with the results of the FBI investigation hanging over him, and subject to periodic fits of depression, Angelos Seferiadis can have seen little to hope for in his future. The post-mortem examination gave the cause of death as undiagnosed diabetes. But when he read Ann's account of how his brother had been found, George must have wondered. Angelos had been reading a book of ancient philosophy before he went to sleep; the book had been left open at a page in which Plato discusses the immortality of the soul. In a drawer beside his bed was found an unfinished letter to Ann, written, to her surprise, in English. Apparently there was also something for George: 'they told me there was a terribly bleak letter ready for posting.' This must be the same as 'the terrible letter intended – it's sticking out a mile – for you,' that Ann mentioned on another occasion. It if ever reached George, this letter does not appear to have been preserved.[88]

It had been, as George soon wrote to console Ioanna, a 'gentle death.' The possibility that it might not have been a natural one is never raised, either in the extant correspondence or in the tributes to their brother published much later by both George and Ioanna. Both do, however, mention their brother's devotion to Shakespeare's *Hamlet*, which he had translated into Greek; Ioanna even says that 'he had his heroes: Ajax and Hamlet,' surely the two most suicidal tragic heroes in literature. George would certainly never have forgotten the day in Paris when Angelos had rushed into their flat, having sliced through his own vein, as an act of defiance against a fellow student who had offended him. And George had been frank enough, in his own student days, to confide in his sister, at length, his own thoughts of suicide.[89]

There is no substantive evidence that Angelos Seferiadis may have taken his own life. But the shadow of a possibility, its outline sharpened by silence, can only have deepened the sense of helplessness and loss that Ioanna and George experienced now and for long afterwards.

At the beginning of May, Maro left for Athens, to help her elder daughter, Mina, prepare for her wedding. George had now completed his two-year tour of duty in Ankara; he could expect news of his next posting at any time. If he wished to confront the ghosts of his childhood, and revisit Smyrna and Skala, he would have to do it soon. Angelos' death no doubt compounded the need to go back, but also his reluctance. The absence of Maro perhaps helped him crystallise his plans; this was not something that he could share with someone close to him, not even with Maro.[90]

The opportunity came about through the veteran Swedish archaeologist Axel Persson, who was now digging at the Hellenistic site of Lavranda (ancient Labraunda) in south-west Turkey. There was a certain irony in this, not lost on George: Persson had been the excavator of the citadel of Asine, and had therefore unwittingly provided the inspiration for George's most famous poem; as a result, the visit to his own buried past could not avoid being linked, in his mind, not only with that poem, but also with the archaeological traces of Hellenism on these shores. He had met Persson for the first time in Athens in 1947, and again in Ankara, and had taken an immediate liking to him.[91]

George now teamed up with the Swedish ambassador in Ankara, Eric von Post, for a two-week archaeological tour of the Aegean coast. Von Post was interested in buying antiquities; but he was also travelling officially, in a chauffeur-driven jeep, with George as his unofficial companion. It was still an arduous journey, through country where tourism at the time was unknown; but the sometimes comically over-zealous attention of local officials, as described by George, undoubtedly smoothed their path. For the ambassador, the focal point of the trip was to be their visit to the Swedish excavations at Lavranda; for George, it was to be Smyrna and, if possible, Skala. His feelings were perhaps mixed on being told, before leaving Ankara, that Urla Iskelesi (Skala) now lay within a prohibited military zone.[92]

They set off from Ankara on 22 June. On the first part of the journey, it rained incessantly. The roads were frequently all but impassable, accommodation primitive. Proud of his newly acquired driving skills, George took the wheel of the jeep and safely negotiated the steep hairpin bends of the mountain pass between Ushak and Denizli. They reached the sea at Marmaris, opposite Rhodes; George had his first sea-bathe in almost three years. Today a brash tourist centre, the tiny fishing hamlet of Marmaris in those days was incapable of producing even the portion of freshly grilled fish that George craved.[93]

To reach Lavranda, high up on the Boz Dağ mountain range (Tmolos in Greek) they had to leave the jeep behind; it was a steep climb on horseback to the site. He slept under canvas, and more soundly than at any time since Poros, when he had been writing '*Thrush*.' 'I'm finding myself again,' he wrote in his diary; 'a new man.' He and von Post spent three days at Lavranda with the Swedish archaeological team. By now George felt confident enough with Persson to broach the candidature of Sikelianos for the Nobel prize, only to learn that it been torpedoed by the Greek government – presumably on political grounds. At almost exactly the same time, and unknown to George, Valaoritis was writing prophetically to Katsimbalis from London: even if 'our great poet,' Sikelianos, should fail to win the Nobel, 'Seferis won't fail to carry it off.'[94]

After Lavranda, they travelled constantly, all the while coming closer to the world of George's own childhood. He was struck not only by the ancient monuments and inscriptions in Greek, but by the sound of Greek being spoken in some of the villages they passed. Even the 1923 Treaty of Lausanne had not finally eradicated the Greek language from Anatolia; in his travels George often encountered Muslims from Macedonia or Crete, refugees like himself who had been displaced in the opposite direction. The exchange of populations had been made on the basis of religion, not language; and many of the Muslims from Greece, particularly those from Crete, spoke only their regional dialect of Greek. It moved George deeply to hear the language of *Erotokritos* spoken in the streets of Bodrum (ancient Halikarnassos), even if the local church had been turned into a

287

butcher's shop, and local memory could recall no more than that it had once been a cinema. 'Not,' George added in his diary, 'that we've treated the mosques [in Greece] any differently.'[95]

They reached Izmir late on Saturday, 1 July. It had already been getting dark as they passed the ancient site of Ephesus, in those days a good two hours' drive away. George was beginning to suffer from the exhaustion of constant travelling. It was the breeze, and the scent of herbs, that alerted him first as they approached the outskirts of the city from the south. 'My God,' he asked himself, 'what am I about to do?'

Soon the jeep drew up outside the Commercial Club, once the Sporting Club, on the 'Quai.' Although gutted by the fire of September 1922, it had been rebuilt and remained in use until it was demolished, a few years after George's visit, to make way for the headquarters of NATO's south-eastern command. It was a Saturday evening in a provincial city; a dance was going on downstairs. After dinner, the visitors took a turn along the waterfront, where they met two diplomatic colleagues from the Netherlands. Together, they looked for the house where George had been born, and had lived for the first fourteen years of his life. They found only waste ground. As though to console him, one of the Dutchmen murmured: 'The Greeks say that the Turks set fire to Smyrna; the Turks say that the Greeks did it. Who can know the truth?'

288

At the time, George said nothing. Later, reflecting on this remark, as the 'moral' of the whole story of his return, he would add: 'The evil thing happened; what matters is who redeems the evil.'[96]

Next morning, the summer sunlight on the sea, and the twin peaks of the mountain that rises to the west of the city, called the Two Brothers in Greek, were as they had always been. As George described this first sight of modern Izmir in daylight, the city, like a ghost, had lost its shadow.[97]

George now learned that he could visit Skala after all. He and von Post set off in the jeep at eight in the morning. It was a Sunday; there was traffic making for the coastal villages. Once again, George was gripped by a sensation close to panic. 'I know the crisis is going to come and I can't gauge the consequences of what I was so thoughtless as to embark upon; that I've done something like a provocation to the dead, a violation of the nature of things.' As they went, he talked to his companion about where they were going, and its significance for him; but it was only at the mention of the ancient name for Skala, Clazomenae, that the Swedish diplomat showed real interest. Essentially, at this moment of 'crisis,' George was alone, as he had no doubt wanted to be.

It was a day of perfect stillness. The little harbour with its semi-circle of stone-built houses was almost deserted. The 'little house,' that his grand-mother had left him in her will, was a ruin, locked up and deserted, though the outhouses behind it were still intact. The shop next door had collapsed; but beyond it his grandmother's house had been enlarged and now seemed to be the home of someone of consequence. He walked right round the harbour; the old wooden jetty had gone, though the stumps still remained, protruding from the water. The harbour that had once been a hive of activity now contained only 'three dormant boats;' George exchanged greet-ings with the single fisherman in sight. Otherwise the only people he saw in the entire visit were a couple of soldiers and a group of children that ran out of one of the derelict houses 'like large rodents.'

The Greek church had been turned into a school. They drove up to the main town of Urla (Vourla in Greek), where George recognised nothing. But they met a guard from the fever hospital, the former Ottoman quar-antine station on the peninsula next to the harbour of Skala, and he offered to take them there. They all went swimming, and the guard took them to the cave that had been the church of St John. George saw once again where     289
the subterranean altar had been, and the stones that had been blackened by the candles of Christian worship. The guard knew the old story, that had been current in George's childhood, about a lost secret passage leading to the mainland. 'You can chase away the gods sometimes, but the gestures of worship don't disappear so easily,' he commented.

All in all, and including the ten-minute drive to and from Skala to Vourla and out to the peninsula of St John, George must have spent no more than two hours at Skala. Exactly as he had foreseen, years ago when he wrote the poem 'The Return of the Exile,' everything that he remembered from before the age of twelve had shrunk in memory:

> The landscape was the inside of a sphere, and the things enclosed in this sphere, and I with them, had diminished and shrunk and fallen apart, so as to become a broken mock-up of the past, forgotten on a shelf.

As they left, to have lunch farther down the coast at Kokaryali (birth-place of Aristotle Onassis), George understood how it was that Lot's wife, in the Old Testament, had turned into a pillar of salt when she looked back.

He would return twice more to Smyrna; but never again to Skala.[98]

Two days later George and his travelling companion were back in Ankara. They had covered 2,876 kilometres, presumably not including the ascent on horseback to Lavranda and a day's excursion by boat from Bodrum to the Greek island of Kos.[99]

His diplomatic duties in Turkey were now all but over. As soon as Maro returned from Athens, they set about packing up the house; from the end of July they were once again homeless. He had been promoted, for the second time in two years; but there was no certain word from the Ministry about where he would be sent next. Rome, London, and Alexandria were all possibilities; before long he was complaining that in the eyes of the Ministry he was *'bon pour l'Orient,'* meaning in effect that he was still on the sidelines.[100]

While this was going on, he and Maro found time for a three-day visit, postponed from the previous summer, to the rock-cut monasteries of central Anatolia, near Kayseri (Caesarea), in the region known in Greek as Cappadocia. They travelled with George's junior colleague Angelos Vlachos and his wife Ninette; a fifth was the military attaché of the embassy, who this time would provide the obligatory jeep. Here, where the Orthodox monastic tradition had flourished for centuries, far from cities or the influences of learning, George sought and found something of the underlying popular culture of Byzantium, an equivalent of *Erotokritos*, Makriyannis and Theophilos of later centuries. It had been from here, too, as he no doubt also remembered, that the first recorded Seferis had taken a wife, in the early nineteenth century.[101]

On 27 July 1950, Katsimbalis wrote to tell him that his collected poems had been published by Ikaros, in Athens. From day to day George was expecting word from the Ministry. His exile in the Anatolian 'steppe,' and his long-postponed return to his birthplace should both, now, have been behind him; a chapter of his life had closed. But here, his hopes proved premature.[102]

During the hiatus that followed through August and September, George and Maro spent a fortnight in Istanbul. Then, on 13 October, they were on the train from Ankara to Izmir. Back in July, George had spent barely twenty-four hours in the places he had known as a child. This was surely rather less than he had promised himself when he had first come to Turkey.

290

Seizing the opportunity afforded by some minor official business, he decided to take Maro to Izmir for ten days.[103]

It was perfect late-autumn weather; they stayed, as he had done before, at the former Sporting Club. Armed with *Murray's Handbook* of 1898, he led Maro through the streets, most of them unrecognisable. They were shown the stumps of masonry and a mass of wild herbs where the Greek Orthodox cathedral of St Photini had been; it reminded George of London in 1944. The edges of the city – the streets near the Point, the old Ottoman administrative centre, and the slopes of Mount Pagos – had been untouched by the destruction of 1922; he pointed out to Maro the distinctively 'rococo' decorations of the villas of well-to-do Greeks and Europeans of old Smyrna that had survived. They spent time with his aunt, Beba Farkouch, and her family at Budca, in the southern suburbs of the city; he found a friend in Sherif Remzi, a merchant in figs whom he had first met in July. This genial Turkish businessman and candidate for parliament had been provoked by the line in *The Waste Land* about 'Mr Eugenides, the Smyrna merchant,' into becoming a lifelong admirer of T.S. Eliot; in the cavernous recesses of his warehouse, while telephones rang and the year's harvest from the Menderes (Meander) valley was disposed about the world, George and Remzi talked poetry.

He took Maro to Ephesus. The ancient site, its harbour now landlocked and miles from the sea, its Hellenistic theatre and the Christian basilica dedicated to St John, became the emblem, in his mind, for all the ancient Greek cities of the Anatolian seaboard whose ruins he had visited that summer; cities that had been abandoned or had declined at about the same time as the pagan Greco-Roman civilisation of antiquity had given way to Christianity. It seemed to George, now, that the Smyrna he remembered, of thirty years ago, had much more in common with these ruins of the distant past, than with Izmir now. 'I don't feel hatred,' he wrote in his diary, after looking at the ruins of St Photini, 'what I feel most strongly inside me is the opposite of hatred: an attempt to *accommodate* in my mind the mechanism of catastrophe.'[104]

George and Maro departed from Izmir, the traditional way, by sea. They were bound for Istanbul, Ankara, and before long, at last, for Athens. As the ship, the *Iskenderun*, slipped through the waters of the Gulf of Smyrna in the early afternoon of 24 October 1950, George found himself sailing out along the course that used to be taken by the old steamer, with its drunken Armenian captain, on the short trip down to Skala. With his eyes, he followed the 'cart-track' on which the family had made its slow progress down

291

the coast at the start of each summer holiday. Surprisingly quickly, he recognised the three islands off Skala.

That night, in his diary, writing with his brother's pen, he confessed that at the sight his eyes had filled with tears.[105]

# 10
# Paradise Found
# 1951–1955

It was the revelation of a world and even the experience of a human drama that, beyond the exigencies of everyday dealings, is the measure and judge of our humanity. . . . It is a strange thing to say today: Cyprus is a place where the miracle still functions.

(Author's note to ...*Cyprus, Where It Was Ordained For Me...*, September 1955, Famagusta)[1]

## A time of transition

Six months after that departure from Izmir, George and Maro arrived at London's Victoria Station on the boat-train from Paris. The three-day journey, by ship and train, via Marseille and the French capital was still, at the beginning of the decade, the normal means of travel from Athens. Maro was recovering from an emergency operation for appendicitis. On 20 April 1951, George took up his duties as Counsellor at the embassy in London. It had been, he recorded with undisguised irritation, the most exhausting transfer of his career; he had been in professional limbo for nine months. Since December, he had been in Athens, except for a brief holiday with Maro in the Peloponnese and a final return to Turkey to hand over to his successor, in March. This, except for the briefest of visits, near the end of his life, was George's last contact with the country of his birth.[2]

Since the end of the civil war, in October 1949, a centrist government had been elected in Greece; it included Tsatsos' brother Mistos (Themistocles) and Kartalis; probably, however, it was the general change in political climate, rather than the direct intervention of his friends, that had brought George in from the cold – temporarily, as things would turn out.

His life in London, now, was very different from what it had been in the early 1930s. He and Maro could afford to move into a flat at 7 Sloane Avenue, SW3, a fashionable address and one of two in the city that today bear a blue plaque to commemorate his stay there. When he had lived in London before, he had been unknown and had no contact with the British literary world; then, even Katsimbalis' efforts to secure him an introduction to T.S. Eliot had fallen through. Now, since the publication of *The King of Asine and Other Poems*, George at once found doors open everywhere. One of the first people he met was Eliot.

It happened at the end of May, at an impromptu dinner party given by Stephen Spender. No sooner had George and Maro arrived, than they were being greeted by the great man, with a glass of champagne in his hand. 'I was watching George as he was introduced, the unexpectedness of it moved him deeply,' Maro reported to Katsimbalis afterwards. It was she who had the opportunity to talk to Eliot first. She was seated at his table, and spoke to him in French; Maro's English was always limited, while French was, literally, her mother tongue. Before George came over to join them at the end of dinner, Maro had already, in her forthright way, gone straight to the heart of the matter. 'Since he's translated you,' she said to Eliot, 'many people think he also imitates you.' This was a sore point with George: only five days previously, he had been incensed to receive the book by Timos Malanos, *The Poetry of Seferis*, whose main thrust is precisely this. To Maro's pleasure and relief, Eliot replied, 'I don't think so at all, *mais absolument pas!*'[3]

It was the first of five meetings between the two poets over the next year and a half. With the exception of this first one, George kept a meticulous record of their conversations; on Eliot's death, in 1965, he would publish the edited extracts of these and a few later diary entries as his personal obituary.[4]

Soon, in addition to Spender, who had hosted the party that May, George had renewed a number of old acquaintances and made others: they included W.H. Auden ('that dry, athletic poet'); E.M. Forster, who had known Cavafy in Alexandria; Louis MacNeice, whom George found rather colourless: 'not the sort to get on well with Katsimbalis;' and Dylan Thomas, who was predictably drunk but redeemed himself in George's eyes by the single-mindedness with which he talked about poetry. Another was Reggie Smith, husband of Olivia Manning, whom he had last seen in Jerusalem during the 'Flap' of 1942; 'so many years didn't seem to have matured him greatly,' George noted dryly. Several friends whom he had made at the British Council in Athens after the war were in London at this time: Rex Warner, Maurice Cardiff and (briefly) Steven Runciman. Two young Greeks also contributed greatly to the warmth of George's reception in England: Nanos Valaoritis, who had done so much to make *The King of Asine* a reality; and at Cambridge, George Savidis, who was then a student at King's College, and would soon become an energetic supporter and trusted friend.[5]

Despite all this, the beginning of August, 1951, found George in a bleak mood. Because, presumably, of the distance and cost of travel, there was no question of taking summer leave in Greece. The veteran poet Angelos Sikelianos had just died; George read a moving tribute to him on the BBC Greek Service. Back home after the broadcast, he could hardly restrain his grief. Sikelianos had been not only the acknowledged greatest of Greek poets since the death of Palamas; he had at one time been close to George's sister, and had presided, with the grand benevolence of a *deus ex machina*, over the first days that George and Maro had spent together. 'He's not made to the world's measure,' George had marvelled in his diary some years before, 'the world is made to his.'[6]

At the beginning of August, with the prospect of a long weekend ahead of him, George sat down to begin organising his papers for the first time since coming to London. It was just over two months since Malanos' book about him had arrived. He wrote to Katsimbalis, that weekend, that he was 'boiling over with rage – at the calumny of it.' Not only did Malanos accuse him of imitating Eliot; he had included extracts from George's private letters from the war years. Malanos may have felt that there was sufficient precedent for this after the publication of George's letters to others about the poem '*Thrush*,' but George, always punctilious in such matters, saw it as a betrayal of trust. Behind all this, as he no doubt realised, Malanos' book was the sequel to the quarrel that had begun in the aftermath of the political and professional crises of spring 1944. On the other hand, *The Poetry of Seferis* is a serious study, only the second book (after the one by Karantonis) to be devoted entirely to George's work; and Malanos' bewildered surprise at his friend's reaction was not entirely feigned.[7]

George took the opportunity afforded by the long weekend to pen the last letter that he ever wrote to Malanos, a curt demand for the return of the original calligraphic manuscripts of *Logbook II* that, back in 1944, Malanos had generously seen through press for him. It was the bitter end of a friendship that had never been wholehearted on either side, but had at times been both close and productive. At the same time George began to compose a long and intemperate rebuttal of Malanos' argument, which he asked Katsimbalis to publish in the *Anglo-Hellenic Review*. To his credit, Katsimbalis, always better attuned than George in matters of public relations, refused.[8]

295

Returning to the embassy on Tuesday, 7 August, George found a telegram addressed to him from Paris. It was from Thérèse: Stelios Seferiadis had passed away at four o'clock the previous afternoon. There had been no one at the embassy on the Monday evening to contact George with the news. Stelios had died of a stroke, apparently the last of several. 'He didn't suffer,' George wrote to Ioanna the same day, having already despatched a telegram to Athens.

None of his children was with Stelios Seferiadis when he died. Ioanna, the most faithful, had seen him for the last time the previous summer. By that time Angelos was already dead, though Ioanna had concealed this from him. George had not seen his father for five years. The international lawyer, amateur man of letters, and former university professor died in obscurity and relative poverty, in the Parisian suburb of Ezanville, where he would be buried, surrounded by a French family with whom George had 'nothing in common.' It was because of the French relatives, George confided to Ioanna, that he had decided not even to go to the funeral.[9]

George responded curtly to the condolences of his friends. His relationship with his father had been troubled since at least his late teens. Stelios had made demands on him that he had always resented bitterly; but stern and irascible as he was, and perhaps unreasonable in his last years, Stelios had been a loving father. More able than George in the professional sphere, less talented in poetry, Stelios, too, had devoted his considerable abilities and energies to both throughout his life. George's rigorous attempts to separate these worlds in his own life had led him instinctively to try to exclude his father from the one that he valued the more highly. Where poetry was concerned, father and son had always circled one another warily, neither prepared to acknowledge the other's gift. But George was filial enough to be moved, even if there is also a touch of *Schadenfreude* in this, when he learned that Cavafy had once declaimed some of his father's lines, with the comment, 'They're by some poet from Smyrna: the finest forgotten verses I know.' George always remembered this; at the time, in the bitter turmoil of his feelings that August, it cannot have been far from his mind that the source of this rather backhanded poetic tribute to Stelios Seferiadis had been none other than Malanos.[10]

As, indeed, with his Alexandrian friend and sometime mentor in Egypt, so with his father: the extremity of George's rejection may owe something to a troubled conscience. To both men, in very different ways, George owed more than latterly he was prepared to acknowledge (a decade later, he would remove the dedication to Malanos from the second edition of his

*Essays*). In the case of his father, the nearest he came to acknowledging this was in a letter to Ioanna, written from Ankara three years before Stelios' death:

> It's strange, how much this man has hurt me. It's perhaps the greatest sorrow I feel in my life. And even now, after so much learned and suffered, I ask, why? why?[11]

In London, George was, as usual, wryly observant of his surroundings. Among some six thousand guests at the royal garden party in the grounds of Buckingham Palace, he was shocked to see the great and good of the land queuing patiently for 'a cup of coffee and some dreadful cake.' The noble demeanor of a visiting black African dignitary, juxtaposed to the vulgar, mass-produced clothes he was wearing, set George thinking about what was valuable in the 'mire' that was 'transitional Britain.' The gentlemen's club where Louis MacNeice invited him for his second meeting with Eliot impressed him by its shabby, down-at-heel condition:

> 'A very good place,' they say. 'Good' in London often has a mysterious sense in this extraordinarily transitional period of its history.[12]

297

These thoughts came to a head when George met Eliot again, a year later, at the offices of the publishing firm Faber and Faber, where Eliot was director. When he arrived at 24 Russell Square (a legendary address in literary circles in those days), George was shown into a small waiting room, with parcels of books heaped round the floor; the clerk took him to the lift.

> He pressed the button for some time. No response. There are places here – perhaps the ones that strike you most – where everything seems to be worn out by the years; it's a surprise if anything works.

To the despair of the unfortunate clerk, who had to accompany him, George impatiently decided to abandon the lift and walk up three flights of stairs. He found Eliot in the director's office: 'a cell, we'd have called it in the days of Palamas. You could hardly get three visitors into it.' The 'cell' was long and narrow; but the obligatory tea and biscuits were laid out.[13]

In the presence of its acknowledged greatest poet, George saw at the heart of the once-powerful British empire the symptoms of a 'spent power,' of an empire on the cusp of decline, that he had diagnosed so vividly among the weeds and ruined walls of Constantinople, and elsewhere in his travels in Anatolia. It was an intuition that would stay with him and deepen during the next few years, years that would be crucial in his own, and his country's, relationship with Great Britain.

For a time after his father's death, George seems seriously to have considered giving up his career and his public responsibilities in order to live as a writer. The repressive shadow of Stelios was no longer there to force him back into the path of duty; but a stronger reason would seem to have been the real temptation afforded by his experience of literary London. After George had given a highly successful reading at the ICA (Institute of Contemporary Arts), flanked by Louis MacNeice and Rex Warner, Maro wrote to Katsimbalis a spirited account of the occasion, and went on:

> After things like that I'm racking my brains trying to think of ways and means, what we might do for George to able to change his life. But there's nothing to be done; this way he'll go on frittering himself away between a boring desk and the worm that gnaws him.[14]

She ended by asking Katsimbalis to help, though it is not at all clear what she was hoping he might be able to do.

298

Evidently, George and Maro were seriously discussing a change of direction at this time, since he wrote to Ioanna shortly afterwards that 'to earn your bread today by writing is a greater slavery than the career.' At least, he went on, in the service of the Ministry, he had complete independence in the things that mattered to him most. George was as divided on the issue as he had ever been; in diaries and letters at this time, he reverts to the complaints of his earlier years about serving 'two masters.'[15]

Perhaps surprisingly, he confided this new restlessness to Eliot. But if he had hoped for encouragement from the doyen of English letters, who had himself held down a demanding job in publishing for many years, and at sixty-four showed no sign of retiring, George was to be disappointed. Eliot told him severely:

> One must have another job. You cannot devote yourself to poetry alone, because I believe that a great part of poetic creation is unconscious and there must be times when one is occupied with other things.[16]

And on another occasion, when George told him that 'it was high time for me to begin to think of ridding myself of the Service, so as to be able to work at last,' Eliot looked at him with concern: 'Ah! be careful,' he said. 'That could be dangerous.'[17]

What George did not reveal to Eliot, or probably to anyone else in England, was that ever since his father's death, at the same time as he toyed with a change of career, he had also been furiously trying to accelerate his promotion at the Ministry. For reasons that remain obscure, but can perhaps be guessed, George had renounced whatever inheritance would otherwise have passed to him from Stelios' estate.[18] From the autumn of 1951, he was acutely anxious about money. In the cause of his promotion he mobilised Ioanna and Kostakis; he enlisted the support of his former ambassador at Tirana and Ankara, Pericles Skeferis. He even wrote, formally and at length, to the new foreign minister, Evangelos Averoff-Tosizza. Leaving the service, as he explained to Ioanna while these efforts were at their height, would be an option only if they failed.[19]

The decision was taken by the Ministry at the end of June, 1952, just over a month after George's plea to Averoff. This suggests that the plea was effective, very probably thanks to the mediation of Ioanna. But what his masters in Athens awarded with one hand, they took away with the other. George had already, it seems, been warned that promotion would mean a new posting, away from the great metropolitan embassies. When, at the end of August, he learned his fate, it was to be promoted to Minister Plenipotentiary grade II, but with immediate transfer to Beirut. George was once again, in the eyes of his superiors in Athens, *bon pour l'Orient.*[20]

To sell up and move before the end of the year, as the Ministry required, would be financially ruinous, he complained to Katsimbalis. Afterwards, Maro would recall their abrupt departure from London, after only eighteen months, as a 'tragedy;' in order to make ends meet, they had even to sell their car. To Ioanna, at the time, George complained that the appointment had been 'stitched up' in such a way that he could not refuse it; 'you shouldn't treat a secretary this badly,' he railed.[21]

George and Maro left London on 9 November 1952. It was a low-key and rancorous end to a posting that had begun with such high hopes. Possibly George had been the victim of the new shift towards the Right in the Greek government: a general election that month would confirm power in the hands of the Greek Rally party, recently founded along Gaullist lines by Field-Marshal Papagos, that with American backing had come to dominate the coalition government since early spring. But it is hard to see what other outcome George could realistically have hoped for. He had not been so frustrated with his professional career for many years; but neither could he afford the financial consequences of giving it up in order to live by writing.[22]

The financial pressures the couple suffered at this time must, of course, be seen in context; who in the British literary establishment, at which George looked with such longing, could afford to live in Sloane Avenue? But George was the child of both his parents in this, and always seems to have seen a certain standard of living as his due. At the same time, he no doubt felt that he owed nothing less to Maro, whose deep and enduring sense of financial insecurity must in part, at least, have been the legacy of her years as the wife of the profligate Londos.

On their way back to Athens, George and Maro enjoyed a fortnight's holiday in Venice. Back in Greece, a rainy weekend at Delphi in December brought George close to the spirit of Sikelianos, the inspirer of the pre-war Delphic Festivals. Then on Christmas Eve, he and Maro embarked once more, bound for Beirut and George's first posting as Head of Mission.[23]

### Bon pour l'Orient

On the way, the SS. *Aeolia* put in at Alexandria, and at Limassol on the south coast of Cyprus. Alexandria, with its wartime memories, was 'without interest now.' Two days after Christmas, George had his first sight of Cyprus, when the ship rounded the low-lying southernmost point of the island, Cape Gata. This name is supposed to commemorate the heroic cats belonging to the local monastery of St Nicholas, that had once saved the monks from a plague of poisonous snakes. This moment and this legend would become the basis of a poem finished sixteen years later, 'The Cats of St Nicholas.' At the same time, the chief steward on board reminded George powerfully of the effete 'young men of Sidon' in a poem by Cavafy, so providing him with the germ of another poem to which in due course he would give a Cypriot setting: 'Pedlar from Sidon.' That same afternoon, George and Maro spent two hours ashore at Limassol. As he entered these waters for the first time, it is quite likely that George was already mentally preparing himself for the revelation that was to come.[24]

But now his course was set further east. George and Maro spent New Year, 1953, in the Hotel St Georges in the Lebanese capital. To Ioanna, he had just written, 'my god, what a difficult year it's been.' Sixteen months later he would write to Henry Miller, 'my first year over here as been one of the hardest of my life.' On the other hand, Steven Runciman, who spent a month in Beirut in 1953, much of it in the company of George and Maro, recalled of George and his time there:

It was a post which I think he enjoyed. It involved no serious political worries at that date; and Beirut was still a pleasant city in which to live. Moreover, the Greek Ambassador, in those countries where there was a large native Orthodox population, enjoyed a special position. In the eyes of the Orthodox believers the King of Greece was heir to the Emperor of Byzantium, God's viceroy on earth; and the Greek Ambassador was thus entitled to royal honours. George fully appreciated that historic role.[25]

In Beirut, George and Maro soon moved into a spacious apartment in the rue Georges Picot. Here, they were able to accommodate the younger members of their respective families, who came to visit. English friends who passed through, and whom they took travelling with them, apart from Runciman included C.M. (Monty) Woodhouse, the Leigh Fermors, and Osbert Lancaster; among Greek friends and colleagues, Xydis and Vlachos were warmly welcomed.[26] At the same time, George renewed acquaintance with the French archaeologist, Henri Seyrig, who in 1929 had been secretary of the French School of Archaeology in Athens, and had accompanied him in showing Edouard Herriot around the archaeological sites of Greece. Seyrig was now director of the French Archaeological Institute in Beirut.    301
It had been a chance remark of his, during that trip in 1929, that had furnished George, many years later, with the epigraph for 'Thrush;' from now on, Seyrig would be a firm friend. Another was the young Greek writer Th.D. (Boulis) Frangopoulos, who was earning his living in a Greek shipping office in Beirut; before long, Frangopoulos had established a reputation as a writer of novels, poems and plays; a decade later he would collaborate with Rex Warner in the translation of George's selected essays.[27]

George's accreditation was not only to the government of Lebanon, but also to those of Syria, Jordan, Iraq, and to the Orthodox Patriarchate in the old city of Jerusalem, then part of Jordan. The one country in the region that was closed to him, because of the tensions after the first Arab-Israeli war of 1948, was Israel. George had to spend a good deal of his time travelling throughout the region, shuttling among Beirut, Damascus, Amman, Baghdad and Jerusalem. Just as in Turkey, in these areas too, George found a particular fascination in the ruins of Greco-Roman antiquity. Cities such as Palmyra, Seleucia, Byblos, Baalbek and Jerash, even Babylon, had adopted the Greek language and Greek styles of architecture after the conquests of Alexander the Great. The 'shells' of ancient theatres, in the mountains and deserts of the Levant, made George feel strangely at home.

Many of these cities survived as dazzling ruins; the Greek and Roman public buildings of Palmyra and Jerash are grander, and in a better state of preservation, than any in Europe. Others, such as Seleucia on the banks of the Tigris, as George had already written in the poem 'Last Stop,' had 'become grazing ground for water-buffaloes / and fields for sugar-cane and maize.' He went to the site of Seleucia in May 1953, during his first official visit to Baghdad. 'The sun was setting,' he recalled, years later; 'nothing whatever remains today. Only the green of the river bank and the sound of a reed-pipe.'[28]

What struck George most forcefully on these travels in the Levant was something more than the well-worn theme of the transience of worldly power. After having come to face to face, in Turkey, with the vanished world of his own childhood, these discoveries were for him more than mere archaeological curiosity. As he had written to Lorenzatos before leaving Ankara, 'I've acquired the habit of murmuring aloud the names of cities that have sunk out of sight.' This was not just melancholia: George was already beginning to wonder about the process of decay and renewal, at once in the short span of a human life, and in the *longue durée* of history. In his youth, he had written, partly echoing Gide, 'We give birth to statues with every passing moment;' later, the fixed immobility of 'the friends who no longer know how to die' had haunted the poems of *Mythistorema*. Now, in the relics of an irrecoverable past, whether his own or that of an entire civilisation, he saw the signs of a process at work. Ancient civilisations rose and sank. The naive-seeming question was also urgent: 'how do we replace these things?' It was a question that would increasingly preoccupy George throughout his last years.[29]

302

The beginning of an answer came to him at the 'cave of Adonis,' near Beirut. Here George was struck, as he had also been at Ephesus, by the continuity from the old pagan worship to the Christian one that had ousted it centuries ago. The site, sacred in ancient times to Aphrodite, had become a place where Lebanese Christians still brought votive offerings for the Virgin Mary. A year later George experienced the same intuition more strongly while following the liturgies of Holy Week in Jerusalem. In the sound of the clapper-board summoning the Orthodox faithful to church, he heard repeated the cry of the pagan priestess Cassandra to Apollo: 'the surge of a tradition that is stronger than we are,' he tried to describe it.[30]

But the worn-out empires whose traces George found so haunting on these travels were not only ancient ones. The Arab states to which he was accredited had only recently emerged from paternalist, European control:

the French mandate over Lebanon and Syria had ended in 1944; the kingdom of Iraq was the oldest-established of the four, the successor to the British mandate in Mesopotamia in 1937, while the Hashemite Kingdom of Jordan had been born out of the partition of British-mandated Palestine and the creation of Israel in 1947. Only in Jordan would the constitutional arrangements put in place at the time of independence endure for longer than a few years (and indeed are still in place in the early twenty-first century). In all four countries the signs of rapid and sometimes chaotic transition were apparent; their élites still looked to France and Britain respectively, while the waning influence of these European powers was palpable. In Lebanon, Syria, Jordan and Iraq, George saw, much more starkly than he had in London, the same unmistakable and irreversible signs: the powers that had for so long ruled the destiny of peoples like the Arabs or the Greeks were in full retreat. What would come to replace the once unchallenged cultural supremacy of France and the world-wide reach of British imperial might?

Driving across the desert, on his first visit to Baghdad, he noted (in English) in his diary: 'There is no landlord to the desert. The desert is a sea. Largely cocacola-ized [sic] countries.' Coca-cola was then a novelty in these parts, already synonymous with the spread of American influence and capital. Just as the Americans had succeeded the British in Greece in 1947, so the new super-power was visibly doing here in the Middle East. Spending the night at a rest-house that seemed unchanged since British rule, George noted the 'puritan' absence of mirrors in the bedrooms: 'one wouldn't be astonished to see an old gentleman eating his dinner with his bowler hat on.' On a later visit to Baghdad, he would note that although the British still owned the Iraqi oilwells, the American embassy had twice the personnel of the British, and the first university in the country had been founded by American Jesuits.[31]

The Jordanian capital, Amman, struck him, on his first sight of it, as 'a village wearing modern make-up at the bottom of a hole.' Two years later, back in Amman for the wedding of King Hussein, he would describe the festivities as 'a terrible example of the "civilisation" that's fashioned in these parts out of half-settled Bedouins and coca-cola.'[32]

All these experiences would form the background to the book of poems that George would produce while he was based in Beirut. But neither the experiences themselves, nor the landscape in which most of these poems would be written, appear in them directly. It was, instead, the revelation of Cyprus and its people, during three private visits there, in 1953, 1954 and

303

1955, that would prove to be at once the crowning experience of these years, and the unifying theme of the volume to which George would give the title, ...*Cyprus, Where It Was Ordained For Me*...[33]

### Annus mirabilis

Cyprus had been part of the Ottoman empire, since its conquest from the Venetians in 1571, until 1878. In that year, the island had been leased by the Ottomans to Great Britain, as part of the settlement of the recent Russo-Turkish war, at the Congress of Berlin. When the Ottoman empire entered the First World War, in 1914, Britain formally annexed Cyprus, but the following year offered sovereignty to Greece, as part of a series of inducements and threats designed to bring Greece into the war. The Greek government of the day refused the offer, and it would never be repeated. In the Treaty of Lausanne, in 1923, after the Greek defeat in Anatolia, the boundaries and claims of the new Turkish Republic were agreed and internationally recognised; Cyprus lay outside them, and this state of affairs was finally incorporated into the Locarno Agreement of 1925. At the same time, Cyprus became formally a Crown Colony of Great Britain.

Six years later, in October 1931, Greek Cypriots urging union with Greece burned down Government House in Nicosia. The British responded with harsh measures; although feelings ran high in Greece at the time, the government of Eleftherios Venizelos pragmatically distanced itself from the aspirations of the Greeks of Cyprus. Since then, many Cypriots had served as volunteers under British command in the Second World War. Although some of the restrictions imposed after the insurrection of 1931 had since been alleviated, by the late 1940s Cypriots still had very little say, beyond the local level, in the administration of their island.

By this time, British withdrawal from long-prized overseas possessions, such as India, was giving impetus to expectations that before long Cyprus would be united with Greece. Since 1878 the proportion of the population had been stable, with about eighty per cent Greek-speaking Orthodox Christians and most of the rest Turkish-speaking Muslims. An unofficial plebiscite conducted among its members by the Orthodox Church in Cyprus, in 1949, produced a 96.5% return in favour of union, for which the Greek word, that would soon become an explosive slogan, is *enosis*. Further political impetus came a year later, in the election of the young and charismatic Michael Mouskos as Archbishop Makarios III. Following the old Ottoman system, the archbishops in Cyprus retained the title 'ethnarch,' or leader of their community; the ethnarch by tradition, if no longer in law,

304

was expected both to represent the temporal interests of his flock, and to exercise a strong political influence beyond the ecclesiastical sphere.

By the autumn of 1953, when George and Maro went to Cyprus to spend just over a month there, the British colonial government and Greek-Cypriot public opinion were on a collision course. The previous year, a campaign of painted slogans all over the island had shown just how strong were the sentiments of the majority for *enosis*; in the summer and early autumn of 1953, just before George's visit, the British Foreign Secretary, Anthony Eden, on a visit to Athens, had replied brusquely over the issue to the Greek prime minister, Field-Marshal Papagos. Attitudes were hardening on both sides, but there was as yet no serious hint of the violence that was to come. Cyprus could still be described, by the British Labour politician Richard Crossman, as 'the only amiable police state I have ever visited.'[34]

It is hard to tell to what extent George's visit to Cyprus in 1953 was premeditated, and what expectations he may have had before he went. At this time he numbered among his friends only one Greek Cypriot. This was the lawyer and landowner, Evangelos Louizos, who had become a member of Katsimbalis' circle while a student in Athens in the 1930s, and had helped to finance Katsimbalis' periodical, *Ta Nea Grammata*; George had encountered Louizos again briefly in Egypt, during the war. On the other hand, 305 two of his British friends were now working in Cyprus. Maurice Cardiff, whom he had got to know at the British Council in Athens after the war, had since been transferred to Nicosia. And Lawrence Durrell had retreated to the picturesque village of Bellapais, in the Pentadaktylos hills, and was earning a living teaching at the island's most prestigious high school, the Pancyprian Gymnasium. It seems to have been Cardiff who first thought of inviting George to Cyprus. George was fully sensitive to the potential for political embarrassment in accepting such an invitation.[35]

A few months later, the Cypriot poet, and secretary to Archbishop Makarios, Nikos Kranidiotis, sought him out in the Middle East. Kranidiotis had recently begun discovering George's work, and was soon to publish a book, warmly praising it, in Cyprus. But as Kranidiotis recalled their first meeting, he had also gone to enlist the political support of Minister Plenipotentiary Seferiadis for the archbishop's cause. George's reply was austerely diplomatic:

You ask me now, after a world war, after a terrible civil war, for us to turn against our allies, against those who today support us in the Truman doctrine and so forth. You're absolutely right. But Greece has a lot of problems. Personally I agree entirely with your ideas, that the Cypriots, as developed Greeks, should have complete self-determination.

The upshot of the meeting was another warm invitation to visit Cyprus soon, though Kranidiotis did not say that George accepted it.[56]

Katsimbalis, who had heard via Ioanna of George's plans, wrote to warn him against going, although by the time the letter reached him he was already in Cyprus. He too, wrote Katsimbalis, had received an invitation from Louizos. He was too busy to take it up, but thought to alert George to a phonecall he had had from the Foreign Ministry. An intellectual with such well-known ties to Britain (Katsimbalis had only just given up the editorship of the *Anglo-Hellenic Review*) would 'strengthen the British position' by going to Cyprus. Katsimbalis worried that George might create difficulties for himself with the Ministry if he went.[37]

By the time he arrived at Nicosia airport, on 6 November 1953, to be met there by both Louizos and Cardiff, as well as the Greek Consul General, George had had time to work out his strategy:

On the official Greek side: they're terrified I'll overdo my contacts, especially with the British (no need: I know very well what I'm going to do). On the British, spontaneous friendship for sure, . . . but the unpleasant thing is that, *here*, . . . you can't see it without the political tinge given by the official position of an old British friend and the anti-British feeling of the Cypriots.[38]

There was no question, then, of George leaving behind either his official role, or his political conscience, in going to Cyprus.

There were other considerations, too, that must have weighed with him. That summer, Katsimbalis had been urging him 'to declare [his] presence in the world of literature.' It had been seven years, after all, since George had published a new poem. George replied with what may have been a veiled hint of plans already taking shape. As on other occasions in the past, George was certainly suffering from exhaustion at the end of his first summer in the Middle East. But it was not until October that he asked the Ministry for a month's leave, and not until the end of the month that he seems to have decided definitely to spend it in Cyprus.

There was, finally, a practical reason. To cover the ninety miles or so that separate Beirut from Cyprus was only 'an hour by plane or a night on the

306

boat.' To Ioanna, a week before setting out, he apologised for not coming to Athens:

> Never mind that the journey [to Athens] is expensive and while on leave we get only half a salary. That's the reason we plan to go to Cyprus.[39]

Whatever the precise mix of reasons that had brought him there, once in Cyprus George set about discovering the island with passionate intensity. Not since he had had the task of showing Edouard Herriot around the ancient sites of Greece had he taken on such a gruelling itinerary – and this one was entirely voluntary. In the space of five weeks, he and Maro were taken by Louizos in his car to every corner of the island. Indefatigably, George discovered archaeological sites from Mycenaean to Early Christian; Louizos introduced him to the painted churches of the Troödos mountains, to crusader castles and cathedrals, to Turkish mosques and the dervish monastery outside Larnaca that is one of the holy sites of Islam. Everywhere they went, George met and talked to the islanders; he took notes; he took one hundred and forty-five photographs.[40]

Cyprus, he found, was 'Greek, without a Greek policeman or civil servant;' he discovered there that expanded sense of Hellenism, beyond the limits and the limitations of the Greek state, of which he had been able to trace only the ruins, during his travels in Anatolia and the Middle East:

307

> from here one experiences Greece as (suddenly) spacious, broader. The sense that there exists a world where people speak Greek: a Greek world, but one that doesn't depend on the Greek Government – and this last contributes to this sense of spaciousness.

He worried immediately, on his very first evening at the Ledra Palace Hotel in Nicosia:

> Question: are we worthy to administer Cyprus, without damaging this world, making it better without turning it into a Greek provincial backwater, like Corfu or Thessaloniki?[41]

It was a subtle observation, and it was typical of George's sense of wonder at this newly discovered world: Corfu and Thessaloniki had each had a long and distinctive history and character before being absorbed into the Greek state, respectively in 1864 and 1912; George was more sensitive than most, to the levelling potential of state organs and bureaucracy.

But for him, the issue went still deeper than the unresolved political future of Cyprus. The island that in ancient times had been sacred to Aphrodite, goddess of sexual love, even before his arrival seems to have provoked in him a peculiarly sensual fascination. 'There's a sensuality about this place, it's drenched in it,' he wrote in his diary, again on that very first evening: the narrow lighted doorways of the backstreets of Nicosia had reminded him of brothels. Either before leaving Beirut, or on the plane, he had been reading Herodotus' account of sacred prostitution in the ancient Near East, later to be worked into the poem 'In the Goddess's Name I Summon You.' One of his first evenings in Cyprus was spent at Durrell's unfinished house at Bellapais. With Durrell, he discussed this story from Herodotus; their talk strayed to other bizarre manifestations of Aphrodite in Cyprus, such as the unusually high percentage of hermaphrodite births in the island. Something of this discussion left its traces in both Durrell's travel-book about Cyprus, *Bitter Lemons*, and George's poem 'Pedlar from Sidon.'[42]

On a visit to the prehistoric archaeological site of Engomi, in the Bay of Famagusta, as he wrote to Philip Sherrard not long afterwards, George found:

308

> no interest in the ruins; but the plain had an extraordinary flatness under the clouds. At the west the dome of a little byzantine church, at the other end the mountains. The diggers, mainly women, were digging. One of them a young very beautiful girl was handling her spade with such a rhythm, that one had the feeling that <u>her</u> naked body was emerging out of the movement — the actual Aphrodite.[43]

It was here, on the flat plain among the ruins, while the clouds that had brought a recent rain squall towered over the Pentadaktylos hills in the sunset, that George had the initial experience that would give him the poem named after the site, 'Engomi.' It was probably the only one of the poems that came out of that visit to be actually begun in Cyprus; the last to be completed, it occupies the climactic final position in his next volume. There, the visionary moment is expanded to become an epiphany, in which the pagan Aphrodite becomes fused with the Virgin Mary, a composite emblem of love ascending to heaven. But on that first afternoon at Engomi, these intimations of love transcendent had a sharply sensual edge. It was, it seems, the raunchy bachelor Louizos who drew George's attention to the bare legs of a girl excavator working in the archaeologists' trench. And the brief entry in his diary for that date, which includes the first sketches for the poem, ends with an abrupt juxtaposition: it may have been the somewhat taurine appearance of Louizos himself, taken together with the crudeness of his observation to George, which set the latter thinking of the stud bull that Louizos kept on his estate (the 'mechanism of copulation,' as he called it), and which George later photographed in action.[44]

Another of the group of poems later dedicated to Cyprus has the indicative title, 'The Demon of Fornication,' extracting gory, as well as sensual details, from the fifteenth-century *Chronicle* of medieval Cypriot history by Leontios Machairas. All in all, the traditional associations of Cyprus with the goddess of love figured large in George's initial response to the island, and there was nothing tame or abstract in their manifestations in his thinking. It is as though, at the most elemental level, George experienced in Cyprus a dramatic rejuvenation of the biological instinct for life.

Above all, what appealed to George in Cyprus was the sense of homecoming. Laconically, his diary notes: 'I've come across customs that I'd known only as a child;' among the 'Details on Cyprus' described in the poem of that title was the practice of painting decorations on dried gourds, called *kolokes*. Another was the wooden well-wheel, that no doubt reminded him of his grandmother's garden at Skala; its name, in the Cypriot dialect, was a survival of much greater antiquity. Nor was it only the idyllic aspects of the island that brought George face to face with the world of his childhood: concluding one of his frequent and frank discussions with Maurice Cardiff about British policy and its likely consequences, he warned: 'That reminds me of my earliest years, under the Turks.'[45]

309

Not only did George recognise this world and feel at home in it, as he had never expected to do again; just like the home that he had lost as a child, this one, too, lay under threat. The British colonial authorities, with their 'obstinacy and lack of imagination,' without knowing it risked repeating the historical role of the decaying Ottoman empire, half a century before. Even the presence of the Turkish Cypriots, maintaining their mosques and their different traditions with dignity among their Greek neighbours, must again have seemed to George an impossible survival of the day-to-day realities of those early years. 'I can't imagine Cyprus without the Turks being there as well,' says the Greek Cypriot hero of the unfinished novel that he began to write a year later. And to Kranidiotis, at this early stage, George would stress the need to win over the Turkish Cypriots, if the campaign for *enosis* were to be successful.[46]

As he would write to Ioanna a little later:

> I've fallen in love with this place. Maybe because I've found there things still living, that have been lost in that other Greece . . . perhaps because I feel that this people has need of all our love and all our support.[47]

This sense of solidarity with an idealised 'people' builds not only on George's sentiments during the Second World War, but also, as Ioanna would immediately have recognised, on the shared admiration of brother and sister for the 'feudal' generosity and grandeur of their grandmother, benignly presiding at Skala over their own young lives and those of the 'simple' villagers to whom George always felt that he belonged.

This first visit to Cyprus was a triumph for George in another way, too. Although his contacts with his British friends were scrupulously limited to the informal, no such constraint affected his dealings with the Greek-Cypriot community. Kranidiotis was not the only Cypriot man of letters to whom the name of George Seferis was already becoming well known in 1953. Within days, George had made the acquaintance of the painter Adamantios Diamantis who, with his French wife Antoinette, was also a close friend of Cardiff, and with whom George was to maintain an affectionate correspondence for the rest of his life. Another new friend was Kypros Chrysanthis, a doctor and poet, who also wrote regularly for one of the Greek Cypriot newspapers. George visited schools and gave informal, impromptu talks and readings of his poems, which were warmly received in the local Greek press. One of these was at the Pancyprian Gymnasium. Durrell reported to Henry Miller:

> It was so lovely too to see Seferis again after so many years, as gentle and as humorous as ever. . . . [h]e was brought down as a distinguished poet and given an ovation, so I was able to be present as a master. He made a touching address to the boys, full of thoughtful things very gently said.[48]

It seems that George was in relaxed mood at these and other semi-public occasions. Just as in London, two years before, when he had found himself lionised by the literary establishment, so too, in Cyprus, he was more gratified than he would readily have admitted to find himself and his work the object of public admiration.[49]

Writing to Katsimbalis just a week after their return to Beirut, Maro reported enthusiastically on the reception George had been given in Cyprus, and went on:

Cyprus has filled him with ideas, but these ones too will have to stay bottled up until the blessed day comes when he can be liberated from the millstone of the Ministry.[50]

Maro may have been surprised, and was surely gratified, by what happened next. Beginning on Christmas Day, just a week after she had written these words to Katsimbalis, and a fortnight since their return from Cyprus, George suddenly found a way to free himself from the 'drudgery.' It came about, as he explained it, 'not as the result of a decision but insensibly, being so much caught up in the true life.'[51]

'And you see the light of the sun, as the ancients used to say.' This line had first appeared in his diary in the summer of 1946, and so links the new burst of creativity with the mood of revelation that had given birth to 'Thrush.' It now became the opening line of 'Agianapa I,' the poem that was to head his next volume and was written on that day. George had visited the deserted beach at Agianapa, with its Venetian-built monastery, on the morning of his visit to Engomi; he had photographed Maro and Louizos there, under the giant, ancient sycamore with which, less than two weeks later, 'Agianapa II' would begin. (Nothing existed, then, of the brash and overcrowded tourist resort that has grown up since the 1980s.) In the intervening days, four more poems, all to do with places in Cyprus, were written in rapid succession.[52]

But this was only the beginning. The revelation of Cyprus had unleashed what George was soon calling, in his diary, an 'orgasm of writing' (the metaphor no doubt reflecting the sensuality he still associated with the island). He now set himself to rewrite and complete the novel that he had abandoned almost twenty-five years before, *Six Nights on the Acropolis*. It was, he now realised, the 'sensual part' that had been missing from his earlier attempt; it was this that he now felt able to supply. He surrendered himself to the 'automatism of memory' that had just been released in him. 'Driving power,' he marvelled, in English, during the first month of writing: 'tremendous.'[53]

In its completed form this novel, based on George's erotic and artistic quest of his late twenties, owes its existence and some, at least, of its memorable details to the aftermath of his discovery of Cyprus. The 'mechanism of copulation' is there, in the form of allusions to the Minotaur, to Minos' queen Pasiphae, and the mechanical bull built to satisfy her, according to the myth; so, too, at the end of the novel, is the first realised form of the apotheosis of sexual love, fully achieved a year later in the final form of 'Engomi.' No doubt the symbolism of Good Friday, and the conjunction of the Epitaphios procession with the first coupling of the lovers in the novel, owe something to George's experience of Holy Week in Jerusalem, during a brief, enforced interruption of writing.

*Six Nights* was finished in Beirut on 15 August 1954, the feast of the Virgin Mary, that had once been his mother's nameday. Maro, at the time, was away in Athens; George was laid up with a swollen foot, and could not go out. 'I worked on it . . . like a madman – in waking and in sleeping. . . . I slept only four hours a night and felt no tiredness – no small thing in this climate.' Already, he had finished two more poems with Cypriot themes and settings ('Salamis in Cyprus' and 'In the Goddess's Name I Summon You'), and begun to draft a third ('Helen'). And as though that were not enough, three days after finishing *Six Nights*, George was writing to Maro that he was embarking on another novel, which he announced to her as 'Stratis Thalassinos in Cyprus.'[54]

312     From the end of his first visit to Cyprus, right up to the start of his second, in mid-September, George had been writing fast and furiously. It was a liberation such as he had only very rarely experienced, and never for such a sustained period: 'a few weeks in South Africa and when I was writing "Erotikos Logos",' were the comparisons he made at the time. He might have added the weeks on Poros when he wrote *'Thrush.'* Though he had much yet to do in his life, including the final creative burst the following July that would complete the volume *...Cyprus, Where It Was Ordained For Me...* , George would never again experience such a sustained access of creative energy as during the *annus mirabilis* that had begun with his first discovery of Cyprus.

### The serpent in the garden

On 28 July 1954, the future of Cyprus was debated on the floor of the House of Commons in London; on the same day, in Nicosia, a stern proclamation from the Cyprus Attorney-General announced the beginning of a crackdown against sedition. The Commons debate was often afterwards taken as the point when armed conflict between Cypriot supporters of *enosis* and the British authorities became inevitable. One word, used by the junior Colonial Office minister, Henry Hopkinson, in answer to a question about future constitutional arrangements in Cyprus, inflamed almost all Greek opinion, and has never been forgotten since: the word was 'never.' Although there was a slight element of ambiguity in the phrasing, and the government spokesman, caught wrong-footed, had exceeded the terms of his brief, what was widely understood to have been said was that a change of sovereignty in Cyprus could *never* be contemplated.[55]

George possessed the transcript of the debate in the weekly *Hansard*. As well as Hopkinson's inflammatory words, he marked in it a number of other interventions. One of the most heavily marked is this, which came from the government benches:

> There never was any great enforced demand for Enosis or to go back to join the Greek people, that is to say, a desire by the Greek people in Cyprus to be affiliated with Greece. They have no history or traditional background nor have they ever been part of Greece at any time.[56]

The signs of a propaganda campaign in Cyprus itself, to promote this view, had already deeply disturbed George the previous autumn; now it had the sanction of the governing party in Britain. Although Greek counter-claims, both before and since, have often been equally strident and unsupported, here lay the deepest challenge, not just to Greek political aspirations, but to George's personal revelation of a homecoming to the lost world of his childhood. In his eyes, it was precisely the *differences* from the present-day Greek state that guaranteed the ancient and indigenous character of Cypriot culture as part of Hellenism.

Also marked by George, in the transcript of the debate, were the observations of the Labour member and future cabinet minister, Richard Crossman:

> Even when under the great influence of this Metropolis they remain obstinately convinced of their grievance and remain in favour of Enosis; they feel Greek; they are Greek — even if the Honourable Gentlemen say 'No, no, gentlemen — with time and trouble we shall teach you not to be Greek'.[57]

The final insult to Greek sensibilities came at the end of the debate, when Hopkinson's minister, Oliver Lyttleton, summoned to the House to contain the damage, referred to Greece as a 'friendly but unstable ally;' George additionally marked, from this speech, the words: 'to plunge into

313

things like Enosis when there is no democratic basis for the formation of public opinion is very dangerous.' It was, of course, precisely this democratic basis that the British Conservative government had determined to deny to the Cypriots.[58]

Within days of the debate in London on 28 July, George had finished the poem 'Salamis in Cyprus.' Salamis in antiquity, standing on the Bay of Famagusta, had been the largest city in Cyprus. George had visited the extensive ruins, with Maro and Louizos, the previous November; some of the most impressive of these date from the first Christian centuries. Here was yet another visible sign of a decayed imperial power (that of Rome and its Christian continuation in the East, Byzantium). The archaeological site becomes the setting for the poet to hear a voice, that is in part the voice of George's beloved hero of Greek independence, Makriyannis:

> Earth hath not handles
> that they may take her upon their shoulders and depart
> nor can they, however much they thirst
> make the salt sea fresh with half a dram of water.
> And these bodies
> fashioned of a soil they know not,
> have souls.
> They gather implements to change them,
> they will not be able; they will only undo them
> if souls can be undone.
> The husk is not slow to ripen
> it does not take very long
> for the yeast of bitterness to swell,
> it does not take very long
> for evil to raise its head,
> and the sick mind that empties
> does not take very long
> to fill with madness,
> *there is an island...*[59]

314

Crossman's argument in the recent parliamentary debate is given to the prophetic voice in the poem; but the tone has become apocalyptic. The warning is not only against what George saw as the cruel and misguided educational and propaganda policy of the colonial government in Cyprus; he foresaw, with the clarity he had brought to other crises, exactly the dehumanising process that leads to terrorist violence. The final line quoted alludes to another imperial power, that of the Great King of Persia, Xerxes, subject of Aeschylus' play *The Persians*, from which it is quoted, and the rout of the Persian forces at another Salamis, the island close to Athens, in 480 BC.

The poem now turns to invoke specifically the 'friends from the other war,' implicitly the British and George's personal friends among them, who had fought alongside his countrymen in World War II. The last part of the poem offers two potential solutions. One is fatalistic, echoing George's own attitude in earlier years: 'the will of the powerful who can change it? / who can make himself heard?' But 'yes,' replies the other, more authoritative: the messenger is already on his way, and however long he takes, he will bring:

> to those who sought to chain the Hellespont
> the terrible message of Salamis.

This was the message brought to the Persian king Xerxes in the denouement ('catastrophe' in ancient Greek) of Aeschylus' play: the ancient sin of *hubris*, of overstepping the laws of nature, will inevitably find its punishment. The poem's last line again belongs to Aeschylus, in the language of those ancient Greeks with whom it had been claimed in the British parliament that the Cypriots of today had no connection: '*there is an island.*'

As soon as the poem was finished, George sent it to Petros Haris, the editor of *Nea Estia*, a long-running, traditionalist and rather staid publication with which he had broken off relations in the early 1930s. The nominal publication date was 1 September, but Katsimbalis, who was in Paris at the time, was already astonished to see George wearing the mantle of 'national poet,' and wrote to tell him so, on 25 August. George wrote back at once to explain:

As you see, it's a cry addressed to my friends – my friends from Britain, a cry of love. I'd have burst if I'd kept it bottled up inside me. . . . In Cyprus . . . there's a cold, subterranean mechanism that operates undisturbed and bastardises everything. I felt it as a personal humiliation, I mean as a person, I'm not talking politics . . . And I'd be delighted if *Salamis* could be translated and published in London.[60]

In this George was to be disappointed. Later in the year, Katsimbalis broke the news to him that John Lehmann had turned down Rex Warner's translation of the poem. It was, Katsimbalis reported Lehmann as saying, 'the *worst* poem Seferis has ever written, because it's a "topical" poem.'[61]

In the strict sense this is true; but 'Salamis in Cyprus' has endured because it is also a great deal more. Like many of George's poems, it had been provoked by a unique combination of personal and political circumstances, but irrespective of the conditions out of which it arose, the poem offers a powerful diagnosis of the causes of all wars, the nature and effects of divided loyalties, and George's long-standing and still developing concept of a 'natural' justice, founded in the presocratic philosophers and Aeschylus.

George's own loyalties were about to be more severely tested than ever. Lawrence Durrell, he learned that August, had just accepted a government post in Cyprus, as Director of Information Services. Maurice Cardiff, who as Director of the British Council was less compromised with government policy, had given Durrell due warning that if he took up this appointment, he would lose all his Greek friends. George, for one, would never fully forgive his old friend for this betrayal; it was none other than the declared philhellene, who had once come close to volunteering to fight in the Greek army against Mussolini, who was now in charge of 'undoing souls,' and persuading the Greeks of Cyprus that they were not Greeks after all. To Katsimbalis, George expressed his disgust:

> As for Larry, to hell with him; he's taken on the Information there. In today's conditions you understand what that means – *gauleiter.*[62]

George was not perhaps best informed about the precise responsibilities of Nazi officials, but the general thrust of the charge strikes home. Before long, indeed, it would become a commonplace in Greece to compare British actions in Cyprus with those of the Nazi occupiers during the war, although George as a rule eschewed such excesses.

Still in August 1954, George was writing to Diamantis in Cyprus to plan the details of his next visit to the island. This time, and in the new conditions that prevailed there, it was imperative for him 'to pass entirely unnoticed;' Cardiff, for his part, Diamantis reported, 'fully sympathises with your wish to be left alone,' and would be out of Cyprus for part of the time that George planned to visit. In the event he did meet Cardiff again ('I love him always and respect him,' George wrote to Katsimbalis afterwards), but he avoided Durrell, except for a single meeting when Durrell turned up, drunk, along with Cardiff. At this time George began warning his friends

316

of what he saw as Durrell's duplicity: Durrell must be prevented from trying to exploit old friendships 'for this evil enterprise.' George was particularly concerned lest Henry Miller, who around this time had suggested to Katsimbalis a reunion in Cyprus, should 'fall into the trap.'[63]

Other British friends stood firmer, and for the time being there were no further rifts. Cardiff himself wrote to George, 'The stupidity of the B[ritish] in Cyprus has been unsurpassed – and the only thing to do is to forget about [it]. I hope to go somewhere else soon.' Osbert Lancaster had written on behalf of the Greek cause in *The Times*, and was a welcome guest with George and Maro in Beirut. To Joan Rayner, Paddy Leigh Fermor's wife, George would write affectionately at the end of the year: 'you are perhaps my last friend in England.' The letter continues:

> I feel sad, sad about the Cyprus affair – but putting aside government and politics etc – do you really think that I care so much about what sort of a helmet the policeman in the streets of Famagusta is going to wear? The awful thing, for me is that, owing to various intricacies of our age, a machine is set there transforming some thousands of men into bastards [another allusion to the 'propaganda war' in which Durrell was involved].[64]

317

In September 1954, the case for the union of Cyprus with Greece was officially presented by the Greek government to the United Nations Organization in New York.[65]

On the 15th of that month, George and Maro began their second visit to Cyprus, which would last for a month. As George recounted the visit afterwards, to Katsimbalis, they saw the half of the island they had not seen before. In fact, staying this time as the guests of Louizos at Famagusta, they revisited many of the same places. Once again, George took a prodigious number of photographs; but this time he had also come armed with some of the reading matter he had been assiduously acquiring since his last visit: the guidebook in English by Rupert Gunnis, George Hill's *History of Cyprus*, the historical accounts in Greek by St Neophytos the Recluse (of the twelfth century), and the fifteenth-century *Chronicle* by Leontios Machairas. This time he was meticulous in matching up places with descriptions and historical accounts; he also made systematic notes on the Cypriot dialect as he heard it in use.[66]

It was partly his observations on the contemporary language that caused George to exclaim in his diary, '*Enosis* – it already exists, on the cultural level – the point is not to lose it.' What infuriated him most was the repeated official British claim that the Cypriots were not Greek; though at the same time he remained dourly critical of the abilities of those in Greece with responsibility for directing policy.[67]

Although George's feelings about the island and its people remained as strong as before, there was a heavier atmosphere about this second visit. This time, the political situation forbade any public appearances; there could be no repetition of the warmth of his reception by audiences and young people. On his first visit he may have been too busy to write letters; now he avoided writing to his friends, while he was in Cyprus, because he believed his letters would be read by the British censors. A more mundane, but no doubt pervasive, annoyance was toothache, that lasted throughout the visit, until in the last week he consented to have two teeth drawn.[68]

Emblematic of these changes, since the year before, was his return to Engomi. The archaeologists had gone; the site was deserted. The flatness of the plain he still found 'superb;' but there was no sign now of the young girl labourer whose bare legs had so excited Louizos a year ago. Instead, exploring part of the ancient walls that had been cleared since the previous year, he encountered a large snake ('longer than my stick') moving sinuously to right and left through the cropped grass, 'with careless impunity.' He noted that in the local dialect, it was called a 'monster.'[69]

When he returned to the poem that he had begun writing at Engomi the previous year, George would add this bleakly sinister image as the conclusion to the poem, and to the volume, ...*Cyprus, Where It Was Ordained For Me...*

### ...*Cyprus, Where It Was Ordained For Me...*

The novel about Cyprus that George had announced to Maro in August 1954 reached some hundred and twenty pages before he abandoned it. The story is somewhat vestigial; it is transparently based on his own experience of coming to Cyprus as an outsider from Greece, and on the personality of his host there, Evangelos Louizos. A fictional love intrigue has been added. The provisional title of the novel was to be the name of the Cypriot character, *Varnavas Kalostefanos*. This is not a real surname, but is derived from the traditional good wishes uttered at a Greek wedding. Varnavas Kalostefanos is, or ought to be, the story-book character who 'lives happily ever after.'

It is not clear when, or precisely why, George gave up work on *Varnavas Kalostefanos*. He last refers to the novel in his diary during January 1955, but at that time seems to have been still pressing on; the latest date that

318

appears in the manuscripts is 22 February. That the attempt counted for something with George, even after he had given it up, is shown by his choice of the code-name 'Varnavas,' for secret correspondence with Cyprus during the conflict that followed. It has been suggested that George turned away from the novel once his plans had crystallised for the book of poems that he would dedicate to Cyprus. But by the first months of 1955 the impetus of the previous year was no longer there; the routine of diplomatic work had reasserted itself. It is also quite possible that what put an end to George's hopes for his optimistically-named hero was the start of the campaign of violence by EOKA (National Organization of Cypriot Fighters), which set off a series of coordinated bomb explosions in the main towns of Cyprus on 1 April. The conflict with Great Britain over the future of the island had entered a new phase.[70]

What George had grimly prophesied in the poem 'Salamis in Cyprus' was rapidly, by the spring of 1955, coming to pass. From now on, there was to be no stopping the slide into a true state of terror in the island. The armed revolt that now began is usually known in English as the 'Cyprus Emergency' (a state that did not formally begin until November); in Greek as the 'Cypriot Struggle.' It lasted for almost four years, with even longer-lasting damage to Anglo-Greek relations and much worse consequences for Cyprus itself, as well as for relations between Greece and Turkey. It was to divide George from almost all his English and several of his Greek friends; among many similar casualties was the *Anglo-Hellenic Review*, whose editorship had in the meantime passed from Katsimbalis to Savidis, and which published its last issue in 1955.

That year, Archbishop Makarios passed through the Middle East on his way to take part in the Afro-Asian summit in Indonesia. The archbishop spent the weekend of Orthodox Easter in Beirut, where he officiated at the midnight celebration of the Resurrection in the Greek church. George was in the congregation. Two weeks later, on his way back from the Far East, Makarios spent four days at Bhamdun, outside Beirut. George had met the ethnarch twice before, on his first visit to Cyprus, and already been deeply impressed by him. He noted the dates of these more recent meetings in his diary, and at the end of June received a florid letter, in which the archbishop expressed 'our deepest gratitude, for your kind support and divers attentions to our person vouchsafed us at your hands.'[71]

Later in the year, to Ioanna, George gave a warm account of his feelings for Makarios, whom he seems again to have visited during his final stay in Cyprus, at the end of September:

319

It's a great relief to see a real man. In his ancient cathedral precinct, without any guards, with just his senior archimandrite and a secretary. . . . 'Even if they deport me,' he said to me, 'to a place where I can be heard, I shall keep up the same things, and if I am kept in isolation I shall still keep up the same things, and if I should return to Cyprus after ten years, I shall still keep up the same things.' May God help him. He's a little over forty. Last year at Jerusalem I met his father (who'd come over as a pilgrim [for Easter]). A simple islander, like the ones I used to know at Skala.[72]

In this way George's admiration for the ethnarch of the Greek Cypriots was profoundly linked to his identification of Cyprus with his own lost world of childhood.

Now that there was dynamite going off in Cyprus (as he put it), Katsimbalis wrote to George:

I'm ready to blow up, myself, about our friends the British... They're shits and bastards every one of them (and I don't make exceptions, only Rex [Warner] and Osbert [Lancaster] – perhaps).[73]

With Paddy Leigh Fermor, who was living in Athens while working on the first of his classic travel books about the country, *Mani*, Katsimbalis added that he was embroiled in 'Homeric quarrels.' A few months later, that great diner-out pointedly refused a dinner invitation from the Leigh Fermors, to their great distress, as Joan wrote to inform George.[74]

Katsimbalis' opinion and manner of expressing it were shared by many people in Greece at the time, not least by the newspapers and radio. But George, although there was no question about where his sympathies lay, could still see both sides. 'It's not worth blowing up about the British,' he wrote back to Katsimbalis that summer:

They're British; and if we were in their shoes I don't see many among us who would be ready to acknowledge the right of the other side. The great thing is how *we* respond to the business.[75]

The decisive response, on the British side, to the EOKA campaign of violence was an apparently indirect one, though George would not have missed its significance from the first. This was to internationalise the conflict. Foreign Secretary Harold Macmillan, on the last day of June 1955,

320

announced a forthcoming conference in London, to which representatives were invited from the governments of Greece and Turkey, but not from the Cypriots. Given that the Ottoman empire had ceded the administration of the island as long ago as 1878, and that its successor, the Turkish Republic, had renounced all claim to it in the Treaty of Lausanne in 1923, it was blatantly obvious that Turkey was being involved for the most cynical of reasons, as a counterweight to pressures from Greece and from the Greek majority in Cyprus. The authoritative diplomatic history of the conflict by Robert Holland, based mainly on British and US official documents, refers to the 'high-risk nature of this gambit, and its not entirely respectable nature.'[76]

George, from his own perspective, would always insist that it had been a mistake, on the Greek side, not to enlist the support of the Turkish Cypriot minority; but the government of Turkey was another matter. George does not seem ever to have harboured animosity towards Turks as people; but what he called the 'mechanism of catastrophe,' whose effects he had seen in Smyrna, was indissolubly bound up, in his mind, as it was in that of many Greeks of his generation, with the Turkish state and its formidable military strength.

The Tripartite Conference was due to open, after some delay, at the end    321
of August; its consequences mark the beginning of a new chapter in the history of Greece, Turkey and Cyprus, and would leave an indelible mark, too, on George's writing and thinking from that time on. It may be no more than a coincidence, but it is a striking fact that the final creative burst that produced the volume of poems, ...*Cyprus, Where It Was Ordained For Me* ..., including the overall conception of the volume and its title, began on the day after the announcement of the Tripartite Conference, and ended shortly before the representatives gathered in London. The writing of the poems occupied George for the whole of July; at the beginning of August, he wrote to Savidis, to announce the collection and its title. Then on 23 August, less than a week before the conference was finally due to open, he had finished all the revising and typing, and the 'little book' was ready for the printer.[77]

Many years before, George had suddenly seen his way to finishing 'The King of Asine,' and gone on to hasten into print his poetic 'testament,' before Greece could be engulfed by World War II. It is possible that a similar impetus underlay the final stage of this book, dedicated to a Cyprus that was already under threat of disappearing, and hustled through press before the calamity fell.

To this final stage of writing belong two of the longer poems of the collection: 'Helen' (which had been begun the previous summer) and 'In the Kyrenia District.' One set in the ancient world, the other in the modern, both hark back caustically to memories of the Second World War, as a just war fought by allies, in a shared and noble cause, since revealed to be a sham. 'Helen' additionally invokes the world of ancient myth, seen from an angle that is new to George's poetry, that of the fifth-century BC Athenian dramatist Euripides. According to ancient reputation a misanthrope and a cynic, Euripides is credited with having introduced a wry scepticism into the more hieratic world of his predecessors, Aeschylus and Sophocles. The old gods are no longer to be trusted in Euripides' plays; the heroes of old are brought down to earth and turn out to be either ridiculous or cruel; the sufferings of women and children in wartime are contrasted to the arrogance of the victors.

'Helen' is based upon Euripides' play of that title. According to the play, the most beautiful woman of ancient legend was wrongly named 'Helen of Troy;' she never went to Troy at all. The gods sent a phantom there in her image, and it was for this phantom that the most famous war in all Greek mythology, the War of Troy, was fought. Adopting the persona of Teucer, one of the characters in Euripides' play, George adapts this discovery to the landscape and the circumstances of Cyprus in 1954 and 1955. Teucer had been been exiled from his native Salamis, to become the founder of the Cypriot city of that name, that George had already invoked in a poem. It is Teucer, the poem's mouthpiece, who in a line from Euripides' play, speaks of 'Cyprus, where it was ordained for me to live,' the phrase that George would adopt, in the original ancient Greek, as the title of the volume.

Euripides is also present in the epigram 'Pentheus,' whose hero is dismembered by the frenzied worshippers of Dionysos, the Bacchae, in Euripides' play of that title. This fate is closely echoed in the last of the poems to be conceived, 'Euripides the Athenian.' Here the dour, traditional misanthrope whose tragedy it is to perceive, but to be unable to alter, the inherent weaknesses that make humanity the prey to capricious gods, is clearly a version of George himself:

> He was crabby, his friends were few;
> the time came and he was torn apart by dogs.[78]

The source for these details is the ancient biography of Euripides; but the repetition of the motif of dismemberment in two short poems from the collection is striking. It seems likely that Euripides, his disillusion and the fate that he is supposed to have shared with the hero of one of his own plays (Pentheus), now seemed to George, in the summer of 1955, emblematic for the terrible clarity of vision, and for the clash of powerful and irreconcilable forces, that are among the fundamental themes of ...*Cyprus, Where It Was Ordained For Me*...

But the crowning position in the volume George reserved for 'Engomi,' the poem that he had begun that afternoon with Maro and Louizos back in November 1953, and to which he now put the finishing touches. Out of the immediate intimations of love both sacred and carnal that he had experienced on that day, George weaves together a composite vision that alludes at once to the Apocryphal Gospels and to earlier moments of epiphany in Modern Greek poetry, notably by Solomos, in the nineteenth century, and by George's immediate predecessor Sikelianos. As the speaker watches the excavators at work exposing the foundations of an ancient city, time miraculously comes to a standstill. He watches as a female figure, from among those digging, 'ascends the light' and disappears into heaven. She is at once the sensual Aphrodite of pagan antiquity, and the Virgin Mary as depicted in Byzantine icons; it is, the poem declares, 'a motionless dance.'

This conclusion to ...*Cyprus, Where It Was Ordained For Me*... follows and builds upon the end of George's previous volume, *'Thrush,'* that had also ended with the symbolic rebirth of the goddess of love in the modern world. But here there is a simplicity and directness in the way in which the vision is presented, such as George very rarely achieved in any of his other poems. Drawing on this small corner of the Hellenic world, George found himself able to create on the page, more fully and compellingly than ever before, the intimate and organic unity of landscape, people, history and myth, for which he had striven ever since *Mythistorema* twenty years before. 'Engomi' was George's fullest poetic affirmation so far. But the poem, in its final form, ends not with the vision based on his first visit to the site, but with the nonchalant 'monster,' the snake, and the desolation of his second visit there, when he found the site deserted: 'here where much time is taken up with dying.'

The relative simplicity and the directness of the seventeen poems which make up ...*Cyprus, Where It Was Ordained For Me*... are without precedent in George's poetry. Out of the 'revelation' of Cyprus and the *annus mirabilis* that followed, George had come closer than at any other time of his life to achieving that 'grace' of being able 'to speak simply.' Also unique in this collection is his successful assimilation of the opposed voices of his most illustrious predecessors, Cavafy and Sikelianos. There is still a wealth of literary and historical allusion in these poems; but more than ever this is assimilated, so that recognising the points of reference adds progressive depth to a surface largely without the formidable obstacles to understanding, of which critics of George's earlier work had complained. These poems are full of the sights, sounds, touch and smell of real places and lived moments; in a small number of pages they also weave together a pageant of the whole history of Cyprus, from prehistoric times to the 1950s. Even the cadences of the Cypriot form of the Greek language, unfamiliar to most Greeks, and culled from different epochs, add, as it were, grace notes to the volume.[79]

That summer of 1955, George was busy planning for his next period of leave. This already encompassed Cyprus, but from an early stage his thoughts had been leading him further west. The islands of the Dodecanese, lying close to the southwestern coast of Turkey, had been ceded to Greece in 1947, after thirty-five years of Italian occupation and a brief transitional administration by the British. The largest of these islands, Rhodes, had a significant Turkish minority. The whole group lies much closer to the Turkish mainland than does Cyprus; but in this case, union with Greece had aroused none of the objections that now blocked *enosis* for Cyprus. George had occasion to know this, since most of the details of the transfer of sovereignty for the Dodecanese had been concluded during the regency of Archbishop Damaskinos. No doubt, in the current climate, he was curious to see another part of the Greek world that had until recently lain outside the jurisdiction of the Greek state. No doubt, too, the same practical motives obtained as before: Rhodes, the capital of the Dodecanese, is only about half as far from Beirut as Athens.[80]

George and Maro left Beirut on 30 August, stopping briefly in Cyprus on their way. In Rhodes, George sought out the young novelist Nikos Kasdaglis, whose powerful novel of the German occupation had just been published in Athens, and had attracted his attention. George impressed Kasdaglis with his enthusiasm for 'the alleys and cobbled lanes, the mosques and the Turkish neighbourhoods, the medieval houses' of the old town of Rhodes, to which his host introduced him by night. Mentally, George was no doubt weighing these impressions against his first evening in Nicosia two years before, and imagining a different future for his beloved Cyprus. It has to be said that, today, the once picturesque Turkish quarter of Rhodes is in a poor state of repair and its Turkish population has greatly declined since the 1950s. But the Dodecanese in modern times has never known the intercommunal violence, or the armed interventions, that have disfigured the recent history of Cyprus.[81]

During the week that followed, George and Maro were joined, in quick succession, by Katsimbalis, Savidis and Antoniou. Far away in London, the representatives of Great Britain, Greece and Turkey had at last convened and the Tripartite Conference was under way. In Rhodes and on holiday, out of touch with diplomatic channels, George was dependent on the newspapers, which arrived late from Athens, and on the radio.

On 6 September, a wave of anti-Greek violence swept through those enclaves in Turkey where there was still a Greek presence – principally Istanbul, whose population had been exempt from the exchange of populations in 1923. Greek businesses were set on fire, churches desecrated; even in Izmir, which no longer had a Greek population, the Greek consulate was burned down and attacks were made on the families of Greek army officers seconded to NATO headquarters. Greek reports were quick to point the finger of accusation at the Turkish authorities, who had done nothing to quell the violence, even, it was said, inciting the rioters. It would soon be accepted by the British Foreign Office, too, that the demonstrations had had the unofficial backing of the government of Adnan Menderes, and had been intended to back up the uncompromising stance of its foreign minister, Fatin Zorlu, at the London conference. If the Foreign Office plan had been to divide and rule, it had succeeded in unleashing forces that had not been foreseen in Whitehall, with consequences that could not now be controlled. The Menderes government had done more than accept the British government's invitation to re-acquire an interest in the island that lay outside the territory of the Turkish 'National Pact' established by Atatürk; through the violence unleashed on the streets, it had laid an uncompromising claim, from which no Turkish government since has found it possible to retreat. There was also an immediate backlash in Greece, where rioters set ablaze the British Institute in Athens. In London, the Tripartite Conference broke up in disarray.[82]

From this moment a new urgency, even a stridency, enters George's diaries and letters about Cyprus. With his poems finished, it seems as though he now deliberately sought to play a part on the diplomatic stage; and it would not be long before he was back in Athens for talks at the Ministry and with the beleaguered British ambassador, Sir Charles Peake (whom he had met with T.S. Eliot in London).[83]

But first, continuing his travels around the Dodecanese, in the words of the last book of the Bible, the *Book of Revelation*, also known as the

325

*Apocalypse*, George found himself 'in the isle that is called Patmos.' It had been here, near the site of the fortress-monastery founded in the eleventh century, that St John the Divine had been inspired by his vision of the end of all things. The day was 16 September; it was just ten days since the wave of violence had been unleashed in Turkey, threatening the very heart of the Orthodox Church, the Ecumenical Patriarchate in Constantinople. Years later, George recalled that moment as the one when he had determined to translate the *Apocalypse* into Modern Greek. In the unearthly stillness of dawn at the monastery on Patmos,

> I was again overwhelmed by feelings I had been given, before, by the Greek light, by that terrible blackness that I'd felt very strongly behind the azure, when in October '44 I came home to my country.

Another such moment had been when the German Stukas dive-bombed the lemon-groves of Crete, in the spring of 1941. He went on, implicitly placing the events of September 1955 in the same category of horror:

> The Furies were once again lying in wait behind the sun, just as Heraclitus imagined them. A mechanism of self-destruction was there, in motion, destroying every manifestation of good will.[84]

326

The translation of the *Apocalypse* would not appear for another eleven years; its first draft, though, was done, as an act of 'despair,' in May 1956, that is, before George left Beirut. That same moment on Patmos, in the recent shock of the violence in Turkey, must also mark the beginning of George's own private, or 'secret' apocalypse, the *Three Secret Poems*, eventually finished and published in 1966, along with the Biblical translation.[85]

With the two Georges, Katsimbalis and Savidis, George and Maro travelled to other islands of the Dodecanese, including Kos and Leros. Then on 23 September they sailed for Cyprus; it was presumably on this voyage that George was on the bridge with his friend Tonio (Antoniou) as the ship rounded Cavo Gata, and he associated the sound of the ship's bell with the old story of the Cats of St Nicholas, that had saved the monastery from vipers.

For the remainder of the month, George yielded to the hospitable pressure of Louizos, with whom he and Maro stayed longer than they had at first intended. These were the days when the American consul in Nicosia was reporting, to his superiors back home, 'a grimness and tension . . .

which is difficult to describe but strongly felt.' On 29 September, George was in the centre of Famagusta; a strike had been declared and demonstrators were on the streets. Teargas was fired to disperse them, and George, watching from the fringe and not in the best of health, was overcome by the fumes. Louizos, who was with him, had to call a doctor. But George was undeterred. To Savidis, he summed up the mood of this last visit: 'Astonishing atmosphere: youthful vigour, faith, and this amazing spirit of a people suddenly waking up to its own self.' It was against this background, in Louizos' ramshackle old mansion ('a house all but turning into a plant'), that George wrote the brief dedicatory preface to ...*Cyprus, Where It Was Ordained For Me...*, from which the epigraph to this chapter is taken.[86]

George and Maro left Cyprus on 3 October, the same day as the unfortunate governor, Sir Robert Armitage, who was about to be replaced by the more formidable Field-Marshal Sir John Harding. Except for the briefest of visits in 1969, George never returned to the island where his mythological alter ego, Teucer, had been 'ordained' by the gods to live.

Back in Beirut, George at once sent the manuscript of his book of poems to Savidis in Athens. It seems that he had already decided to have them printed privately, rather than by Ikaros, his publisher since 1944, and instructed Savidis accordingly. This provoked a rupture in several relationships. The publishers protested; Katsimbalis felt himself upstaged, and took George severely to task, ostensibly on behalf of Nikos Karydis and Alekos Patsifas, the slighted proprietors of Ikaros:

327

> Seferis, Seferis, (I'm reminding you yet again, even if you do shout and scream) that very often you are not, but not, straight in your dealings with people who have served you well and have loved you.[87]

The rift would widen, and there is surely more at stake in this appeal by Katsimbalis than the good opinion of George's publishers. It may not be accidental that Savidis, who in many ways resembled a more youthful version of the Colossus himself, came more and more, from this time on, to take over Katsimbalis' old role as George's trusted publicity manager. But Katsimbalis' 'big stick' had not lost all its legendary power: ...*Cyprus, Where It Was Ordained For Me...* was after all published by Ikaros, which remains to this day the loyal publisher of George's poetry and essays in Greek.

Scarcely had he finished making these arrangements, from Beirut, than George found himself summoned by the Ministry for consultations in

Athens. He arrived in early November, and stayed for six weeks. While there, he was taken ill with a stomach ulcer. He had been suffering for some time, at least since his return from Cyprus to Beirut; a few months later, he would attribute his illness, at least in part, to the events of 6–7 September. At the time, George responded well to the drugs prescribed, and seems to have continued working. But it was the onset of a condition that would return, to dog him intermittently for the rest of his life; and he can never since have failed to associate it with the moment when he had finished his poems about Cyprus, and with the 'darkness behind the light,' that September, out of which his final book of poetry would be born.[88]

George was back in Beirut by the second half of December. ...*Cyprus, Where It Was Ordained For Me*... appeared, in Athens, on the last day of the year. It bore the dedication: 'To the World of Cyprus, [in] Memory and Love.'

# 11
# '... And Lost Again and Again'
# 1956-1961

There is only the fight to recover what has been lost
And found and lost again and again: and now, under conditions
That seem unpropitious. But perhaps neither gain nor loss.
For us, there is only the trying. The rest is not our business.

(T.S. Eliot, *East Coker*)

### 'The yeast of bitterness'

The poems that George published at the end of 1955 and dedicated to Cyprus have in recent years become the most discussed part of his *oeuvre*, more intensively analysed and admired than any other. But in the months following their first publication, long-trusted friends such as Katsimbalis and Lorenzatos expressed reservations which George could not fully forgive. For these profoundly metropolitan spirits, the subject-matter of George's latest collection was a wilful aberration, if not a distraction. To Savidis, a loyal supporter and the most perceptive early reader of the poems, he confided that *...Cyprus, Where It Was Ordained For Me...* had been written for Cyprus, not for the sophisticated metropolis; it was 'a work of local character.'[1]

These responses by his friends highlight a latent tension inherent in George's response to Cyprus. He himself was no Teucer. Coincidentally, while he and Maro had been in Athens in December 1955, the opportunity had arisen to buy a plot of building land close to the centre of the city. There, behind the ancient stadium, in the Pangrati district, at no. 20 Agras Street, the couple's first and only permanent home would be built in the coming years. The purchase of the site was sealed only eleven days after *...Cyprus, Where It Was Ordained For Me...* was ready for distribution to the bookshops. However much he might idealise the simple, traditional life of small communities, such as that of Skala or of Cyprus as he had first found it in 1953, George himself seems not to have been at ease, for long, outside big cities. This tension, the origins of which go back to his earliest years, would profoundly affect not only the reception of his poems, but also the final phase of his professional career, that was now about to begin.[2]

Beyond the immediate circle of his friends, George's latest book of poetry was at first almost entirely ignored; soon, it became the object of abusive criticism. This had little to do with the quality of the poems, but with what was seen as their political stance. George's haste to publish on the last day of 1955, ensuring that as the year of publication, had been fully justified. Even so, the 'world' of Cyprus had already changed by the time the book was published. Already, in early 1956, and increasingly during the years that followed, the nuanced balance of these poems, the tormented clash of loyalties, and above all their allusive commentary on the causes of any and every war, not just this one, were jarringly out of tune with the public mood in Greece. George had suffered in this way before; now, while his English publisher had refused 'Salamis in Cyprus' on the grounds that it was too political (and implicitly, that it was anti-British), almost all his readers in Greece rejected ...*Cyprus, Where It Was Ordained For Me*... on the grounds that the poems were not political *enough*, and were far too conciliatory to the colonial power. It would not be until Savidis published his detailed and penetrating study, six years later, by which time the Cyprus crisis was over, that the poems' true stature would begin to be recognised.[3]

In the meantime, from Beirut, George was following events in Cyprus closely. His own attitude, by the early months of 1956, had hardened considerably, and this was clearly a response to events in the island. The new Governor of Cyprus, Field-Marshal Sir John Harding, had declared a State of Emergency at the end of November. EOKA (the National Organisation of Cypriot Fighters) was proscribed; mass arrests and punitive blockades of villages and neighbourhoods became routine. The death sentence became mandatory for anyone caught carrying arms; the first executions, under these laws, were carried out that summer. But the measure which provoked greater and more lasting anger than any other, among the Greeks of Cyprus and Greece, was the arrest of Archbishop Makarios at Nicosia airport as he was about to board a plane for Athens, on 9 March; Makarios was then deported and held a prisoner in the Seychelles for just over a year.

On the day of Makarios' arrest, and before the news broke, George began a letter to Osbert Lancaster:

Yes, Osbert, it is horrible to have been both right and totally ineffectual. And this horror, which, as you can well imagine, I share with you, is bound, alas, to increase till the last climax. 'We are like the chorus of the ancient tragedy, watching but unable to stop the action' a common friend told me last autumn. Indeed we are; with the difference that we moderns know that at the moment of the curtain we shall be all included – the just and the unjust – in the indiscriminating catastrophy [*sic*]. . . . Our world seems to me a nightmare where gaily and lightheartedly, and painlessly we are cutting our limbs in order to feed and maintain the wild beasts around us. Osbert, Osbert, what is left to say, and what is the use of writing such letters.

A postscript announces that he has just been telephoned the news about Makarios. In unmistakable anger, and drawing on a rather crude image which goes all the way back to his disgust at the return to Greece of King George II in 1935, George goes on:

Unbelievable: But what Russian Iago has skillfully suggested to brush up the dusty tradition of deporting negro kings from Uganda to the Seychelles? Two years ago the problem was not enosis but how to unite Greece to Cyprus. Now the problem appears to be who first among the mighty ones is going to push Cyprus and Greece behind the Iron Curtain. Strange competition. The pity of it.[4]

331

George's newfound anger was similarly vented to Maurice Cardiff, who came over to Beirut from the British Council in Nicosia for what must have been an uncomfortable weekend in May. George recorded their arguments in his diary, and wrote a testy summary to Joan Rayner (wife of Paddy Leigh Fermor), in reply to a sympathetic letter from her shortly afterwards:

Cardiff . . . was saying . . . that greece appeared to him to have abandoned the West and become eastern in the sense that [she] preferred the violent way . . . to the constitutional way by negotiation. I tried to explain to him a) that negotiations were always made impossible; b) that it is not Greece that abandoned the West, neither in 1940, nor after the Liberation, but that it is the West which abandoned her in the name of a factor which we can hardly call western, the Turkish. And c) that those who are called Cypriot terrorists appeared on the stage after years and years of hearing that Cypriots are not Greeks because they have no guts, that they are quite pleased with the situation because they show no sign of real reaction, and finally that no respect is due to those who are not able to fight for their dignity.[5]

In an abandoned draft of this letter, George had gone further, to describe EOKA, that in British eyes was a terrorist organisation, as

> for the whole of Greece a resistance movement of the pure type[:] of the type which has been experienced by Paddy [Leigh Fermor, *whose wartime record in occupied Crete was legendary*] and so many others when we were fighting together.[6]

It has been said that before leaving Beirut, George even took the oath of allegiance to EOKA. This seems unlikely, not least because of George's own temperament; he consistently refused overt political allegiances, and only on very rare occasions subscribed to any form of communal action. In any case, EOKA was a closed organisation, very few of whose members were recruited outside Cyprus. But there is no doubt that, during this early phase of the crisis, George approved the campaign of violence initiated by EOKA; he always referred to its leader, Colonel George Grivas, by his *nom de guerre*, Digenis, a name whose heroic resonances go back to the middle ages. This was a measure of how far George had come since the summer of 1954, when he had written of the dire consequences that would follow, should the 'yeast of bitterness' rise. Although he seems to have retained his respect for Grivas throughout the conflict, there is no evidence that George ever dealt with him directly. The codename 'Varnavas,' under which he corresponded with the Greek consulate in Nicosia, was one of a number of such codenames agreed between EOKA and Greek officials, several of whom were markedly less sympathetic to the campaign of violence than was George.[7]

The letter to Mrs Leigh Fermor at the end of May seems to have been George's last contact with any of his English friends for just over a year. On 2 June, he drafted a letter to Joan's husband, Paddy, along similar lines, but did not send it. From the midnight news bulletin on Athens radio, the previous day, he had learned that he was being posted back to the Ministry, to take charge of the Second Political Directorate, with responsibility for Cyprus. George was now in the eye of the storm.[8]

George had known since the beginning of the year that he could expect a new posting soon; he had completed three years in Beirut. As usual, intense lobbying had been going on behind the scenes, involving his family in Athens. Since the death of the prime minister, Field-Marshal Papagos, the year before, elections had been won by the right-wing successor to the

Greek Rally party, the National Radical Union. The new prime minister was Constantine Karamanlis, a dynamic figure who at forty-eight was younger than most of his predecessors in office had been. George's brother-in-law, Kostakis Tsatsos, was already close to Karamanlis, and would serve him loyally and efficiently for the remainder of both men's long careers; since the February election, Tsatsos had been in the confidential position of minister to the prime minister.

George's intermediary on the spot was Maro, who stayed in Athens until the beginning of May. Relations between Maro and George's family were already brittle; Kostakis was understandably anxious not to be seen to be too blatant in preferring a member of his wife's family. But Ioanna reportedly told Maro that it was 'now or never,' if George wanted to ask a real favour of Kostakis. At the time, the Ministry seemed set to send him next to Cairo; George had already made it known that he would refuse, citing medical advice (his ulcer was still troubling him) and, at least privately to Maro, the fact that he had had enough of the Arab world.

Taking a cool look at the openings that were likely to be available, George thought that he would prefer Moscow; it was confirmation of this posting that he was expecting, when the news came through of his recall to Athens. In all this, the post that George had in his sights was London. There, he confided to Maro, even though it would cost the couple financially, 'I'd be prepared to go so as to help those lads that are getting killed [in Cyprus], if I could.' Ioanna and Kostakis, and therefore their friends in the Foreign Ministry, certainly knew, both from George directly and through Maro, that the 'favour' George would have liked to ask was to be directly involved with the Cyprus issue. There was, however, for the time being, no vacancy in the key position at the London embassy. Vasilios Mostras, the incumbent, had in any case just been recalled, in protest at the arrest of Makarios, so for the time being there was no role for an ambassador there.[9]

At the end of May, the Karamanlis government had narrowly survived a vote of censure in parliament over its handling of Cyprus. The foreign minister was the obvious casualty, and into the post Karamanlis drafted a recent convert from the centre-left, Evangelos Averoff-Tosizza (Averof-Tositsas). Son of an influential land-owning family from Metsovo in northwest Greece, Averoff had broad interests in literature and the arts, and had been part of the Kydathinaion Street circle since before the war. He had been briefly Under-Secretary for Foreign Affairs in 1951–2, in which capacity George had appealed to him about his promotion that had then been pending. With receding hair and a clipped, military moustache, Averoff struck Sir Charles Peake, British ambassador at the time of his appointment, as 'a frightened man;' Peake 'doubted whether he [Averoff] had the qualities necessary to carry a settlement of the Cyprus issue through the Greek Chamber.' The British Foreign Office clearly did not expect the new appointment to last; neither, according to Averoff's own account, did he himself. In the event, Averoff was to hold on to his post for eight years and would become the principal instigator, on the Greek side, of a settlement to the Cyprus crisis. The fortunes of the Averoff ministry were also crucially to shape the closing stages of George's diplomatic career.

One of Averoff's first acts in office was to appoint George to the Directorate of the Ministry with responsibility for Cyprus.[10]

One of the things that most irked George about his profession was the absence of consultation before a change in posting was announced. This is a professional hazard accepted by most diplomats the world over; but George had complained bitterly about it since at least the early 1940s. He found it an affront to the dignity of his office. Now, hearing of this latest appointment on the radio news, his immediate reaction was fury. In a hurried exchange of telegrams with Averoff on 1 June, it was agreed that he would come to Athens for talks before accepting. When he arrived at Athens airport six days later, he was gratified to be greeted by the head of personnel himself: the Ministry, he noted in his diary and to Maro, was 'terrified I'll refuse.' In this way George was mollified; he found himself immediately surrounded by an atmosphere that reminded him of the time of the regency, and he entered upon ten days of intensive talks with gusto. There had never been any question of him refusing.[11]

In Athens, George talked not only to senior officials, but also to MPs with an interest in Cyprus and to newspaper editors, who were among the most vociferous supporters of *enosis*, and a source of anxiety to the government. He talked, inconclusively, to his old friend Kartalis, still the leading figure in the centre-left opposition, although by now seriously ill; the left had been putting pressure on the government, for months, to take a tougher line over Cyprus. He had long confidential talks with Kostakis Tsatsos; he was disappointed, but not surprised, to find his brother-in-law principally preoccupied with the party-political aspect of the crisis. Averoff, the new foreign minister, was not in Athens when George arrived. This irritated him, and he responded to their first official meetings with reserve.

334

The climax of George's ten-day visit to Athens came on Tuesday, 12 June, when he was called to a secret meeting at the house of Karamanlis. Also present were Averoff, the Permanent Secretary for Foreign Affairs Pericles Skeferis (under whom George had served in the past and who had always thought highly of him), and Kostakis Tsatsos. From now until the Cyprus conflict was about to enter its closing stages, George would be at the heart of the inner group of politicians and officials responsible for determining the policy of the Greek government. At this stage, George was determined that clandestine support for the armed struggle in Cyprus should continue. It is no wonder, then, that for the next twelve months he found it impossible to meet British officials, and even his own British friends, in any but the most formal circumstances.[12]

At the same time, George harboured no illusions about the nature of the task facing him:

> This job that they want me to do is a form of chaos – you can't judge in advance what you'll be able to give to it – you have to shut your eyes and jump, believing in what you believe in.[13]

335

### The eye of the storm

Back in the Middle East, George embarked during July on a hectic round of diplomatic farewells. On his way to Baghdad, his aircraft was diverted to Tehran because of a dust storm; at the time he was reading, with increasing bitterness, the letters of Gertrude Bell, written from the same region during the First World War. 'What a dreadful world of broken friendships we have created between us,' he quoted Bell as writing in January 1918. And George commented in his diary:

> How many British people who have known Greece must be thinking like that now, after the indescribable damage done by Eden.[14]

The days of Sir Anthony Eden as British prime minister were already numbered. Later that same month, the nationalisation of the Suez Canal by the Egyptian leader, Abdul Gamal Nasser, would precipitate the ill-fated invasion of Egypt by British and French forces at the end of October; the ignominious withdrawal that followed was widely seen, both in Britain and throughout the world, as marking the end of that country's imperial fortunes. George seemed already to prefigure these events in a conversation with an elderly cosmopolitan lady in Jerusalem:

> I said to her, . . . 'when you've run out of gold, and you're no longer strong enough to crack the whip (I was thinking of the British), you ought not behave as though you still had them, but have the imagination to think of something else.'[15]

George left Beirut for the last time on 30 July, 1956, with Maro, to take up his new post at the Ministry in Athens. They travelled by way of Port Said and Alexandria. There they renewed their friendship with an ailing Nanis Panayotopoulos, and snubbed Malanos, who was not to be forgiven for his book about George.[16]

Back in Athens, the immediate task facing George, during the summer and autumn of 1956, was to help prepare his government's brief for the Eleventh General Assembly of the United Nations. Cyprus itself had no representation in that international forum, as it was not a sovereign state. In each of the previous two years, the Greek government had assumed the responsibility, on behalf of the Greek Cypriot community, to have the issue of self-determination for Cyprus placed on the UN agenda. There had been an inconclusive discussion in 1954; in 1955, further discussion of Cyprus had been shelved. In those relatively early days of the United Nations Organisation, rather more weight was attached to the resolutions reached there than has often been the case since; there was a real and general belief in Greece and Cyprus that a resolution in New York in favour of self-determination was all that was needed in order to make *enosis* a reality. George would certainly not have believed that matters were so simple, but he probably did place more faith in the results of his country's efforts at the United Nations than would be justified by events. It is indicative of his thinking at this time, and prophetic of what was to come, that George would soon be urging Averoff not to dissipate Greek efforts at the United Nations by entering into parallel negotiations, either through NATO, or directly with the Turkish government.[17]

The Assembly of the United Nations should have opened in September 1956; it was delayed because of the larger crisis of Suez. While British forces were withdrawing from Egypt, and British international prestige plummeted, George took off from Athens airport, with a delegation of ministers, MPs and officials headed by Averoff, for New York; there, they would be joined two days later by Karamanlis himself. That was in November

1956. Two months later, George was again in America, for longer this time, to prepare for the committee sessions at the UN which finally took place in February 1957. These two visits were George's first experience of the New World.[18]

The delegation was housed at the Plaza Hilton Hotel, on Fifth Avenue, facing the south side of Central Park. George had a room on the eleventh floor, with a television set in it (this must have been a novelty to him; some years later he would 'wonder with horror what will happen when television arrives' in Greece). The transatlantic flight, with a short stopover in Rome, and his first experience of travelling across time zones had taken their toll on George's health: even at official functions he could drink only milk, because of his ulcer. But his first impressions of New York, in late autumn sunshine, were of lightness and airiness; the skyscrapers he found not overwhelming, but graceful in their proportions. When he returned in January, it was to a grimmer cityscape, when it snowed for two days without stopping and the temperature plunged to minus sixteen, reminding him of Ankara.[19]

Not all of George's time in America was spent in work. In November, he escaped to Providence, Rhode Island, where his niece, Ioanna's daughter Despina, was living. In New York, and also in Washington, where he went twice with Averoff in January, he was invited to concerts and operas conducted by Dimitri Mitropoulos, whose distinguished career as musical director of the New York Philharmonic was now in its last, 'strained' phase. George spent several congenial evenings with Mitropoulos and his long-term correspondent Katy Katsoyanni, who was with him at this time. In New York he went to cinemas and theatres, to the Museum of Modern Art, and was bemused to be entertained to breakfast at the Stock Exchange on Wall Street. A strip-tease show in Greenwich Village, within the limits of nudity permitted at the time in New York City, seemed to him an atavistic throw-back to more primitive rites. But the high point of George's first experience of America was his meeting, in Washington, with the French poet and diplomat Saint-John Perse, whose work he had read and admired for almost thirty years, and who at the time was working as an advisor to the Library of Congress. Saint-John Perse would be awarded the Nobel Prize in 1960, three years ahead of George.[20]

Despite all this, George's overall impression of America, in February 1957, was not an enthusiastic one. After the vibrancy of New York, he found Washington DC dismal ('like leafing through the architectural sketches of

337

a very diligent student'); he thought of its monuments as mausolea waiting to close round their over-wealthy incumbents. The Americans themselves, he felt, at least as he saw them in their nation's capital, had failed to liberate themselves from their British colonial past; all the spontaneity he found to admire among the citizens of Washington was concentrated in a group of black children he and Averoff came across playing in a park. 'The other thing I felt,' he wrote to Maro,

> is that the Americans are a people that has never suffered in its life — how can they possibly understand us, those other peoples that have suffered so much.[21]

All these experiences and impressions were, of course, on the margins of what had brought George to America. In November, Karamanlis and Averoff had been successful in persuading the General Assembly to place the Greek motion on its agenda. George was pleased with Averoff's performance, in particular. A much reproduced photograph shows the prime minister and the foreign minister in the front row, Karamanlis looking pleased with himself and his eyebrows even larger than the cartoonists delighted in depicting them, while Averoff half turns to answer an urgent intervention from George, whose head has appeared from the row behind like a bespectacled jack-in-the-box.[22]

In February, the task facing the Greek delegation was altogether tougher. When the debate opened in the Political Committee of the UN on the 18th, there were two draft resolutions on the table. One was from Greece, the other from Great Britain, condemning Greece for its support of terrorism in Cyprus. Since the start of the year there had been intense lobbying by both sides. George was well satisfied with his delegation's preparations; a crucial, and for him satisfactory, 'turning point' had been reached when Averoff, in his opening speech, agreed to take the hard line that George proposed. At the end of the second day's debate, George sat up late with Averoff working over the text of his reply for the next day. 'We're joining battle with spirit (*kefi*) and panache,' he wrote to Maro. 'It's the first time since the war that my career has given me such a sense of satisfaction.'[23] When it was over, he reported:

> Even *I* think we've achieved something good. A significant step. . . . [But] don't be proud of your husband; there are other things that your husband can do; these are just a little jewel, a tiny contribution to

338

reduce the suffering of that world [of Cyprus] that we came to know and love.[24]

From the diplomatic point of view, these sessions at the United Nations, and the arduous preparations that preceded them, were George's finest hour. For almost the only time in his life, he was working closely with a strong and effective politician who was both willing to heed his advice and in a position to act on it, in a cause which at the time coincided with George's own most deeply held principles. To reach this point, he had had to overcome strong opposition from within the Greek delegation, several of whom were prepared to be more conciliatory in the face of British, Turkish, and latterly also American pressure. In practical terms, though, the 'significant step' achieved by Greece at the United Nations in February 1957 was largely illusory. By 26 February, when the vote was taken in the General Assembly, both resolutions, the Greek and the British, had been withdrawn, to be replaced by a compromise that was purely 'anodyne.' But, as George had already confessed to Maro, the satisfaction he felt during the debate was 'irrespective of the outcome;' he had given of his best, and helped to achieve the best that could be achieved in the circumstances.[25]

Before he left New York, on the last day of February, George took a taxi to the address on the Upper West Side, close to the Hudson River, where his brother Angelos had rented a room when he first came to America after the war. It was a bleak neighbourhood, particularly so in the piercing cold of that February day. Walking alone down West 88th Street, George had vividly before his mind's eye

> the silhouette of a man tormented, a sensitive man in America, in that wretched house, coming and going, questing, reciting verses. That loneliness that I dared not approach any closer.

It was now that he compared these 'returns to the past,' such as his return to Skala and Smyrna had been, to a 'descent into Hades.'[26]

When he reached Athens, after a flight via Gander and Paris, it was to find that work had begun in his absence on levelling the site, on the steep hill behind the Stadium, where building was about to begin on the house in Agras Street.[27]

One way in which the vote at the United Nations in February 1957 did have an influence on wider events was in the timing, if not the fact, of the British

339

decision to release Archbishop Makarios from detention in the Seychelles. This happened on 6 April.[28]

Makarios was still prevented by the British authorities from entering Cyprus; on his release, he headed for Athens instead. Amid scenes of wild jubilation, the archbishop arrived in Athens during Orthodox Holy Week, on Wednesday 17 April. It was a grey, windy day. George was present at the airport to welcome him; an American-style cavalcade, in open cars, then made its way to the Grande Bretagne hotel in the centre of Athens, which became Makarios' headquarters for the next two years. A photograph shows George, in an overcoat and almost completely bald, bowing to kiss the archbishop's hand with a degree of devotion that seems to attract the notice of the surrounding clerics and officials, while Makarios, caught in profile, smiles his famous enigmatic smile.[29]

While Makarios was still on his way to Athens, George had learned that the key post of ambassador to London was about to become vacant, and would be his. These events were very closely linked.

Throughout the time of Makarios' exile, the London embassy had been headed by a *chargé d'affaires*. The ambassador, Vassilios Mostras, had only just been allowed by the Greek government to return to London, on the news of Makarios' release. Mostras had a reputation for being pro-British, and on his arrival made an emollient speech which drew down the full wrath of the Greek press. On 11 April, Mostras tendered his resignation, and the following day received a telegram from Averoff asking him to seek *agrément* (the formal approval on behalf of the British Crown) for his successor. George Seferiadis, although he still held the lower rank of Minister Plenipotentiary, had learned three days before, that he was to head the London embassy, with the title of Ambassador.[30]

Not long afterwards, George and Maro went out to dinner in Plaka with Angelos Vlachos (now consul in Nirosia, from where he had been recalled for the arrival of Makarios) and Dimitris Nikolareizis, the *chargé d'affaires* from London. Vlachos found George far from enthusiastic about his new appointment. As he recorded many years later, George looked 'anxious and awe-struck;' it was Maro whose eyes 'flashed with gratified ambition.' Vlachos' portrait of George at this moment bears the hallmarks both of hindsight and of personal animus, but should not be discounted altogether:

I was watching Seferis carefully and thinking that this languid individual, whose way of walking down the street was enough to conjure up in

340

my mind the 'voluptuous East,' where it takes a man two hours of day-dreaming to down a cup of coffee, would be up against the Turkish ambassador to London, Nuri Birgi, who was the exact opposite of George: short, thin, with a mobile, intelligent face, crafty and active, affable, open-hearted and generous, humorous and quick-witted; his English, too, was perfect.

Both George and Vlachos had known Birgi in Ankara; as a negative catalogue of the qualities George was supposed to lack, this list is both eloquent and diplomatic. But it was Vlachos, not George, whose nerves would be shattered before the Cyprus crisis was over. If George was not enthusiastic about his impending responsibilities, this is surely because he had already recognised, and accepted, the most demanding professional challenge of his career.[31]

In the days that followed, a somewhat different view of the impending ambassadorial appointment was being passed around the Foreign Office in London. The request for *agrément* was approved, but with the rider that 'the change [of ambassador] can scarcely be welcome to us.' A minute by Sir Frederick Hoyer-Millar, Permanent Under-Secretary of State, adds:

341

> I am sorry that the present Ambassador is leaving and I am afraid that we shall lose on the exchange and that M. Seferiadis may be rather a nuisance here. However, perhaps in fact he will do less harm here than he would in Athens.

A few days later, the British ambassador in Athens, Sir Anthony Lambert, summed up his own impressions of Ambassador Seferiadis, based on extensive dealings with him over the past few months:

> Despite the fact that he is slightly hard of hearing, I have, on the whole, found him pleasant to deal with. He considers problems seriously and carefully and does not get excited. On the other hand, he has the reputation of being an ardent Enotist. I would not say myself that he is a fanatic, but there is no doubt that he is convinced of the rightness of the Greek claim to Cyprus and would pursue it stubbornly within the now familiar limits of preserving Anglo-Greek friendship. He is thus a very different type from his predecessor in London and is likely to present his Government's case much more forcefully and tenaciously.[32]

So far as it goes, this seems accurately to sum up the spirit in which George was about to embark on the final stage of his career – except that the deafness noted by the ambassador was probably a professional mannerism. There is no evidence that there was ever anything wrong with George's hearing.

### A time of trial

George could not take up his appointment in London immediately. The second international forum, after the UN, for which he had to help prepare his government's brief was NATO. The NATO Council was due to meet in Bonn, the West German capital, from 2 to 5 May 1957. George accompanied Averoff, by way of Strasbourg, where they lodged protests with the Council of Europe against the curtailments of civil liberties by the British in Cyprus. The NATO meeting was another minor breakthrough for Greece, since the new Secretary-General, the Belgian Paul Henri Spaak, was markedly more sympathetic than his British predecessor had been. Although repeated attempts at mediation by NATO, and by Spaak in particular, would all prove fruitless, it was at this meeting that a possible compromise solution to the Cyprus crisis began to be seriously canvassed. This was that instead of being united to Greece, as the Greeks wanted, or partitioned, as the Turkish government was now ever more insistently demanding, Cyprus should become an independent state.[33]

This was the political background against which Ambassador Seferiadis arrived in London to take up his duties on 15 June 1957. Eleven days later, he wrote to his sister, with restrained pride, that he had presented his credentials to Queen Elizabeth II at Buckingham Palace; Ioanna wished that their father could have lived to see 'his dream come true.' He paid his first call on the Foreign Secretary, Selwyn Lloyd. The new prime minister (since January) was Harold Macmillan. George always had a high personal regard for Macmillan, a sentiment which seems to have been to some degree mutual. The two had first met when Macmillan served in Churchill's entourage in Greece at the time of the violence in Athens in December 1944. On a later occasion, visiting London with Damaskinos, while Macmillan's party had been in opposition, George had relished being able to converse confidentially, in French, with Macmillan, over the head of the Labour prime minister, Clement Attlee. It would have been entirely natural, in these circumstances, for the new ambassador to pay a courtesy call on the prime minister soon after his arrival. But it is a measure of the diplomatic sensitivities of the time that the Foreign Office intervened to forestall him. Politely, George was asked to withdraw his request to call on Macmillan.

Professionally, his stock had never been higher. A confidential Foreign Office memorandum records first impressions there: 'M. Seferiades is intelligent and agreeable. He is a strong supporter of Enosis but is anxious to preserve Anglo-Greek friendship.' Congratulating him on his promotion to Minister Plenipotentiary Grade I, which came through at the beginning of September, Ioanna relayed to him the high praises for his work that she had heard, not only from his minister, Averoff, but from the US ambassador in Athens, George Allen.[34]

Still, for George and Maro, this was the beginning of a testing time. The present-day Greek embassy, in Holland Park, had not yet been built; all the functions of the embassy were carried out from what is today the ambassador's residence, the five-storey house at 51 Upper Brook Street, on the corner of Grosvenor Square, that had been gifted to the Greek state by Helena Schilizzi, the second wife of Eleftherios Venizelos. George had worked in the building before; now he was faced with the prospect of carving out of the antiquated 'interior of a mausoleum' a modern home fit for himself and Maro, where they could also entertain in appropriate style. The domestic staff were a constant source of irritation; elaborate and time-consuming arrangements to bring over their former cook from Beirut, for instance, foundered when the man left after only a few months, to go back to his Lebanese girlfriend.[35]

Maro seems to have been unusually on edge just after they moved in; it was she who now had to bear the brunt of establishing not one but two households, since work was progressing at the same time on the house in Agras Street. In order to oversee the building work in Athens, Maro had to leave George on his own, during the next year and a half, for periods of up to three months. Their correspondence during these times of enforced separation testifies to the care and attention to detail that both lavished on their future home in Athens. The building work came to a finish early in 1959; until then, Maro, while she was in Athens, lived in the ground-floor flat at Kydathinaion Street. Without George there to keep the peace, there was frequent friction between Maro and Ioanna on the floor above; they communicated by telephone. When the time came, and against George's advice, Maro moved her belongings into the new house before the builders had properly finished.[36]

All this time, the situation in Cyprus was deteriorating further. EOKA continued its work of assassination and sabotage, interspersed with

343

unilaterally declared truces and a campaign of passive resistance; large numbers of Greek Cypriot men were now being held by the British army, without trial, in detention camps. The replacement of Field-Marshal Sir John Harding, as Governor, by Sir Hugh Foot, who had radical leanings and family connections to the Labour opposition in Parliament, had altered the style but not the substance of British policy on the ground. A new and still more deadly factor had entered the equation at the end of 1957, with the start of intercommunal terrorism. EOKA now had a Turkish rival, which enjoyed the clandestine support of the Turkish government, just as EOKA did of the Greek. For the first time, Turkish Cypriots and Greek Cypriots were now killing one another on the streets. In such a climate, the intransigence of both governments, the Greek and the Turkish, reached a new pitch. The international dimension introduced into the conflict by the British at the beginning, in order to counter the threat to their sovereignty from EOKA, had at last come home to claim a place in the hearts and minds of Cypriots. Although not all the players recognised it at the time, the nature of the conflict had changed drastically by the middle of 1958; the real threat to Greek and Greek-Cypriot interests came no longer from the colonial power, but from the Turkish-Cypriot minority and its militarily strong backers in Ankara. In these new circumstances, George's earlier hardline support for the EOKA campaign vanished; to continue the armed struggle against the British would only be to play into the hands of the Turks.[37]

By the summer of 1958, a new diplomatic impasse had been reached. No solution was likely to be effective if it did not have the support of the Greek and Turkish governments; but neither government would now accept any solution that was also acceptable to the other. It was now that the British side moved to impose a solution that was tortuous in its complexity, but had the political advantage, in the eyes of its proposers, that it could be implemented even without the agreement of the other parties concerned. This was known as the 'Macmillan Plan.' A first version of this plan had been proposed in the summer of 1957 but nothing had come of it. A modified version had then been concocted, amid great secrecy, early in 1958. It was this plan that was presented to the British parliament by Macmillan on 19 June. The substance of this plan was an interim status for Cyprus known as 'tridominium': while Great Britain would retain sovereignty, this would now be exercised in 'partnership' with the governments of Greece and Turkey, through their respective Representatives who would have an executive role alongside the British Governor.[38]

The determination of Macmillan and the British government to impose this plan quickly, ahead of a general election in Britain the following year, marked the beginning of the endgame of the Cyprus crisis.

As part of this strategy, the details of the Plan were given to the Greek and Turkish governments ahead of the announcement in Parliament. George had consistently badgered the Assistant Under-Secretary of State at the Foreign Office, Sir Archibald Ross, for advance notification of the British government's intentions. On this occasion, at least, his insistence was rewarded (although Ross kept from him the intention to give the Turkish government a twenty-four hour start). Once it was unveiled, the Macmillan Plan was robustly rejected by the Greek government; in his own representations to Ross, George emphasised the sticking point that 'tridominium' would give to Turkey rights over Cyprus which had been expressly renounced in the Treaty of Lausanne in 1923. To Ioanna, George wrote:

> I'm making desperate efforts; . . . I haven't stopped for a moment, all these last days . . . [*He had been lobbying the Labour Opposition, in preparation for a debate in the House of Commons later that week.*] I have the feeling that this time it's not just Cyprus but the fate of Greece itself that's hanging in the balance. And behind all that there is a Nemesis which has already begun to work; a Nemesis that, in the way of these things, strikes down the just with the unjust.[39]

For his sister, who had experienced as he had the effects of Turkish military power unleashed in their homeland of Anatolia, there was no need to spell out the nature of the Nemesis that George feared. In a private meeting with Selwyn Lloyd, the Foreign Secretary, soon afterwards, he protested that 'this was the beginning of Turkish re-occupation of Cyprus and what they [the Turkish government] wanted now was not partition but the whole of the island.' Shortly after that meeting, the British authorities in Cyprus launched 'Operation Matchbox,' a sweep against EOKA which all but ignored the equally murderous activities of the rival Turkish guerrilla group, TMT. George protested his 'astonishment that . . . [the British] reaction to Turkish violence had been to seize 1,200 Greeks,' and ended his interview with Ross with the pronouncement that the 'sibyl had by now burnt all her books.' According to an ancient Roman tradition, the Cumaean Sibyl, refused the price she demanded for her books of prophecy, progressively burned them, to offer the remainder for sale at the original price.

The analogy between this story and the successive British offers to the Greeks over Cyprus seems first to have been drawn, in an off-duty moment, by the Foreign Secretary, Selwyn Lloyd; it became something of a running joke in George's exchanges at the Foreign Office that summer. It was an irony of the position in which he found himself, that his own deep knowledge of the classical past was effortlessly shared among the British officials and politicians with whom he had to deal; such light-hearted erudition would never have been acceptable on his own side.[40]

On 7 August, Macmillan set out with his Foreign and Colonial Secretaries for direct talks in Athens and Ankara. George was summoned to Athens, to be in attendance at Macmillan's meetings with Karamanlis and Averoff. But the British European Airways flight on which he and his press attaché, Alexandros Xydis, were booked was delayed for several hours. While he was waiting at the airport, a message reached George from Macmillan's office, offering him a lift to Athens in the prime minister's specially commissioned RAF Comet. Telephone calls ensued; the Foreign Office intervened to say that there was no spare seat on the Comet. Then, when Macmillan himself arrived, with his entourage, at the airport, he sent his car for George. A photograph shows Macmillan bare-headed, striding out and evidently talking loudly, while he hustles forward a slower-moving George, whose brow is deeply furrowed, between his thick-rimmed spectacles and bowler hat. It is said that George's 'disappearance,' for several hours, caused consternation among Greek officials, until the missing ambassador emerged from the RAF jet on to the tarmac at Ellinikon airport, in the wake of Macmillan's party.[41]

Back in London after attending the talks between Macmillan and Karamanlis, George was summoned to a meeting with Macmillan, who had in the meantime returned after going on to Ankara, for similar talks with the Turkish government. According to Macmillan's memoirs,

> [Seferiadis] was very charming and rather sad. For he clearly feels that his government are behaving weakly and foolishly. . . . [R]eally he had little to say. He did however add that perhaps the return of Makarios to Cyprus would be now the only way out. He said, quite frankly, that his presence in Athens made the government's position impossible.

What George actually said, according to the prime minister's own minute of this conversation, was rather different. Asked for the view of the Greek government, if the British were to allow Makarios to return to Cyprus, the Ambassador said that it would help[,] but if the Archbishop was allowed to come back he hoped that he would be given a position of responsibility; the atmosphere in Athens was quite unreal.[42]

The British prime minister could hardly have been expected to know that George had adapted the refrain from Eliot's *The Waste Land,* 'unreal city,' to depict the British-dominated chaos of the Middle East in 1942, shortly before the battle of El Alamein. The situation that George was now trying to convey was one in which, as he had summed it up in his service diary earlier in the year, 'you've got involved in a game where all the players (these are the rules of the game) say the opposite of what they think – *all of them.*'[43]

Perhaps it was inevitable that the 'gloomy' ambassador should have acquired the reputation in Whitehall of being 'notorious[ly] . . . hard to understand.'[44]

None of these representations, whether from George in London, from the Greek government in Athens, or through NATO in Paris, was sufficient to dent the British government's determination to push through the Macmillan Plan. Neither was the unexpected concession by Makarios, in an interview with the British Labour member of parliament Barbara Castle, on 24 September, that the Greek Cypriots would after all be prepared to accept independence, on certain conditions, as a preferable alternative. The date set for the implementation of the Plan was 1 October 1958. Neither the Greek government nor any Greek-Cypriot organisation was prepared to cooperate. The Turks had by this time approved the plan, and now designated their consul in Nicosia as the official representative of the Ankara government in Cyprus; the Greeks refused to appoint a representative of their own. A sense of 'grim expectation' descended on Cyprus. The British embassy in Athens warned that the Greek government might now leave NATO, break off diplomatic relations, or resign. George, 'very despondent,' repeated none of these threats to Ross when he came to see him at the Foreign Office at the end of September. On the other hand, the Greek Ambassador had, as Ross reported,

347

communed with his own heart on many occasions and the thought had struck him that he personally could not stay on in London. The harm which would be done was irreparable. So much bitterness and hatred would be created. . . . As he left the Ambassador asked me to remember that he was a mild man and not prone to exaggeration: I must take his remarks as seriously as if he had shouted and banged the table.[45]

### 'There is an island'

In Cyprus, EOKA responded to the implementation of the Macmillan Plan by launching a new campaign of violence, which claimed forty-five lives and left another 370 people injured during 'Black October.' Yet another round of negotiations among NATO ministers in Paris, the same month, proved fruitless, and brought Averoff to the brink of resignation.[46]

By the time that Cyprus was yet again debated at the United Nations, at the start of December 1958, the cut and thrust of claims and counter-claims in the Political Committee, and the passing of a worthy but tooth-less resolution, had come to be little more than a familiar ritual. George, in London, cannot have been awaiting the telegram from his ministry, announcing the outcome, with more than routine interest. Even he, at the beginning, can have had no inkling of what had begun, in the corridor of the United Nations building in New York, at the end of the last session of the Political Committee on 4 December. When he did, he was horrified.

It had already been the custom, at the United Nations, for the Greek and Turkish delegations to indulge in some diplomatic banter and ironic mutual congratulation backstage, in the intervals between their formal confonta-tions. George himself had been at the receiving end of the bullying charm of the Turkish foreign minister, Fatin Zorlu, during one of these informal exchanges after the 1957 debate. But when Zorlu approached Averoff this time, something completely unexpected happened. The upshot was that the two foreign ministers agreed to secret talks on the future of Cyprus from which everyone, including their own officials and the British colonial power, should be excluded. The first of these talks took place two days later, after the full session of the Assembly, on 6 December. As George had dryly to concede to Ross at the Foreign Office, while both men were essentially in the dark, 'M. Zorlu and M. Averoff had exchanged "Turkish delights" in New York.'[47]

On 16 December, George flew to Paris. Averoff had summoned him to be in attendance at the annual meeting of NATO foreign ministers. Zorlu would be there, as would Selwyn Lloyd, the British Foreign Secretary. Ross can only have been confirming George's unspoken fears, when he had ended their meeting, the day before, by saying that 'everything would depend on the contacts which would undoubtedly take place in Paris in the next couple of days.'

Averoff had in the meantime briefed Karamanlis in Athens about the diplomatic breakthrough in New York. If the British could be persuaded to abandon the Macmillan Plan, the preliminary basis for agreement between the foreign ministers ran, why should not Greece and Turkey amicably work out a constitutional framework for an independent Cyprus? Averoff was now ready to meet his Turkish counterpart again, on the fringe of the NATO meeting; their talks would be exploratory and wide-ranging; neither government would be bound by their outcome. To ensure this, Averoff and Zorlu again met with no officials present. According to Averoff, it was also agreed at the outset that no papers would be exchanged, though each would keep his own notes of their discussions. Out of these meetings, which took place on 16 and 17 December, emerged a set of proposals which Averoff and Zorlu then unveiled before the British Foreign Secretary the next day. This meeting on the 18th was the only one at which officials were present; on the Greek side these were George and the ambassador to NATO, Michael Melas.

Averoff says that he had briefed George and Melas the night before, at George's insistence, and that he did so only on the basis of his rough, hand-written notes of his discussions with Zorlu. There was, however, in exis-tence by the end of the next day, a sixteen-point plan for the constitution of an independent Republic of Cyprus, known as the 'Paris sketch.' Averoff's account of these events includes a dramatic digression: while their talks had been going on, it was Zorlu, of all people, whose intervention had been crucial in saving from the gallows two Greek Cypriots condemned to death in Nicosia; British sensibilities, however, required that the role of the Turkish foreign minister in the affair must remain totally secret. Whether or not this demonstration of Turkish good will was shared with George and Melas at the time, Averoff's later account elides the existence of the 'Paris sketch,' along with the probability that the draft agreement on the table in Paris on 18 December was largely, if not wholly, the brainchild of Zorlu.[48]

349

In hindsight, the sudden change of tactics by the Turkish government over Cyprus can be explained in geopolitical terms. The overthrow of the regime in Iraq, a few months previously, and continuing tension between Turkey and Syria, were potentially far greater threats to Turkish interests than Greece or Cyprus; of even greater importance, probably, was the inten-sification of the cold war confrontation over Berlin at the end of Novem-ber 1958. The balance of interest for the government of Turkey would be better served by a speedy settlement of differences with Greece, and espe-cially by closing ranks within the NATO alliance. In these circumstances, it all at once became possible for the Turkish government to make the minimal concessions necessary to break the deadlock.[49]

But this was not the light in which Ambassador Seferiadis saw matters. This was, after all, the same Turkish government that had instigated the anti-Greek riots of September 1955 in Istanbul, and whose repeatedly and stridently stated position on Cyprus was that the island should be partitioned between the two communities. What George suddenly saw staring him in the face, as he sat up late at the Hotel Bristol, on the nights of 18 and 19 December, with his notes on the 'Paris sketch' in front of him, was not the heaven-sent breakthrough that would solve the insoluble question of Cyprus. For him, the issue went far deeper than whether or not the new expressions of good will by the foreign minister of Turkey were sincere. George saw once more, as he had seen on the island of Patmos, in September 1955, while news of the mob violence in Istanbul was still fresh, 'a mechanism of self-destruction . . . in motion, obliterating every manifestation of good will.'[50]

Averoff spent the day after the meeting with Selwyn Lloyd at Versailles. George had a chance to discuss his anxieties with him only for half an hour in the morning, as they travelled out from the centre of Paris together. That night, George composed a detailed 'service memorandum' for Averoff. In it, with devastating foresight, he wrote:

350

> The absolute veto accorded in particular circumstances to the [Greek Cypriot] President and the [Turkish Cypriot] Vice-President concedes to Turkey the right to immobilise the working of the Cypriot State whenever she likes and to open the door, on the excuse that the constitution is incapable of working, either to a new push towards its demands for partition, or for military intervention . . .

It was a short critique, but it was damning. It concluded: 'If I were compelled to accept the preliminary draft as it stands, or to re-examine the possibility of cooperating [with the British] in accordance with the Macmillan Plan, I would opt for the latter.'[51]

Averoff left Paris on the morning of 20 December, with George's memorandum in his briefcase. At the same time, George left for London. Twenty-four hours later, he received a telephone call from Averoff in Athens. The foreign minister clearly did not mince his words. Their effect on George, that Sunday morning, was 'to make me weigh up my opinions again and again, to interrogate the objectivity of my judgement from every angle.' The view that he had expressed in his memorandum, George now wrote in a long and considered reply to Averoff on Christmas Day, had the advantage of being based on 'pure good faith;' as he had done in previous crises, George stressed that his actions were untainted by personal aspirations, either political or material. The disadvantage, he confessed with a touch of sarcasm, was that the view he had expressed in his memorandum was also, inevitably,

> influenced by the experience that I have gained in working on the Cyprus crisis and particularly as regards the mentality and political reactions of the Turks and the British. How else could it be? If there are matters which require this experience, obtained at such cost, to be re-evaluated, I do not know what these are.

George sent this more formal statement of his objections to the Paris proposals via the diplomatic bag to Averoff at the Ministry; by adding a file-number, even although it also carried the highest secrecy classification, he committed the unpardonable sin, in the eyes of its recipient, of making his objections to the talks a matter of record.[52]

Retribution followed swiftly. Averoff himself took the trouble to reply in a long, personal letter on New Year's Day, which in a friendly but firm tone rebuts George's objections and ends with a clear statement of the minister's determination to see the negotiations through to the end. It was from his brother-in-law, Kostakis Tsatsos, that George learned of the 'deep displeasure' of his minister; Tsatsos (himself also with a portfolio in the government) further reprimanded him for exceeding the duties of a senior civil servant. But these, and a further exchange of letters with Averoff lasting for several months, were only on the surface. From now on, Averoff simply thrust his ambassador in London aside.[53]

By the middle of January, George was becoming desperate. He begged Averoff for the information he urgently needed in order to brief British MPs, the Press, and the Foreign Office. On 17 January, Averoff was once again in Paris, for further secret talks with Zorlu. George tried unsuccessfully to reach him by phone at the Hotel Bristol. Two days later, Maro was on a plane to Athens. The flight went via Paris, where George had arranged for an embassy courier to be at the airport, so that she could hand over a copy of the letter he had addressed to Averoff in Athens, the week before. When Maro reached Kydathinaion Street, she was questioned by Ioanna: was George in Paris with Averoff? 'I told her that Averoff hadn't phoned to ask you,' Maro reported to George the same day. While Averoff was still

351

in Paris, George dashed off yet another long, handwritten letter to him; Macmillan himself, he complained, had been asking the other day, 'how's it going?' – and George had had no choice but to be evasive. 'How far is this thing going to go?' he demanded. 'The matter is in crisis and the London Embassy to all intents and purposes has been shut down.'[54]

It was the last time that Maro stayed in the flat at Kydathinaion Street. The atmosphere must have been more tense even than usual. Ioanna wrote to George soothingly, but hinted at exceptional strain in the household, and at a rift between Kostakis and Averoff, either caused or exacerbated by George's conduct; to Maro, Ioanna gave a strong hint that she thought her brother ought to resign. Maro reported to George, in characteristically undiplomatic language, that the government was 'scared stiff' of him; there may have been some truth in this, which may, in turn, help to explain Averoff's attitude. The negotiations between Greece and Turkey were still a closely guarded secret; in the hands of the opposition, or the Press, George's recent exchanges with Averoff would have been enough to blow not just the negotiations but the whole government sky-high.[55]

The crisis, in this acute phase, was short-lived. On Thursday 22 January 1959, George cancelled his engagements for the latter part of the day, claiming to be unwell, and spent the afternoon and evening composing letters and telegrams. It seems that until then he still believed that his own actions could help to avoid the 'tragedy' that he saw coming. By midday the next day, with the responses coming in, that belief was shattered. He knew, now, the outcome of Averoff's latest round of talks with Zorlu in Paris: that agreement on an independent Cyprus would soon be sealed by a summit meeting of the Greek and Turkish prime ministers. He knew, too, that Zorlu, on his way back from Paris to Ankara had made a brief stop, the evening before, at Athens airport, an unprecedented thing for a Turkish minister to do. But what, more than anything, must have put an end to George's hopes, was the behaviour of Makarios. The archbishop, who the week before had returned to Athens from a visit to the United States, had given his blessing to the proposals. Incredulous, George could not at first believe that Makarios had been fully briefed; if he had, had he fully taken in what was being proposed?[56] As George expressed his feelings to Ioanna:

We're up against people who're calculating and controlled and perfectly organised. We, on the other hand, set sail like the little coastal traders in the first years of independent Greece [*i.e. the 1830s*], without life-rafts, loaded to the gunwales, at the mercy of God. So be it. I'm certain that one day they'll remember me.[57]

The historic series of meetings took place at the Hotel Dolder, outside Zurich, from 6 to 11 February 1959. The Greek ambassador to London was not invited to attend, although his Turkish opposite number, Birgi, was. It was only the day before that George learned the timing or the venue of the summit; he wondered whether to cancel an invitation from Maurice Bowra to Oxford, but then: 'I thought that if I'm to sit here endlessly waiting, I'll never be able to do anything.'[58]

After intense negotiation and last-minute brinkmanship, a series of accords was signed at Dolder on 11 February. From George's point of view, these terms were even worse than the ones that he had seen in Paris, since they provided for a token contingent of Turkish troops (as well as a larger one from Greece) to be stationed in independent Cyprus. It was to this development, as well as to the imminent transfer of the talks to London, that he was referring when he wrote to Maro, in a touchingly transparent, improvised code:

News from Switzerland this afternoon: the child's getting worse; the 353
doctors from Athens have done the most unforgivably stupid things. . . .
It's unbelievable what mistakes people can make and once they've taken
the downward path they seem determined to roll all the way to the
bottom. Now it's not improbable that they'll bring the child here (in a
matter of days). You know what the doctors *here* are like. May God lend
a hand. Don't say anything of this to the relatives; it can't do any good.[59]

It was now, in the course of a sleepless night, that George seriously considered resigning his post. But he did not resign. To have done so, as he would later explain it, would have to have been a gift only to the far right and the communists. 'I decided to stay and salvage what could still be salvaged. I wanted to help Makarios. I stayed.' But Makarios had already given his assent, in advance, in the outcome of the Zurich talks, even though he, like George, was excluded from them. Makarios was now past help; George knew this.[60]

As George saw it, the signing of the Zurich accords between the Greek and Turkish prime ministers on 11 February sealed the fate of Cyprus. When the parties began to converge in London, at the end of that day, for talks that would last throughout the following week, George was once again the loyal civil servant, the obedient servant of ministers. What had been intended by the protagonists as a series of formalities, in London, to give legal and constitutional substance to the agreements reached at Zurich, would turn, instead, into a week of high drama. George and his embassy would be at the centre of the action.

In London, the February days were cold and foggy. The final round of talks was scheduled to begin at Lancaster House on the 17th. At this late stage, and for the first time, representatives of the Greek and Turkish communities of Cyprus were hastily summoned to attend. At the Greek embassy, Averoff dictated a bullying telegram to Athens for Makarios, which went out over the signature of George Seferiadis. It was presumably George's embassy that had made the arrangements for the delegations from the Greek government and from the Greek Cypriots to stay at two of London's most famous hotels. The archbishop and his entourage were booked into the Dorchester, overlooking Hyde Park; Karamanlis, Averoff, and their staff were housed at Claridge's, at an equal distance from the embassy but in diametrically the opposite direction.[61]

354
Makarios arrived on Sunday 15 February. George was at the airport to meet him, and accompanied him, amid tight security, to the Dorchester. At the end of the previous week, consternation had broken out among the Greek delegation; the archbishop was threatening, after all, to reject the terms that had been agreed at Zurich. As soon as George delivered him to the Dorchester, Makarios was subjected to intense pressure from Averoff, several of his officials, and finally from Karamanlis when he too arrived. Divisions between the Greek government and the Greek Cypriot point of view, represented by Makarios, went back at least to the time of the archbishop's release from the Seychelles; now they came to a head. At the London conference, the overriding political imperative for the Greek government was to extricate itself from a conflict that it could not win; for the Greek-Cypriots, on the other hand, what was at stake was their centuries-old identity as Greeks, which had first been systematically undermined by the British, and now, potentially, was under threat from the Turks.

Faced with these choices, George's deepest loyalties were bound to be with the Cypriots, as representatives of the wider Hellenism in which he had always believed, and against what he saw as the short-term pragmatism of his own government. It is hard to tell exactly what part was played by George in the concerted efforts of the Greek delegation to put pressure on Makarios, during these crucial days in London; George was certainly present at several acrimonious meetings, of which some record has been preserved, but there is nothing to indicate how, or even whether, he intervened. Walking in Grosvenor Square in the fog, after midnight on one of those nights, he confided to his press attaché, his friend Alexandros Xydis, 'his bitterness at the pressures being exerted on the Cypriots from all sides, the complacency and anti-Cypriot bias of certain of his colleagues, and his thoughts of giving up his post.'[62]

The Greek and Turkish prime ministers were due to arrive in London on Tuesday 17 February. The night before, George hosted a dinner at the embassy; it was a limited success, as several of his parliamentary guests had to return to the House of Commons to vote in a division. Late that night, he sat up, writing to Maro in Athens. Everything was ready for the final round of talks, at Lancaster House, tomorrow. 'I wish always that I could be wrong in what I'm saying – the bitterest thing is when events prove you right.' He was again having difficulty sleeping. It was, he continued, like reliving the days of Cava dei Tirreni, in 1944.[63]

The next day, the fog was thicker than ever. George met Karamanlis at Gatwick airport, where he left Vlachos behind to form part of the welcoming party for Adnan Menderes, the Turkish prime minister. It transpired later that the two premiers had exchanged greetings when both their planes touched down at Rome on the way; Karamanlis had refused the offer of a lift from Menderes, thereby most probably saving his life. The aircraft carrying the Turkish prime minister and his entourage now crashed on its approach to Gatwick in dense fog. Menderes himself survived, to be pulled out of the branches of a tree and offered tea and first aid by a local farmer; more than half of those aboard the Turkish plane were killed.

While this was going on, George accompanied Karamanlis, who went straight to the Dorchester. A bruising confrontation with Makarios followed. Then came dinner at 10 Downing Street, the official residence of the British prime minister, which George attended along with Averoff and Karamanlis. Because of the crash at Gatwick, the dinner started late. In the absence of his Turkish guests, Macmillan took advantage of the situation to exercise his 'theatrical sense of lazy, but deadly, power.' What, Macmillan asked Averoff, would happen if the British security forces in Cyprus were to arrest Grivas tonight? Averoff replied that all negotiations would be at an end. But the Greek foreign minister was sufficiently rattled that as soon as dinner was over, he hustled George back to the embassy, where together they sent an urgent coded message to the consulate in Nicosia, to alert Grivas to the danger. Macmillan, no doubt relishing the moment, gave

355

instructions to his security chief not to pursue the EOKA leader, and went shortly afterwards to pay his respects to Menderes, who had in the meantime been transferred to the London Clinic.[64]

It was against the background of these upsets that, on the second day of the Lancaster House talks, Makarios claimed centre-stage. Going back on the earlier promise of acquiescence extracted from him by Averoff and Karamanlis, the archbishop inveighed against several key terms of the Zurich accords. These were the same terms to which, in the earlier 'Paris sketch,' George had also objected: the right of veto exercised by the Greek president and the Turkish vice-president; the percentage of Turkish Cypriots in key institutions (which was higher than their percentage in the population); and the 'servitudes' which still limited the self-determination of the nominally independent republic. Averoff records the consternation in his own delegation when Makarios, under intense pressure to put his signature to the agreements, replied, 'If you want me to give an answer now, I say "no".' None of the eye-witnesses mentions the reaction of Ambassador Seferiadis.[65]

The next day, when Makarios had after all bowed to overwhelming pressure and put his signature to the agreements, Karamanlis hosted a reception at Claridge's. Makarios reportedly teased him, and the group of officials clustered round him: 'Did you really think I wouldn't sign?' 'Then why did you go through all that?' demanded Karamanlis. 'I had my reasons,' was the characteristically enigmatic reply.[66]

Makarios never said what these reasons were. From George's point of view, nothing had been gained by the archbishop's stand; it had been intensely embarrassing for the Greek delegation to find itself allied with the British and the Turks in facing down Makarios. But the archbishop's reputation for political shrewdness had been well earned. Faced with a *fait accompli* at the London conference, Makarios had forced the divisions between the Greek Cypriots and the Athens government into the open. Whatever happened next, it would be a matter of record that he had agreed to the terms only under intense pressure from Athens.

George was standing by when this exchange took place, and left the reception soon afterwards. It was not the first time that a political leader had failed to live up to his own high hopes. Writing to Maro two days later, he recalled the words of a colleague a year ago, at the time when divisions between Makarios and the Greek government had become acute: 'you'll have to drink the cup to the bottom.' 'I drank it, I think,' George wrote to Maro, 'and I came through.'[67]

The independent Republic of Cyprus was born on that day, 19 February 1959, with the signing of what became known as the Zurich-London Agreements. The new republic would have a Greek president and a Turkish vice-president; its independence was to be guaranteed by a treaty binding Great Britain, Greece and Turkey; Britain was to retain its military bases, which would remain British sovereign territory in perpetuity.[68]

All the participants at the London conference proclaimed victory – even Makarios, whose rallying cry, in Ancient Greek, 'we have won,' provoked a sardonic echo in George's diary. In diplomatic language, George stated to John Profumo, the Minister of State at the Foreign Office, shortly after the agreements were signed, his own view that 'Greece had perhaps given up more than she could afford to give up, particularly in agreeing to intervention in certain circumstances by one power acting alone.' (This last was a clear reference to Turkey.) George's assessment was echoed by Harold Macmillan, in his memoirs, who from his own vantage point noted, with some satisfaction, that the Greeks had '*not* had the best of the bargain. They could have done better by accepting the Radcliffe plan [tabled in 1956] *or* the Macmillan plan.'[69]

A year and a half would pass before the new Cypriot state would become a reality. During that time, George would be intensely involved in successive rounds of negotiations over the fine tuning of the agreements. In these talks, he would exert himself tirelessly to limit what he saw as the damage done, particularly over the Turkish military presence in the island and the size of the British bases. But the concessions he was able to win were trivial when set beside the atavistic processes that George believed had been set in motion by the agreements themselves.[70]

Even before Cyprus became formally independent (on 16 August 1960), the government of Adnan Menderes in Turkey would be ousted by a military *coup*; Menderes and most of his cabinet, including Zorlu, would be put on trial and publicly executed a year later. In December 1963, the Cyprus constitution would break down, exactly as George had predicted, and the next year, amid violent clashes, the Turkish Cypriots would retreat into enclaves. In 1967, it would become the turn of Greece to experience a military dictatorship, which almost at once would move to the brink of war with Turkey over Cyprus. Then in 1974 another *coup* by the Greek military, this time in Cyprus, would bring about the 'particular circumstances' in which, as George had foreseen back in December 1958, the Turkish army could legitimately intervene under the terms of the Zurich-London Agreements. Averoff, in his memoirs, written after these events, would concede

357

that a weakness of the agreements had been to permit the unilateral military intervention of one of the signatories in certain circumstances. But according to Averoff, this 'oversight' had only been pointed out 'much later;' it was, on the contrary, the main ground of George's memorandum delivered to the foreign minister in Paris on the morning of 20 December 1958, and suppressed in Averoff's memoirs. The consequence of these events, today, is the de facto partition of Cyprus along a cease-fire line policed by United Nations troops; almost half of the island, at the start of the twenty-first century, was still inaccessible to the eighty per cent of its population who are Greek Cypriots.[71]

Not even George, of course, could have foreseen how the 'mechanism' he had diagnosed would work itself out in detail. But within days of the agreements being signed, he was again considering his own position at the embassy, and before long would be asking Averoff to recall him to Athens. At the end of the year he noted in his diary, 'The worst thing is that I'm working now without faith.' Taking stock on his sixtieth birthday, he confessed that since the time of the agreements, 'my interest in the service has been greatly blunted. We [Greeks] aren't fit for great things.'[72]

A measure of the personal and collective sense of failure that George felt, after February 1959, is that when he brought out the next edition of his *Poems*, and included the collection that he had dedicated to the 'world' of Cyprus, he changed the title, from ...*Cyprus, Where It Was Ordained For Me*... to *Logbook III*. The symbolic homecoming implied by the earlier title had proved a bitter illusion; the voyage was resumed. The last of these poems to be completed, some years later still, ends with the line: ' "Steady on her course!" impassively echoed the helmsman.'[73]

### The poet's share

Even during the difficult times just past, George had not forgotten or been forgotten by his British friends. Soon after his arrival in London, he was dining with Maurice Cardiff, now back in London from the British Council in Nicosia, and Osbert and Karen Lancaster. Rex Warner was at this time working on the second book-length translation of George's poems into English; George's feelings for Warner were as warm as ever, even though he privately professed to misgivings about his friend's knowledge of Modern Greek.[74]

Thanks, in part, to Savidis who had been a student there, George was on excellent terms with the Provost of King's College, Cambridge, Noel Annan, and with the college's most distinguished literary Fellow, E.M.

Forster. At the end of 1957, George had been the guest of honour at the Founder's Day feast at the College; Annan in his speech of welcome declared:

In King's all of us think with sorrow of the division between Greece and Britain over Cyprus – I myself think of it with shame. But one thing is certain – political problems are transitory and in the world of the spirit, of art and of poetry, England will always be a colony of Greece.

On a later visit, George took a set of more than twenty photographs of Forster in the garden of the Old Vicarage at Grantchester, outside Cambridge, that had once been the home of the poet Rupert Brooke. When King's celebrated Forster's eightieth birthday in January 1959, George and Maro were among the official guests. Coming at the height of his own personal crisis over the Cyprus negotiations, this occasion was 'one of the best moments in this country and of our lives here,' as George noted in his diary.[75]

With the ending of the Cyprus Emergency and the relaxation of tension, it was at last possible for George to savour to the full the life of a high-ranking diplomat and man of letters at the turn of the new decade. His rather formal, but by George treasured, exchanges with T.S. Eliot now resumed. Eliot had written to congratulate him on his appointment, but had parried George's invitations, professing diffidence before one of such exalted rank; in all probability, Eliot's traditionalism in his adopted country did not lend itself to sympathy for the Greek cause in Cyprus while the Emergency lasted. Now that it was over, George met Eliot again, along with his new wife, in the company of Maurice Bowra. From then on, they would meet at intervals of a few months, until George left London; on many of these occasions, George would once again keep a respectful record of their conversations.[76]

Beginning in 1959, George and Maro spent three Christmases at the home of Osbert and Karen Lancaster at Henley-on-Thames, outside London. An extended series of travels around Great Britain, in the spring of 1959 and early summer of 1960, took them to the Channel Islands, and then to Scotland. In Edinburgh, often called the 'Athens of the North' for its neo-classical architecture, George observed, without comment, the 'Doric columns that look as though they're made of charcoal,' and was bemused by the total shut-down of the Scottish presbyterian sabbath. On the west coast, he and Maro were the guests of Warner and his family, at

Craignish House not far from Oban. The mist and rain made George think painfully of Greece. From Oban they continued their journey northwards, to visit another old friend: Steven Runciman, who owned and lived on the small island of Eigg. Runciman, a Byzantinist and a fine raconteur, enchanted George with his spooky tales, and seems to have convinced his guest that he had second sight.[77]

Only with Durrell was George never fully able to overcome, afterwards, the bitterness he had felt at the time of the Cyprus crisis. 'Although Seferis did not break off contact with Larry,' writes Durrell's biographer, Ian MacNiven, 'it is doubtful that their relationship ever recovered fully.' In common with many Greeks, George had been outraged at the portrayal of Cyprus and the Greek Cypriots in Durrell's semi-fictionalised account of his experiences there, *Bitter Lemons*, when he read it shortly before taking up his post in London. He only began to read *The Alexandria Quartet* in 1960, three years after its first volume, *Justine,* had been published, and he was unimpressed, though he never said so in public. Indicative of his feelings towards Durrell after Cyprus, and after the success of the *Quartet*, was George's reply to an invitation to visit Durrell and his third wife in Paris, at the end of his service at the London embassy: 'I have been following your literary successes very eagerly, with many interrogation marks when thinking of Larry the poet whom I used to know.' This is certainly barbed, but George ended by wondering if they might not meet again in Greece, as indeed they did, on at least two subsequent occasions.[78]

In the spring of 1960, George carried off an unusual diplomatic achievement. This was the repatriation to Greece of the remains of one of the best known Greek poets of the nineteenth century, Andreas Kalvos, who had spent his last years in England and was buried in a small village churchyard in Lincolnshire. It was George's initiative to have his illustrious predecessor exhumed; a glum liturgy in the Orthodox mortuary chapel in London was recorded by the BBC, before the coffins containing Kalvos and his English wife were flown by Olympic Airways to Athens, for re-burial in Kalvos' native island of Zakynthos. George had always been puzzled by Kalvos' small but enduring poetic output of the 1820s, written during the Greek War of Independence. Romantic passion, the fire of patriotism, love of liberty and nature, as George read Kalvos' *Odes*, are overlaid by a thick formal carapace of neoclassical rhetoric and an artificial language. Kalvos, for George, was an enigma, a poet without a face, a voice 'struggling to speak, from behind a curtain.' The enigma was not solved when George was shown the photographs from the exhumation; there, he saw 'a very large skull and the lower jaw in such a position as to suggest a mouth gaping like an abyss as though he was yelling at full strength.' In this rather shocking glimpse, the poet as living man becomes more remote, more elusive than ever; but the image is eloquent of how George himself thought about poetry. For a poet to fall silent for half a century, as Kalvos had done after the 1820s, was a strange and frightening idea to him.

The repatriation of Kalvos' remains was not merely a sentimental act, a belated fulfilment of that poet's own implied wish: 'Death is sweet only / When we lie in our fatherland.' As such, it was of course appreciated in Greece. But without the influence that George was in a position to wield, it could not have been done at all. And its greater importance was that it raised awareness, even if only for a time, that there had been a great modern Greek poet who had died in England. Some months afterwards, a memorial plaque to Andreas Kalvos and his English wife was set up in the village church of Keddington, where they had lived and died. The Dean of Lincoln Cathedral, leading the Sunday morning service when the plaque was unveiled, prayed 'that through the inspiration and work of poets and all kind of artists the nations of men may be drawn closer together in sympathy and understanding.'

361

Even at this moment of reconciliation, though, the shadow of the Cyprus settlement was not far away. The arrival of Kalvos' bones in Greece, in March 1960, provided the occasion for the first of a series of vicious attacks in the far-right newspaper *Estia*. This was an attack not only on the Zurich-London Agreements in general, but also specifically on George, who had allegedly conspired with Averoff to 'sacrifice the liberty of Cyprus to Turkish cannibals [sic].' Later in the year, the ceremony in Lincolnshire fell just two days before the official celebration of the independence of Cyprus, on 16 August.[79]

On vacation in Greece, that summer, George called in at Ikaros, the bookshop run by his publisher. 'Records are what sell,' the proprietor told him, 'nobody's interested in buying books these days.' His own latest book, *...Cyprus, Where It Was Ordained For Me...* had not sold at all. 'Why?' George asked himself, in exasperation, in his diary.[80]

No doubt he shared this exasperation with his friends, of whom the most influential was the ebullient and well connected George Savidis. It may well have been thanks to a gentle nudge from Savidis that, soon after his return to London, in the autumn of 1960, George for the first time met the popular composer Mikis Theodorakis. Before long, the musical setting of four of

George's poems, by Theodorakis, with the general title *Epiphania*, would have its first public performance, followed by a record release.

Theodorakis was not only a talented and popular composer, but also a prominent member of the United Democratic Left, the parliamentary front for the outlawed communists, and the main opposition party at the time. What would become, before long, the 'new wave' in Greek popular music had sparked a long-running, and sometimes vituperative, controversy in the press during 1960; both the principal musical instrument for these settings, the bouzouki, and the gritty voice of Grigoris Bithikotsis, at the time had a strongly proletarian flavour. So far Theodorakis had set poems by his fellow-Marxist, the poet Yannis Ritsos; it was by no means an obvious step for the Greek ambassador in London to follow suit.[81]

Theodorakis in his memoirs recalls the moment of vindication, after George had returned permanently to Greece, when he and Savidis took him round the tavernas of Plaka, so that he could hear for himself his own words issuing from juke-boxes and being sung, impromptu, around pavement tables and open-air courtyards. According to Theodorakis, 'perhaps for the first time in his adult life, the great Seferis was like a small child, laughing and glowing with happiness.' But George's initial reaction to the recording would be far less favourable:

362

> I didn't much like it; maybe that's the fault of freezing London. 'Denial' seems better than the rest which seem to me a bit garbled, missing the meaning. But even in 'Denial,' the lack of a pause before the word 'wrong' makes nonsense of the last verse. Unfortunately, Th[eodorakis] thinks he knows everything . . . forgive me, my dear George, but I've a different idea of the craftsman.[82]

George's objection to the 'missing semi-colon' that punctuates the penultimate line of the poem 'Denial' would quickly become public knowledge, and has since become notorious, without doing anything either to dampen enthusiasm for the song or to change the way that it is sung. Whoever it was that first had the idea of making popular songs out of his poems, whether it was Savidis, or Theodorakis, or George himself, stung by the remark of his publisher that summer day in 1960, the result was a spectacular success. Since then, verses by almost every major Greek poet, living and dead, have been set to music, in the 'new-wave' style pioneered by Theodorakis and Manos Hadzidakis; today, the sound of the bouzouki, and the characteristic rhythms of this music, are almost synonymous, worldwide, with Greece itself. Among Greeks the world over, Theodorakis' setting of 'Denial' has come to acquire the status of an unofficial national anthem.[83]

Already by this time, George had begun to receive honours in England. On 18 February 1960, opening the morning mail, he found an invitation from the Vice-Chancellor of the University of Cambridge to accept an honorary doctorate of that university. George might have guessed that it had been the Provost of King's, Noel Annan, who had proposed him. What he is unlikely to have known is that before doing so, Annan had quietly sounded out the Foreign Office. An internal Foreign Office memorandum is revealing of the regard in which George was held there:

> Throughout his mission in London, Seferiades has always conducted himself as a true friend of Anglo-Greek understanding. We do not think that any lingering echoes from the Cyprus question would make it in any way undesirable that he should be honoured for his achievements as a poet at Cambridge next summer, and his friends in the FO would all be delighted that he should receive an honorary degree.[84]

363

When the ceremony took place, on 9 June 1960, the university's public orator had prepared the commendation not in the customary Latin but in ancient Greek. It was, George wrote to Ioanna, not for himself that he felt the honour of this occasion, but on behalf of the 'world that I'd loved.' This was a reference to Skala, whose fishermen and peasants figured in the speech among the formative influences on George's work.[85]

At the end of the same week, George was at the BBC to read five poems on the Third Programme, with links by the poet Cecil Day Lewis; the programme was produced by Louis MacNeice. Then in the autumn, Rex Warner's translation of the *Poems* was published. This was a larger and more representative selection than the earlier *King of Asine and Other Poems*, and for the first time included both *'Thrush'* and the greater part of the collection dedicated to Cyprus. At the same time, the newly formed collaboration of Edmund Keeley and Philip Sherrard resulted in the anthology *Six Poets of Modern Greece*, in which George was also strongly represented. The Warner translation was launched with a reading at the ICA (Institute of Contemporary Arts) in November; the next day Max Reinhardt hosted a reception in honour of the book, to which Eliot came, looking old and tired, and told George, 'You are a master now.' A few months later, the *Poems* of George Seferis, translated by Rex Warner, would become the first book by a foreign author to win the annual Foyle Prize. Accepting the award, George would speak warmly of his long-standing British friendships; for Ioanna he would proudly copy out, in full, the letter of congratulation he had received from Harold Macmillan.[86]

But a greater honour than any of these was already beginning to be talked of behind the scenes. The Nobel Prize for Literature had always eluded Greece, even though writers of the stature of Palamas, Sikelianos and Kazantzakis, as well as several lesser figures, had at various times been proposed. The possibility that a suitable recipient for this overdue award might be Seferis had first been privately suggested by Nanos Valaoritis in a letter to Katsimbalis ten years before. In 1956 a French newspaper had named George as a potential candidate for the prize. But it was not until early in 1960, in the aftermath of the Cyprus settlement and of George's confrontation with Averoff, that the idea took hold within the small circle that consisted of Ioanna, her husband Kostakis Tsatsos, and Averoff, of using diplomatic channels to promote George as a candidate for the prize.[87]

What happened next is worth examining closely, because it must have been the origin of the persistent libel that would surface in the Greek press, within days of George winning the prize, three years later, and has never been fully laid to rest: namely, that George 'sold out Cyprus in order to win the Nobel.' The motivation of his sister and brother-in-law scarcely needs to be questioned. But what of Averoff? Averoff would remain foreign minister until June 1963; all the evidence suggests that he had felt George's opposition, at the crucial stage of the Cyprus negotiations, keenly as a personal betrayal. Politically, Averoff never forgave George; but as the inaccuracies and elisions of his memoirs prove, Averoff's conscience was not entirely clear. In the summer of 1959, Averoff seems still to have perceived the existence of George's formal letter, with its secret file-number, as a threat; George found himself under intense pressure to withdraw it, so that the dissonant voice on the Greek side would not remain on the record. This, predictably, George refused to do; not for nothing had he written to his sister, at the height of the crisis, 'I'm certain that one day they'll remember me.'

This makes it quite likely, during the summer of 1959 and into the following year, that Averoff, or even the government at large, still feared the political damage that could be done if George's objections to the Zurich-London Agreements were ever to become public. If this was so, then supporting him for the Nobel Prize might have seemed an effective means of ensuring his discretion, and the timing is certainly suggestive. On the other hand, if Averoff or anyone else ever did make such a calculation, it would have been a gross misjudgement of George's character. More probable is that Averoff, who in the crucial exchange of letters had made a point of addressing George by his literary pseudonym, saw a subtle kind of revenge in promoting him for the Nobel: Ambassador Seferiadis had let the Minister down badly, but the poet Seferis could yet be of service to his country. From Averoff's point of view, a Nobel Prize for George would be nothing less than 'poetic' justice.[88]

At first, when Ioanna sounded him out, in April 1960, George may have been tempted. 'No,' he responded, 'I don't have an idea, and deep down I think that I don't want to have an idea.' Already, he foresaw what was likely to happen. He recalled for her the conversation he had had with the Swedish academician Axel Persson, whom he had met at Lavranda, in Turkey, ten years before, about Sikelianos' candidature, which had apparently been torpedoed by the Greek government. His old arch-enemy in the service, Alexis Kyrou, would move heaven and earth to frustrate any moves on his behalf. Reluctantly, he told his sister, 'it's not worth losing your beauty-sleep over it. If it's to be Greece's turn, let it come, and it doesn't matter who the chosen one is.' Ioanna was not put off by this response, and the topic continued to be discussed until early the following year. 'Don't talk to Vangelis [Averoff, *the familiar form of his Christian name*], any more about the Nobel and suchlike,' George would write definitively to Ioanna in January 1961. 'He can't do anything anyway, and talk like that just stirs up envy.'[89]

There, on the face of it, the matter rested. But a seed had been sown. What George rejected, in 1960, and again at the beginning of the following year, was the means proposed, not the end of the prize itself. Since the issue of the Nobel had first been raised, he had already begun work on preparing the second, and much expanded, edition of his *Essays*, first published in wartime Cairo and long unobtainable. By the start of 1961, at the same time as he was decisively rejecting Ioanna's proposal, he was in contact with Ikaros about a third edition of his *Poems*, which for the first time would include ...*Cyprus, Where It Was Ordained For Me*... If George was to be considered for the highest literary award in the world, he intended it to be strictly on his merits as a poet.[90]

While the Cyprus Emergency had lasted, George had written only a single poem, an unfinished sketch on the appropriately gloomy theme of 'Seleucia on the Tigris' – the Greek city founded by Alexander the Great, of which no trace remained when he had visited the site in modern Iraq. Before assuming his responsibilities for Cyprus, at the Ministry in 1957, he had begun translating the last book of the Bible, the Apocalypse, or Book of Revelation, which tells of the end of the world. This, too, had been a project born out of despair over political events. At the same time, on a less sombre note, he had also begun working on another book of the Bible which traditionally has been admired for its literary character, the love poem from the Old Testament known as *Song of Songs* (or *Song of Solomon*). In 1960, George took up these translations again: the *Song of Songs* was finished that Easter; the *Apocalypse* a year later. At the same time he re-read, with Maro, some of his old translations from the 1920s, with a view to reworking them, and embarked on others.[91]

These were hesitant steps: translations, rather than new writing of his own, and both involved taking up something already started. George's first, equally tentative, foray into verse after the end of the Cyprus crisis was again conceived as a sequel to an earlier group of poems, 'Sketches for a Summer, II,' and petered out after only one and a half of the projected twenty-four poems had been drafted. Dating from September 1959, these no doubt derived from his first summer holiday with Maro, back in Greece, since the crisis had begun. A year later, he was still looking backwards rather than forwards: an exercise called 'Countries of the Sun' is a variation on a line from *'Thrush.'*[92]

366

In the immediate aftermath of these turbulent years, it seems that George was not yet ready to break upon the new ground that he would mark out in the poems and essays of his last decade. But the conviction was growing upon him that the time remaining to him was limited; so, too, was his determination to use that time in the best way that he knew.[93]

On his sixtieth birthday (29 February 1960), he was entertaining thoughts of retiring early. 'I'll pick up my pen once more,' he wrote in his diary on that day. 'Out of practice as I am now, stuck with a lot of old habits, I don't know how I'll make out – but I've got to try.' This prospective 'change,' as he began to call it, was becoming a matter of urgency; to Ioanna he confided his anxiety to achieve 'some good work still, before senility takes over.' In May 1960, he summed up the position starkly:

> I must be able to concentrate, without interruption. The way I'm living now, that's impossible. I've only got a few years left; there's no tomorrow; it's now that I've got to make the final effort. I've given the best years of my life to the service, that's all over.[94]

But the 'change' that George now longed for was slow in coming. Ioanna seems to have persuaded him not to retire until he had been promoted to full ambassadorial rank, which would enhance his pension. This final promotion would not come through until December 1960.[95]

A month after that, the forthcoming official visit to London by Prime Minister Karamanlis and Foreign Minister Averoff seemed to George to afford the opportunity to close a chapter in his own life, as well as in that of the nations that had been so bitterly so divided by the Cyprus crisis. He wrote to Averoff: 'This [visit] is a watershed that signals the restoration of Greek-British relations to their long-standing atmosphere of friendship.' It was, he added, the moment for him to bow out as ambassador, and be transferred back to Athens.[96]

In the event, Averoff kept him at his post for another year and a half. But when the time did come for him finally to leave the London embassy, a sympathetic article in the *Manchester Guardian* echoed George's own sense of an ending:

the fact that Seferiades leaves London with Anglo-Greek relations restored to their traditional amity owes something to his sad patience. ... Perhaps Seferiades is one of the last of the old school of scholar diplomats — men in whom there has survived a touch of the Renaissance amplitude of spirit and wide horizons of learning, combined with complete professional accomplishment.[97]

—Όπου κι' άν πάω ή Έλλάδα με πληγώνει...

'Wherever I travel Greece wounds me,' or 'Travel wherever I might, it is Greece that causes me pain.' The opening line of the poem 'In the Manner of G.S.' provides the caption for this cartoon by the prolific political cartoonist Kostas Mitropoulos, published in the magazine *Tachydromos* in April 1966, when George and Maro were involved in a road accident outside Corinth.

# 12

# A Time for Renewal
# 1961–1971

The question is not what things have come to an end, but what we who are alive, like every living thing, amid decay and change, substitute in place of those things that we think have come to an end.

('Delphi,' August 1961)[1]

### Intimations of mortality

Within a few days of putting his request to be relieved of his duties in London, George had begun writing poetry again. During the last week of January 1961, he embarked in earnest on what would become the first of the *Three Secret Poems*, 'On a Ray of Winter Light.' This was the first real manifestation of the 'change' that he had been so earnestly anticipating; but it also coincided with the start of an exceptionally difficult period in both his public and his private life.[2]

Professionally, during the first six months of the year, George was at full stretch organising a series of high-level visits from Greece. Karamanlis and Averoff came in February; hard on their heels came King Paul and Queen Frederica. George had never been at ease in his dealings with the Greek royal family. 'Officially,' this was supposed to be an unofficial visit; but still he was called upon to introduce the king and queen to selected representatives of the British intelligentsia, a task to which he responded with a mixture of humorous resignation and annoyance. The royal guests left on 19 March; but for the next few months George was considerably taken up with arrangements for other members of the dynasty.[3]

At the same time, his personal life came under intense strain, of a kind that he had not experienced for many years, in all probability not since before his marriage to Maro. In general, the couple's relationship was remarkable for its closeness and durability over thirty-five years; but George was not without susceptibility to the charms of younger women. A casual affair, in the summer of 1958, while the Cyprus conflict had been at its height, had provoked Maro to recall, not long afterwards, a time when: 'the miracle had gone. I would look at you and feel lifeless and indifferent. The world had gone black all round me.' The rift on that occasion, though it may have gone deep, was soon healed. What happened during the first half of 1961 was apparently more serious. According to a story that is as persistent as it is inconsistent in its details, George became infatuated with a young woman employed at the embassy; Maro attempted suicide. There is naturally no proof of what happened exactly; but there is documentary evidence for a crisis, consistent with this outline, which began in March and came to a head in June 1961. At the end of that month, George wrote to Ioanna:

> there have been moments here, this past month, when I've thought my nerves were going to break for good — and I'm not one to exaggerate, as you know. In even worse shape than me, from nervous exhaustion, is Maro.[4]

A much-needed respite for the couple came in the form of an extended summer holiday, which they spent together in Greece. Their house in Athens was now finished, George wrote to the Cypriot painter Diamantis: 'we're hoping to live in it a bit more this summer.' In fact, it had been just over two years since the building was completed, though it was not yet fully ready as their permanent home.[5]

370

From Athens, George and Maro went first to Delphi, whose ancient sanctuary of Apollo had been a place of pilgrimage for him since at least his late twenties. As well as going all over the site, they made the arduous ascent, on muleback, to the Corycian Cave, high on the slopes of Mount Parnassus. 'The mountain air was a resurrection,' as George described it. The cave itself he associated with the primitive, orgiastic rituals of a time before the worship of Apollo had become established at Delphi, and also with the Orthodox iconographical tradition that depicts the birth of Jesus in a cave. 'Just like all things human . . . Apollo's oracle had its beginnings . . . , and it had its end.' Before the heyday of the Olympian gods, the 'furies of the earth' had been worshipped here; after their decline and the coming of Christianity, the centre of worship had moved a few kilometres, when the monastery of St Luke had been founded in the eleventh century. 'Nature,' observed George, 'abhors a vacuum.'[6]

The process of renewal that George saw at work here, in the *longue durée* of the life of religions, he also experienced in a personal, immediate way, coming out of the Corycian Cave:

Only when you go in deep and come back, do you see, like a blessing, the rays of the sun slanting in from the mouth of the cave and striking pink and green sparks from its walls. You're happy to be born again into the warmth of the sun, and certainly no poorer; you know that there exists something more, behind those things.[7]

What this 'something' was is perhaps suggested by the final section of *On Stage*, the second of the *Three Secret Poems*, written a year and a half later: the affirmation of a presence that is at once sensual and divine, and eludes any formal statement of religious belief ('an aura of holiness' is how he cautiously summed up the experience, at the end of the essay on Delphi). At a purely personal level, and in the context of the visit to the cave that August, it is possible also to see in these lines a reaffirmation, in retrospect, of George's feelings for Maro:

> And yet there, on the other shore
> below the dark aspect of the cave
> suns in your eyes birds on your shoulders
> you were there; compassionate
> of the other toil that is love
> of the other dawn that is presence
> of the other birth that is resurrection;
> and yet there, you came to be once more
> in the immense dilation of time
> moment by moment like drops of resin
> stalactite and stalagmite.[8]

371

Before leaving London, George had accepted a commission to write a short essay about Delphi for a 'coffee-table' book that was being produced in German. After Delphi, he and Maro headed for the Aegean and the island of Amorgos, which in those days was little frequented by tourists. There, during the last week of August and the first of September, he wrote up his diary of the visit to Delphi. It was not the first time that he had produced an essay in this way; it would not be the last. This one was finished very quickly, and inaugurates the series of deeply reflective essays that, despite the ostensible diversity of their subject matter, explore the nature of change, survival and renewal that provides this chapter with its epigraph.

The precipitous island of Amorgos George described to Rex Warner as 'perfectly naked and lovely like Eve; but after London, after Athens, and

Tourist-ridden Delphi . . . it is a gift of the Gods.' The new, or renewed, insights that suddenly fell into place in the essay may have been no less the gift of those humbler gods who inhabited the simple island landscape, where once again George made friends among the peasants and fishermen, like those he had known at Skala. It certainly appears that the process of renewal, that had begun at the cave above Delphi, continued against the benign backdrop of Amorgos, where the path to the monastery of the Virgin Mary ('Chozoviotissa'), built into the island's sheer cliff, smelt powerfully of mule-dung.[9]

But George's troubles were not over. The situation he had left behind in London had yet to be fully resolved; the ambivalence, as well as the intense sensuality, of his feelings can be guessed from a set of pornographic couplets and a pornographic pastiche of a scene from his beloved sixteenth-century Cretan romance, *Erotokritos*, all written within a few days of his and Maro's return from Amorgos to Athens. Pornographic doggerel had been a source of high-spirited amusement to George before; it seems to have been Durrell who had first introduced him both to the English limerick, and to its characteristically schoolboy extension into the pornographic. Most of George's limericks of this type had been written in Pretoria in 1941. Almost all the rest of the small collection of his sexually explicit verse, edited posthumously by Savidis, was written during these few days in September 1961.[10]

Earlier in the summer, in addition to his other difficulties, George had been experiencing trouble with his prostate. Back in London, with Maro, in October, the symptoms recurred, and he was advised to have the gland removed. The operation was performed in November. He spent three weeks in a private clinic in Queen Anne's Gate. Ioanna came over from Greece; together they discussed the recent election there. Karamanlis had been returned to power, but amid allegations of vote-rigging that would tarnish the last government of the National Radical Union and contribute to its premature end two years later. They also discussed George's translations from the Bible.[11]

On 8 December 1961, the first day when he was allowed out of doors, for a brief walk in Hyde Park, George wrote the lines that in due course he would place at the start of 'On a Ray of Winter Light,' the first of the *Three Secret Poems*:

> Leaves of rusted tin
> for the poor brain that saw the end . . .[12]

372

It marks a bleak beginning; even after the glimpses of renewal at Delphi and on Amorgos, the 'change' in which George had placed such high hopes must have seemed as far off as ever.

## Faces of change

Back in June, a group of 'those who love Seferis and admire his literary work' had taken the initiative to commission a volume of essays in his honour. The gesture had been timed to mark the thirtieth anniversary of the publication of his first book, *Turning Point*, that had just passed. Presented as the collective work of its twenty-three contributors, who are listed alphabetically on the cover, the volume has a title that means at once *For Seferis* and *About Seferis*, and was published in January 1962. According to its preface, which is unsigned but transparently the work of Savidis, its preparation was supposed to be a secret from the dedicatee; in fact, there is evidence that Savidis was not only the invisible master of ceremonies on this occasion, but also sought George's approval for much of his behind-the-scenes work as commissioning editor and copy-editor.[13]

The publication of *For Seferis* brought to a head a crisis in George's friendships that had been simmering for several years. It had always been Katsimbalis, Miller's 'Colossus of Maroussi,' who had acted as George's unofficial literary agent and publicity manager. There had been a tussle between the two Georges, Katsimbalis and Savidis, over the publication of *...Cyprus, Where It Was Ordained For Me...* Then Katsimbalis had been lukewarm about the poems. Now, in 1961, in the arrangement of the volume, Katsimbalis is respectfully given the last word; the 'Colossus' had long ago found his own literary métier in the humble assiduity of the bibliographer, and the volume closes with sixty pages of dry but invaluable tribute in this form. But immediately preceding it, crowning the volume as its longest contribution, at just over a hundred pages, comes Savidis' brilliant exposition and vindication of *...Cyprus, Where It Was Ordained For Me...* In a perfectly self-effacing way, Savidis, with this volume and his own contribution published in it, had capped the combined achievement of Katsimbalis and Karantonis thirty years before, when *The Poet George Seferis* had been rushed out to boost the success of George's first book of poems.

George by this time had unlimited confidence in Savidis' abilities, and indeed also in his loyalty. If there were pragmatic benefits to this relationship, on both sides, these had long since been overlaid by a genuine intimacy and trust. Despite the difference in their ages (Savidis was twenty-five years younger than George), their correspondence, from the mid 1950s onwards, is frequent, good-humoured, and full of vitality. It was as though in this high-spirited Cambridge graduate, whose conversation was as inexhaustible as his love of good food and wine, an extrovert dedicated to literature, with experience and all-important connections in the world of Greek publishing, George had found a younger incarnation of the 'Colossus of Maroussi' as Katsimbalis had been thirty years before. In the company of Savidis and his wife Lena, George seems to have felt himself rejuvenated. After his return to London in October 1961, he was regularly exchanging letters and confidences with Savidis. To Katsimbalis he had not written for months. Now, with *For Seferis* published, in February 1962, the first that Katsimbalis heard about George's recent operation was via Louizos in Cyprus. It was too much:

> I'm not going to write any more, because for a while now I've been forming the impression (confirmed after our last meeting in the summer), that what I write is a matter of indifference to you, if not an annoyance. All my life I've tried not to be a nuisance to my friends. I don't know how well I've succeeded. But when I get wind of it in time, I concede at once and retire inside my shell. Whoever wants me, knows where to find me – and will find me the same and unchanged even at 63 years old![14]

374

George was shocked. 'I'm literally speechless; I make the sign of the cross with both my hands,' he wrote back by return. But he must have known what the real bone of contention was, and his justification is more brusque than emollient:

> Sometimes a person gets tired and loses patience, but to damage old friendships because of such insubstantial rubbish is a sin against nature. It's childish to continue this conversation.[15]

Soon after, George returned permanently to Greece and on the surface, at least, the old intimacy seemed restored. But Katsimbalis would keep his promise; although there are a few short notes and postcards from George to Katsimbalis after this date, Katsimbalis would never again put pen to paper to write to George. It was effectively the end of a correspondence that had lasted almost forty years.

Although he had nominally returned from sick leave in January, two months after his operation, George's recovery was slow. During the first months of 1962, he found himself beset by a series of minor complications and additional ailments. These included exhaustion and severe rheumatic pains that for months made it impossible for him to spend more than short intervals seated at a desk.[16]

In February, he penned a lengthy plea to the Prime Minister himself, Constantine Karamanlis; to the grounds for being recalled to Athens, that he had already set out for Averoff the year before, he now added the condition of his health. By the end of May, he was well enough to resume his official engagements (he had just attended the opening of the new Coventry Cathedral); but he had still received no reply to this renewed request to be relieved of his duties. A reminder to Averoff, by official telegram, at last produced the response for which he had waited so long.[17]

George and Maro left the London embassy for the last time on 20 August 1962. From now until retirement he would be 'at the disposal' of the Ministry in Athens, which meant, in effect, that for the first time since the age of eighteen, he was his own master. The 'change' for which he had been preparing for the last two years was at last upon him. The days of the ambassadorial chauffeur-driven limousine, and of regularly crossing Europe by air in the first-class cabin, were over. George departed from Upper Brook Street, with Maro at his side, at the wheel of their small Volkswagen 'beetle.'[18]

They travelled slowly through France, and were met at Marseille by George and Lena Savidis, who had come specially from Athens to accompany them home. In this way, George retraced the route that he had taken often in his youth. The wireless operator on the ship to Piraeus was Nikos Kavvadias, a younger poet whom George knew well, and who enabled him to exchange fraternal greetings in Morse code with his old 'seafaring friend,' Captain Antoniou. As he sailed back into his own familiar Aegean waters, George had every reason to feel that he was once more among friends.

It was now that he and Maro moved permanently into their new home at number 20, Agras Street. Built on a site carved out of the flank of the hill that forms one side of the ancient stadium, the house is based upon the simple box-shaped design of traditional Greek island houses; its whitewashed exterior and blue shutters belong to the Cyclades, not to Athens. An English visitor, soon after it was finished, was struck by the 'mermaid street-lights by John Craxton and a dolphin [door-] knocker.'[19]

There was still much work to be done, before the house would be fully habitable. This took up the whole of September. A belated summer holiday, in October, at the resort of Kamena Vourla near Athens, gave George 'the first opportunity of looking and finding myself a rather useless man and more ignorant than in the past,' as he expressed it to Warner. Over Christmas and New Year, the house was still full of 'workmen, painters and carpenters,' George wrote wistfully to Osbert Lancaster, recalling their shared Christmases at Henley.[20]

Already, during his summer vacations, he had come to realise that the Greece to which he would be returning to live was not quite the country he had left, five, ten, or forty years before. Even before his return in 1962, George had had the sense of being '*depaysé*' in Greece. When he had been back for six months, writing to Diamantis, he had to concede: 'I haven't felt the change so far at all; it comes slowly.' To his diplomatic colleague Angelos Vlachos he put it more bluntly: 'my first impressions here remind me what a difficult country this is to live in. Sometimes I feel as though I'm sur-rounded by madmen.' And to Rex Warner, after a year:

> it isn't an easy job to settle in one's own country after so many years. ... [T]he truth is that with the onslaught of tourists and other para-phernalia the country has changed a great deal and I'm hunting for places which I can subjectively recognise.[21]

The most graphic symptom of this difficult acclimatisation was a night-mare that caused him to leap out of bed, screaming, in the small hours of a hot August morning, during that first summer back in Greece. He was on the Acropolis, but this was happening a long time in the future; it seemed that, in the meantime, 'civilisation had progressed a long way.' A crowd had gathered before the west façade of the Parthenon; with the excitement of football supporters, they were awaiting the result of a contest. George, the visitor to the future, was the only one not to know the latest stroke of genius of the Greek government: now that no one had any need of these 'old stones' any more, the contest was to auction off the temples of the Acro-polis to the highest bidder. To a roar of applause, the auctioneer's hammer came down: the favourite had won. The temples were now the property of an American toothpaste manufacturer:

> Then I saw the Parthenon horrifically stripped bare, without pediment, without entablature, its columns hammered smooth and shiny, to repre-sent giant tubes of toothpaste.[22]

By this time, George had begun writing again. In the spring of 1963, he had the experience, for the first time in his life, as he expressed it to George Theotokas, of 'having all my papers around me in the same place.' He was working on a translation of T.S. Eliot's verse drama, *Murder in the Cathedral*. At the same time, and not coincidentally, he was also writing the second of the *Three Secret Poems*, which has the title 'On Stage,' and whose central theme is again the dramatic representation of a murder. The poem transfers the sacrilegious murder of Archbishop Thomas Becket, in Eliot's play, to the shell-like space of an ancient Greek theatre, such as he had seen in ruins on his travels in Turkey and the Levant, but also as living theatres, in the annual festival performances at Athens and Epidauros. In the poem, the lights go down, 'as though for some notorious murder.' No places are mentioned; it is not specified who is murdered either, though there are hints of the murder of Clytemnestra by her son Orestes to avenge the death of his father Agamemnon, and also of the deranged violence of the sixteenth-century Cretan tragedy *Erofili*, that George had seen performed in the Herod Atticus theatre in Athens in September 1961.[23]

Explaining his rendering of the title of Eliot's play into Greek, George invoked the 'horror of a murder in the house of God.' The ancient theatre which is the setting for 'On Stage' has a different aura of sanctity from Eliot's cathedral. However, this setting, too, in lines from the final chorus of Eliot's play that could have been written by George himself at this time:

> . . . is holy ground, and the sanctity shall not depart from it
> Though armies trample over it, though sightseers come with guide-
>     books looking over it . . .

In both *Murder in the Cathedral* and 'On Stage' there is a strong link between murder and ritual sacrifice. Eliot's religious commitment required the dead archbishop, at the end, to be vindicated and venerated as a saint and martyr. His killers, too, appear on the stage, are given names, and have the opportunity to defend their action. 'On Stage,' by contrast, invokes the different horror of an unwitnessed crime repeated throughout history:

> No one is guilty, but has vanished.
> Who was it that fled
> hoofbeats thudding on slabs?
> They have dispensed with their eyes, not to see.
> No one bears witness any more, to anything.[24]

377

In Greek, ancient or modern, one who bears witness is a 'martyr.' In this way George parts company with Eliot (and indeed with a play that had been written before the Second World War). Instead, 'On Stage' follows a cyclical course, from sunlight to darkness and violence, and then back into the light in a moment of 'rebirth,' such as George had experienced at the cave above Delphi, a year and a half before.[25]

Although he would soon see the translation of *Murder in the Cathedral* through to completion, George was dissatisfied with what were, at the time, two *Secret Poems*. It is almost certainly to these that he was referring when he continued his letter to Theotokas: 'I hadn't the courage to go any further in this confabulation with myself – I'll need to look at them again some time.'

There was another reason why the summer and autumn of 1963 were not conducive to creative work. Talk of the Nobel Prize was once again in the air; this time there was to be no escaping it.

### The Nobel and after

By the end of 1962, George's *Poems* and *Essays* were in print in Greece, in new editions that included everything of importance that he had published to date. There were already two book-length translations of his poetry in print in English, as well as the selections in the Keeley and Sherrard anthology. Now, at the end of 1962, a bilingual edition of his poetry appeared in German, at the same time as his essay on Delphi that had been commissioned the previous year. Volumes of his translated poetry were in preparation or in press in Italy, France and Denmark, to appear during 1963. At the end of 1962, George handed over to Savidis a short collection of previously unpublished poems, which was announced by Ikaros at the start of the new year with the title *Book of Exercises II*. By September of that year, although the *Secret Poems* had been shelved, George had no fewer than four other books ready for publication: the translation of *Murder in the Cathedral*, his collected translations of French and English poets, and the two books of the Bible translated into Modern Greek that he had finished in London.[26]

In the meantime, in February 1963, George had been approached by Börje Knös, the doyen of Swedish neo-hellenists and the promoter of Sikelianos and Kazantzakis for the Nobel Prize in their day. Knös requested his permission to publish a selection from his poems translated into Swedish, with the collaboration of the Swedish poet Johannes Edfelt; he also enclosed several pages of queries on which he sought George's elucidation. Although

378

naturally nothing was said directly to George, when the translators approached a leading Stockholm publisher in May, Edfelt was confident enough to cite the 'well-known fact . . . that Seferis has been among the candidates for the literary Nobel Prize for a long time.' What had once been conspiratorially whispered among the political friends of Ioanna and Kostakis Tsatsos in Athens, was now gathering momentum, and in a far different arena.[27]

The annual ceremony for the award of the year's Nobel prizes takes place in December. The Swedish translation of George's poems would be unlikely to be published in time to influence the judges for that year. It may have been for this reason that an extract appeared in Sweden in July, accompanied by a sympathetic introduction to George's work by another staunch admirer in that country, Dr Sture Linnér. Linnér had recently come to Greece as Permanent Representative of the United Nations Development Programme. He had had firsthand experience of the country during the Second World War, while working for the Swedish Red Cross. It would be surprising if in this capacity he had not made the acquaintance of Ioanna Tsatsou. Linnér, like Knös, was a dedicated philhellene; he had a Greek wife and spoke the modern language well. Later, he and George would become firm friends; it seems that they first met that summer.

379

During the summer and early autumn of 1963, Linnér became a tireless promoter of George's cause. He came to the house in Agras Street and recorded an interview with him that became the basis for a broadcast on Swedish radio in September. According to an enthusiastic and deferential letter he addressed to George the following month, Linnér had been busy in Stockholm lobbying on his behalf and had high hopes. Just how influential these well-intentioned efforts could have been is impossible to know – the full story of how the first Greek Nobel Prize came to be won will not be known until 2013, when the Swedish Academy opens its archives for that year.[28]

By the middle of October, rumour was rife in Athens that the announcement of the prize was imminent, and that the new Nobel laureate would be George Seferis. George himself had retired from the fray, the previous month, to take refuge among the simple peasants and artisans of the Cycladic island of Paros. But he was to be allowed no peace. A violent recurrence of his stomach ulcer forced him and Maro to cut short their holiday. The first onset of this condition had coincided with a bitter moment in his own and his country's history; now he was once again laid low on the eve of his greatest public triumph.[29]

Thanks to Linnér, George knew that the announcement of the winner was to be made on Thursday 24 October. His friends gathered early that morning at Agras Street; Maro had taken the precaution of laying in a supply of champagne – though when the moment came, George would be unable to celebrate with anything stronger than milk. George and Lena Savidis took charge and commandeered the telephone. The 'long hours of anxious waiting' lasted all morning. For all the rumours that George was the favourite, there were other distinguished names in the field (eighty-one according to the newspaper *To Vima*); probably the best known was that of Jean-Paul Sartre.[30]

The telegram from Anders Osterling, Permanent Secretary of the Swedish Academy, was received in Athens at seven minutes past one; the official announcement followed some hours later. Recalling that day, thirty years afterwards, Savidis was bitter about the grudging reception of the news by all but a small band of close family and friends: congratulations from fellow-writers were slow to arrive, or backhanded; the expected posse from the press corps failed to materialise. Among the small and trusted circle, the perception was that the award had come despite, rather than because of, the attitude of the Greek government; crucial support, they believed, had come from T.S. Eliot and Saint-John Perse.[31]

380

Whatever the truth behind these guesses, it is clear from the official citation, broadcast on radio that evening, that the award was made to Seferis as a *Greek* poet, and in some measure as a form of amends for previous neglect of that country by the Academy:

> This year's Nobel prize for literature has been awarded to the Greek poet Giorgos Seferis . . . Seferis's poetic production is not great in size, but because of its unique thought and style, and its beauty of language, it has become a lasting symbol of all that is indestructible in the Hellenic acceptance of life. Now that Palamas and Sikelianos are dead he is today the representative Hellenic poet, carrying on the classical heritage . . . It has given the Swedish Academy great pleasure, through this prize to Giorgos Seferis, to pay tribute to the Greece of today, whose wealth of literature has perhaps waited far too long for its laurel wreath in this connexion.[32]

Despite Savidis' disappointment at the response from the public, the award did receive generous coverage in the Greek press during the days that followed. In Britain the announcement was carried by all the major newspapers, where more interest seemed to be generated by the rumoured value of the prize (in the region of £18,000) than by the literary achievement of the recipient. But the response was not universally favourable. In Sweden itself, one liberal newspaper complained that the Nobel Prize had become 'an old-age pension for the diplomats of literature,' only vouchsafed to those 'who are safely well-behaved' (George was the third diplomat to win the prize, after Claudel and Saint-John Perse). In Greece this sentiment was echoed more vociferously still by the left, who affected chagrin that the award had gone not to Sartre or Neruda but to a fellow-Greek of the wrong political persuasion. At the opposite end of the political spectrum, the right-wing newspaper *Eleftheros* for the first time put about the libel that George had 'sold out Cyprus to win the Nobel.'[33]

Among George's friends, surely the most bizarre response to the news was on the ship that had brought him back to Greece, where Nikos Kavvadias was still the wireless officer: 'he festooned the *Apollonia* with flags and sent a telegram: "We have sacrificed every crocodile on board." '[34]

The weeks that followed were full of intense activity. Arrangements had to be made for George and Maro to attend the award ceremony in Stockholm on 10 December; would he be prepared to give a lecture there? At first he demurred, and had to confess to the precarious state of his health. But yes, he *would* give a lecture. Did he wish to nominate friends or other family members to be included in the official arrangements? Those that George chose were presumably those to whom he felt he owed the most at this moment: George and Lena Savidis and Sture Linnér. There was a tight schedule to be arranged, that included visits to Uppsala, where he wished to lay a wreath at the grave of Dag Hammarskjold and meet the Greek Orthodox bishop, and to Linnér's home town of Lund, where he was to meet students and staff at the university.[35]

On 6 December, George, Maro and their small entourage left Athens by air for Stockholm. On the 10th, at the official dinner following the award ceremony, he gave a short speech of acceptance; the following day, in a lecture addressed to the Swedish Academy, he elaborated on some of the ideas he had touched on in that address. Both of these were written directly in French; together they make a powerful statement of George's ideas about the Greek tradition and the value of poetry in the modern world. It was here that he made his most categorical statement of his humanist belief: 'When . . . Oedipus encountered the Sphinx, and she put to him her riddle, his answer was: man. That simple word destroyed the monster.' More challengingly, perhaps, he also claimed the discovery of man, in this humane

sense, as the great and distinctive achievement of Hellenism: 'another characteristic of this tradition [of the Greek language] is its love for humanity
[or: humane-ness]; its rule is justice.'[36]

In the longer lecture, George gave examples from the literary tradition
in support of his assertion the previous evening, that 'the Greek language
has never ceased to be spoken. It has undergone many alterations, like every
living thing, but there is no gap [in its history].' In his earlier interview
with Linnér for Swedish radio, he had gone further, to compare the Greek
tradition, as a whole, to a 'continent as big as China.' Towards the end of
this lecture, George gave his fullest statement yet of the nature of tradition and change, as he understood these ideas that were much preoccupy-
ing him at this time:

> I shall not say that we are of the same blood [as the ancients] – because
> I have a horror of racial theories – but we still live in the same country
> and we see the same mountains ending in the sea. Perhaps I may have
> used the word 'tradition,' without drawing sufficient attention to this
> evidence that tradition does not mean habit. Tradition is interesting, on
> the contrary, for its power to break habit; that is the means by which
> it demonstrates its vitality.[37]

382

There was nothing self-contradictory in George's quest, during these last
years of his life, for the mainsprings of renewal in the depths of his own
and his country's past.

By Christmas, George and Maro were back in Athens. He wrote to Steven
Runciman, 'We were back here two days ago, after an exhausting air trip
. . . Putting aside our return Odyssey due to fog, our Stockholm visit devel-
opped [sic] in a satisfactory way. I am longing now to get out of this situation.' To Rex Warner, he summed up his feelings at the start of the New
Year: 'The fact is that the Nobel affair was a sort of tornado which left a
great amount of dust. This I'm clearing out now in order to feel a human
being again.' February 1964 found George and Maro once again at Delphi,
seeking what he called, in French, '*désintoxication.*' 'Everything that I've
done in the past gives me the nausea,' he explained to Warner, 'and I feel
that I have to turn my back to all that in order to clean[se] myself and
proceed, if I may, a little bit further.'[38]

In all the upheaval of the past few months, perhaps the most revealing
moment came when George replied to the affectionate congratulations of
a now nonagenarian Marie-Louise, the mother of Jacqueline:

I don't have a moment to experience the joy [you mention]. It's rather the joy of those close to me who make me think of it at all. Yes, I've often thought of Angelos. And of my father; this would have given *him* more pleasure than it does me. May God keep you.[39]

In the wake of the Nobel, other honours and invitations followed. An honorary doctorate from the Aristotle University of Thessaloniki, at the time the only university in Greece outside Athens, became the occasion for George to deliver a lecture on language and poetry that includes one of the most memorable statements of his poetics: 'The end point to which the poet reaches out, is to be able to say "Let there be light," and for there to be light.'[40]

On this visit to the city, George either made or renewed acquaintance with one of its greatest literary luminaries, the novelist and poet Nikos Gabriel Pentzikis. At once a committed adherent of the French and English literary modernism in which George, too, had been formed as a poet, Pentzikis had also formed a deep attachment to the spirituality of the Orthodox Church. Two years after this, urged by Zissimos Lorenzatos, who had come to share these interests, George would struggle to keep an open-minded diary of his encounter with Pentzikis' Joycean magnum opus, *The Novel of Mrs Ersi*; characteristically, he would lose patience not with Pentzikis' elaborately mannered mysticism, but when he caught him out misquoting from Mallarmé.[41]

383

In the summer of 1964, George and Maro were the guests of Maurice Bowra at Oxford, where he was awarded his second honorary degree in Britain. He had had another severe ulcer attack at the end of May; as he wrote to his Italian translator, Filippo Maria Pontani,

the worst aspect [of these pains] is the way they sap your morale, and the medicines turn you into a permanent imbecile – all this time I've been incapable of any sort of work or thought.[42]

At Oxford in July, Bowra was 'extremely worried' about the state of George's health, and afterwards commended 'the heroic way in which you went through all the ordeals.' Once again, as in Stockholm at the Nobel ceremony, George found himself obliged to ask for a glass of milk, while everyone else was drinking champagne. He was too ill, afterwards, to go on and visit Pontani in Rome as he had planned, but he did spend ten days in Paris, where he renewed his acquaintance with Saint-John Perse. Back in Greece, there was a convivial reunion on Hydra, at the house of the painter Nikos Hatzikyriakos Ghika, now married to Rex Warner's former wife, Barbara. The company included the Katsimbalises, the Leigh Fermors, and Bowra from Oxford. 'You can well imagine the conversation in the company of the three most talkative men I ever met in my life,' George wrote to Warner afterwards. He was now beginning to feel distinctly better.[43]

Next month, in August, the new centre-left government of George Papandreou passed a law limiting the years of continuous service for civil servants; it was part of a deliberate purge of the 'old guard' by an incoming government. George soon found himself one of many, 'endowed with exceptional qualities,' in the words of the personal letter he received from the prime minister, whose services were now regretfully to be dispensed with, due to the 'urgent necessity for renewal of the staff of the Administration.' This phrase may have roused a sardonic chuckle in George; he, too, was in pursuit of renewal, and his duties at the Ministry had for some time been nominal in any case. He does not seem to have taken this news badly, but there was a further irony in the situation that could not have escaped him: the final termination of his service came at the hands of the same prime minister who had first held that office twenty years before, in 1944; one of Papandreou's first acts, then, had been to sack George from his post as Press Director for the Greek government in exile.[44]

In September, George was well enough to accept an invitation from the Union of Antiquarian Booksellers in Barcelona to give a talk at the opening of the annual book exhibition. He and Maro spent a fortnight in Spain. During three days at Toledo ('three weeks wouldn't have been enough,' he wrote to the painter Diamantis in Cyprus), he paid homage to the great Cretan artist of the Renaissance, Dominikos Theotokopoulos, better known as El Greco. It was a 'pilgrimage' that he had been promising himself for years, ever since a small portrait of a saint by Greco in the National Gallery in London had been one of the few consolations of his first months in England, in 1924. The experience surpassed all his expectations.[45]

By the end of 1964, George had received invitations to lecture in America and Japan; with Maro he was planning a round-the-world trip, but as he confided in his diary, 'I feel no enthusiasm – either for expressing myself in a foreign language (I find I've had enough of that) – or for lecturing to foreign audiences, who have no idea about this strange thing called Greece.' He did, on the other hand, enjoy the experience of meeting and talking to new people. In the event, George dithered during the first months of 1965;

he never went to Japan, but he and Maro did spend three weeks in America in June. While there he received an honorary degree from Princeton, paid his respects to Rex Warner, who was now teaching at the University of Connecticut, and gave a reading at the Guggenheim Foundation in New York City. Plans were by this time well advanced for the first complete English translation of his poems. The translators were Edmund Keeley and Philip Sherrard, whose earlier anthology, *Six Poets of Modern Greece*, had been well received in Britain and the USA. Keeley, who was on the Princeton faculty, had already negotiated a contract for the translations to be published by Princeton University Press. Keeley's intervention had no doubt also helped to secure George's honorary degree there; it was certainly crucial in persuading him finally to go to America to receive it.[46]

It had been, George wrote to Sture Linnér on his return, 'the first trip where I felt on the loose and free to see things and talk to people.' Among those he met were the poets Archibald MacLeish, one of whose poems he had translated as far back as 1938, and Robert Lowell; he also renewed his acquaintance with Sir Hugh Foot, who had earned George's respect during the difficult days when Foot had served as the last Governor of Cyprus.[47]

But George was rapidly tiring of official honours. Earlier the same year, the announcement of a vacant Chair of Literature at the Academy of Athens had left him largely indifferent, despite pressure from some of his friends. The Academy has its own rituals, one of which is that candidates are expected to canvass the existing members in order to be elected. This, after some acrimony, George refused to do; when a year later the Academy decided not to elect him, he vented his feelings to Linnér:

385

> Your beloved Academy of Athens has rejected the proposal of three of its members ... to elect me as a member. I'm thankful for that; I wouldn't have had much in common with those plesiosaurs.[48]

In September 1965, he turned down the offer of a Visiting Professorship at the University of Illinois for the following year. The day after he wrote to the Dean to refuse this latest honour, George and Maro went down to Piraeus and boarded a ship for the Cyclades. Their destination was Delos, the island that had been sacred to Apollo in ancient times. The protracted process of 'change' that George had longed for since his days in London, and which had begun at the sanctuary at Delphi, was at last about to be accomplished.[49]

## A hidden Apocalypse

That summer of 1965, in Athens, had been hot in more senses than one. In July a new political crisis had burst upon Greece. George was no longer professionally involved, of course. He had given himself over wholly to poetry since returning from London; only the previous month, at Princeton, he had protested to a disbelieving Sir Hugh Foot, 'politics doesn't interest me any more.' Then in July, the young King Constantine II dismissed his prime minister, Papandreou, without calling a new election; instead, a group of MPs from Papandreou's party, the Centre Union, was induced to support a precarious parliamentary majority under a prime minister acceptable to the king. In protest, there were strikes and violent demonstrations in Athens throughout July (the 'July Events,' as they became known). While the summer sun flared over Attica, the political world of Greece was convulsed with the signs of imminent dissolution. The remark of a taxi driver went to the heart of the matter, for George: 'don't you understand, sir, words have lost their meaning in this country;' as always, it was the intuitions of the simple and the uneducated that won his admiration.[50]

'Summer in Attica was as hot as burning resin.' So begins the essay that includes George's diary account of the visit to Delos that September. That image of cataclysmic heat would soon become the central axis of the third of the *Three Secret Poems*, 'Summer Solstice.' This would be George's final large-scale poetic testament. There are no direct references anywhere in the *Three Secret Poems* to political issues. But it is very likely that the poetic counterpart, in this poem, to Eliot's 'unimaginable zero summer' in 'Little Gidding,' the last of the *Four Quartets*, had been suggested to George by the literal and political heat of Athens, that summer of 1965.[51]

The island of Delos, for which George and Maro now set out, had boasted a thriving city in Hellenistic times. It is no longer inhabited; tourists visit by motor-boat from the nearby island of Mykonos, and are not allowed to stay overnight. George and Maro were able to stay at the small tourist pavilion used by the French Archaeological School; from four in the afternoon they had the ruins to themselves, 'shut in until next morning with these ruins hallowed by the years,' he wrote with humble gratitude.

He had accepted a commission from a friend of Savidis, the Italian art-publisher Enzo (Vicenzo) Crea, for an essay on the Homeric hymns. This made the circumstances of the visit to Delos strikingly similar to the ones that had sent him to Delphi four years before. The Homeric hymns had been addressed, in the seventh and sixth centuries BC, to gods whose worship had been ousted by the coming of Christianity, a thousand years later. 'The gods are born immortal,' George concluded his essay on the *Hymns*, 'but they die.' Reading an ancient inscription in the temple of Zeus, whose ruins crown the highest point on Delos, he had noticed that the faithful pagan, in order to enter, had been required to abstain from meat and sexual intercourse from the day before, just like the Orthodox faithful approaching communion. 'This last instruction,' he commented, 'shows that the ancient gods knew their work was done, and were preparing to hand over to others.' On Delos, as at Delphi, it was the process of renewal, through the *longue durée* of history, that appealed to George. From this he concluded that:

> The ancient forms of worship have not been extinguished altogether in Greece. Anachronism? I would rather have that anachronism . . . until today's modernised man finds something valid to put in its place.[52]

During the last months of 1965, George was hard at work on this essay, and also on another commission: to commemorate the seven hundredth anniversary of the birth, in Florence, of the poet Dante Alighieri. This chance combination of circumstances had the effect of concentrating his thoughts on poetry as the expression of religious belief ('No doubt this year starts as [a] theological year for me,' he wrote to Warner the following March). The beliefs themselves, in George's thinking, were relative, time-bound and part of history: 'I was born into the Greek Orthodox tradition; into the tradition of the great Anatolian Fathers, that was my fate; I did not choose it.' (It is indicative that he did not say, 'into the Greek Orthodox *faith*.') This marks a crucial difference between George and the later Eliot, with whom the poetry he was writing at this time was in dialogue. Eliot, after his conversion to Anglo-Catholicism, could and did share the articles of religious faith that bound Dante to the Catholic readers of his own and later times; George could not. 'In Dante,' George insisted, 'the image of God is an indissoluble part of the image of *man*: the one without the other would hardly be able to function.'[53]

In June 1966, George rounded off what had become a triptych of essays on religious subjects with the 'prologue' to his translation of the biblical *Apocalypse*. At the same time, and against the background of these interests, the fourteen short sections that make up the poem 'Summer Solstice' had now taken shape. The *Three Secret Poems* would appear, simultaneously with the translation of the *Apocalypse*, at the end of the year.[54]

The midsummer rituals with which 'Summer Solstice' begins and ends recall memories of George's childhood at Skala. But this is no ordinary midsummer. The sense of imminent ending is caught in the very first section of the poem, and the accelerating rhythms that follow compound the urgency; the moment is approaching for the 'sun to stop' (this is the root meaning of the word 'solstice,' in Greek as in English). The *Three Secret Poems* as a whole draw on the biblical *Apocalypse*, not least in their organisation into sections in multiples of the 'mystical' number seven, and in their provocative title, the exact antithesis of 'revelation.' But at the heart of 'Summer Solstice' lies a concept which the ancient Stoics derived from Heraclitus, the philosopher that George revered most of all. This is the belief that the universe is periodically consumed by fire, out of which a new universe is born.[55]

In this way, 'Summer Solstice' differs fundamentally from the Christian *Apocalypse*, from Dante's *Commedia*, and from Eliot's *Four Quartets*, although it is linked to all of them through a rich texture of allusion. In all of these, the end is at once transcendental and final: nothing can come after it. 'Summer Solstice,' by contrast, envisions a corrupt and degraded world coming to an end, just as the poet's own life, having 'seen many moons and suns,' is approaching its natural end. There is no palliative for the pain of physical dissolution, and no escape for the soul into an afterlife. But the end of a life, and even the ending of a world, are still not final. At the moment when the pulse stops, when the sun 'oversteps his measure,' in Heraclitus' words, and the world is consumed in fire, comes the 'birthpang of resurrection.' It is the moment, in the popular rituals of Skala, when the molten lead of the *klidonas* tells fortunes for the future; after the 'torment' of the fire:

> call the children to gather the ashes
> and sow them like seeds.
> All that has passed has rightly passed.[56]

The *Three Secret Poems* end with a cyclical process, a conflagration that like the summer solstice itself is part of a pattern of natural recurrence. If George possessed a religious belief, it was probably closer to that of the Stoic philosopher who was also emperor of Rome (another 'servant of two masters,' if ever there was one) Marcus Aurelius, than to the Christianity of St John the Divine, Dante, or T.S. Eliot.[57]

George was apprehensive about the reception of his new poems. 'I don't know if they're good,' he confessed to Nikos Karydis, one of the partners in the Ikaros publishing house. 'I mean, I don't know if the interaction between poet and reader will be there.' Friends put this down to the shadow of the Nobel. George may have known of Eliot's opinion: 'The Nobel is a ticket to one's funeral. No one has ever done anything after he got it.' But the real nature of his anxiety, at the end of 1966, went much deeper. It was the anxiety of the dedicated craftsman who looks back on a life's work, and he had already given it expression in a key central section of 'Summer Solstice':

> The white paper is a harsh mirror
> it returns to you only that which you were.

A poet's whole life is nothing, the section continues, without the leap of faith, without the risk taken of trusting to that unpromising and uncompromising 'void.' Only there – 'perhaps' – might you hope to 'find what you thought was lost.' The section concludes:

> Your life is what you gave
> this void is what you gave
> the white paper.[58]

389

It is a bleak epitaph; life and work stripped bare to the bone.

By the time that George was putting the finishing touches to 'Summer Solstice,' the political crisis had been dragging on for over a year, with no sign of a resolution in sight. A hysterical climate had developed; everywhere there were stories of conspiracies by sinister forces of the far left and far right. By the first months of 1967, there were rumoured to be no fewer than three secret plots, by different groups of army officers, to take over the country.[59]

George's political allegiances had long since ceased to be bound by the horizons of political parties. On this occasion, his old Venizelist antipathy to the monarchy was no doubt revived; but he had no personal sympathy for Papandreou, either. What distressed him most was that 'after a whole lifetime rocked by military putsches, dictatorships, changes of political system, disasters and despair,' nothing seemed to have changed in Greek political life.[60]

In October 1966, the novelist George Theotokas, who along with George and Katsimbalis had made up the 'three Georges' from the end of the 1920s, died after a sudden illness. In a heartfelt personal tribute, George gave voice to his despair about the political situation. He had just been asked by a 'middle-aged writer,' would he please sign a manifesto against dictatorship?

> I refused. 'Then we're going to let the dictatorship happen?' he asked me. I said to him, 'Dictatorship will be the *coup de grâce* for the country. But I believe that dictatorships are not stopped by the manifestos of intellectuals.'[61]

At the end of 1966, while the rumours flew, and the newspaper *To Vima* announced the *Three Secret Poems* of George Seferis as 'the most important cultural event of recent months,' George was once again deadly accurate in his political prophecy. These were the last months of political freedom that he would ever experience in his own country.[62]

**Dictatorship**

It was time, indeed, as George had written at the end of 'Summer Solstice,' to begin to 'gather the ashes,' to 'sow the seeds' for those who would come after. Just as he had done in 1940, faced with the end of the pre-war world, he set to, during the first months of 1967, to publish what remained to be published of his 'testament' as a poet. Taking a break, as was his habit, after an intensive bout of work, he and Maro spent a few days in Delphi in early February, in the snow. It had been only since the summer of 1965, as he announced to Durrell, that he had been 'function[ing] normally as a pen-holder.' To Linnér, at greater length, he added that he now had two new books almost ready, that he expected would be printed before the summer. These were a much expanded third edition of his *Essays,* and a volume of his diaries, to be called *Days of 1945–1951.*[63]

The title was a form of homage to Cavafy; he had begun transcribing his old diaries, with the help of Maro, during idle hours in Ankara at the end of the 1940s, while he had also still been struggling with his unfinished book on Cavafy. Soon, he would have two further volumes, containing these earlier diaries, in a definitive form ready for publication. Another form of testament to the past, that George did not mention to Linnér, was the volume of his brother's poems that he was also preparing and to which he contributed an afterword. That these projects were closely linked in his mind is confirmed by the dedication of *Days of 1945–1951:* 'to the memory

390

of my brother Angelos,' dated 19 January 1967, the anniversary of his death.[64]

On the morning of Friday, 21 April 1967, Greeks woke up to find tanks and soldiers occupying the main streets and squares of all major towns; the telephones had been cut off; the radio played military marches, alternating with folk tunes and patriotic popular melodies. The nightmare, that had been talked about so much that few still believed in it, had become a reality. Strict censorship was imposed; just as in 1936, articles of the constitution were abrogated. Some of the first decrees of the new military rulers provoked more incredulity than anger: gatherings of more than five people were prohibited, whether in public or in private; long hair for men and mini-skirts for girls were banned – and this in the late 1960s. Through official pronouncements and a hobbled press, the reality of the new situation took some time to sink in.

It was not, in the event, the king or his generals who had taken over, although faced with a *fait accompli* they would acquiesce in the new regime. The plotters had been military men of middle rank; this is why the regime soon came to be dubbed abroad, collectively, as 'The Colonels.' The most senior among them was Brigadier Stylianos Pattakos, who would become minister for the interior; Colonel George Papadopoulos would soon emerge as prime minister and the regime's 'strong man.' These were petty, vainglorious men, of limited education, their political ideas restricted to the slogans of their military training. The 'Colonels' were the butt of countless jokes in Greece while they ruled. But their grip on power was absolute, and brutally enforced. In the first days after the *coup*, thousands of leftists, and of those whose friends or family were suspected of leftward leanings, were rounded up. Many would be sent into internal exile in prison-camps on Aegean islands, in a revival of a practice that went back to the early 1930s and had reached a peak at the end of the civil war. Strict censorship was introduced, and applied not just to the mass media; nothing could be printed in Greece without first obtaining a stamp of approval from the censor's office.

From the first, George was under no illusions. In his tribute to Theotokas, published just four months previously, he had contemplated the political upheavals of his lifetime, and concluded: 'When a country doesn't get ahead in forty years, that means it's falling back headlong.' In his pocket diary, against the date 21 April 1967, he noted sarcastically: 'We're getting ahead amazingly.'[65]

For some months after the *coup,* George went to ground. In common with most reputable writers, he refused to submit his work to the censors; while the hope remained that the regime would not last, he would be silent, or would publish abroad. His plans to publish his essays and diaries were immediately shelved, although he did not abandon work on them until later in the year. He made an exception only for the book of his brother's poems, which appeared in July; Angelos, being dead, was above being compromised with the regime. Even private correspondence was liable to be opened and read; for the next two years, George all but stopped corresponding on anything but the most practical matters.[66]

In what may have been a guarded reference to the new situation in Greece, in the course of a letter to Edmund Keeley in October 1967, he confessed, 'I don't feel in a very good mood for creative work.' This was an understatement; only the previous week, George had put away the nearly completed new edition of his *Essays*; it is probable that this was also the point at which he finished and set aside the editorial work on the volume of his diaries that would become *Days 2*, covering the period of his consular service in London. 'What's the use of a writer who stops writing,' he despaired in his diary, soon afterwards, 'even if it's for the good of his country?' Sensitive to the hint in the letter, Keeley began to explore the possibility of an invitation for George to spend a semester or longer at the Institute for Advanced Study at Princeton.[67]

392

The invitation from the Institute reached George at the end of November 1967. 'I must confess,' he wrote to Keeley, 'that I felt the need of some sort of ventilation.' A few weeks later, and before he had definitely decided to go to Princeton, another invitation arrived. This was probably the highest honour, after the Nobel prize, he ever received – to become Charles Eliot Norton Professor of Poetry at Harvard University for the academic year 1969–1970. Exactly why George decided to accept the invitation from Princeton, while turning down the one from Harvard is not entirely clear; the timing would easily have allowed him to accept both. His formal letter to the Dean of Arts and Sciences at Harvard became the occasion for his first overt declaration against the regime in Greece: 'since last spring a censorship is functioning in my country; and my belief is that no written work can prosper without freedom of expression.' He could not, he went on, enjoy the benefits of freedom of speech, abroad, that were denied to him and his fellow-countrymen at home. 'The condition of the emigrant does not attract me; I want to stay with my people and share its vicissitudes,' he concluded.[68]

It might have been more consistent to have declined the invitation from Princeton too, since all these grounds applied equally. No doubt George was torn, but two factors may well have been decisive for him. Even though his letter to the Dean at Harvard was a personal, not a public, statement, the Charles Norton Professorship itself was very much in the public eye; his refusal of it a matter of record. This was the nearest to an open denunciation of the regime in Greece that George was prepared to make at this stage. Then at Princeton, it emerges from a touching aside in his letter to Keeley, he would have friends.[69]

In Greece itself, conditions had worsened by the end of 1967. In November the Colonels had come very close to provoking war with Turkey over Cyprus; the implacable mutual hostility between the military rulers of Greece and President Makarios of Cyprus would eventually lead to an open rift, with calamitous results for both. Then on 13 December, King Constantine had staged a bungled *coup d'état* and been forced to flee the country; in the aftermath, the Colonels were able to strengthen their grip. It was becoming daily harder to believe, as many had done at the beginning, that the regime was only a passing aberration.

The early months of 1968 found George in poor health. One day, he collapsed in the street, narrowly escaping being run over by a car; he was unconscious for two hours, and had to spend a week in hospital. 'Thank God all the checks were favourable,' he was able to write to Linnér, recalling another set of tests in Stockholm, at the time of the Nobel, 'except one: that five years have elapsed since then.' It turned out that he had suffered a 'vascular episode;' it left George with a greater feeling than ever that his body was beginning to fail him.[70]

Despite this, he was well enough to spend almost two months in Italy in May and June. He and Maro would be leaving for America at the end of September. In the meantime, he had been approached at least twice on behalf of prominent members of the left, who were being persecuted by the regime. The composer Theodorakis had brought George a tape of a new set of his poems that he had set to music while imprisoned by the regime, and tried to persuade him to join him in demanding the right to a public performance. One of the first decrees of the regime had been to ban all music by Theodorakis, since he was a known and outspoken leftist, and had been an MP of the United Democratic Left in the last parliament. George knew there was no hope of such a request being granted, and declined to make what seemed to him a pointless gesture. At the same time, he wondered about the composer's motives. It may have been recalling this

393

occasion that Maro remarked disapprovingly of the way that the penultimate poem of *Mythistorema* had been set to music: 'Theodorakis makes it sounds like a tarantella.'[71]

In September he was approached again, this time on behalf of the Marxist poet Yannis Ritsos, who was under house arrest and about to undergo surgery. Could George intervene with the authorities, to persuade them to allow Ritsos' wife to visit him in hospital? He had never met Ritsos, but was both moved and embarrassed by the request, soon afterwards withdrawn. Already, before he left for three months at Princeton, George knew that the world of political involvement, that he had thought he had left behind him for ever, was closing round him once more. He was a public figure, a Nobel laureate. How long could he maintain his present silence?[72]

The Institute for Advanced Study is housed in a low complex of buildings surrounded by the New Jersey woods. The centre of Princeton is a half-hour's walk or a short taxi-ride away. Living in Spartan simplicity with Maro in one of its small apartments, George called it an 'oasis within an oasis, within another oasis;' he was moved by the sight of so many young people ('beards and girls with very short skirts'), and by the black and grey squirrels, that were almost tame. Occasionally, he and Maro watched television in the apartment of one of the other fellows; 'we, thank God, have no such deadly machine.' During the three months that they stayed at Princeton, Keeley found George

> in particularly good spirits because he felt that his visit had served for a kind of rejuvenation: an interlude free from the political tensions that had been building up for some months in Athens and the occasion for both reflection and performance.[73]

As part of the terms of his fellowship, George had taken up again the project of translating into Modern Greek the 'myths and legends' contained in Plato's dialogues, that he had begun and abandoned as long ago as 1929. (The results of these labours would be published long after his death.) But a time for reflection it undoubtedly was, and for performance, too: accompanied always by the indefatigable Keeley, George gave readings and responded to questions at Harvard, Princeton and Rutgers universities, at Pittsburgh and Washington DC, and at the YMCA Poetry Center in New York City. On the last occasion, he was introduced to his audience by Senator Eugene McCarthy, who had run unsuccessfully for the Democrat nomination in the presidential election of that year, on an anti-Vietnam-war ticket, and was also a poet. George responded warmly to McCarthy, and was particularly moved to find that the senator had dedicated a poem to him; 'Jumping Ship,' from McCarthy's collection published that year, is an American response to 'In the Manner of G.S.' Then, before leaving America, George recorded a long interview with Keeley, that ranges widely across his life and work.[74]

But even on the other side of the Atlantic, there was no escaping the political realities that George had left behind in Greece. While he was at Princeton he maintained a notebook, separate from his diary. To this he gave the title *Manuscript Oct. '68,* obviously harking back to that earlier act of political stock-taking, from the vantage point of distant exile, the *Manuscript Sept. '41,* that he had written in Pretoria. By comparison with that earlier testament, the 1968 *Manuscript* is disappointing: disjointed and inconclusive. Its real theme is the dilemma with which George had been faced before he arrived at Princeton, and which tormented him during the three months that he spent there: to speak out or not, and if so, how?[75]

A crucial turning point seems to have been his reading in New York, on 2 December. Keeley recalls the occasion:

395

During the question period following the New York reading, Seferis was asked directly about his feelings regarding the situation in Greece, and when he refused to answer the several probes of this kind, the murmured dissatisfaction on the part of some in the audience clearly disturbed him. At dinner in his honor that evening he explained his reason for not answering some of the questions, a position related to his refusal to become an emigrant: he didn't think it was right to criticize his government while he was safely abroad in a foreign country at a time when others were suffering in Greece for their opposition to the Colonels' regime. . . . Seferis hadn't made this position clear to his audience, some of whom clearly thought he was evading the issue, as did some at the dinner table even after hearing his explanation.[76]

A few days later, in his interview with Keeley, George again twice side-stepped similar gentle probing.[77]

The nature of George's dilemma at the end of 1968 is most succinctly encapsulated in the two-line epigram (it is hardly a poem) with which *Manuscript Oct. '68* ends. It was written, probably, on the eve of his departure with Maro from Princeton at the end of the year. The question it asks is answered by its title:

Out of Stupidity
*Greece*: bang! *Christian*: bang! *Hellenes*: bang!
Three words dead. What did you kill them for?[78]

That spring, the regime in Greece had adopted the slogan, *Greece of Christian Hellenes*, that suddenly began to appear everywhere on hoardings, on public transport, in official buildings, even on hillsides. The underlying historical unity of the pagan Hellenic and the Orthodox Christian traditions, and the paramount importance of both as the heritage of Greeks in the modern world, had been articles of faith for George all his life. It was this all-inclusive, accumulated, and specifically non-racial, non-nationalistic historical and cultural consciousness that he had used the Nobel ceremony in Stockholm as a platform to proclaim to the world. Hijacked by the language and the mentality of the parade-ground, these precious words, in the epigram, are shot dead.[79]

But George's dilemma remained unresolved. According to Maro, in conversations after his death, his decision to make a public statement had been taken before they left America at the end of 1968. She herself, ever forthright where he was guarded, was apparently in no doubt that he should do so. But the *Manuscript* was probably not finished until after he had returned to Greece, and still contains no sign of a resolution. According to Robert Keeley, Edmund's younger brother, who was at that time serving as First Secretary and Political Officer at the American embassy in Athens, and one of the few people outside his immediate family in whom George confided on this matter, George 'agonized throughout January and February 1969.'[80]

In the meantime, at the beginning of February, George finished the poem, 'The Cats of St Nicholas.' Its starting point had been his first sight of Cyprus at Christmas in 1952, but he had left it unfinished when the rest of his poems dedicated to Cyprus went to press three years later. Now, he took it up again; the folktale of the cats that had saved a monastery from an invasion of poisonous snakes, in the final version, becomes a bleak parable for the age: after months, years, and ages of vicious fighting, the forces of good prevail, only to be destroyed themselves:

What would you expect of the poor things
fighting and taking in, day and night,
the poisonous blood of the serpents?
Centuries of poison; generations of poison . . .

'In writing the poem,' he would explain a few months later to Eugene McCarthy, 'I had in mind the evil unconsciously absorbed if I may put it so...'[81]

George could not, of course, publish this poem in Greece. That summer, he gave a copy to Edmund Keeley, who published it in translation in England soon after; he also sent it to Cyprus, the only other country where he could hope to have it published in his own language. But even 'The Cats of St Nicholas,' published abroad, did not amount to the kind of public statement that friends and critics alike expected of Greece's only Nobel laureate. The poem's political reference is implicit and oblique; its criticism is no more overt than in many poems of *Logbook I*, that had been published, under similar conditions of censorship, in 1940. Something more was needed, and George knew it.[82]

All his life, George had moved cautiously. He had never been one to seek the limelight; he abhorred the empty rhetoric of political slogans and promises. There is no doubting George's private, and profound, contempt for the regime of the Colonels; but it had been a conscious decision, as he confided to Robert Keeley, to put all involvement in politics behind him, once he had returned to Athens and retired from the diplomatic service. Above all, as Keeley recalls, he was 'fearful of being used by any political party or faction.'[83] At the same time, while younger and politically committed friends, acquaintances and perfect strangers were putting pressure on him to act, there were many of his generation, including some of his friends, who had lived through more destructive upheavals in the life of the nation, and remained condescendingly tolerant towards the new regime. In making public his personal antipathy, George would not necessarily be speaking for all, or even for a majority, of his fellow-countrymen. In addition, given his background, and even allowing for his lifelong frustrations with the Ministry of Foreign Affairs, he must have been acutely sensitive to the professional ethics of a lifetime: for a trusted higher civil servant to criticise the government of his country in public is the one unforgivable transgression.[84]

But the overriding reason for George's reticence, in the late 1960s under the Colonels, just as under Metaxas in the late 1930s, surely goes back to long-held *aesthetic* beliefs. Although he had long ago rejected the model of the poet in his ivory tower, George had always equally distanced himself from the opposite extreme of the *poète engagé*, or politically committed poet. To make a direct political statement, *as a poet*, would run counter to everything he had always believed about the nature and role of his art;

tacitly, he would be conceding that the 'world of the house in the country,' at Skala, and the 'world of the house in the city,' that he had striven all his life to keep apart, could not be so separated. There is a sense in which the act that would make George into a hero in the eyes of so many, then and since, could not avoid being also a deeply personal admission of defeat.[85]

It was not until the middle of March 1969 that George announced to Robert Keeley, at one of their private meetings, that he had decided to act. He showed Keeley the text that he proposed to distribute, with his own translations of it into English and French. All that remained was to determine the means and timing of its release. Later that month, George and Maro were due to spend a few days in Delphi, with the Italian publisher Enzo Crea. To Ioanna, he confided that he had three possible dates in mind. The first was the day after his return from Delphi. Ioanna interrupted him, 'Never mind the second. You'll give it on the first, the soonest possible.' And so the date was agreed: Friday 28 March.[86]

George now went into action with great secrecy. Even Savidis, who was with him and Maro at Delphi, had no idea what was afoot. George's statement had to carry the authenticity of his own voice, speaking in his own language. So he read it aloud on tape, and had the tape smuggled to London, to be broadcast on the Greek-language service of the BBC. On the morning of the day when the broadcast was due, printed copies were also distributed, by Maro and trusted friends, to every newspaper (except the far-right *Estia*), press agency, and foreign correspondent in Athens. Shortly before noon on the 28th, the time for secrecy was over. The previous autumn, George had refused to speak out from the safety of America; now he disdained to hide away from the expected retribution of the dictatorship.

While copies of his statement were being distributed, he took up his position in Zonar's patisserie, a regular haunt for writers and intellectuals on Panepistimiou Street, in the centre of Athens. There he was soon joined by Maro, on her way back from the newspaper offices nearby. As the news quickly spread, the patisserie filled up with friends, acquaintances, and supporters. By the time that Robert Keeley received George's telephone call at the American embassy, authorising him to forward his text to the State Department via an official telegram, it sounded to him as though George had thrown a party. Later in the day, the BBC Greek Service broadcast George's voice, reading in Greek, from London; his statement was also heard on Radio Paris and the West German station, Deutsche Welle, broadcasting from Cologne.[87]

For all the enthusiasm that it unleashed among opponents of the regime, George's 'Statement,' as it has come to be known ever since, is a dour document. It is not a clarion-call to resistance from below, but a withering rebuke delivered as though from a great height: 'This anomaly must cease. It is the nation's command.' The tone is solemn, invoking in different words the unstoppable 'mechanism of catastrophe' that George had identified in other historical crises that he had experienced. The traces are clear, in the text, of the deep reluctance with which it had been dragged from him: almost half of it consists of an oblique justification for his earlier reticence. It ends, 'I return now to my silence. I pray God never again to place me under such necessity to speak.'[88]

It was still, in all the circumstances, an act of real courage. Almost as important, it was quickly seen as such, and has been ever since, even by those most exasperated by George's previous ambivalence. After the musical settings of his poems by Theodorakis, this hugely influential stand against the Colonels remains today the best known event in George's life.[89]

The explanation for his long-delayed action that he gave to Robert Keeley in some ways testifies with greater immediacy and urgency than does the more formal 'Statement' itself, to the passion and depth of feeling behind it.

399

I came to this decision alone. I don't know what changed my mind: Perhaps my visit to America and its freedom last fall, perhaps my talks with Senator McCarthy. But there is one thing that makes it urgent: These young people are losing so much, they are not learning and they are being filled with awful propaganda. We cannot afford to lose a whole generation. That is why I have spoken out, and now I feel at ease.

To his translator Edmund Keeley he said, 'I ended up ready for anything but expecting nothing. The only emotion I felt once I'd made the decision to speak was intense liberation.'[90]

From the regime, the response was characteristically inept. The foreign newspapers, which usually circulated freely in Athens, published only extracts from the 'Statement;' it was the regime's own propaganda organs which a few days later carried the full text, as their editorialists rounded on the perpetrator with predictable fury. Suddenly, newspapers that were normally only bought by supporters of the regime and public employees had to rush out extra editions. Though the attacks were wounding, they were not new; it was claimed that George had 'sold out Cyprus to win the

Nobel prize;' he was a secret communist, in the pay of foreign governments. But thanks to them, what he had said, and above all the fact that he had said it, reached every Greek household at home and abroad.[91]

A more oblique response was the sudden announcement, at the beginning of April, of a national anthology of short stories to be serialised in all the newspapers. Much was made of the fact that several of the writers to be included were well known dissidents, some even in prison; in this way the Colonels aimed to show the world that freedom of expression did, after all, exist in Greece. Some of the contributors, whose permission to reproduce their work had not been asked, also noted wryly that almost half of their number were dead. In April, eighteen writers signed a public statement denouncing the proposed anthology; it ended, in notably Seferian style:

> We honour George Seferis, because he was the first to draw attention to the dangers that are increasing while the present situation continues. We hope that the voice of the great poet will not be proved to be the voice of a Cassandra.[92]

George was now the focus for literary protest against the regime. On 3 October 1969, preventive censorship was abolished, to be replaced by a complex set of laws that were in effect a form of self-censorship. The first test of these laws came the following summer. A group of writers, mostly in their thirties and forties, brought out an anthology of prose, poetry and literary criticism that in various indirect ways criticised the regime and in particular the institution of censorship. Some of these writers, such as the novelists Rodis Roufos and Th.D. (Boulis) Frangopoulos, had been friends of George since the 1950s; others made his acquaintance now. Obedient to the letter, but not to the spirit, of the current press law, that bizarrely required exact conformity between the title of a publication and its content, the volume was entitled *Eighteen Texts*. The names of its contributors were listed alphabetically on the plain front cover. The only exception, set in larger type some way above the rest, is the name of George Seferis, who is honoured as the patron of the entire venture. The first of the *Eighteen Texts* is his poem, 'The Cats of St Nicholas,' that in this way first came to be published in Greece.[93]

*Eighteen Texts* appeared in July 1970 and sold out so quickly that the volume had to be reprinted many times. Not the least remarkable aspect of this first literary assault on the dam of censorship was that it encompassed a broad political spectrum; it was not, like other forms of organised resistance that existed at the time, confined to the left. Nor was it a youthful protest; almost all the writers who took part were already established; the young would follow shortly, through a door that had already been opened. It must be very doubtful whether this protest would have happened at all, still less in the politically inclusive manner that it did, had it not been for George's 'Statement' in March 1969; everything else followed from that. It is also worth noting that no other writer of George's generation either made a public protest or participated in the *Eighteen Texts*.

### Valedictory

In April 1970, George made his annual application to the Foreign Ministry for the renewal of his and Maro's diplomatic passports. The privilege of travelling with these documents, rather than with ordinary passports issued by the Ministry of the Interior, had been granted to George and his wife on his retirement, along with the title of 'Honorary Ambassador,' as was customary. This time, the application was refused. George reacted angrily to the refusal, not so much as a personal slight, as because 'it would bring discredit on all former civil servants who had served their country in a capacity similar to his.' The foreign press again became involved, when 401 prominence was given to reports that the Nobel laureate had been denied a passport by the Greek government. The Minister of the Interior, Brigadier Pattakos, was able to deny the stories, on the technical grounds that George had never applied for a passport from Pattakos' ministry. By this time George had had to cancel his plans to travel to Padua, where his Italian translator, Pontani, had arranged a celebration to launch a collection of essays and tributes, in honour of his seventieth birthday.[94]

Later in the summer, a three-page letter arrived from the regime's Foreign Minister, Panayotis Pipinelis. George had forfeited the right to his honorary title and to a diplomatic passport, because his 'Statement' had been broadcast over Soviet Radio and so constituted 'propaganda against the nation.' Pipinelis had been a former diplomat; George had often had professional dealings with him in the past. In a further ironic twist, by the time this letter reached George, six weeks after it had been written, its author had died; it was a macabre and literal manifestation of the 'dead hand' of the regime.[95]

By this time, George's physical condition was giving cause for concern. Photographs show deep wrinkles on his forehead; his huge eyes are still bright and alert, but full of sadness; he leans for support on a stick. Ever since his operation in 1961, he had experienced a dragging on the left side; now it became so pronounced that his left leg was all but paralysed. In July, while swimming with Edmund and Mary Keeley near Marathon, he lost his footing under water and almost drowned. After hospital tests, he was advised by a French doctor, in October, to seek treatment in Paris.[96]

There was now nothing for it, but for Maro to present herself at the notorious Security Headquarters in Bouboulinas Street, behind the National Archaeological Museum, and brandish the newspaper, from back in May, in which Pattakos had denied refusing them passports. 'Now who's telling lies, us or Mr Pattakos?' she demanded of the officer in charge. Ten days later, the couple left Greece, travelling 'like ordinary mortals, with ordinary travel documents.' George felt the humiliation keenly.[97]

In Paris, they stayed in an inexpensive hotel in the Latin Quarter. From there, George sent a nostalgic picture postcard to Katsimbalis, whom he had first met in the same neighbourhood half a century ago. Through his French publisher, he had been put in touch with the journalist and writer Anne Philipe, the widow of the well-known actor Gérard Philipe; during the weeks that George and Maro spent in the rue Tournon, where she was their neighbour, Anne Philipe became a friend. Six months later, on a visit to Athens, she recorded a long taped interview with him, part of which would appear in *Le Monde* on the eve of his death.[98]

In the meantime, the results of five days of hospital tests were better than might have been expected: a spinal operation might bring some improvement, but the risks outweighed the likely benefits. The condition was not a threatening one; the symptoms could be relieved by medication, exercise, and physiotherapy. George and Maro returned to Athens in the middle of December, considerably relieved.[99]

Thursday 25 March 1971, was the day of the Annunciation; it was also the Greek national day, commemorating the start of the War of Independence in 1821. In Athens, there would be military parades all morning; it was a day to be elsewhere. George and Maro went with the poet George Pavlopoulos and another friend to Sounion, the promontory an hour and a half's drive from the city, where the ruined marble columns of the temple to Poseidon have been a famous landmark since ancient times. There, by chance, they met the English poet and translator, Peter Levi. Over lunch in a beach taverna, George demonstrated his skill in English and Greek limericks. Levi recalled, 'He was happy that day, although there was a black undercurrent of things that we all avoided mentioning.'

402

After lunch, they climbed the hill opposite the ancient temple. This was an ordeal for George, but he was full of enthusiasm. The men began arguing about the spiky bushes that were in brilliant yellow bloom on the slopes: were they caltrop or gorse? Pavlopoulos recalled the popular name, in Greek, from an old folk song. 'That reminds me of something,' said George. 'I don't know . . .' And he would say nothing more, all the way back to Athens. That night, as George explained afterwards to Pavlopoulos, he had found the word he was looking for: it was *aspalathoi*. In one of the legends told by Plato, in the *Republic,* a notorious tyrant had been condemned to pay eternally for his crimes, in the Underworld, by having his skin stripped from him by these spiky bushes.[100]

George's last poem, 'On Aspalathoi,' commemorates that spring day at Sounion, a day of both religious and political 'annunciation.' At the heart of the poem lies:

> One word in Plato I think, lost in the runnels of the mind;
> the name of the yellow bush
> has not changed since those times.[101]

The last word of the poem is 'tyrant.' In the poem, it is nature itself, true to the dictum of the ancient philosopher Heraclitus, that punishes for all time the usurper of absolute power who exceeds his ordained 'measures.'[102]     **403**

In the summer of 1971, plans were well advanced for George's long-postponed return to Cyprus. Tickets had been issued for him and Maro to travel on the *Apollonia,* the ship where their friend Nikos Kavvadias was the wireless operator. A fortnight before they were due to sail, George wrote to the Cypriot poet Hebe Meleagrou:

> I say *if* [I come to Cyprus], because the last few days I've begun to feel so unwell, I can hardly stand, and if we're insisting on [staying with Louizos at] Famagusta, it's because we hope the sea-bathing will do me good.

It was to be his last letter.[103]

A week later, on 22 July, George was admitted to the Evangelismos Hospital in Athens. The ulcer from which he had suffered at moments of crisis over the last fifteen years had recurred, more violently than ever.

The first of two operations was carried out at the beginning of August. Then came a severe haemorrhage, and a second operation. As George's condition worsened, Maro stood guard outside his ward; even Ioanna, it seems, found it difficult to approach her brother. After a series of complications, a tracheotomy was performed; the operation enabled George to breathe, but he would never speak again. Ioanna was haunted by 'that look of a wounded animal,' in his 'enlarged eyes.'[104]

Jacqueline Pouyollon, now long since married, with a career behind her, and herself in poor health, came to Athens and stayed at Kydathinaion Street; but Ioanna could not allow her to go to the hospital. Jacqueline left Athens without seeing George again.[105]

George Seferis died on the afternoon of Monday, 20 September 1971.

Two days later, the little Church of the Transfiguration of the Saviour in Kydathinaion Street had filled up long before the funeral service was due to begin. Soon the sunken courtyard of the church, with its flowering oleanders and tall cypresses, was also full. The overwhelming majority of those who crowded into the church and the surrounding streets were young people and students. Inside the church, wreaths had arrived from the exiled king of Greece, from Archbishop Makarios, President of Cyprus, but also from groups of political prisoners held in jails up and down Greece, from prominent detainees and exiles such as Mikis Theodorakis, the actress (later Minister of Culture) Melina Mercouri and her husband, the film director Jules Dassin. It is said that the Security Police had removed the inscriptions from some of these, but relatives of the signatories had been able to replace them in time. Not least remarkable is the fact that the arrival of the wreaths, and the names of their senders, were printed in the next day's newspapers.

The funeral liturgy began at 4 pm. To the consternation of many inside the church, Archbishop Hieronymos of Athens and All Greece, an appointee of the regime, arrived to officiate. Apart from the archbishop, the ambassadors of Great Britain and of Cyprus, and other members of the foreign diplomatic corps, there was no official presence; a solitary wreath from the Ministry of Culture and Sciences was scarcely noticed among so many of which bore the names of the most infamous prisons in the land.[106]

When the obsequies were over, the coffin was carried out of the church and placed in the back of the waiting hearse. At a walking pace, surrounded by mourners, George began his last journey along Kydathinaion Street. There were cheers and shouts; people began to sing the national anthem. Soon the hearse had reached the wide boulevard, Amalias Avenue; in the open space in front of Hadrian's Gate and the massive columns of the Temple of Zeus, the crowd spilled out until the traffic was stopped in both directions. Spontaneously, here and there, in snatches, then with gathering momentum until the whole street was ringing with it, emerging from the throats of the crowd came the forbidden music of Theodorakis. It was the first of the *Epiphania* settings, that had given George such misgivings when they had first been performed and recorded ten years before: the poem called 'Denial' (or 'Renunciation'), that begins, 'On our own secret seashore.' The chorus swelled to a climax (oblivious, as always, of George's 'lost semi-colon' in the final verse):

> Such heart we put into our lives,
> such passion, love and long-
> ing when we started; wrong!
> And so we changed our lives.

Written a little over forty years earlier, it had been George's renunciation of his love for Jacqueline. Today, while crowds of young people took to the streets, under the watchful eyes of hundreds of police in uniform and as many more informers in plain clothes, the words and music together took on a whole new meaning. It was a hymn of hope that carried George through the streets to his final resting place in the Athens First Cemetery. As one eye-witness described it at the time, 'with the song rising up, up, the sadness began to lift too and we floated along as if on air, the stream widening as we went along until it flooded the cemetery.'

There were more crowds at the cemetery; more flowers had already been laid at the Seferiadis family grave. According to the press reports, 'people who had never set eyes on Seferis were weeping.' As the coffin was laid to rest, the crowd broke into a burst of applause, a common custom in Greece at the funerals of the famous. There were cries of 'Immortal!' and the strains of 'Denial' rose once more among the cypress trees, as the shadows lengthened.[107]

George had always maintained that his first and greatest inspiration had been the speech and the songs of the fishermen and peasants of Skala, the truest representatives, for him, of the Greek people. Now, in a way that he could scarcely ever have expected, and of which he might not wholly have approved, George Seferis in death had reached the audience to which he had always insisted that his poetry belonged: the people.

405

# Acknowledgements

Many people who knew Seferis have been generous with their time, with information, and with moral support for my project over the years. Among them I must single out Anna Londou, who lived much of the story told in the latter half of this book, and brought to life her experiences in talking to me. I am no less grateful to: Eleni Cubitt, Dimitris Daskalopoulos, Mark Dragoumis, Edmund Keeley, Robert V. Keeley, John Leatham, Zissimos Lorenzatos, Despina Mylonas, Anna Sikelianou, Lydia Stefanou, Lili Theotoka-Alivizatou, Nanos Valaoritis, Mario Vitti, and Alexandros Xydis. To these names should be added the following, who are no longer living: Nikos Kranidiotis, George Savidis, Maro Seferi, Ioanna Tsatsou, and C.M. Woodhouse (Lord Terington).

Many more people helped me to gather material, gain access to archives, and to find my way through the complexities of Seferis' surviving papers, particularly at the Gennadius Library. Here, the largest debt of all is owed to Katerina Krikos-Davis, who has stood by me throughout, not only as academic consultant for the Seferis papers at the Gennadius, as a distinguished and meticulous commentator on Seferis' work, and a colleague of many years' standing, but also as a friend and a sharp-eyed reader of an earlier full draft of this book. At the Gennadius Library, I am additionally grateful to the Director, Haris Calligas; to her predecessor, David Jordan; to the former Chairman of the Managing Committee, Professor Alan Boegehold; to the academic consultants who have worked on the new material in the archive, Katerina Kostiou and Theano Michaelidou; and to the archivists, Natalia Vogeikoff-Brogan and Maria Voltera, whose patience and goodwill were truly inexhaustible.

At the Vikelaia Municipal Library, Heraklion, Crete I was greatly assisted by Frida Hatzaki; it is a matter of sadness that I never met Nikos Yannadakis, the librarian there who had first charge of the Library of George and Maro Seferis, and had arranged for me to have access to all the material I needed, but who was already terminally ill when I visited in 1997. Other debts in Greece are to Manos Haritatos, Director of the Hellenic Literary and Historical Archive (ELIA); to Dr Photini Tomai-Constantopoulou, Director of Diplomatic and Historical Archives of the

Foreign Ministry, and her obliging assistant Dora Gota; to Dionysis Kapsalis, Director of the Cultural Foundation of the National Bank (MIET), and the capable archivist of the photographic collection there, Voula Livani, who provided most of the photographs; and to Rhena Spanou, in the Public Relations Department of the Ministry for Press and Mass Media. In London, at the Greek embassy, the moral and practical support of Victoria Solomonides, Nikos Papadakis, and (going back some years) Katerina Boura was invaluable. On matters to do with the Nobel prize, and the Swedish language, I am deeply grateful for the enthusiastic assistance of Bo-Lennart Eklund, of the University of Gothenburg.

In addition, I have been helped in ways too numerous to name by: Philip Carabott, Nadia Charalambidou, Diskin Clay, Dimitris Daskalopoulos, Natalia Deliyannaki, Sarah Ekdawi, Elena Frangakis-Syrett, Stathis Gauntlett, Liana Giannakopoulou, Dimitri Gondicas, Denise Harvey-Sherrard, Renée Hirschon, Chryssi and Katerina Karydi, Denis Kohler, Peter Mackridge, Elli Mylonas, Dimitris Papanikolaou, Michalis Pieris, Mika Provata David Roessel, Bengi Rona, Avi Sharon, Maria Stasinopoulou, Niki Tsironi, Dimitris Tziovas, Nasos Vayenas, Christopher Williams, Yorgos Yatromanolakis, and Yorgos Yeoryis.

Preliminary work for this book was done during a year-long sabbatical
leave from King's College in 1994–5; the bulk of the writing was made possible by a second sabbatical from September 2001 to September 2002. I am grateful to my colleagues in the Department of Byzantine and Modern Greek Studies, to the Head of the School of Humanities, Dr David Ricks, and to the Principal, Professor Arthur Lucas, for these 'windows,' without which the book could never have been written. I have also benefited from the Small Grants Fund of the School of Humanities, which awarded me travel grants for study in Greece, in 1994 and 2001. The final stage of writing, between September and December 2002, was generously funded by the Arts and Humanities Research Board, through its competitive Research Leave Scheme. I am grateful to the Board for the support received, and to Edmund Keeley and Peter Mackridge, who generously backed me in my pursuit of funding for the project.

I am grateful for permission to quote the following copyright material: the Icaros Publishing Company, Athens, for all quotations from the *Poems*, *Essays*, and other works by Seferis published by them (in my own translations); Penguin Books, for the remark of T.S. Eliot quoted by Peter Ackroyd in his biography, *T.S. Eliot* (Hamish Hamilton 1984); Faber, for the lines quoted from T.S. Eliot's poems, *The Waste Land*, 'Marina,' and 'East

Coker,' and from *Murder in the Cathedral*, for citations from *The Durrell–Miller Letters 1935–80*, edited by Ian MacNiven (1988) and from Ian MacNiven, *Lawrence Durrell, A Biography* (1999); AOL Time Warner Books Group for the quotations from John Lehmann, *In My Own Time* (1969); and New Directions Publishing Corporation for the passages from Henry Miller, *The Colossus of Maroussi* (all excerpts © 1941 by Henry Miller).

For permission to reproduce unpublished material (in my own translation, where the original is in Greek or French) I am grateful to Anna Londou (George Seferis papers in the Gennadius Library, Athens; the Library of George and Maro Seferis, Vikelaia Municipal Library, Heraklion, Crete; George Seferis Photographic Archive, Cultural Foundation of the National Bank (MIET), Athens); Despina Mylonas (Tsatsos family archive), and the editors of several works-in-progress, of which details appear in the section, 'Abbreviations and Sources.' I am also grateful to the following institutions for permission to reproduce unpublished material which they hold: American School of Classical Studies, Gennadius Library, Athens; Cultural Foundation of the National Bank, Athens (MIET); Hellenic Literary and Historical Archive (ELIA); Hellenic Republic, Ministry of Foreign Affairs, Service of Diplomatic and Historical Archives; Princeton University Library, Department of Rare Books and Special Collections (Selected Papers of George Seferis); Public Record Office, Kew; Vikelaia Municipal Library, Heraklion, Crete.

Several people read the book in draft, in whole or in part, and made useful comments, corrections, and suggestions: Edmund Keeley, Katerina Krikos-Davis, Peter Mackridge, an anonymous peer reviewer for the Press, and my editor, Adam Freudenheim, whose early enthusiasm for the project sustained me through difficult times, and has been matched throughout by a firm rein that has done much to keep this book within manageable proportions. I would also like to thank my agent, Jonathan Pegg of Curtis Brown, who had faith in me, and in Seferis, from an early stage in the writing. None of this, finally, would have been possible without the support of my family: of my wife Fran, and our two sons, to whom this book is dedicated.

408

# Greek Names, Transliteration, Translation

There is no consistent or satisfactory way of representing modern Greek words and names in the Latin alphabet. Where a well-established English equivalent exists, I have used that (e.g. 'Athens', not 'Athina', 'Athinai', or 'Athine'; 'King Constantine', not 'Konstantinos'); where individuals have adopted a particular spelling of their names in English, I have respected it, with inevitable loss of consistency (though the family name 'Seferiadis' may appear in the sources alternatively as 'Seferiades' or, in French, Séfériadès); finally, where no such clearly established precedent exists, I have aimed for a compromise between representing the sounds of the Greek and its appearance on the page. Where divergences are significant (for example, with initial soft 'g', which can be represented either as 'g' or as 'y'), cross-references have been supplied in the index.

Family names in Greek, in their masculine form usually, but not always, end in 's'; the equivalent feminine forms end in either 'i' or 'ou'. The wife or daughter of Stelios Seferiadis has the surname 'Seferiadi' or, in older, more formal sources, 'Seferiadou', denoting literally 'of Seferiadis'. Similarly, names of streets and squares in Greek are almost invariably in the genitive case: 'Stadiou Street' literally means 'Street of the Stadium [*stadion*]'. Exceptions, in everyday usage, are the two main squares in the centre of Athens, known simply as 'Syntagma' ('Constitution') and 'Omonia' ('Concord'). The former often appears in English-language sources as 'Constitution Square'; I have retained the Greek.

In Greek, the position of the stress in a word or name is important, and not usually predictable unless it is written in Greek characters, where the stress is marked. I have resisted the temptation to clutter up my English text by including these accents, but have added them to personal names in the index, which may also therefore serve as a guide to pronunciation.

Finally, all translations, unless otherwise indicated, are my own, except for the titles of Seferis' published poems. For these, to avoid confusion, I have retained the translated titles as they appear in George Seferis, *Complete Poems*, translated, edited and introduced by Edmund Keeley and Philip Sherrard (Princeton: Princeton University Press; London: Anvil

Press Poetry, 1995), even where I also suggest an alternative rendering. Greek has been retained, in the notes, only in the titles of source material, and very occasionally where I felt that precision was required beyond what could be rendered by a translation.

410

# Sources and Abbreviations

## I. Published sources

*Antigrafes* = George Seferis, *Αντιγραφές*,
ed. G.P. Savidis (Athens: Ikaros, 1978,
first edition 1965) [*Transcriptions*
(Translations from French and
English)]

AP = Γιώργος Σεφέρης – Anne Philipe:
*Συνομιλία*, trans. [from French]
with preface by Nikos Bakounakis,
introduction by Panos Paionidis
(Athens: Kastaniotis, 1991)
[*Conversation*]; edited extract
published in *Le Monde*, 27 August
1971

Aronis = Nikolaos Ch. Aronis,
*Αναθυμήματα από την εφηβεία του φίλου
μου Γιώργου Σεφέρη*. Εκδόσεις Ενώσεως
Σμυρναίων, 24 (Athens: Union of
Smyrniots, 1984) [*Recollections from the
Early Years of My Friend George
Seferis*]

D1–3 = George Seferis, *Δοκιμές*, 3 vols. Vols
1–2, 3rd ed., ed. G.P. Savidis (Athens:
Ikaros, 1974; reprinted with minor
corrections, 1981); vol. 3, ed. Dimitris
Daskalopoulos (Athens: Ikaros, 1992)
[*Essays*]

Daskalopoulos, *Ergographia* = Δημήτρης
Δασκαλόπουλος, *Εργογραφία Σεφέρη
(1931–1979)* (Athens: ELIA [Hellenic
Literary and Historical Archive], 1979)
[includes detailed descriptions of GS's
editions]

IT = Ioanna Tsatsou, *Ο αδερφός μου Γιώργος
Σεφέρης* (Athens: Estia, 1973) [*My
Brother George Seferis*]

Keeley/int. = Edmund Keeley, 'Postscript:
A Conversation with Seferis' [1968], in
Keeley, *Modern Greek Poetry, Voice and
Myth* (Princeton University Press,

1983), 180–217 (first published: *Paris
Review* 50, 1970)

Kohler = Denis Kohler, *L'Aviron d'Ulysse:
L'Itinéraire poétique de Georges Séféris*
(Paris: Les Belles Lettres, 1985)

KS = George Seferis, *Complete Poems*, trans-
lated, edited and introduced by Edmund
Keeley and Philip Sherrard (Princeton:
Princeton University Press; London:
Anvil Press Poetry, 1995)

KT = Konstantinos Tsatsos, *Λογοδοσία μιας
ζωής*, 2 vols (Athens: I Ekdoseis ton
Filon, 2000) [Autobiography]

Kyd9 = Ioanna Tsatsou, *Κυδαθηναίων
9*, 2nd, expanded, ed. (Athens:
Astrolavos/Evthyni, 1994; first
published 1993) [*No. 9, Kydathinaion
Street*]

KypEp = *"Κυπριακές" επιστολές του Σεφέρη
(1954–1962): από την αλληλογραφία του με
τον Γ.Π. Σαββίδη*, ed. Katerina Kostiou
(Nicosia: Πολιτιστικό "Ίδρυμα Τραπέζης
Κύπρου [Cultural Foundation of the
Bank of Cyprus], 1991) [*'Cypriot' Letters
of Seferis (1954–1962); From His
Correspondence with G.P. Savidis*]

M1–7 = George Seferis, *Μέρες*, 7 vols; 1–5
without editorial material or index; vol.
6 ed. Panayotis Mermingas; vol. 7 ed.
Theano Michailidou (Athens: Ikaros,
1975–1990) [*Days* (diary)]

Maro/diary = Maria Stasinopoulou (ed.),
*Ανέκδοτες ημερολογιακές σελίδες της
Μαρώς Σεφέρη*, *Diavazo* 142 (April 1986),
73–8 ['Unpublished Pages from a Diary
by Maro Seferi']

Maro/int. = Maro Seferi, *Αναμνήσεις από
τη ζωή μου με τον Σεφέρη*, *I Lexi* 53
(1986), 190–205 ['Memories from My
Life with Seferis']

MIET album = Οι φωτογραφίες του Γιώργου Σεφέρη (Athens: Μορφωτικό Ίδρυμα Εθνικής Τραπέζης [Cultural Foundation of the National Bank], 2000) [*The Photographs of George Seferis*]

P = George Seferis, Ποιήματα, ed. G.P. Savidis, 8th ed. (Athens: Ikaros, 1972, not significantly changed in subsequent reprints) [*Poems*]

PE1–2 = George Seferis, Πολιτικό ημερολόγιο, 2 vols, ed. Alexandros Xydis (Athens: Ikaros, 1979; 1985) [*Political Diary*]

PE2.XI = πηρεσιακή σταδιοδρομία, appendix XI in PE2, pp. 182–192, ed. Alexandros Xydis [GS's professional curriculum vitae]

PE3 = Σελίδες απο το ανέκδοτο Πολιτικό Ημερολόγιο Γ´ (1956–1960), ed. Yorgos Yeoryis [Georgis], *Ta Nea: Prosopa* 48 (5 February 2000), 22–3

S/Apost = George Seferis and George Apostolidis, Αλληλογραφία 1931–1945, ed. Vasiliki Kontoyanni (Athens: Ikaros, 2002) [*Correspondence*]

S/Diam = Adamantios Diamantis and George Seferis, Αλληλογραφία 1953–1971, ed. Michalis Pieris (Athens: Stigmi, 1985) [*Correspondence*]

S/Kar = George Seferis and Andreas Karantonis, Αλληλογραφιά, 1931–1960, ed. Fotis Dimitrakopoulos (Athens: Kastaniotis, 1988) [*Correspondence*]

S/Keeley = George Seferis and Edmund Keeley, *Correspondence, 1951–1971*, ed. Edmund Keeley (Princeton University Press, 1997 = *Princeton University Library Chronicle*, vol. 58, no. 3 [Spring 1997])

S/L = Γράμματα Σεφέρη – Λορεντζάτου (1948–1968), ed. N.D. Triantafyllopoulos (Athens: Domos, 1990) [*Seferis – Lorenzatos Letters*]

S/M1 = [George] Seferis and Maro [Seferi], Αλληλογραφία Ά (1936–1940), ed. M.Z. Kopidakis (Heraklion, Crete: Βικελαία Δημοτική Βιβλιοθήκη [Vikelaia Municipal Library], 1989) [*Correspondence, vol. 1*]

S/Mal = G[eorge] Seferis and T[imos] Malanos, Αλληλογραφία (1935–1963), ed. Dimitris Daskalopoulos (Athens: Olkos, 1990) [*Correspondence*]

S/T = George Theotokas and George Seferis, Αλληλογραφία (1930–1966), ed. G.P. Savidis (Athens: Ermis, 1981) [*Correspondence*]

Stas/Chron = Maria Stasinopoulou, Χρονολόγιο, εργοβιογραφία Γιώργου Σεφέρη (1900–1971) (Athens: Metaichmio, 2000) [*Chronology, Life and Works of George Seferis*]

TetEuth = Περιγραφή του Γιώργου Σεφέρη, *Tetradia Efthynis* 25 (1986) [*Description of George Seferis*]

TGB = George Seferis, Τετράδιο γυμνασμάτων, Β́, ed. G.P. Savidis (Athens: Ikaros, 1976) [*Book of Exercises, II* (posthumous poems)]

X41 = George Seferis, Χειρόγραφο Σεπ. '41, [ed. Alexandros Xydis] (Athens: Ikaros, 1972) [*Manuscript, September 1941*]; reprinted in D3 but without the first editor's notes

X68 = George Seferis, Χειρόγραφο Οκτ. '68, ed. P.A. Zannas (Athens: Diatton, 1986) [*Manuscript, October 1968*]; reprinted in D3 but without the first editor's notes

Yannadakis = Nikos Yannadakis, Κατάλογος βιβλιοθήκης Γιώργου και Μαρώς Σεφέρη (Heraklion: Vikelaia Municipal Library, 1989) [*Catalogue of the Library of George and Maro Seferis*]

6N = George Seferis, Έξι νύχτες στην Ακρόπολη, ed. G.P. Savidis (Athens: Ermis, 1974) [*Six Nights on the Acropolis*]

## II. Unpublished sources

CO = Public Record Office, London, Colonial Office papers

ELIA = Ελληνικό Λογοτεχνικό και Ιστορικό Αρχείο [Hellenic Literary and Historical Archive], Athens: George Seferis papers

FO = Public Record Office, London, Foreign Office papers

G = George Seferis Papers, Gennadius Library, American School of Classical

Studies at Athens [catalogued by Th.D. Frangopoulos, 1975] (see below for files listed)

GN = George Seferis Papers, Gennadius Library, American School of Classical Studies at Athens [current catalogue, in progress, cited for material acquired since 1996] (see below for files listed)

M8 = George Seferis, *Μέρες*, vol. 8 (possibly to be issued as vols. 8 and 9), ed. Katerina Krikos-Davis (Athens: Ikaros, forthcoming). References by permission of the editor

MIET = Μορφωτικό 'Ιδρυμα Εθνικής Τραπέζης [Cultural Foundation of the National Bank], Athens: George Seferis photographic collection. Photographs reproduced by permission of Anna Londou and Dionysis Kapsalis, Director

Princeton = Department of Rare Books and Special Collections, Firestone Library, Princeton University: Selected Papers of George Seferis (C0816)

S/Sherrard = George Seferis and Philip Sherrard, correspondence, ed. Denise Sherrard (Athens: Romiosyni, forthcoming). Quoted by permission of the editor

S/Kats = George Seferis and George Katsimbalis, correspondence; edition by Dimitris Daskalopoulos in progress (citations from typescript prepared by the late G.P. Savidis). Quoted by permission of George Savidis and the editor

S/M2 = Maro [Seferi] and George Seferis, *Αλληλογραφία Β (1944–1959)*; edition by Maria Stasinopoulou in progress. Quoted by permission of the editor

S/Val = Nanos Valaoritis, correspondence with George Seferis and George Katsimbalis, introduction by Avi Sharon, edited with notes by Lila Theodosi (Athens: forthcoming). Quoted by permission of Nanos Valaoritis

StS/cv1945 = Stelios Seferiadis, curriculum vitae enclosed with letter to GS dated 15 September 1945, in G.III.106

Tsatsos/ = Archive of Konstantinos and Ioanna Tsatsos (in the possession of the Tsatsos family): GS = George Seferis papers; IT7 = Ioanna Tsatsou papers (folder 7: George Seferis correspondence); StS = Stelios Seferiadis papers. References and citations by permission of Despina Mylonas

YPEX = Hellenic Republic, Ministry of Foreign Affairs, Service of Diplomatic & Historical Archives, Athens: London Embassy papers (1957–1963)

Vik. (GS cat.) = Βικελαία Δημοτική Βιβλιοθήκη [Vikelaia Municipal Library], Heraklion, Crete: Library of George and Maro Seferis. Library catalogue number follows 'Vik.' 'GS cat.' refers, where relevant, to GS's own numbered record of books acquired between 1923 and 1948 (title page: Γιώργος Σεφεριάδης. Βιβλία μου (αριθμημένη σειρά). Παρίσι1923). Bibliographical information in Yannadakis (see published sources)

Vik./Dip. = Uncatalogued, numbered diplomatic files, kept with the above

413

## George Seferis Papers, Gennadius Library, American School of Classical Studies at Athens. Catalogue by Th.D. Frangopoulos, 1975

*Prefix 'G' (Gennadius) has been added to the file numbers of the archive*

| | |
|---|---|
| G.I.67 | Faculté de Droit, Paris |
| G.I.73 | Certificates and basic biographical details |
| G.I.118 | Medical examinations |
| G.II.5 | Newspaper cuttings 1930–64 |
| G.II.15 | Newspaper cuttings 1967–70 |
| G.II.19 | Newspaper cuttings 1951–55 |
| G.II.25 | Newspaper cuttings: T.S. Eliot |
| G.II.27 | Newspaper cuttings: Valéry and Gide |
| G.II.51 | Newspaper cuttings: Palamas Prize (1946) |

| | | | |
|---|---|---|---|
| G.II.53 | Newspaper cuttings: Palamas Prize, 'Cliques', Theophilos | G.VIII.134 | *Days 1* |
| | | G.VIII.144 | *Logbook [I]* |
| G.II.126 | Miscellaneous printed matter 1914–18, 1918–19 | G.VIII.146 | *Mythistorema, Gymnopaidia* |
| | | G.VIII.147 | *'Thrush'* |
| G.II.127 | Printed mattter 1: 1919–25 | G.VIII.148 | *Book of Exercises* |
| G.III.14 | Correspondence with Ioanna Tsatsou (1948–1949) (sealed) | G.VIII.149 | *...Cyprus, Where It Was Ordained For Me... [Logbook III]* |
| G.III.16 | GS to his mother (Despo Seferiadou) | G.VIII.154 | 'Note-Book (Prose), October 1931–32 or 33' |
| G.III.22 | Angelos Seferiadis to GS | G.VIII.157 | *Turning Point* |
| G.III.75 | Death of GS's father (sealed) | G.VIII.158 | 'Prose, 1936–40' |
| G.III.85 | GS to Angelos Seferiadis | G.VIII.159 | *Days 2* |
| G.III.102 | Ioanna Tsatsou to GS (1929–1962) | G.X.6 | National Radio Station, 1945–6 |
| G.III.104 | Student friends and relatives | G.X.24 | Edouard Herriot, visit to Greece [1929] |
| G.III.105 | Despo Seferiadou to GS (1913–1925) | G.X.39 | Service correspondence 1958–61 |
| G.III.106 | Stelios Seferiadis to GS (1915–1946) | G.X.40 | Service file, 1937–45 |
| | | G.X.41 | Service file, 1945–65 |
| G.IV.43,44 | Correspondence with Takis Papatsonis, and cuttings (1948) | G.X.42 | Service file, 1926–36 |
| G.IV.82 | BBC (1959–1960) | | |

| | |
|---|---|
| G.IV.87 | Correspondence with G. Apostolidis (1955–1962) |
| G.V.2 | Academy of Athens |
| G.V.4 | National Theatre |
| G.V.33 | Correspondence with friends and acquaintances (1926–1930) |
| G.VII.117 | Final illness and death |
| G.VIII.13 | *Days 5* |
| G.VIII.32 | Angelos Seferiadis (correspondence and cuttings) |
| G.VIII.36 | 'Notes on reading' (1934–46) |
| G.VIII.54 | *Apocalypse* |
| G.VIII.56 | 'Poetic drafts 1918–1924' (may not be published) |
| G.VIII.57 | Poems 1916–24 (may not be published) |
| G.VIII.66 | School exercise books 1914–18 |
| G.VIII.88 | *The Cistern* |
| G.VIII.133 | 'The Cats of St Nicholas' |

**George Seferis Papers, Gennadius Library, American School of Classical Studies at Athens. Current catalogue of material acquired since 1996**

*Prefix 'GN' (Gennadius: New) has been added to the file numbers of the archive*

| | |
|---|---|
| GN.I.A3 | 'Scattered notes, 1918–1925' |
| GN.I.A11 | *Logbook II* |
| GN.I.A16 | *Three Secret Poems* |
| GN.I.B1 | 'Alyis Vayias,' 1923 |
| GN.I.B25 | *Six Nights on the Acropolis* (by permission of Katerina Krikos-Davis) |
| GN.I.B54 | *Varnavas Kalostefanos* |
| GN.I.E7 | Note-Book 1948–50 |
| GN.II.A | Correspondence (subfiles: Antoniou, Aronis, Birtles, Bowra, Cardiff, Leigh Fermor, Linnér, Makarios, Runciman, Skeferis) |

## Sources and Abbreviations

| | | | |
|---|---|---|---|
| GN.II.B7 | Ioanna Seferiadou [Tsatsou] to GS, 1919–27 | GN.II.D1 | Nobel correspondence |
| GN.II.B13 | Amaryllis Dragoumi to GS, 1936–40 | GN.II.E | GS correspondence, copies and drafts (files 1–21) |
| | | GN.III.D1 | Pocket diaries (files 1–10) |

# Notes

## Preface

1 Edmund Keeley, *Inventing Paradise: The Greek Journey, 1937–47* (New York: Farrar, Straus and Giroux, 1999), 60–77; David Roessel, *In Byron's Shadow: Modern Greece in the English and American Imagination* (Oxford University Press, 2002), 262–8.

2 Roderick Beaton, *An Introduction to Modern Greek Literature*, 2nd ed. (Oxford University Press, 1999), 252–95.

3 Mark Twain, *Autobiography* (New York, 1924) I 2, twice cited in GS's free Greek translation, and mis-attributed to Emily Dickinson (6N.261; M6.195); M1.21: 2 October 1925; cf. M1.42, citing Valéry, 'Je suis né plusieurs.'

4 P.300 = KS 210: *Three Secret Poems* III, 8.

5 Full bibliography, compiled by Dimitris Daskalopoulos, forthcoming. For files in the Gennadius Library, see p. 413–15.

6 D2.229; cf. pp. 385–7 above.

## 1   Exile from Paradise (1900–1918)

1 X41.8–9.

2 Population estimates for this period vary wildly; there are no reliable figures. See *Murray's Handbook: Asia Minor, Transcaucasia, Persia* (London: Sanforth, 1898), 71; this was the guide used by GS when he returned to Smyrna in 1950, in which the proportion of Greeks to Muslim Turks (more than 50% Greeks, less than 25% Turks) is probably exaggerated. Despite wide discrepancies in figures, all accounts agree that the Greeks were the largest single group in a population of between 200,000 and 250,000. There is a useful summary in the notes to the Greek edition of Charles de Scherzer, *Smyrne: Σμύρνη*, trans. and ed. X. Baloti, 2 vols (Athens: Istoritis, 1995), 1, 310–11.

3 The figure for the Jewish population, given in the locally produced 'History of Beth-Israel Synagogue' (Midhatpaşa Caddesi 265, 35280 Izmir – the only synagogue still functioning) is much higher than in any of the European accounts of the period, but is presumably based on community records.

4 Edmond Boissonas, *Smyrne: photographies* (Geneva: Boissonas, 1919), reproduced, along with the photographs of George Horton, American Consul in Smyrna, in *Smyrna: The City of Smyrna Before the Destruction* (Athens: Nea Synora, A.A. Livani, 1991), with Greek and English text; see also *Smyrna: Metropolis of the Asia Minor Greeks*, published by Ephesos on behalf of the Cultural Foundation of the Bank of Cyprus, 2001. For city plans, with text in Turkish only, see Çinar Atay, *Osmanlı'dan Cumhuriyet'e Izmir planları* (Ankara: Ajans Türk Basin ve Basim, 1998). For description see Marjorie Housepian Dobkin, *Smyrna 1922: The Destruction of a City* (London: Faber, 1972, reprinted

New York: Newmark, 1998), 103–7; historical background in Michael Llewellyn Smith, *Ionian Vision: Greece in Asia Minor 1919–22* (London: Allen Lane, 1973), 21–34. On the commercial background see Elena Frangakis-Syrett, 'Commerce in the Eastern Mediterranean from the Eighteenth to the Early Twentieth Centuries: The City-Port of Izmir and its Hinterland,' *International Journal of Maritime History*, 10 (1998), 125–54.

5  For the period up to March 1924, when Greece adopted the Gregorian (western) calendar it is usual to give dates in two forms: Old Style/New Style (abbreviated to OS/NS). NS dates in the 20th century are thirteen days later than OS. The date of George's birth did not exist in the western calendar, in which 1900 was not a leap year.

6  IT 13–14; M5.196; 211; Atay, *Osmanlı'dan Cumhuriyet'e Izmir planları*, 51.

7  M2.61–5; GS's manuscript notes in G.I.73; an annotated transcription of these notes, with some discrepancies, supplied by the Tsatsos family; genealogical tree by Elli Mylonas dated 28 July 1992. For *'sefer,'* see H.C. Hony and Fahir Iz, *A Turkish-English Dictionary*, 2nd ed. (Oxford: Clarendon Press, 1957) (quoted); amplified but not significantly different in James W. Redhouse, *A Turkish and English Lexicon* (Constantinople: A.H. Boyajian, for the American Mission, 1890), 1061. For GS's self-description as a wanderer throughout his life, see e.g. IT 233: GS to Ioanna, 23 December 1923 ('We are [like] Sinbad the Sailor...'), and M6.237: 24 July 1956 (quotation from Plutarch as 'epigraph for Seferis').

8  Stelios Seferiadis, *Απ' το συρτάρι μου (1895–1912)* (Athens: Pyrsos, 1939), 7–9; G.I.73: transcribed with brief explanatory note by GS.

9  IT 21; Christos Solomonides, *H δημοσιογραφία της Σμύρνης* (Athens: privately printed, 1959), 90; idem, *Ακαδημαϊκοί της Σμύρνης* (Athens: privately printed, 1966), 111.

10  S/T 14–15 [1964].

11  Solomonides, *Ακαδημαϊκοί*, 105; StS/cv1945; G.I.73 (quoted).

12  M2.49: 29 February 1932.

13  IT 15–16; cf. Aronis 13.

14  IT 14–15; G.III.16 (correspondence with mother).

15  G.I.73.

16  IT 10.

17  G.I.73.

18  Stas/Chron 13; D3.241 (Angelos).

19  Solomonides, *Ακαδημαϊκοί*, 105.

20  Solomonides, *Ακαδημαϊκοί*, 129; D1.365.

21  Solomonides, *Ακαδημαϊκοί*, 114, where an extract from the poem is quoted.

22  Nikolaos Ch. Aronis, *Από την ιστορία της παιδείας στη Σμύρνη: το χρονικό της Σχολής Αρώνη* (Athens: privately printed, 1963), 42–45 and 45–6 n.

23  X41.10 (referring to 1913–14).

24  IT 17–18; 19.

25  Aronis (*Από την ιστορία*) includes a line-drawing of the building, and gives the address as Alhambra 9. This was the name of the street, now known by a number, like most of the smaller streets of Izmir, that bounds the French consulate on its southwestern side (Atay, *Osmanlı'dan Cumhuriyet'e Izmir planları*, 51).

26  Full details of the reorganised curriculum are given in Aronis, *Από την ιστορία*, 49–52 and n.

27  Tsatsos/GS.

28  IT 149; Aronis 12 (where the date is given, wrongly, as 1914).

29  AP 55; IT 16.

30  Tsatsos/StS: GS to Stelios, 2 June
    1908.

31  Tsatsos/StS: GS to Stelios,
    September 1908: Anni est sure
    que je pourrai suivre des leçons de
    quatrième cours et que ma chère
    maman perdra son mari et moi je
    serai très content si elle le perdra. Et
    vous mon cher papa en seriez vous
    content?

32  X41. 7–9 (continuation quoted as
    the epigraph to this chapter).

33  See pp. 288–90.

34  IT 25–7.

35  GN.II.E16: GS to Warner, 20 May
    1961.

36  See p. 363.

37  GN.II.E 16: GS to Warner, 20 May
    1961 (quoted); IT 54; 6N.31; see
    also pp. 172–3 above.

38  Rena Stavridi-Patrikiou: personal
    communication (houses on
    waterfront); Keeley/int. 185;
    M4.21–2; IT 27.

**418**  39  M5.199–201; IT 25–9; 53–5; cf.
    P.60–1 = KS 19: *Mythistorema* 15;
    P.64 = KS 21: *Mythistorema* 17, lines
    2, 16–17. The term το πίσω σπίτι, in
    letters from Ioanna to GS when she
    returned to Skala, must refer to this
    house; the larger one facing the sea,
    in which the family seem often to
    have stayed in these early years, is
    not identifiable (GN.II.B7: Ioanna to
    GS, 15 September 1919; 3 September
    1921).

40  M2.64.

41  Maro/diary 74: 12 September 1941.

42  M2.63–4; M5.201; Keeley/int.185;
    M5.225.

43  M4.21–2; M5.195–6; AP 21; P.87–9 =
    KS 42–3: 'Reflections on a Foreign
    Line of Verse,' written 1931, lines
    15–18.

44  Christos Solomonidis, Της Σμύρνης
    (Athens: privately printed, 1957),
    130–9; M2.64–5.

45  Ioanna says that Stelios went to
    Samos in 1908 to help Sofoulis (she

does not say how) in the abortive
revolt of 12 May (IT 19); but if
he had, this would probably have
disqualified him from the rather
different role he did play, in Samos,
in 1912. She also says that in 1912,
when the first Balkan war broke out
in Macedonia, Stelios was ready to
go and fight as a volunteer. In fact,
Stelios was in Samos, exercising his
diplomatic and linguistic skills in
the service of the French consul-
general at Smyrna (see below).

46  On the political and diplomatic
    background to these events, and
    the stand-off between Sofoulis and
    the prime minister, Eleftherios
    Venizelos, see P.J. Carabott, 'The
    Temporary Italian Occupation of
    the Dodecanese: A Prelude to
    Permanency,' *Diplomacy and
    Statecraft* 4 (1993), 285–312
    (pp. 298–9).

47  Kostas I. Ptinis, Αγώνες ελευθερίας:
    συμβολή στην ιστορία της Σάμου
    1900–13, 2nd ed. (Samos, 1994), 241;
    325–31. In the curriculum vitae
    which he sent to GS in 1945, Stelios
    describes his role as *Juriste attaché à
    la Délégation anglo-française-russe,
    chargé de pacifier l'île de Samos
    (1912) et de rédiger une nouvelle
    constitution* (StS/cv1945).

48  Solomonides, Ακαδημαϊκοί, 109; 121.
    Thanasis Papathanasiou, Τα παιδικά
    χρόνια του Γ. Σεφέρη στη Σμύρνη
    (1900–14) (Athens: Kastaniotis,
    2001), 195, cites the Ilios
    Encyclopaedia (n.d., vol. 16, p. 959)
    for the information that Stelios was
    legal counsellor at the French
    consulate during these years.
    Despite its title this book gives no
    information specific to GS or his
    family that is not elsewhere
    available.

49  X41.7; IT 33. Neither is very specific
    about dates, but the 'last two
    summers,' when the family did not

move out to Skala in early June, must be 1913 and 1914, before their departure for Athens in August 1914.

50 Philip Mansel, *Constantinople: City of the World's Desire, 1453-1924* (London: Penguin, 1997), 367-8; Andrew Mango, *Atatürk* (London: John Murray, 1999), 118-22.

51 G.III.16: GS (from Lycée Aroni, Smyrna) to Despo at Grand Hôtel Doré, 3 Blvd Montmartre, Paris, 5 May 1913; X41.9; IT 23-4.

52 X41.9; for the boating expedition see IT 29.

53 X41.7; AP 21; IT 33-4; KT 193.

54 IT 34-5; Aronis 14; cf. M8 appendix; Aronis 15 (photograph).

55 G.VIII.66: D. Goudis, *Η έκθεσις των θερινών εξετάσεων των μαθητών της Β'. του Προτύπου Γυμνασίου* (Athens: privately printed, 1915), 7-8.

56 G.VIII.66, dated 2 March 1915. Below this verse appears a copy, in GS's hand, of his headmaster's monogram, perhaps suggesting that Goudis, not he, may have been its author.

57 These are the books and exercise-books that GS preserved (G.VIII.66).

58 M1.19-20; AP 41-5; S/M1.156-7. Aronis lists Solomos, Kalvos, Palamas, Corneille, Racine, Hugo and Rostand, all of whom GS 'knew by heart' (Aronis 14). Aronis is not a wholly reliable witness to GS's reading, since he wrongly includes T.S. Eliot among the authors read by GS as a student in Paris (Aronis 28).

59 IT 36; Aronis 21; cf. KT 193-4. One of Despo's brothers, Kokos, it seems was also in Athens and a near neighbour (Aronis 13).

60 On the constitutional crisis of 1915 and its consequences see Douglas Dakin, *The Unification of Greece, 1770-1923* (London: Benn, 1972), 209-10; Llewellyn Smith, *Ionian Vision*, 35-61. The dates in these

and other historical accounts of the period in English are New Style, from which 13 days have to be subtracted to give the dates in use in Greece at the time.

61 The only direct source for Stelios' short-lived appointment in 1915 is IT 35, but on this she is clear and unambiguous, and what she says fits both with the political developments and with surviving correspondence which shows that Stelios established himself in Paris not, as she rather vaguely implies, during 1916 (IT 36-7), but at the beginning of December 1915. Both Solomonides, *Ακαδημαϊκοί* and StS/cv1945 mention Stelios' appointment to the university only in 1919. Tsatsos also mentions the appointment in 1915, but here is probably following Ioanna (KT 186).

62 G.III.106: Stelios to GS, 11 December 1915. It is often not possible to tell, in family correspondence between Athens and Paris, whether the old or the new calendar is being used. Stelios sometimes gives double dates, in the form OS/NS, as was normal in official correspondence; GS, his mother and Ioanna never do.

63 G.III.106: Stelios to GS, 6/19 July 1917. A good number, probably the majority, of Stelios' letters to GS are preserved in the Gennadius archive; of GS's letters to his father only the few drafts or copies that he kept are there. The letters that Stelios received, if they are extant, will be in the possession of the Tsatsos family. Very few, however, have so far been identified and catalogued.

64 Aronis 12-14; IT 35. On Ioanna's relationship with Aronis see chapter 2. For Aronis' life (1895-1986) and other details, see Manos Eleftheriou in *I Lexi* 53 (1986), 438.

65 Aronis 12. The programme, which includes the date of the

419

performance, is in the file, now closed, which contains GS's first poems (G.VIII.57). Aronis gives the day as 'St John's' (i.e. 7 January), but the year as 1915 and also includes Stelios among the audience, which would have been true for 1915 but not 1916, the date on the programme. Ioanna does not mention the *Emancipation*, and names the girl only as Melpo (IT 37).

66 GN.I.A3: file 'Notes 1919–24' ('first verse . . .'); IT 37; diary and poems in G.VIII.57, which may not be published; the file is currently closed.

67 GN.II.A (subfile Aronis): Yannis [surname unknown] to GS, 30 August 1916 ('unforgettable time'); cf. Aronis 22; G.III.16: GS to Despo, 12 August 1916 (misdated by GS to '1915;' correct date from postmark) and 19 August 1916; cf. IT 36. In a letter to Aronis, from Paris, GS recalls with unexpected intensity: 'every evening when I accompanied you, dear God be praised for leaving me the memory,' GN.II.A (subfile Aronis): GS to Aronis, deleted draft, no. 13 in file, wrongly dated '1918;' probably written April 1919. In the autobiographical novel *Six Nights on the Acropolis*, the hero, Stratis, answers the question, 'Do you go to the brothel?': ' "I think I have twice altogether," I answered. "The first time when I finished High School, and the second, much later, out of solidarity not to leave a friend in the lurch" ' (6N.22).

68 X41.12 (quoted); Dakin, *Unification*, 214–15 (dates converted to OS).

69 X41.10 (quoted); X41.11; 69–70; cf. Aronis 21–2. Further details graphically presented in G.VIII.57: 'Diary of 1916,' 18 and 19 November [Old Style] = M8 appendix.

70 X41.12; 21.

71 G.I.73, no. 5317: school leaving certificate; GN.II.E1: GS to Stelios (draft), 16 May 1917. It is not clear whether a fair copy was sent, or the letter was abandoned in draft.

72 IT 35–6; Tsatsos/StS: Stelios to Despo, 22 August 1917 (quoted).

73 G.II.126: press cutting, 12 November 1917 (NS); G.III.106: Stelios to GS, 12 January 1918 (NS).

74 IT 38.

75 Aronis 22.

76 G.II.126: press cuttings. Some of these are annotated. The front page of *Patris* for 27 April 1917 has an enthusiastic 'Hurrah!' (Ζήτω) scrawled on it in GS's handwriting. GN.II.E1 contains a draft of GS's response to his father's ballad, with the upper part of the page, perhaps containing a superscription, cut off.

77 IT 38–41; M4.85–6; GN.II.A (subfile Aronis): GS to Aronis, 24 June 1918 (long draft letter); D2.12. M8 appendix (date of arrival, for which IT 41 gives 'the last days of July'). Address in Paris, M7.54: when GS passed through in 1957 the building had been turned into the 'Ceramic Hotel.'

**2   A Student in Paris (1918–1925)**

1 GN.III.D1.

2 D2.12.

3 IT 41; 43 ('That autumn I understood that his passion was going to be poetry'); cf. M8 appendix; G.II.126; G.II.127 (press cuttings).

4 TetEuth 203–4. Dated 'Paris – July 1918.'

5 'Sonnet;' for publication see n. 50 below. The first and last lines of this poem are also copied in the fragmentary letter to Aronis discussed below, dated September 1918. The published dateline, 'Paris, June 1918,' is obviously incorrect. In

reality, the poem must have been written at some point between late July and September. This and other poems mentioned in this chapter are preserved in G.VIII.56; the contents of this file may not be published, but much of the material has already appeared in print, from other sources. Only the published sources are quoted here.

6 TetEuth 189.

7 GN.II.E1: September 1918.

8 GN.II.A (subfile Aronis), fragment of a draft letter dated September 1918, no. 14; file attached to this letter. Later GS recalled, in a letter to Ioanna, both his impetus to write during those first two months in Paris and this incident (IT 154: GS to Ioanna, 25 March 1922).

9 IT 41–7 (p. 41 quoted); D2.12, recollection amplified in 6N.258–9 (discarded diary entry); cf. M8 appendix for GS's moves in November 1918 and March 1919.

10 GN.II.B7: Ioanna to GS, a very rich collection of letters from May 1919 to the end of 1922; G.III.106: Stelios to GS, 6 November 1918.

11 G.II.127: cutting from *Neos Kosmos*. For an overview of Venizelos' efforts in the wider context of the conference, see Margaret MacMillan, *Peacemakers: The Paris Peace Conference of 1919 and Its Attempt to End War* (London: John Murray, 2001), 357–76.

12 GN.II.A (subfile Aronis): no. 13 on file, undated (GS has later added the date '1918,' but other details date this draft letter almost certainly to late March or April 1919); GN.II.A (subfile Aronis): GS to Aronis (draft) 19 February 1919.

13 IT 51 (where the episode is wrongly assigned to 'the end of May'), but see IT 79; GN.III.D1: 2 May 1919.

14 Michael Llewellyn Smith, *Ionian Vision: Greece in Asia Minor*

*1919–22* (London: Allen Lane, 1973), 86–101; MacMillan, *Peacemakers*, 440–4.

15 G.III.16: GS to Despo, 17 May 1919.

16 GN.II.B7: Ioanna to GS, 16 May 1919 [OS], written just after their arrival at Smyrna, which must therefore have been around the 27th or 28th NS.

17 GN.III.D1: 5 May 1919; IT 56. GS was now living at 2, rue de la Sorbonne. The address appears on letters and official documents, from which it appears that he stayed there until July 1920. For the landlady's name see G.III.16: GS to Despo, 12 December 1919; cf. M8 appendix.

18 GN.II.B7: Ioanna to GS, 7 May 1919; 23 October 1919; 3 January 1920; 21 March 1921 [all dates OS].

19 GN.III.D1: 13 May 1919; 13 June 1919; IT 55: GS to Ioanna, 4 August 1919.

20 GN.II.B7: Ioanna to GS, 3 May 1919; 1, 6 and 15 September 1919 [all dates OS].

21 IT 59: GS to Ioanna, 10 October 1919; IT 60: GS to Ioanna, 19 October 1919; IT 64: GS to Ioanna, 16 November 1919; G.III.16: GS to Despo, 7 and 22 October 1919; 12 December 1919; 4 January 1920.

22 GN.III.D1: 12, 16, 17, 18, 26 December 1919 (the last quoted).

23 IT 81; 132; cf. M8 appendix. The relationship was briefly revived, apparently for the last time, during the first months of 1922.

24 G.III.106: Stelios to GS, 4 June 1919; G.I.67: [Professor] André Weisz to 'Monsieur Séfériadès, Professeur à l'Université d'Athènes, 19 Bd Haussmann, Paris,' 4 July 1919; G.I.67: notification of examinations on 2–3 July 1920; cf. IT 80.

25 Llewellyn Smith, *Ionian Vision*, 128–9; MacMillan, *Peacemakers*, 460–1.

26 G.III.16: Stelios to GS, 10 August 1920; IT 46. Ioanna specifies 'Sèvres' but places the event in spring 1919 and includes Angelos (who in the summer of 1920 was in Smyrna) in the party.

27 KT 248; cf. IT 47, both of whom associate the event, wrongly, with the previous year. For a factual account, see Xydis in X41.70 (who gives the date, Old Style, as 30 July); Dimitris Pournaras, *Ελευθέριος Βενιζέλος* (3 vols, Athens: Eleftheros, n.d.), vol. 2, 463–4. GS preserved an autographed photograph, from a Greek newspaper, of Venizelos sitting up in bed in a Paris hospital, dated 18 August 1920 (G.II.127).

28 Llewellyn Smith, *Ionian Vision*, 144; Douglas Dakin, *The Unification of Greece, 1770–1923* (London: Benn, 1972), 228. Dates here are New Style; the corresponding dates in use in Greece at the time (Old Style) are thirteen days earlier.

29 StS/cv1945; GN.II.B7: Ioanna to GS, 19 November 1920; 3 and 11 December 1920 [OS]; IT 88. See also cutting from *Le Temps*, which singles out Seferiadis as a notable loss, dated 20 December 1920 (G.III.16: GS to Despo, 31 December 1921 [sic]).

30 IT 90–3; 104; 124; 127; 162; full text of these letters in Tsatsos/IT7; cf. M8 appendix; photographs in MIET (several with brief messages in French).

31 Poniridy: IT 87, 84, 159; singled out and praised in a letter to Ioanna of 24 October 1920 (IT 87); Adamos: IT 112–13; Aronis 28. GN.II.B7: Ioanna to GS, 27 October 1920 [OS], on receipt of these photographs.

32 GN.II.B7: Ioanna to GS, 21 March 1921 [OS].

33 IT 115, 117; 121; 124–5; 128: GS to Ioanna, 20 May 1921 (quoted); GN.II.E1: GS to Stelios, 21 June 1921 (draft letter, quoted); cf. IT 129–30.

34 G.III.16: GS to Despo, 9 August 1921, giving his arrival as 15 July; IT 138.

35 IT 134–5: GS to Ioanna, from Sceaux, 11 August 1921; GN.II.B7: Ioanna to GS, from Skala, 14 [/27] August 1921; G.III.16: GS to Despo from Sceaux, 4 October 1921.

36 G.III.16: GS to Despo, 1 April 1920; also several letters from March.

37 Llewellyn Smith, *Ionian Vision*, 198–236.

38 G III.16: GS to Despo, from Sceaux, 31 October 1921; cf. IT 139. G.I.67: André Weisz to Stelios, 28 October 1921.

39 IT 139–43; IT 142: GS to Ioanna, 16 November 1921 (quoted).

40 GN.II.A (subfile Aronis), no. 14: 'From the time when I changed[:] 1920 June;' cf. pp. 32–3 above; IT 76–9; cf. IT 60; D2.12–13, which places GS's first acquaintance with the poetry of Laforgue during his first winter in Paris in 1918–19.

41 G.I.67: reader's card dated 20 June 1920; cf. AP 51–2 (Bibliothèque Nationale); on GS's reading at this time, Kohler 45–84; 131–85; cf. S/Keeley 90; D3.263–4 (Proust); G.II.27 (cuttings).

42 Georges Séfériadès [= Seferis], *Jean Moréas, conférence faite à Paris pour l'Association des Etudiants Hellènes, le 18 mars 1921*. Texte établi, présenté et annoté par Polyxène Goula-Mitakou, traduit en collaboration avec J.-P. Bouniol (Athens: privately printed, 1990), 28; G.I.67: *Association des Etudiants Hellènes de Paris*, Carte de Membre Actif, 1920–21, dated October 1920. For Adamos' role, see *Jean Moréas*, 13; IT 112.

43 IT 73: GS to Ioanna, 9 January 1920, but the year should surely be 1921: compare IT 74–5, all of which belongs to 1921, not 1920.

44  *Jean Moréas*, (lecture delivered 18 March 1921). For the description of the MS see pp. 14–17; line numbers refer to the edition.

45  *Jean Moréas*, 30; 36, lines 180–5; 40, lines 295–300; 42, lines 311–13 (cf. IT 110–12); 44, lines 363–5 (quoted). The ground is traversed in more detail, but with a surprising similarity of coverage and approach, in what seems to be the standard modern work on Moréas: John Davis Butler, *Jean Moréas* (The Hague: Mouton, 1967).

46  *Jean Moréas*, 34, lines 163–4; cf. GN.I.A3: file 'Notes 1919–24' and p. 27 above; *Jean Moréas*, 48, lines 462–5.

47  *Jean Moréas*, 54, lines 557–61.

48  *Jean Moréas*, 54–8.

49  *Jean Moréas*, 80–2, lines 1070, 1074–6, 1078–80; cited edited form in IT 112.

50  The text of the poem and details of its publication in *Vomos*, 1–2 (25 January 1922), 14 are reproduced by G.P. Savidis, Εφήμερον σπέρμα (Athens: Ermis, 1978), 35; text only in TetEuth 193.

51  IT 151: GS to Ioanna, 20 February 1922; D3.66. *Ulysses* was first published by Beach in Paris on 2 February 1922.

52  IT 142. The address appears in correspondence first as Mavromataion 2, later as Kyvelis 2. Cf. S/T 14: the 'old apartment block,' in 1929, is surely not the anonymous though fairly elderly concrete apartment block which stands on the site today.

53  G.III.22: GS to Angelos, 2 March 1922. For the decision that Angelos should study in Paris see G.III.16: GS to Despo, 5 February 1922, in which he touchingly expresses the hope that we'll 'make a family again;' cf. IT 160.

54  Llewellyn Smith, *Ionian Vision*, 254–5.

55  G.III.16: GS to Despo, 22 April 1922.

56  G.III.16: GS to Despo, 2 March 1922; GS to Stelios (draft or copy), 15 March 1922; GS to Despo, 8 May 1922.

57  IT 122; 126; GN.II.B7: Ioanna to GS, 17 February 1922 [OS] (quoted).

58  G.III.16: GS to Despo, 22 April 1922; G.III.106: Stelios (Paris) to GS (Dresden), 3 July 1922.

59  G.III.16: GS (Paris) to Despo (Dresden), 11 July (letter) and 16 July 1922 (telegram); IT 163–4 (quoted).

60  IT 164–68. In his pocket-diary, GS has noted the departure of his mother and Ioanna against the last date of the wrong month (GN.III.D1: 31 July 1922). GS's first letter to Despo (see next note) was written on 3 September; M8 appendix gives what must be the correct date of departure, 31 August.

61  GN.II.E1: GS to Despo, 3 September 1922.

62  Marjorie Housepian Dobkin, *Smyrna 1922: The Destruction of a City* (London: Faber, 1972, reprinted New York: Newmark, 1998), 120–208; Llewellyn Smith, *Ionian Vision*, 284–311; the earliest eye-witness account that GS must have read is René Puaux, *La Mort de Smyrne* (Paris: La Revue des Balkans, 1922; Greek translation Athens: Eirmos, 1992). The facts as given here are accepted by Andrew Mango, *Atatürk* (London: John Murray, 1999), 343–7, who also places them judiciously in the context of contemporary and subsequent Turkish perspectives.

63  G.III.16: GS to Despo, 17 September 1922.

64  G.III.105: 22 September 1922 (telegram); IT 174–5.

423

424

65 Llewellyn Smith, *Ionian Vision*, 312–36; G.III.16: GS to Despo, 13 December 1922; X41.19.

66 IT 201–2: GS to Ioanna, 28 November 1922 (quoted); cf. IT 182: GS to Ioanna, 2 November 1922. For the poem, 'Nocturne,' see IT 183–4.

67 IT 178–9; G.III.16: GS to Despo, 18 November 1922; G.III.106: Stelios (Athens) to GS (Paris), 31 December 1922 [/12 January 1923].

68 IT 215 (quoted). The only published source for Jacqueline's surname is Aronis 29, where it appears misspelt as 'Pouillolon,' here corrected from GN.III.D9: GS's Paris address book. Date of first meeting, GN.I.B1, on which see below.

69 GN.II.E2: GS to Edouard Herriot (draft), 7 November 1932 (quoted); for GS on Jacqueline's father see M1.82; M2.86–7; G/Apost 157: GS to Apostolidis, 28 September 1932.

70 MIET: photographs at Bois de Boulogne, 9 February 1923; at Le Vésinet (with Aronis and his wife Androniki, including those reproduced by Aronis), 12 October 1923; G.III.106: Stelios to GS, 20 January 1923; G.III.16: GS to Despo, 13 February, 5 March and 18 April 1923; Despo to GS, 15 June 1923.

71 IT 165 (episode at the Ritz); GN.II.A (subfile Aronis): Aronis to GS, 23 March 1923 (quoted); GN.II.B7: Ioanna to GS, 6 April 1923 [OS]; Aronis 27; 37; IT 159 (quoted). It is no doubt revealing of Ioanna's feelings, fifty years later, that she never mentions the presence of Aronis and his wife in Paris.

72 IT 217: GS to Ioanna, 27 March 1923; cf. MIET album, no. 3; Ministry of Culture, Multimedia exhibition (2000), 32; Aronis 31.

73 Aronis 29 (quoted); M1.13–14; Kohler, 25: 'une jeune femme destinée à devenir une brillante pianiste' (no source given).

74 GN.I.B1: title page, dated 11 March 1923, followed by 4 double pages dated 13 March (p. 4r quoted); second draft dated 24 March (on unhappiness in her company and parting); IT 219 (quoted).

75 IT 226–8; 232. On GS's attitude to marriage see pp. 122; 184–5 above.

76 M2.45: 23 February 1932. Jacqueline's age is given as eighteen in GS's letter to Ioanna of 17 February 1923 (IT 215), and this is surely correct.

77 G.III.16: GS to Despo, 31 March 1923; IT 219–20 (quoted). Postponement of examinations, G.III.16: Despo to GS, 15 June 1923.

78 Aronis 37–8.

79 G.III.16: GS to Despo, 18 May and 18 July 1923; IT 220–1: GS to Ioanna, 23 July 1923. MIET contains several photographs which show that GS, Angelos and Stelios were together in Brittany, one is published in *I Lexi* 53 (1986), 189; MIET: prints of Jacqueline marked on the back 'Spa, August 1923.'

80 G.III.16: GS to Despo, 15 September 1923; IT 226; M4.107; for the illness see G.I.118: summary medical history (report on medical examination, 5 October 1970), and M8 appendix; G.III.16: GS to Despo, 17 October 1923; '*Notre premier anniversaire*,' GN.III.D1: 20 October 1924.

81 G.III.16: GS to Despo, 22 November 1922; Aronis 35 (quoted).

82 IT 239; D3.237–45.

83 GN.II.B7: Ioanna to GS, 18 January 1920 ('because before long it will be your turn to go through this competition'); G.III.16: GS to Despo, 6 January and 26 February 1924 (the latter quoted).

84 GN.III.D1: 12 July 1924; 26 June 1924 (quoted); GN.II.E1: GS to Stelios, 16 December 1924 (dated draft, quoted). G.X.42 confirms that GS's highest academic qualification

was the *Diplôme de Licencié en Droit* (or bachelor's degree), awarded on 27 October 1921.

85 G.III.16: GS to Despo, 12 June 1924 (quoted); cf. 16 June, 6 July 1924.

86 IT 235; GN.III.D1: 14 April 1924. The poem is preserved in GN.I.A3.

87 GN.III.D1: 3 July 1924; G.III.16: GS to Despo, 6 July 1924 (photographs of this occasion in MIET); GN.III.D1: 23 July 1924 (departure of Marie-Louise and Jacqueline), 1 and 2 August 1924; Aronis 38; cf. IT 239 (who makes no mention of Aronis or his wife).

88 G.III.16: GS to Despo, 12 August 1924; S/L 67–8: GS to Lorenzatos, 26 May 1949.

89 Maro/int. 197.

90 G.III.16: GS to Despo, 1 September 1924; G.III.85: GS to Angelos, 1 September 1924; GN.III.D1; GN.II.E12: GS to Joan Rayner, 24 December 1954 (quoted) = Fotis Dimitrakopoulos, Σεφέρης, Κύπρος, επιστολογραφικά και άλλα (Athens: Kastaniotis, 2000), 156–8; M3.104 (quoted).

91 M1.37; G.III 16: GS to Despo, 25 September 1924.

92 G.III.104: Petros [Adamos] to GS, 12 October 1924; GN.III.D9: Paris address book.

93 G.III.16: Stelios to GS, 26 October, 3 November 1924 (on finding an English teacher); GN.III.D1 (press announcements of concerts). El Greco, M1.37; M2.33; D1.101; D2.10. Other memories, M3.129, also recalled at M1.37 and 6N.70.

94 G.III.85: GS to Angelos, 7 October 1924; M1.27–36.

95 G.III.85: GS to Angelos, 16 October 1924; GN.II.E12: GS to Joan Rayner, 24 December 1954 (see n. 90); GN.I.A3: 11 November 1924.

96 P.15–16 = KS 237–8; G.VIII.157, nos 6053–4.

97 GN.II.E1: GS to Stelios, 16 December 1924 (undated, unfinished

pencil draft of the letter that bears this date).

98 GN.III.D1; M1.82; G.III.16: Despo to GS, 29 January 1925 (quoted).

99 GN.IV.B9: 15 June 1919 (article by P. Loti in *Information*); 9 [/22] June 1919 (reply by Stelios in *Journal des Hellènes*). Return to Greece, M1.7; M2.49.

3   **Servant of Two Masters (1925–1931)**

1   Yorgos Yannakopoulos (ed.), *Refugee Greece: Photographs from the Archive of the Centre for Asia Minor Studies* (Athens: A.G. Leventis Foundation, Centre for Asia Minor Studies, 1992); Dimitri Pentzopoulos, *The Balkan Exchange of Populations and its Impact on Greece* (London: C. Hurst, 2002, with a new introduction by Michael Llewellyn Smith; first published 1962); Renée Hirschon (ed.), *Crossing the Aegean: An Appraisal of the 1923 Compulsory Population Exchange between Greece and Turkey* (Oxford and New York: Berghahn, 2003).

2   D1.77 (Ford buses). Political background, George Th. Mavrogordatos, *Stillborn Republic* (University of California Press, 1983), 30–4; Richard Clogg, *A Short History of Modern Greece*, 2nd ed. (Cambridge University Press 1986), 124 ('opera bouffe,' quoted). GS's commentary, X41.16–18; G.VIII.159: GS to Lou[kia Fotopoulou], 16 April 1933 ('Mr Kronos, having nothing else to do, was so kindly disposed to communism that finally communism came to Greece. According to the new ideas, Modern Greek men and women would change sleeping partner every night so as to counteract the sense of duration in sexual relationships, which belongs to the outmoded atavism of the bourgeoisie.')

425

3  G.VIII.134: signed note, dated 1967, on the cover of the edited typescript of *Days 1*; cf. S/L 106; 110–11 (reworking in 1949–50); M6.39 (reworking in the 1950s); 6N.255–62 (Savidis). The surviving early drafts of this novel (GN.I.B25) are temporarily in the possession of Dr Katerina Krikos-Davis, to whom I am grateful for the opportunity to examine them. Published evidence for the nature and content of the novel before it was abandoned in 1930 can be found in S/M1.191–2 and Nadia Charalambidou, Μια εξερεύνηση γύρω από το φεγγάρι, τις Έξι νύχτες στην Ακρόπολη και την επικοινωνία. Μια περίπτωση διακειμενικότητας, in Πρακτικά Συμποσίου Σεφέρη (Αγία Νάπα, 14–16 Απριλίου 1988) (Nicosia, 1991), 79–147, see p. 137 n. 95. On the relationship between M1 and 6N, see Nasos Vayenas, 'Seferis' *Six Nights on the Acropolis:* The Diary as Novel,' in Roderick Beaton (ed.), *The Greek Novel, A.D. 1 – 1985* (London: Croom Helm, 1988), 54–62; Alexandra Samouil, *Ο βυθός του καθρέφτη: ο André Gide και η ημερολογιακή μυθοπλασία στην Ελλάδα* (Crete University Press: Heraklion, Crete, 1998), 241–58; Roderick Beaton, 'Seferis and the Novel: A Reading of *Six Nights on the Acropolis,' Byzantine and Modern Greek Studies,* 25 (2001), 156–84, see pp. 167–9.

4  M1.20: 27 September 1925; M1.13: 22 August 1925.

5  M1.40: 3 January 1926; cf. 6N.16; X41.11–12; M1.95: November 1927; part of the same passage also appears at 6N.35; cf. S/M 1.191–2: GS to Maro, 14 May 1937.

6  D1.168 (1941, quoting D.I. Antoniou).

7  Begun in September 1925 (M1.15), published *Nea Estia* 4 (1 and 15 July 1928), 600–3; 652–5. On the imperfections of this version see Kohler, 177–9. The version included in *Antigrafes* was substantially revised in 1963.

8  G.VIII.145 (fair copy of *Paludes*); cf. M1.79. Translation of *Le Prométhée mal enchaîné*, S/L 36; M7.146. Other translations, M1.63: 1 June 1926; M1.89–91: September 1927; M1.79–81: 10 October 1926. Translations destroyed: M1.79; 89–91: September 1927.

9  See esp. M1.79–80; 89–91; cf. IT 257–8.

10  GN.III.D1: 19 March, 12 December 1926 (Poniridy); cf. IT 246; MIET (photographs).

11  M1.10; 11; 13–14; 39; 78; 82; 84–5 (where she is called 'Bi'); 6N.65–66; 97–8 ('F'). M1.72: 15 August 1926 (quoted).

12  GN.III.D1: 5 March 1926.

13  IT 301: GS to Ioanna, 23 February 1932; the significance of this passage is obscured in context, since Ioanna gives her own version of the later stages of GS's relationship with Jacqueline, on which see below. 'Tragic experience . . .' M2.99: 29 January 1932. 'Introspection,' M2.32: 20 December 1931.

14  6N.227; M1.26: 30 December 1925; P.60–1 = KS 19: *Mythistorema* 15, lines 16–19.

15  G.III.106: Stelios to GS, 27 November and 22 December 1924 (postponements); Matthew 6.24, 31–2 = M1.10–11: 12 August 1925 (quoted).

16  IT 246–7; M1.40: 8 February 1926.

17  M1 passim; M5.171; for Alain, see Kohler, 149–59; for Rilke, see n. 34.

18  Homer, S/Keeley 90; S/Kar.153. The first two volumes of Bérard's edition and translation of the *Odyssey* (1924) appear as Vik. (GS cat.) 558–61 [1924–1925]; see also

19 Yannadakis, 357. Makriyannis and Solomos, IT 247; AP 77–8.

19 M1.63–4; IT 248; GN.III.D1: 7 June 1926 (house taken); 12 June 1926 (Stelios' departure); GN.III.D1: 11 November 1926 (Stelios' return).

20 M1.74: 24 August 1926; Mavrogordato, *Stillborn Republic*, 33–4; IT 248–51; M1.77.

21 IT 251–3. M1 gives very little indication of these events, but see M1.63; 76; nothing of GS's family life is carried over into 6N.

22 M1.72: 15 August 1926 (quoted); M1.82: 26 October 1926.

23 IT 253; G.X.42: undated handwritten 'service diary;' GN.III.D1: 21 December 1926.

24 X41.70; PE2.XI; G. X.42 (as previous note). The statue by Theodoros Papayannis was erected 2001, after photographs from the late 1960s.

25 IT 262.

26 Anna Sikelianou, *Η ζωή μου με τον 'Αγγελο* (Athens: Estia, n.d.), 50–1; 56; Maro/int. 201; Kleon Paraschos, *Προβλήματα λογοτεχνίας* (Athens: Zarvanos, 1964), 103–5 (first published 1939); S/M1.348. For her musical interests and tastes see Loukia Fotopoulou, *Μουσικές σελίδες* (Athens: Ippalektryon, 1939).

27 Respectively: 6N.39; 37; 130; 19; 42; 37 (all noted by Charalambidou, *Μια εξερεύνηση*, 118–19); 6N.66–7; 113.

28 Lou's bisexuality is already implied in the allusions to *Corydon* (Gide's testament in favour of homosexuality) included in the published version of M2:125, 126. For explicit references in the original letters, see G.VIII.159: GS to Lou, 3 February 1933 ('I'm really sorry about your girlfriend; I felt it as though she'd been mine'); 2 April 1933 = M2.117: after the first sentence on *Corydon* the original letter continues: 'I've a lot of work

to do yet on this aspect of your character.' GS's promiscuity during the summer of 1927, GN.III.D1: 13 August 1927 ('What do you think of Sofia? I hope I'm going to love her too.') Following this four pages have been excised. Other entries at this time consist of the names of different girls. See also IT 268.

29 M1.69–70: 15 and 16 July 1926 (since the incident narrated in the latter entry happened 'the other day in the afternoon,' the feelings described in the former must be in part the *consequence* of the incident narrated in the latter); 6N.37–8. The fantasy elaborated in the poem 'Automobile' may derive in part from this, in part from the related entry at M1.73: 9 August 1926; P.12 (KS 234) = G.VIII.157, nos 6005–8, where the earliest (very rough) draft of 'Automobile' bears the date '10 August 1926. Kifisia;' cf. M1.71: 12 August 1926 ('This month I've begun an exercise-book of *contrerimes*'). For GS's gloss on this poem see S/Kats 12 November 1931 = *Nea Estia*, 108/1278 (1980), 1369; S/Apost 353: GS to Louis Roussel, 13 November 1932.

30 6N.61–9; cf. 268 (fictionally, the action takes place in 1928); GN.III.D1: 1–5 April 1927; M1.87: 2 April 1927; Anna Sikelianou: interview (LF's semi-basement and address); George Savidis: interview (explanation of 'cistern' in M1). See also 6N.61 (description of Salome's 'semi-basement); 6N.244, where another basement is metaphorically called a 'cistern;' the immediately juxtaposed word φωτισμένα (lighted) is one of many coded puns on the name Fotopoulou in the novel. A further link between Lou and the word 'cistern' comes from Wilde's *Salomé*, in which John the Baptist's

427

428

prison is called a *citerne* (see
S/M1.173 and 176 n. 2).

31  GN.III.D1: 11 May 1927 ('Loukidi,'
Lou's married name); 'Lou' for the
first time on 4 June; cf. 8 June,
where the indication 'June–Aug.
1926' seems to confirm the period of
their first acquaintance.

32  IT 259. Ioanna and Stelios left
Athens for Paris on 11 June 1927
(GN.III.D1), which places Ioanna's
first meeting with Jacqueline just
after the middle of June.

33  IT 212; cf. IT 262; 268–9. See also
S/Apost 95: GS to Apostolidis, 31
March 1932, quoted on p. 111.

34  Stratis' introspection in the novel,
6N.226–8. Negative aspects of
Salome, 6N.24 ('*amorale*'); 6N.66;
236 (she calls her breasts 'wolf-cubs,'
λυκοπούλα); 6N.65 (nipples as 'dog-
teeth,' σκυλόδοντα); 6N.120
('labyrinth'); 6N.185–93 (Minotaur).
Wilde's *Salomé*, IT 103: GS to
Ioanna, 9 February 1921 and
6N.163–5. Another literary link
between the names 'Lou' and
'Salome' comes from the life and
work of Rilke, who had just died,
and on whom GS kept a number
of cuttings, from 1926 and 1927;
thematically, some of these can be
linked with *The Cistern* (GN.IV.B11).
Rilke had had a passionate affair
with an older woman, Lou Andreas-
Salomé, to whom he had later
dedicated poems; see Stéphane
Michaud, *Lou Andreas-Salomé.
L'Alliée de la vie* (Paris: Seuil, 2000).
There is an uncanny biographical
parallel with the use to which
Lawrence Durrell would later put
the same literary precedent, see Ian
MacNiven, *Lawrence Durrell, A
Biography* (London: Faber, 1999),
588.

35  M1.95–9: 26 December 1927; cf.
107–8: September 1928. On GS's use
of this Latin text, in 6N and

elsewhere, see Michael Paschalis,
Σεφέρης και Απουλήιος: η μετάφραση
των Μεταμορφώσεων και οι 'Εξι νύχτες
στην Ακρόπολη, Dodoni: Philologia
(University of Ioannina), 30 (2001),
80–106.

36  'Princess Lu,' M1.91–3: 1 October
1927. For the Far Eastern
connection: white as the colour of
mourning (M1.91); see also M1.119
and the haiku addressed to 'Lou'
(M1.109). An unpublished portion
of a letter to Lou, soon after GS's
arrival in London in 1931, further
confirms the identification
(G.VIII.159: GS to Lou, 12
September 1931. PS: 'I'm thinking
of the little princess of China'). The
episode, and the story, are recalled
in M2.53: [GS to Lou], 11 April
1932; M2.89–90: [GS to Lou], 18
September 1932; and M2.134: [GS to
Lou], 4 May 1933. Later, when the
'Stratis Thalassinos' poems were in
press, after Lou's death, GS noted in
his diary 'The princess of China
would have been pleased' (M3.169:
15 February 1940). The prose
poem, 'Nijinsky,' P.111–3
= KS 65–6; Nasos Vayenas, Ο ποιητής
και ο χορευτής: μια εξέταση της
ποιητικής και της ποίησης του Σεφέρη
(Athens: Kedros, 1979), 60–76. In
*Six Nights,* too, Stratis, on first
seeing Salome naked, had been
suddenly reminded of the Russian
dancer (6N.66).

37  P.10 = KS 232: 'Slowly You Spoke';
G.VIII.157, nos 6001 (MS); 6106
(typescript): epigraph = *Odyssey* V
225–8.

38  S/T 119–21: Theotokas to GS, 28
November 1932; cf. S/Apost 95: GS
to Apostolidis, 31 March 1932; P.37–9
= KS 255–9: *The Cistern*, lines 2,
111–5; see also pp. 112–13 above.

39  M1.122–4: 31 July 1930; although
the original has not been preserved,
a letter with this date and

description ('letter in vain') is listed in G.VIII.159 among the letters to Lou (see also n. 83).

40 M1.68; M2.28, 83 (Poniridy); G.V.33: Adamos to GS, 28 October 1925; Aronis 11; 38–44; cf. *I Lexi* 53 (1986), 438; M1.137 (Aronis).

41 S/Kats: GS to Katsimbalis, 31 March 1937; Katsimbalis to GS, 14 August 1951 (on the deaths of their respective fathers).

42 G.P. Savidis, *Εφήμερον σπέρμα* (Athens: Ermis, 1978), 291–7; Theodore Stephanides, Σε ανάμνηση του Γιώργου Κ. Κατσίμπαλη, *Nea Estia*, 108/1278 (1980), 1406–8; Angelos Katakouzinos, Γιατί δεν έγραψε ο Γιώργος Κατσίμπαλης; *Nea Estia*, 108/1278 (1980), 1398–1405.

43 First acquaintance: Stelios to GS, 5 May 1922, refers to the young Katsimbalis, who was then studying at Montpellier, in terms that reveal he and GS had not yet met (G.III.106). Recollections, respectively, S/Kats: GS to Katsimbalis, 18 December 1931 and Katsimbalis to GS, 1 January 1932 (the latter = Savidis, *Εφήμερον σπέρμα*, 294); Katsimbalis to GS, 6 December 1924 = Dimitris Daskalopoulos, 'Αγαπητέ μου Γιώργο': η αλληλογραφία Γ.Κ. Κατσίμπαλη – Γιώργου Σεφέρη (1924–1970),' in M. Pieris (ed.), Γιώργος Σεφέρης: φιλολογικές και ερμηνευτικές προσεγγίσεις (Athens: Patakis, 1997), 219–25, see pp. 221–2; S/Kats: Katsimbalis to GS, 27 November 1927. See also D1.77–8; M1.79: 13 October 1926 (the latter referring presumably to both father and son), but the emphasis before 1927 is on the father.

44 IT 297; Henry Miller, *The Colossus of Maroussi* (Harmondsworth: Penguin, 1950; 1st ed. 1941), 40–3; Edmund Keeley, *Inventing Paradise: The Greek Journey, 1937–47* (New York: Farrar, Straus and Giroux, 1999), 51–4.

45 Miller, *Colossus*, 31; 32.

46 Keeley, *Inventing Paradise*, 53–5.

47 Keeley/int. 199 (1968).

48 S/T 11–13; 26 (the relationship after WWII); IT 271–2; D2.293–305.

49 P.87–8 = KS 41; cf. S/T 18. The poem was first published in May 1935. (But see p. 43 above for GS's earliest, unpublished experiments with free verse.)

50 S/T 76–85: GS to Theotokas, 26 January 1932; Theotokas to GS, 1 February 1932.

51 S/T 13.

52 G.A. Apostolidis, Τον καιρό της Στροφής, in *Για τον Σεφέρη, Τιμητικό αφιέρωμα στα τριάντα χρόνια της Στροφής* (Athens: Konstantinidis and Michalas, 1961), 15–17; S/Apost 14–15 and passim. Photographs: MIET album, no. 19; S/Apost 26.

53 IT 298: GS to Ioanna, 2 November 1931; M2.78: [GS to Lou], 3 July 1932; S/Apost 164: GS to Charoula Poseidon, 25 October 1932; S/M1.94: GS to Maro, 21 January 1937; S/M1.210: GS to Maro, 4 June 1937. The house in Agras Street, S/Apost 11–13; G.IV.87; many references also in S/M2.

54 M1.104–5: 8 March 1928; but see PE2.XI, which gives the dates of this mission as 24–29 March. For the disparaging reference to human activity, see also D1.58, both passages probably derived from Marcus Aurelius, *Meditations* II.16: 'For a human soul, the greatest of self-inflicted wrongs is to make itself . . . a kind of tumour or abscess on the universe . . . ,' trans. Maxwell Staniforth (Harmondsworth: Penguin, 1964).

55 M1.106: 1 April 1928; P. 14 = KS 236. The first draft of this poem is dated, in the MS, 20 March 1928 (G.VIII.157; no. 6010).

429

430

56 IT 263–9; cf. KT 194; Mavrogordato, *Stillborn Republic*, 36–41.

57 D1.167 (1941); see K. G. Karyotakis, Ποιήματα και πεζά, ed. G.P. Savidis (Athens: Ermis, 1972), 205–6 (for the poem 'Preveza').

58 IT 43; 95–6; 103; 158; G.II.5: newspaper cuttings on attempted suicides, dated between 1921 and 1930.

59 IT 264; M1.107.

60 M3.132; 6N.21; 264; S/Kats: GS to Katsimbalis, 14 April 1958 ('Mathios Paskalis was born in Athens the summer of the dengue fever'); cf. S/Apost 70–1: GS to Apostolidis, 20 December 1931; M2.96: [GS to Lou,] 26 January 1933.

61 Compare the name with GS's rendering of Apuleius' 'Byrrhena' at M1.97. Probably this was also the addressee of the poem 'Scholia' (P.19–20, omitted from KS), described at IT 269; earliest preserved draft dated 10 June 1928 (G.VIII.157, nos 6046–8). For the whereabouts of Lou see GN.II.E1: GS to Loukia Fotopoulou, 26 July 1928 (the only letter preserved from before 1930, and strictly formal).

62 P.81–2 = KS 39–40, lines 9–10; 19–20. First published as the opening poem in *Book of Exercises* (1940); cf. IT 264; M1.107. The manuscript has the dedication, on the back: 'For Verina, the companion who was forgotten [or: who forgot herself] along with me. M.P.' (G.VIII.147, no. 4130).

63 M1.109: 9 May 1929.

64 Haiku, M2.20: [GS to Lou,] 3 November 1931; S/Kats: GS to Katsimbalis, 14 January 1932; P.90–3 = KS 44–7: 'Sixteen Haiku'; M1.109–10; 133; 135. Pantun, P.83–4 = KS 263–4: 'Pantoum,' first published in *Nea Estia*, 11 (January 1932), 59–60; earliest dated draft, entitled 'Old Songs, 1,' 31 January

1931 (G.VIII.157, no. 5996); cf. M2.29.

65 According to a note dated 15 August 1954, *Six Nights* 'began in the summer of 1926 (26 May)' (6N.256). This unusually precise recollection may have been prompted by the account of a visit to the Acropolis by moonlight which appears in M1.60, with the date 'Saturday 28 May 1926.' However, 28 May was a Saturday not in 1926 but in 1927; the entry in M1, on which the later recollection is surely based, has almost certainly been misdated in the transcription and editing of the diary. If this is so, then the visits to the Acropolis by moonlight began at the same time as the relationship with Lou (as is also the case with Stratis and Salome in the novel), and the novel was begun shortly afterwards. Confirmation for this comes from GN.I.B25, where the cover of the folder containing the early drafts bears the date '1927–1930.' Dated references to the novel's progress are found at M1.94–5: November 1927; M1.103: 26 January 1928. According to 6N.256, the first draft 'faded out around 1930.' In fact, 1930 is the date of the latest events in GS's life to be used in the story (see below); the last reference to the first draft comes in S/Apost 33: GS to Apostolidis, 21 September 1931 (GS intends, but apparently fails, to 'work a little on my "novel-with-many-characters"').

66 M1.107: 20 September 1928; IT 265–6; KT 186–8.

67 P.17–18 = KS 239–40, lines 1–4; 10; 13–16; G.VIII.157, nos 6049–52 (title: ζκίνημα). Cf. pp. 32–3 above.

68 IT 273: GS to Ioanna, 27 June 1929. Later in the summer, Ioanna spent two weeks in Paris and saw Jacqueline often (IT 278).

69 G.X.24, from which the above narrative is drawn; drafts of George's letters to Herriot, and photographs, in GN.II.E1. See also IT 275: GS to Ioanna, 19 July; 14 September 1929; E. Herriot, *Sous l'olivier* (Paris: Hachette, 1930), 316.

70 D3.92–3; Kohler, 224–7; Denis Kohler, *Georges Séféris*, series: *Qui êtes-vous?* (Lyon: La Manufacture, 1989), 11–12.

71 IT 280; M1.115: 29 October 1929; cf. M1.111 (quoted, rejected from the final poem); the title 'Stopping' (Σταμάτημα), links the poem in this form to 'The Mood of a Day' (entitled 'Starting Out;' see p. 87); G.VIII.157, no. 6016 (MS dated 18–28 October 1929).

72 P.13 = KS 235; MS dated 18 October 1929 (G.VIII.157, no. 6000).

73 IT 262; 283; KT 188–9. Photographs of Ioanna in 1920 and 1930 in KT, plate opposite 225; contrast opposite 209.

74 Details respectively in KT 20–1; 67–8; 121; 123; 178–80; 'womanizer,' KT 39; 421–4 and passim; see also editors' note, KT 10.

75 G.III.85: GS to Angelos, 15 June 1930 (quoted). M1.120: 21 June 1930; G.X.42: 22 July 1930, confirming a month's leave from the 28th, cut short on 12 August; M1.121–7; IT 283–6; KT 189.

76 IT 307: GS to Ioanna, 29 June 1932 ('happiest interludes'). On Skiathos and Sotiris, M1.127 (quoted); M2.32; 6N.221–3, 228–30, 232–5; IT 285; GN.I.E7: draft start of new essay on Makriyannis, dedicated to the memory Sotiris N. Stamelos, 'in memory of Skiathos 1930;' P.87–9 = KS 42–3; P.189 = KS 137; also recalled at S/M1.115: GS to Maro, 7 February 1937.

77 *Odyssey*, M1.125; IT 286, 307. *Ulysses*, S/T 14, which shows that GS read both the *Odyssey* and

Joyce's modern re-enactment during 1930; see also M2.81; M4.10; D1.20; 340. *Ulysses* (in the French translation of 1930) = Vik. 3087 (GS cat. 852); with the book is an advertising leaflet dated by GS to 10 December 1929; the book shows signs of having been carefully read; it must have been acquired during the first half of 1930.

78 M1.122–4: [GS to Lou,] 31 July 1930 (see also nn. 39 and 83).

79 IT 286.

80 'Bilio's island,' 6N.219–39 (details shared with M1 describing Skiathos, but also memories of Skala, e.g. 6N.222: the three uninhabited islands; 6N.237: the open cave). Lala is described: she is twenty-two in 1927 (Jacqueline's age) (6N.39); well-built (6N.38–9; 80; 159); her voice is crystalline (6N.130); she speaks slowly, her words emerging 'round like beads' (6N.81, 233); she is notable for her air of calm (6N.127; 202), serenity (6N.9–10; 236), innocence and naiveté (6N40, 50, cf. 29, 79); but also profoundly perceptive (6N.175; 189–91) (all these details listed by Charalambidou, Μια εξερεύνηση, 118–19). Lala tends to be silent while others are speaking (6N.12). All these characteristics are consistent with the accounts of Jacqueline by Ioanna and Aronis, and with Jacqueline's appearance in photographs. Only Lala's blonde hair (6N.39) does not fit. Her affinity with trees (6N.162–3; 242) closely echoes the imagery of *Mythistorema* 15, one of the group of poems written around the time of Jacqueline's marriage (see pp. 125–6). For 'Lili,' see Charalambidou, Μια εξερεύνηση, 137 n. 95; for 'Krinoula,' p. 55 above.

81 PE2.XI: 10 December 1929; S/Kats: Katsimbalis to GS, 26 April 1930;

431

IT 286: GS to Ioanna, 15 August 1930.

82 M1.128.

83 Mission to Geneva, PE2.XI: 5 September to 8 October 1930; G.X.42. GS preserved a set of typewritten memos and press cuttings of the debate on the Briand plan: 'Documents rélatifs à l'organisation d'un régime d'union fédérale européenne' (Vik.Dip. 16 b). 'Letters to Lou,' G.VIII.159 contains a list of letters to Lou, of which the first three are described as 'letters in vain.' The first (dated 31 July, Skiathos) must be the source, no doubt edited, of the letter with this date and heading in M1.122–4; the second is dated 15 August, the word 'Geneva,' written against it, has been deleted (GS did not go to Geneva until the following month); the third is dated '16 September, Geneva.' None of the originals has been preserved, and there is now no trace of the second and third.

84 M1.129: 21 September 1930; IT 287: GS to Ioanna, 1 October 1930 (quoted); G.X.42: 27–28 September; 3–5 October 1929 in Paris; S/Apost 195: GS to Apostolidis, 14 July 1933 (quoted); cf. the haiku with the title 'Geneva' in which the same images appear (M1.133: 6 January 1931).

85 M2.136–7: 17 June 1933; M3.180: 5 March 1940, the last with reference to the poem 'The Sentence to Oblivion' (P.183–4 = KS 132–3; dated November 1939 in G.VIII.144). The title of this poem repeats a line from *Mythistorema* 7 (line 33), which itself can be connected to Jacqueline (see pp. 125–6 above); the strange image of the swans murdering the 'village-girls' (χωριατοπούλες) may not be unconnected with the dream in which 'Bi' (Jacqueline) appeared as a 'village-girl' (M2.141: 9 February

432

1934). Salome's body like a swan, 6N.62.

86 M1.130–1; G.VIII.157, no. 5996.

87 P.30 = KS 249–50: 'Erotikos Logos' III, lines 21–8

88 P.32 = KS 252: 'Erotikos Logos' V, lines 1, 4, 12. The last two stanzas of the poem appear as the first epigraph of this book.

89 M1.131; dates in G.VIII.157.

90 Rejected epigraph for *Turning Point* used for *The Cistern*, P.33 = KS 255; cf. M2.33. Alternative titles, G.VIII.157, no. 5998: Γυμνάσματα. – Παραφωνία. – Εξαγορά. – Φόρος υποτελείας. . . . Δευτέρα Παρουσία. Looking back, many years later, GS doubted whether critics would have recognised the 'humour' contained in 'Homage,' M8: 28 October 1967 = *Anti* 64 (1977), 19. A series of possible epigraphs is also listed. On the ambiguity of the eventual title, AP 37; Daskalopoulos, *Ergographia*, 27.

91 'Looking for a pseudonym,' M1.136: March 1931; cf. IT 282–3; 288; G.VIII.157, nos 6060–1. Apostolidis later remembered both the decision to publish and the search for a pseudonym as belonging to 1931: G.A. Apostolidis, Τον καιρό της Στροφής, 16. GS's copy of *Ulysses* in French, Vik. 3087 (GS cat. 852), see n. 77. A 'turning point' indeed, this volume has also been stamped with GS's old monogram and (later) with the 'official' mermaid and the name 'Seferis.'

92 M1.134: 18 January 1931; cf. M1.135: 22 January 1931; M1.137: 25 May 1931.

93 Daskalopoulos, *Ergographia*, 23, 26; G.VIII.157 (distribution lists).

94 S/T 58: Theotokas to GS, 31 October 1931; cf. M2.59; Daskalopoulos, *Ergographia*, 27–8; S/Keeley 186; cf. AP 37–8. The figure of 90 copies comes from a

later note on p. 2 of the distribution lists in G.VIII.157 (dated 29 September 1938).

95 Daskalopoulos, *Ergographia*, 27. Nine of these reviews, with two more that were prompted by the appearance of Karantonis' book at the end of 1931, are reprinted in *Nea Estia, Αφιέρωμα στον Γιώργο Σεφέρη*, 92/1087 (15 October 1972), 1552–68. On the critical reception of this and subsequent works by GS, see Antonis Drakopoulos, *Ο Σεφέρης και η κριτική: η υποδοχή του σεφερικού έργου (1931–1971)* (Athens: Plethron, 2002).

96 See S/Kats: GS to Katsimbalis, 30 August 1931 (= *Nea Estia* 1980), p. 1356. Palamas' letter is reprinted in *Nea Estia* 1972, Αφιέρωμα, 1562–4.

97 Cryptography, G.X.42: undated 'service diary.' Stratis defends his activity as a poet: 'I don't know how else to express my emotion' (6N.8); 'I want nothing else but to speak simply, to be given this grace' (P.201 = KS 146–7: 'An Old Man on the River Bank,' 1942); cf. p. 213 below.

98 S/Kar 16; G.P. Savidis, Από την ανέκδοτη αλληλογραφία Γ.Κ. Κατσίμπαλη-Γιώργου Σεφέρη, *Nea Estia*, 108/1278 (1980), 1354–78.

99 PE2.XI: 5 May 1931; M1.137: 9 August 1931; IT 290.

4 **Wayfarer the seafarer (1931–1934)**
1 G.VIII.154, no. 5947.
2 Tsatsos/IT7: GS to Ioanna, 23 February 1932; cf. IT 301; S/Kats: GS to Katsimbalis, 1 March 1932 (punctuation added).
3 Frontispiece to *Days 2*, dated '1932;' GN.III.D2: 1932, 1933; the unit of measurement is not given, but in the information section printed at the beginning of the diary, the relevant items of the British imperial system have been marked.

4 G.VIII.159 contains a fair copy of GS's letters to Lou from 24 August 1931 to December 1932, copied by Maro. There is also an A5 loose-bound notebook containing GS's own handwritten transcription of the letters chosen for inclusion in the published diary, with a series of further extracts marked to be integrated, and GS's introductory note reproduced in M2.8–9 and dated 1967. The first page lists letters with dates, indicating which ones have been used, and which 'lost or destroyed' (no. 6241). This list appears to derive from the tally recorded at the time in GN.III.D2: between August 1931 and February 1933, GS wrote 83 letters to Lou, between 20 February 1933 and June 1933, a further 42. A pencil list, in Maro's handwriting, identifies diary entries for inclusion in *Days 2*; none of these survives in its original form. G.VIII.159 contains, in a separate file, the original letters (about half of the total listed), against which the edited version was collated by the editor of *Days 2*, D.N. Maronitis, with the advice of Maro, after GS's death. The file was then sealed until 1980.

5 Mark Mazower, *Greece and the Inter-War Economic Crisis* (Oxford: Clarendon Press, 1991), 151–76; Vik.Dip. 11, title in (later) red crayon: 'Economy. 1932.' Cf. IT 294–5; 296–7; 302–3, 310 (only the last of which implies any degree of involvement by GS). GS's economic difficulties, G.X.42; IT 302: GS to Ioanna, March 1932; S/Apost 111: GS to Apostolidis, 1 May 1932; cf. 174: GS to Apostolidis, 15 January 1933. Financial support for Lou is explicitly discussed in G.VIII.159: GS to Lou, 18 September 1932; 3 February 1933, among many other references in the unpublished

433

portions of this correspondence. From March 1932, GS was remitting to Lou £2 a month (GN.III.D2).

6 IT 298; cf. 193–5; the evidence for GS's interest in Cyprus before the 1950s is fully presented and assessed in Savvas Pavlou, Σεφέρης και Κύπρος (Πολιτιστικές Υπηρεσίες Υπουργείου Παιδείας και Πολιτισμού, Σειρά Διδακτορικών Διατριβών, no. 2, Nicosia, 2000), 35–139. Vik.Dip. 24a (headed 'Cyprus') contains an earlier letter from Achilles C. Aimilianides, of the National Organisation of Cyprus, a semi-secret group whose avowed aim was union of Cyprus with Greece. Aimilianides was a long-standing correspondent of Stelios (Tsatsos/StS: Achilleus Aimilianides to Stelios Seferiadis, 1924–1938). Also in the vik. file are the leader page of *The Times* for 23 November 1931, which praised Venizelos for the scrupulous stand taken by the Greek government; and the official British government report on the events (March 1932).

7 Described in M2.79; cf. references to the 'academic pediment' which reminded him of the paintings of de Chirico (M2.136; 137; cf. P.135 = KS 86: 'Notes for a "Week": Sunday'). The hospital also appears in P.126 = KS 77–8: 'Tuesday.'

8 S/T 101–2: GS to Theotokas, 9 May 1932; M2.16: [GS to Lou], 13 October 1931; cf. M2.81: [GS to Lou], 23 July 1932; S/Apost 47–8: GS to Apostolidis, 2 November 1931.

9 S/Kats: GS to Katsimbalis, 23 January 1932; S/T 95: GS to Theotokas, 24 April 1932 (cf. S/Apost 139: GS to Apostolidis, 27 June 1932).

10 M2.15–16: [GS to Lou], 13 October 1931; cf. S/Apost 41: GS to Apostolidis, 8 October 1931.

11 G.VIII.159: GS to Lou, 13 October 1931.

12 GN.I.B1, on which see pp. 55, 85 above. 'Anastasis' (Anastasios), unlike 'Alyis,' is a real Greek name, but especially in this demotic form also recalls the root meaning of the word ανάσταση (resurrection); in this way its symbolism belongs together with that of the earlier aliases, Alyis Vayias and Mathios Paskalis.

13 First appearance of the name 'Stratis,' G.III.85: GS to Angelos, 7 October 1924, and p. 62 above.

14 S/Kats: GS to Katsimbalis, 14 April 1958; cf. M2.54: [GS to Lou], 16 April 1932. Yorgos Yatromanolakis (ed.), Παραλειπόμενα του κ. Στράτη Θαλασσινού, *Anti* (period B), no. 715 (9 June 2000), 43–5 (p. 44 quoted) = G.VIII.154, no. 5936, dated 17 October 1931.

15 G.VIII.159: GS to Lou, 29 November 1931. Later in the correspondence, M2.120–4 reproduces a long letter from Stratis Thalassinos addressed to a male friend, presumably GS. The letter which appears in M2.124–7 (16 April 1933) was also originally signed 'Stratis Thalassinos,' and enclosed with a letter from GS to Lou (G.VIII.159: GS to Lou, 11 April 1933).

16 Another sketch, dated '1931' and seemingly written soon after the first, begins: 'Coals – S.T. is writing again . . .' (G.VIII.154: no. 5938, numbered III, changed to II); cf. M2.23–4, 33 (poem dated 23 December 1931), 60, 66. It is in the same way that the imagined figure of Nijinsky is introduced in the prose poem of that title (also attributed to Stratis Thalassinos): 'He appeared as I was watching the lighted coals in the grate' (P.111 = KS 165–6; G.VIII.147, no. 4158; cf. M2.35).

17 M2.80–1: 23 July 1932; M2.29: [GS to Lou], 16 December 1931; P.105–23 = KS 59–73.

18 M2.30: [GS to Lou], 16 December 1931 ('last week'); GN.II.A (subfile Antoniou): Antoniou to GS from Barry Dock, South Wales, 15 December 1931. GS describes Antoniou variously as 'second' or 'third' captain (M2.30–1; D1.47); 'navigation officer': Antoniou's c.v. sent to GS enclosed with a letter of June 1954 (GN.II.A, subfile Antoniou).

19 M2.30: [GS to Lou], 16 December 1931; Henry Miller, *The Colossus of Maroussi* (Harmondsworth: Penguin, 1950; 1st ed. 1941), 38. For George's two public tributes to Antoniou see D1.47–9 (1936, entitled 'Our Seafaring Friend' – the Greek adjective is θαλασσινός) and D1.166–72 (1941). S/M1.79: GS to Maro, 7 January 1937 ('a friend who has the gift of expressing himself in monosyllables').

20 Edmund Keeley, *Inventing Paradise: The Greek Journey, 1937–47* (New York: Farrar, Straus and Giroux, 1999), 56–60; MIET album, no. 78 (photograph).

21 D1.47–9; P.57–8 = KS 16–17: *Mythistorema* 12, 13; cf. P.130 = KS 81–2: 'Notes for a "Week":' Thursday,' lines 32–4; P.48 = KS 8: *Mythistorema* 5, esp. lines 9–10, cf. M2.29–30.

22 M2.27: [GS to Lou], 13 December 1931.

23 M2.26: [GS to Lou], 3 December 1931, quoting Alain [= Emile Auguste Chartier], *Vingt Leçons sur les Beaux-Arts* (Paris: Gallimard/Nouvelle Revue Française, 1931), 293; cf. S/Apost 57: GS to Apostolidis, 5 December 1931, and n. 2. Relevant excerpts from chapters 4, 7 and 20 of Alain's book appear, with Greek translation,

as an appendix in S/Apost 313–47.

24 Respectively: Alain, *Vingt Leçons*, 289 (cf. D.50: 'I am not a philosopher. My job is not with abstract ideas, but to listen to what the things of the world tell me, to see how they are interwoven with my soul and my body, and to express them'); *Vingt Leçons*, 191–2; 186–7 (cf. D1.102–3); these and other passages discussed by Kohler, 152–6.

25 D2.10 (1948); T.S. Eliot, *Collected Poems, 1909–1962* (London: Faber, 1963), 115–16.

26 S/Kats: GS to Katsimbalis, 15 March 1932. The first mention of Eliot in GS's correspondence is in a letter to Karantonis on 15 December 1931 (S/Kar 59). He first mentions Eliot to Katsimbalis on 14 January 1932, by which time he had already begun to translate two of Eliot's poems.

27 Kleon Paraschos in *Eleftheron Vima*, 4 July 1931, reproduced in *Nea Estia, Αφιέρωμα στον Γιώργο Σεφέρη*, 92/1087 (15 October 1972), 1558.

28 Eliot, *Collected Poems*, 115–16; Lyndall Gordon, *T.S. Eliot: An Imperfect Life*, revised ed. (London: Vintage, 1998), 11–13; 163–4.

29 S/Kats: GS to Katsimbalis, 14 January 1932; IT 316; M2.108–9: [GS to Lou], 24 February 1933.

30 M2.32–3: [GS to Lou], 20 December 1931; TetEuth 211: GS to Tsatsos, 23 January 1932.

31 Jean Baruzi, *Saint Jean de la Croix et le problème de l'expérience mystique*, 2nd ed. (Paris: Alcan, 1931 = Vik. 4764, GS cat. 1368), 65–6, citing *Noche del Espiritu*, 'commentaire du vers 1 de la strophe II' (quotation marks indicate the actual words of the *Dark Night*); the Spanish original follows. Copied by GS in Baruzi's French, but without quotation marks or

435

punctuation, in S/Kats: GS to Katsimbalis, 14 January 1932; and in GS's Greek translation, again without quotation marks, and omitting the word *métier* (vocation or profession), in M2.34: 31 December 1931. Cited again, and explicitly linked to his reading of 'Marina,' in D2.23 (1948).

32 Anne Philipe, 'Entretien avec Georges Séféris,' *Le Monde* (27 August 1971), 12; cf. AP 46 (rather free Greek translation).

33 S/Kats: Katsimbalis to GS, 9 January 1932; GS to Katsimbalis, 14 January 1932; TetEuth 212: GS to Tsatsos, 23 January 1932.

34 IT 301; cf. p. 69 above. The first passage by Eliot that GS sent to his sister was from *Ash Wednesday*, one of the poems written after Eliot's very public religious conversion. In general, later, GS always distanced himself from Eliot's Anglo-Catholicism, see M2.108: [GS to Lou], 28 February 1933; D1.25–7; D2.14–15; see also pp. 377–8; 387–8 above.

35 S/T 106: GS to Theotokas, 14 June 1932.

36 D1.122: 'Monologue on Poetry' (1939) (quoted). Cf. P.17–18 = KS 239–40: 'The Mood of a Day,' line 10 [September 1928]; P.92 = KS 45: 'Sixteen Haiku,' no. 9 [1928–1931]; P.221–3 = KS 163–5: 'Thrush': 'Sensual Elpenor,' esp. lines 18–24, and p. 274 below.

37 Correspondence and Lou's comments, G.VIII.88: nos 2425–9. Date of early drafts, M2.17; G.VIII.88: no. 2409 (title, outline of numbered stanzas, dated 'Athens, 1931'); cf. M1.137: 25 May 1931.

38 M2.17 (quoted); 39–40; 40–1; 42–3; 51.

39 IT 304: GS to Ioanna, 21 March 1932; G.III.22: Angelos to GS, 25 March 1932.

40 S/Apost 95: GS to Apostolidis, 31 March 1932. Ioanna mentions Jacqueline's proposed marriage only in the context of GS's brief visit to Paris three months later, on which see above, p. 116.

41 S/Kats: GS to Katsimbalis, 16 April 1932; IT 305: GS to Ioanna, 16 April 1932; the fullest account in S/Apost 100–101: GS to Apostolidis, 10 April 1932.

42 G.VIII.159: GS to Lou, 20 April 1932 (nothing of this letter appears in M2); M2.59–60: 8 May 1932 (diary).

43 Among GS's books in the Vikelaia Municipal Library is the handbook of metrics by Th. Stavrou, *Νεοελληνική μετρική* (Vik. 1650, GS cat. 937), which from its position in his chronological list must have been acquired while he was in the first stages of working on this poem (early in 1931). The sections relating to the eleven-syllable metre have been intensively marked in red ink; there are few marks elsewhere.

44 Andreas Karantonis, *Ο ποιητής Γιώργος Σεφέρης* (Athens: Estia, 1957), 108 (original emphasis; essay first published in *Ta Nea Grammata*, 1936); on the lost letter see S/Kar 21 and n. 86–7; 91. For the cryptic significance of the 'cistern,' see p. 75 above.

45 6N.69; *Inf.* XXXIV 91–3; G.VIII.88, nos 2417; 2425 = S/Apost 105 (epigraph transcribed and MS sent to Apostolidis, 20 April 1932). Cf. M2.58: [GS to Lou], 30 April 1932, describing the *Epitaphios* in London the previous day, and explicitly linking it to the poem. The paragraph ends, in what is surely a private allusion, 'how far off now is that other *Epitaphios*' (G.VIII.159); in the published version, άλλος (other) has been replaced by άγιος (holy).

46 P.33–9 = KS 255–9.

436

47 S/Apost 105: GS to Apostolidis, 20 April 1932; S/Apost 108: Apostolidis to GS, 30 April 1932; cf. M2.58: [GS to Lou], 30 April 1932.

48 Respectively: S/T 114: Theotokas to GS, 10 July 1932; S/Kar 83–4: Karantonis to GS, 1 July 1932, and S/Kar 85–90: Karantonis to GS, 19 August 1932; S/Kats: Katsimbalis to GS, 21 June 1932.

49 S/Kats: Katsimbalis to GS, 11 July 1932.

50 S/Kats: Katsimbalis to GS, 8 October 1932 (original emphases).

51 IT 311: GS to Ioanna, 13 October 1932.

52 M2.78: [GS to Lou], 3 July 1932; S/Apost 142: GS to Apostolidis, 1 September 1932; S/Apost 144–6: Apostolidis to GS, 11 September 1932; S/Apost 159: GS to Apostolidis, 13 October 1932 ('You've done me a great favour, letting me dedicate it to you. No one else would have wanted it'); cf. Daskalopoulos, *Ergographia*, 31–2. Distribution list, G.VIII.88, no. 2433 = Stas/Chron, 28, and Ministry of Culture, Multimedia exhibition (2000), 42.

53 M2.80–1: 23 July 1932.

54 G.III.106: Stelios (Adelphi Hotel, Paris) to GS, 1 and 6 July 1932 and IT 312. On GS in Paris: M2.83: [GS to Lou], 3 August 1932 ('no beautiful girl . . . ,' G.VIII.159). On Angelos' studies: D3.241. There are references to Angelos' financial and possibly other difficulties in G.III.85. IT introduces Jacqueline's proposed marriage at this point, as the reason for GS's visit to Paris (IT 309), but when next GS refers to Jacqueline it is clear that they had not met since April (see next note).

55 S/Apost 157: GS to Apostolidis, 28 September 1932 (quoted) and 158 n. 4; GN.II.E2: GS to Herriot (draft), 7 November 1932; IT 311–12; M2.86–7: 29 August 1932. cf.

S/Apost 95: GS to Apostolidis, 31 March 1932 ('a soul terribly alive and shaped by me – I'm certain of it') and IT 316: GS to Ioanna, 22 February 1933 (final quoted paragraph).

56 P.109–10 = KS 63–4: 'Fires of St John,' [4] July 1932 (G VIII.148, no. 4151); S/Apost 175: GS to Apostolidis, 15 January 1933; cf. M2.84; 95; 98; 100.

57 G.VIII.159: GS to Lou, 18 September and 22 October 1932.

58 S/Apost 166: Apostolidis to GS, 10 November 1932; S/Apost 169: GS to Apostolidis, 15 November 1932; S/Apost 173: GS to Apostolidis, undated [approx. 10 January 1933, datable from reference to flu]; cf. M93: 5 January 1933.

59 S/T 119–20: Theotokas to GS, 28 November 1932.

60 G.VIII.159: GS to Lou, 29 March and 30 April 1933; cf. S/Kats: GS to Katsimbalis, 14 October 1933.

61 M2.99 refers to 'a month,' but GN.III.D2 notes her arrival on 18 November. See also M2.133: [GS to Lou], 4 May 1933 (British Museum, perhaps also referring to the Victoria and Albert); M2.91: 'December, Kew Gardens. Paphiopedilum. Cypripedilum [sic, for *-pedium*]. 65°;' recalled in G.VIII.159: GS to Lou, 13 March 1933 and P.124 = KS 76: 'Notes for a "Week": Monday,' lines 4–5.

62 GN.III.D2: 1 January 1933 ('Hotel Montana, 28 rue St Benoît'); M2.93: 4 January 1933; G.VIII.159: GS to Lou, 4 February 1933 ('moments when we quarrelled. Why?'). MIET: a photograph showing Lou, standing alone and looking miserable in a Paris park, is dated '2 January 1933.'

63 G.VIII.159: GS to Lou, 22 January 1933.

64 G.VIII.159: GS to Lou, 29 January, 3, 4, and 8 February 1933.

437

65 M2.100: [GS to Lou], 29 January 1933; M2.102: [GS to Lou], 4 February 1933.

66 M2.105–6: 13 and 14 February 1933.

67 All these letters are listed in G.VIII.159, no. 6241, corresponding to the numbers recorded in GN.III.D2: pocket-diary for 1933. No. 1 in the new sequence is dated 20 February 1933. Only the letters dated 8, 20, 24 February, 2, 4, and 5 March have been preserved in their original form in G.VIII.159; it is impossible to tell whether the remainder of the passages which appear in M2.105–12 are extracts from letters that were then destroyed, or from a diary. M2.107: 21 February 1933 (quoted).

68 M2.110: 25 February 1933 (quotation marks round this passage perhaps indicating an extract from a letter to Lou).

69 M2.107: 23 February 1933; IT 315: GS to Ioanna, 22 February 1933.

70 M2.112: 4 March 1933 (continuing the metaphor established in M2.106); G.VIII.159: GS to Lou, 26 June 1933 (quoted).

71 Respectively, G.VIII.159: GS to Lou, 5 March 1933 ('Dawn, Sunday'); 7 March 1933; M2.112: [GS to Lou], 4 March 1933 (quoted).

72 G.VIII.159: GS to Lou, 4 March 1933.

73 P.46–7 = KS 6–7: *Mythistorema* 4, line 41; P.60–1 = KS 19: *Mythistorema* 15, line 15 (quoted); P.71 = KS 28: *Mythistorema* 24, line 6.

74 G.VIII.159: GS to Lou, 29 March and 11 April 1933.

75 Swans, P.43 = KS 3: *Mythistorema* 1, line 12; M2.97; 109; 137. Almond trees, P.70 = KS 27: *Mythistorema* 23, line 2; M2.115: [GS to Lou], 13 March 1933; cf. IT 76: GS to Ioanna, 20 March 1920.

76 George Th. Mavrogordatos, *Stillborn Republic* (University of California Press, 1983), 41–5; cf. IT 319; S/Kats: Katsimbalis to GS, 5 March 1933 (quoted).

77 M2.114: [GS to Lou], 11 March 1933.

78 G.VIII.159: GS to Lou, 7 March 1933; S/Apost 128: GS to Apostolidis, 10 June 1932; cf. S/Apost 70–71: GS to Apostolidis, 20 December 1931; P.290 = KS 204–5: *Three Secret Poems* II 6, line 2.

79 G.VIII.159: GS to Lou, 10 May 1933 and subsequent letters; M2.124; 14 April 1933 (*The Waste Land*); P.124–35 = KS 76–86: 'Notes for a "Week";' G.VIII.148, no. 4090.

80 P.128 = KS 79–80: 'Wednesday,' lines 11–13; P.134 = KS 84–5: 'Saturday,' lines 34–42; P.130 = KS 81: 'Thursday,' lines 1–7 (quoted).

81 G.VIII.159: GS to Lou, 26 June 1933; S/Apost 195: GS to Apostolidis, 14 July 1933.

82 P.69 = KS 26: *Mythistorema* 22 [December 1933], line 15; P.43 = KS 3: *Mythistorema* 1 [1 June 1934], line 14; P.66 = KS 23: *Mythistorema* 19, [6 August 1934], lines 4–5; P.67 = KS 24: *Mythistorema* 20 [January 1935], line 9; P.55 = KS 4: *Mythistorema* 10 [20 October 1934], lines 5–6, cf. P.44 = KS 4: *Mythistorema* 2 [7 September 1934] (dates from G.VIII.146: chronological list).

83 M3.10: 23 July 1934.

84 P2.XI; S/Kats: Katsimbalis to GS, 22 October 1933; IT 321–2.

85 S/T 123–4: GS to Theotokas, 14 November 1933; cf. M2.139–40; S/T 121: GS to Theotokas, 4 November 1933; cf. S/T 122–3.

86 S/T 125: Theotokas to GS, 20 November 1933; S/T 124: GS to Theotokas, 14 November 1933.

87 M2.139: 12 November 1933; M2.140: 22 November 1933; cf. D2.9; PE2.XI (departure from London consulate);

S/Kats: GS to Katsimbalis, 28 October 1933. GN.III.D2 (pocket-diary for 2–4 October 1933) suggests that Ioanna had been the intermediary in renewed contact with Jacqueline.

88  M2.141: 9 February 1934; P.52–6 = KS 12: *Mythistorema* 8 [9 September 1934]; M3.95: 9 February 1938 (quoted).

89  Dates in G.VIII.146 (see n. 93 below), from which this title for the discarded poem also comes. It was published posthumously with a title which can be translated as either 'Last Dance' or 'Final Chorus' (TGB 60 = M3.14: Ο τελευταίος χορός). Jacqueline's marriage, IT 326–7.

90  G.III.106: Stelios to GS, 14 November 1932 announces the purchase of the plot of land; cf. IT 312–13; M2.141: 12 February 1934; M3.9: 16 April 1934.

91  IT 324; Kyd9.13–16.

92  GS's professional responsibilities, PE2.XI: 13 April 1934; cf. M3.9: 16 April 1934; PE2.XI: 27 August 1934. Political background, Mavrogordatos, *Stillborn Republic*, 46–8. GS's later commentary, X41.18–19 (quoted).

93  G.VIII.146 contains a complete set of drafts of the twenty-four poems finally included in the volume, most of them dated; a chronological list of twenty-five poems, numbered 3–27, with dates against each; and three draft versions of the author's note on the title. Some of this material has been transcribed by Yoryis Yatromanolakis and made publicly available in lectures. So far the only published notice is H "ποίηση-μοντάζ" του Σεφέρη, *To Vima: Nees Epoches* (7 May 1995), B4. The poem that would be published as no. 21 is dated in the chronological list: 'Delphi, April 1934;' cf. M3.10–11: 16 December

1934 (quoted) and S/Kar 152: GS to Karantonis, 24 December 1949.

94  KT 185 (quoted); IT 326–7 (cf. IT 214); M3.11: 16 December 1934; S/Kar 152: GS to Karantonis, 24 December 1949.

95  G.VIII.146: *Mythistorema* 13 and 2, both drafted 7 September 1934; *Mythistorema* 12 and 14 drafted respectively on the following two days. It is not clear how long GS spent on Spetses. The poem 'Description' (P.96 = KS 50, published in *Book of Exercises*, 1940) has the dateline 'Spetses, August 1934,' cf. IT 214. Poems 19 and 3 of *Mythistorema* are dated, respectively, 6 and 8 August, and so may also have been written on Spetses.

96  S/T 20–21.

97  M3.10–11, 13: 16 December 1934 and 1 April 1935; G.VIII.146, nos 4023–5. The draft prefaces are undated, but since the title *Mythistorema* appears in them, they must have been written between December 1934 and March 1935.

98  P.314 = KS 277 (included in the first and all subsequent editions).

99  G.VIII.146, which numbers the poems up to 27, does not include the 'unused drafts,' nos 1 and 3, which appear in M3.13–15; the latter of these is dated 'Oct. '34–March '35.' Since the list in the file is chronological, and begins at 3, it must be assumed that the discarded nos 1 and 2, of which there is no trace in G.VIII.146, must predate December 1933. If these were not destroyed, they must have been two of the poems, written between April and about July 1933, later published as 'Notes for a "Week".' The poems of *Mythistorema* were not numbered in the first edition (just as the numbering was removed from the stanzas of 'Erotikos Logos' and

439

*The Cistern* in their published form), but are numbered in all subsequent editions.

100  M3.13: 1 April 1935; Daskalopoulos, *Ergographia*, 34–6.

101  P.71 = KS 28; G.VIII 146: 13 December 1934.

## 5  The Scales of Injustice (1935–1937)

1  *Ta Nea Grammata*, vol. 1, no. 1 (January 1935) opens with a long interview with Palamas, followed by GS's poem 'The Cistern' (effectively published for the first time, since the first edition had been a private one); PE2.XI (promotion).

2  G. Benekos, *Τὸ κίνημα τοῦ 1935* ([Athens:] Yiannikos, [1965]), see esp. pp. 101–4; George Th. Mavrogordatos, *Stillborn Republic* (University of California Press, 1983), 48–51; GS's later commentary, X41.20.

3  The fullest, though by no means exhaustive, study is Nikos Orfanidis, *Η πολιτική διάσταση της ποίησης του Γιώργου Σεφέρη* (Athens: Astir, 1985).

4  IT 334; PE1.262: 19 September 1944; X41.20–22.

5  KT 242–6; IT 334–6.

6  IT 335: GS to Ioanna, 'Sunday' (undated); P.97–8 = KS 51, dated 'Pelion, 19 August 1935'; on the poem's title see editor's note, P.322. Antoniou's ship, GN.II.A (subfile Antoniou).

7  P.99–101 = KS 52–3, dated 'Summer 1936'. For the first line and an early draft of the opening see M3.19–20: 12 August 1935 ('Zagora').

8  M3.19–28. Dante, D2.249; cf. KT 246; G.VIII.36 (file headed: 1934–46 Σημειώσεις από διαβάσματα, including cosmological drawings of Dante's universe); for evidence that GS had read at least the *Inferno* before this, see Vik. 3498, GS cat. 602, probably acquired early in 1927, with annotations, esp. on

Canto 3, which may have been used in the early drafts of *Six Nights*; also M2.48 and p. 113 above on the abandoned epigraph for *The Cistern*. Freud and Heraclitus, M3.24: 31 August 1935; D2.330 (1970).

9  X41.21 (quoted); cf. Bert Birtles, *Exiles in the Aegean: A Personal Narrative of Greek Politics and Travel* (London: Gollancz, 1938), 13–14. Plebiscite and voting figures, Mavrogordatos, *Stillborn Republic*, 51.

10  PE1.7–9, editor's preface. The earliest of these notebooks has no title, but only the cryptic last letter of the Greek alphabet (omega); later they are referred to in the MSS as 'service' or 'professional' diaries (υπηρεσιακά). The two volumes so far published, which cover, although not continuously, the period 1935–1952, owe their title *Political Diary* (Πολιτικό ημερολόγιο) to their editor, Alexandros Xydis. The poem was first published in TGB 64–6 (line 30 quoted); on publication, see editor's note, TGB 133–41, and esp. p. 136. Abyssinian references, S/T 129–31: Theotokas to GS, 9 July 1935.

11  X41.24 (quoted); 20–2 (p. 22 quoted).

12  P.73–8 = KS 29–34: 'Santorini,' 'Mycenae'. G.VIII.154, nos 5939–40: prose sketch by 'Stratis Thalassinos,' numbered 3; G.VIII.146, no. 4079: typescript of *Gymnopaidia* with handwritten epigraph, 'Gymnopédie 1. Erik Satie;' cf. M2.58. For this and other musical allusions, see Polina Tambakaki, '*Γυμνοπαιδίες: Γιώργου Σεφέρη – Ερίκ Σατί* (Athens: Oriolos, 2002).

13  P.78 = KS 34, lines 26–32. It is by persuading him to tread on purple, the colour of royalty, that Clytemnestra, in Aeschylus' tragedy *Agamemnon*, lures her husband, the

440

king, on his return to Mycenae, into offending the gods, so setting the seal on his murder and the cycle of vengeance that follows; the sparse-growing weeds allude to one of the most famous poems on the Greek War of Independence, 'The Catastrophe of Psara' (1824) by Dionysios Solomos. The reference to snakes is a direct quotation from a traditional lament, depicting the world of the dead. The most telling detail of all is the *'evening* of the return': Agamemnon's fateful return to Mycenae in Aeschylus' play happens in the morning; in 'Syngrou Avenue II,' the scene is set for the arrival of King George II as the sun is setting. G.VIII.154, no. 4081: original dateline for *Gymnopaidia*; when it was first published, both in *Ta Nea Grammata* and as a separate pamphlet, in 1936, the poem had no dateline at all.

14 Birtles, *Exiles*, 88. For the date of the meeting, see also GN.II.A: Birtles to GS, 24 February 1936, thanking him for the meeting 'the other day.'

15 Birtles, *Exiles*, 65–8; X41.22 ('At that time you felt without support, surrounded by people who had nothing in their minds but to set up intrigues or to steer clear of traps'). On GS and the left in the 1960s, see pp. 392–9 above; for critiques of his political attitudes since the late 1980s, and a critical response, see Roderick Beaton, 'Reading Seferis's Politics and the Politics of Reading Seferis,' *Kampos: Cambridge Studies in Modern Greek* 9 (2001), 1–35.

16 M3.31–2: 26–27 March 1936; cf. P.168 = KS 115: 'The Container of the Uncontainable,' where the mourning bells, described on that occasion, are transposed to

Constantinople two years later; X41.22.

17 Mavrogordatos, *Stillborn Republic*, 51–3.

18 Kyd9.47; 50; 60–1; 65–6; 67–8; 74; IT 332–3; KT 149; Stratis Myrivilis, *Τα παγανά* (Athens: I Fili tou Vivliou, 1945).

19 S/M1.9–10; 125; 127; 143; Maro/int. 203.

20 Miranda Zannou-Papadopoulou, *Μια οικογένεια, δύο αιώνες: το χρονικό της οικογένειας Ζάννου* (Athens: privately published, [1998]), 67–71. I am grateful to Katerina Krikos-Davis for making this rare publication available to me. See also S/M1.30–2, n.4. There are minor discrepancies between these two accounts.

21 Lou: inferred from 6N.65 (quoted); cf. 6N.166: 'the first time I've felt at my side a person of my race'); Maro: S/M1.72; 200.

22 Zannou-Papadopoulou, *Μια οικογένεια*, 76; S/M1.156 n. 1; 238: GS to Maro, 6 July 1937 (date of marriage to Londos); S/M1.243 n. 2; S/Mal. 181 n. (on Londos); Maro/int. 202; Anna Londou: interview; Mark Dragoumis: interview. Quotation from S/M1.253–4: GS to Maro, 12 July 1937.

23 Zannou-Papadopoulou, *Μια οικογένεια*, 74–5.

24 GN.II.B13: Amaryllis Dragoumi to GS, 13 July 1936. The correspondence begins on 17 June.

25 Anna Londou: interview.

26 IT 341; M3.33.

27 Tsatsos' infidelities, KT 422; 549; cf., in characteristically forthright style, S/M1.345: Maro to GS, 3 August 1939.

28 Vik. 2523 (GS cat. 1153), handwritten dedication in GS's copy of *The Last Orphic Dithyramb*, dated 10 November 1932.

441

29 KT 165; cf. the special double issue
of *Ta Nea Grammata* in honour of
Palamas: vol. 2, nos 5–6 (May–June
1936).

30 IT 340–1; Kyd9.53; cf. George's later,
less specific, account in D2.98–9.

31 S/Kats: GS to Katsimbalis, 17
September 1936; S/M1.32: GS to
Maro, 21 November 1936; IT 343;
Kyd9.54–5. In the first, but not
the second of Ioanna's accounts,
she adds that Sikelianos was
accompanied by Palamas' daughter,
Nausicaa. It is clear from S/M1.26,
however, that Sikelianos was
actually staying on the island, and
there is no further mention of the
presence of Nausicaa Palama. For
George's comments on Sikelianos'
poem, see S/M1.104: GS to Maro, 30
January 1937, and n.1. cf. P.137–9;
140–2.

32 Mavrogordatos, *Stillborn Republic*,
51–4; John S. Koliopoulos, *Greece
and the British Connection 1935–1941*
(Oxford University Press, 1977),
10–12; 38–46; John V. Kofas,
*Authoritarianism in Greece: The
Metaxas Regime* (East European
Monographs, Boulder/Columbia
University Press, New York, 1983),
42–5; Nicos C. Alivizatos, *Les
Institutions politiques de la Grèce à
travers les crises 1922–1974* (Paris:
Pichon, 1979), 58–72. For additional
background to this and the next
chapter see Robin Higham and
Thanos Veremis (eds), *The Metaxas
Dictatorship: Aspects of Greece
1936–40* (Athens: Hellenic
Foundation for Defense and Foreign
Policy [ELIAMEP], 1993) and P.J.
Vatikiotis, *Popular Autocracy in
Greece 1936–41: A Political
Biography of General Ioannis
Metaxas* (London: Frank Cass,
1998), 153–64; 185–201. Tsatsos'
brother's deportation, IT 345–6; KT
265. GS's perspective, X41.18–25.

33 M3.65: 8 July 1937 (quoted); also
recalled at S/M1.184: GS to Maro, 9
May 1937; S/M1.240 and 244: GS to
Maro, 6 and 8 July 1937. Date of
GS's arrival on Aegina, S/Kats: GS
to Katsimbalis, 1 September 1936.

34 S/M1.26; recalled by GS at
S/M1.95: GS to Maro, 25 January
1937; S/M1.125: GS to Maro, 16
February 1937 (cf. 127–8 n. 4).

35 P.138–42 = KS 89–93; P.150 = KS
100; P.279 = KS 199; for the
significance of the Peak: S/M1.34
(and n. 2); P.303 = KS 212.

36 M3.34: 17 September 1936.

37 S/Kats: GS to Katsimbalis, 17
September 1936.

38 GN.II.B13: Amaryllis Dragoumi to
GS, 20 and 26 September 1936.

39 S/Kats: Katsimbalis to GS, 25
September 1936; GS to Katsimbalis,
13 October 1936 (quoted); S/M1.27
n. 3; S/M1.63–4 n.2; cf. S/M1.10
('little gazelle' and Stelios' attitude);
S/M1.124 n. 1 (Maro: 'George never
did learn the reason that the
minister would not give him leave
[to return to Athens]. I knew, but
didn't want to hurt him'); G.III.106:
Stelios to GS, 24 December 1936.

40 P.102–3 = KS 54–5; cf. S/M1.124 n.1.
Mavroudis described, X41.33.

41 P.137–9 = KS 89–91: 'A Word for
Summer,' line 60 quoted (the word
here translated as 'lines,' στίχους, in
context can refer equally to a
military line-up and to lines of
verse); P.148 = KS 98: 'Epitaph'. The
editor of S/M1, drawing on Maro's
recollections, states that the
relationship with Loukia Fotopoulou
was 'breathing its last' by 1935
(SM1.9); on George's side there is no
clear sign of her presence between
the summer of 1933 and this poem,
more than three years later; but
there is evidence that she was badly
affected by this final break
(G.III.104: Melpo Axioti [Loukia's

442

cousin] to GS, 24 January 1937).

42  PE2.XI: 21 October 1936; S/M1.51: GS to Maro, 5 December 1936; S/M1.238–9: GS to Maro, 6 July 1937; cf. P.141 = KS 92–3: 'Epiphany, 1937,' lines 31–5; M3.35–8: 8 November 1936 ('Il Dolce Nido') with minor changes = S/M1.103–10 and n.; cf. S/M1.235: GS to Maro, 3 July 1937.

43  S/M1.121: GS to Maro, 13 February 1937.

44  M3.38–9; S/M1.27–8: GS to Maro, 17 November 1937; S/M1.49: GS to Maro, 3 December 1936; cf. S/M1.214: GS to Maro, 6 June 1937; P.183–4 = KS 132–3: 'The Sentence to Oblivion', lines 1, 25–8 (the placid lake); P.157–8 = KS 107–8: 'Fine Autumn Morning,' line 2 (quoted).

45  S/M1.28–9: GS to Maro, 17 November 1936; cf. M3. 38–40; IT 347: GS to Ioanna, 18 November 1936 (without reference to Maro); P.140 = KS 92–3: 'Epiphany, 1937,' lines 6–9 (quoted).

46  M3.48–9; S/M1.163; 179–80; 181–2; MIET album, nos 11–15; S/M1.33: GS to Maro, 21 November 1936; S/Kats: Katsimbalis to GS, 1 February 1937 (quoted). Korça is the modern Albanian spelling; soon after his arrival there, GS noted eight different written forms of the name (S/M1.71: GS to Maro, December 1936).

47  S/T 140: GS to Theotokas, 12 December 1937; S/M1.69: GS to Maro, 17 December 1936. Serious references to the politics of the Greek community are confined to September, during the two-month break in the relationship with Maro, M3.73–5: 14 September 1937; M3.83–4: 27 September 1937.

48  Style of life, S/M1.71; 146; 148; cf. P.155 = KS 105–6: 'Mathios Paskalis Among the Roses,' lines 1, 11.

Caricatures, M3.43–5; 50–1; 54–63; S/M1.59; 119–20. *Lycée Français*, M3.78: 20 September 1937. May rebellion, S/M1.198–9: GS to Maro, 20 May 1937, and editor's note.

49  S/Apost 225–6: GS to Apostolidis, 2 June 1937.

50  S/M1.11 (editor's introduction), where the intermediary for the informal letters is not mentioned. For indications that it was Amaryllis ('Marouli') see S/M1.93; 270, probably confirmed by GN.II.B13: Amaryllis Dragoumi to GS, 18 January 1937 ('You're a great egoist, my dear friend, if you seriously wish to conscript all of us into the service of the "little one" you're in love with.')

51  S/Kats: Katsimbalis to GS, 12 August 1936 (the first from Paris); GS to Katsimbalis, 31 March 1937; D1.81 (GS's obituary for K. Katsimbalis, first published *Ta Nea Grammata*, April 1937; cf. S/M1.149; 152). S/Kar 142–3: Karantonis to GS, 12 April 1937 (Katsimbalis' return to Athens). On the impact of censorship on *Ta Nea Grammata* (which GS never mentions at the time) see S/Kar 110: Karantonis to GS, 4 December 1936. S/Kats: Katsimbalis to GS, Katsimbalis to GS, 19 September 1936 and 17 January 1937 (difficulties, and GS's contributions).

52  S/Kats: GS to Katsimbalis, 2 and 20 September 1937; IT 357: GS to Ioanna, 12 September 1937; cf. M3.105; 138. The first four poems in *Logbook [I]* were written between June and September 1937, in Korça (G.VIII.144).

53  D1.47–81; D3.272–7; S/Kats: Katsimbalis to GS, 12 December 1936. The non-standard term Δοκιμές (δοκιμή being closer to the original meaning of the French *essai*) first appears in S/Kats: GS to

443

Katsimbalis, 7 January 1937; cf. IT
350: GS to Ioanna, 25 January 1937;
S/Kar 119: GS to Karantonis, 30
January 1937; cf. S/Kar 130. On GS
as essayist, see Nikolaos K.
Petropoulos, *Ο ποιητής ως
δοκιμιογράφος: οι 'Δοκιμές' του
Γιώργου Σεφέρη μέσα στην παράδοση
της ευρωπαϊκής δοκιμιογραφίας*
(Athens: privately published, 2000).

54 S/M1.161: GS to Maro, 18 April
1937; S/Kats: GS to Katsimbalis, 5
September 1936 (Makriyannis);
S/M1.165: GS to Maro, 20 April
1937; M3.85–92: 22 November 1937
(Cavafy). G.VIII.158 contains notes
for projected essays on Romos
Filyras, Pericles Yannopoulos, Ion
Dragoumis, and aspects of the
Greek language.

55 S/M1.62: GS to Maro, 15 December
1936.

56 S/M1.114: GS to Maro, 3 February
1937; cf. S/M1.123–4. GS in Athens
in March, M3.42; IT 351–2 (without
mention of Maro); S/M1.135–6 n.1.
Plans for June 1937, S/M1.214–7.

57 The trip lasted from 18 to 27 June
1937 (M3.68–9; S/M1.222–4 and n.
2); for GS absent without leave see
S/M1.267: GS to Maro, 19 July 1937.
The aftermath is reported in M3.71;
S/M1.226–9 and n. 1: GS to Maro,
30 June 1937 (p. 228 quoted).

58 S/M1.229–32: GS to Maro, 2 July
1937; S/M1.235: GS to Maro, 3 July
1937 (citing her telegram, quoted);
S/M1.240–1; GS to Maro, 6 July
1937 (quoted).

59 S/M1.245; 246; GS to Maro, 8 July
1937; S/M1.268: GS to Maro, 19 July
1937; cf. the first reference to
decisions having to be made for the
future, S/M1.184: GS to Maro, 9
May 1937; S/M1.208–9: GS to
Maro, 4 June 1937; S/Apost 231–2:
GS to Apostolidis, 19 [July 1937]
(quoted). The month and year of
this letter, missing in the original,

have been supplied by the editor,
who wrongly gives the former as
'June'.

60 GN.III.D2: 24 July 1937. GS's
departure from Korça is wrongly
dated 21 July in M3.69. The official
document handing over the
consulate is dated the 26th (G.X.40
and see below). Meeting in Athens
recalled by Maro, S/M1.269 n. 3
(quoted).

61 Tsatsos/IT7: GS to Ioanna,
'Monday' [2 August 1937], date
inferred from those which follow
(quoted); S/M1.269 n. 3.

62 IT 356 (quoted). GS's letters from
Pelion are preserved in Tsatsos/IT7;
hers to him in G.III.102. 'Clélia'
may have been the same person as
the 'beautiful woman' with whom
George had gone riding on Pelion,
while staying with Ioanna and her
family in the summer of 1935, so
provoking a mild scandal in the
neighbourhood (IT 336).

63 IT 356 (GS's letters described); see
also IT 348: 'he wrote with errands,
requests and references to women;'
cf. his injunction to Maro to deposit
his letters to her with Ioanna, *sealed*
(p. 151 above).

64 M3.72–3; P.159–60 = KS 109–10, see
esp. lines 1–11. The poem has the
published dateline 'Pelion – Koritsa,
summer – autumn '37;' but GS's
handwritten chronological list of the
poems that make up *Logbook [I]*
dates it to '20 August 1937'
(G.VIII.144). This list is published
with commentary by Yoryis Yatromanolakis, *'Ο Βασιλιάς της Ασίνης': η
ανασκαφή ενός ποιήματος* (Athens:
Stigmi, 1986), 20, where the Greek
numeral 8 denoting the month in
the entry for this poem has been
wrongly transcribed as '10').

65 Tsatsos/IT7: GS to Ioanna, 10
August 1937; P.159–60 = KS 109–10,
lines 21–3; 31–4.

66  G.X.40: GS to Ministry, 8 July 1937, requesting leave of 'one week,' approved; 26 July 1937: hand-over of consulate from GS to replacement; 3 August 1937: hand-over from replacement to GS.

67  GN.III.D2; M3.69; S/M1.269: GS to Maro, 17 August 1937 and n. 1; G.III.102: Ioanna to GS, 17 and 23 August 1937 (with annotations by Maro, which probably date from after GS's death).

68  S/M1.270: Maro to GS, 26 August 1937, and n. 1; GN.II.B13: Amaryllis Dragoumi to GS, 9 September 1937; GN.III.D2: 9 September 1937 ('Girlfriend,' with drawing which may be of a waste-paper basket); last of several mentions on 16 September 1937.

69  G.III.106: Stelios to GS, 9 September 1937; S/Kats: GS to Katsimbalis, 20 September 1937; S/Apost 235: GS to Apostolidis, 25 September 1937; three letters to 'Marouli' [Amaryllis] are noted in GS's pocket-diary (GN.III.D2); cf. her replies (GN.II.B13); G.X.40: Mavroudis to GS (transcribed telegram), 30 September 1937; M3.84: 7 October 1937; S/M1.270–1 n. 1 (quoted).

70  G.X.40: Nikoloudis, order of the day no. 35, 20 October 1937 (...Επιτροπής προς επεξεργασίαν των καταρτιζομένων υπό των υπηρεσιών του καθ' ημάς υφυπουργείου σχεδίων νόμων).

71  Koliopoulos, *Greece and the British Connection*, 57; legislation in detail in Alivizatos, *Les Institutions*, 324–38.

72  M3.84–5; S/M1.272 n. 1; M3.94; PE2.XI and X41.72 (editor's note). GS's precise title was Διευθύνων το παρά τω Υφυπουργείω Τύπου και Τουρισμού Τμήμα Εξωτερικού Τύπου. G.X.40: 7 December 1937, Personnel Department to GS, with GS's note added: 'I started on 4 December 1937'; cf. IT 358.

73  ELIA: GS to Georgios Roussos, 20 May 1943 (typed carbon copy), pp. 2–3, on which see further below, pp. 221–2; G.X.40: Pericles Skeferis to Ministry, 15 December 1937.

74  GN.III.D2: 10, 14, 17 December 1937 (Maro); S/M1.18; cf. 279–80 n. 4. They lived for a year in Adrianou Street, then in Monis Asteriou, which intersects with Kydathinaion at the end of the block that includes number 9 (Anna Londou: interview).

6  'A Generation Sacrificed' (1938–1941)

1  ELIA: GS to Georgios Roussos, 20 May 1943 (typed carbon copy), pp. 2–3; for the context of this letter see pp. 221–2 below; cf. PE1.164–5: 26 March 1944; X41.72, n. 27 (editor's note) and Alexandros Xydis, Ο πολιτικός Σεφέρης, in A. Argyriou et al., Κύκλος Σεφέρη. Βιβλιοθήκη Γενικής Παιδείας, no. 10 (Athens: Etaireia Spoudon, 1984), 105–123, see p. 112.

2  G.X.40: GS to Nikoloudis, 6 May 1938. The decree assigning GS temporarily to the duties of M. Vatalan, Director of Internal Press, is dated 17 April.

3  Under-Ministry for Press and Tourism, Ο απολογισμός μιας διετίας: 4η Αυγούστου 1936–1938. Publications of the Under-Ministry of Press and Tourism, no. 21 (Athens: Pyrsos, 1938), 211.

4  Lincoln MacVeagh, *Ambassador MacVeagh Reports*, ed. John O. Iatrides (Princeton University Press, 1980), 119–22; PE1.15: 5 January 1938.

5  John S. Koliopoulos, *Greece and the British Connection 1935–1941* (Oxford University Press, 1977), 71–3; John V. Kofas, *Authoritarianism in Greece: The Metaxas Regime* (East

445

European Monographs,
Boulder/Columbia University Press,
New York, 1983), 125–6.

6 Kofas, *Authoritarianism*, 126–9; 104
(quoted); cf. Nicos C. Alivizatos, *Les
Institutions politiques de la Grèce à
travers les crises 1922–1974* (Paris:
Pichon, 1979), 328–33.

7 PE1.15–16; M3.94–6: 12 December
1937; 5 January and 13 March 1938
(quoted).

8 Koliopoulos, *Greece and the
British Connection*, 71–3; Kofas,
*Authoritarianism*, 125–6; MacVeagh,
*Reports*, 124–6.

9 M3.96: 'end of March' 1938
(debased: παρακμασμένη). The entry
begins 'Official funeral,' which
must refer to the obsequies for
Michalakopoulos, on 28 March,
which MacVeagh noted that the
staff of the Foreign Ministry
attended.

10 X41.50.

11 P.171–2 = KS 120–1: 'The Last Day,'
lines 26–8.

12 Publication history, Daskalopoulos,
*Ergographia*, 52–3. GS's comments
on censorship, M3.165; M4.367–8.
For discussion of the poem's date see
Yoryis Yatromanolakis, *'Ο Βασιλιάς
της Ασίνης': η ανασκαφή ενός
ποιήματος* (Athens: Stigmi, 1986),
19–20; resolved by a fair copy
in manuscript (probably one of
the seven inserted in copies of
*Logbook*), on display in the Vikelaia
Municipal Library, Heraklion, dated
'12.2.38' and signed. The poem's
eventual place in *Logbook [I]*,
whose arrangement is close to the
order in which the poems were
written, confirms that this was not
an oversight on GS's part. For GS's
prophecy of a new war, see the
epigraph to this chapter, which
dates from 1935.

13 Edmund Keeley: personal
communication.

14 G.VIII.144; cf. Yatromanolakis, *'Ο
Βασιλιάς της Ασίνης'*, 20; G.X.40:
announcement of promotion, 12
March 1938, citing *Government
Gazette* for 5 March in which the
royal decree of 26 February appears.
It is possible that GS chose this date
in hindsight, for a poem that he
worked on over a longer period
that spring.

15 P.163–5 = KS 113–14, lines 49–54,
published dateline 'Athens, spring
'38.' The translation retains the
form of the original, in which a
regular four-stress metre is used
for all lines except the last.

16 Respectively: D1.159; 157.

17 D1.139; further elaborated, D1.264–7
[1945].

18 M3.28: 6 September 1935; M3.49: 9
May 1937 (...το Έθνος μαζεύτηκε
μέσα στα όρια του ελλαδικού
κράτους...).

19 X41.44; M3.95: 5 January 1938
(quoted).

20 M3.97–8: 5–14 April 1938;
S/M1.275–82; the papers from the
meeting, including GS's opening
speech, in French, are preserved
in Vik.Dip. 12.

21 M3.98: 14 April 1938; P.166 = KS
115: 'The Container [*Chora*] of
the Uncontainable.' The title is a
mystical title for the Virgin Mary,
from which the Byzantine name of
the church derives; in context the
phrase could also be understood as
'The country of that which does not
(or cannot) have a country.' The
poem itself seems to derive from a
detail of GS's account of Venizelos'
funeral; cf. M3.32: 27 March 1936
('The metallic sound of bells shines
out here and there, like a coin
dropping'), and can be read as GS's
obituary on the 'Great Idea' of
restoring Constantinople as the
capital of a greater Greece,
championed by Venizelos.

22 GS's side of the dialogue is reprinted in D1.82–165; both sides in G. Seferis and K. Tsatsos, 'Ένας διάλογος για την ποίηση, ed. L. Kousoulas (Athens: Ermis, 1975). Relations between the two men at the time, IT 365; cf. S/M1.329: GS to Maro, 12 July 1939. Censorship, M3.165: 26 January 1940.

23 D1.98.

24 D1.101 (quoted). 'Hellenism' used elsewhere by GS, M3.247. The language of this whole passage closely shadows key terms earlier used in *Mythistorema*, and also (if more moderately) the peroration of the lecture on Moréas, quoted on p. 46 above.

25 See, authoritatively, the dictionary definitions of Yorgos Babiniotis, Λεξικό της νέας ελληνικής γλώσσας (Athens: Kentro Lexikologias, 1998). Another recent dictionary (Tegopoulos-Fytrakis, Μείζον ελληνικό λεξικό, 1997) additionally cites this text by GS as authority for the subsidiary meaning of the word as 'Greek language and literature,' in addition to 'Greek civilisation...' See also D.G. Tsaousis (ed.), Ελληνισμός – ελληνικότητα· ιδεολογικοί και βιωματικοί άξονες της νεοελληνικής κοινωνίας (Athens: Estia, 1983).

26 D1.99.

27 D1.101.

28 D1.102.

29 Respectively: M3.97–8; D1.101; Tsatsos in 'Ένας διάλογος, 59.

30 D3.93 (1944); 167 (1963).

31 S/M1.285: GS to Maro, 8 July 1938; S/M1.291: Maro to GS, 14 July 1938 (quoted); S/M1.296: Maro to GS, 22 August 1938 (quoted); KT 262–3; Anna Sikelianou, Η ζωή μου με τον 'Αγγελο (Athens: Estia, n.d.), 65–70; 95; 131–3.

32 S/M1.294: Maro to GS, 22 August 1938; cf. S/M1.289 n. 1; 297

n. 1; MIET album, no. 23, cf. no. 24.

33 IT 358; on marriage and residence among Anatolian Greeks, see Renée Hirschon, *Heirs to the Greek Catastrophe* (Oxford: Clarendon Press, 1988), 106–22. Maro's whereabouts, Anna Londou: interview.

34 IT 358; 365–6; KT 194–5. Ioanna disposes of her father's remarriage in a single sentence, without naming his wife (IT 366), although elsewhere she conceded that the unnamed Thérèse 'was good and took care of' Stelios during his final illness (IT 364); Tsatsos gives an unkind vignette, which is inaccurate about dates, and may be about other things as well.

35 Stelios Seferiadis, Απ' το συρτάρι μου (1895–1912) (Athens: Pyrsos, 1939): GS's copy in the Vikelaia Municipal Library.

36 S/M1.308: GS to Maro, 25 September 1938; M3.103–5 (30 September 1938 quoted).

37 M3.113: 10 April 1939.

38 S/M1.318: GS to Maro, 21 May 1939; cf. M3.120–2.

39 TGB 70–3 (and notes pp. 156–7); cf. M3.120–2; S/M1.314–17 and notes 1–4 (pp. 317–18).

40 S/M1.328–9: GS to Maro, 12 July 1939; cf. S/M1.337–48; M3.126–7; GN.III.D2: 1939; Anna Londou: interview.

41 M3.125–6: 3 August 1939; cf. S/M1.342–3: GS to Maro, 2 August 1939, and n. 2.

42 IT 54.

43 Cutting preserved in G.II.5, on which see also M4.140. Quotation from Jonathan Barnes, *Early Greek Philosophy* (Harmondsworth: Penguin, 1987), 74–5.

44 S/M1.348–50; M3.130: 31 August 1939; M3.129: 25 August 1939 (quoted).

45 M3.130: 30 August 1939.

46 Ian MacNiven, *Lawrence Durrell, A Biography* (London: Faber, 1999), 216–24.

47 Henry Miller, *The Colossus of Maroussi* (Harmondsworth: Penguin, 1950; 1st ed. 1941), 49, 108. For all his legendary contempt for the sexual taboos of his day, Miller stopped short of risking embarrassment to his friend by any mention that Maro so much as existed: 'Seferiades,' in the *Colossus*, lives an 'austere bachelor' life without attachments. Writing to Miller several years later, George told him he was married, and reminded him that he had met Maro at his flat in Kydathinaion Street; see *Labrys* 8 (1983), 56: GS to Miller, 7 December 1948.

48 Miller, *Colossus*, 36; Miller may have had in mind the evening described by GS in M3.141–2: 24 October 1941. Reading and meeting described, M3.131: 2 September 1939 (quoted); Miller, *Colossus*, 40–43; 51–2; cf. Keeley/int. 198–9.

49 Keeley/int. 200–1 (1968); GN.II.E6: GS to Angelos, 14 December 1948 (quoted).

50 George Thaniel, *Seferis and Friends*, ed. G. Phinney (Stratford, Ontario: Mercury, 1994), 132; *Labrys* 8 (1953), 57: GS to Miller, 8 May 1954.

51 Miller, *Colossus*, 57–9 and see p. 271 above. Photo: MIET album, no. 32.

52 M3.146; 145: 16 November 1939; Thaniel, *GS and Friends*, 120.

53 P.180–2 = KS 129–31, lines 10, 31–7; dateline 'Hydra – Athens, Nov. 1939;' G.VIII.144 specifies 19 November (list reproduced in Yatromanolakis, 'Ο Βασιλιάς της Ασίνης', 20). See also Edmund Keeley, *Inventing Paradise: The Greek Journey, 1937–47* (New York:

Farrar, Straus and Giroux, 1999), 76–7.

54 Keeley, *Inventing Paradise*, 87; cf. Keeley/int. 200; Thaniel, *Seferis and Friends*, 105. For Miller's father, see Miller to GS, December 1939: 'It seems my father is on his last legs – they urge me to hurry back' (Princeton 1.28), though the reason given in the *Colossus* is that the American consul had ordered him back because of the war. On the GS/Miller correspondence, see Thaniel, *Seferis and Friends*, 135–6.

55 MacNiven, *Durrell*, 218–22 (quoting Stephen Spender on Spencer); M4.26; 39.

56 M3.239; 244–6: 28 September 1940; S/M1.401–2: GS to Maro, 11 September 1940; *Labrys* 8 (1983), 52: GS to Miller, 8 October 1940; Miller, *Colossus*, 180; 214; MacNiven, *Durrell*, 222, 225, 227, 584; Keeley, *Inventing Paradise*, 166. The Argentina, M3.261. For Nimiec as British spymaster see the document cited in n. 65 below.

57 M3.147: 27 November 1939 (cf. M3.149–50); Gerald Durrell, *Birds, Beasts and Relatives* (London: Fontana, 1971; first published 1969), 43; cf. MacNiven, *Durrell*, 137–8.

58 M3.168; for Kambas see also M3.180; M4.79, 81, 82, 83, 106; for Valaoritis see also M3.163; Nanos Valaoritis, ['Autobiography'], *Contemporary Authors*, vol. 186 (2001), 402–3.

59 M3.115–16: 16 April 1939; cf. S/M1.335–6: GS to Maro, 18 July 1939; 337 n. 9. See also M3.218; 237–8; 244; 247; M4.21; 26; S/M1.277: GS to Maro, 26 July 1940; Alan Sheridan, *André Gide: A Life in the Present* (Cambridge, Mass.: Harvard University Press, 1998), 418; 530; 533; cf. André Gide, Robert Levesque, *Correspondance 1926–1950*, ed. Pierre Masson (Lyon:

60 Presses Universitaires de Lyon, 1995), 295.

60 Koliopoulos, *Greece and the British Connection*, 154–5.

61 X41.34–7; M3.164: 4 January 1940.

62 M2.114: [GS to Lou,] 11 March 1933 (and see p. 122 above); M3.75: 14 September 1937; M3.195–6: 24 May 1940.

63 M3.261–2: 5 November 1940; M3.264: 3 December 1940.

64 FO371/23782: [David Wallace, Press Attaché], memorandum enclosed in Athens Despatch, no. 485, 17 November 1939, cited and summarised in Koliopoulos, *Greece and the British Connection*, 154–5. A year later, the journalist Clare Hollingworth, who would have scathing things to say about the operation of press censorship in Greece, was surely echoing her briefing by Wallace: 'The Director of Foreign Press, George Seferiades, a man of high culture, an intellectual and poet, translator of the poems of T.S. Eliot into modern Greek, did his best, but the difficulties of the position were too much for him,' Clare Hollingworth, *There's a German Just Behind Me* (London: Secker and Warburg, 1942), 152–3. During the Greek-Italian war of 1940–1, when 'strict impartiality' was still the rule between the British and the Germans, GS invited the representative of the British Royal Air Force to exhibit photographs taken on a recent bombing raid against Italian positions in Albania, alerting him at the same time to the presence, in the audience, of a German correspondent. See T.H. Wisdom, *Wings over Olympus: The Story of the Royal Air Force in Libya and Greece* (London: Allen and Unwin, 1942), 84.

65 M3.252; X41.37; Vasos Mathiopoulos, Ο Γ. Σεφέρης στο στόχαστρο του ναζισμού, *I Lexi* 72 (1988), 116–18: *Chef der Sicherheitspolizei und des SD* to Foreign Ministry, Berlin, 10 September 1940 (facsimile and Greek translation).

66 M3.206: 19 June 1940 (original emphasis); X41.41–2.

67 M3.164–5: 26 January 1940; S/T 24: GS to Theotokas, 16 June 1940.

68 First epigraph, GN.I.B25. The extract from a ship's log, preserved among the early drafts of *Six Nights on the Acropolis*, in which the phrase appears repeatedly, is dated 16–20 November 1926; an undated accompanying letter refers to its receipt by the Greek embassy in London on 1 March 1927. I am grateful to Katerina Krikos-Davis for bringing it to my attention. Second epigraph to *Logbook [I]* cf. Henry Gifford, *Poetry in a Divided World: The Clark Lectures 1985* (Cambridge University Press, 1986), 7–8.

69 M3.167: 1 February 1940; M3.169: 15 February 1940.

70 M6.55: 11 October 1952, reproduced with minor changes in D2.203; Keeley/int. 195 (1968); for the drafts see Yatromanolakis, Ό Βασιλιάς της Ασίνης, 24–6; 66–8.

71 Respectively M3.241: 18 September 1940; M3.237: 10 September 1940. The poem first appeared in the periodical *Neoellenika Grammata* of 27 July 1940, and then in *Logbook* which went into circulation on 31 August.

72 P.185–7 = KS 134–6 ('Asini'). With the substitution of 'winter' for 'summer,' lines 32–7 conflate Lou's death back in August with that other August in Kifisia, when 'Princess Lu' had flown like a bird and turned into a dead sparrow; the

curious 'dog-teeth' are Salome's aggressive nipples in *Six Nights* (6N.65); line 37 alludes to the unglorious passage to the underworld of the slain suitors, at the end of the *Odyssey*.

73  P.185–7 = KS 134–6, lines 45–50; 58–60.

74  M3.185–191: 26–29 April 1940 (Good Friday-Easter Monday).

75  S/M1.374 (departure for Trapeza in July); S/M1.396: Maro to GS, 20 August 1940.

76  S/M1.384–6: Maro to GS, 22 July 1940.

77  S/M1.387–91: GS to Maro, [28 July 1940]. Dated only 'Sunday,' the letter has been published out of sequence with the date '11 August' supplied by the editor. The actual sequence of events can be reconstructed: 22 July, Maro writes to GS; Sunday 28 July is the actual date of S/M1.387–91, which is his reply and ends by proposing that she should come to Athens to discuss things; 2 August, Maro has received his reply to her letter of the 22nd two days ago, and is coming to Athens the following Tuesday (S/M1.386); 7 August (Wednesday), GS writes in his diary that Maro has been in Athens 'since yesterday' (M3.221); 9 August (Saturday), she leaves GS to talk to Londos' sister in Kolonaki and return direct to Trapeza (S/M393); 13 August, Maro reports to GS developments which had not been discussed while she was in Athens, and he takes her to task in his reply of 19 August (S/M1.391–4).

78  S/M1.10 ('the poet or your children'); S/M1.391–2: Maro to GS, 13 August 1940; cf. S/M1.393–7.

79  X41.40–3; M3.226: 15 August 1940 (quoted, original emphasis).

80  M3.229: 31 August 1940; Daskalopoulos, *Ergographia*, 45–56.

According to the colophons, *Book of Exercises* was printed in only a hundred copies, *Logbook* in three hundred. Two separate notes, dated 28 August 1940 and preserved with the manuscripts of *Logbook,* indicate that there were actually 200 copies printed of each (G.VIII.144, nos 3897, 3898).

81  S/M1.410: GS to Maro, 25 September 1940; M3.243: 26 September 1940 (quoted).

82  S/M1.411: Maro to GS, 27 September 1940; S/M1.412: GS to Maro, 29 September 1940 (quoted).

83  M3.258–9: 28 October 1940 (quoted). Metaxas and his ministers, X41.47; PE1.19 and later note, quoting Metaxas' diary (published 1950).

84  X41.51–3.

85  X41.45 (quoted); cf. P.J. Vatikiotis, *Popular Autocracy in Greece 1936–41: A Political Biography of General Ioannis Metaxas* (London: Frank Cass, 1998), 164–81; Koliopoulos, *Greece and the British Connection*, 167. Tsatsos' exile, KT 267–8; IT 368; M3.133: 7 September 1939.

86  S/T back cover; 26; M4.7: 6 January 1941 (Theotokas); M4.40: 12 March 1941 (Angelos); M4.170: GS to Miller, 25 December 1941 (on Katsimbalis, in English, original emphasis); MacNiven, *Durrell*, 226 (Stephanides); M4.30: 27 February 1941 (Antoniou); Anna Londou: interview; S/Mal. 181 n. (Londos); G.I.73: 14 February and 14 March 1941 (GS called up).

87  KT 279, cf. Koliopoulos, *Greece and the British Connection*, 167 and n. 2; M3.264–5: 3 December 1940 (quoted).

88  M4.19; 21–2 (memories of Skala, Sotiris, etc.); M4.23; 24; 28; 30; 36 (Maro's experiences).

89  M3.261; M4.11, but see PE1.283 n.6 (location of Under-Ministry); X41.74

450

n. 52 (press conferences); M3.262: 10
November 1940 (quoted).

90  M3.256: 18[?] October 1940; M4.27:
19 February 1941 (quoted), cf.
Keeley/int. 193–4.

91  Koliopoulos, *Greece and the British
Connection*, 216–7. GS lists four
others as 'fixers' (M4.16: 29 January
1941).

92  M4.20: 20 February 1941.

93  M4.40: 14 March 1941.

94  M4.29; 34–5; for the Tatoi
meeting of 22–23 February, and
its consequences, see Koliopoulos,
*Greece and the British Connection*,
235–62.

95  M4.49–50: 6 April 1941; X41.65–6
(official Greek translation, my
emphases).

96  M4.53: 10 April 1941; PE2.XI:
certificate dated 9 April 1941.

97  KT 196; S/M1.11 (GS's words, as
recalled by Maro, quoted).

## 7  The Second Exile (1941–1943)

1  Olivia Manning, 'Poets in Exile,'
*Horizon*, 10/58 (1944), 275.

2  John S. Koliopoulos, *Greece and the
British Connection 1935–1941* (Oxford
University Press, 1977), 268; 277.
First mention of evacuation, M4.54:
11 April 1941.

3  M4.55: 16 April 1941.

4  Patricia Storace, *Dinner with
Persephone* (London: Granta,
1997), 320; 359; see also Penelope
Delta, *Αναμνήσεις, 1921*, ed. Alekos
P. Zannas (Athens: Ermis,
1996).

5  M4.54–60.

6  GS on the German blacklist, M4.61;
X68.43 and n. Means of evacuation,
ELIA: GS to Georgios Roussos, 20
May 1943, pp. 5–6; cf. PE1.28.
G.X.40 contains a handwritten note
authorising embarkation of GS
and wife, unsigned, but stamped
'Ministry of Foreign Affairs,' dated
22 April 1941.

7  For the reminiscence of the voyage
by another Englishman, the classical
scholar A.R. Burn, who had recently
met GS, see George Thaniel, *Seferis
and Friends*, ed. G. Phinney
(Stratford, Ontario: Mercury, 1994),
13.

8  M4.66; 81; 247–8.

9  Procopis Papastratis, *British Policy
towards Greece during the Second
World War 1941–1944* (Cambridge
University Press, 1984), 2–5; M4.68:
27 April 1941 (Maniadakis); M4.72:
30 April 1941 (quoted); M4.84: 14
May 1941 (police).

10  M4.75: 6 May 1941 (quoted, original
emphases); M4.76 (Cretan peasants);
M4.68; S/Mal 113 (*Erotokritos*).

11  M4.68: 29 April 1941; PE1.26: 28
April 1941; G.X.40: 2 May 1941
(*Government Gazette*); M4.78: 9
May 1941 (Nikoloudis).

12  PE1.28: 13 July 1941; ELIA: GS to
Roussos, 20 May 1943, p. 5; G.X.42
(1930).

13  M4.81–2: 12 May 1941; cf. M4.92: 24
May 1941; PE1.28.

14  M4.66: 25 April 1941; M4.72: 30
April 1941; M4.80: 11 May 1941.

15  M4.83–4: 14 May 1941.

16  M4.85–7: 16 May 1941; cf. D1.166–7.

17  M4.87–8: 16 May 1941.

18  M4.88–90: 17–19 May 1941; M4.107
('mouldy taste'); PE1.27. For the
pelican see also the poem 'Kerk Str.
Oost, Pretoria, Transvaal' (P.195 =
KS 143, lines 14–17) and S/Mal
72–75: GS to Malanos, 14 November
1941, where GS gives a different
interpretation of the reference to
the 'humiliated prime minister.' But
his 'explanations' for Malanos are
often tongue-in-cheek and on this
occasion perhaps also dictated by
prudence. Contrast the editor's note
at P.330. In the first edition, the
ink-drawn pelican is almost bald,
and comically huffy and
disgruntled; a series of sketches for

452

this image, preserved with the MSS for *Logbook II*, bears witness to the influence of Edward Lear (GN.I.A11, nos 31–4).

19    M4.92–6: 27–31 May 1941; 103 (quoted).

20    M4.107–8: 27 June 1941 (GS: 'Daniel' for 'Danial').

21    P.191 = KS 139, lines 11–14. Earlier draft dated 11 September 1941 sent to Malanos (S/Mal 56–7; cf. pp. 204–5 above).

22    S/Kats: Katsimbalis to GS, 16 October 1932; GS's comments on Cavafy at this time: M4.87; 101; and in retrospect: D2.363–9 (1960). For his views before this: S/Mal 32: GS to Malanos, December 1935; M3.85–92 (1937). GS on Cavafy's homosexuality, M3.87; S/M1.165; AP 24, 25. All the relevant published texts, as well as GS's unpublished anthology of Cavafy's poems, are included in G.P. Savvidis, *Ο Καβάφης του Σεφέρη*, vol. 1 (Athens: Ermis, 1984). E.M. Forster, 'The Poetry of C.P. Cavafy,' first published in idem, *Pharos and Pharillon* (1923), reprinted in *The Mind and Art of C.P. Cavafy: Essays on His Life and Work* (Athens: Denise Harvey & Co., 1983), 13 (quoted).

23    M4.94; 100; S/Mal 10–11 (editor's introduction); 27 (Panayotopoulos).

24    M4.94: 28 May 1941; recalled at M4.100–101.

25    Papastratis, *British Policy*, 7–8; C.M. Woodhouse, *The Apple of Discord: A Survey of Recent Greek Politics in their International Setting* (London: Hutchinson, 1948), 118–121. Woodhouse's book has the advantage of drawing closely on the author's personal involvement in many of the events; Woodhouse was a fluent Greek speaker and also a good friend of GS; it is only in dealing

with the actions and attitudes of the communists that Woodhouse loses the finely balanced objectivity that characterises the rest of his study (which was written while the Greek civil war was at its height, and the Cold War in its early stages). For additional material on the politics of the Greek government in exile, not cited below, see Emmanuel Tsouderos, *Διπλωματικά παρασκήνια, 1941–1944* (Athens: Aetos, 1949); Ilias Venezis, *Εμμανουήλ Τσουδερός*, 2 vols (Athens: privately printed, 1966); Vangelis Hatziangelis, *Το όγδοο τάγμα* (Athens: Rappas, 1994); A. Korantis, *Πολιτική και διπλωματική ιστορία της Ελλάδος (1941–1945)* (Athens: Estia, 1987).

26    M4.78: 9 May 1941 (Nikoloudis described); M4.96–8; PE1.26–7: 17 and 22 June 1941; cf. PE1.115; ELIA: GS to Roussos, 20 May 1943, p. 6.

27    M4.102: 17 June 1941; M4.169: GS to Miller, 25 December 1941 (quoted). On Durrell, see Thaniel, *GS and Friends*, 78 and Gordon Bowker, *Through the Dark Labyrinth: A Biography of Lawrence Durrell* (London: Sinclair-Stevenson, 1997), 146. See also S/Mal 48: GS to Malanos, 26 June 1941 (Liddell); M4.106–7; 108: 27 June 1941 (Spencer; Papadimitriou); for Papadimitriou in the evacuation and in Cairo see Manning, 'Poets in Exile,' 273.

28    M4.104–5: 27 June 1941; M4.113: 3 July 1941 (quoted, in English).

29    M4.110–12; PE1.27: 30 June 1941 (quoted).

30    M4.116–7: 7 July 1941. Some of the material discussed in the following pages is available in English, in George Seferis, *South African Diaries, Poems and Letters*, ed. with introduction by Roy Macnab (Cape Town: Carrefour Press, 1990).

31 M4.118: 8 July 1941; PE1.29–30: 27 July 1941 (Tsouderos described); M4.124: 27 July 1941.

32 PE1.28: 13 July 1941. For the term 'service diary,' and the published title 'political diary,' see p. 136 above.

33 M4.120–1: 13 July 1941; M4.122 ('ghastly'); cf. M4.139: 27 September 1941. The official confirmation from Tsouderos of Nikoloudis' position, with GS as his 'first secretary,' did not come through until 4 August 1941 (G.X.40).

34 M4.128: 3 September 1941; M4.206: 13 April 1942 (quoted); S/Mal 55: GS to Malanos, 2 October 1941; S/Mal 72–3: GS to Malanos, 14 November 1941; Maro/diary 74: 13 September 1941. Address of the embassy, S/Mal 138: GS to Malanos, 21 February 1942.

35 M6.134: 15 August 1954; Maro/diary 75: 13 September 1941 (GS's daily routine); 77: 18 November 1941.

36 Maro/diary 77: 12 September 1941; M4.128: 14 September 1941 (both of which give the impression that the poems were written on the 12th). The first version of 'Days of June '41' which was sent to Malanos on 2 October (SMal 56–57) carries the dateline 'Pretoria 11.9.41;' in the first edition of *Logbook II* only the date appears; the standard edition has 'Crete-Alexandria-South Africa, May-Sept. '41' (reflecting the experiences encapsulated in the poem, rather than the date of writing). 'Postscript,' in all editions, has this date but no attribution of place. On the dating of these two poems see also Katerina Krikos-Davis, *Διαβάζοντας τον Σεφέρη: το 'Ημερολόγιο Καταστρώματος Β' και το πεζογραφικό έργο του ποιητή* (Athens: Ikaros, 1989), 184. It does not seem to have been noticed before that Maro's account quite clearly distinguishes the writing of *two* poems on the same evening.

37 P.192 = KS 140; Maro/diary 74: 13 September 1941.

38 Maro/diary 75: 16 September 1941.

39 P.193–4 = KS 141–2: 'The Figure of Fate,' lines 16–17.

40 X41.61–2.

41 M4.150: 15 December 1941 (quoted), cf. Krikos-Davis, *Διαβάζοντας τον Σεφέρη,* 71 (flowers); Maro/diary 76: 12 November 1941 ('colony,' quoted); M4.198–9: 17 March 1942 (Dr Ley). See also S/Mal 50: GS to Malanos, 16 August 1941; M4.193: 8 March 1942.

42 M4.159: GS to Durrell, November 1941. See also M4.122; 144; S/Mal 56: GS to Malanos, 2 October 1941; TGB 76. The more salacious limericks appear in Mathios Paschalis [*sic*, for 'Paskalis,' = George Seferis], *Τα Εντεψίζικα,* ed. G.P. Eftychidis [= Savidis] (Athens: Leschi, 1989), 13–28. More innocent ones, with other light verse, were collected into the illustrated album that GS presented to Maro's granddaughter, Daphne Krinou, in 1961, and which was subsequently published in facsimile as George Seferis, *Ποιήματα με ζωγραφιές για μικρά παιδιά* (Athens: Ermis, 1975), see pp. 8–44.

43 P.189 = KS 137 (the epigraph was originally an untitled *calligramme,* reproduced on p. 224 above); P.207 = KS 151, where the title is rendered as 'Calligraphy'. See also TGB 108–119.

44 S/Mal 50: GS to Malanos, 16 August 1941 ('Say what you like . . .') The copying of the Cavafy canon was done between 18 October and 11 November 1941 (M4.145; M4.161 = S/Mal 64–7); work on the book continued sporadically until February 1942 (M4.147–8; 176; 179; 188). The draft preface, dated 18

453

454

October 1941, was first published by
G.P. Savidis, *Εφήμερον σπέρμα*
(Athens: Ermis, 1978), 255–6,
reprinted in Krikos-Davis,
*Διαβάζοντας τον Σεφέρη*, 41–2. For
GS's choice of publication method
in 1944, see Savvas Pavlou,
Η κατάργηση της τυπογραφίας.
Ιδεολογικές και τεχνολογικές ερμηνείες,
*Mikrophilologika* (Nicosia, Cyprus),
5 (1999), 40–4, and pp. 228, 237
above.

45 *Personal Landscape* 1 (January
1942), 10 = M4.159: GS to Durrell,
November 1941 ('We are going
backwards . . . mythology'); Princeton
1.5: Durrell to GS: 3 February 1942.

46 Respectively, Maro/diary 77: 26
January 1942 (cf. M4.179–80: 26
January 1941 and S/Mal 137: GS to
Malanos, 21 February 1942); G.X.40:
Papadakis/Tsouderos to GS, 23
January 1942, at 23.20, GS's hand-
written transcript with note, Ελήφθη
24.1.42 ώρα 11; M4. 80: 26 January
1941 (quoted). The change was
cautiously welcomed by the British
Foreign Office, see FO371/33161
(R4208), 15 June 1942, H.
Hopkinson, Minister of State's
Office, Cairo, to FO: 'M. Tsouderos
has further been at pains to improve
the Greek Propaganda Service in
the Middle East. For this purpose
M. Seferiadis, who had been a senior
official in the Ministry of Press and
Tourism in Athens, was transferred
from the staff of the Greek Minister
at Pretoria to that of M. Collas, late
Greek Minister at Bucharest, who
had been entrusted with Greek
propaganda work at Cairo. It is
hoped that this service will ensure a
steady flow of accurate news about
the Greek armed forces, and other
Greek affairs in the Middle East,
for the benefit of the Greek trans-
missions from London and Cairo,
and Greek publicity generally.'

47 PE1.39: 29 January 1942; M4.181–6
(p. 185 quoted); Maro/diary 78: 18
February 1942; cf. *Labrys* 8 (1983),
53–4: GS to Miller, 7 March 1942.

48 Anna Londou: interview; M4.170:
GS to Miller, 25 December 1941;
G.III.85: GS to Angelos, 1 March
1942; S/Apost 246: Apostolidis to
GS, 28 April 1942. On copies of GS's
letters see M4.156: GS to Nanis
Panayotopoulos, 24 October 1941;
GN.II.E contains approximately 1400
of these, dated between August 1941
and the eve of GS's death.

49 PE1.40–1: 11 March 1942; PE1.43–6:
1 April 1942. The fullest account of
conditions in occupied Greece can
be found in Mark Mazower, *Inside
Hitler's Greece* (New Haven and
London: Yale University Press,
1993).

50 M4.206–10.

51 M4.210–14.

52 Ioanna Tsatsou, *Φύλλα κατοχής*
(Athens: Estia, 3rd ed., 1976, first
published 1965).

53 M4.216: 29 June 1942.

54 Respectively, PE1.46: 8 July 1942;
FO371/37244 = *The Greek Gazette*
(London), vol. 29, nos 333–335
(May 1995), 6–14.

55 Papastratis, *British Policy*, 51–8.

56 PE1.46–8: 8 July 1942; M4.215–7
(p. 216: 29 June 1942 quoted). For
Kollas ('quite incompetent,' in the
confidential opinion of Leeper) see
FO371/37244.

57 P.201 = KS 146–7: 'An Old Man on
the River Bank,' lines 16–19; cf.
S/M1.75: GS to Maro, 27 December
1936 ('Sometimes I speak to you [i.e.
in letters], the way I would to an old
friend. This is your grace, and I
thank you for this gift.')

58 M4.273: 1 January 1943; M4.309: 11
October 1943.

59 Artemis Cooper, *Cairo in the War,
1939–1945* (London: Hamish
Hamilton, 1989), 190–201; M4.215;

217–223 (p. 218: 30 June 1942 quoted); cf. PE1.49: 17 July 1942.

60  M4.229–231.

61  P.203–6 = KS 148–50. The all-but-finished draft sent to Malanos a month later bears the date '23 July' (S/Mal 160–3: GS to Malanos, 10 August 1942), though GS's diary for the next day reports that the poem was 'stuck' (M4.233: 24 July 1942). Compare line 1 of this version ('Jerusalem, unreal city') with *The Waste Land*: 'Unreal City,/Under the brown fog . . .' (lines 60–1); 'Jerusalem Athens Alexandria/Vienna London/Unreal' (lines 373–6).

62  On the *Struma* see M4.228: 18 July 1942, and a possible allusion in P.203–6 = KS 148–50, lines 26–30; the suggestion is made by Christopher Williams, *Readings in Eliot: Allusion as Technique in the Poetry of George Seferis* (unpublished doctoral thesis, King's College London, University of London, 1997), 121. The quotation is from M4.215: 26 June 1942.

63  M4.233–7 (pp. 236, 237 quoted). Collapse of European civilisation and the need to save 'man' instead, M4.223–4: 6 July 1942. For a comparable use of a public notice, in English, see 'Neophytos the Recluse Speaks Out' (P.259–60, not included in KS) and ch. 11 n. 4.

64  PE1.51: 27 July 1942; M4.238: 27 July 1942; PE2.XI.

65  Ian MacNiven, *Lawrence Durrell, A Biography* (London: Faber, 1999), 247; M4.253–4: 7 and 11 October 1942; PE1.53–4 (quotations); 67; 68.

66  M4.282; D3.242; Tsatsou, *Φύλλα*, 49–53; 56–7; 165; cf. KT 192.

67  S/Mal 181, n. 1 and 3; PE1.93: 20 January 1943; Anna Londou: interview (Mina and Anna in Athens).

68  PE1.56–9; 62; 68–75; 78–9; 81; 82; 87 (quoted); for background see Papastratis, *British Policy*, 67–9.

69  Panayotis Kanellopoulos, *H ζωή μου* (Athens: D. Yiallelis, 1985), 63. See also Papastratis, *British Policy*, 90–104.

70  PE1.98–100: 14 March 1943; Panayotis Kanellopoulos, *Ημερολόγιο* (Athens: Kedros, 1977), 385–8; Papastratis, *British Policy*, 74–85.

71  PE1.93–4; 96–7; Kanellopoulos, *H ζωή μου*, 70–74; FO371/37244 = *Greek Gazette*.

72  PE1.102: 17 March 1943.

73  GS on Tsouderos, PE1.118: 14 April 1943 (quoted, original emphasis). The new government was sworn in on 24 March (Kanellopoulos, *Ημερολόγιο*, 421). Consequences for GS, PE1.112: 3 April 1943 (transfer to Tehran); M4.287: 14 April 1943 (shopping for move to Ankara); PE1.119: 18 April 1943 (signed decree delivered to GS).

74  PE1.114; 115; 117; *Colossus*, PE1.48–9: 8 July 1942.

75  FO371/37244 = *Greek Gazette*.

76  PE1.115: 7 April 1943. The Greek word δημοκρατικός, used of GS here, means both 'democratic' and 'republican;' here, as often, it could be understood in either sense, or in both.

77  Lecture on Palamas, M4.285: 7 March 1943; D2.386. The address given in March was only half the length of the version he gave in Alexandria four months later, that appears in D1.214–27 (M4.293: 14 June 1943); for the original version having been commissioned, AP 65. Lecture on Makriyannis: S/Mal 176: Malanos to GS, [May 1943]; S/Mal 178: GS to Malanos, 23 May 1943; cf. M4.289–90; D2.386; text = D1.228–63.

78  D1.263.

455

79　M4.289–90: 16–21 May 1943; PE1.120: 19 May 1943; PE1.121: 23 May 1943; cf. PE1.122: 27 June 1943, where GS reflects on the 'hatred' aroused in Tsouderos by 'my defence these last three months: self-defence against slander.'

80　Kanellopoulos, *Ημερολόγιο*, 448 (quoted); M4.291–2: 23 May 1943.

81　ELIA: GS to Roussos, 20 May 1943, p. 2.

82　In his verbal apologia to George Papandreou (PE1.210–1: 27 April 1944), which at this point runs close to his earlier letter to Roussos, GS stated his principles as 'liberal and democratic [or republican],' but omitted any mention of 'people's rule' (*λαοκρατία*).

83　PE1.120: 22 May 1943; PE1.122: 4 June 1943; PE2.XI: 4 June 1943.

84　P.208 = KS 152, lines 15–20 (published dateline: 24 June 1943); cf. Krikos-Davis, *Διαβάζοντας τον Σεφέρη*, 123–7.

85　M4.300: 26 July 1943 (Mussolini arrested).

86　M4.302 (quoted); P.209–10 = KS 266; the diary entry dates the genesis of the poem to 5 August 1943; Krikos-Davis, *Διαβάζοντας τον Σεφέρη*, 128–37. The Greek word θεατρίνοι, used in the title, is heavily loaded, and I have tried to bring this out in my slightly free rendering of the first line. GS's line-drawing is reproduced as the cover and frontispiece of PE1; for Tsarouchis see M5.23: 13 December 1945; edition described by Daskalopoulos, *Ergographia*, 72–5.

**8　'The Pain-Perpetuating Memory of Pain' (1943–1944)**

1　M4.307: 29 August 1943. On the political background and the delegation from the partisans see Procopis Papastratis, *British Policy towards Greece during the Second World War 1941–44* (Cambridge University Press, 1984), 104–12; C.M. Woodhouse, *The Apple of Discord: A Survey of Recent Greek Politics in their International Setting* (London: Hutchinson, 1948), 150–8. For additional background see ch. 7, n. 25.

2　M4.303: 12 August 1943.

3　C.M. Woodhouse: interview (quoted); Ioanna Tsatsou, *Φύλλα κατοχής* (Athens: Estia, 3rd ed., 1976, first published 1965), 38; 50; 54; 102–5; 125–8; and Kyd9.74; Komninos Pyromaglou, *Ο Γεώργιος Καρτάλης και η εποχή του, 1934–57* (Athens: Istoriki Erevna, 1965); cf. FO371/43754: Leeper to FO, 11 July 1944.

4　P.211 = KS 153: 'Here Among the Bones' (published dateline 'August 1943'). In the first edition the dateline is '1 August;' but this is surely incorrect, as the *antartes* did not arrive until the 9th, and GS did not meet Kartalis until the 12th.

5　PE1.123; M4.303–4 (p. 303 quoted: 22 August 1943).

6　M4.307: 19 September 1943 (Kartalis' safe arrival in Greece).

7　PE1.124–6: 24 October 1943.

8　Daskalopoulos, *Ergographia*, 59–60; M4.296: 23 June 1943; M4.310: 27 October 1943; M4.329: 24 March 1944. For Malanos' assistance and support in the early stages of planning the volume see S/Mal 185; 188.

9　GS's preface reproduced, D3.111–12. For the fullest account of the edition, see S/Mal 247–8 n. 3. The first mention of *Akritika* in GS's diary is M4.316–17: 12 December 1943; cf. S/Mal 205: Malanos to GS, 3 January 1944. See also M4.323; PE1.158. Although the handwritten colophon dates the publication to March 1944, GS was chivvying Malanos on the subject at the end of June (S/Mal 246–7: GS to Malanos,

27 June 1944); the edition was still not ready for circulation in early July (S/Mal 249–50: Malanos to GS, 4 July 1944 and GS's reply), and was eventually published while GS was in London with Kartalis (13 July–13 August), see S/Mal 253: GS to Malanos, 22 August 1944. On Apkar see S/Mal 48: GS to Malanos, 25 June 1941 and n. 1.

10 GN.II.E4: GS to Durrell, 29 January 1944 (draft). GS's letters to Durrell are now in the Collection of Southern Illinois University at Carbondale. D3.113–4: 'Mathios Paskalis: His Ideas About Poems' ('Mathaios Pascal' in *Personal Landscape* vol. 2, part 3 [1944], 2). Originally written in English; original emphases.

11 D3.148 (1961).

12 The translation carries the addition 'II' to the title; this was the original title of the poem before Durrell re-titled its predecessor 'Coptic Poem,' see George Thaniel, *Seferis and Friends*, ed. G. Phinney (Stratford, Ontario: Mercury 1994), 77; 102 n. 1. The translated poem was dropped from *Logbook II*, from the 2nd edition (1945) onwards, but is included in *Antigrafes*.

13 'The King of Asini' [sic], *Personal Landscape* vol. 2, part 3 (1944), 9–10; Thaniel, *GS and Friends*, 88–9: Durrell to GS, 29 March 1944 and undated [1944]. These letters are now in the Princeton collection (Princeton 1.5). The translation is unsigned, but 'we' in Durrell's letters implies collaboration, which must have been with Spencer. The collaboration with Nanos Valaoritis could not have begun before the end of August 1944, see M4.347–8: 27 August 1944 and Nanos Valaoritis, Μοντερνισμός, πρωτοπορία και Πάλι (Athens: Kastaniotis, 1997), 17–18.

14 Jonathan Bolton, *Personal Landscapes: British Poets in Egypt During the Second World War* (London: Macmillan 1997), xviii, xix (quoted). See also Roger Bowen, *Many Histories Deep: The Personal Landscape Poets in Egypt* (Madison, NJ: Fairleigh Dickinson University Press, 1995); Gordon Bowker, *Through the Dark Labyrinth: A Biography of Lawrence Durrell* (London: Sinclair-Stevenson, 1997), 142–7 and Preface, n. 2.

15 Ian MacNiven (ed.), *The Durrell-Miller Letters 1935–80* (London: Faber, 1988), 174–5: Durrell to Miller, 22 August 1944. A year later, in the epilogue to *Prospero's Cell*, Durrell would remember warmly, among his fellow-exiles in Egypt, 'Maro, the human and beautiful, in her struggle against apathy . . . the solemn face of Seferiades with its candour and purity,' Lawrence Durrell, *Prospero's Cell* (London: Faber, 1975; 1st ed. 1945), 143; cf. Thaniel, *GS and Friends*, 87.

16 M4.332: 10 May 1944; for the proposal see S/Mal 229–30: Malanos to GS, undated [May 1944]; GS response in S/Mal 232; 234; finally 239: 13 May 1944.

17 GN.II.E4: GS to Durrell, 8 February 1944 (draft); part cited by Ian MacNiven, *Lawrence Durrell, A Biography* (London: Faber, 1999), 286.

18 M4.321: 30 January 1944.

19 PE1.136: 7 January 1944; PE1.152: 8 February 1944 (quoted); cf. M4.328: 30 January 1944. New job designation, PE2.XI; cf. PE1.309: GS to George Papandreou, 28 April 1944, para. 2. Also quoted: Angelos S. Vlachos, Μια φορά κι ένα καιρό ένας διπλωμάτης..., 6 vols (Athens: Estia, 1985–8), 1.155–6.

20 For a detailed account of the politics behind the April mutinies

see Papastratis, *British Policy,*
165–77.

21 PE1.161: 24 March 1944; Woodhouse,
*Apple of Discord,* 187; PE1.166–7: 30
March–1 April 1944.

22 PE1.168–9: 3 April 1944.

23 PE1.170–1: 4 April 1944. On the
events of the naval mutiny, see
Mark C. Jones, 'Misunderstood and
Forgotten: The Greek Naval Mutiny
of April 1944,' *Journal of Modern
Greek Studies,* 20/2 (2002), 367–97.

24 PE1.169–78: 4–6 April 1944 (S.
Venizelos, p. 171 quoted); PE1.182–3:
8 April 1944.

25 PE.174: 5 April 1944 (quoted);
PE1.184–5: 8 April 1944; PE1.299
n. 43.

26 Respectively, PE1.185: 9 April 1944;
PE1.196: 13 April 1944 (quoted);
PE1.189: 9 April 1944 (quoted).

27 Artemis Cooper, *Cairo in the War,
1939–1945* (London: Hamish
Hamilton, 1989), 293–304;
PE1.203–4: 23 April 1944;
PE1.191–2: 11 April 1944, reported
dialogue, GS to Nikolareïzis
(quoted); cf. the very similar
sentiments at PE1.196: 13 April 1944.
'Anglo-Greek war,' PE1.202: 18 April
1944.

28 PE1.208: 25 April 1944. The quoted
phrase, from Aeschylus' *Agamemnon*
(line 180: μνησιμήμων πόνος) also
appears in his next poem, 'Last Stop'
(cf. epigraph to this chapter).

29 PE1.206: 25 April 1944 and PE1.211:
27 April 1944 (murder of Psarros);
PE1.193: 11 April 1944 (the Russians
at Odessa); PE1.199: 13 April 1944;
see also PE1.200–1; 204; 207.

30 PE1.206: 25 April 1944 (quoted). GS
reports hearing that Papandreou
had been expressly brought out
from Greece by the British, who had
despaired of Venizelos (PE1.229: 8
May 1944), but see Woodhouse,
*Apple of Discord,* 188–9, who gives
a different explanation.

458

31 Contemporary and subsequent
opinions of Papandreou's first
premiership, Lincoln MacVeagh,
*Ambassador MacVeagh Reports,* ed.
John O. Iatrides (Princeton
University Press, 1980), 508–9 (28
April 1944: 'His personality has
completely revolutionized the Greek
Foreign Office, which now has
something vital and expansive in
it'); Panayotis Kanellopoulos, *Η ζωή
μου* (Athens: D. Yiallelis, 1985), 75;
G.M. Alexander, *The Prelude to the
Truman Doctrine: British Policy in
Greece 1944–1947* (Oxford University
Press, 1982), 19; 51; and Christos
Tyrovouzis, Η πρώτη πρωθυπουργία
του Γεωργίου Παπανδρέου και το
συνέδριο του Λιβάνου. Ιστορικο-
πολιτικοί όροι, in P. Petridis and G.
Anastasiadis (eds), *Γεώργιος
Παπανδρέου: 60 χρόνια παρουσίας και
δράσης στην πολιτική ζωή*
(Thessaloniki: University Studio
Press, 1994), 323–43. Papandreou's
programme announced on 27 April
1944, Woodhouse, *Apple of Discord,*
189. On the Lebanon Conference
and Charter, see n. 42 below. GS's
view, M4.333: 23 May 1944;
PE1.233: 23 May 1944; PE1.234–6.

32 GS on Papandreou, PE1.233–4: 24
May 1944; PE1.234: 8 July 1944
('histrionically . . . '); PE1.236–7: 12
July 1944 ('like a drunk'); PE1.238:
19 July 1944. Negative comments on
Papandreou reported, PE1.208: 25
April 1944; PE1.211: 27 April 1944
('straw-man'); PE1.216: 30 April
1944 ('Tsouderos').

33 PE1.210–16; text of letters in
PE1.309–14; 315.

34 PE1.254: 21 August 1944 (quoted);
PE1.216: 30 April 1944; PE1.224:
6 May 1944. Angelos Vlachos'
comment on GS's dismissal is
characteristically ungenerous: 'How
could the hypersensitive, timid and
rather amateurish Seferis, for all his

35 PE1.221: 3 May 1944.

36 PE1.174; 179; 185; M4.331: 10 May 1944 (quoted); P.45 = KS 5: *Mythistorema* 3, lines 9–10 (quoted). On the visual symbol see Katerina Krikos-Davis, Διαβάζοντας τον Σεφέρη: το Ἡμερολόγιο Καταστρώματος Β' και το πεζογραφικό έργο του ποιητή (Athens: Ikaros, 1989), 27 and n. 55. For description of the first edition of *Logbook II*, see Daskalopoulos, *Ergographia*, 63–9. The reprint of 1973 is now almost as rare (*Ergographia*, 153). See also pp. 208–9 above.

37 GS and Maro visited Tsouderos and his wife privately in their flat at Zamalek, apparently united by their antipathy to Papandreou (PE1.231–2: 11 May 1944). GS's personal relations with Tsouderos seem to have improved markedly from the beginning of February 1944, that is after Roussos' resignation from the government, PE1.147–8: 1 February 1944; PE1.148: 7 February 1944.

38 S/Mal 229: Malanos to GS, [May 1944]; S/Mal 231–2: GS to Malanos, 9 May 1944 and cf. M4.331–2: 10 May 1944; S/Mal 235: GS to Malanos, 12 May 1944 (quoted).

39 S/Mal 235–6: GS to Malanos, 12 May 1944.

40 S/Mal 237–8: GS to Malanos, 13 May 1944 ('interaction': επιμεζεία). GS would elaborate his position a little more in response to a public debate in *Nea Estia*, a little over a year later; see D1.264–7, first published 1 August 1945 (D2.386).

41 S/Mal 243: Malanos to GS, 17 May 1944 ('You don't shut me up . . .'); cf. S/Mal 245: Malanos to GS, 19 May 1944. S/Mal 312: Malanos to GS, 28 December 1949 (quoted); cf. p. 295 below.

42 On the Lebanon Conference, and particularly the role of Leeper behind the scenes, see Papastratis, *British Policy*, 177–86. For the text of the Lebanon Charter, in English, see Woodhouse, *Apple of Discord*, 305. GS, Kartalis and news from Greece, PE1.232–3: 23 May 1944; M4.322–3: 23 May 1944.

43 M4.333–5; PE1.233–7. For a historical assessment of Kartalis' mission see Prokopis Papastratis, Ο Γεώργιος Καρτάλης στην Κατοχή, in Εταιρεία Σπουδών Νεοελληνικού Πολιτισμού και Γενικής Παιδείας (Ιδρυτής: Σχολή Μοραΐτη) [Society for the Study of Modern Greek Culture, Moraitis School], Ο Γεώργιος Καρτάλης και η δύσκολη δημοκρατία (Athens: [Moraitis School], 1998), 55–84; see pp. 71–6; for the phrase 'oriental secretary' and a slightly different, positive, assessment see Alexandros Xydis, Ο πολιτικός Σεφέρης, in A. Argyriou et al., Κύκλος Σεφέρη (Athens: Moraitis School, 1980), 103–23, see pp. 114–15.

44 S/Mal 150: GS to Malanos, 13 July 1944 ('surprise,' in English); S/Mal 150–1: Maro to Malanos, 14 July 1944; PE1.237 = M4.334: 12 July 1944.

45 M4.334–6: 14–15 July 1944.

46 PE1.237–46; M4.338–9: 19 July 1944 (quoted; cf. PE1.244: 5 August 1944); M4.342–5. Vlachos (Μια φορά, 1.214) noted that Kartalis drank heavily.

47 John Lehmann, *In My Own Time* (Boston and Toronto: Little, Brown, 1969), 382; for background see Avi Sharon, 'New Friends for New

459

460

48 M4.342 (Powell and Russell);
M4.344 (Connolly); S/Mal 253: GS
to Malanos, 22 August 1944.

49 M4.64: 23 April 1941; M4.106: 27
June 1941; M4.334: 14 July 1944;
M4.340–2: 24 July 1944; Woodhouse,
*Apple of Discord,* 195.

50 S/M2: GS to Maro, July 1944;
M4.337–9.

51 PE1.240–1: 1 August 1944;
PE1.244–5: 7 August 1944; PE1.243:
3 August 1944 (quoted); Papastratis,
Ο Καρτάλης στην Κατοχή, 76.

52 Papastratis, Ο Καρτάλης στην Κατοχή,
73.

53 Papastratis, Ο Καρτάλης στην Κατοχή,
78 (citing PE1.262: 19 September
1944); PE1.243–4: 3–4 August 1944;
PE1.317 n. 136.

54 Tsatsos and A. Seferiadis, PE1.239:
26 July 1944; M4.345: 14 August
1944. Valaoritis, M4.347–8: 27
August 1944; Nanos Valaoritis,
['Autobiography'], *Contemporary
Authors,* vol. 186 (2001), 405–7 and
idem, Μοντερνισμός, πρωτοπορία και
Πάλι (Athens: Kastaniotis, 1997),
17–18.

55 PE1.246–58 (p. 258 quoted: 30
August 1944); M4.347–8. According
to Vlachos, 'The most miserable [at
this news], inexplicably to me,
almost whingeing, was George
Seferis' (Μια φορά, 1.203–4).

56 M4.349–54 (p. 354 quoted: 11
September 1944); PE1.259–60;
S/Mal 255–60. On 'Last Stop' see
immediately below; cf. P.228–9 = KS
168–70: 'Thrush' III, lines 70–1; cf.
P.239–42 = KS 177–9: 'Helen', lines
16–19.

57 M4.356–62 (on becoming a monk:
24 September and 4 October 1944);
M4.360 ('Greek landscapes').

58 PE1.261–7 (p. 262 quoted);
M4.357:17 September 1944; Vlachos,
Μια φορά, 1.196–7; 208–9.

59 PE1.318 n. 159; Papastratis, Ο
Καρτάλης στην Κατοχή, 77–8.
Vlachos (Μια φορά, 1.214) probably
reflects the majority view at Cava
when he describes Kartalis' press
conference as 'an unforgivably hare-
brained act.' PE1.269: 1 October
1944 (quoted). Cf. FO371/43754,
handwritten comment on Minute
R15338: 'Mr Kartalis has got into
hot water all round. A recent Most
Secret paper shows that the King
has complained to Papandreou
about his broadcasts as giving an
erroneous impression of the internal
situation in Greece.'

60 PE1.279–80: GS [to Kartalis], 7
October 1944 ('I'm writing all this
to you not because I've any desire to
see your ugly mug again, but
motivated by thoughts altogether
objective'). In the event, Kartalis did
not resign, but would rejoin the
government in Greece and keep his
post until its dissolution in
December.

61 PE1.271: 4 October 1944.

62 Papastratis, Ο Καρτάλης στην Κατοχή,
79.

63 TGB 84–5: Το απομεσήμερο ενός
φαύλου, dateline 'Cava dei Tirreni,
7.10.1944.'

64 PE1.277: GS to Nikos [Pantelidis];
GS to Panayotopoulos and Malanos,
both 23 September 1944 ('odyssey').
P.212–5 = KS 154–7: 'Last Stop,'
lines 20–2, cf. M4.362: 1 October
1944. In the first preserved draft of
the poem, the word 'islands,' at the
start of line 8, replaces the earlier
'mountains of Aegina' (GN.I.A11).
Moonlit nights in 1939–41,
M3.125–6: 3 August 1939; cf.
S/M1.342–3 and n. 2. (see p. 172
above); M4.53: 11 April 1941;
P.191 = KS 139, lines 10–11; see also

Krikos-Davis, Διαβάζοντας τον
Σεφέρη, 148–9.

65 PE1.260: 10 September 1944; P212–5
= KS 154–7: 'Last Stop,' lines 31–40.

66 P.212–5 = KS 154–7: 'Last Stop,'
respectively line 44 and GS note;
lines 82, 83–8; compare the whole
tenor of the Watchman's speech and
first chorus of the *Agamemnon* (see
also note 28 above and epigraph to
this chapter), as well as the author's
preface to Makriyannis' *Memoirs*.
See the abridged translation by H.A.
Lidderdale, *The Memoirs of
General Makriyannis* (London:
Oxford University Press, 1966), 5.

67 P212–5 = KS 154–7, lines 89–95;
cf. M4.30: 26 February 1941 and
Krikos-Davis, Διαβάζοντας τον
Σεφέρη, 164; 193 n. 119, and p. 189
above. The poem's published
dateline is 5 October, but in fact it
must had been begun on the voyage
from Alexandria (M4.354; 355: 11
and 13 September 1944), was not yet
finished on 16 October (M4.366),
and according to GS's much later
account would be finished in Athens
(AP 66). It is the only poem of
*Logbook II* of which substantial
manuscript versions survive; a note
on one of these indicates that the
poem was finally revised as late as
July 1946, although there is nothing
to indicate the extent of this
revision (GN.I.A11). Conceivably, the
poem's intimations of civil war to
come are not so prescient after all.
'Last Stop' was first published in
1947, and not incorporated into
*Logbook II* until the *Poems* of 1950
(Daskalopoulos, *Ergographia*, 78;
84–8).

68 M4.366–70 (p. 369 quoted); Peter
Levi, *The Hill of Kronos* (London:
Collins, 1980), 152 (quoted).

69 Papastratis, *British Policy*, 206;
Alexander, *Prelude*, 61–2; Mark
Mazower, *Inside Hitler's Greece*

(London and New Haven: Yale
University Press, 1993), 340–51.

70 Anna Londou: interview; published
interview in *Eleftherotypia* (Sunday
Supplement), no. 10, (20 January
2002), 8–12; Keeley/int. 186; cf. AP
38; Tsatsou, Φύλλα, 89–91; 171.

71 Alexander, *Prelude*, 50–1; *Labrys*
8 (1983), 55: GS to Miller, 7
December 1948 (quoted).

72 For these events, see Alexander,
*Prelude*, 77–91; Mazower, *Inside
Hitler's Greece*, 352–3; 368–72;
David Close, *The Origins of the
Greek Civil War* (London and New
York: Longman, 1995), 137–41; the
fullest account, including many
photographs, is by Lars Baerentzen,
'The Demonstration in Syntagma
Square on Sunday 3rd December
1944,' *Scandinavian Studies in
Modern Greek* 2 (1978), 3–52.

73 M4.374: 7 December 1944 (quoted);
cf. M4.378: 18 December 1944;
Alexander, *Prelude*, 79; Mazower,
*Inside Hitler's Greece*, 352.

74 M4.373–80 (M4.378: 20 December
1944 quoted).

**9 Descent into Hades (1945–1950)**

1 D2.283–4. The italicised words are
from *The Revelation of St John the
Divine* (or *Apocalypse*), 1.9, cited by
GS in the original New Testament
Greek, here given in the Authorized
Version.

2 *Labrys* 8 (1983), 55, in English.

3 M4.380–1: 25 December 1945.

4 Winston Churchill, *The Second
World War, Vol. 6, Triumph and
Tragedy* (London: Cassell, 1954),
273–9; G.X.40: Leeper [to GS], 26
December 1944.

5 G.M. Alexander, *The Prelude to the
Truman Doctrine: British Policy in
Greece 1944–47* (Oxford University
Press, 1982), 86–7; M4.381–2.

6 Ioanna Tsatsou, Φύλλα κατοχής
(Athens: Estia, 3rd ed., 1976, first

published 1965), 82: 24 March 1943;
Kyd9. 83–4; 99; KT 297 (quoted).

7   M4.382–3: 30 December 1944.
    Here, as often, the word
    δημοκρατικός (translated as
    'republican') is ambiguous, but
    probably refers to Damaskinos'
    known Venizelist background, rather
    than to a commitment to the
    democratic process. Damaskinos'
    angina, Tsatsou, Φύλλα, 158.

8   M5.16 = PE2.17: 24 May 1945;
    PE2.XI.

9   M5.11–16; PE2.15–17.

10  There is a traditional-style
    biography of Damaskinos by the
    novelist Ilias Venezis (Athens: Estia,
    1981). For background, see
    Demosthenes Koukounas, O
    αρχιεπίσκοπος Δαμασκηνός (Athens:
    Metron, 1991), which reproduces a
    large number of documents, chiefly
    from the period of the Occupation;
    additional details in Yorgos N.
    Karayiannis, Η εκκλησία από την
    Κατοχή στον Εμφύλιο (Athens:
    Proskinio, 2001).

11  GS's disillusion with the left is
    explicit in M4.382: 20 December
    1944. On the critical attitude of the
    left to his work see M.5.18: July
    1945 and X. Kokolis, Το έργο του
    Σεφέρη και η αριστερή κριτική,
    1931–1950, in idem, Σεφερικά μιας
    εικοσαετίας (Thessaloniki: Paratiritis,
    1993), 211–24; see pp. 216–9.

12  Alexander, Prelude, 78–9; 90; 103–4;
    133; PE2.110; cf. 129–32. Leeper's
    own memoir of these events,
    published when many of the
    protagonists were still alive, conveys
    an engaging enthusiasm and has
    some vivid details, but is
    understandably somewhat bland on
    the politics; Reginald Leeper, When
    Greek Meets Greek (London: Chatto
    and Windus, 1950). No Greek
    officials are mentioned by name,
    and there is sadly no trace of

Leeper's close working relationship
with GS.

13  Steven Runciman, 'Some Personal
    Memories,' Labrys 8 (1983), 47–9,
    p. 47 quoted. The British Institutes
    were re-amalgamated with the
    British Council offices in Athens and
    Thessaloniki in 1950, see Jon
    Stallworthy, Louis MacNeice
    (London: Faber, 1995), 376–7;
    382–4.

14  Avi Sharon, 'An Anglo-Hellenic
    Colossus,' Anglo-Hellenic Review, 21
    (Spring 2000), 3–4. Apart from its
    name, this periodical, published in
    English by the Anglo-Hellenic
    League in London, has no
    connection with its predecessor.

15  Nanos Valaoritis, ['Autobiography'],
    Contemporary Authors, vol. 186
    (2001), 406–7; S/Val: Valaoritis to
    GS, 27 May 1945 ('best known...');
    10 December 1945 ('Seferis book').
    See also Avi Sharon, 'New Friends
    for New Places: Facets of England's
    Rediscovery of Greece,' Arion,
    Third Series, 8/2 (2000), 42–62.

16  M5.16: 8 May 1945; cf. M5.18: 12
    August 1945.

17  Alexander, Prelude, 125–33;
    PE2.17–24; esp. p. 23: 26 August
    1945.

18  PE2.26–8; 29; 30; 33; 39; 40; 42; 43.
    Damaskinos had official meetings
    with Bevin on 7, 17, and 18
    September. GS was present only at
    the last of these (PE2.43 and n.);
    the private meeting proposed by GS,
    at the house of the MP Francis
    Noel-Baker (who had a house on
    Euboea and spoke Greek), never
    took place (PE2.32–3).

19  PE2.35: 13 September 1945.

20  FO371/48280; minute by Orme
    Sergeant, 14 September 1945,
    summarising 'the Regent's version
    of the conversation as given to Sir
    R. Leeper' (quoted). Alexander
    (Prelude, 135) over-interprets this

source when he says 'the meeting ended on a discordant note.' Leeper's later published account plays down the significance of the meeting, and naturally includes no hint of his conversations with GS (*When Greek Meets Greek*, 178–80).

21 PE2.37: 13 September 1945.

22 GS and Damaskinos in Paris, PE2.9 (photograph): 20 September 1945; PE2.43: 22 September 1945.

23 M5.17: 3 June 1945; PE2.49–50: 1 October 1945; PE2.56: 22 October 1945 (quoted); PE2.57: 24 October 1945; M5.25: 'Christmas 1945;' GN.II.E5: GS to Stelios, 30 September 1946. See also KT 195, where this event is dated during the Occupation and elided with the sale of the house in 1948, on which see below. PE2.56 ('dispersal'); D3.242, from where it appears that Angelos left in 'spring 1946.'

24 PE2.62–3.

25 PE2.53–4: 16–17 October 1945. Karayiannis, Εκκλησία, 66–7, reproduces some of the newspaper headlines and cartoons. See also PE2.62: 31 October 1945 ('He holds a strong hand of cards and is losing them. He's playing badly'); PE2.54: 16 October 1945; '*Sésame, ouvre-toi,*' PE2.61: 31 October 1945.

26 Alexander, *Prelude*, 143–5; 150–3; PE2.50: 1 October 1945; PE2.59: 28 October 1945; PE2.64: 2 November 1945 (quoted); PE2.68: 22 November 1945. Damaskinos at Kydathinaion Street, PE2.61: 31 October 1945; PE2.66: 18 November 1945.

27 PE2.60: 28 October 1945; cf. PE2.49: 1 October 1945; PE2.67–8: 20 November 1945.

28 Alexander, *Prelude*, 188–94; PE2.87–98.

29 PE2.223–4, n. 29 (editor's note). On Kyrou, see PE1.18–19.

30 Keeley/int. 212; PE2.109–10: 28 September 1946.

31 See, for example, Alexander, *Prelude*, 143–7 and *passim*; David Close, *The Origins of the Greek Civil War* (London and New York: Longman, 1995), 183–4; 189–99. That GS did appreciate the importance of the economic issue, and realised that vital opportunities were being wasted, is clear from PE2.68–9: 22 November 1946; but it is indicative of GS's pre-war, Venizelist mind-set, that the 'favour' he urged Damaskinos to press for, in London, was not economic aid (he may have assumed that would come anyway), but territorial (see above). On what would nowadays be called 'confidence building,' GS's service diary is silent, although the third part of the poem '*Thrush*,' discussed below, shows how deeply he was aware of this need too, at least in theory.

32 National Theatre from 14 February 1945 (G.V.4; D2.310) to 10 May 1946 (G.V.4; M5.32; cf. S/L 134); National Radio from 9 July 1945 to 6 May 1946 (G.X.6). For poems, see TGB 9–14 (first published in M5.12–14; 24; 31); TGB 86–8; M5.17: July 1945 (the first draft of what, 21 years later, would become *Three Secret Poems* II.6); M5.18–19; 30. Essay = D1.268–319 (cf. D2.386; M5.31: 11 March 1946). GS wearing glasses, M5.23: 13 December 1945.

33 Ian MacNiven, *Lawrence Durrell, A Biography* (London: Faber, 1999), 322–3, citing Durrell to Stephanides, c. March, 1946; M5.31: 21 April 1946; M5.33: 5 May 1946.

34 M5.33–4: 24 May 1946 (quoted). Robert Levesque, *Séféris. Choix de poèmes traduits et accompagnés du texte grec avec une préface.* Collection de l'Institut Français d'Athènes (Athens: Ikaros, 1945); cf.

463

Daskalopoulos, *Ergographia*, 70–1;
M5.15: 23 April 1945. GS and
leftwing criticism, Kokolis, Το έργο,
217–8, citing *Rizospastis*, 14 April
1946, with commentary.

35  M5.36–7: 29 May 1946; D2.55
(1949).

36  M5.46: 6 August 1946
(demobilisation); M5.44: 29 June
and 1 July 1946 (landscape); M5.33:
12 May 1946 (another world);
M5.37–8: 2 June 1946 (eternity,
quoted). On the last see D1.122 and
p. 110 above; also M5.41–2: 17 June
1946; M5.105: 13 July 1947
('I had the feeling I'd seen a
moment of eternity').

37  M5.38–9: 4 June 1946.

38  Notes for '*Thrush*,' M5.52–6 = TGB
15–17. Visit to Poros, M5.47: 11
August 1946. Death of Nikolaos
(Nelos) Dragoumis, M4.147: 4
November 1941. Shipwreck, M5.51:
16 August 1946 (quoted); cf. Andreas
Karantonis, Ο ποιητής Γιώργος
Σεφέρης (Athens: Estia, 1957),
149.

39  PE2.107–12; S/M2: GS to Maro, 25
September 1946.

40  M5.47–8; 50; GN.II.E5: GS to
Durrell, 4 October 1946. Cf. M5.51:
2 October 1946.

41  Stage on a journey, M5.70: 24
October 1946; M5.75: 31 October
1946, cf. D2.34. GS and Maro in
1936, this appears to be the meaning
of M5.47: 13 August 1946; cf. D2.34
and p. 145 above. Miller on Hydra,
see pp. 175–6 above and *Colossus*, 61
('. . . sat up with a bottle of whisky
talking to Ghika about the monks in
Tibet . . .'). Miller on Poros,
*Colossus*, 57–8 (quoted).

42  A copy of *The Simple Way* by Lao
Tze, given him by Durrell, was one
of the handful of books that GS had
with him in South Africa (M4.120:
13 July 1941). The book is Laotze,
*The Simple Way* (1929) = Vik. 3799;

GS cat. 1754; inscribed: 'Lawrence
Durrell, 1937. Corfu: Greece;' with a
note in Maro's handwriting that the
annotations are by Durrell. Also in
Pretoria, at the same time as the
*Colossus*, GS read *Some Sayings of
the Buddha*, introduction by F.
Younghusband (World's Classics,
1939 = Vik. 1867, GS cat. 1660),
inscribed: '16.9.41.' See also
M5.43–4: 26 June 1946 (quotation
from I.A. Richards, *Mencius on the
Mind*, also reproduced in the notes
to the first edition of '*Thrush*'); cf.
M5.145: 17 September 1949. See also
M5.71–7 for references to Zen and
the Japanese poet Basho. See also
TGB 89–92 and Nasos Vayenas, Ο
ποιητής και ο χορευτής: μια εξέταση
της ποιητικής και της ποίησης του
Σεφέρη (Athens: Kedros, 1979),
277–83.

43  M5.56–7; 59.

44  M5.60–66; M5.67–8: 21 October
1946 (original emphasis); see also
Edmund Keeley, '*Nostos* and the
Poet's Vision in Seferis and Ritsos,'
in Peter Mackridge (ed.), *Ancient
Greek Myth in Modern Greek
Poetry: Essays in Memory of C.A.
Trypanis* (London and Portland, Or:
Frank Cass, 1996), 81–96; and idem,
*Inventing Paradise: The Greek
Journey, 1937–47* (New York:
Farrar, Straus and Giroux, 1999),
239–47.

45  M5.74: 28 October 1946; M5.76: 31
October 1946 (original emphasis).

46  1) Robert Levesque, *Permanence de
la Grèce* (Les Cahiers du Sud, 1948),
337–8, reprinted in Kohler, 777–8
(note 69); Karantonis included a
Greek translation in his essay on the
poem for the *Anglo-Hellenic Review*,
January-February 1950 (= Ποιητής,
148; 151–2). A draft of the original
letter is preserved in GN.II.E5:
GS to Levesque, 1 August 1947. 2)
S/L 177–97 (text enclosed with S/L

464

38: GS to Lorenzatos: 4 September 1948; cf. M5.124). This version of the diary was not published until 1990, but Lorenzatos read it aloud to Karantonis, in order to help him write his article on the poem (S/L 64: Lorenzatos to GS, 22 May 1949; cf. GS's negative reaction, S/L 67–8: GS to Lorenzatos, 26 May 1949). Karantonis' article was first published in the *Anglo-Hellenic Review*, January–February 1950 (=*Ποιητής*, 131–67). 3) D2.30–56: GS to Katsimbalis, 27 December 1949, first published in the *Anglo-Hellenic Review*, July–August 1950; English translation in *Journal of the Hellenic Diaspora*, 7/2 (1980), 5–26. Only part of the text was included in the 2nd edition of D (1962); the decision to restore the full text in the now-standard 3rd edition (which appeared only posthumously, in 1974), was GS's own (D2.353 n.1; cf. D2.387).

47   D2.31–4; 49–52; 55–6; Karantonis, *Ποιητής*, 151–2. Later in the letter to Levesque, GS elaborates on the roles of 'Elpenor' and 'Circe' in Part II of the poem; but there is no mention of Odysseus, and the only authoritative figures from the ancient world mentioned are Socrates and Oedipus, who appear in Part III.

48   P.219–20 = KS 161–2, lines I 1, 40 quoted. On *Galini*, M5.50–1: 16 August 1946; D2.34. For a brief history of the house and its occupants, with recent colour photographs, see Alex Zannou, Οικία Γαλήνη: ο δρόμος είναι ακόμη πολύ στενός *(Γεύση*, summer 2000), 44–57; photography by Christos Potsios. I am grateful to Anna Londou for making this publication available to me.

49   P.221 = KS 163, '*Thrush*' II, subtitle and lines 1–11. Clearly irked that

'some readers are allowing themselves to believe that Elpenor is myself,' GS is surely unjust to his creation, consigning him among 'those blameless people who, precisely because they are facile, are often the best carriers of an evil whose source lies elsewhere' (D2.40).

50   P.221–3 = KS 163–6, lines 31, 26, 54 quoted. In the MS fair copy this section was entitled 'Talking with Circe' (Ομιλία με την Κίρκη) (G.VIII.147). Elpenor's 'visions' recall poems by GS written between 1928 and 1932; cf. Peter Mackridge, Ο ηδονικός Σεφέρης, *Akti* (Nicosia, Cyprus), 5/17 (1993), 43–8. The poem's epigraph (from Plutarch) had first been quoted to GS by the archaeologist Henri Seyrig, on the way to Olympia where he accompanied Edouard Herriot in August 1929 (M1.110). 'Images in the mirror,' in a comparable context, also appear in *Six Nights* (6N.120). The expression 'The world has become a vast hotel' (I 21) had first been used in a letter attributed to Stratis Thalassinos (M2.121: 6 April 1933). One of the prose sketches attributed to Stratis Thalassinos, probably of 1931, narrates an encounter that has affinities with that of Elpenor and Circe in the poem, particularly in its ending: 'We spoke in monosyllables till dawn and then we parted – she towards Hypate, which as the tale of the *Golden Ass* informs us, was once notorious for enchantresses and ghosts, and I towards Athens,' Yorgos Yatromanolakis (ed.), Παραλειπόμενα του κ. Στράτη Θαλασσινού, *Anti* (period B), no. 715 (9 June 2000), 43–5 (p. 45 quoted); cf. P.223 = KS 165, '*Thrush*' II 57–60. From the same group of texts comes the first articulation of

465

the light-dark paradox with which '*Thrush*' ends: 'Mr Stratis Thalassinos, although the day was full of sun, saw everything black' (G.VIII.154, no. 5938, dated 1931).

51 On the 'ivory tower' see pp. 238–9 above. In *Six Nights*, moments before the death of Salome/Bilio, she says to Lala: 'It's all over with the moonlight; Stratis needs the sun' (6N.234).

52 P.228–9 = KS 168–70: '*Thrush*' III 66–75; cf. M3.65: 8 July 1937 and p. 144 above.

53 P.229 = KS 169–70: '*Thrush*' III 75–81. 'scarce knowing...': the non-standard syntax of the Greek alludes to the sixteenth-century language of *Erotokritos* (GS's note).

54 The most important discussions of this poem are: Argyris Argyriou, Προτάσεις για την 'Κίχλη'. Μια πρώτη προσέγγιση, in Για τον Σεφέρη. Τιμητικό αφιέρωμα στα τριάντα χρόνια της Στροφής (Athens: Konstantinidis and Michalas, 1961), 250–91; Nasos Vayenas, Ποιητής, 247–97, and Mario Vitti, Φθορά και λόγος: εισαγωγή στην ποίηση του Γιώργου Σεφέρη, revd ed. (Athens: Estia, 1989), 175–240; also in French as *Introduction à la poésie de Georges Séféris* (Paris: L'Harmattan, 1996), 157–222.

55 M5.80: 4 November 1946; M5.82–3; S/Mal.277: GS to Malanos, 24 December 1946. The lecture was given at the British Institute on 17 December 1946 (D2.386; M5.85, text = D1.324–63). On plans for the book, M5.85: 1 January 1947; M5.86: 20 January 1947; much of the material on Cavafy that GS wrote at this time was eventually included in D1.364–457; the remainder appears in M5.157–71.

56 M5.80: 5 November 1946 (quoted);

cf. M5.81: 9 November 1946. These entries closely anticipate passages of the *Three Secret Poems*, P.279 = KS 199: I 3, line 9; P.298 = KS 208: III 6, lines 1–4; P.303 = KS 212: III 11, lines 1–4; and also D2.246 (1965, quoted); cf. M5.59: 12 October 1946 (collective memory). The phrase 'I am a question of light' also appears, without context, in M7.53: 1 October 1957 and P.280 = KS 200: *Three Secret Poems* I 4, lines 1–2. See also Vayenas, Ποιητής, 326, n. 72.

57 M5.83: 2 December 1946.

58 Poems, M5.77; 79 = TGB 92–3; TGB 94–6. Invitation, GN.II.E5: GS to Amaryllis Dragoumi, 1 November 1946. 'Now the local... ,' M2.82: 14 November 1946; John Lehmann, *In My Own Time* (Boston, Toronto: Little, Brown, 1969), 445 (quoted); Rex Warner, *Views of Attica and its Surroundings* (London: John Lehmann, 1950), 167.

59 GN.II.E5: GS to Katy [Katsoyanni], 21 November 1946. GS's acquaintance with Mitropoulos, D3.180–2; M7.27, 41–2. On preparations for GS's book in English, S/Val: Valaoritis to GS, 4 July 1946, telegram ('Please send consent about translations quickest possible. Love [Bernard] Spencer [and Nanos] Valaorities [*sic*, in English].' See also GN.II.E5: GS to Durrell, 4 October 1946; M5.89: 6 February 1947.

60 M5.46–7: 8 June 1946; M5.86–7: 20 January 1947.

61 Alexander, *Prelude*, 239–40; M5.85–6 (Athens and strike); PE2.XI: 19 April 1947 (duties).

62 Close, *Origins*, 209–10; Alexander, *Prelude*, 244.

63 G.II.51: cuttings dated 1 March 1947. See also *Nea Estia* 41 (15 March 1947), 369 (cited in Daskalopoulos, *Ergographia*, 71). Most of the texts of this and the succeeding disputes

are reproduced in Michalis Pitsilidis, *Οι σκοτεινές πλευρές του Γιώργου Σεφέρη* (Athens: Archipelagos, 2000), 233–308. GS on the Palamas prize, M5.90: 9 February 1947; M5.93–4: 26 February 1947.

64 D2.386; text of lecture = D1.458–66 (p. 460 quoted); I.M. Panayotopoulos, *Οι κλίκες*, *Grammata* (April–June 1947) and Η φυσιολογία της υπερβολής, *Nea Estia*, 480 (1 July 1947). These and other cuttings, G.II.53; GS's replies, D3.278–80; 393–4, reproduced by Pitsilidis (see n. 63 above).

65 Levesque working with GS, M5.15. Texts preserved, with GS's annotations, in G.II.53, cf. Pitsilidis, *Οι σκοτεινές πλευρές*. See also M5.104: 11 July 1947; D3.282–6; 394–5. 'Sans du tout connaître le grec, je m'étais mis en tête de minitier à la poésie grecque actuelle. Tantôt je recourais aux poètes eux-mêmes qui me traduisaient méticuleusement leurs propres oeuvres, tantôt un ami athénien [Katsimbalis] me faisait partager l'émotion qu'il ressentait devant tel ou tel poème' (Robert Levesque, Souvenirs d'un traducteur, *Alif, Revue Trimestrielle: Georges Séféris* (Tunis) 2 (June 1972), 137–40; cf. editor's introduction and commentary in André Gide, Robert Levesque, *Correspondance 1926–1950*, ed. Pierre Masson (Lyon: Presses Universitaires de Lyon, 1995).

66 S/Kats: Katsimbalis to GS, 27 May 1948.

67 PE2.119: 17–18 June 1947; PE2.225 n. 3; PE2.122–3: GS to Syndikas, 30 October 1947.

68 M5.119–20.

69 M5.120–1; 131; S/L 20–7; poem, TGB 23.

70 Previously posted to Izmir, 8 September 1933 and 26 February 1938, cf. M5.213: 17 October 1950.

GN.II.E7: GS to Beba [Farkouch], 2 March 1948. 'Descent into Hades,' M7.43: 28 February 1957.

71 M5.120: 4 February 1948; Angelos S. Vlachos, *Μια φορά κι ένα καιρό ένας διπλωμάτης...* , 6 vols (Athens: Estia, 1985–8), 3.25; S/T 146: GS to Theotokas, 9 September 1948 ('much work'); PE2.XI: 27 April 1948 (delayed promotion); M6.42: 7 February 1952 (statement to Eliot); cf. letter to Miller quoted as the epigraph to this chapter, referring to the 'December events'of 1944. There are indirect allusions to the third round of the civil war in poems written at the time, none of them published by GS (TGB 18–32).

72 Takis Papatsonis, Ο ένδοξός μας βυζαντινισμός, *Nea Estia*, 499 (14 April 1948); 501 (15 May 1948). GS's annotated copies, G.II.25; correspondence, G.IV.43 and 44.

73 Response to Papatsonis, G.IV.43: GS to Papatsonis (several drafts); S/Kats: GS to Katsimbalis, 1 June 1948 = Dimitris Daskalopoulos, 'Αγαπητέ μου Γιώργο': από την αλληλογραφία Γ.Κ. Κατσίμπαλη – Γ. Σεφέρη [22 March 1948–1 June 1948], *Porfyras* (Corfu), 93 (January–March 2000), 253. Cause of civil war, M5.46: 3 August 1946. GS on Byzantium, S/Kats: GS to Katsimbalis, 15 September 1949 (quoted); S/L 89–90: GS to Lorenzatos, 6 October 1949 (quoted); cf. S/L 115: GS to Lorenzatos, 26 November 1950.

74 M5.123: 1 July 1948; S/L 36: GS to Lorenzatos, 26 August 1948; GN.II.E5: GS to Ioanna: 21 August 1948; MIET album, no. 73. Poem, M5.139: 1 August 1949 = TGB 27; title explained, TGB 146 (editor's note).

75 S/L 38: GS to Lorenzatos, 4 September 1948, citing Valaoritis to

467

GS, 22 August 1948; GN.II.E6: GS to Warner, 14 October 1948 (in English, quoted); AP 40 (contrast with reception in France). See also Sharon, 'New Friends for New Places.'

76 G.III.14: 'October 1948–February 1949. Correspondence with Ioanna over house,' file sealed on the instructions of Maro Seferi 'until the death of Ioanna Tsatsou,' and not yet accessible. In his diary, GS refers to 'the greatest bitterness I've experienced at the hands of someone close to me' (M5.136: 4 June 1949). A terse account of events is contained in GN.II.E 6: GS to Angelos, 14 December 1948 (quoted); cf. the more confused recollection of Tsatsos (KT 195). Stelios' health, GN.II.E5: GS to Stelios (drafts in French), 15 May and 23 October 1948; GS to Ioanna, 21 August 1948.

77 S/L 36: GS to Lorenzatos, 26 August 1948; M5.135–6: 4 June 1949; S/L 110–1: GS to Lorenzatos, 15 August 1950 (diaries); M5.101: 2 July 1947; M5.152–3: 15 March 1950; S/L 105–6: GS to Lorenzatos, 8 April 1950 (posterity).

78 M5.133–4 = TGB 25–6; S/L 61: GS to Lorenzatos, 4 May 1949 (quoted).

79 M5.145–7.

80 M5.142 (on Touti); M5.147–8: 14 and 16 October 1949; P.271 = KS 220: 'The Cats of St Nicholas,' lines 8–11 quoted; cf. P.245–6 = KS 180–1: 'Memory I,' line 18.

81 M5.151: 16 January 1950; S/L 91: GS to Lorenzatos, 9 January 1950; Daskalopoulos, *Ergographia*, 84–8. Text on Cavafy, M5.171–5.

82 M5.151: 28 January 1950 (the date when GS learned the news). The bottom half of the page, after the bare announcement of the date and Angelos' name, is blank.

83 G.VIII.32: *Newsweek* (4 September

1950), cutting preserved by GS; Ann Arpajoglu to GS, 5 March 1950. This is how her name appears in English (many years later she would publish a teaching manual of Modern Greek); to GS she signed her letters, Άννα Αρπάτζογλου. GS's letters to her, and to Ioanna, about Angelos' death, GN.II.E8 (1950), in a separate bundle labelled 'Letters about Angelos Seferiadis 28 January to 23 February.'

84 Neither GS (D3.242–3) nor IT (356) gives any details of what Angelos was doing in New York. That he worked for the *National Herald* is clear from G.VIII.32: Angelos to GS, from NY, 16 January 1948; Ann Arpajoglu to GS, 25 April 1950. According to Tsatsos, Angelos was 'cultural attaché at the New York press office' (KT 191); but on 7 November 1947, Angelos wrote to GS defiantly that he would 'not be *attached* to anything;' and if this is the 'state job,' for which GS warns Ioanna that he fears their brother would not be suited (GN.II.E5: GS to Ioanna, 21 August 1948), he can never actually have taken it up, since by that time Angelos had left New York for Monterey. See also M5.229–30: 21 November 1950.

85 G.VIII.32: Ann Arpajoglu to GS, 5 March ('unkindest . . .') and 11 June 1950; cf. KT 191.

86 G.VIII.32: Ann Arpajoglu to GS, 5 March and 26 April 1950.

87 G.VIII.32: Ann Arpajoglu to GS, 14 May 1950; Angelos Seferiadis, Σήμα, με σημειώματα του Γιώργου Σεφέρη (Athens: Ikaros, 1967). GS's afterword to the volume = D3.237–45.

88 G.VIII.32: Ann Arpajoglu to GS, 20 January, 8 February ('they told me . . .'), 24 March 1950 ('terrible letter'). The letter of 8 February quotes the letter found beside

Angelos, in English; in slightly
abridged form, it was reproduced
by GS in D3.244; cf. IT
359–60.

89 IT 362, citing GS to Ioanna, 13
February 1950; cf. D3.244; IT 358
('Ajax and Hamlet').

90 M5.176: 3 May 1950; S/Kats: GS to
Katsimbalis, 30 December 1949.

91 M5.111: 15 September 1947; S/Kats:
GS to Katsimbalis, 14 May 1949; 26
February 1950.

92 M5.179–205 (prohibition on travel
to Skala, p. 197). GS's travelling
companion appears only as 'E' in
M5, identified in Stas/Chron 87;
also in G.VIII.13: 22 June 1950 and
S/M2: GS to Maro, 6 June 1950.
Claës Eric Axelsson Thuröe von Post
was Sweden's ambassador to Ankara,
1945–51, and also a minor poet (Bo-
Lennart Eklund: private
communication).

93 M5.179–87.

94 M5.188: 27 June 1950 (quoted).
GN.II.E15: GS to Ioanna, 9 April
1960 ('Once, on the heights of
Tmolos, I met a Swedish
academician, a member of the
Nobel committee, a delightful man,
God bless his memory . . . He told
me that they'd been ready to give
the Nobel to Sikelianos, when they
were informed that Greece would
regard such an award as a hostile
act'); on this see p. 365 above;
S/Val: Valaoritis to Katsimbalis,
18 June 1950 (quoted).

95 M5.193–4: 29 June 1950. The poem
'Written in Pencil' (M5.190 = TGB
34), that had been written at
Lavranda two days before, parallels
this Cretan influx in 1923 with the
evidence unearthed by Persson and
his team for the strong influence of
the Bronze Age Minoan civilisation
from Crete in the prehistory of the
region (M5.188–93).

96 M5.196–7: 1 July 1950 (details

supplied from G.VIII.13); M5.226:
24 October 1950.

97 M5.197: 2 July 1950.

98 M5.197–203; first published in the
volume of GS's selected essays
(Εκλογή από τις Δοκιμές) in 1966,
with the title 'The Other World'
(along with the extracts from M5
dealing with his return visit to
Smyrna in October). See also
M5.218: 19 October 1950 ('I shan't
have the courage to go back to
Skala. You can't repeat a journey
like that'). For GS's last, brief visit
to Smyrna, in November 1969, see
Katerina Krikos-Davis, 'At the
Smyrna Merchant's: Aspects of
George Seferis as Revealed in his
Personal Diaries,' TLS (20 October
2000), 13–14, and Yorgos Yeoryis,
Γιώργος Σεφέρης: η τρίτη επιστροφή
στη Σμύρνη, Ta Nea: Prosopa (7
October 2000), 8–9.

99 M5.205: 4 July 1950.

100 M5.208–10; S/L 110–1, 114; PE2.XI
(promotion, 14 July 1950); 'bon pour
l'Orient,' S/L 105: GS to Lorenzatos,
5 April 1950; S/Kats: GS to
Katsimbalis, 3 September 1950.

101 D2.57–93; cf. Vlachos, Μια φορά,
3.109–114. For the earlier plan see
S/L 68; 69.

102 S/Kats: Katsimbalis to GS, 27 July
1950.

103 M5.207–9; 210. It is likely that they
travelled with Angelos and Ninette
Vlachos, with whom they had
toured the Cappadocian monasteries
in the summer. Vlachos would have
been on his way to his next posting
(Vlachos Μια φορά, 3.119); Vlachos'
account gives the impression that
he and his wife went with GS and
Maro to Izmir, Ephesus and
Pergamum soon after they all
visited Konya together in the spring
of 1950 (M5.154: 5 April 1950), but
this cannot be reconciled with the
sequence of events in M5 (Vlachos,

469

*Mια φορά*, 3.91–7). While Vlachos' presence is acknowledged (by tactful initial) in GS's account of the visit to Cappadocia, published in 1953, by the time he prepared M5 for publication, in 1967, all trace of his junior colleague had disappeared.

104 M5.210–23; cf. Krikos-Davis, 'At the Smyrna Merchant's;' M5.212: 16 October 1950 (quoted, original emphasis).

105 M5.225–6: 24 October 1950.

## 10 Paradise Found (1951–1955)

1 P.335–6, not included in the notes to KS. The collection was later retitled *Logbook III.*

2 M5.232–40; M.6.21: 20 April 1951 (cited); S/L 119–20: GS to Lorenzatos, 13 May 1951. On GS's last visit to Smyrna, see ch. 9, n. 98.

3 S/Kats: Maro to Katsimbalis, 20 May and 31 May 1951 (the latter quoted); cf. M6.22: 28 May 1951; S/Kats: GS to Katsimbalis, 31 May 1951 = Dimitris Daskalopoulos, Ανέκδοτη αλληλογραφία με τον Γ.Κ. Κατσίμπαλη, *Ta Nea: Prosopa* (5 February 2000), 29. On Malanos' book see M6.21–2: 22 May 1951, and below.

4 D2.190–216; cf. M6.245, n.3.

5 M6.22–3 (Auden, Forster); 35–6 (MacNeice, Thomas, Smith); 40, 47, 56 (British friends from Athens).

6 D2.94–100; M6.24: 2 July 1951; M5.106: 6 August 1947 (quoted).

7 S/Kats: GS to Katsimbalis, 4 August 1951.

8 S/Mal 313: GS to Malanos, 4 August 1951; for GS's initial response expressed to Malanos, and the latter's surprised reaction, see S/Mal 312–3. After this Malanos wrote to GS on a few occasions; the only time when GS replied was by telegram, in response to Malanos' telegram of congratulation when he won the Nobel Prize. It consists of one word,

'Merci,' and is signed 'G. Seferis' (S/Mal 317). S/Kats: GS to Katsimbalis, 23 August 1951 (enclosing the letter with request to publish); Katsimbalis to GS, 15 October 1951. Text of open letter, S/Mal 321–7 and n; substantially revised and abbreviated in D2.353–6, n. 2.

9 IT 363–5; GN.II.E9: GS to Ioanna, 7 August 1951. Shortly before Maro had been taken ill in March, GS was asking for directions for the suburb of Paris where Stelios lived, presumably intending to visit while passing through on his way to London (S/M2: GS to Maro, 17 March 1951); Maro's convalescence postponed their departure, so that it was only possible to spend two hours in Paris, and the visit never took place (M5.239–40: 30 March 1951; M5.242: 19 April 1951).

10 S/L 128–9; S/Kats: Katsimbalis to GS, 14 August 1951 (a moving personal tribute to 'old-man Seferiadis,' enclosing two press cuttings). GS's reply (23 August 1951) ignores this entirely and does not even mention his father. Stelios' 'forgotten verses,' M4.247: 5 September 1942. Recalling the anecdote much later, in very similar words, GS's expressed feelings about his father are warmer, but Malanos as the immediate source has been erased altogether (S/T 169–70: GS to Theotokas, 5 February 1964); recalled again, with additional details, M8: April 1968.

11 GN.II.E5: GS to Ioanna, 21 August 1948.

12 M6.25: 12 July 1951; M6.30: 15 October 1951; cf. his conversation with Forster about the meaning of a reported remark by Cavafy, which implicitly highlights the impoverished condition of post-war Britain (M6.23; D3.142–3;

S/Kats: GS to Katsimbalis, 25 May 1952).

13 M6.48–9: 11 October 1952.

14 S/Kats: Maro to Katsimbalis, 24 November 1951; for the occasion see also M6.35–6.

15 IT 141: GS to Ioanna, 30 December 1951 (quoted); cf. M6.27; 36; S/Kar 175–9: GS to Karantonis, 10 February 1950; ('two masters').

16 M6.42: 7 February 1952 ('unconscious' in English).

17 M6.57: 23 October 1952; cf. Keeley/int. 193–4.

18 According to the outside cover of G.III.75 ('Death of Father,' sealed until the death of Ioanna Tsatsou and not yet opened), GS renounced his inheritance; from the available indications, it seems that what little Stelios had to leave (shortly before his death he had borrowed from his wife against arrears of pension due from Greece) was left to Thérèse.

19 GN.II.E10: GS to Ioanna, letters between October 1952 and August 1952; see esp. 4 May 1952, with reference to Skeferis and 'ovr' efforts; the preserved correspondence between GS and Skeferis (GN.II.A) dates from 1952. GN.II.E10: GS to Averoff (handwritten draft, 8 pp.), 21 May 1952; cf. S/Kats: GS to Katsimbalis, 16 May 1952.

20 S/Kats: GS to Katsimbalis, 16 May 1952; PE2.XI: 27 June 1952 (promotion); S/Kats: GS to Katsimbalis, 20 August 1952. The letter to Averoff (see previous note) indicates GS's explicit willingness to serve 'outside major cities.'

21 S/Kats: GS to Katsimbalis, 20 August 1952; S/M2: Maro to GS, 28 March 1956 ('tragedy'); GN.II.E10: GS to Ioanna, 28 August 1952 (quoted).

22 PE2.XI; cf. M6.59.

23 M6.59–63.

24 P.271–3 = KS 220–2: 'The Cats of St Nicholas.' The poem itself insists that this happened on Christmas Day, but assuming that the ship put in at Alexandria first, the landfall in Cyprus must have been on the 27th (M6.63–4; cf. S/Kats: 26 December 1952, aboard SS. *Aeolia*, off Abukir, having left Alexandria earlier the same day). Cf. G.VIII.133, reproduced in Fotis Dimitrakopoulos, *Γιώργος Σεφέρης – Κύπρος Χρυσάνθης και Οι γάτες τ' άη Νικόλα* (Athens: Kastaniotis, 1995), 140–64; summary contents and text of draft published in Fotis Dimitrakopoulos, *Οι κυπριακοί φάκελοι του Αρχείου Σεφέρη στη Γεννάδειο, I Lexi* 85–86 (1989), 578–93, see pp. 586–8; Savvas Pavlou, *Σεφέρης και Κύπρος* (Πολιτιστικές Υπηρεσίες Υπουργείου Παιδείας και Πολιτισμού, Σειρά Διδακτορικών Διατριβών, no. 2, Nicosia, 2000), 336–7. P.254–5 = KS 271: 'Pedlar from Sidon;' cf. S/Kats: 26 December 1952 (the ship's steward described); Pavlou, *Σεφέρης*, 141 and n.1 (based on an interview with Louizos); M6.98.

25 M6.67; GN.II.E10: GS to Ioanna: 31 December 1952; *Labrys* 8 (1983), 57: GS to Miller, 8 May 1954; Steven Runciman, 'Some Personal Memories,' *Labrys* 8 (1983), 47–9 (p. 47 quoted).

26 M6.173 (Anna Londou; Despina Tsatsou); M6.177 (Mina Londou); M6.87 (Woodhouse); GN.II.A (subfile Leigh Fermor): Joan Rayner [= Leigh Fermor] to GS, 7 May 1954; M6.87–8 (Xydis); KypEp 67–8: GS to Savidis, 15 May 1955 (Lancaster, Vlachos, Leigh Fermor).

27 M6.68; 129; 189; 251 n. 4; see also M7.36; 60; 62–3; 169; 172–4

471

(Seyrig); S/L 156: GS to Lorenzatos, 26 April 1956 (Frangopoulos).

28  D2.176 (1964, quoted); cf. M7.35; AP 53. For the date of the visit see M6.73; M7.292 n.

29  'Sunken cities,' S/L 115: GS to Lorenzatos, 26 November 1950. 'We give birth to statues,' M1.75–6: 6 September 1926; cf. 6N.73 and André Gide, *Paludes* (Paris: Gallimard, 1920, first ed. 1895), 16. 'How to die,' P.66 = KS 23: *Mythistorema* 19, on which see pp. 123 above. Urgent question, phrased slightly differently, S/L139–40: GS to Lorenzatos, 4 August 1952 (on the death of Gide, also explicitly recalling *Paludes*); M6.115: 6 December 1953 (on the Muslim dervish ritual at the *tekke* outside Larnaca).

30  M6.87–8: 25 September 1953; M6.122: 17 April 1954 (quoted).

31  M6.73: 18 April 1953, on the road to Baghdad; M6.231–2: 3 July 1956, Baghdad. He added, prophetically, that the small Iraqi aristocracy nurtured by the British was universally loathed; though in hindsight the efforts by the US mentioned by GS would hardly prove more successful in supporting western interests in that country.

32  M6.90: 6 October 1953 (Amman); cf. KypEp 67–8: GS to Savidis, 15 May 1955.

33  Only two poems, not included in this volume, and published posthumously, refer directly to Lebanon; their titles are the names of hill resorts above Beirut, in which GS and Maro spent part of each summer, and where many of the 'Cypriot' poems were written. 'Bhamdun' is dated 27 August 1953; 'Dhour el Choueir' 14 September of the same year (TGB 99; 100; for the latter, cf. M6.87).

34  Robert Holland, *Britain and the Revolt in Cyprus, 1954–1959*

472

(Oxford: Clarendon Press, 1998), 13–32; quotation from p. 23.

35  Pavlou, Σεφέρης, 89–90; for wartime correspondence see S/Mal 150; 152; 156 (Louizos). GN.II.A: Cardiff to GS, 11 February 1953. The very informal tone of this letter, which does not refer to official engagements, does not bear out the view later publicised by the Cypriot poet Kypros Chrysanthis, that there had been a systematic British plan to lure GS to the island to promote the interests of the colonial government. GS replied to Chrysanthis that 'no one invited me. I came spontaneously,' Kypros Chrysanthis, Η πρώτη παρεπιδημία στην Κύπρο του Γ. Σεφέρη (1963), and GS to Chrysanthis, Easter 1963, reprinted in Dimitrakopoulos, Σεφέρης – Χρυσάνθης, 39–51 (p. 50 quoted).

36  Nikos Kranidiotis: interview; cf. Yorgos Yeoryis, Νίκος Κρανιδιώτης: μικρή σπουδή στην ποιητική του πορεία, Πνευματική Κύπρος (Nicosia), 394, (July-December 1991), 164, and Pavlou, Σεφέρης, 142 n. 1. There is some doubt about the place and precise date of this meeting; cf. Nikos Kranidiotis Δύσκολα χρόνια: Κύπρος 1950–1960 (Athens: Estia, 1981), 262.

37  S/Kats: Katsimbalis to GS, 16 November 1953. No doubt this is connected with efforts by Cardiff and Durrell, in Cyprus, to establish a counterpart of the *Anglo-Hellenic Review* there (see Chrysanthis, Η πρώτη παρεπιδημία, 39–41; Pavlou, Σεφέρης, 141–2 n. 2).

38  M6.98–9.

39  S/Kats: GS to Katsimbalis, 19 August 1953 (overdue appearance in print) and 17 October 1953 (leave requested); cf. M6.99: 6 November 1953 (final paragraph); IT 194: GS to Ioanna, 25 October 1954; GN.II.E11: GS to Ioanna, 29 October

1953 (quoted; one sentence from this letter appears in IT 194).

40 M6.93–117; *Κύπρος: μνήμη και αγάπη. Με το φακό του Γιώργου Σεφέρη*, (Nicosia: Cultural Centre of the Popular Bank, 1990), 12–13.

41 M6.105: 17 November 1953 ('without a Greek policeman'); M6.98: 6 November 1953 (both quotations).

42 M6.97–9: 6 November 1953; cf. M6.107; 116; Ian MacNiven, *Lawrence Durrell, A Biography* (London: Faber, 1999), 403; M6.108; P.254–5 = KS 271, lines 16–18.

43 S/Sherrard: GS to Sherrard, 22 December 1953 (in English).

44 M6.103–4: 13 November 1953; Evangelos Louizos, 'Ενα απόγεμα στην 'Εγκωμη, in *Για τον Σεφέρη. Τιμητικό αφιέρωμα στα τριάντα χρόνια της Στροφής* (Athens: Konstantinidis and Michalas, 1961), 22–3; photographs in *Κύπρος: μνήμη και αγάπη*, nos 115–6 (1955).

45 M6.107; cf. IT 194: GS to Ioanna, 25 October 1954; P.235–6 = KS 175: 'Details on Cyprus' (survivals in Cyprus); M6.111: 1 December 1953 (remark to Cardiff, quoted). On that visit, GS noted that Cardiff seemed anxious to discuss the political situation with him, and some of these conversations are reported in his diary (M6.100; 104–5; 106; 108); cf. S/Kats: GS to Katsimbalis, 15 December 1953 ('I saw Maurice Cardiff and we spoke privately and cordially, but also frankly [σταράτα]'). Recalling these discussions a year later, he said that talking to Cardiff had made him feel like a quisling, and he had said so, explaining forthrightly why he would not set foot inside the British Council, S/T 157: GS to Theotokas, 28 December 1954, translation in *Labrys* 8 (1983), 67–70.

46 M6.104–5: 16 November 1953 (British obstinacy); Pavlou, *Σεφέρης*, 169, citing the unpublished MS of *Varnavas Kalostefanos* (GN.I.B54), p. 29 (quoted, on Turks in Cyprus); Nikos Kranidiotis: interview ('we must be attentive to the Turks [i.e. Turkish Cypriots], their support over Cyprus') on which Kranidiotis commented: 'I don't know how he understood this thing.' See also Kranidiotis, *Δύσκολα χρόνια*, 262.

47 IT 194: GS to to Ioanna, 25 October 1954; cf. similar sentiments to other correspondents, S/Kats: GS to Katsimbalis: 15 December 1953; S/Val = *I Lexi* 134 (1996), 475–8: GS to Valaoritis, 31 December 1953; Fotis Dimitrakopoulos, *Σεφέρης, Κύπρος, επιστολογραφικά και άλλα* (Athens: Kastaniotis, 2000), 147–8: GS to Xydis, 8 February 1954; S/Diam 32: GS to Diamantis, 12 March 1954; *Labrys* 8 (1983), 57–8: GS to Miller, 8 May 1954; KypEp 27: GS to Savidis 16 May 1954; S/L 147–8: GS to Lorenzatos, 29 November 1954; S/T 157: GS to Theotokas, 28 December 1954, translation in *Labrys* 8 (1983), 67–70. See also Pavlou, *Σεφέρης*, 155–6, including some of the relevant extracts.

48 S/Diam 19–20; Dimitrakopoulos, *Σεφέρης – Χρυσάνθης*, 15–38; Ian MacNiven (ed.), *The Durrell-Miller Letters 1935–80* (London: Faber, 1988), 275 (quoted).

49 Pavlou, *Σεφέρης*, 142–54.

50 S/Kats: Maro to Katsimbalis, 17 December 1953.

51 M6.119: 19 January 1954.

52 P.233 = KS 173, line 1 (= M5.40: 4 July 1946). G.VIII.149 (summary in Dimitrakopoulos, Οι κυπριακοί φάκελλοι): 'Neophytos the Recluse Speaks Out,' on 27 December; 'Three Mules,' on 30 December; 'Pedlar from Sidon,' on 2 January

473

1954; 'Agianapa II,' on 5 January. The MSS of 'Details on Cyprus' are undated, but a dated typescript of 14 June 1954 makes it almost certain that this poem, too, had been written at the same time as the others; there is also a typescript of 'Three Mules,' dated to 22 June 1954. These (with 'Agianapa I') must have been the six poems that GS sent to Savidis at the end of July (KypEp 32–3: GS to Savidis, 30 July 1954).

53  M6.119: 19 January 1954 ('orgasm of writing'). On beginning to rewrite *Six Nights*, M6.39. This entry is dated 'Monday, 7 January 1952,' but according to the editor was found on a loose sheet and may have been misplaced. While it is possible that GS made a start on this project in London in 1952, there is no other evidence for this, and the entry would fit more plausibly at the beginning of 1954. Examination of the MS is not conclusive: the loose sheet containing this entry contains the 1952 date in full, and there are notes in Maro's handwriting, directing the editor to insert it at the appropriate place. It is in a different ink from the surrounding entries. Like many of the loose sheets that make up the MSS of GS's diaries, this one may well have been copied from a rougher jotting, and the date erroneously added at that point. 'Driving power,' M6.119: dated only 'Saturday,' between entries for 19 January and 22 February 1954.

54  M6.134: 15 August 1954 (quoted); G.VIII.149 (dates of poems in typescript), cf. Dimitrikapoulos, Οι κυπριακοί φάκελλοι. On 'Helen' see also M6.178: 7 August 1955; S/M2: GS to Maro, 18 August 1954, part published in Michalis Pieris, Συμβολή στο θέμα της κυπριακής

εμπειρίας του Γιώργου Σεφέρη, *Diavazo* 146 (April 1986), 102; reprinted in the collective volume *O Σεφέρης στην Πύλη της Αμμοχώστου* (Athens: Cultural Foundation of the National Bank, 1987), 70, and M. Pieris, *Από το μερτικόν της Κύπρου* (Athens: Kastaniotis, 1991), 171–2.

55  Holland, *Revolt*, 37–8, with citation and comment.

56  Vik.Dip. 22: *Hansard* 299 (23 July–30 July 1954) = *Parliamentay Debates (Commons)*, 1953–1954, vol. 531: col. 524.

57  *Hansard*, col. 541.

58  *Hansard*, col. 552.

59  P.263–5 = KS 190–2, lines 16–34 (the first two lines quoted paraphrase Makriyannis). The only date among the drafts is '2 August 1954.'

60  S/Kats: Katsimbalis to GS, 25 August 1954; GS to Katsimbalis, 27 August 1954 (quoted). There are unexplained details in the timing and place of this publication. GS had also sent the poem to Savidis, and as late as 19 August was writing to Maro, to tell Savidis to hold back publication (presumably in the *Anglo-Hellenic Review*) until the October issue, to coincide with the group of poems that would be appearing then in Cyprus, in *Kypriaka Grammata*. It was only *after* 'Salamis in Cyprus' had appeared in the rival *Nea Estia* that GS refused Savidis permission to publish any of his poems about Cyprus in the *Anglo-Hellenic*, explaining his reasons in terms of British propaganda that the Cypriots were not Greeks (M6.148: 7 October 1954; cf. M6.283 (editor's note); KypEp 56–7: GS to Savidis, 29 November 1954).

61  S/Kats: Katsimbalis to GS, 10 November 1954; Yorgos Yeoryis is probably right that it was to head

474

off this charge that GS added the dateline to the published version, 'Salamis, Cyprus, November '53,' *Ο Σεφέρης περί των κατά την χώραν Κύπρον σκαιών* (Athens: Smili, 1991), 61–2.

62 MacNiven, *Durrell*, 412–3; S/Diam 47–50: Diamantis to GS, 24 August 1954; S/Kats: GS to Katsimbalis, 27 August 1954 (quoted).

63 S/Diam 43: GS to Diamantis, 15 August 1954; already at the beginning of the year GS had announced to Katsimbalis his intention to go back to Cyprus (S/Kats: GS to Katsimbalis, 15 January 1954); S/Diam 48–50: Diamantis to GS, 24 August 1954; S/Kats: GS to Katsimbalis, 13 November 1954; cf. KypEp 56–8: GS to Savidis, 29 November 1954; S/T 157: GS to Theotokas, 28 December 1954. 'Larry [Durrell] was there (drunk), with his wife,' M6.149: 8 October 1954.

64 GN.II.A: Cardiff to GS, undated [early September 1954]; KypEp 32–3: GS to Savidis, 30 July 1954; GN.II.E12: GS to Joan Rayner, 24 December 1954 (quoted) = Dimitrakopoulos, *Σεφέρης, Κύπρος*, 156–8; cf. Pavlou, *Σεφέρης*, 309.

65 Holland, *Revolt*, 42.

66 M6.137–72; *Κύπρος· μνήμη και αγάπη* (photographs).

67 M6.155: 14 October 1954; elaborated in S/T 156–9: GS to Theotokas, 28 December 1954.

68 Pavlou, *Σεφέρης*, 163–4 (no public appearances). Censorship, KypEp 56–8: GS to Savidis, 29 November 1954; S/Diam 59: GS to Diamantis, Good Friday [= 5 April] 1955; S/Diam 186 (editor's note). Toothache, M6.154: 13 October 1954.

69 M6.155: 16 October 1954.

70 Natalia Deliyannaki, *Από το σχεδίασμα του 'Βαρνάβα Καλοστέφανου,' I Kathimerini: Epta Imeres*, (13 October 1996), 16; see also details and bibliography in Pavlou, *Σεφέρης*, 167–73. GN.I.B54 contains 141 pages of drafts and notes in MS, and a typescript of the first 8 pages. An edition has been announced by Deliyannaki. Reasons for abandoning, Pavlou, *Σεφέρης*, 167–73; KypEp 69: GS to Savidis, 15 May 1955. Start of EOKA campaign, Holland, *Revolt*, 52, 55.

71 M6.93; 99–100: 7 November 1953; M6.97: 9 December 1953; GN.II.A: Makarios to GS, 30 June 1955; cf. Michalis Pieris, *Μακάριος και Σεφέρης, I Lexi* 53 (1986), 237–47, reprinted in idem, *Από το μερτικόν*, 205–17.

72 GN.II.E13: GS to Ioanna, 11 October 1955 ('Ένας βρακάς σαν αυτούς που γνώρισα στη Σκάλα). Literally, the *vraka* is the name of the traditional baggy knee-length trousers worn by Greek peasants in the islands; a *vrakas* is one who wears it; see Katerina Krikos-Davis, *Kolokes: A Study of George Seferis' Logbook III (1953–1955)* (Amsterdam: Hakkert, 1994), 130. On Makarios see also S/Kats: GS to Katsimbalis, 2 July 1955 ('[The Cypriots] have got someone, Makarios, whom every time I meet him I respect him the more').

73 S/Kats: Katsimbalis to GS, 18 April 1955. Είμαι μπαρουτισμένος με τους φίλους μας τους Άγγλους . . . Είναι όλοι τους πούστηδες και καθίκια (και δεν εξαιρώ κανέναν εκτός από το Ρεξ και τον Όσμπερτ - ίσως).

74 GN.II.A (subfile Leigh Fermor): Joan Rayner to GS, 1 November 1955.

75 S/Kats: GS to Katsimbalis, 2 July 1955, from Bhamdun = Dimitris Daskalopoulos, Ανέκδοτη αλληλογραφία με τον Γ.Κ. Κατσίμπαλη, *Ta Nea: Prosopa* (5 February 2000), 29.

76 Holland, *Revolt*, 65.

77 G.VIII.149: the final version of 'Helen' (begun August 1954) is dated 1–4 July 1955; the latest date to appear there is 31 July, the date of the final version of 'Engomi.' Evidence partly summarised in Dimitrakopoulos, Οι κυπριακοί φάκελλοι, and Pavlou, Σεφέρης, 188. See also KypEp 83–4: GS to Savidis, 2 August 1955; S/Kats: GS to Katsimbalis, 24 August 1955 (referring to φυλλάδα).

78 P.266 = KS 193. On the identification of GS with Euripides in this poem and in the collection, see Krikos-Davis, *Kolokes*, 54–61.

79 For poem-by-poem commentaries see Krikos-Davis, *Kolokes*, and Christos Papazoglou, *Georges Séféris, Journal de Bord, III, édition commentée* (Paris and Athens: Langues'O/Nefeli, 2002), with bilingual texts and commentary in French.

80 KypEp 83–4: GS to Savidis, 2 August 1955.

81 Nikos Kasdaglis, Ιστορικό μιας γνωριμίας, in Για τον Σεφέρη, 20–21; cf. M6.195; also the rather different details and attitude noted in M6.182.

82 M6.181–2; 292–8 (editor's notes); Holland, *Revolt*, 72–7.

83 There are not many entries between September 1955 and February 1956, but the new tone is first discernible in GS's second reported exchange with the *New York Times* correspondent, Cyrus Sulzberger (M6.182: 28 September 1955; contrast M6.175–6: 29 January 1955) and in the terse notes of his visit to Athens in December (M6.186–7).

84 D2.283–4 (1966); see also epigraph to Part III.

85 GN.II.E14: GS to Joan Rayner, 27 May 1956 (heavily corrected draft), in English. GS writes: 'from mere

despair;' the adjective he had in mind was surely 'sheer.' Cf. S/L 155: GS to Lorenzatos, 26 April 1956.

86 S/Kats: GS to Katsimbalis, 27 September 1955 and KypEp 85: GS to Savidis, 9 October 1955 (Louizos' hospitality; the latter also quoted on 'Astonishing atmosphere'); Holland, *Revolt*, 81 (situation summarised, American consul's report); M6.181: 29 September 1955; Pavlou, Σεφέρης, 164 and n. 1 (testimony of Louizos: GS teargassed).

87 KypEp 83–93; 137–44. It appears that the choice between the two possibilities outlined by GS to Savidis on 2 August was decided against Ikaros during the time when all three were in the Dodecanese together, since it does not appear in the correspondence. There is perhaps an implication of friction during that period. S/Kats: Katsimbalis to GS, 28 October 1955 (quoted).

88 KypEp 89: GS to Savidis, 26 October 1955; M6.195–6: 25 February 1956; G.I.118, medical file: prescription from Athens doctor dated 8 December 1955; summary of past history, dated 28 November 1963, indicates first '*poussée ulcérieure*' in November 1955.

11 **... And Lost Again and Again' (1956–1961)**

1 S/L 152–5: Lorenzatos to GS, 18 April 1956, to which GS replied with blunt directness (S/L 155); by a coincidence which is probably not irrelevant, GS had recently dashed his younger friend's hope of being recognised as a poet, with his comments on Lorenzatos' long poem, *Little Syrtis* (see the immediately preceding correspondence, S/L 149–52, beginning with GS to Lorenzatos, 16 January 1955). See also Savvas Pavlou, Σεφέρης και Κύπρος

(Πολιτιστικές Υπηρεσίες Υπουργείου
Παιδείας και Πολιτισμού Σειρά
Διδακτορικών Διατριβών no. 2,
Nicosia, 2000), 211; KypEp 101; 106:
GS to Savidis, 12 February 1956; 12
May 1956 (quoted).

2   M7.314 n.; S/M2: Maro to GS,
undated (no. 58), gives the date of
purchase as 11 January 1956.

3   Pavlou, Σεφέρης, 214–26; G.P. Savidis,
Μια περιδιάβαση in Για τον Σεφέρη.
Τιμητικό αφιέρωμα στα τριάντα
χρόνια της Στροφής (Athens:
Konstantinidis and Michalas, 1961),
304–408. The volume actually
appeared in January 1962 (see
below).

4   GN.II.E14: GS to Lancaster, 9–10
March 1956 = Labrys 8 (1983),
70–1. The last sentence is quoted
from Shakespeare's Othello, picking
up the allusion not just to Iago but
to GS's poem 'Neophytos the
Recluse Speaks Out;' there GS had
sarcastically referred to the British
publicity posters which used words
from the same play: 'You are
welcome, Sirs, to Cyprus,' but added,
as a mocking commentary, the
remainder of Shakespeare's line, in
which the deranged Moor raves:
'Goats and monkeys' (P. 259–60);
omitted from KS, this poem was
first translated by John Stathatos in
Labrys 8 (1983), 10; see also the
translation by Peter Mackridge,
'Neophytos the Cloisterer Speaks,'
Modern Poetry in Translation, New
Series 13 (1998), 17–18.

5   GN.II.E14: GS to Joan Rayner, 27
May 1956.

6   GN.II.A (subfile Leigh Fermor):
interlinear pencil draft by GS
written on Joan Rayner to GS, 1
May 1956. Cf. M6.206: 13 May 1956
('Cardiff: Why has Greece taken
terrorism to its heart? GS: Because
the Greek people [laos] is stirred by
those who're fighting. . . . [The

Greek government] had to do
something, even if only with words,
when it could do nothing more to
help those people. Otherwise the
Government would have been
accused of treason.')

7   Pavlou, Σεφέρης, 234–5 (GS and
EOKA); PE3: 19 October 1956; 19
March 1959. Contacts between
Grivas and the Foreign Ministry in
Athens, Angelos S. Vlachos, Μια
φορά κι ένα καιρό ένας διπλωμάτης...,
6 vols (Athens: Estia, 1985–8),
4.249–51; Evangelos Averoff-Tosizza
[Averof-Tositsas], Ιστορία χαμένων
ευκαιριών. Κυπριακό 1950–1963, 2
vols (Athens: Estia, 1982), 1.184–5;
244–5. See also the English
translation: Evangelos Averoff-
Tossizza, Lost Opportunities. The
Cyprus question, 1950–63, trans.
Timothy Cullen and Susan
Kyriakidis (New York: Caratzas,
1986).

8   There are no copies or drafts of
letters from GS to his British
friends, after the abandoned draft
letter to Leigh Fermor on 2 June
1956, in the files for 1956–60
(GN.II.E14 and 15). Most of these
friendships were resumed face to
face once George was posted to
London in June 1957; during the
period when he had responsibility
for the Cyprus crisis at the Ministry,
there is no evidence for any direct
contact with British friends. He does
not appear to have responded either
to an undated letter from Leigh
Fermor (presumably May or early
June 1957) asking for the date of his
arrival as ambassador, or to another
from A.R. Burn on the same subject,
George Thaniel, Seferis and Friends,
ed. G. Phinney (Stratford, Ontario:
Mercury, 1994), 34–5: Burn to GS,
13 June 1957. It even appears that
his regular contact with Rex
Warner, who was working

477

throughout this period on his translated *Poems,* was maintained through Savidis (S/M2: GS to Maro, 21 January 1957).

9  S/M2: Maro to GS, 27 March 1956; GS to Maro, 2 April 1956; an extract from the latter = Maria Stasinopoulou, Μαρώ και Γιώργος Σεφέρης, Αλληλογραφία Β́ (*1944– 1959*). Παλίμψηστο (Heraklion, Crete), 11 (1991), 126–40, pp. 132–3 = idem, Ανέκδοτη αλληλογραφία με τη Μαρώ, *Ta Nea: Prosopa* 48 (5 February 2000), 30–1. '*As for London,* have it in mind that the matter must be put in hand with some delicacy and without agitation (με κάποια τέχνη και χωρίς νευρική βία). I don't want people to think – because it isn't true – that I'm taking advantage of Mostras' misfortune so as to take his place' (S/M2: GS to Maro, 4 April 1956).

10  FO 371/123894; Averoff-Tosizza, *Ιστορία*, 1.119. The censure debate ended on 24 May 1956; Averoff was sworn in on 28 May; GS learned of his own appointment at midnight on the night of 31 May–1 June.

11  S/M2: GS to Maro, 27 March 1956 = Maria Stasinopoulou, Ανέκδοτη αλληλογραφία, *Ta Nea: Prosopa* 48 (5 February 2000), 30 (dignity of office); M6.213–16; S/M2: GS (in Athens) to Maro (in Beirut), 9 June 1956 ('terrified...' = M6.216); G.X.41: exchange of telegrams 1 June 1956.

12  M6.216–25; see esp. p. 220 and p. 311 n. 42: 11 June 1956 (coded reference to arms as 'chocolates'); PE3: 19 October 1956.

13  M6.218: 7 June 1956; cf. M8: 26 November 1967.

14  M6.232: 3 July 1956 (Baghdad).

15  M6.235: 13 July 1956 (Jerusalem, conversation with Katy Antonius).

16  M6.239: 1 August 1956; S/Mal 314–15 and n.

17  Robert Holland, *Britain and the Revolt in Cyprus, 1954–1959* (Oxford: Clarendon Press, 1998), 40–4; PE3: 24 November 1956 (GS's advice to Averoff in the context of a meeting of NATO foreign ministers in Paris).

18  M7.27; 289; 291; Pavlou, Σεφέρης, 228; see also Angelos Vlachos, Δέκα χρόνια Κυπριακού (Athens: Estia, 1980), 168–70, and Averoff-Tosizza, *Ιστορία*, 1.152–4.

19  Stas/Chron 107–10; S/M2: GS to Maro, 10 November 1956; extract = Maria Stasinopoulou, Ανέκδοτη αλληλογραφία, *Ta Nea: Prosopa* 48 (5 February 2000), 31; S/M2: GS to Maro, 15–16 January 1957; M7.251: 26 September 1960 (when television comes to Greece).

20  M7.27; 31–43; cf. D3.180–3; for Mitropoulos' career at this time, see William Trotter, *Priest of Music: The Life of Dimitri Mitropoulos* (Portland, Or.: Amadeus Press, 1995), 388; 418–19.

21  M7.31: 27 January 1957; S/M2: GS to Maro, 21 January 1957 = Maria Stasinopoulou, Παλίμψηστο, 11 (1991), 138–9.

22  S/M2: GS to Maro, 15 November 1956; M7.92 (photograph).

23  S/M2: GS to Maro, 19 February 1957.

24  S/M2: GS to Maro, 25 February 1957 = Stas/Chron 110.

25  Holland, *Revolt,* 173 ('anodyne resolution'); cf. Vlachos' assessment as 'a battle in vain' (Μια φορά, 4.324); text of the Indian resolution in full in Averoff-Tosizza, *Ιστορία*, 1.175; on the closing plenary session see also S/M2: GS to Maro, 26 February 1957 = *I Lexi* 53 (1986), 303. GS overcoming opposition from colleagues, PE3: 19 February 1957. Satisfaction 'irrespective,' S/M2: GS to Maro, 19 February 1957.

26 M7.43–7: 28 February 1957 (p. 47
quoted; p. 43: 'descent').

27 Stas/Chron 110; M7. 46
(photograph: April 1957).

28 Holland, *Revolt*, 175–83; cf. Averoff-
Tosizza, Ιστορία, 1.176–83; Vlachos,
Δέκα χρόνια, 181.

29 Holland, *Revolt*, 184–5 (who
describes this moment as 'the
apogee of his [Makarios'] entire
career'). Photograph reproduced in
*Ta Nea: Prosopa* 48 (5 February
2000), 23 (where the wrong date, '8
May,' is reproduced from the back of
the print in MIET).

30 FO 371/130061: Athens to FO, 30
March 1957 (Mostras to return to
London); 11 April 1957, Athens to
FO (Mostras' resignation); YPEX 5.1
(1962): 12 April 1957 (Averoff to
London).

31 Vlachos, Μια φορά, 4.353–4. On
Vlachos' subsequent nervous
breakdown, caused by his service in
Nicosia, see 4.441–50.

32 FO 371/130061: Request for
Agrément for new Greek
Ambassador, W.H. Young, 15 April
1957; F. Hoyer-Millar, 16 April 1957;
Athens to FO, 25 April 1957. These
documents have been published,
with comment, by Krista Anemoudi-
Arzoglou, *Anti*, 367 (26 February
1988), 42–3; cf. Pavlou, Σεφέρης,
238. See also *The Greek Gazette*
(London), 245–6 (February 1988),
which also reproduces a number of
FO minutes relating to meetings
with GS in the summer of 1957.

33 Holland, *Revolt*, 193; 196–7; Pavlou,
Σεφέρης, 240. For GS's informative
vignettes and negative response to
Strasbourg and Bonn see S/M2: GS
to Maro from Bad Godesberg, Bonn,
1 May 1957 = *I Lexi* 53 (1986), 304.

34 IT 19: GS to Ioanna, [26 June 1957]
(Buckingham Palace); PE2.XI
(promotion); FO 371/130084: J.A.
Thomson, confidential internal

memo, 11 July 1957 (quoted);
GN.II.E14: Ioanna to GS, 2
September 1957. GS's previous
acquaintance with Macmillan,
PE2.34: 12 September 1945; cf.
PE2.40, 41, 93–5.

35 S/M2: GS to Maro, 18 September
1957 (quoted), the first of a large
batch of correspondence covering
the next three months, when Maro
was in Athens; on the cook and
other staff see esp. the letters of
November, and M7.65: 16 April
1958.

36 S/M2: Maro (in Athens) to GS, 21
September 1957 ('Now that I think
back to *how* I was in London I'm
appalled, I'm keeping a watch on
myself not to let it happen it
again'). Maro was in Athens from
September to December 1957, for
some time during the autumn of
1958, and for something over a
month from 19 January 1959.
Precipitate move from Kydathinaion
Street to Agras, S/M 2: Maro to GS,
2 and 10 February 1959.

37 Averoff attributes the first
recognition of this new situation, on
the Greek side, to Vlachos during
the meeting with Makarios in
Athens on 17 April 1957, at which
GS was also present. Vlachos, who
might have been expected to claim
the credit if this was true, makes no
mention of it in either of his own
two accounts of that meeting. All
the evidence indicates that the new
reality had in fact been first spelt
out by GS, back in April 1957, if not
even earlier.

38 On the authorship and successive
modifications of the Macmillan
Plan, see Holland, *Revolt*, 236–7;
244–7.

39 FO 371/136308: minute of meeting
between the Greek Ambassador and
Sir A. Ross, 29 May 1958; Ross to
Hoyer Millar, 2 June 1958 (24-hour

479

start for Turks); FO 371/136309: minutes of meetings between the Greek Ambassador and Sir A. Ross, 11 and 16 June 1958; FO 371/136310, 27 June 1958. Macmillan, in his memoirs, states that the Greek tactic of invoking the Lausanne Treaty was new at this time, Harold Macmillan, *Riding the Storm, 1956–1959* (London: Macmillan, 1971), 668; that it was taken seriously in the Foreign Office is proved by a lengthy set of legal advice on the provisions of the treaty, which was assembled shortly afterwards (CO 926/718: Solicitor General to FO, with enclosures, 27 September 1958). GN.II.E15: GS to Ioanna, 22 June 1958 (quoted).

40 FO 371/136310: minute of meeting between the Greek Ambassador and the Secretary of State, 2 July 1958; FO 371/136311: minute of meeting between the Greek Ambassador and Sir A. Ross, 25 July 1958. See Holland, *Revolt*, 267, for the fact that 1,992 Greeks had been taken into custody, and 58 Turks.

41 Maro/int. 198; GN.II.E15: GS to Ioanna, 28 August 1958; M7.91 (photograph); Macmillan, *Riding the Storm*, 674–5; CO 926/716 (arrangements for the PM's visit to Athens on 7 August 1956). Meetings between Macmillan and Karamanlis in Athens, Holland, *Revolt*, 270–2.

42 Macmillan, *Riding the Storm*, 686; FO 371/136312: minute of meeting between the Prime Minister and the Greek Ambassador, 19 August 1958.

43 PE3: 20 February 1958 (original emphasis). On the poem 'Stratis Thalassinos on the Dead Sea' see pp. 214–15 above.

44 FO 371/136308: minute of meeting between the Greek Ambassador and Sir A. Ross, 29 May 1958. 'Gloomy' is a regular epithet for GS in Ross's reports; cf. 'The Ambassador seemed

to me rather less gloomy than usual' (FO 371/136309: minute of meeting on 16 June 1958).

45 Holland, *Revolt*, 283–5; FO 371/136313: Athens to FO, 2 October 1958; minute of meeting between Sir A. Ross and the Greek Ambassador, 29 September 1958 (quoted); cf. minute of meeting on 23 September.

46 Holland, *Revolt*, 289–91; Averoff-Tosizza, Ιστορία, 2.92–4.

47 Holland, *Revolt*, 293–4; Averoff-Tosizza, Ιστορία, 2.134–5; 139–45; FO 371/136314: minute of meeting between Sir A. Ross and the Greek Ambassador, 15 December 1958. Holland, citing this, wrongly attributes the expression 'Turkish delights' (and the 'pique' that he discerns behind it) to Ross. GS and Zorlu, PE3: 26 February 1957. On the character of Zorlu, see Holland, *Revolt*, 74, 76; Macmillan, *Riding the Storm*, 699–700.

48 Averoff-Tosizza, Ιστορία, 2.155–63 (briefing of officials, p. 161). 'Paris sketch,' Stephen G. Xydis, *Reluctant Republic* (The Hague and Paris: Mouton, 1973), 344–50 (including the fullest available account of its contents but no indication of his source or the whereabouts of the document). That such a formal document existed is confirmed by the memo of GS to Averoff (19 December 1958, on which see immediately below), which results from his 'reading of the preliminary draft Constitution for an independent Cyprus drawn up during the recent discussions here . . .' A few days later, the Turkish ambassador in London, Nuri Birgi, read out extracts of what must have been the 'Paris sketch' to Ross but did not offer him the text itself (a further indication of its actual authorship) (Holland, *Revolt*,

298, citing Ross minute, 23
December 1958).

49 Holland, *Revolt*, 269; 292–3.

50 D2.283–4 (1966), see pp. 255, 321,
326 above.

51 G.X.39: GS to Averoff, Hotel Bristol,
Paris, 19 December 1958.

52 G.X.39: GS to Averoff, 25 December
1958 (carbon copy of typed letter),
secret file no. 357918. The text of
this letter, together with that of
Averoff's reply (1 January 1959), is
published with commentary by
Yorgos Yeoryis, Η δικαίωση του
Γιώργου Σεφέρη: η απόρρητη
αλληλογραφία για την Κύπρο, *Ta Nea:
Prosopa*, 105 (10 March 2001), 14–21.
Here, GS's objections are set out less
bluntly than in his memorandum of
19 December. See also M8: 11 May
1971 = Michalis Pieris, Συμβολή στο
θέμα της κυπριακής εμπειρίας του
Γιώργου Σεφέρη, *Diavazo* 146 (April
1986), 113–14; reprinted in the
collective volume *Ο Σεφέρης στην
Πύλη της Αμμοχώστου* (Athens:
Cultural Foundation of the National
Bank, 1987), 70, and M. Pieris, *Από
το μερτικόν της Κύπρου* (Athens:
Kastaniotis, 1991), 171–2, reproduced
in M7.306–7.

53 G.X.39: Averoff to GS, 1 January
1959 = Yeoryis, Η δικαίωση. Tsatsos
to GS, 5 January 1959. The
correspondence in this file continues
into February and is resumed in
July, when news of their
disagreement leaked out, and
Averoff's displeasure was renewed.
Averoff's later account, Averoff-
Tosizza, *Ιστορία*, 2.166–7.

54 G.X.39: GS to Averoff, 12 and 18
January 1959; S/M2: Maro to GS, 19
January 1959; G.X.39: GS to Averoff,
21 January 1959 (quoted).

55 G.X.39: Ioanna to GS, 24 January
1959; S/M2: Maro to GS, 22 and 24
January 1959 (the latter quoted).

56 S/M2: GS to Maro, 22 and 26

January 1959. Averoff-Zorlu talks
and their immediate aftermath,
Averoff-Tosizza, *Ιστορία*, 2.167–8;
Xydis, *Reluctant Republic*, 395–8.
Averoff had his own reasons for
publishing the full text of a
meeting between Karamanlis and
Makarios, with himself present, at
which Makarios gave his consent to
the terms that were about to be
negotiated at Zurich (Averoff-
Tosizza, *Ιστορία*, 2.168–76). This
meeting did not take place until 29
January, but is presented by Averoff
as one of several which began
immediately after the archbishop's
return to Athens on 15 January.

57 GN.II.E15: GS to Ioanna, 29 January
1959.

58 S/M2: GS to Maro, 5 February
1959.

59 S/M2: GS to Maro, 9 February
1959; cf. M7.312–13. The fullest
account of the Zurich negotiations
is given by Xydis, *Reluctant
Republic*, 406–19; see also the eye-
witness accounts of Averoff-Tosizza,
*Ιστορία*, 2.183–7 and Vlachos, *Μια
φορά*, 4.451–61.

60 M8: 11 May 1971 = Pieris, Συμβολή
and M7.306; 312–13; GS in
conversation with the Cypriot poet
Hebe Meleagrou, in May 1971, cited
by Pavlou, Σεφέρης, 274–5 (quoted).

61 Averoff-Tosizza, *Ιστορία*, 2.197–9;
cited with comment by Pavlou,
Σεφέρης, 248–9.

62 Averoff-Tosizza, *Ιστορία*, 2.207–10;
Vlachos, Δέκα χρόνια 248–9;
Vlachos, *Μια φορά*, 4.466 (according
to whom it was himself, Bitsios and
Roufos who accompanied Averoff to
the Dorchester) and 4.469–70;
Dimitris S. Bitsios, *Cyprus, The
Vulnerable Republic* (Thessaloniki:
Institute for Balkan Studies, 1975),
109; Pavlou, Σεφέρης, 250–1; 253–4;
Alexandros Xydis, Ο πολιτικός
Σεφέρης, in A. Argyriou et al., *Κύκλος

481

Σεφέρη. Βιβλιοθήκη Γενικής Παιδείας, no. 10 (Athens: Etaireia Spoudon, 1984), 118 (quoted).

63  S/M2: GS to Maro, 16 February 1959 = M7.312–3.

64  Holland, *Revolt*, 312–13 (quoted); Averoff-Tosizza, *Ιστορία*, 2.225–8; Macmillan, *Riding the Storm*, 694–5.

65  Holland, *Revolt*, 314–16; Averoff-Tosizza, *Ιστορία*, 2.215–16; Vlachos, *Μια φορά*, 4.470–1; Bitsios, *Cyprus*, 110.

66  Averoff-Tosizza, *Ιστορία*, 2.213; Vlachos, *Μια φορά*, 4.471.

67  S/M2: GS to Maro, 21 February 1959 = M7.313 and Stas/Chron 115–16; cf. M8: 16 September 1961; 28 April 1962. Compare also GS's comments on the meeting between Damaskinos and King George (in the same hotel), PE2.37: 13 September 1945, and pp. 262–3 above. GS had not been alone in seeing in Makarios' career, up to this point, strong parallels with the early career of Eleftherios Venizelos (see e.g. Vlachos, *Μια φορά*, 4.342–3).

68  Holland, *Revolt*, 317.

69  M7.100: 28 March 1959, and M7.308 (editor's note); FO 371/144611: minute of a meeting between the Greek Ambassador and the Secretary of State (John Profumo), 24 February 1959; Macmillan, *Riding the Storm*, 698 (original emphases).

70  M7.138–43; 318–19; 322–3 (all relating to January 1960); M7.222; 342 (June 1960) and GN.II.E15: GS to Ioanna, 26 June 1960; Xydis, Ο πολιτικός Σεφέρης, 117; Averoff-Tosizza, 2.256–65; cf. Pavlou, Σεφέρης, 321.

71  Averoff-Tosizza, *Ιστορία*, 2.238–44, see esp. pp. 241–2. Averoff gives a (downbeat) account of GS's letter with the offending file-number of 25 December, but states: 'he [GS]

did not mention these [objections] in Paris, but only made them now, a week later' (Averoff-Tosizza, *Ιστορία*, 2.163). This was untrue, as has been noted by Michalis Pitsilidis, Οι σκοτεινές πλευρές του Γιώργου Σεφέρη (Athens: Archipelagos, 2000), 382 and Yeoryis, Η δικαίωση, 21. In the context of the London conference (11–19 February 1959), Averoff mentions GS *only* as the intermediary of his, Averoff's, contacts with Makarios and Grivas (*Ιστορία*, 2.197–9; 228).

72  M7.96: 22 February 1959; M7.131–2: 31 December 1959 (quoted); M7.152: 29 February 1960 (quoted); cf. M7.181: 17 April 1960 (Easter Day).

73  *Poems,* 3rd edition, April 1962 and all subsequent editions (the former title is retained as the epigraph to the collection); P.271–3 = KS 220–2: 'The Cats of St Nicholas,' line 60, dateline 5 February 1969 (see also pp. 300, 396–7).

74  S/M2: GS to Maro, 29 October 1957 = *I Lexi* 53 (1986), 304–5; S/M2: GS to Maro, 1 December 1957; M7.75–6; 135; KypEp 117: GS to Savidis, 26 July 1959.

75  KypEp 107–12; 154–6 (full text of Annan's speech, quoted); M7.55–6 (1957); M7.72–3: 6 May 1958 and photograph; M7.95: 11 January 1959 (quoted).

76  George's fairly meagre and always very formal correspondence with Eliot, Princeton 1.6. Meetings with Eliot, M7.118: 1 July 1959; D2.190–210; for dates of thirteen further recorded meetings with Eliot between 1951 and 1962, see M7.313.

77  M7.129–31; M7.283–5 (Christmases at Henley); M7.101–114: 24 April ≃ 12 May 1959; M7.193–210: 15–29 May 1960 (M7.194 quoted).

78  Ian MacNiven, *Lawrence Durrell, A Biography* (London: Faber, 1999),

459 (quoted); M7.221: 25 June 1960 (on *Justine*); cf. G.II.19: favourable reviews of *Bitter Lemons* in *Εικόνες* (17 March 1961) and *Le Monde* (18 March 1961) with unmistakably angry underlining and '?' by GS. GN.II.E17: GS to Durrell, 29 July 1962 (quoted), replying to Princeton 1.5: Durrell to GS, 19 July 1962. In the same year GS supplied sleeve-notes for a record of Durrell reading his 'Greek' poems, in which a similar barb can be detected (Jupiter Records, London: 'Poets Reading, no. 6, Lawrence Durrell: Greek Poems,' April 1962), part quoted in Gordon Bowker, *Through the Dark Labyrinth: A Biography of Lawrence Durrell* (London: Sinclair-Stevenson, 1997), 302. For subsequent meetings in 1962 and 1964 (the latter in Corfu), see Bowker, *Labyrinth*, 302, 312, and GN.II.E18: GS to Durrell, 19 July 1964 ('It was good to see you the other day. I remember now September 39: from Corfu to Corfu: a full circle. I take it as a symbol . . .'). In early 1969, GS would decline to be interviewed by Durrell for BBC television, implicitly because of the political situation in Greece at the time (Princeton 1.5: GS to Durrell, 19 [February?] 1969).

79  M7.162–7: 18 March 1960, with photographs (p. 164 quoted); M7.233–8: 13–18 August 1960; D2.112–35 (with additional material, but omitting the details about the skeleton); D2.359: text of commemorative plaque and address by the Dean of Lincoln (sentence quoted also in M7.236). GS's previous thoughts on Kalvos, D1.56–63; 179–210 (D1.79: 'behind a curtain'). *Estia* editorial (mis-dated to 1959) and context, Pavlou, *Σεφέρης*, 262.

80  M7.251: 26 July 1960.

81  P. Petridis, *Ο πολιτικός Θεοδωράκης* (Athens: Proskynio, 1997), 458, mentions a public rift with GS about the time of the October 1961 general election in Greece.

82  Mikis Theodorakis, *Μελοποιημένη μουσική*, vol. 1 (Athens: Ypsilon, 1997), 55. Quotation translated by Dimitris Papanikolaou, to whom I am grateful for making this publication available to me. GN.II.E17: GS to Savidis, 19 January 1962.

83  Dimitris Papanikolaou, 'Setting Seferis' Poetry to Music, Or The Story of the Lost Semi-Colon,' in [Embassy of Greece, London], *George Seferis: Centenary Celebrations* (London, 15–17 May 2000), [pp. 8–11].

84  FO 371/144576: J.M. Addis, 2 November 1959.

85  IT 193: GS to Ioanna, 11 June 1960; cf. M7.213–6 (with photographs); text of the speech, M7.340–1.

86  M7.217: 12 June 1960; correspondence and details, G.IV.82 (radio broadcast); M7.261–2: 10 November 1960 (Eliot, quoted); D3.144–8; cf. 385; GN.II.E16: GS to Ioanna, 19 February 1961 (Foyle's Prize).

87  Bo-Lennart Eklund, 'A Poet Translated with More Pain than Pleasure: Giorgos Seferis' Poetry in Sweden' (unpublished lecture, May 2001); Anita Eklund Lykull and Bo-Lennart Eklund, 'Towards a New Image of Greece. Börje Knös and the Breakthrough of Greek Literature in Sweden,' in *The Problematic Image of Greece. Modern Greek Literature in Sweden* (Gothenburg University, project report no. 2, 1988), 72–6 (in Swedish: English translation kindly supplied by the authors). *Le Figaro Littéraire*, 29 September 1956

484

(Stas/Chron 108). For Valaoritis, see p. 287.

88 Libel, Pavlou, Σεφέρης, 257–86. Pitsilidis, whose avowed aim is to bring to light the 'dark sides' of GS's character and career, concludes, after an examination of the evidence publicly available, that the accusation is not supported (Οι σκοτεινές πλευρές, 388). For pressure on GS to withdraw his filed letter, see G.X.39: Tsatsos to GS, 5 January 1959; GS to Averoff, 19 July 1959; GS to Ioanna, 23 July 1959.

89 GN.II.E15: GS to Ioanna, 9 April 1960; GN.II.E16: GS to Ioanna, 13 January 1961. Ioanna's letters to GS have in general been fairly fully preserved; there are greater than usual gaps for the years 1960 and 1961; neither of the letters to which these two are the replies is extant (G.III.102). It is possible that, in the light of the later libel, either GS himself or Maro thought that these proposals, in which Averoff's name was evidently mentioned, could have been used against him. A year later, Ioanna would raise the matter again, but this time in the context of lobbying in the press and in literary circles. This letter has been preserved (G.III.102: Ioanna to GS, 29 January 1962); GS's reply is as categorically negative as before: 'I think it's best if absolutely nothing is said about my name and I beg you earnestly to stick to this line' (GN.II.E17: GS to Ioanna, 6 February 1962); cf. also M8: 31 July 1968 (recalling 1962).

90 M7.283–5: December 1960 (Essays); M8: 19 January 1961 (Poems) = Katerina Krikos-Davis, 'At the Smyrna Merchant's: Aspects of George Seferis as Revealed in his Personal Diaries,' TLS (20 October 2000), 13–14.

91 M7.54: 3 November 1957 (poem); cf. M7.35; 292 (Seleucia). Song of Songs: M7.177; 180; 181; Apocalypse: for work in 1956, see p. 326; G.VIII.54: GS to Patriarch Athenagoras, requesting permission to publish, 10 July 1961, refers to the translation as having been 'completed some months ago;' cf. IT 77. Other translations, M7.146; M7.159; 162 (Golden Ass); M7.173 (Paludes); M7.206–210; M7.264; 350–1 (Saint-John Perse); M7.271–2 (Yeats).

92 M7.127–8: 20 September 1959; M7.263: 12 November 1960.

93 On medical tests and probably minor ailments, M7.122: 22 August 1959; M7.181; 183; 185: April 1960; M7.211: 2 June 1960; M7.243: 30 August 1960.

94 M7.152: 29 February 1960 (quoted); M7.169: 26 March 1960; GN.II.E15: GS to Ioanna, 9 April 1960 (quoted); 12 July 1960; M7.192–3: 12 May 1960 (quoted).

95 M7.330: n. 5 to p. 169; GN.II.E15: GS to Ioanna, 16 April 1960; M7.222; 226 (correspondence with Ioanna about 'change'); M7.259–60: 4 November 1960 (promotion); PE2.XI: promoted to full ambassadorial rank (Πρέσβυς), 9 December 1960.

96 G.X.39: GS to Averoff, 18 January 1961.

97 YPEX 5.1 (1962): Lena Jeger in the Manchester Guardian (20 August 1962).

12 A Time for Renewal (1961–1971)

1 D2.138; cf. D2.149; 154; 157; 219; 235; 247; 344.

2 GN.I.A16: 28 January 1961; more on this in M8: 23–30 January 1961. The MSS for Three Secret Poems have been published in facsimile, George Seferis, Κρυφά ποιήματα. Τα

χειρόγραφα τετράδια σε πανομοιότυπη
έκδοση (Athens: Ermis, 1975).

3 GN.II.E16: GS to Ioanna, 19 March
1961; cf. M8: entries between
February and May 1961.

4 S/M2: Maro to GS, 18 October 1958;
GN.II.E16: GS to Ioanna, 9 April
and 30 June 1961 (the latter quoted);
M8: brief indications in a small
number of entries between January
and November 1961. In letters to his
sister, GS consistently presents the
nervous exhaustion from which both
he and Maro are suffering as due to
the pressures of his work; but the
precise instructions he gave her for
their reception, before they arrived
in Greece at the end of July, must
have prepared her for something
more personal (4, 17 and 30 June
1961).

5 S/Diam 110: GS to Diamantis, 4
May 1961; cf. IT 207: GS to Ioanna,
30 June 1961.

6 Respectively, D2.143–6; 150; 148–9.

7 D2.146; cf. S/L 169, on avoiding a
comparable experience in Crete, five
years later: 'caves make me lose my
equilibrium, it's that return to birth'
(GS to Lorenzatos, 9 August 1966).

8 P.291 = KS 205: Three Secret Poems
II, 7; stalactites and stalagmites also
in D2.146; for GS's concept of
eternity, as expressed at the end of
this poem, see pp. 110, 269 and the
reformulation of these ideas in
'Delphi,' D2.151. See also M5.221: 21
October 1950, for an early
adumbration of these ideas, in the
context of GS's return to his
birthplace at that time.

9 GN.II.E16: GS to Warner, 2
September 1961; IT 210; GS and
Maro spent from 21 August to 6
September on Amorgos (S/Keeley
105: GS to Keeley, 17 August 1961;
cf. M8).

10 Mathios Paschalis [sic, for 'Paskalis,'
= George Seferis], Τα Εντεψίζικα, ed.

G.P. Eftychidis [= Savidis] (Athens:
Leschi, 1989) 28–40. The only
limerick dated to 1961, which must
have been written on Amorgos (p.
28) is not strictly speaking
pornographic; all the other products
of that September are in rhyming
fifteen-syllable couplets (the verseform of Erotokritos and the tragedy
Erofili, written by Yeoryios
Chortatsis in Cretan dialect at the
end of the sixteenth century). It is
probable that a performance of the
latter, revived in the Herod Atticus
theatre during the Athens Festival
of that year, underlies Three Secret
Poems II 1 and 2 (including a direct
quotation from the play, II 1, line 5);
cf. M8: 16 September 1961.

11 GN.II.E16: GS to Ioanna, 25 October
1961; IT 77–8.

12 P.277 = KS 199: Three Secret Poems
I 1, lines 1–2. GN.I.A16, p. 14: full
draft MS of this section (only),
dated 8 December 1961, prefaced by
a note: 'first moment in the park.'

13 Για τον Σεφέρη. Τιμητικό αφιέρωμα στα
τριάντα χρόνια της Στροφής (Athens:
Konstantinidis and Michalas, 1961
[sic, for January 1962]); see pp. 9–10
for Savidis' (unsigned) preface and
the colophon which identifies Savidis
as the second of two copy-editors.
Publication date, Stas/Chron 121.

14 S/Kats: Katsimbalis to GS, 23
February 1962. For correspondence
with Savidis, see GN.II.E16 and E17.
Only that part of the
correspondence dealing with Cyprus
in the 1950s has been published
(in KypEp); for a description of
the whole see KypEp 19–20 and
Mariliza Mitsou, Η αλληλεγγύη της
διασποράς, I Kathimerini: Epta
Imeres (13 October 1996), 20–21.

15 S/Kats: GS to Katsimbalis, 28
February 1962.

16 Duties resumed 6 January 1962,
YPEX 5.1 (1962). Medical

485

complications, G.I.118 (referral to a consultant physician for exhaustion, 8 February 1962); Nanos Valaoritis, *Μοντερνισμός, πρωτοπορία και Πάλι* (Athens: Kastaniotis, 1997), 88: GS to Valaoritis, 17 March 1962; S/L 164: GS to Lorenzatos, 14 April 1962.

17 G.X.41: GS to President [of Council = Karamanlis], 9 February 1962; Averoff to GS, 29 May 1962 (coded telegram, replying to GS's telegram of the previous day); PE2.XI; GN.II.E17: GS to Ioanna, 28 May (opening of Coventry Cathedral, cf. M8: 25–27 May 1962); GS to Ioanna, 8 June 1962.

18 MIET: unpublished, dated photograph; M8: 20 August 1962.

19 Peter Levi, *The Hill of Kronos* (London: Collins, 1980), 33.

20 GN.II.E17: GS to Warner, 17 October 1962; cf. M8: 11 October 1962; GN.II.E18: GS to Lancaster, 21 January 1963.

21 M7.248: 12 September 1960 (*depaysé*); cf. M7.249–51; D2.150; S/Diam 120–1: GS to Diamantis, 20 February 1963; GN.II.E17: GS to Vlachos, 23 December 1962; GN.II.E18: GS to Warner, 10 October 1963 (quoted).

22 D2.326–7 (1970), based closely on M8: 13 August 1963; GN.II.E18 contains a version in English, with the title 'A dream of G.S.,' that was presumably included in a letter to one of GS's English friends, perhaps Warner, and dated 31 March 1964.

23 S/T 170: GS to Theotokas, 5 February 1964 (referring to 'last spring'). *Murder in the Cathedral* was finished by July (Princeton 1.6: Eliot to GS, 25 July 1963) and published in December 1963 (Daskalopoulos, *Ergographia*, 111). GN.I.A16 preserves four drafts of 'On Stage,' of which only one, which appears to be the earliest, is dated: 1 March 1963. This version

consists of ten sections, of which the material in nos 7–9 was later condensed into other sections (mainly no. 5) or omitted; these sections expand considerably upon the theme of ritual murder. T.S. Eliot, *Φονικό στην εκκλησία*, trans. George Seferis (Athens: Ikaros, 1963), 111 (quoted). The project of translating Eliot's play, originally planned as a collaboration with the poet Nikos Gatsos, is first mentioned in GS's diary just nine days after the performance of *Erofili* (see note 10), which seems to be invoked in the first two sections of 'On Stage' (M8: 25 September 1961).

24 T.S. Eliot, *Murder in the Cathedral*, Part II, lines 631–2 (London: Faber, 1965); P.289 = KS 204: *Three Secret Poems* II, 5, lines 9–13.

25 P.291 = KS 205: *Three Secret Poems* II, 7, quoted above, p. 371.

26 *Poems* (3rd ed.) appeared in April 1962, *Essays* (2nd ed.) in December (Daskalopoulos, *Ergographia*, 103; 104–8). Translations into other languages, Daskalopoulos, *Ergographia*, 110; 203; 204–5; Stas/Chron 125. *Book of Exercises II* was soon afterwards withdrawn, and did not appear until 1976 (TGB 133–4, editor's note). *Murder in the Cathedral* was published in December 1963 (Daskalopoulos, *Ergographia*, 111); the preface to *Antigrafes* is dated 'September 1963,' although the volume itself did not appear until 1965. The Biblical translations, published in 1965 and 1966 respectively, are described as ready for publication, but held up due to 'censorship' by the Greek Church, GN.II.E18: GS to Warner, 19 October 1963.

27 GN.II.D1 (subfile 3): Knös to GS, 18 February 1963; GS to Knös: 20 February 1963; Bo-Lennart Eklund, 'A Poet Translated with More Pain

than Pleasure: Giorgos Seferis' Poetry in Sweden' (unpublished lecture, May 2001), citing Johannes Edfelt to Georg Svensson, vice-president of Bonniers publishing house, Stockholm, 10 April 1963.

28 Eklund, 'A Poet Translated,' citing Bonniers Litterära Magasin, no. 7 (1963). That Linnér's initiative was wholly unconnected with that of Knös is proved by his assumption in that essay, not corrected by the editors, that the accompanying translations were those first published in 1956 by the Swedish poet Hjalmar Gullberg. GN.II.A: Linnér to GS, 19 October 1963; the file also contains a transcript of the interview with some comments by GS, and a c.v. in Swedish, drawn up by Linnér.

29 Stas/Chron 124; D2.153–8 ('Athens, September 1963'). GS's ulcer, GN.II.E18: GS to Papatsonis, 16 October 1963; GS to Durrell, 15 November 1963; G.I.118: medical letter in French, presumably for use in case of a further crisis on his visit to Sweden, dated 28 November 1963. M8: 20 June 1964, apparently recalling the same episode, places it on Poros, not Paros.

30 GN.II.A: Linnér to GS, 19 October 1963; M8: 18 October 1963.

31 G.P. Savidis, Ποια ήταν η αμέση απήχηση του πρώτου μας Βραβείου Νομπέλ; in idem, Φύλλα φτερά. Δοκιμές και δοκιμασίες 1989–1993 (Athens: Ikaros, 1995), 48–9, first published in To Vima, 7 November 1993; cf. G.P. Savidis, Εφήμερον σπέρμα (Athens: Ermis, 1978), 60; GN.II.D1 (subfile 1): Osterling to GS (telegram), 24 October 1963. 'Crucial support . . . ,' Henri al-Kayem, Par Grand vent d'est avec rafales (Paris: L'Esprit des Péninsules, 1999), 57: Nani[s] Panayotopoulo[s] to Henri al-Kayem, 8 December 1963 (for

GS's meeting with al-Kayem in Alexandria see M4.299: 14 July 1943).

32 GN.II.D1 (subfile 1): official English translation of the announcement released to be broadcast on radio after 18.45 on Thursday, 24 October 1963, by Dr Anders Osterling, Permanent Secretary of the Swedish Academy and Chairman of the Nobel Committee.

33 YPEX 17.2 (1963): Seferiades, Nobel Prize, UK press cuttings; Eklund, 'A Poet Translated' (Swedish press comment, quoted); Savvas Pavlou, Σεφέρης και Κύπρος (Πολιτιστικές Υπηρεσίες Υπουργείου Παιδείας και Πολιτισμού, Σειρά Διδακτορικών Διατριβών, no. 2, Nicosia, 2000), 265–6; Stas/Chron 124–5 (Greek press comment); cf. M8: 31 July 1968; 24 April 1969.

34 Diskin Clay: unpublished interview with GS, 5 July 1971 (quoted by permission). The text quoted appears, slightly altered, in the publication of the Gennadius Library, The New Griffon (new series), 2 (1997), with the title "Greek Poets and Strangers," see p. 40.

35 Correspondence and final programme in GN.II.D1 (subfile 1).

36 D2.159–61: GS's own Greek translation of the acceptance speech, which he intended to include in the third edition of the Essays (see D2.361; 387).

37 D3.149–68 (in French), p. 167 quoted. GS himself never published this lecture in Greek, or proposed to include it in his collected Essays, although a Greek translation by Savidis appeared shortly after it was delivered. For its publishing history see D2.361; D3.386. 'A continent as big as China,' GN.II.A (subfile Linnér): typescript (in French) headed by GS, 'Conversation with

487

Linnér. Poor recording – poor photograph. Summer 63.' 'The Greek language . . . ,' D2.159.

38 GN.II.A: GS to Runciman, 27 December 1963; GN.II.E18: GS to Warner, 10 January 1964; 14 February 1964.

39 GN.II.E18: GS to Marie-Louise [Pouyollon], 17 November 1963 (draft). I am grateful to Katerina Krikos-Davis for showing me the letter (undated, and signed only 'Marie-Louise,' and at the time uncatalogued), to which this one responds.

40 D2.162–81 (p. 164 quoted: 16 April 1964); D2.387.

41 M8: 17 April 1964; GN.II.E19: GS to Pentzikis, 27 July 1965; D3.193–236 (1966–7); see pp. 218–9 for Mallarmé misquoted. On the publishing history of this essay see D3.389: it appears that only a few pages appeared during GS's lifetime. For the origin of GS's pseudonym on this occasion (Ignatis Trellos), see the obituary for Eliot by Papatsonis, citing St Ignatius of Tralles (G.II.25: 15 January 1965). See also George Thaniel, *Homage to Byzantium. The Life and Work of Nikos Gabriel Pentzikis* (Minneapolis: Nostos, 1983), 58–61.

42 GN.II.E18: GS to 'Fili' [= Pontani], 26 July 1964; cf. M8: 20 June 1964.

43 GN.II.A: Bowra to GS, 4 August 1964; GN.II.E18: GS to Pontani, 26 July 1964; GS to Bowra, 19 July 1964; GS to Warner, 24 October 1964 (quoted); M8: entries between 25 June and 18 August 1964.

44 PE2.XI, 191 and note, citing G.X.41: George Papandreou to GS, 30 September 1964. See also M8: 5 September 1964.

45 Stas/Chron 126; D2.182–9; 364; S/Diam 146: GS to Diamantis, 16 October 1964 ('three weeks...');

GN.II.E 18: GS to Pontani, 6 October 1964 ('pilgrimage'; 'expectations'); further details in M8: 14 September to 3 October 1964.

46 M8: 9 December 1964 = *Ta Nea: Prosopa* 48 (5 February 2000), 25; translation in Katerina Krikos-Davis, 'At the Smyrna Merchant's: Aspects of George Seferis as Revealed in his Personal Diaries,' *TLS* (20 October 2000), 13–14) (quoted); cf. M8: 19 November 1964; S/Keeley 38–43; 130–53; TGB 43–4 (for the poem 'Letter to Rex Warner,' begun on this visit).

47 GN.II.E19: GS to Linnér, 18 August 1965; *Ta Nea Grammata* 4 (1938), 368–71.

48 Most of the relevant correspondence is preserved in G.V.2; see also KT 386; Stas/Chron 127–8; GN.II.E19: GS to 'Stouropoulos' [= Sture Linnér], in Greek, 23 March 1966 (quoted); further details in M8: 7 and 14 March 1965.

49 GN.II.E19: GS to the Dean, University of Illinois, 9 September 1965; M8: 10 October 1965; D2.228; 236.

50 GN.II.E19: GS to Linnér, 18 August 1965 (quoted); cf. M8: 18 July 1965. Background, Richard Clogg, *A Short History of Modern Greece* (Cambridge University Press, 1986), 184–5.

51 D2.217; cf. P.306 = KS 213–4: *Three Secret Poems* III, 14, lines 8–11.

52 G.P. Savidis, Καστανόχωμα (Athens: Kastaniotis, 1989), 45; D2.217–48; 388. Both essays were written for non-Greek readers, and first published in a foreign language. Respectively, D2.231; D2.247–8; D2.235; D2.219.

53 GN.II.E19: GS to Warner, 1 March 1966; D2.218; D2.266 (my emphasis).

488

54 *Apocalypse* introduction, D2.281–92, dated 'June 1966.' Correspondence, including legal advice re the Church of Greece, G.VIII.54. Date of 'Summer Solstice,' GN.I.A16, p. 61 (draft table of contents dated 'June'). The manuscripts show a great deal of reworking and reordering, but no dates other than this one and '1966' for the 'penultimate' fair copy (p. 73).

55 On the semantic range of the Greek word κρυφά, in the title of these poems, for which there is no exact English equivalent, see Dimitris Dimiroulis, ʿΟ φοβερός παφλασμός᾿: κριτικό αφήγημα για τα ʿΤρία Κρυφά Ποιήματα᾿ (Athens: Plethron, 1999), 16–18. The fullest discussion of the allusions in these poems to Eliot, Dante and the *Apocalpyse* is to be found in Christopher Williams, *Readings in Eliot: Allusion as Technique in the Poetry of George Seferis* (unpublished doctoral thesis, King's College London, University of London, 1997), pp. 240–96. For critical commentary see Kostas Papageorgiou, Σημειώσεις πάνω στα ʿΤρία Κρυφά Ποιήματα᾿ του Γ. Σεφέρη, (Athens: Boukoumanis, 1973); Anthoula Daniel, Τα ʿΤρία Κρυφά Ποιήματα᾿ του Γιώργου Σεφέρη (Athens: Epikairotita, 1988).

56 P.306 = KS 213–4: *Three Secret Poems* III, 14, lines 2; 12–14 (quoted); see also III, 4, lines 6–12 (no afterlife); III, 12 and 13, line 12 ('birthpang of resurrection').

57 Compare the last line quoted above with Marcus Aurelius, *Meditations,* IV 10 ('Whatever happens, happens rightly'). Marcus is a constant presence in GS's poetry from *Mythistorema* onwards, but nowhere more so than in 'Summer Solstice' (compare also III 7, line 21 with *Meditations* VII 59).

58 Nikos Karydis, Σελίδες προσωπικού ημερολογίου, *I Lexi* 53 (1986), 212–15: 27 October 1966 (quoted); 29 October 1966; cf. 19 January 1967. Eliot on the Nobel, quoted in Peter Ackroyd, *T.S. Eliot* (London: Hamish Hamilton, 1984), 290; very possibly repeated in conversation with GS, though not recorded. Quotations from P.300 = KS 210: *Three Secret Poems* III 8, lines 1–2; 20–22.

59 C.M. Woodhouse, *The Rise and Fall of the Greek Colonels* (London: Granada, 1985), 16–17.

60 D2.303 ('since the end of the Putsch of 1935'). Taken together with X41.24, this presumably means: 'since the moment at the end of 1935 when Venizelos accepted the return of King George II;' see p. 136 above.

61 D2.304 (November 1966).

62 Daskalopoulos, *Ergographia*, 132, citing *To Vima*, 22 December 1966.

63 GN.II.E20: GS to Durrell, from Delphi, 7 February 1967; GS to Linnér, from Delphi, 20 February 1967 = Fotis Dimitrakopoulos, Τρία γράμματα του Σεφέρη: στον Καββαδία, στον Κατακουζηνό, και στον Παπασταύρου, in Dimitrakopoulos, Σεφέρης, Κύπρος, επιστολογραφικά και άλλα (Athens: Kastaniotis, 2000), 123–6, where the addressee is wrongly identified as Stavros Papastavrou (Αγαπητέ Στούρε = Sture [Linnér]). For the unfinished preface to the third edition of *Essays*, dated 'February 1967,' see D1.10; D2.379.

64 *Days of 1945–1951* [= M5] was ready for printing on 10 April 1967, but withdrawn from the printer after the imposition of dictatorship on the 21st (M8: 15 October 1967, editor's note). *Days* 1 [= M1]: G.VIII.134 contains the typescript with note, 'The originals have been

489

destroyed. (Organised and copied first in Ankara and then typed 1967).' This work was finished on 22 May (M8: 15 October 1967, editor's note). *Days 2*: M2.7; 8; 61. On Angelos' poems, Daskalopoulos, *Ergographia*, 138; M5: dedication and p. 9 (preface dated 'January 1967').

65 Respectively, D2.303; X68.12. See also the brief entries for Good Friday [= 28 April] and Easter Saturday [= 29 April] 1967 in X68.33–4.

66 X68.29–30: 26 October 1968; refusal to publish in Greece reaffirmed in letters to Senator Eugene McCarthy and Maurice Bowra, respectively on 24 and 25 December 1969 (GN.II.E21). GS did, however, allow Ikaros to reprint two of his books that had sold out during 1969, without allowing the date of reprinting to appear on the books themselves (Daskalopoulos, *Ergographia*, 140–1; cf. Pavlou, *Σεφέρης και Κύπρος*, 349). GS's letters at this time, preserved in GN.II.E20 (1967–8) are mostly practical and make no mention of the political situation. A letter to Warner begun in May 1967 was not finished and sent until October. Cf. S/Diam 153–8 (no letters from GS to Diamantis between 15 April 1967 and 26 January 1969); S/Keeley 165–84.

67 S/Keeley 170: GS to Keeley, 21 October 1967 (quoted); X68.35: undated entry, between 10 November 1967 and 2 December 1968 (quoted); S/Keeley 52; 172: Keeley to GS, 30 October 1967. There is evidence that GS finally abandoned work on his projected diaries and 3rd edition of *Essays* in October 1967: D1.10 (postscript to unfinished preface, dated 14 October 1967); M8: 15 October 1967 = *Anti* 64 (1977), 19.

68 S/Keeley 173: GS to Keeley, 2 December 1967 (quoted); S/Keeley 225–6: GS to Franklin L. Ford, 27 December 1967; for date and text of the invitation (12 December 1967), and a Greek translation of GS's reply, see X68.58–63. GS's reasons are discussed by the editor, Pavlos Zannas, in X68.63–7 and by Keeley (S/Keeley 52–4).

69 S/Keeley 173: GS to Keeley, 2 December 1967 ('I take it for granted that you'll be at Princeton by next mid-September, as we are going to feel rather lost without you and Mary').

70 GN.II.A: GS to Linnér, 15 March 1968; G.I.118: Medical opinion, 16 October 1970; an account of the incident is given by Kostas Tachtsis, Οι δισταγμοί του Σεφέρη, *Anti* 64 (5 February 1977), 22–3, p. 23.

71 Stas/Chron 131; S/Keeley 182; GN.II.E20: GS to Crea, 1 June 1968; X68.44–5 (Theodorakis' proposal); S/Keeley 24–5 (Maro's comment).

72 X68.45–6.

73 Respectively, X68.27–8; Keeley/int. 180.

74 X68.11–17; 27–8; S/Keeley 55–7; 173; Keeley/int. The fables from Plato are published in George Seferis, *Μεταγραφές*, ed. Yoryis Yatromanolakis (Athens: Ikaros, 2000, first published, Athens: Leschi, 1980), 59–189; GS later translated McCarthy's poem into Greek (TGB 127–9); cf. George Thaniel, *Seferis and Friends*, ed. G. Phinney (Stratford, Ontario: Mercury, 1994), 42: McCarthy to GS: 24 March 1970 ('I wish that the reports on the government in Greece were more encouraging and that there was a deeper interest in the United States in restoring liberty in your country').

75 X68.9–17.

76 S/Keeley 55–7; cf. X68.42–4.

77  Keeley/int. 213; 215–6; for Keeley's comments, see S/Keeley 57; Edmund Keeley, 'Seferis's "Political" Voice,' in idem, *Modern Greek Poetry: Voice and Myth* (Princeton University Press, 1983), 95–118, pp. 106–7.

78  X68.53; see also Zannas' note, pp. 88–9. The dateline which immediately follows surely refers to the *Manuscript*, not to the epigram, though Zannas is clearly right that this was the 'poem of two lines' that GS told Keeley was all that he had written at Princeton (Keeley/int. 211). See also X41.19 ('I thought it right [in November 1922] to bring before a firing squad the Six who at the time of the Asia Minor disaster, either *out of stupidity* or through malice had led the Nation to its destruction,' my emphasis).

79  Woodhouse, *Rise and Fall*, 34.

80  Maro/int. 205; cf. Pavlos Zannas, Η θέση μιας άρνησης, epilogue in X68. 57–67, see p. 67 (first published 1977), but contrast IT 197–9. The dateline of X68 is 'Athens summer – Princeton N.J., Christmas 1968' but the closing pages refer to Greece as 'here' (X68.49–50). Robert Keeley: personal communication.

81  P.271–3 = KS 220–2, lines 56–9 (quoted); for the MSS, reproduced in full, see ch. 8 n. 24; GN.II.E21: GS to McCarthy, 24 December 1969. On the poem see Katerina Krikos-Davis, 'Cats, Snakes and Poetry: A Study of Seferis' "The Cats of Saint Nicholas",' *Journal of Modern Greek Studies*, 2/2 (1984), 225–40.

82  'The Cats of St Nicholas' first appeared in Greek, without GS's knowledge, in a Cypriot newspaper on 28 August 1969; see Pavlou, Σεφέρης και Κύπρος, 350–53. Cf. Fotis Dimitrakopoulos, Γιώργος Σεφέρης – Κυπρος Χρυσάνθης και ʿΟι γάτες τʼ άη Νικόλαʾ (Athens: Kastaniotis, 1995), 77–101.

83  Robert Keeley: personal communication. The issue is sympathetically, if briefly, discussed in Tachtsis, Δισταγμοί. For GS's refusal to make a public statement in a different political context (to refute the libel about his conduct at the time of the Zurich-London Agreements over Cyprus), on the grounds that to do so would only be to give ammunition to the far-right newspaper *Estia* and the communists, see M8: 11 May 1971, cited in M7.312–3, n. 118, and Pavlou, Σεφέρης και Κύπρος, 269–85, esp. p. 270.

84  Robert Keeley (personal communication) recalls GS saying, shortly after his 'Statement' had been released, and while people were still congratulating him on it, 'You know, now I am no longer a diplomat.'

85  The fullest statement GS ever made of this position is in D1.264–7 [1945].

86  Robert Keeley: personal communication; IT 198.

87  Robert Keeley: personal communication; George Savidis: interview (GS at Delphi); Yoryis Pavlopoulos, Μνήμες από τον Γιώργο Σεφέρη, *Ylantron* (Nicosia, Cyprus), 1 (November 2001), 17–31, see pp. 22–3 (where the patisserie is named as Floka's), while Maro/int. 205 gives Zonar's; Keeley, 'Seferis's "Political" Voice,' 108–9; Levi, *Hill*, 152–3. The date '28 March 1969' which appears in the published text is often erroneously cited as the date when the 'Statement' was written (see e.g. D3.390).

88  GS's English text, cited from *Labrys* 8 (1983), 82; for the Greek, see D3.261–2. The original is untitled.

89  Eloquent testimony in the documentary film by Stelios Charalambopoulos, *Logbooks: George Seferis* (2002).

90  Robert Keeley: personal communication (extract from memorandum to the US State Department, quoting GS's words); Edmund Keeley, 'Seferis's "Political" Voice,' 109.

91  IT 199; Nikos Kasdaglis, Το έλος· χρονικά (Thessaloniki: Diagonios, 1988), 27. Official backlash, Daskalopoulos, *Ergographia,* 249–50 (nos 800–808); *Labrys* 8 (1983), 83 (English text released by the Greek government, 28 March 1969); Alexandros Xydis, Ο πολιτικός Σεφέρης, in A. Argyriou et al., *Κύκλος Σεφέρη.* Βιβλιοθήκη Γενικής Παιδείας, no. 10 (Athens: Etaireia Spoudon, 1984), 119.

92  Text and signatories, dated 23 April 1969, in Kasdaglis, *Το έλος,* 81–3; for background see pp. 28–85.

93  New press law: GS cut out and kept the announcements in *To Vima* (G.II.15); cf. Robert McDonald, *Pillar and Tinderbox: The Greek Press and the Dictatorship* (New York: Boyars, 1983), 109–10; *Δεκαοχτώ κείμενα* (Athens: Kedros, 1970), translated as *Eighteen Texts: Writings by Contemporary Authors,* ed. Willis Barnstone (Cambridge, Mass.: Harvard University Press, 1972). See also Th.D. Frangopoulos, Το ημερολόγιο των Δεκαοχτώ Κειμένων, in Frangopoulos, *Δίαυλοι* (Athens: Diogenis, 1974), 188–93; Keeley, 'Seferis's "Political" Voice,' 110–113.

94  M8: entries dated between 8 April and 13 May 1970; Keeley, 'Seferis's "Political" Voice,' 110 (quoted).

95  PE2.XI: 192 n. 1; G.VII.117: Ministry of Foreign Affairs to GS, 5 August 1970, enclosing Pipinelis to GS, 30 June 1970 (quoted); G.X.41: D. Papaioannou (Minister Plenipotentiary grade II) to GS, 1 July 1970.

96  On GS's health and appearance, Yorgos Heimonas, Οι τρεις συναντήσεις, *I Lexi* 53 (1986), 187–9; IT 197–8, where the context is the decision, a year earlier, to make the 'Statement;' Ioanna may possibly exaggerate the degree of her brother's infirmity in 1969, but the description in these pages tallies closely with testimony and photographs from early 1970 onwards. Swimming incident, S/Keeley 61–2. Medical condition and advice, G.I.118: Medical opinion, 16 October 1970; Hôpital de la Salpetrière, Paris XIIIe, to GS, 23 October 1970.

97  Maro/int. 205 (quoted); GN.II.E21: GS to Professor Paul S. Lykoudis, Purdue University, 21 December 1970 (quoted); Keeley, 'Seferis's "Political" Voice,' 110; M8: October 1970.

98  S/Kats: GS to Katsimbalis, Scandinavia Hotel, [rue Tournon], Paris, 24 November 1970; AP 13; Στήλη 20-9-71, ο θάνατος του Γιώργου Σεφέρη στον ελληνικό τύπο, 2 vols (Athens: Ermis, 1972), 1.189–90. The interview (actually a series of interviews) was conducted in French; only this edited version has been published in the original; AP consists of a Greek translation.

99  G.I.118: medical report, Hôpital Foch, 26 November 1970; GN.II.E21: GS to Crea, 15 December 1970; S/Keeley 194: GS to Keeley, 15 December 1970.

100  Pavlopoulos, Μνήμες, 29–30; Levi, *Hill,* 174–5.

101  TGB 50 = KS 223, lines 10–12; first published in *To Vima* on 23 September 1971, the day after GS's funeral. The title has also been rendered as 'On Gorse' (Levi, *Hill,* 175; *Labrys* 8 (1983), 19, trans. Peter Thompson). The allusion is to the

myth of Er (Plato, *Republic* 616a), presumably one of the 'myths and legends' on which GS had been working at Princeton, in the autumn of 1968.

102 Most recently formulated in D2.324 (1 February 1970).

103 S/Diam 175: Diamantis to GS, 24 June 1971; Pavlou, Σεφέρης και Κύπρος, 364–5, citing the testimony of Louizos; Στήλη 1.191. GN.II.E21: GS to Hebe [Meleagrou], 14 July 1971 (draft, quoted).

104 S/Diam 177: Diamantis to GS, 4 August 1971 (improvement after operation); IT.228; cf. KT 198 (difficulty of access); IT 17; 229 (description); further details in Heimonas, Οι τρεις συναντήσεις, 189; Thanasis Valtinos, Μέρες του '71,

*Ylantron* 1 (November 2001), 39–41, p. 41; Στήλη 1.9.

105 Aronis 44.

106 Kevin Andrews, '1971. "Angelic and Black Day" – Seferis' Death,' in *idem, Greece in the Dark* (Amsterdam: Hakkert, 1980), 41–58, see pp. 52–3. The story that Maro rose up to bar the archbishop's entrance is sadly apocryphal; it is told by Nikos Kasdaglis, Ο Σεφέρης στη Δωρική κρήνη (Rhodes: privately published, 2000), 27–9; first published in *To Dentro* 90 (1995).

107 Στήλη 1.73–6 (press report from *To Vima*, 23 September 1971); Keeley, 'Seferis's "Political" Voice,' 114–8, citing a letter from the novelist and translator Kay Cicellis (quoted); Andrews, '1971.'

# Guide to Further Reading

**On the historical background**

Richard Clogg, *A Concise History of Greece,* 2nd ed. (Cambridge University Press, 2002, 1st ed. 1992)

John S. Koliopoulos and Thanos M. Veremis, *Greece: The Modern Sequel* (London: C. Hurst, 2002)

**On the literary background**

Roderick Beaton, *An Introduction to Modern Greek Literature,* 2nd ed. (Oxford University Press, 1999, 1st ed. 1994)

**Translations**

*The King of Asine and Other Poems,* translated by Bernard Spencer, Nanos Valaoritis, and Lawrence Durrell, with an introduction by Rex Warner (London: John Lehmann, 1948). The contribution of George Katsimbalis to this volume, though not credited, was considerable. This is very much a poets' translation, and deserves to be read

*Poems,* translated by Rex Warner (London: Bodley Head; Boston and Toronto: Little, Brown, 1960). Contains about half of GS's published output between 1935 and 1955. The translator's deficiencies in modern Greek were compensated by extensive help from GS himself and G.P. Savidis

*Collected Poems, 1924–1955* [Greek and English texts], translated, edited and introduced by Edmund Keeley and Philip Sherrard (Princeton University Press, 1967; London: Jonathan Cape, 1969). At the time the fullest introduction to GS's poetry in English, now superseded (see below)

*Tria Kryfa Poiemata. Three Secret Poems* [Greek and English texts], translated,

with an introduction, by Walter Kaiser (Cambridge, Mass.: Harvard University Press; London: Oxford University Press, 1969). Rather wooden; the first translation of GS's final book of poetry. Several rival versions appeared soon afterwards in magazines; now best approached through the next item

*Collected Poems, Expanded Edition,* [Greek and English texts], translated and edited by Edmund Keeley and Philip Sherrard (Princeton University Press, 1981; London: Anvil Press, 1982). The translations have been revised and the *Three Secret Poems* added. Although some of the translations have been superseded by the next item, the coverage is the same; this remains the fullest introduction to GS's poetry for the reader who appreciates having access to the original Greek alongside a translation

*Complete Poems,* translated, edited and introduced by Edmund Keeley and Philip Sherrard (Princeton University Press; London: Anvil Press Poetry, 1995). The standard English version, to which reference is made throughout the notes to this book

*On the Greek Style,* translated, with an introduction, by Rex Warner and Th.D. Frangopoulos (London: Bodley Head; Boston and Toronto: Little, Brown, 1966; reprinted by Denise Harvey, Athens, 1982). Selections from the *Essays,* based on the 2nd edition of 1962

*A Poet's Journal: Days of 1945–1951,* translated by Athan Anagnostopoulos, with an introduction by Walter Kaiser (Cambridge, Mass.: Belknap, 1974; London: Harvard University Press, 1975). The first volume of GS's diaries to be published in Greek, now known as *Days 5*

**Books on Seferis in English**

Roderick Beaton, *George Seferis*. Series: Studies in Modern Greek (Bristol: Bristol Classical Press; New Rochelle, NY: Aristide Caratzas, 1991)

C. Capri-Karka, *Love and the Symbolic Journey in the Poetry of Cavafy, Eliot and Seferis* (New York: Pella, 1982)

C. Capri-Karka, *War in the Poetry of George Seferis* (New York: Pella, 1986)

Henry Gifford, *Poetry in a Divided World: The Clark Lectures 1985* (Cambridge University Press, 1986)

Rachel Hadas, *Form, Cycle, Infinity: Landscape Imagery in the Poetry of Robert Frost and George Seferis* (Lewisburg: Bucknell University Press; London and Toronto: Associated University Presses, 1985)

Edmund Keeley, *Modern Greek Poetry: Voice and Myth* (Princeton University Press, 1983)

David Ricks, *The Shade of Homer: A Study in Modern Greek Poetry* (Cambridge University Press, 1989)

Ioanna Tsatsos, *My Brother George Seferis*, translated by Jean Demos. A Nostos Book (Minneapolis, Minn.: North Central Publishing, 1982)

495

# Index

Academy of Athens, *see* Athens, Academy of

Adám(os), Pétros, 41, 44, 60–1

Aegina, xv, 27, 30, 141–2, 151, 144–5, 152, 246, 248, 250, 271

Aeschylus, 172–3, 234, 249, 275, 322; *Agamemnon*, 440–1, 458, 461; *Persians*, 314–15

Agianapa (Cyprus), 311

Agras Street (Athens): building of house at, 329, 339, 343; GS's home at, 83, 370, 375, 379

Aix-les-Bains, 30, 94

Akýlas, Michális, 139

Alain (Emile-Auguste Chartier), 71, 83, 106–7, 109

Albania, 145, 146, 148–51, 155–7, 162, 179, 279, 299; invaded by Italy, 171; war between Italy and Greece in, 185, 188–90

Alepoudélis, Odysséas, *see* Elytis, Odysseus

Alexander of Macedon (the Great), 167, 199, 204–5, 301, 365

Alexander: uncrowned king of Greece, 40

Alexandria, 89, 194, 209, 234; GS in, 198–201, 202, 204–5, 213, 245, 300, 336

al-Kayem, Henri, 487

America, *see* USA

Amman, 301, 303

Amorgos, 371–3, 485

Anacreon, 42

Analídi, *see* Angelidi

Anaxagoras of Clazomenae, 17, 172–3

Anaximander of Miletus, 173

Andreas-Salomé, Lou, 428

Andresen, Kirsten, 40

angel(s), 73, 87, 101, 176

Angelídi, Charíkleia (GS's paternal grandmother), 6

*Anglo-Hellenic Review* (Athens), 260, 267, 282, 295, 306, 319, 462, 464–5, 472, 474

Ankara, xv, 84, 279–82, 283–4, 290, 291, 299, 337, 341

Annan, Noel, 358–9, 363

Antoniou, D.I., 67, 105–6, 135, 137, 138, 174, 188, 198, 325, 326, 375

Aphrodite, 275, 308–9, 311–12, 323

*Apocalypse*, 71, 255, 325–6, 366, 387–8

Apollinaire, Guillaume, 208

Apostolídis, George, 83, 97, 110, 111, 113, 115, 116, 117, 122, 123, 149, 152, 155, 210, 268

Apuleius, 76–7, 429, 430, 465

Archaeological Museum, *see* National Archaeological Museum (Athens)

Armenians (in Smyrna), 3, 4

Arnold, Matthew, 167

Aronis School (Smyrna), 12–15

Arónis, Chrístos, 12, 13

Arónis, Níkos, 26–7, 28, 30, 32–3, 34, 35, 37, 55, 56, 58, 60, 78–9

Arpajoglu, Ann, 284–5

Asine, 170, 286

Atatürk, *see* Kemal

Athens, Academy of, 82–3, 385; buildings, 166–7

Athens, University of: GS not enrolled, 29–30; Stelios Seferiadis as professor, 25–6, 57, 170, 419

Athens: as experienced by GS, 65, 67, 172; civil war in, 251–3, 257–9; evacuation from, 193–5; GS's home in, 23–8, 29, 30, 47, 52–3, 83, 126, 133–6, 152, 156–7, 250–79, 336–7, 340–2, 375–405; under occupation (WWII), 210, 211, 216, 226, 250

Attlee, Clement, 262, 342

Auden, W.H., 294

Averoff-Tosizza (Avérof-Tosítsas), Evángelos: foreign minister, 299, 333–4, 338, 340, 342, 346, 348–50, 354, 355–6, 367; GS's relations with, 334–5, 336,

338–9, 350–3, 358, 364–5, 375; member of Kydathinaion Street circle, 139, 333; memoirs, 358, 477, 479, 481, 482
Axióti, Mélpo, 115, 442–3

Baalbek, 301
Babylon, 301
Baghdad, xv, 301, 303, 335, 472
Balfour, David, 233
Balkan Entente, 165, 171–2, 180
Balkan wars (1912–13), 21–2, 25
Balzac, Honoré de, 175–6
Barcelona, 384
Baruzi, Jean, 108
BBC Greek Service, 261, 295, 398–9
Beirut, 299, 301, 302, 308, 311–12, 319, 324, 326, 327, 328, 332, 336, 343
Bell, Gertrude, 335
Benákis family, see Delta
Bevin, Ernest, 261, 262, 265
Birgi, Nuri: Turkish ambassador to London, 341, 353, 480
Birtles, Bert, 138, 440, 441
Bítsios, Dimítrios, 481
Bodrum (Halicarnassus), 287–8, 290
Bonn, 342
Bowra, Maurice, 359, 383, 384, 490
Brémond, Henri, 43, 98
Britain: decline of empire, 297–8, 302–3, 309–10; parliament, see House of Commons
British Council (Athens), 177, 260, 176, 294, 305, 462
British Council (Cairo), 202
British Council (Nicosia), 305, 316, 358, 473
British embassy (Athens), 177, 180, 347
British Institute (Athens), 260, 271, 278, 325, 462, 466
Bucharest, 171–2
Buckingham Palace (London), 297, 342
Budca (near Izmir), 280, 291
Burn, A.R. (Robin), 250, 451, 477
Bursa (Turkey), 283
Byblos, 301
Byron, George Gordon, Lord, 115
Byzantine art, 165, 283, 290
Byzantium (empire), 165, 281, 283, 297–8, 301, 302, 314

Caccia, Harold, 261
Caesarea, see Kayseri
Cairo: 198, 202, 211–13, 215–40, 244–5, 253, 258, 259, 333, 365
calligramme, 208, 224
Cambridge, University of: honorary doctorate for GS, 363; see also King's College
Cape Town, xv, 209–10
Capetanakis, Demetrios, 139, 242
Cappadocia, rock-cut monasteries of, 290, 469–70
Cardiff (GS notionally posted to), 124
Cardiff, Maurice, 276, 294, 305, 306, 309, 310, 316–17, 331, 358, 472, 473, 477
Castle, Barbara, 347
Castoriades, Cornelius, 139
Cava dei Tirreni (near Salerno, Italy), 245–9, 259, 355
Cavafy, C.P., xi, 81, 97, 150, 200–201, 204–5, 208–9, 222, 271, 276, 284, 294, 296, 324, 390, 470–1
censorship, 143–4, 150, 159, 161, 164, 166, 197, 318, 391, 397, 400, 443, 446, 447, 449
Chamberlain, Neville, 170–1
Chania (Crete), 195–7
Channel Islands, 359
Chora (Church), see Kahrye Camii
Chortátsis, Geórgios, 377, 485
Christianity: and paganism, 291, 302, 370–1, 387; GS's attitude to, 9, 43, 108–10, 113, 387–8
Chrysánthis, Kýpros, 310, 472
Churchill, Winston, 217, 235, 240, 241, 252, 257–8, 261, 342
Cicellis, Kay, 493
Cicero, 24
civil war in Greece, 25, 122, 225–7, 251–3, 257–9, 263, 267, 277–8, 280–1, 284, 342, 391
Claridge's Hotel (London), 262–3, 354, 356
Claudel, Paul, 43, 381
Clauzel, Suzon, 36–7, 38, 39
Clazomenae, 17, 172, 288–9
Cocteau, Jean, 172
Codrington, Sir Edward, 23 (see also Kodringtonos Street)

Colonels, regime of (1967–74), 162, 357, 389, 391–405; GS's 'Statement' against, 398–401

*Colossus of Maroussi, The* (*see also* Miller, Henry), 80–1, 105, 174–7, 183, 219, 260, 261, 448

Communist Party of Greece (KKE), 66, 187, 259, 267, 268, 277, 425

Connolly, Cyril, 242, 261

Constanţa (Romania), 171

Constantine I: king of Greece, 25, 29, 40, 52, 262

Constantine II: king of Greece, 83, 386, 393, 404

Constantinople (*see also* Byzantium; Istanbul): capital of Byzantine empire, 165, 168; Ecumenical Patriarchate in, 6, 326; home of G. Apostolidis, 83, 84; home of G. Theotokas, 81; home of Zannos family, 140; traditional songs of, 248

Corfu, 30, 57, 174, 178, 307

Craxton, John, 375

Crea, Vicenzo (Enzo), 386, 398

Crete, 88, 138, 287, 326, 485; Battle of, 195, 198, 199–200, 201, 204–5; Greek government established in, 193, 195–7

Crossman, Richard, 305, 313, 314

Cyprus: as British possession, xii, 304–5; cession to Greece proposed by Damaskinos, 261–2, 263; debated at UNO, 317, 336–9, 348; debated in British parliament, 312–14; 'Emergency' in, xii, 319, 330–2, 334–5, 343–4, 345, 348, 355–6, 359, 365, 367, 369; *enosis* (union with Greece), Greek-Cypriot campaign for, xii, 304–5, 307, 311, 312, 313, 314–15, 324, 334, 341; Greek-Cypriot uprising in (1931), 102, 304, 434; GS plans to return to, 327, 403; GS professionally involved with, 325, 332, 333–4, 335–58; GS publishes in, 397; GS vilified over settlement, 361, 364, 381, 399–400; GS visits (1952), 300, 396; GS visits (1953), 305, 306–12, 314, 329; GS visits (1954), 316, 317–18; GS visits (1955), 319, 324, 326–7, 328; GS's poems dedicated to, 240, 303–4, 311–12, 318, 319, 321, 323–4, 327, 328, 329–30;

independent state proposed, 342, 348–51, 352; Macmillan Plan for, 344–5, 347, 348, 349, 350, 357; Paris meeting over (1958), 348–50; partition of, xv, 345, 350, 357–8; Republic of, 357; Tripartite Conference (London, 1955), 320–1, 325; Turkish Cypriots, 304, 307, 309–10, 321, 344, 345, 354; war between Greece and Turkey threatened over, 357–8, 393; Zurich and London Agreements over, 353–8, 361

d'Annunzio, Gabriele, 142–3

Damascus, 301

Damaskinós: archbishop and regent of Greece, 257–9, 265–7, 280, 324, 342, 463, 482; in internal exile, 268

Dante Alighieri, xiii, 112, 113, 135, 387, 440

Dassin, Jules, 404

Day Lewis, Cecil, 363

de Gourmont, Remy, 43

de Simony, Henry Reynold, 177–8

Debussy, Claude-Achille, 74, 248

December Events (*Dekemvrianá*, 1944), 251–3, 342, 467

Delmoúzos, Aléxandros, 139

Delos, xiv, 88, 385, 386–7

Delphi, 88, 127, 142, 300, 369, 370–3, 378, 382, 385, 387, 390, 398

Délta, Penelope, 151, 194, 195

Democratic Army, 277

demotic Greek, 11–12, 46, 68

Diamantís, Adamántios, 310, 316, 370, 376, 384, 490

dictatorship in Greece, *see* Fourth of August regime; Colonels

Dodecanese, 105, 262, 324, 325–6

*Domaine grec* (Levesque), 278–9

Dorchester Hotel (London), 354, 355

Dostoyevsky, Fyodor, 124

Douglas, Keith, 229

Dragoúmi, Amaryllís (Maro's sister), 141, 145, 146, 149, 155, 183, 270, 271, 272, 276, 443

Dragoúmis, Íon, 39–40, 194

Dragoúmis, Nikólaos (Nélos), 141, 270, 464

Dragoúmis, Phílippos: undersecretary for foreign affairs, 245, 246

Dresden, 49

Drosínis, George, 97

Duncan, Isadora, 142

Durban, 202–3, 205, 207, 210, 250

Durrell, Gerald, 178

Durrell, Lawrence, xi, xiv, 174–5, 177, 178, 202, 215, 228, 229, 230, 245, 267–8, 360, 372, 390, 428, 457, 464, 483; GS corresponding with, 208, 209, 228–30, 271; in Cyprus, 305, 308, 310, 316–17, 472

EAM (National Liberation Front), 217, 222, 225–7, 231, 235, 237, 243, 244, 252, 259

Eden, Anthony, 191, 240, 261, 305, 335–6

EDES (National Republican Greek League), 227

Edfelt, Johannes, 378–9

Edinburgh, 359

Edwards, Harold, 230

Egypt: Greek government evacuated to, 197–8; see also Alexandria; Cairo

Eighteen Texts, 400–1

EKKA (National and Social Liberation), 226–7, 234, 251

ELAS (National Popular Liberation Army), 217, 226, 227, 231, 234, 235, 250, 251, 252, 277

Eleftheros (newspaper), 381

Elgin Marbles, 261

Eliot, T.S., 43, 138, 229, 230, 238, 380, 387, 389; Ash Wednesday, 109, 436; 'East Coker,' 329; Four Quartets, 272, 329, 386, 388; GS's correspondence with, xiv, 359; GS's discovery of, 107–8, 109; GS's lecture on, 271, 276; GS's meetings with, 182, 280, 294, 297–9, 325, 359, 363, 482; 'Little Gidding,' 386; 'Marina,' 107–8, 154; Murder in the Cathedral, 377–8; The Hollow Men, 123; The Waste Land, 122–3, 150, 171, 214–15, 291, 347; translated by GS, see Seferis, George, WORKS (3) TRANSLATIONS

Eluard, Paul, 268–9, 279

Elytis, Odysseus, 139, 189, 198, 268

empire: see Byzantium, Britain

Engomi (Cyprus), 308–9, 318, 323

enosis, see Cyprus

EOKA (National Organization of Cypriot Fighters), 319, 320, 330, 343–4, 345,

348, 355–6; GS's attitude to, 332, 335, 344

Ephesus, 288, 291, 302, 469; see also Heraclitus of Ephesus

Erofíli (tragedy by G. Chortatsis, late 16th century), 377, 485

Erotokritos (romance by V. Kornaros, late 16th century), 19, 196, 267, 287, 290, 372, 466

Estia (newspaper), 266, 282, 361, 398, 491

eternity (GS's concept of), 110, 269–70, 464, 485

Eunostos (abortive periodical), 209

Euripides, 322–3

Ezanville (Paris), 296

Faliron (outside Athens): King George II lands at, 136, 138

Famagusta, 317, 326–7, 403; bay of, 308, 314

Farkoúch, Stefanía (Béba), 280, 291

Fedden, Robin, 177, 202, 228

Federal Bureau of Investigation, 285

Finance Ministry, see Ministry of Finance

Florina, 147

Foot, Hugh: governor of Cyprus, 344, 385, 386

Foreign Ministry, see Ministry of Foreign Affairs, Athens

Foreign Office (London), 180, 212, 219, 242, 244, 259, 261, 263, 334, 347, 351, 454, 460, 480; GS's relations with, 341, 342–3, 345, 346, 363

Forster, E.M., 200, 294, 358–9, 470–1

Fotopoúlou, Loukía (abbreviated by GS to 'Lou'), 73–8, 83, 84, 85, 86, 87, 92, 93–4, 95, 97, 110–11, 113, 115, 127, 140, 141, 146, 149, 151, 442–3; GS corresponding with, 101–2, 103–4, 106, 112, 116, 118–22, 433, 438; remembered by GS, 173, 182, 274; with GS in London, 116–18, 123–4

Fourth of August regime (1936–41), 143–4, 150, 156–64, 158–64, 165, 166, 187, 188, 195–6, 197, 201–2, 206, 212, 215, 217, 226, 268, 275, 397; GS accused of sympathy with, 156–7, 218–22

Foyle Prize (awarded to GS, 1961), 228, 364

Frangópoulos, Th.D. (Boúlis), 301, 400

Fraser, G.S., 229
Frederica: queen of Greece, 159, 369
Freud, Sigmund, 135
Friar, Kimon, 260

Galini (villa on Poros), 141, 183, 270, 272, 273, 276–7, 465
Gátsos, Níkos, 178
Geneva, 93–4, 123, 160, 197
Gennadius Library (Athens): GS papers in, xii, xiv
George II: king of Greece, 136, 138, 144, 159, 190, 193, 202, 217, 226, 231–3, 262–3, 265, 266–7, 441, 482
Gide, André, 43, 71, 124, 279; Corydon, 427; GS meets in Athens, 178; Paludes, 68, 472
Goudís, Dimítrios, 24
Gower Street (London), GS living in, 115, 117, 124–5
'Great Idea, The' 36, 39, 164, 446
Greco, El (Domínikos Theotokópoulos), 62, 96, 108, 168, 384
Greek civil war, see civil war
Greek consulate (London), GS working at, 101–3, 115, 117, 124–5
Greek embassy (London), GS at, 293–9, 342–67, 369–70, 372, 375, 369–70, 372–5
Greek Literary and Historical Archive (ELIA, Athens), xiv
Greek people, see people
'Greekness,' 166–8
Grivas, Colonel George: leader of EOKA, 332, 355, 477
Gullberg, Hjalmar, 487

Hadzidákis, Mános, 362
Hague, The: Stelios employed at, 40, 41
haiku, 86
Hampstead (London): GS living in, 103–4, 115
Hansen, Theophil, 167
Harding, Field-Marshal Sir John: governor of Cyprus, 327, 330, 344
Háris, Pétros: editor, Nea Estia, 315
Harvard University, 162, 392–3, 394
Hatzikyriákos-Ghíka, Níkos, 128, 175, 271, 384

Hellenism, 164–9, 281, 301–2, 307–8, 313, 354, 382, 396
Heraclitus of Ephesus, 135, 173, 234, 326, 388, 403
Herodotus, 308
Herriot, Edouard, 88–9, 116, 301, 307, 465
Hieronymos, Archbishop, 404
Hitler, Adolf, 122, 144, 170, 179, 187, 191, 192, 202, 250
Hölderlin, Friedrich, 131, 181
Holland, Robert, 321
Hollingworth, Clare, 449
Homer, 92, 109, 129; Iliad, 24, 42, 170, 182; Odyssey, 25, 71, 77, 84, 96, 112, 113, 273–5, 450
Homeric hymns, 386–7
Hopkinson, Henry: Colonial Office minister, 312–13
Horizon, 193, 242, 261
House of Commons (London), 312–14, 344, 345, 355
Hove (near Brighton), 60
Hoxha, Enver, 149
Hoyer-Millar, Frederick: permanent under-secretary of state (Foreign Office), 341, 479–80
Hugo, Victor, 25
Huxley, Aldous, 108
Hydra, 128, 175–6, 183, 250, 271, 384

Ikaros publishing house (Athens), 290, 327, 490
Illinois, University of, 385
Institute of Contemporary Arts (ICA, London), 298, 363
Iraq, see also Baghdad, 301, 303, 349, 365–6
irredentism, see 'Great Idea'
Israel, 301, 303
Istanbul, see also Constantinople: anti-Greek riots in, 325–6, 328, 350; GS visits, 83–4, 165, 168, 171, 283, 290, 291
ivory tower, see also poésie pure, 98, 163, 239, 274, 466
Izmir (since 1922, see also Smyrna), xv, 5, 124, 280; anti-Greek riots in, 325–6, 328; GS returns to (1950), 280, 287, 288, 290–2, 293; GS returns to (1969), 469, 470

Jacqueline, *see* Pouyollon

James, Henry, 125

Japan, 384–5

Jerash, 301, 302

Jerusalem, 193, 213–15, 220, 301, 302, 336

Jews: in Smyrna, 3–4, 416; in WWII, 214–15

Johannesburg, 203–4, 207, 210

Jordan, Hashemite kingdom of, *see also* Amman, 301, 303

Joyce, James, 108, 115; *Ulysses*, 47, 92, 96, 431, 432

July Events (*Ioulianá*, 1965), 386

Kahrye Camii, Istanbul (Church of the Chora), 165, 168, 283

Kakoúros, Evángelos, 139

Kálvos, Andréas, xi, 24, 208, 360–1

Kambás, Andréas, 178

Kanellópoulos, Panayótis: deputy prime minister (government in exile), 211–13, 215–18, 232; GS's relations with, 219, 221, 227, 247, 248, 258; in postwar governments, 264–5; member of Kydathinaion Street circle, 139, 188

Kant, Immanuel, 166

Karamáni, Ánna, *see* Sikelianou, Anna

Karamánis, George, 153, 189

Karamanlís, Constantine: GS's relations with, 335, 375; prime minister, 333, 336–7, 338, 346, 348, 354, 355–6, 367, 369, 481

Karantónis, Andréas, 112, 113, 464–5; author, *The Poet George Seferis*, 99, 295, 373; editor, *Ta Nea Grammata*, 128

Kartális, George, 139, 226–7, 234, 240, 264–5, 293, 334; GS's relations with, 247–8, 259; journey to London with GS, 240–4, 261; minister of Press and Information, 240, 247

Karýdis, Níkos: GS's publisher, 327, 389

Karyotákis, Kóstas, 84–5

Kásdaglis, Níkos, 324–5, 492, 493

*katharévousa* (formal Greek), 46, 166–7

Katsímbalis, Constantine, 79, 145–6, 150

Katsímbalis, George (the 'Colossus of Maroussi'), 79–81; and Karantonis, 99, 128; and Henry Miller, 174–6, 229; and Savidis, 373–4; at Maroussi, 80–1, 172–3, 174–5, 248; circle of, 105, 106, 139, 178,

189, 200, 260, 268, 271, 278, 305; commenting on GS's poems, 113–15, 273, 329; correspondence with GS, 86, 101, 103, 104, 107–8, 109, 112, 122, 124, 125, 145–6, 148, 155, 171, 281, 284, 295, 299, 306, 315–17, 320, 327, 374, 402, 465; correspondence with Maro, 294, 298, 311; correspondence with Valaoritis, 287, 364; during WWII, 187, 188; editor, *Anglo-Hellenic Review*, 260, 267, 306, 319; founder, *Ta Nea Grammata*, 128, 129, 133, 143, 150, 244; in Paris, 79–80, 145, 315–16; leader of 'clique,' 278–9, 281; with GS in Greece, 83, 276, 325, 326, 384, 390

Katsoyánni, Katy, 277, 337

Kavvadías, Níkos, 375, 381, 403

Kayseri (Caesarea), 5, 290

Kazantzákis, Níkos, 81, 143, 268, 277, 364, 378

Keeley, Edmund, xiv, 81, 162, 177, 260, 363, 385, 392, 393, 394, 395, 397, 399, 402

Keeley, Robert, 396, 397, 398–9, 491, 492

Kemal, Mustafa (Atatürk), 40, 42, 50, 84, 325

Kew Gardens (London), 118, 121

Kifisiá, 53, 71–2, 74, 77, 84, 85, 166, 170, 173, 194, 206, 211, 212

King's College, Cambridge, 295, 358–9

Kirsten, *see* Andresen

*klídonas* (midsummer ritual), 19, 388

Knös, Börje, 378–9

Kodringtonos Street (Athens): GS's home in, 23, 30

Kóllas, Constantine: press director, Cairo, 209, 212, 215, 454

Kondýlis, General Geórgios, 134, 138

Konya, 469

Korça (Albania), 145, 148–51, 152, 155–6, 165, 179, 181, 184, 200, 443

Koryzís, Aléxandros: prime minister, 190, 193, 194–5

Kos, 290, 326

Kranidiótis, Níkos, 305–6, 309

Kydathinaion Street (Athens): Church of the Transfiguration, 192, 404; circle of Ioanna and Kostakis Tsatsos, 139, 141, 189, 210, 212, 226, 242, 247–8, 251, 265, 333; disagreement over, 282, 463; GS's

502

home in, 126, 133, 134, 152, 157, 170,
183, 192, 250, 252, 261, 266; Maro in,
186, 189–92, 343, 351–2; Stelios in, 186,
263–4
*Kypriaka Grammata*, 474
Kýrou, Aléxis, 266, 365, 463
Kyvelis Street (Athens): GS's home in, 47,
52–3

Laforgue, Jules, 43
Lamartine, Alphonse de, 25
Lambert, Anthony: British ambassador to
Athens, 341
Lancaster, Osbert, 260, 301, 317, 320,
330–1, 358, 359, 376
language question (Greek), 11–12, 46,
166–7
*laós, see* people
Lapathiótis, Napoleon, 97
Lavranda (southwest Turkey), 287, 290,
365
Lawrence, D.H., 108, 115
Le Vésinet (near Paris), 54, 60
League of Nations, 93–4, 160, 197
Lear, Edward, 207–8, 452
Lebanon, *see also* Beirut, 300, 301, 302,
303
Leeper, Reginald (Rex): ambassador to
Athens, 257, 259, 261–3, 265;
ambassador to Greek government in
exile, 212, 219, 225, 226; memoirs, 462
Lefort, Thérèse (Stelios' second wife), 170,
186, 250, 264, 282, 296
Lehmann, John, 242, 261, 276–7, 282,
315–16
Leigh Fermor, Joan, *see* Rayner
Leigh Fermor, Patrick, 260, 301, 320, 332,
384, 477
Leros, 326
Levesque, Robert, 178, 268, 272, 273,
278–9, 464, 465, 467
Levi, Peter, 402–3, 486
Liberal Party: before 1936, *see* Venizelos; in
1946, 264
Liddell, Robert, 177, 202, 230
Limassol, 300
limericks: by GS, 297–8, 372, 402, 453, 485
Linnér, Sture, 379, 381, 385, 390, 393,
487–8

Lloyd, Selwyn: foreign secretary, 342, 345,
346, 348, 349, 350
London: conference on independence for
Cyprus, 353–8; formal seat of Greek
government in exile (WWII), 201, 203,
209, 215–17, 218, 231; GS in, 60–3,
101–25, 168, 241–4, 261–3, 293–300,
342–67, 369–70, 372–5; GS posted to,
99, 101, 293, 333, 340–3; Stelios in, 41;
Tripartite Conference on Cyprus in,
320–1, 325
Lóndos family, 149, 155, 184
Lóndos, Andréas (Maro's first husband),
140–1, 151–2, 157, 172, 183–5, 300;
during WWII, 188, 216
Lóndou, Lía (Andreas' sister), 185, 186, 216
Lóndou, Maríka, *see* Seferi, Maro
Lorenzatos (Lorentzátos), Zíssimos, 272–3,
281, 283, 302, 383, 464–5, 472, 476, 485
Loti, Pierre, 63–4
Lou(kía), *see* Fotopoulou, Loukia
Louízos, Evángelos, 305, 306, 307, 309,
311, 314, 317, 318, 323, 326–7, 374, 403
Loukídi, Loukía, *see* Fotopoulou, Loukia
Lowell, Robert, 385
Lyttleton, Oliver: colonial secretary, 313–14

Machairás, Leóntios: *Chronicle of the
Sweet Land of Cyprus*, 309, 317
MacLeish, Archibald, 385
Macmillan, Harold: foreign secretary,
320–1; GS's relations with, 342–3,
346–7, 352, 364; memoirs, 346, 357,
480; prime minister, 342, 345, 346, 355,
357; *see also* Cyprus: Macmillan Plan
for
MacNeice, Louis, 294, 297, 298, 363
MacVeagh: US ambassador to Greece, 446,
447, 458
Makários III: Archbishop of Cyprus,
304–5, 482; arrest and detention, 330–1;
GS's relations with, 319–20, 353, 404; in
Athens, 340, 346–7, 352, 479, 481; in
London, 354–6; president of Cyprus,
357, 393
Makriyánnis, General, 92, 150, 278, 281,
290, 314; GS's lecture on, 220–1, 222,
228, 237; *Memoirs*, 71, 186, 218, 249,
461, 474

503

Malános, Tímos, 200–1, 204, 208, 209, 220, 228, 274, 295, 296–7, 336, 456, 470; and publication of *Logbook II*, 241, 245; GS quarrels with, 237–40; *The Poetry of Seferis*, 294, 295

Mallarmé, Stéphane, 248, 383

*Manchester Guardian*, 367

Maniadákis, Konstantínos, 190, 196

Manning, Olivia, 177, 193, 195, 215, 230, 294

Maravélia, Charíkleia (mother of GS's maternal grandfather), 8

Marcus Aurelius, 388, 429, 489

Marmaris (Turkey), 287

Maró (GS's wife), see Seferi, Maro; (nickname), 145

Maroussi (Amaroussion), 80, 172–3, 248

Marseille, 63, 71, 293, 375

Mathiós Paskális, see Paskalis, Mathios

Mavrogordátou, Sofía, 151, 194, 195

Mavroudís, Nikólaos: under-secretary for foreign affairs, 145–6, 151, 155, 265

McCarthy, Eugene: US Senator, 394–5, 397, 399, 490

Meleágrou, Hebe, 403, 481

Mélpo, see Stái

Menderes, Adnan: prime minister of Turkey, 325, 355, 356, 357

Mercoúri, Melína, 404

mermaid device, 96, 237, 432, 459

Metaxás, Ioánnis, General, 134, 135, 138, 143–4, 159, 160, 161, 165, 166, 185, 186–7, 188, 190, 196; regime of, see Fourth of August regime

Metsovo, 333

Michalakópoulos, Andréas: foreign minister, 94, 97; death and funeral, 160

Miller, Henry, xi, xiv, 80–1, 105, 310; *Colossus of Maroussi, The*, 219, 229, 260, 271; correspondence with GS, 178, 188, 202, 251, 257, 280, 300, 317, 467; in Greece, 174–7, 183, 448

Ministry of Finance, 171

Ministry of Foreign Affairs, Athens (GS's career at): appointed director, Central Press Service (Cairo), 222; apppointed Press Director (Cairo), 230; appointed to board of National Theatre by, 267; appointed to board of national radio by,

267; 'at the disposal of,' 375, 384; bust of, outside, 73; consular service in London described, 102–3; Cyprus, disagreement over, 350–8; dealings with after retirement, 397, 401–2; entry to, 59, 70–2, 73; exempted from conscription by, 189; in cryptography department, 73, 98–9, 181; posted (notionally) to Ankara, 218; posted (notionally) to Cardiff, 124, 156; posted (notionally) to Izmir, 124, 162, 280, 467; posted to Athens, 126–7, 277, 332–5, 336, 375; posted to Beirut, 299–300, 301; posted to Cairo, 209–11, 215; posted to Korça (Albania), 145–7; posted to London 99, 101–25, 290, 293, 340–3; promotion, 133, 279, 299–300, 343, 367; protests against posting, 146, 151; recalled to Athens for consultation, 325, 327, 334–5; resignation from considered, 298–9, 353, 366; retirement from, 384; seconded from, 156–7, 158, 201–2, 258; transfer requested, 236, 240, 358; unofficial visits to Cyprus and, 306, 324

Ministry of the Interior, 401–2

miracle, 72, 176, 275, 293

Mirambel, André, 97

Mitropoulos, Dimitri, 277, 337

Mitrópoulos, Kóstas, 368

Montaigne, Michel de, 68, 71, 150

Moréas, Jean (Ioánnis Papadiamantópoulos), 43–7, 56, 150, 168; *Stances*, 46, 96; see also Seferis, George, WORKS (2) PROSE: ESSAYS

Móstras, Vassílios: ambassador to London, 340

Moúskos, Michael, see Makarios

musical settings of GS's poems, 90, 147, 361–3, 393–4, 405

Mussolini, Benito, 57, 136, 171, 179, 191, 223, 316

Mycenae, 182; see also Seferis, George, WORKS (1) POEMS: 'Mycenae'

Myers, Brigadier E., 241

Mykonos, 386

Myrivílis, Strátis, 139

Nafplio, 170

Naples, 246

Nasser, Abdul Gamal, 199, 335
National Archaeological Museum (Athens), 47, 52, 269–70, 274, 402
*National Herald* (New York), 284
National Liberation Front, *see* EAM
National Popular Liberation Army, *see* ELAS
NATO: and Cyprus crisis, 342, 347, 348, 349
Naxos, 8, 135
Nazis: GS's reaction to, 122, 179; *see also* *Sicherheitsdienst*; British behaviour in Cyprus compared to, 316
*Nea Estia*, 98, 315, 459, 466, 467, 474
Neruda, Pablo, 381
*New Letters, see Ta Nea Grammata*
*New Testament* (*see also Apocalypse*), 42, 70
New York, 85, 284, 336, 337–9, 385, 394–5, 468
Nicosia, 102, 304, 306, 307, 308, 324, 326, 347, 349; Greek consulate in, 332, 340
Nikolareΐzis, Dimίtrios: chargé d'affaires, London embassy, 340
Nikoloύdis, Theológos: ambassador to South Africa, 201, 203, 209, 215; under-secretary for Press and Tourism, 156, 158, 159, 180, 187, 189, 190, 194–5, 197
Nimiec, Max, 177–8, 448
Nobel Prize for Literature, 277, 287; aftermath in GS's life, 382–3, 389, 392, 397, 399–400; awarded to Elytis (1979), 139; awarded to GS (1963), xi, 229, 380–1, 470; awarded to Saint-John Perse, 337; candidature of GS, 364–5, 378–9; candidature of Sikelianos, 277, 287, 364, 365, 378, 380, 364, 365; GS's acceptance speeches, 169, 381–2, 396, 487
Noel-Baker, Francis, 462
*Nouvelle Revue Française*, 71
November Events (*Noemvrianá*, 1916), 28

Oedipus: and the Sphinx's riddle, 45–6, 381; sons of, and civil war, 274–5
Olympia, 88, 89, 465
Onassis, Aristotle, 289
Osterling, Anders: permanent secretary, Swedish Academy, 380, 487

Otto (first king of Greece), 220
Ovid, 24
Oxford, University of: honorary doctorate for GS, 383

Palamas Prize, 278
Palamás, Kostís, xi, 27, 81, 98, 105, 133, 134, 143, 133, 134, 143, 178, 219–20, 228, 295, 297, 364, 380
Palestine: ruled by British mandate, 214–15, 303
Pállis, Alexander, 97
Palmer, Eva (first wife of Sikelianos), 142
Palmyra, 301, 302
Panayotópoulos, I.M., 278
Panayotópoulos, Nánis, 200–1, 204, 336, 487
Pángalos, General Theódoros, dictatorship of, 66, 71–2
*pantun*, 86
Papadákis, Vassílios: Foreign Ministry official, 94, 195, 197, 201, 203, 209
Papadimitríou, Élli, 202
Papadópoulos, Colonel George: prime minister, 391
Papágos, Field-Marshal: prime minister, 299, 305, 332
Papanastasíou, Aléxandros, 134
Papandréou, George: GS's relations with, 235–7, 240, 248; prime minister (1944), 235, 236, 243, 244, 245, 246, 249, 251, 252; prime minister (1963–5), 384, 386, 389, 456
Papantoníou, Zacharías, 80
Papatsónis, Tákis (T.K.), 171–2, 281, 488
Papayánnis, Theódoros (portrait bust of GS by), 73, 427
Paris: avenue Wagram, 30, 31; GS in, xv, 30, 31–60, 63–4, 116, 118, 125, 263, 293, 348–50, 402; GS nostalgic for, 67–8, 88, 89; GS's parents in, 21, 22; Katsimbalis in, 79–80, 145, 146, 150; Peace Conference in (1918–19), 34, 35–6; rue Bréa, 49, 52; Stelios in, 26, 29–30, 116, 296–7
parliament (British): *see* House of Commons
Parnassus Society (Athens), 27, 143, 267
Paros, 135, 379

505

Pascal, Marie (Maro's mother), 140
Paskális, Mathiós (literary persona of GS), 85–6, 214, 228–9, 277, 453, 485
Pastamantzóglou, see Pesmazóglou
Patmos, 255, 326, 350
Patsifás, Alékos: GS's publisher, 327
Pattakós, Brigadier Stylianós: minister of the interior, 391, 401–2
Paul: crown prince, 159, 221; king of Greece, 369
Pavlópoulos, George, 402–3
Peake, Sir Charles: British ambassador to Athens, 325, 334
PEEA (Political Committee of National Liberation), 231, 243
Pelion, Mount, 134–5, 151, 153–5, 169, 189
Pentzíkis, Níkos Gabriel, 383
people (laós), 189, 196, 220–2, 310, 405
People's Party, 127, 264, 266
Pernot, Hubert, 97
Personal Landscape, 202, 209, 228–30, 238–9, 261
Persson, Axel, 286, 287, 365
Pervigilium Veneris, 275
Pesmazóglou family, 8, 280
Pesmazóglou, Ioánnis (Yángos), 139
Petsális(-Diomídis), Thanásis, 128
Phaleron, see Faliron
Philipe, Anne, 402
Pipinélis, Panayótis: foreign minister, 401
Pirandello, Luigi, 85
Pittsburgh, 394
Plastíras, General Nicholas, 122, 133–4, 136, 143, 264
Plato, 24, 274, 285, 394, 403
Poe, Edgar Allen, 87
poésie pure, 98, 107
poetic language, 164, 383
Poniridy, George, 41, 68, 73, 78, 116
Pontani, Filippo Maria, 383, 401
pornographic verse: by GS, 297–8, 372
Poros, 250; Dragoumis family home on (see also Galini), 140, 141; GS and Maro visit, 145, 183; 'Thrush' written on, 270–2, 276–7, 287, 312
Port Said, 198, 226
Pound, Ezra, 163
Pouyollon, Jacqueline, 53–7, 140, 382; and GS's final illness and death, 404, 405;
and Ioanna Tsatsou, 75–6, 87–8, 92–3; GS breaks off with, 75–6, 79, 83, 127; GS keeps faith with, 61, 68–70, 73, 77, 101, 118; GS meets again, 93–4, 111–12, 113, 116, 123, 125–6; relationship with reflected in GS's writing, 55, 63, 78, 85, 87, 89–90, 95, 125–6
Pouyollon, Marie-Louise, 53–7, 63, 68, 69, 73, 75, 79, 97, 111, 113, 116, 125, 382–3
Powell, Dilys, 242
Presidio of Monterey, see US Army Language School
Pre-Socratic philosophers, 17, 135, 172–3, 234
Press Ministry, see Under-Ministry of Press and Tourism, Athens
Pretoria, xv, 202, 203, 204–9, 210, 215, 238, 249, 372, 464
Princeton (N.J.), 385, 386, 394–6; Institute for Advanced Study, 392–3, 394
Princeton University, 394; honorary doctorate for GS, 385
Profumo, John: minister of state, Foreign Office, 357
Prousa, see Bursa
Proust, Marcel, 43, 154
Providence, Rhode Island, 337
Psarrós, Dimítrios, Colonel: leader of EKKA, 226, 234, 251

Rabelais, François, 71
Ramazan (GS's cat), 283–4
Ravel, Maurice, 74
Rayner (Leigh Fermor), Joan, 301, 317, 320, 331, 332, 384
regency in Greece: see Damaskinos
Reinhardt, Max, 363
Remzi, Sherif ('Smyrna merchant'), 291
Revelation, Book of, see Apocalypse
Rhodes, 324–5
Rilke, Rainer Maria, 71, 428
Rimbaud, Arthur, 43
Rítsos, Yánnis, 362, 394
Romania, 171–2
Roosevelt, Franklin D., 122, 235
Ross, Archibald: under-secretary of state (Foreign Office), 345, 347, 348, 479–80
Rostand, Edmond, 25, 31–2
Roúfos, Ródis, 400, 481

Roussel, Louis, 97

Roússos, Geórgios: deputy prime minister (government in exile), 219–22, 227, 230, 237, 247, 445, 456, 459; named as prime minister, 232

Runciman, Steven, 260, 294, 300–1, 360, 382

Russell, Leonard, 242

Rutgers University, 394

Saint John of the Cross, 108–9, 249

Saint-John Perse (Alexis Leger), 337, 380, 381, 383

Salamis (Cyprus), 314–15, 322

Salamis (Greece), 143, 268–9, 315, 322

Salerno, 245

Salonica, see Thessaloníki

Samos, 20–1, 25, 264

San Francisco, 284, 285

Santorini, 135, 137

Sarantáris, George, 139, 189

Sartre, Jean-Paul, 380, 381

Satie, Erik, 137

Savídis, George, 294–5, 319, 325, 326, 358, 361, 362, 375, 380, 381, 398, 474, 478; and Festschrift for GS, 373–4; and GS's poems about Cyprus, 329, 330, 373; correspondence with GS, 321, 327, 485; editor of GS's posthumous works, 372; relations with Katsimbalis, 327, 374, 476

Sceaux (near Paris), 41–3

Schilizzi, Helena: wife of E. Venizelos, 343

Scobie, Lieutenant-General Sir Ronald, 252

sefer (Arabic/Turkish), 6, 104, 417

Seféri, Maró (María Zánnou, also known as Maríka, first married to Andreas Londos), xiv; and London embassy, 340, 343, 369–70; and T.S. Eliot, 294; at Kydathinaion Street, 189–92, 249; background and first meetings with GS, 140–2, 144–5, 147, 271, 275, 295; children of, 140, 142, 157, 184–5, 194, 198, 205, 211, 216, 250, 272, 286; correspondence with GS, 147, 149–50, 151–2, 155, 171–2, 183–5, 186, 243, 312, 334, 353, 338–9, 355, 356; correspondence with Katsimbalis, 294, 298, 311; described by GS, 213, 241;

developing relationship with GS, 150–3, 156–7, 165, 169–70, 172, 182, 183; diary (1941–2), 204–6, 207, 209–10; GS's poems addressed to, 146, 148, 205, 275, 371; in Athens, 286, 290, 333, 343, 351; interview with, 396, 402; marriage to GS, 192, 193; on Theodorakis, 394

Seferiádi, Élli (GS's cousin), 51, 127

Seferiádis family, 5–11, 23, 25, 52, 126

Seferiádis, Alékos (GS's cousin), 244

Seferiádis, Anastásis (brother of GS's paternal grandfather), 6

Seferiádis, Ángelos (GS's brother), 10; as poet and translator, 10, 58–9, 285–6, 390, 391; correspondence with GS, 91–2; during WWII, 188, 210, 216, 244, 250; early life, 22, 23, 33, 35, 37, 47, 49, 52, 56, 57–9, 60, 286; in Germany, 116, 437; in Greece, 72, 82, 84; in USA and death, 264, 284–6, 339, 463, 468; on distribution list for GS's poems, 97; remembered by GS, 383, 390–1

Seferiádis, Pródromos (GS's paternal grandfather), 6–8, 9, 10

Seferiádis, Socrates ('Uncle Socrates,' GS's cousin), 8, 22, 37, 50, 51

Seferiádis, Stélios (Stylianós) (GS's father), 6–8, 9; and GS's professional career, 59, 70; and house in Kydathinaion Street, Athens, 126, 263–4; and Katsimbalis family, 79; and Palamas, 98; and Pouyollon family, 53–7; and Venizelos, 36, 39, 53, 84; as poet and translator, 6–7, 11–12, 21, 30, 32, 170, 185; at The Hague, 40; attitude to Maro, 146, 170, 184, 186, 192; correspondence with GS, 14–15, 21, 26, 28–9, 30, 34, 39, 41, 54, 59, 61–3, 72, 155, 264, 282; death of, 296–7, 298, 299; in Germany, 48–9; in Paris, 26, 28, 29–30, 31, 94, 116, 170, 250, 282; in Smyrna, 11–15, 163; involvement with Samos (1912), 20–1, 22, 23, 25, 264; on distribution list for GS's poems, 97; pressure on GS to study, 12–13, 38, 41, 59; professor, University of Athens, 25–6, 34, 37, 40, 53, 57, 170; relationship with Despo, 30, 33–4, 71–2

Seferiádou, Ioánna, see Tsatsou, Ioanna

Seféris (Ayinabéyoglou), 5–6, 290

507

Seféris, George (Yórgos): pseudonym, xiii, 46, 62, 66, 84, 96, 141, 432

WORKS. (1) POETRY: 'Actors, Middle East,' 223; 'Agianapa, I,' 311, 474; 'Agianapa, II,' 311, 474; 'Angolo Franciscano, L',' 281; 'Automobile,' 74, 427; 'Bhamdun,' 472; *Book of Exercises*, 86, 150, 155, 181, 185–6, 430, 439, 450; *Book of Exercises, II*, 378, 439, 440, 463, 464, 466, 467, 469, 472, 486, 488, 490; 'Canzona di Ringraziamento,' 283; 'Cats of St Nicholas, The,' 283, 300, 326, 396–7, 400, 471; *Cistern, The*, 75, 78, 96, 97, 98, 110–15, 118, 119, 120, 123, 129, 143, 428, 439, 440; *Collected Poems* (trans. Keeley and Sherrard), 385; 'Companions in Hades, The,' 84; 'Container of the Uncontainable, The,' 441, 446; 'Countries of the Sun,' 366;... *Cyprus, Where It Was Ordained For Me...* , 240, 293, 311–12, 318, 321, 323–4, 327, 328, 329–20, 358, 361, 365, 373, 471, 473–4, 476; 'Days of April, '43,' 222–3; 'Days of June '41,' 199–200, 204–5; 'Demon of Fornication, The,' 309; 'Denial,' xiv, 90, 95, 362–3, 405; 'Description,' 439; 'Details on Cyprus,' 309, 473, 474; 'Dhour el Choueir,' 472; early poems, 27, 32–3, 40, 43, 47, 53, 56, 59, 62, 109–10, 420–1, 423; 'Engomi,' 308–9, 312, 318, 323; *Entepsyzika, see Rude Ones, The;* 'Epiphany, 1937,' 147–8, 443; 'Epitaph,' 146; 'Erotikos Logos,' 90, 95–6, 97, 101, 111, 112, 129, 204, 312, 439; 'Euripides the Athenian,' 322–3; 'Fawning in the Afternoon,' 248; 'Figure of Fate, The,' 206; 'Fine Autumn Morning,' 443; 'Fires of St John', 19, 116; 'Five Poems by Mr S. Thalassinos,' 105; 'Fog,' 62–3; *Gymnopaidia*, 133, 136–7, 181; 'Helen,' 311, 322, 460, 476; 'Here Among the Bones,' 226–7; 'In the Goddess's Name I Summon You,' 308, 311; 'In the Kyrenia District,' 322; 'In the Manner of G.S.', 135, 150, 160, 368, 395; 'Kerk Str. Oost, Pretoria,

Transvaal,' 451–2; *King of Asine and Other Poems, The* (trans. Durrell et al.), 170, 202, 245, 261, 277, 281–2, 294; 'King of Asine, The,' xvi, 182–3, 229, 321; 'Last Day, The,' 161–2; 'Last Stop,' 189, 225, 240, 245, 248–9, 302, 460, 461; 'Les Anges Sont Blancs,' 176; 'Letter of Mathios Paskalis,' 85–6; 'Letter to Rex Warner,' 488; *Logbook [I]*, 131, 150, 161, 181–3, 185–6, 201, 397, 443, 446, 449, 450; *Logbook II*, 92, 205, 207, 208–9, 223, 224, 225, 229, 237, 241, 245, 249, 274, 295, 452, 461; *Logbook III, see... Cyprus, Where It Was Ordained For Me...* ; 'Mathios Paskalis Among the Roses,' 443; 'Memory, I,' 468; 'Mood of a Day, The,' 87, 110; 'Mr Stratis Thalassinos Describes a Man,' 105; 'Mycenae,' 137; *Mythistorema*, 18, 69–70, 72, 92, 97, 106, 114–15, 121, 123–6, 127–30, 133, 137, 237, 240, 273, 302, 394, 432, 439, 447, 472; 'Neophytos the Recluse Speaks Out,' 455, 473, 477; 'Nijinsky,' 77, 434; 'Notes for a "Week",' 123–4, 434, 437, 439; 'Old Man on the River Bank, An,' 213, 222, 433; 'Old Man, The,' 146; 'On a Ray of Winter Light,' 369, 372; 'On Aspalathoi,' 402–3; 'On Stage,' 371, 377–8, 486; 'Out of Stupidity,' 396; 'Pantoum,' 86; 'Pedlar from Sidon,' 300, 308, 473; 'Pentheus,' 322–3; 'Piazza San Niccolò,' 154–5; *Poems* (1st ed., 1940), 97, 181–2, 185–6; *Poems* (2nd ed., 1950), 161, 284; *Poems* (3rd ed.), 358, 365, 378, 482, 486; *Poems* (trans. Warner), 358, 363–4, 477–8; *Poems with Drawings for Small Children*, 453; 'Postscript,' 205; 'Reflections on a Foreign Line of Verse,' 1, 19, 92, 127; 'Return of the Exile, The,' 162–3, 289; 'Rocket,' 96; *Rude Ones, The (Ta Entepsyzika)*, 372, 453, 485; 'Salamis in Cyprus,' 311, 314–16, 319, 330, 474–5; 'Santorini,' 133, 137; 'Scholion,' 430; 'Sentence to Oblivion, The,' 432, 443; 'Sirocco 7 Levante,' 135;

508

'Sketches for a Summer,' 145, 146, 150; 'Sketches for a Summer, II,' 366; 'Slowly You Spoke,' 77; 'Snow Here Is Never-Ending, The,' 280; 'Sonnet,' 32, 47, 420–1, 423; 'Stratis Thalassinos among the Agapanthi,' 207; 'Stratis Thalassinos on the Dead Sea,' 214–15, 347, 480; 'Summer Solstice' (see also *Three Secret Poems*), xiii–xiv, 19, 386–9, 390, 489; 'Syngrou Avenue, 1930,' 82; 'Syngrou Avenue, II,' 136, 440–1; 'Three Mules,' 473, 474; *Three Secret Poems*, 72, 99, 110, 119, 145, 326, 369, 371, 372, 377, 378, 386–9, 390, 438, 466, 484, 485, 486, 489; 'Thrush,' 110, 175, 191, 240, 245, 253, 264, 270–6, 277, 287, 295, 301, 311, 312, 323, 366, 436, 460, 463; *Turning Point*, 46, 74, 78, 85, 86, 90, 95–100, 108, 111, 112, 115, 127, 129, 160, 171, 237, 373; 'Word for Summer, A,' 442; 'Written in Pencil,' 469

(2) PROSE:

DIARIES, xiii; copied and edited by GS, 66, 282, 390–1, 392, 426, 489; *Days 1*, 66, 68–9, 71, 74–5, 76–7, 86, 92; *Days 2*, 102, 112, 392, 433; *Days 3*, 126, 158, 158, 160, 173, 186; *Days 4*, 248; *Days 5 (Days of 1945–1951)*, 295, 311, 390–1, 468, 469; *Days 6*, 474, 476; later diaries, 391, 392, 485, 486, 488, 490, 492; *Manuscript Oct. '68*, 395–6; *Manuscript Sept. '41*, 127, 205–7; *Political Diary* ('service diary'), 160, 203, 218, 227, 233, 235–6, 247, 259, 261, 263, 265, 266, 347, 440, 453;

ESSAYS (*Dokimés*), xi; 150, 443–4; 'A Hellene: Makriyannis,' 220–1, 222, 228, 237; 'A Scenario for *"Thrush"*,' 273, 274, 465; 'Conversation with Fabrice,' 390; 'Delphi,' 369, 370–3; 'Dialogue on Poetry,' 165–9; 'Digressions on the Homeric Hymns,' 386–7; 'Discours de Stockholm, Le,' 169; *Essays* (1st ed.), 227–8; *Essays* (2nd ed.), 296–7, 365, 378; *Essays* (3rd ed.), 390, 392, 465, 489–90; 'Hours of Mrs Ersi, The,' 488; 'Kostis Palamas,' 219–20; 'Monologue on Poetry,' 163–4,

169, 171; *Selections from the Essays* (1966), 469; 'T.S. Eliot – C.P. Cavafy: Parallels,' 271–2, 276; 'The Other World,' 469;

FICTION: 'Alyis Vayias,' 55–6, 85, 93, 104; *Six Nights on the Acropolis*, xiii, 66, 67, 68, 69, 70, 74–5, 76, 86–7, 92, 93, 94, 98, 110, 113, 116, 121, 181, 248, 311–12, 430, 433, 440, 450, 449, 465–6, 474; *Varnavas Kalostefanos*, 312, 318–19;

(3) TRANSLATIONS, 71, 378; *Antigrafés*, 457, 486; 'Apocalypse,' 326, 366, 378, 387–8, 486, 489; Eliot, 122–3, 150, 284, 377–8; Gide, 68; Montaigne, 68; Plato, 394, 403; 'Song of Songs,' 211, 366, 378, 486; Valéry, 68, 86, 98

Seleucia on the Tigris, xv, 301, 302, 365–6

Sèvres, Treaty of (1920), 39–40, 48

Seyrig, Henri, 301, 465

Shakespeare, William, 108, 286, 477

Shepheard's Hotel (Cairo), 212, 225, 253

Sherrard, Philip, 260, 308, 363, 385

*Sicherheitsdienst* (Nazi security service), 180, 195

Sikelianós, Ángelos, xi, 81, 97, 142–3, 145, 189, 268, 295, 300, 323, 324; candidate for Nobel Prize, 277, 287, 364, 365, 378, 380; poems of, published by GS in Egypt, 228, 237

Sikelianú, Ánna (previously Karamani), 169, 189

Sikelianú, Eva, *see* Palmer, Eva

Skála ton Vourlón (*or* tou Vourlá), xv, 8, 15–19, 22; as recalled by GS, 28, 32, 34, 62, 67, 92, 93, 116, 147, 189, 205–6, 291, 309–10, 329, 339, 363, 372, 388, 398, 405; GS returns to, 287, 288–90, 292; Seferiadis family returns to, 37, 172–3

Skéferis, Pericles, 279, 299, 335, 445

Skiathos, 92–3, 95, 189

Sloane Avenue (London), GS living in, 293–300

Smith, R.D. (Reggie), 177, 195, 230, 294

Smyrna (*see also* Izmir): before 1922, 1–5, 7, 11–15, 19, 416–17; destruction of (1922), 5, 51–3, 55, 239, 288, 291, 321; Greek occupation of (1919–22), 35–6, 42, 47–8, 57; GS returns to, *see* Izmir;

509

recalled by GS, 67, 196, 199, 248, 339;
  Seferiadis family returns to, 36, 37
Socrates, 274, 275
Sofoúlis, Themistocles, 20–1, 264
Solomós, Dionýsios, xi, 24, 71, 323, 441
*Song of Songs* (Old Testament), 211, 366
Sophocles, 322; *Ajax*, 286; *Antigone*, 24
Souda (Crete), 195, 197
Sounion, 402–3
South Africa, 201, 203, 207, 210, 214, 245,
  246, 312; *see also* Cape Town;
  Johannesburg; Pretoria
Spaak, Paul Henri: director-general,
  NATO, 342
Spencer, Bernard, 177, 202, 228, 229, 245
Spender, Stephen, 242, 261, 294
Spetses, 127–8
Stái, Mélpo, 27
Stalin, Joseph, 187
Stamélos, Sotíris, 92, 189
Stendhal, 82, 153
Stephanides, Theodore, 174–5, 178, 188
Stockholm, 381–2, 383, 393
Strasbourg, 342
Strátis (fictional persona of GS; *see also*
  Thalassinos, Stratis), 62, 66, 69, 74–5,
  76, 93, 94, 113, 428
Stravinsky, Igor, 74
Suez, 202, 205, 250; crisis, 335, 336–7
Suzon, *see* Clauzel
Swedish Academy, *see* Nobel Prize for
  Literature
Syria, *see also* Damascus, 301, 303, 349
Syros, 135

*Ta Nea Grammata* (*New Letters*), 128, 129,
  133, 136, 139, 150, 171, 200, 244, 260,
  305, 440, 442, 443, 488
Tarousópoulos (brothers), 181–2, 184, 251
Tehran, 335
Tenekés, Yorgákis (GS's maternal
  grandfather), 8
Tenekídis family, 4, 8–9, 25, 52, 58
Tenekídis, Kókos (GS's maternal uncle), 51,
  419
Tenekídou, Ágla (GS's maternal aunt), 54,
  60
Tenekídou, Déspo (Déspina) (GS's
  mother): declining health, 35, 41, 48, 52,

53; final illness and death: 70–1; in
  Athens, 25, 27, 28, 29, 30, 36, 39, 47, 49,
  51–2, 54, 56, 63, 64; in Smyrna, 7–9, 22,
  23; relationship with Stelios, 30, 33–4;
  remembered by GS, 9, 176, 206
Tenekídou, Evanthía Michaláki (GS's
  maternal grandmother), 8, 18, 310
Tenekídou, María (Despo's sister), 8, 9
Thalassinós, Strátis (literary persona of
  GS), 101, 116, 118, 123, 137, 149, 207,
  214–15, 312, 434, 440, 465–6; and
  *Mythistorema*, 129; significance and
  origin of name, 104–5
Theodorákis, Míkis, 90, 147, 361–2, 393–4,
  399, 404, 405
Theóphilos (Hatzimichael), 278, 281, 290
Theotokás, George, 7, 81–3, 97, 103, 110,
  113, 117–18, 136, 137, 143, 153, 181, 188,
  377, 378, 390, 391; *Argo* and genesis of
  *Mythistorema*, 124–5; *Free Spirit*, 82, 85
Thera, *see* Santorini
Thérèse, *see* Lefort
Thessaloniki, 28, 32, 88, 143, 151, 155, 192,
  307; Aristotle University of (honorary
  doctorate for GS), 383
Thessaly, 134–5; *see also* Volos; Pelion
'Third Greek Civilisation,' *see* Fourth of
  August regime
Thomas, Dylan, 294
*Thousand and One Nights*, 25
Tinos, 185
Toledo, 384
Tolo (near Nafplio), 170, 182
Trapeza (near Patras), 172, 183–4, 186, 205
Triantafyllídis, Manólis, 139
Truman, Harry S., 278, 284
Tsaldáris, Constantine: leader, People's
  Party, 264
Tsaldáris, Panayís: leader, People's Party,
  127, 134, 135
Tsaroúchis, Yánnis, 223
Tsátsos, Konstantínos (Kostákis) (GS's
  brother-in-law), xiv, 83, 91–2, 111, 134–5,
  141–3, 188, 210, 244, 264, 299, 333,
  334–5, 364–5, 379; circle of, 139, 189,
  212, 226, 259; correspondence with GS,
  108–9, 155, 351–2; memoirs, 127–8, 169,
  258, 447, 463, 468; public dialogue with
  GS, 107, 165–9, 171

510

Tsátsos, Themistocles (Místos), 144, 293

Tsátsou, Ioánna (née Seferiadou, GS's
sister), xiv, 9–10; and GS's career, 299,
333, 343; and house in Kydathinaion
Street, Athens, 126, 264, 265, 282; and
Jacqueline, 75–6, 87–8, 92, 94, 111, 126,
404; and Maro, 153, 170, 343, 351–2; and
Nobel Prize, 354–5, 379; and Stelios'
last years, 264; children of, 99, 126,
141–2, 337; circle of, 139, 226, 259;
correspondence with GS, 33–4, 37, 41,
42, 43, 44, 47, 48, 53, 55–6, 57, 60, 69,
101, 112, 115, 120, 124, 153–5, 210, 285–6,
296–7, 298, 300, 306–7, 310, 319, 345,
352–3, 363, 364, 366–7, 370, 468, 469,
471, 484, 485; during WWII, 211, 251,
258, 379; early life, 22, 23, 33, 35, 36–7,
39, 49, 51, 53, 55; marriage to K.
Tsatsos, 90–2, 142; My Brother George
Seferis, 12–13, 14, 16, 27, 29, 31, 33, 37,
49, 53–4, 66, 70, 73, 75–6, 80, 82, 87,
88, 89, 92, 93, 96, 109, 134, 153, 165–6,
170, 286, 342, 404, 444, 447, 492; on
distribution list for GS's poems, 97; with
GS, 71–2, 84, 85, 127–8, 134–5, 141–3,
145, 169, 295, 372

Tsírkas, Strátis, 214

Tsouderós, Emmanuel: GS's relations with,
202, 203, 205, 209, 218, 221, 236, 237,
248, 456, 459; in postwar governments,
264; prime minister (government in
exile), 196, 197, 198, 201, 212, 215, 216,
218, 231–2, 454

Turkish Cypriots, see Cyprus

Twain, Mark, xiii

Tzitzifies, see Faliron


Under-Ministry of Press and Tourism
(Athens), 156–64, 165, 178, 179–80, 186,
190–2, 194–5, 197, 222, 454

United Nations Organization: Cyprus
debated at, 317, 336–9, 348

University College London, 102

Upper Brook Street (London), GS living in,
342–67; departure from, 375

Urla Iskelesi (see also Skala), xv, 15,
17–18

Urla, see Vourla

US Army Language School, Presidio of
Monterey, 284, 285

USA: GS in, 337–9, 384–5, 393–6, 398


Valaorítis, Nános, 178, 244–5, 261, 282,
287, 294–5, 364

Valéry, Paul, 43, 56, 68, 98, 107, 114, 181,
183

Várnalis, Kóstas, 97

Váyias (persona of GS), 55–6, 85, 93, 104

Venice, 300

Venizélos, Elefthérios: and 1935 putsch,
133–4, 164; and Greek monarchy, 25–6,
27–8, 30, 66, 136; and London embassy,
343; and Stelios Seferiadis, 29, 36, 39,
53; assassination attempts against,
39–40, 127, 246; death and funeral, 138,
446; electoral defeats, 40, 121–2, 264;
irredentist policies of, 165, 34, 35; last
administration of, 84, 88, 89, 102, 304;
political legacy of, 52, 195–6, 219, 235,
236, 262, 264–5, 268, 482

Venizélos, Sophocles, 231–2, 234

Vikelaia Municipal Library (Heraklion,
Crete): GS's books in, xiv, 170, 436, 441,
446, 447

Villon, François, 71

Vláchos, Ángelos, 230, 246, 280, 290, 301,
340–1, 458–9, 460, 469–70, 478, 479,
481

Vlastós, Pétros, 97

Volos, 151, 153–5

von den Steinen, Helmut, 180

von Post, Eric: Swedish ambassador to
Turkey, 286, 287, 288

Vourla (see also Skala), 8, 289


Wagner, Richard, 74, 204

Wallace, David, 180, 195, 242–3

Warner, Rex: correspondence with GS, 16,
17, 282, 371, 376, 382, 384, 387, 486,
490; in Greece, 260, 276; translator of
GS, 315–16, 358, 363–4, 477–8; visited
by GS, 294, 298, 359–60, 385; with GS
in Beirut, 301

Washington, D.C., 337–8, 394

Weisz, André: professor, Sorbonne, 38,
42–3

Whittemore, Thomas, 283

Wilde, Oscar: Salomé, 76

511

Wisdom, T.H., 449
Woodhouse, C.M., 212, 226, 241, 260,
    261–2, 301, 452

Xýdis, Aléxandros, 209, 236, 247, 266, 301,
    346, 355, 459

Yeats, W.B., 142, 190
Yugoslavia, 171

Zagora, 134–5
Zakynthos, 360–1

Zánnos family, 140, 147, 172, 183
Zánnos, Miltiádes (Maro's father), 140,
    192
Zánnou, Amaryllís, see Dragoumi,
    Amaryllis
Zánnou, Marí(k)a, see Seferi, Maro
Zen, 271
Zog I: king of Albania, 149, 171
Zorlu, Fatin: Turkish foreign minister,
    348–9, 351, 352, 357
Zurich: conference on independence for
    Cyprus, 353, 354